Philosophers of War

Philosophers of War

THE EVOLUTION OF HISTORY'S GREATEST MILITARY THINKERS

Volume 1: The Ancient to Premodern World, 3000 BCE–1815 CE

Daniel Coetzee and Lee W. Eysturlid, Editors

Foreword by Dennis Showalter

 PRAEGER

AN IMPRINT OF ABC-CLIO, LLC

Santa Barbara, California • Denver, Colorado • Oxford, England

Library of Congress Cataloging-in-Publication Data

Philosophers of war : the evolution of history's greatest military thinkers / Daniel Coetzee and Lee W. Eysturlid, editors; foreword by Dennis Showalter.
    pages cm
    Includes index.
    ISBN 978-0-275-98977-4 (hbk. : alk. paper) – ISBN 978-0-313-07033-4 (ebook)   1. War (Philosophy)–History.   2. Military art and science–Philosophy.   3. Military art and science–Biography.   I. Coetzee, Daniel.   II. Eysturlid, Lee W., 1966-
    U21.2.P522 2013
    355.001–dc23   2013014191

ISBN: 978-0-275-98977-4
EISBN: 978-0-313-07033-4

17 16 15 14 13   1 2 3 4 5

This book is also available on the World Wide Web as an eBook.
Visit www.abc-clio.com for details.

Praeger
An Imprint of ABC-CLIO, LLC

ABC-CLIO, LLC
130 Cremona Drive, P.O. Box 1911
Santa Barbara, California 93116-1911

This book is printed on acid-free paper ∞

Manufactured in the United States of America

Contents

List of Entries by Section

I: General Theory

Al-Kufi, Abu-Bakr

Al-Rawandi, 'Ali Abu-Bakr Najm al-Din Muhammad Ibn

Al-Shaybani, Muhammad Ibn al-Hasan

Al-Shayzari, 'Abd al-Rahman

Al-Tarsusi, Mardi bin Ali

Babur, Zahiruddin

Baghdadi Manjaniqi, Ya'qūb Ibn Ṣābir

Bana

Basta, Giorgio, Count of Huszt

Bonaparte, Napoleon

Bueil, Jean V de

Carl, Archduke of Austria and Duke of Teschen

Ch'i Chi-kuang, Senior Commissioner in Chief

Crissé, Turpin de, Lieutenant General Lancelot, Comte de

Ewald, Johann Von

Fazl, Abul

Feuquières, Antoine de pas, Marquis de

Fourquevaux, Raimond de Beccarie de Pavie, Seigneur de

Frontinus, Sextus Julius

Guibert, Jacques-Antoine-Hippolyte, Comte de

Hay du Chastelet, Paul

Herodotus

Ibn Akhi Hizam, Muhammad Ibn Ya'qub al-Khuttali

Kamandaka

IV: Tactical and Operational Theory

V: General Essays

Alphabetical List of Entries

Aineias, called Aeneas Tacticus

Al-Kufi, Abu-Bakr

Al-Rawandi, 'Ali Abu-Bakr Najm al-Din Muhammad Ibn

Al-Shaybani, Muhammad Ibn al-Hasan

Al-Shayzari, 'Abd al-Rahman

Al-Tabari, 'Abd al-Rahman

Al-Tarsusi, Mardi bin Ali

Apollodorus (Apollodoros), Architect

Archimedes of Syracuse

Arrian, Governor of Cappadocia, Lucius Flavius Arrianus (Arrianos) Xenophon

Asklepiodotos (Asclepiodotus) the Philosopher

Babur, Zahiruddin

Baghdadi Manjaniqi, Yaʿqūb Ibn Ṣābir

Bana

Barrin, Rolland-Michel, Marquis de La Galissonière

Basta, Giorgio, Count of Huszt

Biton, Engineer

Bonaparte, Napoleon

Bourcet, Lieutenant General Pierre-Joseph de

Brialmont, Major General Henri Alexis

Bueil, Jean V de

Bülow, (Adam) Dietrich (Heinrich) Freiherr von

Byzantine Military Doctrine

Caesar, Gaius Julius

Carl, Archduke of Austria and Duke of Teschen

Carnot, Comte Lazare Nicolas Marguerite

Foreword

The philosophy of war is usually treated in the context of philosophy as a discipline in the same way military justice is compared to justice, and military music to music. That is to say, it is presented as a red-headed stepchild at best or, more likely, as an illegitimate offspring. Carl von Clausewitz, the West's defining military philosopher and its most familiar figure, barely rates a footnote and an index entry in general histories of philosophy—even those with a German emphasis.

The same point can be made about military thought. Theoretical analysis of war is commonly understood in practical contexts: as a reaction to and a product of, experience. It is correspondingly presented in operational and institutional contexts: its templates are armed forces, states, and societies.

Daniel Coetzee and Lee Eysturlid's two magisterial volumes provide an alternate matrix. *The Philosophers of War* presents in a single compass the intellectual biographies of the world's military thinkers—all of them! Ranging from 3000 BC to the present, the work incorporates general theorists and theoretical specialists from every culture that has practiced war over enough time, and with enough structure, to inspire systematic reflection.

Its expansive structure enhances *The Philosophers of War*'s value by enabling multiple perspectives. The work's two volumes beak at 1815. The theorists presented in Volume 1 range from familiar figures such as Jomini, Sun Tzu, and Thucydides; through such dissertation subjects as Fabius Cunctator and Maurice de Saxe; and to their virtually unknown counterparts from China and South Asia. The encyclopedic format of multiple authors and discrete entries means each subject has his own perspective and voice, as opposed to being fitted into a single editor's matrix. The result is an opportunity for readers unfamiliar with, or dubious about, the existence and nature of the philosophy of war to access a compendium of insights.

The same holds true for the volume's specialized sections. Political and grand strategy; tactical and operational analysis; and siege warfare and artillery—all have their place. Essays on particular subjects ranging from the use of elephants to Southeast Asian naval warfare fill the gaps.

In the period covered by Volume 2, war-making has grown increasingly complex and increasingly compartmentalized. The work responds by including theoretical sections addressing naval and air power. But the "General Theory" category is creatively comprehensive. Henry Kissinger, William S. Lind, and William DePuy appropriately stand alongside Clausewitz and Trotsky. Military management, operational research, and nuclear war expand Volume I's relative battlefield focus—though tactics in general and armored war in particular sustain the analysis of war's sharp end. Pride of place in Volume 2, however, goes to the sections on insurgency and counterinsurgency. The biographic format finds room for Gandhi, Giap, T. E. Lawrence, and Roger Trinquier. The result is a unique compendium of ideas on the nature of a form of war that bids fair to dominate at least the first half of the 21st century.

The Philosophers of War is user friendly in its structure, which enables prompt cross-referencing of personalities, ideas, and references. Further, the editors have assembled a Who's Who of scholars in the field. Some, such as Norman Stone and David Glantz, are readily familiar. The less-familiar essayists, however, are no less competent. Their scholarship combines with Eysturlid's disciplined editing to make *The Philosophers of War* a valuable contribution to the study of war and a worthwhile acquisition for anyone interested in the subject.

Dennis Showalter
Colorado College

Set Introduction

War is a complicated business. Due to the importance that civilized humans have given to it since the very beginning, it simply cannot be taken lightly. For this reason alone the search for the multifaceted answer of how to achieve victory in war has consumed the mental efforts of kings, soldiers, and wise men for millennia. The destructive physical nature of war makes its practice something that demands a civilization's energies and best thinking. When societies have seen war as something to be taken lightly, they have paid for it with military failure. For this reason to unearth the core of any historical period, to understand a society's politics, economics, and especially its social structure and mores, one must study how a society conducts and thinks about war. For how war is conducted is inseparable from how a society thinks about it. To ignore the mental process that is assigned by a culture for the conduct of war is to just see the movement of armies or fleets in a vacuum, obscuring understanding. The student of history cannot, therefore, avoid the study of conflict and those that gave its conduct direction. To understand war we must understand the military thinker, the *Philosophers of War*.

What then qualifies someone as a "philosopher" in the art of war? The general definition often given for that word is of someone that seeks wisdom and is an expounder of a theory or specific area of experience. This being the case the writers and practitioners of war included in this work fit neatly. All of them had, from the course of experience in war, or through the study of it, come to develop theories they felt of merit. In some cases these theories never made it to paper, but their practice was likely dynamic and brought about change. This then is the philosophy part that these writers looked to create a systematic way to get at knowledge about the conduct of war, specific or general. It is for this reason too that many famous military commanders do not warrant inclusion. The simple practice of war, however successful, is not to be equated with the actual study of war. For this reason, great generals such as George Washington or Alexander the Great, to name but two, are not included.

This work, the *Philosophers of War,* is a collection of what might be called professional or intellectual biographies of these individuals that had some originality and impact on their immediate circumstances and on the future. The editors made an effort to be inclusive of both great and minor figures, and to be thoughtful of military practices in societies that were not overtly literate. As with all figures in history, the impact of individuals varies wildly. For this reason the length of specific entries can vary a great deal. The entry on Carl von Clausewitz, perhaps one of three most influential military theorists of any time, runs over 8,000 words. In contrast, a Russian field marshal who was Clausewitz's contemporary, Alexander Suvorov, wrote little and had only a localized impact, warrants a short entry of 300 words.

The intention of this two-volume set is to provide the user with a twofold tool. It is the sincere hope of the editors that the users will see themselves as accessing a tool of reference and also a book of military biography. In the first case the user will be able to find an exhaustive list of military thinkers from the ancient world to the present, each thoughtfully organized to allow for comparison. Next, the entries are broken up first by chronology, with writers appearing before 1815 in the first volume, and those thereafter in the second. Then the writers are organized thematically. Where the military philosopher wrote broadly, he is in a general grouping. The famous Chinese military writer Sun Tzu wrote broadly on military, political, and moral issues, so he transcends a single theme. Otherwise writers are grouped by their specific focus, for example, Osama bin Ladin is in the category titled *Insurgency.*

Having come to the work as one of reference, the user can now see that a second and hopefully even more rewarding option is possible. If the readers were interested in the topic of insurgency, for example, they could begin to read the entries in that section, gaining a broad education in insurgency theory from the key writers in that area of study. The reader would see the time frame of insurgency emerge, the areas, if any, of geographic concentration, and the problems faced by writers of insurgency theory. This collection of writers would allow for a general reading as well as making it a source if doing research. For this reason the intellectual biographies and the organization of the work give it multiple potential uses.

STRUCTURE OF THE ENTRIES

Each entry is generally structured to look alike. As mentioned, the intention is to allow the user to make relatively easy comparisons between them. To facilitate the user getting at the information they want, this layout will speed their research. Each subsection of an entry compliments the overall entry.

The Logic of Entry Structure:

Name: The full name and dates for the theorist.

Significance: Why is this individual worth investigating?

Context: What time frame or in what situation as this individual active?

Biography: This is a short synopsis of this person's life, both professional and personal. Especially as it pertains to what they wrote.

Influences: What other writers, or what events, molded this person.

The Theory: What did this writer actually have to say about war or how did they practice war in an original manner that had some impact on the future?

Descendents: Who can the historian say with some certainty was impacted by the work or practice of this theorist?

See Also: What other entries are there in this work that pertain or have similarities to the entry at hand?

Further Reading: This section contains useful bibliographic material to allow for further research. The less famous theorists often have little written about them, and the work here in the encyclopedia represents the work of the scholar writing the entry.

Finally, as mentioned earlier, it is the intention of the editors that someone doing research might pick up one of these two volumes to find a specific theorist. Having found that person in a specific section, he or she would then see that there as a wealth of individuals who had written about their topic, and they would end up, back at their study table, pouring over that section to see who else was of interest and of use to their research. Facilitated by the common organization of each entry, the reader would have found theorists, book titles, and ideas that they would not have found in a traditionally organized work of reference on the topic.

Introduction to Volume 1

The first volume of *Philosophers at War* is intended to bring the user sources on the writings and practice of war from the earliest period of civilization to the end of the Napoleonic Era. The intention here is to provide a useful separation between the premodern and modern period—for the purpose of understanding the actual theorizing on war this separation is vital. Before 1815 works on war were not engaged in any systematic or academic fashion, but rather as the writer, be he a king, commander, or philosopher, felt inclined. Therefore, expertise is not easily measurable in any modern or academic sense and often theorists covered multiple, even disparate, topics. For example, the works of **Niccolò Machiavelli** covered everything from politics, to tactical dispositions, to a history of the papacy. He was one of many early writers to engage so broadly. Further, the entire period before 1815 was often limited by the ability to effectively publish and distribute such writings, and often the work was not intended for a general audience. **Frederick the Great** had no intention of his *Instructions* being public, whereas **Julius Caesar's** *Commentaries* on the Gallic wars was a work meant for open consumption.

The range of time then, a period that covers some 3,000 years, experienced changes, but retained certain fundamental similarities that allow such a grouping to make sense. It was only in the last 400 years of this three-millennium timeframe that gunpowder came into use. Therefore, weaponry, although diverse, was powered by human muscle, with combat a "face-to-face" affair. Transportation was tied to foot and horse on land and wind or oars at sea. Finally, the primary logistical struggle for all these writers was the tyranny of food supplies, the movement of ammunition and fuel surpassing food only after 1914. Because supply was such an overwhelming issue, the walled city and the siege, whether the attack or in the defense, were often focal points of campaigns.

Another issue encountered in the period before 1815, and especially before 1400, is a lack of literacy. Many famous commanders and innovators in war never put pen to paper. Rather they practiced new and often bold ideas, which influenced future use and memory through actual practice rather than transmission through writing. Several of the practitioners listed, **Genghis Khan,** for example, left no written record, but were clearly innovators in the art of war. The first volume ends with a series of essays that will give the user the ability to better understand the practice of war in places where conflict had limited record and are well served by a summary. Titled "General Essays," these overviews will allow the user to insight into often missed military cultures, the entry on **Indian chariot use** being an excellent example. The discrete organization of theorists by field rather than alphabetically is intended to allow the user to browse through all the work on a single topic rather than just seek a single entry.

I

General Theory

This section describes those writers who engaged with the general topic of war, whether they actually wrote about war or simply practiced it. The writers tend to cover all the main concerns, from politics to strategy to tactics, as can be seen in the works of **Sun Tzu, Herodotus,** and **Timur.** For the theorists in this section the goal is to find a method that will give the reader the information necessary to put together the elements of conflict necessary to achieve success.

Al-Kufi, Abu-Bakr
(Thirteenth century CE, writing about early eighth century CE)

Significance: Hindu scholars of ancient India viewed the world, including human life, as *maya* (illusion) and had a certain disregard for history. But Muslim scholars such as Abu-Bakr had a keen desire to know the course of human affairs and to record the past. Information about medieval India proliferates with the outpourings of the Arab authors from the ninth century onward. In a flowery language, they describe the collapse of Hindu India due to the onslaught of the Muslims. Though written from the victor's perspective and tinged with chauvinism and xenophobia, these accounts clarify military theory and praxis. The *Chach Nama* depicts the introduction of new military techniques by the Arabs into India during their conquest of Sind between 711 and 713. It is particularly useful in establishing changes to Arab warfare that had occurred since their explosion from the Arabian Peninsula in the seventh century, and their subsequent interaction with the Persian and Byzantine military civilizations.

Context: During the seventh century CE, the Umayid Caliphate emerged as a global power, and between 622 and 748, it included Arabia, Iraq, Persia, Syria, and northern Africa. The Persian Sassanid Empire was overrun and Islamic forces reached as far as Afghanistan in the east. The Arabs had started pillaging the coast of Sind from 637, but there was no pan-Indian polity to check them. Indeed, from

775 to 1018, tussles between the Rashtrakutas, the Gurjara-Pratiharas, and the Palas weakened India's western defense. As a result, Sind was an independent regional Hindu kingdom on the eve of Arab invasion.

In 712, Al-Hajjaj, the governor of *Ajam* (Iraq) under Caliph Walid, was in charge of expansion east of Iran. Among the expeditions that he authorized was the one against Sind under Muhammad-bin-Qasim. Initially, the Caliph was not eager to attack Sind, but Hajjaj assured him that the expedition would be rewarding, and that if any economic loss occurred, Hajjaj would personally repay the Caliph's treasury.

Biography: *Chach Nama* (also known as *Tarikh-i-Hind* or *Wa Sind* or *Fath Nama*) was written toward the end of the eighth century. The original author was an Arab intellectual who was appointed by Muhammad Qasim as the *Qazi* [Chief of Justice] of the town of Alor. His original name is unknown to us. Abu-Bakr-al-Kufi, who lived in Delhi during the 13th century, translated *Chach Nama* from Arabic into Persian. The translation was dedicated to Nasir-ud-din Qubacha (a lieutenant of Muhammad Ghori) in 1216.

Influences: Because Arab tradition cherished democratic ideals, the Arab chroniclers treated history as a biography of nations, and narrated incidents related to the common mass. The *Qazi,* while writing *Chach Nama,* depended on oral testimonies of the persons who had participated in the invasion of Sind.

The Theory: *Chach Nama* tells us that the Arabs introduced *manjaniqs* (trebuchets, catapults, or mangonels) and armored cavalry at the western end of the Indian subcontinent. The effective and novel combination of cavalry, artillery (using naphtha), new siege warfare techniques, and river boats, allowed the Arabs to comprehensively outfight Sind's Hindus.

The Arabs' superiority in siege warfare, using *manjaniqs,* naphtha fire, and mining, nullified the defensive value of the Hindu forts. The Arabs had learnt to use *manjaniqs* by copying the Byzantine trebuchets, and had employed them during the sieges of Taif, Damascus, and Mecca. Muhammad Qasim, the master of the author of the *Chach Nama,* himself used *manjaniqs* during the Sind invasion in 711–712 while besieging the port of Debal. Five *manjaniqs* together with their ammunition were transported by sea to Debal. Then, the *manjaniqs* were transported from Debal to Brahmanabad on boats along the Indus. A *manjaniq* required 500 men to work it. Each machine had a pivot, and while the strongest men pulled back one *palla* (beam) with special cords, the other *palla* moved forward and struck the stone ball. The artificially shaped stone balls (usually round or oblong) thrown by the *manjaniqs* shattered forts' stone walls. These weapons were unknown on the Indian subcontinent. Once the walls of the forts were breached by the *manjaniqs* and mining, Arab infantry used scaling ladders for assaulting the garrisons.

Arab cavalry warfare, in both shock and missile styles, also greatly surpassed Hindu techniques. *Chach Nama* implies that India lacked good horses, and this enabled the Arabs to repeatedly defeat the Indian forces. Al-Beruni (January 970–September 1038) who entered the service of Muhammad-bin-Subuktagin, the ruler of a small principality in Afghanistan, noted in his *Kitab-ul-Hind* that even in his day, the Turks were celebrated for their horses, whereas the people of Hind (India) did not breed good horses. The Hindus, asserts Al-Beruni, lacked knowledge about feeding the horses properly. The net result was that most of the horses became lame after some time. Al-Beruni implied that Hindu domestic horses bred in places such as Mabar (Malabar) were of such poor quality that India could be conquered by the Muslim rulers with their superior cavalry. Importing horses from overseas became a strategic necessity for Hindu rulers by the mid-eighth century. Arab merchants brought horses from the Persian Gulf in ships and sold them to the Hindu kings for gold. Thousands of horses were exported by the Arab horse dealers from islands such as Kis, Fars, Katif, Lahsa, Bahrein, Hormuz, and Kilahat. One problem was that the muscles of the horses imported from Arabia became damaged due to the long-distance overseas voyage. In terms of speed and stamina, the Arabian horses were no match for the Central Asian steppe horses. The Hindu kings could not import horses from Central Asia because that region was dominated by the hostile Turks, who repeatedly invaded India through the Northwest Frontier passes.

Another primary reason for the collapse of Sind in the 710s, as implied in *Chach Nama*, was the fact that Dahir, the ruler of Sind, lacked a navy, which could have functioned as the first line of defense.

Application: The Arabs invaded Sind during the rule of King Dahir (679–712), whose defense emphasized positional warfare and the use of elephants. An Arab expeditionary force under the leadership of a 17-year-old Arab general named Muhammad Qasim (the son-in-law of Al-Hajjaj) was sent from Iraq by ships and disembarked at Debal (either modern Karachi or a place near Thatta). From Debal, Qasim moved into Nerun. He crossed Indus by constructing a bridge of boats. Qasim also used a flotilla of boats for conveying the soldiers along the Indus. About 6,000 Syrian cavalry in iron armor constituted the core of the land army. In addition, the Arab force had 6,000 armed camel riders, and for logistical duties there were 3,000 Bactrian camels. The Arabs recruited 3,000 infantry from the Buddhist Sind tribes.

Initially Dahir thought that the Arabs would leave after capturing a few frontier forts. But when Qasim continued to advance, Dahir met the Arab forces at Raor. In a battle fought in June 712, discharge of naphtha (probably Greek fire) and a frontal charge by armored cavalry eviscerated Dahir's elephant-centric army. Dahir, leading his troops from an elephant-mounted *howdah* (box-like chair), was killed.

Dahir's son Jaisiya resorted to positional warfare, as he realized that in open battles, Qasim's cavalry would defeat the Hindus' slow-moving elephant-oriented forces. One of Dahir's queens named Rani Bai moved into the great fort of Rawar with 15,000 soldiers, but to no avail. The fort fell after the garrison suffered 6,000 casualties. The fort of Brahmanabad fell with a loss of 16,000 men out of the 40,000-strong garrison. Within three years, Qasim had captured the whole of Sind.

Descendents: After the Arab invasion, some Hindu powers maintained considerable naval forces. Around the 11th century CE, some of the big ships manufactured by the Hindus weighed 2,300 tons. Such a river navy in Dahir's hand could have checked Qasim's march along the Indus. Moreover, it would have allowed Dahir to react quickly to the Arab invasion by transporting troops in ships from his capital to Debal.

Later Muslim invaders of India copied the new weapons introduced by the Arabs. For example, Mahmud Ghazni (999–1030) used naphtha both in land and river battles. In 1027, Mahmud constructed a flotilla of 1,400 boats at Multan. On each boat, he stationed 20 men armed with bows, arrows, and naphtha. The Jats collected 4,000 boats. But, in the naval battle, the Jats were defeated because of naphtha fire and superior construction of Mahmud's boats. Each of Mahmud Ghazni's boat had an iron spike in the front and on both sides. While explosion of naphtha disorganized the Jat boats, the spikes were used for ramming and sinking them.

The Delhi sultans adopted Qasim's use of a riverine navy for transporting troops. Firuz Shah Tughluq (1351–1388), while campaigning in Sind between 1361 and 1362 used boats to transport his army comprising 90,000 cavalry and 480 elephants along River Indus to Thatta.

Mahmud Ghazni copied Qasim's use of camels as baggage animals. In 1025, during the Somnath expedition across the desert of Rajasthan, Mahmud employed 30,000 camels loaded with corn and water.

The use of *manjaniqs* spread from Sind into India. Sultan Alauddin Khalji (1296–1316) of Delhi used the *manjaniqs* for capturing the forts of Ranthambor (1301) and Mandu (1305). By the 14th century, even the Hindu defenders were using smaller *manjaniqs* known as *iradas* (which were placed inside the forts) against besieging Muslim armies.

See also: Use of Elephants in Indian Warfare

Further Reading

The History of India as Told by Its Own Historians: The Muhammadan Period, ed. from the Posthumous Papers of the late H. M. Elliot, by John Dawson, vol. 1. 4th ed. New Delhi: D. K. Publishers, 2001.

Nizami, K. A., ed. *Politics and Society during the Early Medieval Period: Collected Works of Mohammad Habib,* vol. 2. New Delhi: People's Publishing House, 1981.

Rizvi, S.A.A., *The Wonder that was India,* vol. 2, *A Survey of the History and Culture of the Indian Subcontinent from the Coming of the Muslims to the British Conquest, 1200–1700.* 1987, reprint, New Delhi: Rupa, 1999.

Kaushik Roy

Al-Rawandi, 'Ali Abu-Bakr Najm al-Din Muhammad Ibn
(Late 12th century CE)

Significance: Al-Rawandi's one surviving major work was written in Persian and discussed general military theory.

Context: Al-Rawandi was active in the dying days of the Great Seljuq Sultanate, and saw the rise of the Khwarazmshah dynasty.

Biography: Al-Rawandi's education, at Hamadan in western Iran between 1174 and 1184 CE, focused upon the Hanafi school of Islamic law. He traveled widely and became a skilled calligrapher. He conceived of a book combining an anthology of poetry with a history of the Seljuq Turks, which he would present at the Great Seljuq Sultanate court. Unfortunately, when it was completed around 1205, a new Khwarazmshah dynasty was in power. Al-Rawandi moved to the smaller but still Seljuq Sultanate of Rum. He presented his *Rahat al-Sudur wa-Ayat al-Surur* to Sultan Kay Khusraw I around 1207 CE. It is the only one of his works that is known to survive.

The Theory: The *Rahat al-Sudur* discusses how kingship should be conducted. Al-Rawandi uses the historical narrative as a framework upon which to hang anecdotes, wise sayings, poetic quotations, and examples of correct procedure. He described this *majmu'a* or "compilation" as a morally edifying and practical guide to life at court and on campaign. Militarily, the most interesting part of the *Rahat al-Sudur* deals with the final years of the Great Seljuq Sultanate, when it was dominated by the military *atabeg* or "rulers' father-figure" Muhammad Jahan Pahlavan. Al-Rawandi analyses Pahlavan's failures, offering the *atabeg* as a negative role model because his policy of benefiting his corps of *mamluk* professional soldiers resulted in corruption, which then attracted the predatory Khwarazmshahs. The *Rahat al-Sudur* also includes sections on archery, horse riding, and chess. Another chapter explains *Al-ghalib w'al-maghlub*, a form of fortune telling that supposedly predicted the results of potential clashes between rivals.

Application and Descendents: Al-Rawandi was not highly regarded in Seljuq Turkey after his death. However, his *Rahat al-Sudur wa-Ayat al-Surur* was used by later Persian historians and was translated into Turkish during the reign of the Ottoman Sultan Murad II (1421 and 1446–1451 CE).

See also: Mubarakshah, Fakhr-i Mudabbir; Naṣûḥ bin Karagöz, called Matrakçı, Matrâqî, Silâḥî, etc.; Usama Ibn Munqidh

David Nicolle

Al-Shaybani, Muhammad Ibn al-Hasan
(749–805)

Significance: Muslim jurisprudence has always had an "etiquette of war," which encompassed when armed conflict is justified, legitimate targets of deadly force, permissible weapons of war, treatment of prisoners of war, division of booty, cessation of hostilities, and other topics relevant to initiating, conducting, and ending armed conflict. Al-Shaybani was among the first to develop a coherent framework that drew from Muslim legal tradition and specifically addressed the conduct during armed conflict (al-Siyar).

Context: During the time of Harun al-Rashid, it was accepted practice for government officials to seek the counsel of learned "men of religion." These consultations conferred legitimacy to the subsequent policies, and forced theologians to develop practical solutions through Sharia reasoning. In accordance with the accepted practice of Sharia reasoning, the religious scholars scoured the sacred texts, reviewed past examples, and used reasoning to derive new laws.

Biography: Al-Shaybani lived in Iraq. He was born in al-Wasit, a military town, and to a military family. But he was more interested in perusing an intellectual career than a military one. He moved to Kufa and studied under the famous theologian Abu Hanifa (d. 767), and later under Abu Yusuf (d. 795). By the time of his own death, he was considered one of the early masters of the Hanafi school (along with Abu Hanifa and Abu Yusuf). He was also served as qadi (judge) in Harun al-Rashid's court.

Influences: The Sharia's scope encompassed not only an individual's relationship with other individuals and the state, but also an individual's private thoughts and relationship with the divine. In addition to a legal system, it also included ritual practices and moral standards. Hence, it was a comprehensive code of behavior covering ritual, ethics, and law that regulated both the private and public spheres. Throughout the medieval period this basic doctrine was elaborated and systematized in a large number of commentaries. The voluminous literature this exercise produced constituted the traditional textual authority of Sharia law.

Conduct in war, conditions necessary for armed conflict, and those necessary for its cessation, permissible weapons of war, treatment of prisoners of war, distribution of booty, and other issues related to armed conflict also fell under the Sharia's purview. These were collected under the subheading al-Siyar, which addressed the conduct of war.

The Theory: Al-Shaybani realized that was is a gap between the precedents set during the time of the Prophet (in the seventh century) and questions of subsequent generations. He argued that the space had to be filled by the reasoning of the learned. With this line of reasoning, al-Shaybani and his colleagues started a trans-generational conversation evaluating Sharia reasoning. Later, scholars reached a consensus that the task of providing guidance on the Sharia lay in interpreting the Koran and reports of prophetic practice, considerations of precedents set by earlier generations, and scholarly reasoning.

Al-Shaybani thought of the world as being divided into Dar al-Islam (lit. "House of Peace"), which were the lands ruled by the rightful caliph, and Dar al-Harb (lit. "House of War"), which were lands not controlled by the rightful caliph. He also divided people living in the Muslim territories. First were the Muslims who had an obligation to pay taxes, and respond to a call to arms. The al-dhimmi (protected people) had an obligation to pay tribute to the Muslim ruler, and expected to be protected from invaders. The al-bughat (rebels) were Muslims who challenged the authority of the caliph. They were to be brought back into the fold of Islam if possible. The al-muharribun were the brigands and highwaymen from whom the residents of the territory deserve protection. Finally, the al-murtadd (apostates) who turned away from Islam, and needed to be called to repent or be punished. Within these groups, people were classified as combatants (all men able to bear arms), and noncombatants (women, children, elderly, and disabled—unless they take up arms). Using this classification, al-Shaybani answers three main questions: When is fighting justified? Who are the targets of fighting? How is fighting concluded?

Fighting was justified when there was just cause and presence of right intension. As al-Shaybani assumed that war was a rule-governed activity, he further stipulated that the directive to fight must come from a legitimate authority. Just causes for war needed to entail at least one of the following:

- Fighting to spread Islamic hegemony. This entailed either direct territorial control, or receipt of annual tribute from the territories. One consideration was: does armed conflict necessitate a military threat, or was merely refusal to convert or pay tribute sufficient for armed conquest. The religious scholars realized that the end goal is to spread Islamic hegemony. Conquest can serve that end, but it was a by-product, not an end in itself. War was fought for a purpose, and if that purpose was better served by other means (such as persuasion or diplomacy), then there was no need for armed conflict. Hence, war was justified only when nonmilitary means are exhausted. Furthermore, an army that gave the enemy a second chance acted commendably, as there was another opportunity to avert further destruction.
- Fighting to discipline al-dhimmis, was to be directed only to those al-dhimmi who violated their agreement with Muslim authorities.
- Fighting to bring Muslim rebels back into the fold of Islam had the goal of limiting rebellion and reconciling with other Muslims.
- Fighting to discipline the brigands was to secure the safety and property of those who had entrusted the government to provide them protection.
- Fighting apostates was to either have them repent for their transgression or to bring them to justice.

The target of fighting mirrored the categories of people above. In short, legitimate targets were those groups who resisted the legitimate aims of the established caliph (i.e., legitimate authorities of Dar al-Islam). Thus, in addition to hostile armies, al-dhimmis who violated their agreements, rebels, brigands, and apostates were legitimate targets of military action. However, not everybody among the enemy was a legitimate target of deadly force. Only those who posed a military threat could be subjected to direct and intentional killing.

How fighting ended depended on the identity of the combatants, and the location of the fighting. Fighting against Muslims was more restricted than it was against non-Muslims. The end goal of fighting was to reach reconciliation (the goal was primarily religious, not political or economic).

Treatment of captives depended on the location. Combatants captured in Dar al-Harb may be spared or killed (depending on the commander's judgment). If they were spared, they become part of the booty and were transported to Dar al-Islam for distribution. Noncombatants were transported to Dar al-Islam for distribution. If a means of transport was not immediately available, and the captives could not walk, then the commander was obliged to arrange for suitable transport. Booty was removed from Dar al-Harb and brought to Dar al-Islam before distribution. Hence, a soldier had to wait until the Muslim forces return (with the captured treasure) before it was distributed. The emphasis was on equitable distribution of booty.

Al-Shaybani also addressed concerns regarding unintentional killing of non-combatants. In a just war, noncombatants were immune from direct and intentional killing, but that did not mean that they were immune from all harm. Al-Shaybani took the position that as long as care was taken to aim at combatants, any deaths of noncombatants is an indirect effect of legitimate action. This line of reasoning was used to justify the use of fire, water, and other methods of mass destruction during warfare. Al-Shaybani reasoned that the goal of extending Muslim hegemony was good. The actions necessary to further the goal were also good, provided that the fighters conducted themselves with good intensions, and avoided killing non-combatants. However, the enemy could not be allowed to take advantage of these good intensions through measures that would curtail the army's ability to carry out its legitimate goal. Hence, fighters engaged in legitimate military actions did not incur the guilt of the foreseen, yet unintended consequences of their military actions. Al-Shaybani further reasoned that although war was not the first or most desirable means for of extending Islamic hegemony, it was sometimes necessary. Hence, it should be used only when it is necessary, and hostilities should cease as soon as possible.

Application: The Hanafiyah school (in which al-Shaybani is considered among its masters) was the official system of Islamic interpretation of the Abbasids, Seljuks, and Ottomans. Al-Shaybani's thoughts on conduct of war were used by later Muslim empires, specifically the Ottoman, Safavid, and Moghul, in formulating official policy. In contemporary times, the Hanafiya school of thought is dominant in Central Asia, India, Pakistan, Turkey, and countries of the former Ottoman Empire. Using al-Shaybani's work as a starting point, scholars have debated issues of human rights, and the rights of non-Muslim nations to exist. Although differences exist, al-Shaybani's work has been extended to affirm human rights, and recognize lands that are neither Dar al-Islam nor Dar al-Harb, but neutral states.

Descendents: The generation after al-Shaybani saw the rise of other schools of thought. Some of these restricted the tools available to scholars to address issues of the time. For instance, precedence traceable only to the Prophet were authoritative. Precedence established by previous scholars were binding only if they could garner the consensus of the entire Muslim community. The Shafi school viewed the entire world as Dar al-Islam (at least in theory). This meant that the question of a just war took on a different cast. The requirements for armed conflict were relaxed, and the division of booty became more lenient. As a result, it became easier for the state to wage war.

Further Reading

Johnson, James Turner, *The Holy War Idea in Western and Islamic Traditions.* University Park: Pennsylvania State University Press, 1997.

Peters, Rudolph, *Jihad in Classical and Modern Islam: A Reader.* Princeton: Markus Wiener Publishers, 1996.

Muhammed Hassanali

Al-Shayzari, 'Abd al-Rahman

Significance: Al-Shayzari's work focused on military statecraft and broad strategy.

Context: Al-Shayzari was one of three scholars who wrote treatises on different aspects of warfare for Salah al-Din, Saladin, or his immediate successor in the late 12th and early 13th centuries CE.

Biography: 'Abd al-Rahman al-Shayzari was born before 1128 CE, probably in central Syria. The correct form of his full name was probably 'Abd al-Rahman Ibn Nasr Ibn 'Abd Allah al-Shayzari. He was said to have been a *qadi* Islamic judge in Tiberius, which Saladin retrieved from the Crusaders in 1187 CE. Al-Shayzari reportedly also worked as a physician in Aleppo. His nonmilitary writings show that he knew a great deal about the medical professions. He died ca. 1193 CE.

The Theory: Al-Shayzari's *Al-manhaj al-masluk fi siyasat al-muluk* or "The Proper Course for the Policy of Kings," written for Saladin, is an Arabic example of the genre known as "Mirrors for Princes." Five of its 20 chapters are on military matters, whereas another concerns the Christian Crusader enemy. One deals with a ruler's overall military policy and the organization of his troops. Others describe how to inspire a spirit of *jihad* ("lesser *jihad*" or religiously motivated warfare) among military personnel, the strengths and weaknesses of the "polytheists" or

Crusaders, ways of stopping the "machinations" of the enemies of Islam, the legally correct division of booty among those participating in a campaign, and actions calculated to keep the ruler's army united.

Application and Descendents: Whether al-Shayzari's military writing had any later impact is unknown, though *Al-manhaj al-masluk fi siyasat al-muluk* was quoted in Ibn Qadi Shuhba's biography of Saladin's predecessor, Nur al-Din.

See also: Al-Tarsusi, Mardi bin Ali; Usama Ibn Munqidh

David Nicolle

Al-Tarsusi, Mardi bin Ali
(12th century)

Significance: Al-Tarsusi wrote a military manual for Salah al-Din titled "Instruction of the Masters on the Means of Deliverance in Wars from Disaster, and the Unfurling of the Banners of Information: On Equipment and Engines which aid in Encounters with Enemies." In it we find the first clearly written record of a counterweight trebuchet. The manual also records using "naft" (a petroleum-based resin and sulfur, similar to Greek fire), which al-Tarsusi suggests can be placed inside blown eggshells and thrown from horseback.

Context: During the 12th century, Salah al-Din was fighting back the Crusades and reclaiming some of the territories lost during the earlier Crusades. The Crusaders built heavily fortified citadels to defend their conquered lands. Hence, to gain back the lost territories, Salah al-Din needed methods that would penetrate such heavily fortified structures.

Influences: Stone-throwing artillery has been around since ancient times. Both the Greeks and Romans used such engines to hurl stones at their enemies. Their war engines were powered by either torsion (a wound rope, as in the onager) or tension (a drawn bow, as in the oxybeles). The traction trebuchet was the first to employ principles of gravity and leverage to hurl a projectile.

The Theory: The earliest trebuchet designs were a type of rotating-beam engine powered by a team of human beings. A team of haulers pulled down on a network of ropes attached to the rear of the machine's throwing arm; an engineer loaded ammunition into the sling. The engineer could also provide some "whip" by adding his own weight to the throwing arm to retard its movement momentarily as the crew began its release. Designs ranged from a two-person quick-fire model to those requiring a crew of 250 personnel and were capable of hurling a 60 kg projectile more than 70 meters.

The trebuchet's simple design meant that precision parts (gears, locks, and precision frames) were not required. It also meant that it was not subject to as many catastrophic failures as it did not "cock" components in high-energy states of tension or torsion. As a result, traction trebuchets could be built in the field almost entirely out of rough-cut lumber and used natural stones. By the sixth century, Byzantium and Middle Eastern armies were using traction trebuchets in their military campaigns.

A trebuchet essentially consisted of a heavy frame that supported a pivoted asymmetric beam. Attached to the long end of the beam was a sling in which the operator placed a heavy rock. Attached to the short end were ropes that the hauling team pulled moving the short end downward, causing the long end to move upward. As the long end moved through its upward and forward arc, the sling released the rock, which now acted as a devastating projectile, and—if aimed correctly—collided into the intended target.

Although a trebuchet could be easily build on site, was capable of hurling heavy projectiles relatively long distances, and probably had impressive firing rates (just under four rounds per minute), it was not without its limitations. Coordinating a team of humans to pull with the same force in the same direction every time was challenging. Elementary physics of projectile motion would show that range is a function of the force on the short end of the arm. Hence, variation (in either magnitude or direction) of this force would directly impact range and accuracy. In addition, the best "pulling position" was directly under the short arm, which limited the physical size of the hauling team, and in turn limited the machine's range. A large hauling team placed additional constraints on the trebuchet's geometric considerations further limiting the machine's range of motion, and ultimately restricted its range.

Tarsusi wrote a military manual circa 1187 for Salah al-Din, and in that manual described a hybrid trebuchet. He claimed that his design had the same hurling power as a traction machine pulled by 50 men due to "the constant force [of gravity]." His design was more efficient than that using a large hauling team. As members of the hauling team pull in slightly difference directions, they cancelled out opposing forces (i.e., neutralized part of each other's efforts), and ultimately required more energy output to ready the machine.

Tarsusi's designed his hybrid trebuchet with a counterweight (possibly an iron plate forged directly to the short end of the pivoted beam). Constant force on the counterweight meant lower variation in the downward pull, which led to greater accuracy and better range. Hauling teams that used the counterweight design were smaller than those that used an equivalent performing traction design. The hybrid design also included a sling that gave the projectile more "whip," further increasing the projectile's range. Tarsusi also mounted the frame on wheels making it easier to move around in the battlefield. The added mobility of mounting the hybrid trebuchet on wheels, and the modified design that took advantage of the launching arm's entire range of motion made it a formidable piece of artillery on the battlefield—especially when it was used to take down fortified walls.

Application: Improved firing power was certainly the primary advantage of the hybrid trebuchet. This was proven during the siege of Damietta in Egypt in 1218 when it was used to hurl stones weighing a couple hundred kilograms at the city walls.

Descendents: European engineers encountered the trebuchet during the Crusades. They adopted and improved it during the subsequent centuries. They reasoned that if a small counterweight provided advantages, then a large one would provide even more advantages. This line of reasoning taken to its logical conclusion led to the counterpoise trebuchet.

Unlike traction and hybrid trebuchets, counterpoise trebuchets were powered by "falling weights." These were either stationary weights, or hanging buckets filled with sand, rocks, or rubble from the short end of the beam. The use of gravity meant consistent launching forces, hence, greater accuracy. The absence of a pulling team gave engineers greater design flexibility. This flexibility was leveraged to create even greater throwing arcs, which in turn meant that larger projectiles could be hurled greater distances with improved accuracy.

The counterpoise enhanced the trebuchet's destructive power, but greater artillery power came at a price. These machines needed elaborate block and tackle systems to raise the heavy ballast box; hence, they could only be fired three or four times per day. However, the counterpoise's power gave these war machines a new role in battle. Smaller trebuchets were now used to support troops scaling castle walls or targeting structures within a walled city; counterpoise trebuchets could effectively be used to destroy well-fortified walls, which in turn sparked an architectural arms race.

The various variations of the trebuchet were used not only used for hurling rocks but also horses, cows, barrels of sand, human heads, and even live prisoners. In addition, they were used not only by the attackers, but also by the defenders in attempts to destroy the attackers' siege machines. Their devastating power dominated the military landscape until gunpowder forced them into obsolesce.

Further Reading
Nicolle, David, *Saladin and the Saracens.* New York: Osprey Publishing, 1986, ISBN 0850456827.

Muhammed Hassanali

Babur, Zahiruddin
(February 14, 1484 CE to December 26, 1530 CE)

Significance: The autobiographical *Babur Nama* (*Memoirs of Babur*) tells us that Babur created a combined-arms approach by integrating Timur's *taulqama* cavalry tactics with an Ottoman-style use of matchlocks and field artillery. He also hints at decentralized battlefield command, in that his officers knew whom to attack without detailed instructions in mid-battle. This, the Germans later called *Auftrag-staktik*. Against the composite cavalry-artillery military culture of Babur, neither the Afghans nor the Rajputs had any answer, and his lethal techniques resulted in the foundation of the Mughal Empire in north India. Babur's methods also hint at techniques used by his major influence, the Ottomans, further west.

Context: By the 1520s, the Delhi Sultanate under the Lodhi dynasty (1451–1526) was failing to establish its sway over north India. Peripheral provinces such as Bengal and Punjab had become independent, and the Rajputs were challenging Muslim rule in the Ganga–Jamuna *doab* (the region in north India between Rivers Ganga and Jamuna). Delhi had also lost control over northwest India, and hence, import of Central Asian horses had ceased. As a result, the Lodhi army became dependent primarily on elephants and infantry. Political turmoil and military weakness of the Delhi Sultanate gave Babur an excellent opportunity to invade India. Babur copied artillery from the Ottomans, who were most famed in the non-European world for manufacturing such weapons. The slow-moving Lodhi army and the technologically inferior Rajput forces were easy victims for the firepower-heavy, yet maneuverable, Mughal army.

Biography: In 1494, Babur, a Turkish warlord, inherited the kingdom of Ferghana, a strip of land between Khiva and the desert of Takla Makan, from his father Sheikh Omar. Babur lost this ancestral kingdom, but not his zest for life: he liked dry fruits, wine, women, hunting, and fighting. Babur even composed Turki verses, which he read to his retainers before the onset of a great battle, and left us his autobiography, originally written in the Turki language, entitled *Tuzuk-i-Baburi*. When translated in Persian, it came to be known as *Babur Nama*. In 1504, Babur occupied Kabul. The Afghans were disunited and fought against each other. Moreover, the Afghans mostly relied on infantry equipped with spears. Babur's horse archers easily defeated them. Next, Babur invaded India and fought three battles, which resulted in the replacement of Afghan rule with the Mughals in the Ganga–Jamuna *doab*.

Influences: Babur's military theory was influenced by Central Asian and West Asian traditions. *Babur Nama* gives us information regarding the organization of the Mughal army: the smallest unit was 10 men under an officer; next came a unit of 50 soldiers (which was composed of five 10-soldier units) commanded by a superior officer. This organizing principle had originated with the Mongol Chingiz (Genghis) Khan. Babur also learnt the *taulqama* charge from the Uzbek leader Shaibani Khan, who had, in turn, copied it from Timur. The lesson was learned the hard way: in May 1501, Shaibani defeated Babur at the Battle of Sar-i-Pul near Samarkhand. Shaibani's horse archers simultaneously attacked both the flanks and rear of Babur's army. The Uzbek archers shot their arrows from horseback while they galloped around Babur's soldiers. Babur's army disintegrated and he escaped to Samarkhand, from where he moved into Kabul. During his sojourn here, Babur acquired firearms from the West Asian Muslims. About his next battle at Khanwa, fought on March 17, 1527, Babur writes: "We imitated the *ghazis* of Rum (Ottoman Turks) by posting matchlock men and cannoneers along the line of carts that were chained to one another in front of us." This technique was known as *tabur-jangi* in Turki (*Babur Nama,* vol. 2, p. 564). Babur depended on Ottoman gunners for manning his field guns, and his memoir even gives an account of gun casting by the Ottoman gunners in his pay.

The Theory: Babur's autobiography details the tactics and technology used by him in decisive battles. Chain-mail armor was issued to the heavy cavalry. Composite bows made of wood (later steel); horn and sinews were used by his horse archers. Generally, the length of such a Mughal composite bow was four feet. It was the use of mounted archers, rather than the guns, which was the principal factor behind Mughal victories. Armed with composite bows, a mounted archer could fire six times faster than a matchlock man, and in the 16th century, an arrow shot by such bows had more range and accuracy than a musket shot. Again, whereas a matchlock man offered a static target to the enemy, the mounted archer was mobile. By contrast, typical cannon could fire a maximum 16 times in a day—and several guns burst while firing.

Babur introduced special mounted officers in the battlefields for carrying orders to the commanders of the different contingents. He emphasized strict discipline among his soldiers: those soldiers who raped and murdered ordinary inhabitants were flogged to death. Babur also took care of his men and shared the same hardship with them during campaigns. Such acts endeared him to the ordinary soldiers.

Application: On April 12, 1526, the Mughal and Lodhi armies fought the First Battle of Panipat. Ibrahim Lodhi deployed a thousand-armored elephants, 20,000 cavalry equipped by the state and 20,000 cavalry mounted on Indian horses that were raised by the chiefs. In addition, Ibrahim had 30,000 infantry armed with pikes, swords, and bows. Since the Delhi Sultanate had lost control over Kabul, the Lodhi army did not possess horse archers. Babur, by contrast, had 12,000 horse archers and 13,000 musketeers and gunners. Babur positioned the mounted archers at his two flanks.

The Mughal left wing under Mahdi Khwaja was the first to engage the Lodhi force. Due to the arrows shot by the archers, the elephants opposed to Khwaja were forced to retire. In addition, the noises produced by the guns deployed at Babur's center unnerved the Lodhi soldiers. Then the Mughal mounted archers attacked the Lodhi army from both the flanks and the rear. The shower of arrows made Ibrahim's soldiers fall back on their own center. Soon, the Lodhi soldiers were massed so tightly that they could move neither forward against the Mughal army, nor retreat in an orderly manner. Ibrahim, along with 50,000 of his soldiers, died. Babur captured Delhi and took the title of *Padshah* (emperor).

However, Babur had to defeat the Rajputs before he could establish control over north India. He clashed with the Rajputs under their chief Rana Sanga at Khanwa. The battle started on the morning of March 17, 1527. The Mughals had about a thousand baggage carts placed in a linear formation and tied in Turki fashion with thongs of raw hide, to form an entrenched camp. Between every two carts, the distance was about 40 feet. *Mantlets* (movable shields) were placed in the gaps. Behind the *mantlets* were wheeled tripods from which the foot musketeers fired. The mortars and falconets were placed in the second line. Ustad Kuli was in charge of the guns at the 10,000-strong center. The right wing of the Mughal army under Prince Humayun was 5,000 strong, and the left wing 3,000 strong. At both the wings were placed *taulqama* parties of 1,000 horse archers each.

The Rajputs made a frontal attack, but the charge was destroyed by the Mughal mortars and handguns. The Rana was severely wounded by an arrow shot by such a Mughal mounted archer marksman ordered to pick off enemy commanders, and he fainted on the battlefield and was taken to safety. Two hours later, he awoke to learn that the Mughals were victorious.

After the defeat of the Rajputs, the Afghans rallied in Bihar, and Babur directed his force against them. On May 6, 1529, at the Battle of Ghagra, mortars and matchlocks gave victory to the Mughals. *Babur Nama* notes that in this battle, the Afghans of Bengal used *bans* (rockets) comprising combustible ingredients in bamboo cases against the Mughal army. The Mughals adopted the use of *bans* from the Afghans. The *bans* were considered by the English traders of Balasore Factory as more dangerous than grenades.

The combination of horse archery and gunpowder weapons (matchlocks and field guns) remained the basis of Mughal army under Babur's successors. Humayun maintained 5,000 matchlock men. The Mughal field guns were of two types. One type of guns discharged stone shot and another type discharged shot made of brass.

Things started going wrong for the Mughals after Babur's death in 1530, when his eldest son Humayun ascended the throne. In 1539, the Afghan warlord Sher Shah defeated the Mughals at the Battle of Chausa. Humayun escaped but was defeated again in 1540 at Bilgram. Several factors were responsible for the Mughal defeat. First, due to the treacherous behavior of Mirza Kamran, the governor of Kabul and Humayun's half brother, Humayun was not able to deploy horse archers in his battles against Sher Shah. And following Babur, Sher Shah used mortars made of copper and maintained matchlock men.

Descendents: Babur Nama influenced the production of *Jahangir Nama,* which describes the military achievements of the Mughals between 1605 and 1627. The region beyond the Northwest Frontier was held by the Uzbeks, the traditional enemy of the Mughals. Campaign against them was not feasible. Also, east of Bengal, the unhealthy jungles and Arakan Yoma range discouraged expansion into Burma. So, the Mughals decided to expand in Deccan. Akbar started the process and Jahangir continued this. *Jahangir Nama* tells us that in 1608, Mahabat Khan, a Mughal general, was given 12,000 cavalry, 2,500 foot musketeers, and 80 cannons, plus camels and elephants and ordered to proceed to Deccan. Here, the rocky, mountainous terrain made high-speed cavalry warfare nonpracticable. So, the Mughals had to rely more on foot musketeers and artillery. As in Babur's time, the muskets were fired from wooden tripods.

See also: Fazl, Abul; Timur, Amir (or Tamerlane or Timur the Lame)

Further Reading

Babur, Zahiruddin Muhammad, *Babur Nama,* tr. by A.S. Beveridge, 2 vols. 2nd ed. New Delhi: Saeed International, 1989.

Lane-Poole, Stanley, *The Emperor Babur.* Delhi: Sunita Publications, 1988.

Kaushik Roy

Baghdadi Manjaniqi, Yaʿqūb Ibn Ṣābir
(554–626/1159–1229)

Significance: Baghdadi was responsible for making and using devices or machines by which stones, dead animals that had epidemic diseases, and sometimes even sewage were thrown up to enemies' line. Those machines were called *manjaniq*. The title "Manjaniqi," attributed to *manjaniq,* given to Baghdadi, indicates that he had a great experience in practicing as well as making those machines. In addition, he knew mathematics well to calculate the distance of the army to enemy lines or walls and to form the settlement of those machines in a way that shooting would be accurate. By his carrier and his expertise, he could help the Abbasid army to protect city Baghdad against different attacks. It is said that in the period of the Crusade (11th to 13th centuries), the industry of making and using advanced catapults or *manjaniqs* optimized in wars. Thus, those who had the knowledge or the experience in the art, such as Baghdadi, who lived during that period, can be considered of special significance.

Baghdadi was also the head of a group were responsible for planning a tactic for the army. The tactics included the organization of soldiers, offering a plan for besieging castles of enemy, the definition of places for the settlement of the horseback, the personnel who employed catapults, and the composition of military movements. As historical sources have pointed out, Baghdadi had written a chapter in his book on each part of military engineering.

Context: During his life, there existed many competitions and battles between local and central powers in Islamic territories. In 573/1177, Iraq fell under the domination of a local dynasty of Saljuq princes, the last of whom was Ṭughril II (r. 573–590/1177–1194). Two major dynasties of the Middle East were weakened; the Ayyubids (r. 564–648/1168–1250) in Egypt and Syria were preoccupied with the struggle against the Crusaders, and the Khārazmshahs in Persia with their wars against other Turkish dynasties and then against the Mongols. In this power vacuum, al-Nāṣir Li Dīn Allah, 34th Abbasid caliph (r. 575–622/1180–1225) was trying to restore the lost authority of the caliphate in Baghdad. He increased his authority by arranging an army of his own and by making temporary alliances with Muslim and non-Muslim partners to consolidate the caliphate against all kinds of military, political, and ideological attacks. Baghdadi could gain position and legitimacy in the court of al-Nāṣir by serving to his army and by composing some poetry for the majesty of caliph. Showing himself as an emulator of Alid sentiment (attributed to Ali, the son-in-law of the Prophet Muhammad and the first Imam of Muslim Shiite School), using some Sufi teachings, al-Nāṣir called himself a mediator between God and the people. He was also engaged in transmitting some traditions attributed to the Prophet Muhammad. He by reorganizing some comradely federal groups of men, called *Futuwwa* groups, could gain popularity among Sunnite and Shiite people and consequently could decrease their long conflicts. The caliph imagined that philosophers' ideas and their followers may lead to inner disintegration of the society. At the time, Shahāb al-Dīn Suhrawardī (d. 587/1191), a great Iranian philosopher, because of his ideas in religious and political matters, was killed and his body was burnt by the decree of jurists and by the order of the Ayyūbid Sultan Ṣalāḥ al-Dīn in Aleppo.

Al-Nāṣir, to dominate his competitors, firstly made an alliance with Khārazm Shah to get military support against Ṭughril II, from the Saljuqids, and then after falling of the reign of Saljuqs (590/1194), the caliph found himself confronted with a new power in Sultan Muhammad Khārazm Shah. Because the caliph could not solve his conflict with Khārazm Shah, it is said that he had entered into negotiations with Mongols to encourage them to attack Persia. Even though the details of actual events are not completely clear, one of the greatest tragedies in Islamic history began with the Mongol invasion against the Khārazmids. Al-Nāṣir's successors were weak and when the Mongols, having already conquered Persia, appeared before Baghdad in 656/1258, the last caliph al-Muʿtaṣim was unable to offer any serious resistance and then the city was invaded (See *Encyclopaedia of Islam*, second version, s. v. "Nāṣir Li-Dīn Allah, Abu 'L ʿAbbās," vol. 7: 996b ff.).

Biography: Baghdadi originally was from Harran, close to the board of Turkey and Syria, but born in Baghdad in 554/1159. It is mentioned in an unusual report that he was born in 593/1196 and died in 675/1276. A little is known on his life and the whole information that is available was quoted non-chronologically by his contemporary biographer Ibn Khallakān (d. 680/1281) concentrating on quoting Baghdadi's poems by which he praised the Abbasid caliphs or he reproached Sufi's ideas and behaviors. Later biographers, more or less, repeated what would be found in Ibn Khallakān's work. Baghdadi at first was employed as an ordinary member of the army, working in the group of whom used *manjaniq,* but later he was known as a famous engineer, in the narrow sense of the word, champion and maker of different weapons such as sword and *manjaniq.* Even it is reported that he became toward the end of his life the head of engineers and nobody could compete with him in the skills. Among his poems, one can find two in which he introduced himself as a lover and an innovator of making and using *manjaniq* to kill the enemy and to expand the Muslim territory. It is said that he was honorable, good tempered, and well spoken.

Two books are attributed to him; one of them is a collection of his poems *Maghānī al-Maʿānī* and the other one which, according to biographers, remained incomplete is *ʿUmdat al-Sālik fī Siyāsati al-Mamālik [The Principle of Disciple in the Policy of Countries]*. The latter, which a little content of it is quoted in later works, in accordance with historical sources, concerns military matters such as the history of wars, how to use the weapons especially *manjaniq,* how to organize the army, how to engineer the war, how to compose military moves, etc. A copy of this book, as far as we know, is not available but in the later military works it is frequently mentioned as one of the essential references in this field.

Influences: The relevant sources are silent on mentioning the names of Baghdadi's instructors as well as his disciples in the military field. They, however, introduced some people as his teachers and his students in literary fields, especially in the task of composing poems, which are beyond of the scope of this study.

Further Reading

The earliest Baghdadi's biography written by Ibn Khallakān, *Wafayāt al-Aʿyān wa Anbāʾu Abnāʾ al-Zamān*. Ed. By Ihsān ʿAbbas, Beirut: Dār al-Thiqāfa, n. d., vol. 7: 36–46. Latter biographers more or less reproduced the information in their works. Then, most historical primary sources by which one can gain information concerning the context of the caliphate in Baghdad and its relation with other local governments at the time are in Arabic or Persian. However, reading following articles is suggested:

Bosworth, C.E., "The Political and Dynastic History of the Iranian World," in *The Cambridge History of Iran*. Ed. by J.A. Boyle, Cambridge: Cambridge University Press 1968, esp. 167–178, 183–202.

The Encyclopaedia of Islam, second version. s. v. "Nāṣir Li-Dīn Allah, Abu 'L ʿAbbās" by Angelika Hartmann, vol. 7: 996b ff. Leiden: Brill, 1960–2004.

Furthermore for knowing the role of 'manjaniq' in the Muslim army, see, *ibid.,* s. v. "Mandjanīḳ" by D.R. Hill, vol. 6: 405–406.

Saeid Edalatnejad

Bana
(ca. seventh century CE)

Significance: Bana was the first known Sanskrit prose writer to write in praise of his patron. The chronicle, entitled *Harsacharita,* furnishes historical details about Harsavardhana or Harsa (606–648 CE), the ruler of Kanauj and, together with the Chinese traveler Hsuan-Tsang's account, provides the best literary source concerning immediate post-Gupta Indian history. Bana had access both to the royal court and familiarity with the low castes in the north Indian society. He throws light on army structure, and on weapons, logistics, and objectives of war, with particular focus on the importance of elephants and horses, and on the control of various contingents on contemporary Indian battlefields.

Context: Bana portrays Harsa's kingdom as a decentralized realm. Unlike the Maurya Empire, the Gupta Empire, which came into existence during fourth century CE, was characterized by small kings with considerable autonomy. A major portion of the Gupta Empire was ruled by feudatories and Gupta civil administrative fabric was weak. In contrast to the Maurya monarchs, the Gupta emperors did not possess a large standing army, and troops supplied by the feudatories comprised a large portion of the Gupta army. The Guptas also did not enjoy a monopoly on elephants and horses, two crucial instruments for waging warfare in India.

As soon as Gupta central government was weakened due to the invasions of the Huns, the feudatories proclaimed independence. After the Gupta collapse in the sixth century CE, numerous small principalities, based upon earlier feudatories, dotted the subcontinent. Most prominent of these was the Pushyabatis of Thaneswar. Post-Gupta regional kingdoms were characterized by decentralized administrative structures and feudalism. Its political expression was the *samanta* system, in which the king was at the top and below him was a hierarchy of *mahasamantas* (big vassals) and *samantas* (small vassals). The *samantas* were ranked in accordance with the size of land granted to them and their ranks in the court. The practice of assignment of land in perpetuity and the creation of fiefs became more common. The grantees discharged administrative duties in lieu of land assignments, and gradually replaced the centralized bureaucracy initially created by the Mauryas. Sub-infeudation was seen more often. The landed intermediaries acquired the right of imposing various taxes and *vishti* (forced labor). Peasants, artisans, and merchants were transferred along with the land to the grantees, had to obey the commands of the grantees, and had to remain attached with the donated land. Decline of commerce and de-urbanization resulted in autarchic village economies, which strengthened the landed magnates' stranglehold over the polity and economy. The net result was parcellization of sovereignty. Royal dynasties did not have fixed capitals—the monarch was always on the move to deter dangerous feudatories.

Harsacharita also deals with the invasion of the Huns, who occupied Bactria and threatened India during the reign of the Gupta monarch Kumaragupta (415–454 CE). Toward the end of fifth century CE, the Huns entered India. They were excellent archers and skillful horsemen, and probably used metal and wooden stirrups. This triggered a Hindu military response, including the use of saddles and saddle clothes on horses. The paintings on the Ajanta caves show that in fourth century CE, bits were used for controlling the horses. The dissolution of the Gupta Empire coincided with the establishment of the Hun kingdom in northwest India.

Biography: Bana, also known as Banabhatta, was born in a family of intellectuals, whose forefathers had enjoyed the patronage of the Gupta monarchs. Bana imbibed the knowledge of the *shastras* (religious literature) and the *puranic* (genealogical lists of the mythical as well as ancient historical kings of India) tradition. After the death of his father, Bana mixed with undesirable characters and became a sort of wanderer. While wandering across north India, Bana was introduced to Harsa. Initially, Harsa, who himself was a poet, was skeptical about Bana's abilities, but he later honored him.

Influences: Bana's concept of interstate relationship is derived from Kautilya's *Arthashastra,* written around 300 BCE. Bana divides states into three categories: friends, neutrals, and enemies. Bana's vision of empire as a loose federation of allies dominated by the *vijigishu* (the universal ruler or the ideal monarch) is similar to that of Kamandaka in *Nitisara,* written in the century before *Harsacharita.* Like Kautilya and Kamandaka, Bana does not accept the compartmentalization of warfare into conflict with external powers and internal pacification. In agreement with them, he argues that external threat and internal insurgencies act and react with each other, and that some internal rebels should ideally be co-opted by the paramount power.

Unlike Kautilya, Bana is a proponent of *dharmayuddha* (just war). Bana, in the novel *Kadambari,* writes that Kautilya was wicked and cruel. The execution of the Maurya Emperor Brihadratha in 187 BCE, by his *senapati* (commander in chief) Pusyamitra Sunga, writes Bana, is an example of the worst form of *kutayuddha* (unjust war).

Bana is also influenced by Somadeva Bhatta, who wrote *Kathasaritsagara* around 500 CE. *Kathasaritsagara,* a collection of tales, throw light on contemporary society, polity, and morality. *Kutayuddha* is propounded in parts of *Kathasaritsagara,* and Bana advises that, although an ideal king should not conduct *kutayuddha,* he must be aware that his enemies might practice such warfare. Bana advises that the *vijigishu* should follow righteous warfare stipulated in certain tales of *Kathasaritsagara.* The threat of using force and alliances are the mechanisms for expanding state power. Initially, a defeated ruler should be allowed to rule as a vassal. But, if he revolts, he should be killed.

In central India, most of the Hindu kings' armies, says Somadeva Bhatta, relied on elephants. The best elephants, says Bana, following Somadeva Bhatta,
were acquired from Kamrup (Assam). *Harsacharita's* discussion on the role of
elephant doctors in the army is influenced by the discussion in *Agni Purana* (a
collection of verses by unknown authors composed around 500 CE). The king,
says *Agni Purana,* should appoint people with special training to look after the
war elephants.

Bana, following Somadeva Bhatta, also emphasizes the mobility of the cavalry.
Somadeva Bhatta compares good horses with gods and *Kathsaritsagara* hints at
the danger posed by the cavalry of the *yavanas* (Indo-Greeks, Kushanas, and the
Sakas) along northwest India. Indian kings are warned to maintain grasslands for
their own cavalry.

The Theory: Bana's *Harsacharita* is a historical fiction. He is not a historian but
a poet and an epic bard, decorating his tale with fancy and fantasy, and adding
spicy romantic tales and adventure stories. In contemporary Sanskrit literature,
the idea to be conveyed was concealed beneath the verbiage of metaphors, imag-
eries, adjectives, and complicated adverbs. Bana's prose is a typical example of
stylistic pleonasm, and he created a new style of prose writing by applying all the
rhetorical devices of kavya (poetry) to prose. However, in Sanskrit terminology,
Harsacharita is categorized as an *akhyayika,* which means a story somewhat ro-
manticized but rooted in authentic historical tradition. As the outline of the tale is
factually correct, it is a useful source for inferring the doctrines of force structure
and utilization of Harsa-era Indian armies.

Harsacharita is divided into eight chapters and the narrative follows a linear chronology. Chapter 4 discusses the story of Prabhakarvardhana, the ruler
of Thaneswar from 585 to 606 CE, who checked the Huns and defeated the
rulers of Sind, Gujarat, and Gandhara (Kandahar in Afghanistan). Prabhakarvardhana's queen Yasomati gave birth to two sons named Rajyavardhana
and Harsavardhana (Harsa) and a daughter named Rajyashri. The latter married Grahavarman of the Maukhari family, who ruled at Kanyakubja. Chapter
5 tells us that when Rajyavardhana and Harsha were engaged in fighting the
Huns, Prabhakarvardhana died. Meanwhile, the king of Malava (central Punjab) assassinated Grahavarman, and kidnapped Rajyashri. Chapter 6 portrays
how Rajyavardhana and a cavalry contingent numbering 10,000 attacked the
Malava king. Harsa, with main body of the army, composed of infantry and elephants, followed behind. The king of Malava was defeated. Then Sasanka, the
king of Gauda (Bengal), invited Rajyavardhana for a meeting where Sasanka
treacherously killed Rajyavardhana. Bana thoroughly criticizes this expression of *kutayuddha.*

After the murder of his elder brother, Harsa manipulated the ministers to confirm his succession. Then to legitimize his succession, Harsa resolved to avenge
the death of Rajyavardhana. Although Harsa's *senapati* Simhananda applauded

the king's decision, the chief of his elephant division warned him against the treachery and political intrigues of the vassal rulers.

An account of Harsa's military campaign is given in Chapter 7. Like a *vijigishu*, Harsa after ascending the throne followed the policy of *digvijaya*. The literal meaning of *digvijaya* is conquering the world, but its actual meaning is establishing a pan-Indian empire. Harsa set out with a huge army, captured Kanauj and extended his sway over eastern India and Kalinga (Orissa). Harsa's tributary rulers included those of Nepal, Jalandhar (Punjab), Kashmir, Valabhi and Kamrup.

Bana refers to the conches, kettledrums and various types of banners for commanding the various military units in the battlefield. Under Harsa, the war elephant department was placed in the charge of Skandagupta (not to be confused with the last great Gupta Emperor Skandagupta). On top of the elephants iron plated *howdahs* (box-like seating arrangements) were placed from which the warriors discharged arrows at the enemy soldiers. Elephants were acquired, writes Bana, by the forest rangers employed by Harsa. The rangers had emissaries who collected information about the movement of the elephant herds. In addition, the autonomous forest tribes occasionally presented elephants to their political overlord, Harsa. Sometimes elephants were taken from the defeated rulers and also as tributes from the tributary kings. Harsa's army maintained elephant doctors. For training the young elephants in battles, figures of elephants were used.

Occasionally, a cavalry contingent was used for rapid pursuit of the enemy and for making sudden attack. Mounted archers on Kamboja (Gandhara) horses are mentioned in *Harsacharita*. The riders were equipped with bows with leather quivers tied at their back, and wore soft dark trousers and tunics with Chinese cuirasses. The king commanded on the battlefield by riding on horses, and not on chariots as was the practice in the Vedic era. The best horses were acquired from Kamboja, Sindhu (Indus region), and Persia (Iran). Because Kamboja and Sindhu were under the control of the Huns, continuous clashes occurred between the Harsa's kingdom of Thaneswar and the Huns.

For logistical purpose, Bana mentions utilization of camels. Oxen and hired porters were also used for conveying supplies. In accordance with the custom of *vishti*, villagers were forced to provide supplies for Harsa's military camp. The infantry was used for collecting provisions from the villagers and for preparing the road through which the army marched. Many village headmen appealed to Harsa for protection of their crops from the rampaging soldiers.

The foot soldiers, says *Harsacharita*, wore half-sleeved tunics, trousers or *dhoti*, waistband, and sandals with ankle straps. From Gandhara sculpture, it is clear that the sandals resembled those worn by Roman legionaries. Long swords, round shields, spears, and daggers were the principal infantry weapons. The shield was made of leather and circular in shape. In general, the soldiers were protected with armor. However, the arrows used by the Huns were dangerous and penetrated even the armor. The wounds were dressed with long white bandages. Forts protected by moats and rock walls are also mentioned in *Harsacharita*. After victory in a campaign, overseers were appointed to take charge of the booty.

Harsa wielded power over a feudalized realm. As evident from *Harsacharita*, Harsa ruled from various camps to deter the feudatories from rebelling. His standing army was small and it was supplemented during campaigns by the contingents bought by his *samantas, srenibalas* (soldiers provided by guilds), and semiautonomous tribes. For example, a forest tribe named Sabaras in central India had their own army. Harsa allowed them autonomy in internal administration and in return the Sabaras had to provide military contingents for Harsa's campaign, where they were placed under one of his commanders. The combat effectiveness of such a composite army was bound to be low.

Bana describes Harsa's army breaking camp at dawn before marching. Barrack superintendents were in charge of the camp. Thousands of torches were lit to dispel the darkness of early morning, and were accompanied by shrill words of command from the marshals. The horses were saddled and the elephants were loaded with a cargo of utensils. High born nobles' wives, other women, large number of other noncombatants, and numerous baggage animals accompanied Harsa's army, which was not capable of quick mobility. Abandoned grain was looted by the local poor when the army marched off.

Hsuan-Tsang wrongly ascribes the presence of a chariot corps in Harsa's army—Bana does not refer to it. In the post-Gupta period, for the big military powers within India, chariots had become useless. This is evident from the accounts of other Chinese travelers and Muslim chroniclers. According to Yuaan Chwang, who visited north India during the first half of the seventh century CE, the force structure of Harsa during his accession included 5,000 elephants, 29,000 cavalry, and 50,000 infantry. Toward the end of his life, Harsa increased the size of his army, and the elephant and cavalry corps were expanded much more compared to the infantry. Hsuan-Tsang and Bana agree that Harsa increased the number of cavalry from 20,000 to 100,000. Each elephant was probably accompanied by four to six soldiers, and the total number of elephant soldiers in Harsa's army numbered 60,000. The increase in the number of elephants was stimulated by Harsa's enemy Pulakesi II's reliance on elephants.

Bana, being a court poet of Harsa, could be accused of writing a biased account of his patron. Even Hsuan-Tsang, the Chinese Buddhist pilgrim, was pro-Harsa, because Harsa embraced Buddhism. Therefore, a critical comparison of *Harsacharita* and Hsuan-Tsang's account is not helpful. Certainly, *Harsacharita* exaggerates the achievements of Harsa. In his career, Harsa suffered many defeats, which were glossed over by Bana. For example, Harsa clashed with Pulakesi II of the Chalukya dynasty, the ruler of Badami (Karnataka), sometime between 630 and 633 CE, partly over access to elephants, and Harsa was defeated. Harsa's campaigns in west India also did not bring much success. Far from establishing a pan-Indian empire, Harsa, despite the assertion of Bana, could not be justified in taking his title of *sakal uttara patha natha* (lord of north India).

Application: Harsacharita's description of an increase in the size of elephant corps was justified by events following the collapse of Harsa's empire, when the Rashtrakutas of Deccan, the Palas of Bengal, and the Gurjara-Pratiharas of west India fought for domination of Kanauj. The wide plains of north India and Punjab were suited for large-scale, mobile cavalry battles. However, elephants and infantry were more suitable than cavalry in the mountainous and forested region of central India, especially along the Vindhya Mountain range where most of the battles occurred. In the post-Harsa era, soldiers with bows and arrows from the *howdahs* decimated the infantry. The elephants were also used to storm fortresses, and were designated as mobile forts.

The tri-polar army comprised infantry, cavalry, and elephants, as described in *Harsacharita,* became the typical force structure of post-Harsa Hindu armies. Al-Utbi commented that in 1001 CE, the army of Jaipala, Raja of Bhatinda, was composed of 300 elephants, 12,000 horses, and 30,000 foot. In *Tabaqat-i-Akbari,* Nizamuddin Ahmad places the strength of Chandella's army in 1019 CE at 390 elephants, 36,000 horses, and 145,000 infantry.

Bana's description of a cavalry force as an independent tactical arm, both for long range reconnaissance and as a strike force, was emulated by the Gurjara-Pratiharas. In 851 CE, Sulaiman noted that the Gurjara-Pratihara King Mihir Bhoja employed large numbers of cavalry in a tactically independent mobile capacity, thereby checking the expansion of the Arabs from Sind. The Gurjara-Pratihara's cavalry was considered the best among the Indian powers because of that power's proximity to the sources of supply.

The use of camels as beasts of burden for the army, as advocated by Bana, increased with time. The Gurjara-Pratiharas maintained a camel corps that supported their armies when it fought the Arabs of Sind in the desert of western Rajasthan. The camels were acquired from Gujarat. From the eighth century CE onward, camels became an essential part of the Rajput armies operating in Rajasthan. Most of the camels were procured from Sind.

The trend toward the "privatization" of warfare strengthened in the early medieval era. Business corporations such as the guilds of silk weavers in west India maintained private soldiers. In fact, several traders' corporations in south India such as *Vira-Valanjiyas* (made up of low-caste communities) and *Kaikollars* (silk-weavers' guild of Tamil Nadu) provided armies when the Chola and Sri Lankan monarchs went to war.

Descendents: Some later writers within the Hindu intellectual tradition, in contrast to Bana, gave more importance to cavalry. The Jain intellectual Somadeva Suri (not to be confused with Somadeva Bhatta the author of *Kathasaritsagara*), writing in 10th century CE in his *Nitivakyamitra,* noted that cavalry provides mobility and that, to emerge victorious, a king must be strong in cavalry. The Chalukyan Emperor Somesvara (1127–1138 CE) comments in *Manasollasa* that a strong cavalry force is essential for conducting offensive and defensive campaigns. Somesvara, following Bana, wrote that the best horses came from Sind and Kamboja, but by his time, due to the Arab invasion of Sind in the eighth century CE, good horses were also imported from Arabia. Kalhana's *Rajatarangini* (composed between 1148 and 1150 CE in Sanskrit) describes how the rulers of Kashmir expended vast treasure in buying horses from Afghanistan and Central Asia. The Suleiman Mountains west of Indus also became famous as a horse-breeding area.

From *Harsacharita,* it is clear that Harsa's army depended on organized looting and forced contributions from the countryside. By contrast, Sukra's *Sukranitisara,* written around the ninth century CE, recommends a well-organized state-supported logistical infrastructure. Sukra also focuses on the linkages between operational efficiency and logistical sufficiency. To prevent indiscipline, says Sukra, the soldiers were not to be allowed to engage in plundering, and the ruler is advised to open markets inside the camp for distributing supplies to the soldiers.

See also: Hindu Tradition of Just and Unjust War; Kamandaka; Kautilya; Use of Elephants in Indian Warfare

Further Reading

Banabhatta, *The Harsacharita,* tr. by E. P. Cowell and P. W. Thomas, ed. by R. P. Shastri. Delhi: Global Vision Publishing House, 2004.
Devahuti, D., *Harsha: A Political Study.* Oxford: Clarendon Press, 1970.
Jha, D. N., *Early India: A Concise History.* New Delhi: Manohar, 2004.
Sandhu, Gurcharn Singh, *A Military History of Ancient India.* New Delhi: Vision Books, 2000.

Kaushik Roy

Basta, Giorgio, Count of Huszt
(1544–1607)

Significance: He was the first known Early Modern European theorist who published on light cavalry operations.

Context: Basta served the Emperor Rudolf during the "long" Turkish War 1591–1606. Too little is known of military thinkers of the late 1500s to give a picture of Basta's intellectual milieu.

Biography: Basta, the Imperial governor in Transylvania in the early 1600s, was of likely Albanian descent, and is a figure of some controversy in the Balkans. Although successful, he was also notorious for his ruthless efforts to root out Protestants from Transylvania.

Descendents: Included are potentially Wallenstein, Montecúccoli, other Thirty Years commanders, and "petit guerre" practitioners.

Further Reading
Basta, Giorgio, Count of Huszt, *Maestro di campo generale* (Venice, 1606).
Basta, Giorgio, Count of Huszt, *Guerro della cavalliera leggiere* (Venice, 1612).

Erik A. Lund

Bonaparte, Napoleon
(1769–1821)

Significance: Napoleon ranks as the first master practitioner of modern war. He was only in part its inventor. Many of the changes he wrought in 20 years of European conflict derive from in the ideas of Pierre-Joseph de Bourcet (1700–1780), Comte Jacques de Guibert (1743–1790), General Jean-Pierre Duteil (1722–1794) and his younger brother Chevalier Joseph du Teil (1738–1820), and the French Revolutionary reformer Lazare de Carnot (1753–1823). However, his systematic application of those ideas makes Napoleon the most important innovator of the 19th century.

From 1802 onward, in which he initially became First Consul and later emperor, Napoleon was simultaneously the sovereign of France and its supreme military commander. Combined with his extraordinary military, political and administrative talents, this situation facilitated the closest integration of national policy with the prosecution of war; sped the implementation of decisions; and enhanced Napoleon's ability to revise his diplomacy in response to changing military conditions. The Napoleonic Wars are an appropriate label for a period of transformation, above all of the scale of European warfare. Campaigns typically involving ten of the thousands of troops came to consume hundreds of thousands.

Napoleon was not foremost a military theorist. He wrote about and discussed what he understood as the principles of war, yet he never gave them coherent and comprehensive expression. He was both a gifted and a studied practitioner of military campaigning and battlefield tactics, with an intuitive grasp of the relationship between tactical and strategic dimensions of war. He was, most importantly, a genius of practical innovation, able to recognize the utility of new ideas and discard tradition unsentimentally. He is noted specifically for the introduction of the combined-arms *corps d'armée* and the quadrilateral formation of *bataillon carré*. Applied together, this gave his strategic maneuvering flexibility, aimed at forcing his opponent to accept decisive battle and thereupon to face Napoleon's annihilating aggression. Between 1804 and 1809 in particular, Napoleon chalked a series of spectacular victories that revolutionized European warfare and began its evolution toward the total wars of the 20th century. Napoleon's shocking success greatly stimulated the theories of Clausewitz and Jomini, under whose pen a Napoleon legend first took shape. It remains compelling for many students of military history today.

Context: The French Revolution created the circumstances in which a soldier of Napoleon's abilities and background—an opportunist of aristocratic origin with neither loyalty to the aristocracy nor love of democracy—could prosper professionally. The revolution coincided with changes in thinking about the conduct of war during the last decades of the monarchy. The military literature of the late Enlightenment proposed reforms in both military institutions and practices. These, although partly implemented by the *ancien Régime,* were given new vigor by the Jacobin leadership and the directory. Not only did the revolution need to defend itself, but its export throughout Europe was also integral to republican ideology. The critical feature of both imperatives—and the cornerstone of war as Napoleon prosecuted it—was the adoption by the directory of universal conscription. This produced French armies of an unprecedented size and posed new organizational problems, which recent military literature answered in part, but which had to be mastered and refined in the application.

Fortunately for Bonaparte's generation of French officers, the revolution occasioned war between France and much of the rest of Europe. The size of the army's staff expanded and the avenues of upward mobility for officers increased. The Revolutionary Wars provided opportunity for new talent to prove itself. Of these, Napoleon was the foremost: British Prime Minister William Pitt exaggerated only slightly with his observation that initially, Napoleon was the revolution's "child and champion."

Biography: He was born Napoleone da Buonaparté in Ajaccio on Corsica in 1769 to parents descended from lesser Tuscan nobility. At age 10, Napoleon was sent to a religious school at Autun in Burgundy and from there to a cadet school at Brienne in Champagne, where as a withdrawn but industrious student he demonstrated a facility in history, mathematics, and geography. At 15, he was nominated as a *boursier* for the *École Royale Militaire* on the Champs de Mars in Paris. Whereas the average cadet at the *École Militaire* required from two to three years to complete the curriculum, Bonaparte completed its passing out examination after one year. At 16, he was commissioned as a second lieutenant in the royal corps of artillery and was stationed with the La Fère artillery regiment in Valence-sur-Rhône.

In 1787, the regiment moved to Auxonne. Here, it functioned as depot for the School of Artillery commanded by Major General Jean-Pierre Duteil, among the most distinguished gunnery experts in the French army. Napoleon was thus able to learn the latest technical and tactical developments in artillery. His zeal prompted Duteil to nominate him to serve on a committee tasked with determining how explosive rounds might be fired from long-barreled guns. Duteil became first a formative influence, and then a friend and advisor. In addition, Napoleon tackled a strenuous self-education in the lives of Alexander, Hannibal, Caesar—training his memory by composing a digest of every book he read—while familiarizing himself in a particularly timely fashion with Rousseau's ideas in the *Contrat Social.* By the outbreak of the revolution, Napoleon had supplemented his military instruction with an education in history and a sense of the political ideas behind the upheavals of his time. When in 1791 the new National Assembly ordered all officers to sign a pledge of allegiance, Napoleon declared himself for the republic.

In August 1792, Napoleon was promoted to captain. The following year, Revolutionary France, now at war with Britain, the Netherlands, and Spain, sent him to assist in the recapture of Toulon from Royalist forces backed by British and Spanish units. Though a junior commander, he organized its artillery and contributed to the victory all out of proportion to his rank. The assault, which he planned and led with reckless physical courage, launched Napoleon's military career. A promotion to *général de brigade* followed. Napoleon's career was then imperiled with the fall of Robespierre in July 1794 and the arrest of Jacobin sympathizer. Even after his release, he was not restored to his former artillery command. Rather, his next engagement tested his loyalty to the Convention by pitting his guns in its defense against the royalist rising of the 13 Vendemiaire in Paris. The "whiff of grapeshot" with which Napoleon put the rising to flight was a pivotal event for both the republic and himself. As the reward, Napoleon sought and received command of France's beleaguered army in Italy. A major command in Lazare Carnot's reformed army—and the raw material of an entirely new war machine—came into the hands of the republic's most gifted general. The Napoleonic era of warfare got properly underway.

Influences: Along with the large conscript army initially conceived in Carnot's *levée en masse,* Napoleon also inherited a substantial legacy of 18th-century doctrinal thinking and military reorganization. He employed and refined these in rapid, flexible, and massively destructive offensive operations.

Napoleon had absorbed the ideas of Marshal Count Maurice de Saxe on increasing the mobility and maneuverability of armies, and creating self-contained, all arms "legions"—in substance the forerunner of the "division." Saxe also envisaged the use of swarms of skirmishers to precede the main infantry assault on an enemy force. After 1750, these principles became common to French battle tactics.

Direct and important influences include Bourcet and Guibert. The former insisted that an attacking army should advance in parallel columns to converge at the critical time and place for advantage of weight in numbers. The latter stressed maximum battlefield maneuverability and advised that a campaigning army must live off the country it occupied.

Napoleon also learned from Jean-Baptise de Gribeauval, who rationalized the distribution of the calibers of cannons according to their use for siege, infantry, or cavalry support. This reduced the weight of equipment without loss in firepower or range. Napoleon's instructor at Auxonne, General Jean-Pierre Duteil, taught this system to his star student. His younger brother, Jean "the Chevalier" du Teil, Bonaparte's immediate superior at Toulon, promoted the use of light and rapid horse artillery to support cavalry in the French army, in imitation and improvement of their use by Frederick "the Great" in the Prussian army during the Seven Years'

War. Although Bonaparte read Frederick's biography during his time at Auxonne, the king's direct impact on Bonaparte is difficult to measure.

The Theory and Application: Napoleon was therefore primarily a synthesizer of the ideas of his predecessors, and a brilliant practitioner, who refined and improved the theories of preceding generations.

His first use of strategic maneuver with combined-arms forces—and first stage of the incremental development of a Napoleonic "theory" of war—came in the Italian campaign of 1796–1797. His recovery of a badly deteriorated French situation initially involved an offensive to strike Austro-Piedmontese forces. This divided them and subsequently allowed him to rout the Austrians alone at Lodi. In this engagement, he confronted the Austrians with two divisions after executing a forced march of 115 kilometers in two days, and completing a *manoeuvre sur les derrières* of the Austrian army. He later repeated the maneuver at Bassano near Mantua and personally led an assault of grenadiers across a bridge at Arcola. Ultimately, he directed his army in three separate columns to concentrate at Rivoli to defeat another Austrian army and thereafter open up a strategic offensive against Austria itself.

Napoleon's Egyptian campaign of 1798 was notable for impressive forced marches, but also for the spectacular victory over the Mamelukes in the Battle of the Pyramids. However, after Nelson destroyed the supporting French fleet at Aboukir Bay, it became an early episode in strategic overextension.

Napoleon seized power from the Directory in the *coup d' etat* of 18 Brumaire in 1799, as the war of the Second Coalition threatening France with invasion. With Italy lost and France's position in Germany imperiled, Bonaparte began to fashion a new instrument of warfare with a reorganization as sweeping as the constitutional and administrative reforms he imposed on the nation as First Consul. The centerpiece of change was the establishment of multidivisional army corps, both in Italy and along France's frontier on the Rhine. A corps typically consisted of two or three divisions, including infantry and cavalry, of 8,000 men each. Each division broke down into two brigades, each brigade into two regiments, and each regiment into two battalions. Commanded by a single general, a corps featured such a mixture of infantry, cavalry, artillery, engineers, and service troops. This made it capable of independent operations. Its size, self-reliance and unity of command made it the basic maneuver element of all Napoleonic armies.

Napoleon instructed his chief of staff, General Louis-Alexandre Berthier, to assemble an army of reserve some 60,000 strong at Dijon. The reorganization began formally on March 1, 1800, when Napoleon instructed General Jean-Victor Moreau to divide his army of the Rhine into four corps. By 1805, French corps were stationed all over Western Europe so that they could be brought together to deliver battle anywhere with the necessary speed and weight of numbers.

The first test of these forces was the campaign of April–June 1800 in northwestern Italy, which climaxed at Marengo. Napoleon used five different passes through Switzerland, and the campaign achieved Bonaparte's fundamental goal—despite some severe logistical problems—of presenting the Austrian army in Italy with French forces converging on it from the west, north, and east. However, at the climatic engagement Napoleon divided his forces to prevent an Austrian escape and was caught at a disadvantage when they instead attacked. A desperate battle was won with the timely arrival of French reinforcements, but a strategic masterpiece was nearly squandered. Although Marengo was thereafter considered the first great "Napoleonic" victory, its execution was flawed. After Napoleon destroyed the main Austrian army at Hohenlinden, the Peace of Lunéville of 1801 secured for France the left bank of the Rhine.

A more impressive piece of maneuver and encirclement came at Ulm in southern Germany during the war against the Third Coalition in October 1805. The campaign involved seven corps totaling 200,000 men in an unprecedented effort in coordinated marching. It took the main force from jump-off points around the middle Rhine and lower Main Rivers into Swabia and Bavaria in an easterly and then southerly direction toward the Upper Danube. Simultaneously, six mounted divisions screened its size and direction. This encouraged the Austrian commander, General Karl Mack, to believe that the French were invading Bavaria by way of the Black Forest. As he marched west toward Ulm to engage, the main French forces swept south in a wide arc east of Ulm. They cut Mack off from a supporting Russian army and then caught his army in a pocket formed by the convergence of the French corps. After futile breakout attempts, Mack surrendered his army. For this prize Napoleon paid with only 1,500 dead and wounded. The Ulm encirclement was essentially a repeat of *manoeuvre sur les derrières* at Piancenza in 1796 with vastly improved communications and coordination.

Ulm was atypical of Napoleonic battles in its comparative lack of bloodshed. Usually, the initial dispersal and ultimate concentration of forces, as witnessed at Marengo and Ulm, kept an opponent guessing as to size and disposition of French armies, until he was suddenly presented with a numerically larger and singularly aggressive enemy. Skirmishers and sharpshooters went ahead of the main force to further mask intensions.

Ever the artilleryman, Napoleon took care both to concentrate massive fire from his guns on key points of the enemy columns. Unnerving enemy troops with smoke and thunder was as important as killing them—and usually the prelude to killing them in large numbers. Once powerful infantry columns had revealed a weak point in the enemy position with repeated bayonet attacks, Napoleon would pitch into it with his reserves until the enemy buckled, whereupon he would send in his cavalry to achieve deep penetration of the enemy ranks, followed by panic and their destruction.

With the hard marches of his dispersed army corps, Napoleon sought, above all, their sudden concentration for a decisive battle that would conclude an entire campaign with a crushing victory of strategic consequence. Austerlitz was such a victory. There, on December 2, 1805, he sought to draw a numerically superior Austro-Russian Allied army to take the offensive against him by feigning weakness in first occupying and then conceding the high ground of the Pratzen Heights.

After ordering the corps of Bernadotte and Davout to converge on Austerlitz by forced march, he lured the Austro-Russian army into a trap. The Allies fled to escape envelopment, but a third of the Allied army was destroyed, breaking the Third Coalition.

The thorn in this success was Britain, whose navy shattered the combined fleets of France and Spain off Cape Trafalgar in October 1805, ending the chances of a French invasion of Britain and exposing France to strategic vulnerability as long as Britain opposed Bonapartism. However, this vulnerability was not terminal to military success on the continent until Napoleon tested the limits of his way of war in Russia and Spain.

In the meantime, Napoleon's advantage lay with strategic maneuver, battlefield tactics, and, not least of all, a superior army. Its basic unit, the corps, was typically commanded by a marshal, a rank created by Napoleon upon his elevation to emperor in May 1804. The title *Maréchal de l'Empire* was restoration of the royalist *Maréchal de France*. It was initially bestowed upon 18 of his leading generals, and by 1815 Napoleon had created 26 marshals. True to its revolutionary roots, the *Grande Armée* had a strong meritocratic bent. Marshals came from diverse social backgrounds, yet were uniformly brave and experienced. In fact, marshals, generals, and other officer ranks routinely displayed the same reckless disregard for danger that made the emperor's reputation. This boldness both greatly increased the combat effectiveness of the army and contributed to high casualty rates among officers. Although only two marshals, Davout and Massena, are thought to have had the intellect for independent command at the highest level, most were infused with the Napoleonic temperament: audacious, hyperactive, impatient. Down the ranks, the officer corps possessed many experienced veterans from the royal and Revolutionary armies. Admission to officer rank could be had through military school, transfer from foreign regiments taken into French service, or spot promotion on the field. Although few spot promotions subsequently rose higher than captain, the *Grande Armée* offered its men greater opportunities for promotion than any other national army.

The French army's total strength in 1805 was 176,000 men in 20 divisions and 11 cavalry divisions in 7 corps and 286 field guns. Under the Jourdain Law, dating to 1798, approximately one and a half million men were conscripted between 1800 and 1815. The organizational effort required to move hundreds of the thousands of troops in separate corps over unfamiliar countryside and along roads of variable quality according to the season required thorough planning and crisp staff work. When successful, it orchestrated the corps' convergence for the *masse de rupture,* upon which Napoleon relied for a truly crushing victory. In 1796, Berthier wrote a staff manual that became the procedural bible for the French army and established a standard of command and control routinely superior to that of its principal foes.

When after Austerlitz Napoleon turned his attention to Prussia, he was able to trump his enemy with both the size and the quality of its army. Whereas by September 1806 Prussia had 130,000 troops for the defense of its southern frontier,

Napoleon ordered a concentration of 208,000 *Grande Armée* troops for his Jena campaign. The Prussians, victorious over Austria and France in the Seven Years' War, were steeped in the tradition of Frederick the Great, one of Napoleon's influences. However, the mobility and tactical elasticity first developed the French Revolutionary army, and now given systematic application and refinement by the *Grande Armée,* confronted a Prussian army obsolete in outlook. It was drilled in the doctrine of rigid formation, deliberate maneuver, and volley firing, and had its mobility impaired by its magazine system of cumbersome baggage columns. In invading Prussia, Napoleon achieved the strategic advantage of surprise by concentrating his army behind the natural screen provided by the Thuringian forest, and, emerging from the screen into open country, marched north into the heart of Prussia. This placed him on the rear of the enemy. Although Napoleon made mistakes regarding the disposition of the enemy forces, and the Prussians fought well, the resulting confrontation of Jena-Auerstädt was a catastrophe for the Prussian army.

At this point, the size and quality of Bonaparte's army itself became as important as its commander's art of maneuver. With the Prussians broken, he became concerned to bring their Russian allies to decisive battle almost on any terms, confident that his war machine could smash any opponent with pure offensive power. This is essentially what happened at Friedland in 1807. A victory afforded as much by Russian blunder as Napoleonic guile, Friedland had little of the elegance of victories from Marengo to Jena. It introduced the tactic of massed artillery plowing the ground for an infantry assault, but it was also the first battle in which a major portion of Napoleon's army was not French but drawn from allied and occupied powers. This problem with manpower was the first indication of the overstretch that was Napoleon's undoing.

Friedland ended the Fourth Coalition. However, the severity of the terms imposed on Prussia gave a fresh spark to Prussian, ultimately German, nationalism, and Napoleon's creation of the continental system increased the stakes of continuing conflict with Great Britain. As the attempt to strangle Britain economically led to war with Portugal and Spain, it amounted to an error in grand strategy. Indeed, the Peninsular War occasioned the emergence of guerrilla war and made it possible for Britain to inflict significant continuing harm on French armies in Spain all out of proportion to the small direct military effort required. Austria rejoined hostilities against France prematurely 1809: the fact that the "Spanish ulcer" imposed on Napoleon a two-front, east–west war turned out to be of little help to Vienna. As a strain on French resources, however, the continental bridgehead Britain acquired in Iberia amounted to a decisive, though slow motion, defeat for Napoleonic warfare.

Meanwhile, the lessons taught to Prussia at Jena-Auerstädt prompted conscription, the creation of a new type of general staff and, ultimately, the emergence of the Carl von Clausewitz as the preeminent scholar of the "science" of Napoleonic arms. Although they did not resort to conscription, Austria, Britain, and Russia all increased the size of their armies and eroded France's manpower advantage. By the time Napoleon decided on his disastrous invasion of Russia, the number and professionalism of armies arrayed against him had changed dramatically. Napoleon was thus unable, even at Borodino in September 1812, to extract a decisive victory from a bloodbath that cost him 33,000 men against 44,000 Russians—in part because his enemy had learned how to inflict grievous losses on an invading army while using the strategic depth of Russia to deprive him of a final showdown. Napoleon had marched in 1812 with 600,000 men against Russia, only 270,000 of whom were French. The retreat from Moscow left 300,000 dead and another 200,000 captured.

The Sixth Coalition orchestrated by Britain also included Austria, Prussia, Sweden, Russia, and the smaller German states of Bavaria, Saxony, and Württemberg. After his last truly great victory at Wagram in 1809, Napoleon was still able to produce remarkable feats of arms on the battlefield, but many of these were essentially brilliant rearguard actions. After Wellington's victory at Vitoria in Spain in June 1813, France was threatened by invasion from the north and south. At Leipzig in the same year, three allied armies totaling 335,000 men converged on 190,000 French, to inflict a defeat that opened up a path to Paris. The Hundred Days that led to Waterloo represented the last hurrah of Napoleonic pluck, but little more.

Napoleon Bonaparte developed strategies and operational practices made possible by the great political upheaval of his time. Between 1804 and 1809 in particular he applied them to the development of a way of war for nation-in-arms and, for a time, struck France's enemies with awe. More than any other leader he recognized that delivering an annihilating blow at an enemy's fighting power represented the shortest route to the achievement of war-sustaining political and economic objectives. As the dimensions of his strategic chess board expanded, however, the army organization and command system that served Napoleon well until Friedland unraveled in the face of wholly dissimilar wars fought simultaneously in theatres as far apart as Russia and Spain. France's enemies grew stronger, and the coordination of separate army corps that was possible in Italy and Germany—especially when engaging enemies sequentially—was fatally impaired by the limited means of communications available. However, the circumstances of the Revolutionary Wars that had encouraged a younger Bonaparte to hazard campaigns of an unprecedented scale had shaped his conception of war so completely that by 1809 there was no place in his imagination for limited strategic goals achievable by more modest military means. That a remorseless pragmatist like Bonaparte should even contemplate a project so irrational as an invasion of Russia is testimony that the Napoleonic system had become the master of its creator.

Descendents: Napoleon's most direct intellectual descendent was Baron Antoine Henri de Jomini (1779–1869). A Swiss national who volunteered for the French army and became an aide to Marshal Michel Ney, Jomini was present at Ulm and later served on Napoleon's general staff at Jena and Eylau. Jomini also saw action in Spain and Russia before defecting to Tsar Alexander in 1813. His explanation for the breakthrough in warfare that France had accomplished under Napoleon was so compelling to subsequent generations—above all for its theoretical clarity and elegance—that he contributed in equal parts to a better understanding of Napoleon as well as to Napoleonic mythology. Self-consciously "scientific" in his pursuit of objective and timeless principles of modern war, he drew from Napoleon certain cornerstone principles: that strategy is the key to all warfare; that strategy is controlled by invariable scientific principles; and that offensive action should mass forces against weaker enemy forces at some decisive point if strategy is to lead to victory. The debt to Napoleon is obvious, but the theorist's preoccupation with tidiness equally so. Still, Jomini is noteworthy for having offered that war was less a science than an art, and it was his legions of disciples in succeeding generations who oversimplified his principles to the point of distorting the Napoleonic legacy.

Carl von Clausewitz (1780–1831), who experienced Napoleonic warfare through the lens of Prussia's humiliation, is Jomini's equal as interpreter of the events of 1796 to 1815, but his superior in transmitting a "philosophy" of war that powerfully influenced generations of Prussian and German officers in particular. Apart from depicting war as an essentially political act and creature of state policy, Clausewitz appreciated the effectiveness with which Bonaparte had repeatedly applied his intellect and energy to the utter destruction of an enemy's army as the sole legitimate object of a commander's strategy. Equally, Napoleon demonstrated for Clausewitz that moderation and conventional propriety, common to the military conflicts of the 18th century, would henceforth have no place in the prosecution of war. Rather, the true and essential nature of war as rediscovered and revealed by Napoleon involved the commitment of all resources and every possible violence to achieve comprehensive victory. This interpretation of the Napoleonic legacy became orthodoxy for generations of Prussian officers. It was applied successfully in 1866 and 1870—but disastrously in 1914, possibly because variations of Clausewitz's ideas had also come to dominate the doctrines of so many of Germany's enemies.

Among practitioners, the Union commander Ulysses Grant, not the Confederate Robert E. Lee, stands out as the ablest agent of Napoleonic reasoning in the American Civil War. Grant's campaign against Vicksburg in 1863 was a sweeping *manoeuvre sur les derrières* of the Confederacy and a colossal strategic coup for the Union. Possibly the least Napoleonic personality to ever command an army, Grant nonetheless waged a war of annihilation into the heartland of the Confederacy.

Grant, however, was not the self-conscious student of Napoleon found in Helmut von Moltke (1800–1891). As chief of the Prussian general staff, von Moltke in part succeeded in institutionalizing the "Napoleonic secret" for massive offensive operations. He created the Great General Staff, and used railways to bring about surprise concentrations of troops in overwhelming strength, as in 1870 against a French army whose understanding of Napoleon was inferior to his own.

In a much more diffuse way, the sense that Napoleon had started an evolution of western arms toward total war—a remorseless evolution without alternatives, regardless of circumstance and technological change—actually blighted the military imagination well into the 20th century. Because Napoleon had acquired a mythological status, either as the one true father of modern war or as the inspired interpreter of the timeless verities of war, his name was invoked to justify new schemes for bloodletting in the western front, 1914–1918, that bore little or no relationship whatever to the instincts that first made a reputation at Marengo in 1796.

See also: Bülow, D.; Carnot, L.; Clausewitz, C.; Frederick II ("the Great"); Gribeauval, J.; Guibert, J.; Jomini; Moltke "the Elder", H.; Saxe, M.; Scharnhorst and Gneisenau

Further Reading

Blanning, T.C.W., *The French Revolutionary Wars, 1787–1802*. London: Arnold, 1996.
Esdaile, Charles, *The Wars of Napoleon*. New York: Longman, 1995.
Howard, Michael, *War in European History*. New York: Oxford University Press, 1976.
Liddell Hart, B. H., *Strategy*. London: Faber & Faber, 1954.
Marshall-Cornwall, James, *Napoleon as a Military Commander*. London: B. T. Batsford, 1967.
Paret, Peter (ed.), *Makers of Modern Strategy from Machiavelli to the Nuclear Age*. Princeton: Princeton University Press, 1986.
Rothenberg, Gunther E., *The Napoleonic Wars*. London: Cassell, 1999.

Carl Cavanagh Hodge

Bueil, Jean V de
(1406–1477)

Significance: Jean de Bueil's work describes the changes in European social and military affairs taking place during the Anglo-French "Hundred Years" War.

Context: Jean de Bueil wrote during the Hundred Years' War when both the social structure and military affairs of Western Europe were undergoing a significant transformation.

Biography: Jean de Bueil was born ca. 1405/1406. His father and uncles were killed at Agincourt (1415) whereupon he became Seigneur de Montrésor and Comte de Sancerre. He fought his first battle at Verneuil in 1424 and earned the nickname *le Fléau des Anglais* ("Scourge of the English"). He campaigned with Jeanne d'Arc in 1429 in the Loire Valley and relief of Orléans. De Bueil was Charles VII's lieutenant in Anjou and Maine in the late 1430s and took part in the defeat of the Swiss in the battle of Saint-Jacques in August 1444. Named *Amiral de France* (Admiral of France) in 1450, he was one of the senior captains at Castillon in 1453. Dismissed by Louis XI in 1461, he withdrew from court but was received back into the king's grace in 1469 on account of his military experience and prowess. He died in 1477.

Influences: Influenced primarily by his experiences as a participant in the Hundred Years' War, Jean de Bueil was no doubt familiar with the Classical Greek and Roman military writers. It is possible that he drew upon the work of his near contemporaries, such as Christine de Pizan.

The Theory: Jean de Bueil's military treatise, *Le Jouvencel* (*The Youth*), was written ca. 1461–1468. It takes the form of a romance in which a poor noble youth rises steadily in the knightly class only to be disillusioned in the end by foppish courtiers and a fickle king. The tale is clearly autobiographical, and "the youth" embodies Jean de Bueil's own values of knightly honor and love of battle. The author argues forcefully for the continued military supremacy of the knightly class, but recognizes that warfare is changing due to the growing use of gunpowder weapons and the increasing utility of trained infantry. These changes indeed signaled the declining military importance of heavy cavalry. He offers some advice on the use of "machines," such as using light artillery firing between the shots of the heavy bombards to prevent the enemy's restoration of damage. He also advocates flank protection on the march and provides a clear expression of the psychology of courage in battle, but continues to advocate the static, defensive use of infantry rather than their taking the offense.

Application: There does not appear to have been any direct application of Jean de Bueil's military wisdom, although some 17th-century war memoirists, such as François, the duke of La Rochefoucauld, and Roger de Rabutin, the count of Bussy, echo his views on the ideal military leader.

Descendents: Despite continued enthusiasm for the domination of warfare by the knightly class, by the mid-15th century, the age of the heavily armed mounted warrior was drawing to an end in Europe, and modern warfare, dominated by infantry, firearms, and artillery, was dawning.

See also: Machiavelli; Pizan.

Further Reading

Chan Tsin, Matthieu E., "Jean de Bueil: Reactionary Knight (France)." Ph.D. dissertation, Purdue University, 2005.

"The 'Companions' of Jeanne d'Arc and Others," pages 4–5 [Online, March 2006] at URL http://xenophongroup.com/montjoie/compgns.htm#bueil.

de Bueil, Jean, *Le Jouvencel.* Ed. C. Favre and L. Lecestre. 2 vols. Paris: 1887–89. Reprinted, Paris: Slatkine, 1996.

Szkilnik, Michelle, "The Plight of a Warrior in Changing Times" [Online, December 2005] at URL http://oregonstate.edu/dept/humanities/ Newsletter/Spring%2005/Szkilnik.htm.

Charles R. Shrader

Carl, Archduke of Austria and Duke of Teschen
(1771–1847)

Significance: Interpreter and practitioner of Napoleonic-era grand strategy

Context: Nineteenth century.

Biography: Archduke Carl was younger son of Archduke Leopold, Grand Duke of Tuscany and subsequently Holy Roman Emperor Leopold II, brother to Emperor Francis II, grandson to Maria Theresa, and foster son to Duke Albert of Saxe-Teschen. A slightly built epileptic, he was originally intended for a career in the Church. However, his adoption by the childless Duke Albert led to military training under the military theorist Karl Friedrich von Lindenau. The outbreak of the French Revolutionary Wars saw his appointment as a general in the Habsburg army. Modest success as a column commander saw his rapid promotion as a royal family member. In 1796, he successfully defeated and drove French forces from Germany, although this success was nullified by Napoleon's concurrent victories in Italy. Carl would again command forces in 1798, 1805, and 1809. His greatest military moment came with his defeat of Napoleon at the battle of Aspern-Essling in 1809, although defeat a month later at Wagram led to his permanent retirement. From 1809 to his death in 1847 Carl wrote extensively on military strategy, operations, and tactics, as well as histories of the Napoleonic Wars.

Influences: Karl Friedrich von Lindenau, who experienced the Wars of Frederick the Great, was Carl's most immediate influence. However, Carl's writings mention his love of the classics, especially the work of Tacitus.

The Theory: Carl described war as "the greatest evil that can befall a state." From this tenant, he drew his work on strategy, army operations, and tactics. He must be considered a practitioner and advocate for *limited warfare,* having rejected the efforts of the French Revolution to unleash, as he saw in it "the energies of a people's war." His most original contribution was the creation of the use of geometric lines, called baselines, off which armies could safely operate.

The Application: Realistic about the nature of the Habsburg state and its manpower and resources, Carl attempted to write theory and manuals that were essentially updated and more humane versions of 18th-century practice. He wanted to create literature that would allow officers of modest ability to become professional practitioners, competent if not inspired. In many ways, Carl's work, enshrined as doctrine for the Habsburg military throughout the 19th century, did nothing to inspire reform or modernization.

Descendents: Apart from his son, Archduke Albrecht, Duke of Teschen, he informed the intellectual tradition of the Habsburg general staff.

See also: Bonaparte, Napoleon; Clausewitz, C.; Jomini; Khevenhüller; Lindenau

Further Reading

Charles, Archduke of Austria, *Ausgewählte schriften weiland Sr. K. hoheit Erzherz. Carl v. Österreich*. Vienna and Leipzig, 1862.

Charles, Archduke of Austria, *Grundsätze der höhern Kriegskunst für die Generäle der österreichischen Armee*. Vienna: n.p., 1806. Reprinted Osnabrück: Biblio-Verlag, 1974.

Charles, Archduke of Austria, *Grundsätze der Strategie erlautert durch die darstellung des Feldzugs von 1796 in Deutschland*. Vienna: J. V. Degen, 1813.

Eysturlid, Lee W., *The Formative Influences, Theories and Campaigns of the Archduke Carl of Austria*. Westport, CT: Greenwood, 2000.

Rothenberg, Gunther E., *Napoleon's Great Adversaries: The Archduke Charles and the Austrian Army 1792–1814*. Indiana University Press, Bloomington, 1982.

Lee W. Eysturlid

Ch'i Chi-kuang, Senior Commissioner in Chief
(1528–1588)

Significance: Ch'i Chi-kuang's successful leadership of Chinese forces and recorded principles helped reform and invigorate the military forces fielded by the late Ming dynasty (1550–1644).

Context: The Ming dynasty entered a period of decline for much of the 16th century and faced threats from Japanese pirates (Wokou) and multiple Japanese invasions during the Sino–Japanese Korean War (1592–1598).

Biography: Born into a hereditary military family in 1528. Ch'i recruited, trained, equipped, and led Chinese forces against Japanese pirates from 1555 to 1565, and is credited by historians with ending the piracy threat. He died in 1588.

Influences: Ch'i's writings evoke a system of rewards and punishments written in the *Seven Military Classics* by theorists such as Sun Tzu and Wu-Tzu. Ch'i dictated that a squad leader's death would result in the execution of the remaining soldiers and also advised a system of group and individual rewards.

The Theory: Based on Ch'i's experience against Japanese pirates in southern China, and his training of soldiers, he wrote *The New Book Recording Effective Techniques* (Chi-hsiao hsin-shu) and later wrote the *Record of Military Training* (Lien-ping shih-chi) to assist other leaders in creating disciplined forces that could effectively assert the government's desires.

The Mandarin duck formation (Yuan Yang Zhen) consisted of an 11-person unit led by a squad leader with two teams of five: one multiple tipped spear person to entangle the enemy weapon, one shield person to protect him, two spear people to assist in thrusting at the entangled enemy, and one sword person for additional combat power. A single cook accompanied the unit.

Ch'i directed that squads repeatedly drill in coordinating their individuals' respective and mutually supportive functions. Although the function of individual members remained the same, the specific configuration could be changed between three different models.

Soldiers who faced different types of enemies, such as nomadic horsemen and regular Japanese infantry, benefitted from Ch'i's disciplinary guidelines and grappling techniques. The formation's lack of gunpowder and missile weapons and its creation in the mountainous and jungle terrain of southern China made the formations itself less adaptable on the plains of northern China.

Application: Ch'i successfully applied the duck formation against Japanese pirates where his soldiers earned a reputation for bravery and ferocity in close combat. Li Ru-song, another leader of Chinese forces credited Ch'i Chi-kuang's teaching for "total victory" in the Sino–Japanese Korean War and specifically praised the southern troops in his theatre. The Koreans were so impressed with the skill of Chinese soldiers trained with these methods that they trained exclusively from Ch'i's manual for much of the 17th century.

Descendents: The conquest of China by the barbarian Manchus in 1644 placed indigenous Chinese infantry as auxiliary soldiers in support of Manchu forces. The increase in quality, power, and effective range of firearms quickly made this theory obsolete.

See also: Sun Tzu

Morgan Deane

Crissé, Turpin de, Lieutenant General Lancelot, Comte de
(1716–1795)

Significance: A military *philosophe,* de Crissé attempted to create one of the first modern theories of warfare. He sought to make operations exact and scientific.

Context: Writing during the French Enlightenment, Turpin de Crissé represents that tradition among military thinkers of creating a comprehensive body of military theory, universal in nature, which could guide warfare. For the French army this was particularly attractive, as it had done poorly in the War of the Austrian Succession (1740–1748) and in the Seven Years' War (1756–1763).

Biography: Turpin de Crissé was born in 1716, and became a hussar officer in the French army. In 1748, he became a brigadier general and served widely in Germany during the Seven Years' War. Promoted as lieutenant general in 1780, he won the distinguished Cross of Saint-Louis in 1787. He wrote widely on philosophy and education, and published commentaries on Caesar, Vegetius, and Montecúccoli. He died in Vienna in 1795.

Influences: Ancient military history held particular sway with Turpin de Crissé, as did the writings of Raimondo Montecúccoli. Vauban provided many theoretical underpinnings.

The Theory: Turpin de Crissé's military theory is found in the two-volume *Essai sur l'art de la guerre* (1754–1757). He examines nearly every facet of military affairs. From a theoretical standpoint, the arguments concerning the nature of the study of war are paramount. Unlike many contemporaries, he did not condemn prejudice and tradition for the shortcomings in the military art. War was like no other science, because its rules were difficult to discern and to apply. Intense study and the quality of "genius" were necessary for successful application.

Turpin de Crissé's theoretical approach is noteworthy. One of the first attempts to address operational art systematically is found under the rubric "Plan of Campaign." In it, he proposes to apply Vauban's methods of siegecraft to general military operations. A general must advance toward an objective and fortify his forces once engaged. Then he must methodically advance against the enemy using zigzagging trenches and parallels.

Application: These theories contributed to the growth of military literature during the French Enlightenment. Although its contemporary influence is difficult to discern, he provided a methodology for understanding the study of war and was one of the first to develop the study of operational art. Understanding campaigns as sieges of enemy forces or even nations, proved prophetic of World War I at least.

Descendents: The *Essai* was translated into English, German, and Russian in his own lifetime and de Crissé became standard reading for a generation of military thinkers.

See also: Montecúccoli, R.

Further Reading
Gat, Azar, *The Origins of Military Thought from the Enlightenment to Clausewitz.* New York: Oxford University Press, 1989.

Patrick J. Speelman

Ewald, Johann Von
(1744–1813)

Significance: Ewald's work is a competent summary of previous literature on the tactics of irregular detachments (what today would be called "special forces" or "special operations"), enriched by his extensive practical experiences both in Europe and America. Nevertheless, Peter Paret argued that Ewald's work illustrates the fact that the American War of Independence influenced European thinking about small wars very little.

Context: Ewald experienced the Seven Years' War on the side of Prussia. Then, in 1776, Ewald was among the 14,000 Hessians who were sent to America by the Landgrave of Hesse to fight for the British against the American insurgents in the American War of Independence. Later finding employment in Denmark, he helped keep this country out of the Napoleonic Wars.

Biography: Johann Ewald was born in Kassel on March 30, 1744, as the son of a post office employee and a grocer's daughter. He joined the military of Hesse as a cadet in 1760 and took part in the Seven Years' War. He was promoted in 1765, but his further career was blighted by the fact that he was a commoner. In 1770, he lost his left eye in a duel, but resumed his duties in 1771.

In 1776, as captain of a contingent of special forces (*Leibjäger*), Ewald was sent to America with a Hessian regiment, arriving in New-Rochelle on October 22, 1776. Ewald took part in all the subsequent campaigns; in 1777, he was awarded the Hesse-Cassel decoration *pour la vertu militaire*. He and his regiment became prisoners of war after the capitulation of Cornwallis at Yorktown on October 17, 1781. He was released on parole, and found himself on Long Island as an invalid, having contracted a nervous fever, not recovering until the end of the war. He returned to Hesse in 1784, and was moved to the infantry regiment of Heinrich Wilhelm Maximilian von Dittfurth as a captain. It was in this capacity that he published his *Abhandlungen über den Kleinen Krieg* (1785), followed by a series of other books of a mainly technical–tactical nature.

As further promotion was not forthcoming, he offered his service to the Danish monarch and, in 1788, he became lieutenant colonel and chief of a *Jäger* corps, which he built up, henceforth calling himself "von Ewald," and found a Danish spouse; his descendents were Danes. He was promoted several times in the following years and, in 1803, he was appointed to the command of a corps in southern Holstein. In 1806, he and his corps took part in a skirmish against the French under Murat and Soult, which persuaded the French to respect Danish neutrality. In 1807, Ewald was posted to Zeeland and, during 1809–1813, to Holstein. The Danish monarch accommodated the French by agreeing to the German anti-French partisans out of Danish territory; Ewald was thus part of the contingent that stormed Strahlsund in 1809, where the Prussian partisan captain Schill was killed. Ewald was promoted to lieutenant general in the same year.

Ewald's division was supposed to join the Grande Armée in Napoleon's Russian Campaign of 1812, but it eventually remained in Holstein. Ewald was tanken ill in 1813, had to resign his command in May, and died in Landstelle near Kiel on May 28, 1813 (the date given elsewhere as June 25 is probably his funeral).

Influences: Inter alia, Ewald drew on the publications of the French pioneers of literature on small wars: Grandmaison, Jeney, Folard, Turpin de Crissé, De la Croix, and Jacques François de Chastenet, Marquis de Puységur's work on war, which were widely read in his time after their posthumous publication, as well as Henry Lloyd, and the less famous Friedrich Christoph von Saldern. Ewald drew on the usual Classical texts such as Vegetius for other quotations and examples.

The Theory: Ewald's works concern tactics rather than strategy. Using the terminology of our own times, Ewald urged the need for self-reliance, terrain analysis, adaptability, innovation, and the use of combined forces. He emphasized discipline, and the need to treat the local population well. It is perhaps here that we have a hint of an early inkling of the need to win the hearts and minds of locals in a context where special operations were increasingly being turned, on one side, into insurgency, and on the other, in which Ewald found himself, into counterinsurgency. Otherwise, there is little evidence that Ewald grappled with the strategic, let alone political, aims of the wars in which he fought.

Application: As an active commanding officer, Ewald himself had plenty of occasion to put his own prescriptions into practice; Selig and Skaggs found that they were echoed or independently derived from the earlier works that influenced Ewald by other fellow officers in the German-speaking world.

Descendents: Selig and Skaggs found that Ewald's book was used by the British commander Sir John Moore during the Peninsular War. When Clausewitz lectured his students on small wars (by which he still meant special operations), Ewald's works were among the publications on which he drew.

Further Reading

Ewald, Johann, *Diary of the American War: A Hessian Journal,* trs. and ed. by Joseph Tustin. New Haven: Yale University Press, 1979.

Ewald, Johann, *Gedanken eines hessischen Offiziers über das, was man bei Führung eines Detachements im Felde zu thun hat.* Cassel: Johann Jacob Cramer, 1774.

Ewald, Johann von, *Abhandlung von Dienst der leichten Truppen.* Flensburg/Schleswig und Leipzig, 1790 and 1796.

Ewald, Johann von, *Belehrungen über den Krieg, besonders über den kleinen Krieg, durch Beispiele großer Helden und kluger und tapferer Männer.* 3 vols. Schleswig: J. G. Röhß, 1798.

Ewald, Johann von, *Gespräche eines Husarencorporals, eines Jägers und leichten Infanteristen über die Pflichten und den Dienst der leichten Soldaten.* Altona: Hammerich, 1794.

Ewald, Johann von, *Vom Dienst im Felde für Unteroffiziere...* Schleswig: J. G. Röhß, Christiani & Korte, 1802.

Hauptmann Johann Ewald: *Abhandlung über den kleinen Krieg.* Cassel: Johann Jacob Cramer, 1785; trs into English by Lieutenant A. Maimburg (London 1803), and again by Robert A Selig and David Curtis Skaggs: *Treatise on Partisan Wafare.* New York: Greenwood Press, 1991.

Paret, Peter, "Colonial Experience and European Military Reform at the End of the Eighteenth Century," originally published in 1964, re-published in *Historical Research* Vol. 37 No. 95 (2007), pp. 47–59.

Selig, Robert A. and David Curtis Skaggs (eds. and trs.), *Treatise on Partisan Wafare,* trs. of Ewald's *Abhandlung über den kleinen Krieg.* New York: Greenwood Press, 1991.

Beatrice Heuser

Fazl, Abul
(1551–1602)

Significance: Abul Fazl, a courtier of the Mughals, provides key information on Mughal-era warfare on the Indian subcontinent. The *Akbar Nama* records important battles of his patron Akbar's reign (1542–1605), and is based on information denied to scholars working outside the court. *Akbar Nama* gives a particularly detailed description of the Second Battle of Panipat, fought in 1556 between the warlord Hemu's Suri army and the Mughal army under Bairam Khan, acting as regent of young Akbar. The battle ensured Mughal rule of north India until the first half of the 18th century.

Context: Abul Fazl's life was dominated by struggles for north India between Hindu and Islamic warlords. One such warlord was Hemu (full name Hem Chandra), who was a Brahmin fighting for Afghan lords, and whose life provides a glimpse into war making in 16th-century India. Hemu's family was engaged in the trade of saltpeter, one of the chief components of gunpowder, which explains Hemu's familiarity with firearms. Manpower shortages suffered by the Islamic Suri dynasty, cut off from Mughal-dominated Afghanistan and faced with Mughal resurgence after the death of the Suri ruler Sher Shah, forced them to enlist Hindus such as Hemu. During their campaigns, the *Modis* (Hindu businessmen) supplied the Suri's Afghan troopers. Hemu took employment under one such *Modi,* who used to work for Islam Shah, son of Sher Shah. Islam Shah promoted Hemu to the post of the superintendent of market, his job being to supply Islam Shah's soldiers. Impressed by his organizational abilities, Islam Shah appointed him as minister of food and civil supplies. The rapid rise of Hindus such as Hemu was partly because of Islam Shah's suspicion of the Afghan nobility. Hemu was given the additional post of espionage chief. In 1553, Islam Shah was succeeded by Mubariz Khan. Adil Shah, a nephew of Sher Shah, opposed him. Hemu offered his service to Adil Shah, and he was appointed prime minister. Subsequently, Hemu also became the commander in chief of Adil's army. His main enemies were the Mughals. Hemu established a base in eastern India, while the Mughals were busy reestablishing their authority in Punjab. He became the power behind the throne of Adil Shah.

Biography: Abul Fazl, the son of Shaikh Mubarak, was born in Agra in 1551. He was well educated: religion and philosophy were his favorite subjects, and he was fluent in both Arabic and Persian. In 1574, Fazl entered the service of the Mughal Akbar and became the latter's confidant. Fazl became the author of *Ain-i-Akbari* and *Akbar Nama.* The former is an extremely thorough statistical study of Akbar's empire. Akbar's son Salim assassinated Fazl in 1602.

Fazl's work showers extraordinary attributes upon *Padshah* Akbar, overlooking the latter's limitations. He overlooks the campaigns in which the imperial forces were defeated. Nonetheless, he provides descriptions of important battles, from which contemporary theories of war can be gleaned.

Influences: Abul Fazl tried to combine the Persian and Arabic traditions in his work. He wrote in an ornate style, and resorts to rhetoric to hide Akbar's weaknesses. As a court chronicler, Fazl also ignores individuals who were opposed to Akbar's policies. However, *Akbar Nama* marks a break from the Persian tradition, by incorporating accounts of ancient India and the reigns of Hindu rulers. Fazl possessed *Zafar Nama* (*Book of Victory*) by Sharafuddin Yazdi, which records the military exploits of Tamerlane and was written 30 years after Timur's death. *Akbar Nama* is a blend of religion, politics, society, and warfare, which rotates around the persona of Akbar.

The Theory: Fazl's descriptions of battle allow insight into contemporary theories of war, particularly as applied by Hemu and his main enemies. Abul Fazl notes that prior to the Second Battle of Panipat, Hemu had won 22 battles.

Hemu's logistical system was in advance of his times. He understood that without ample supplies of cash soldiers, horses, or elephants could be not maintained. Elephants were particularly costly. Pillage and plundering alienated the civilian population, which resulted in potential security loss and required garrisoning. Foraging also destroyed soldiers' discipline, and prevented rapid concentration of the force. Hemu ordered his soldiers to buy provisions in cash, and while campaigning, loaded treasure on elephants and horses. Hemu's use of forts and his logistical capacity caused Brahmins, Rajputs, and the Afghans from Bihar and Uttar Pradesh to flock to his banner.

For example, Fazl writes that poor rainfall and devastation caused by continuous warfare created a famine around Delhi between 1556 and 1557. Hemu's logistical tail was, however, so robust that while encamped at Bayana, 50 miles southwest of Agra, he was able to feed 500 war elephants with rice, sugar, and butter when the people of Delhi and Agra were suffering from a shortage of cereals. These elephants gave Hemu victory in his first encounter with the Mughals. Hemu's logistical talents allowed him to crisscross the subcontinent from Bihar to Punjab swiftly.

Hemu, like Babur was a tactical innovator. Hemu realized that Mughal superiority rested on artillery and horse archery. He copied Mughal artillery and achieved parity at the technological level. However, he could not acquire mounted bowmen of Central Asia because the horse markets of Kabul remained under the loose supervision of the Mughals. So, Hemu attempted to synthesize the ancient Hindu tradition of using elephants with the gunpowder technology introduced in north India by the Mughals. Hemu's policy of deliberately enticing the enemy flanks away from their center by ordering controlled retreat of his own flanks, exhibited not only strict discipline of the troops but also the high quality of generalship on his part. Hemu's tactic of concentrating a select corps and then throwing it against a particular point of the enemy's center, especially when the enemy's flanks were hanging in thin air, was a tactically effective ploy.

Application: In 1556, the Mughal cause seemed hopeless. While Hemu threatened them from the east, Sikander Suri, operating from the Siwalik Hills, was attempting to cut Mughal communications with Kabul. Then Muhammad Sulaiman, Akbar's cousin an governor of Kabul, declared his independence. The Mughal army was theoretically under the 13-year-old Akbar, but Bairam Khan was the *de facto* ruler. Bairam Khan was forced to divide the Mughal army into three battle groups to deal with the various threats. One battle group under Tardi Beg Khan was left in Delhi to meet Hemu.

Hemu advanced from Chunar and reached the outskirts of Delhi, where he deployed 50,000 cavalry, 1,000 elephants, 51 cannons, and 50 falconets. He enjoyed numerical superiority over the Mughals. Hemu's force and the Mughal army were technologically similar—the firepower advantage that Babur possessed had vanished by this time. The quality of Hemu's artillery, says Fazl, was the same as that of the Ottomans.

On October 7, 1556, Hemu clashed with the 5,000-strong Mughal detachment under Tardi Beg and the clash was termed as the Battle of Delhi. The Mughal army was divided into four wings: vanguard, center, right wing, and left wing. The Mughal vanguard started the battle by attacking Hemu's right wing. Rai Husain, the commander of Hemu's right wing was killed, along with 3,000 men. This encouraged the Mughal left wing to advance. The right and left wings of the Mughals attempted the classic *taulqama* tactic of outflanking the enemy by destroying its wings.

Hemu's tactical novelty was to launch an attack toward the enemy center with a select corps of troops. He deployed this elite contingent near the center under his direct command. Meanwhile, Hemu's wings deliberately started retreating to entice the Mughal wings to pursue them. At this juncture, when the Mughal center was separated from their advancing wings, Hemu launched his select corps, consisting of 3,000 horses and 300 elephants against the Mughal center and smashed it. When the Mughal wings returned to the battlefield they saw that their center had disintegrated, and they retreated. However, Hemu did not pursue the defeated enemy, because he thought that the Mughals were conducting a tactical retreat before launching a counterattack with the mounted archers. In reality, the defeated Mughal army was in no position to counterattack. Hemu occupied Delhi and in defiance of Adil Shah, crowned himself as Raja Bikramaditya.

When news of this disaster reached the Mughal camp in Punjab, most of the *amirs* (chieftains) were for going back to Kabul to reorganize. However, Bairam Khan exhibited iron determination, concentrated all possible soldiers, and marched to Karnal. Hemu started from Delhi. The Mughals and Hemu again clashed at Panipat, 53 miles from Delhi.

Just before the battle, Hemu's artillery was captured by the Mughals. However, Hemu still enjoyed numerical superiority. The Mughals managed only 10,000 cavalry. Besides 30,000 Rajput and Afghan cavalry, Hemu possessed 500 war elephants. Hemu relied on his armored war elephants for launching the decisive attack. His army was divided into four groups: the right and left wings, center, and the select corps. Just before the beginning of the Second Battle of Panipat, Hemu distributed treasure and issued land grants generously among his soldiers.

The Mughal army's military doctrine was evolving. The Mughal commanders learned from the past mistakes and anticipated Hemu's probable tactics. Hence, Mughal deployment at the Second Battle of Panipat was more complex than Tardi Beg's deployment during the Battle of Delhi. The Mughal contingent of *Altmash* (advance guard) appeared for the first time in their battle order at the Second Battle of Panipat. It was stationed between the vanguard and the center to prevent isolation of the center from the advancing vanguard. For bringing pressure on the enemy's wings, the right and left wings were strengthened with *uqci* (special contingent of mounted archers). Again, in case of an enemy charge against the Mughal center, the rear guard and the reserve would provide succor.

On November 5, 1556, the Mughal vanguard, along with the right and left wings, charged Hemu's left and right wings. The Mughals tried to implement the *taulqama* tactic of destroying the enemy's flanks and then surrounding it from the rear. The Mughal center was not eager to make a charge at the elephants—Fazl emphasizes the destructive capacity of Hemu's elephants, trained to disorder the cavalry. So, the Mughal vanguard attacked Hemu's elephants from a distance with horse archers. The mounted archers were able to pick off the fighters seated in the *howdahs* at long range and shot at the elephants' legs. However, the elephants were able to retain their place in the battlefield.

Hemu's tactics during the Second Battle of Panipat was similar to that implemented during the Battle of Delhi. His right and left wings conducted an ordered retreat to encourage the Mughal left and right wings away from the battlefield. When the Mughal center was isolated from the advancing wings, Hemu launched his select corps against the enemy center with the objective of smashing it. The Mughals had anticipated Hemu's charge, and had dug a ditch for protecting their center. The select corps crossed this ditch and created panic in the Mughal center. At this point, a chance arrow pierced Hemu's right eye. He lost consciousness, was captured, and then beheaded.

Upon the loss of their paymaster, Hemu's men relinquished victory. No clear-cut chain of command existed to provide unified leadership after the fall of Hemu, and his men fled. Akbar and Bairam Khan did not win the battle because of any exceptional military capabilities. Both were absent from the battlefield, leaving the fighting to the Mughal *amirs*. Mughal victory resulted from Hemu's accidental death.

Descendents: The Mughals captured 120 of Hemu's war elephants. The rampage caused by Hemu's elephants impressed Akbar and his *amirs,* and hence, after the Second Battle of Panipat, elephants became an integral part of the Mughal order of battle. In the post-Akbar era, horse archery, firearms, and war elephants constituted the core of the Mughal army. During the Battle of Khajwa, fought on January 5, 1659, both Aurangzeb and his brother Shah Shuja used elephants. Aurangzeb won this battle due to his numerical and firepower superiority, plus treachery among Shuja's generals. Later in 1659, during the Battle of Giria between Shah Shuja and Aurangzeb's general Mir Jumla, the former used light artillery carried on the backs of the elephants. Such guns were known as elephant swivel guns.

Hemu proved that money is the sinew of warfare. The use of ready cash while campaigning, a principle followed by Hemu was also adopted by the Mughals.

Akbar Nama influenced *Padshah* Shah Jahan (1628–1658) to have a similar work written for his reign. Shah Jahan deputed Abdul Hamid Lahori for this task. Like all court chronicles, *Shah Jahan Nama* employs hyperbolic praise of Shah Jahan and the narrative is given to rhetorical excesses. However, *Shah Jahan Nama* provides us with important military details interspersed with vital political information on its era.

See also: Use of Elephants in Indian Warfare

Further Reading

Fazl, Abul, *The Akbar Nama,* 3 vols., tr. from the Persian by H. Beveridge, 2nd ed. New Delhi: Saeed International, 1989.

Khan, Iqtidar, Alam, *Gunpowder and Firearms: Warfare in Medieval India.* New Delhi: Oxford University Press, 2004.

Pant, G. N., *Horse & Elephant Armour.* Delhi: Agam Kala Prakashan, 1997.

Sarkar, Jagadish, Narayan, *The Life of Mir Jumla: The General of Aurangzeb.* New Delhi: Rajesh Publications, 1979.

Kaushik Roy

Feuquières, Antoine de pas, Marquis de
(1648–1711)

Significance: Feuquières, a combat officer in Louis XIV's army, analyzed contemporary generalship and developed a sophisticated theory of strategy and operational art.

Context: France's uneven success during the Wars of Louis XIV spurred Feuquières to dissect the reasons for operational and strategic success and failure.

Biography: Feuquières gained his first military experience as an aide-de-camp to Turenne. He served during the Dutch Wars and during the Nine Years' War, but his tendency for criticizing political rivals at Court precluded him from service in the War of the Spanish Succession, despite his combat experience and excellent command record. He contented himself with critical analysis of ongoing campaigns and worked on his *Memoires* until his death in 1711. His work was published posthumously in French in 1731 and 1740, in English (1736), and German (1738).

Influences: Feuquières drew from the extensive combat experience. He credited Turenne, the Duke of Luxenbourg, and Villars as exemplary, condemned Villeroi, and rendered a mixed judgment of Boufflers, William of Orange, Catinat, and others. In contrast to many of his contemporaries, Feuquières was not interested in Classical Antiquity.

The Theory: Feuquières did not use the terms grand strategy, strategy, operational art, and tactics, but he seems to have understood the concepts. He believed that success in war depended upon a commander's ability to maintain freedom of action while limiting that of his opponent. He emphasized seizing the initiative and believed in using deception and gaining relative advantages over an enemy that in aggregate could prove decisive. Feuquières understood something close to what Clausewitz called friction—the difficulty of controlling situations in war. This situational fragility provided both opportunity and liability. Feuquières advocated minimizing risk, but regarded prudence and vigor as complementary.

Feuquières believed that most conflict could be classified under five "constitutions": "offensive war," "defensive war," "war between equal powers," "auxiliary war," and "civil war." By "offensive war" and "defensive war" Feuquières sometimes seems to have meant the acting on the strategic attack or defense, respectively. Occasionally in his *Memoires,* however, he uses the terms not to refer to a side's intentions, but rather its cumulative advantages or disadvantages relative to the opponent. For example, by "defensive war" he sometimes meant a situation in which a commander suffered at a disadvantage of force size, terrain, or logistical conditions even if that commander's intent was still offensive. By "war between equal powers," Feuquières meant a situation in which neither side enjoyed a clear strategic advantage, regardless of raw indicators of combat power. "Auxiliary war" and "civil war" meant military effort in support of an ally, and internecine conflict, respectively.

Feuquières argued that a commander should maintain or change the "constitution" of a war to his advantage; in a "defensive war," a commander should seek to convert or "improve" it into a "war between equal powers." He could do this by denying the enemy options, while retaining his own freedom of action—in other words, by seizing or maintaining the initiative. Use of deception enhanced a commander's ability to seize the initiative. For example, Feuquières advocated pretending to disperse one's main force and tempt the enemy into dispersing also, while actually retaining the ability to reconcentrate more rapidly than the enemy. He also advocated obscuring one's intentions by positioning a force where it could strike multiple targets.

Feuquières believed a commander's decision to seek battle should depend on whether victory might help change the war's "constitution." Strategic choice meant manipulating an enemy into sacrificing freedom of action. One consequence of victory in a battle was a limiting of an enemy's future strategic-level options. A battle did not have to end the entire war, therefore, to be decisive. Despite this nuanced approach, Feuquières nevertheless wrote a good deal on set-piece combat. He distinguished between larger set-piece field actions and smaller-scale "encounters"—fights between forces each of several battalions detached from a main army.

Feuquières recognized that few generals in his day would make policy, but clearly believed that a field commander's understanding of the grand strategic implications of his strategic- and operational-level decisions should guide him. He addressed logistics and offered tactical analysis of battles and encounters. Yet, unlike other authors of the period, he seemed less interested in training and military administration. For Feuquières, victory in war depended less upon applying some new tactical scheme or universal principles than on making decisions more quickly than an enemy could react, denying an enemy options and maintaining one's own freedom of action.

Feuquières hesitancy to identity fundamental laws for understanding war diverges from some trends of the "Military Enlightenment." Though he does contextualize his examples in explanation of principles, his work is more a narrative interwoven with reflections and recent military history. Yet the desire to classify "species" of war, as well as commentary on how to "improve" an operational situation, comports with Enlightenment epistemology.

Application: Feuquières's conceptions of the "species" of war entered contemporary strategic debate in Britain, with its tradition of vigorous public debate on the conduct of war. Field Marshal Lord Ligonier supposedly formulated plans during the War of the Austrian Succession based upon these principles. Napoleon drew from Feuquières in planning for the Italian campaigns, but later revealed he did not always agree with Feuquières.

Descendents: Extensive commentary on Feuquières is difficult to find. Frederick the Great did, however, call Feuquières's *Memoires* a classic, and had a translation made for his officers. Voltaire remarked that many historians of the Nine Years' War followed Feuquières's narrative, and he found Feuquières's strategic analysis cogent. Clausewitz mentioned Feuquières, approving of his effort to substantiate generalizations about warfare with concrete historical examples, yet also doubted his impartiality. Although historians such as Macaulay drew on Feuquières as a historical source, he figured only marginally in 19th- and 20th-century military thought. Feuquières's conception of the initiative does, however, echo in modern theories of operational art, for example, John Boyd's "OODA-loop."

See also: Crissé; Folard; Maizeroy; Picq; Saxe, M.

Further Reading

The outline of Feuquières's career can be found in *Biographie Universalle* (1968–) 14:72–73. Feuquières's *Memoires* have been reprinted in facsimile in the 20th century, as part of the Greenwood Press West Point Military Library Series. Jean Colin, Ira D. Gruber, Azar Gat, and Christopher Duffy have all considered his military thought.

Mark Danley

Fourquevaux, Raimond de Beccarie de Pavie, Seigneur de
(1509–1574)

Significance: Fourquevaux was one of the very first western authors in one work comprehensively to have discussed warfare both on the higher level of strategy and ethics, and on the more frequently discussed lower levels of tactics, fortifications, logistics, recruitment, morale, and psychological warfare. Fourquevaux was also one of the first explicitly to write about counterinsurgency, that is, how to deal with "rebels." His rules to be observed by soldiers in war are an early forerunner of the Hague and Geneva Conventions of the 20th century.

Context: The Great Italian Wars of 1494–1559, which besides directly affecting also the south of France drew in all the major European powers, form the background to Fourquevaux's writing.

Biography: Raimond de Beccarie de Pavie, baron de Fourquevaux, descended from a noble Italian family that had recently moved to the south of France to escape the Guelf-Ghibelline wars. From 1527, Fourquevaux fought for the French king in northern Italy and southern France. Around 1548, he began to be deployed on French diplomatic missions, first to Scotland and in Ireland, and later in Savoy, northern Italy, Bohemia, and Spain. Later he was put in charge of the defense of several French and Italian cities against sieges and uprisings. He thus combined military and diplomatic experience, and wrote not only for the military practitioner but also fort politically aware decision makers.

Influences: Similarly to Machiavelli's *Discourses on Livy,* Fourquevaux's *Instructions* built on the wisdom of the Ancients, drawing statements and examples from the works of Polybius, Frontinus, and Vegetius, from which Fourquevaux constructed his own book. He also drew on Antonio Cornazano's *Opera bellissima delarte Militar* (1493), and Machiavelli's *Art of War,* on which Fourquevaux's *Instructions* are in part modelled, significantly adding chapters of a more strategic–political nature absent from Machiavelli's book. Fourquevaux reiterated just war theory as found in many other works before from St Augustine of Hippo's writings to the 16th century.

The Theory: By building on antique texts, Fourquevaux provided a comprehensive discussion of warfare on the political, strategic, and tactical levels, including many subareas of warfare, such as fortifications and siegecraft. In addition to reiterating classic just war theory, the *Instructions* debate the ethical problem of what to do if a third party is threatened or attacked, repeatedly France's problem in the Italian wars. He weighed offensive or defensive strategies (he inclined toward the latter), when to seek, and when to avoid battle. Although condoning stratagems or ruses, he urged firm adherence to all promises given to allies or defeated enemies, and the enforcement of strict discipline and observance of rules of engagement among one's own soldiers. In his section on counterinsurgency he urges clemency. The *Instructions* list rules to be observed in war, an early codex of *ius in bello* trying to impose restraints on war by enforcing good discipline among soldiers.

Descendents: Fourquevaux was a widely read author in the second half of the 16th century. The *Instructions* were first published anonymously, leading to the false attribution to another French diplomat, Guillaume du Bellay. Reprinted several times, they were translated into Spanish, Latin, German, and English.

Further Reading

For excerpts, see Beatrice Heuser (ed. and trans.), *The Strategy Makers: Thoughts on War and Society from Machiavelli to Clausewitz.* Santa Barbara, CA: Praeger/ABC-CLIO, 2010.

Beatrice Heuser

Frontinus, Sextus Julius
(ca. 35–103 CE)

Significance: Frontinus's military work is an important guide to Greek and Roman military ruses, tricks, and ploys up to the second century CE.

Context: Frontinus wrote at the end of the first century CE at the height of Roman military and political power.

Biography: Sextus Julius Frontinus, a member of the Roman patrician class, was born ca. 40 CE. He was possibly educated in Alexandria. In 70, he served as urban praetor, and he was consul three times: in 72/73, 98, and again in 100. From 75 to 78, he was governor of Britain where he subdued the Silures and other hostile tribes of Wales and prepared the way for his successor, Agricola. He was a member of the College of Augurs, and served as proconsul in Asia in 86. In 97, the Emperor Nerva appointed him to the important position of superintendent of the aqueducts (*curator aquarum*) in Rome, and he subsequently wrote the definitive work on the water supply of Rome, which survives in only one manuscript. He died in 103 CE.

Influences: Frontinus was familiar with many Greek and Roman military writers and historians from whom he drew his collection of stratagems.

The Theory: Frontinus's principal treatise on military theory, entitled *De re militari (On Military Affairs)*, probably written ca. 78, is lost, but an appendix to that work, perhaps written ca. 84–96, survives. The *Strategemata (Strategems)*, a work in three books to which a fourth book by another author is appended, is not a systematic treatise on military affairs, but rather a collection of more than 500 examples of military stratagems (ruses, ploys, and tricks) drawn from Greek and Roman history and intended for the use of Roman officers. Among the topics addressed were: concealing one's plans, escaping from difficult situations, distracting the attention of the enemy, quelling mutinies, arousing an army's enthusiasm for battle, creating panic in the enemy's ranks, ambushes, concealing reverses, surprise attacks, inducing treachery, pretended retirements, sending and receiving messages, and sorties.

Application: Identifying any actual application of the stratagems directly attributable to Frontinus is problematical, especially as he collected them from other sources, but his readers no doubt sought to apply them on occasion.

Descendents: During the Middle Ages, Frontinus was considered one of the leading Classical authorities on military affairs, and his *Strategemata* was one of the more popular Classical military texts circulating during medieval times. It is often found in manuscripts with the work of Vegetius and other ancient military writers.

See also: Vegetius

Further Reading
Frontinus, *The Strategems and the Aqueducts of Rome.* Translated by Charles E. Bennett and edited by Mary B. McElwain. Cambridge, MA: Harvard University Press/London: William Heinemann, Ltd., 1969.

Gundermann, Gerhard (Ed.), *Quaestiones de Iuli Frontini Strategematon Libris.* Fleckeisen Jahrbuch Supplementband 16. Leipzig: 1888.

Thayer, Bill, "The Life and Works of Sextus Julius Frontinus" [Online, January 2006]. Lacus Curtius website at URL http://penelope.uchicago.edu/Thayer/E/Roman/Texts/Frontinus/life and works*/html.

Charles R. Shrader

Guibert, Jacques-Antoine-Hippolyte, Comte de
(1743–1790)

Significance: De Guibert was the principal theoretician of the reform of French infantry tactics. His ideas informed the codification of the French infantry drill system, published as the *reglement* of 1791, which remained in use throughout the Revolutionary and Napoleonic Wars (1792–1815) until 1830.

Context: The Seven Years' War (1756–1763) was an unhappy experience for French arms. Defeat in Europe at Rossbach (1757) and Minden (1759), and the loss of important colonies in India and North America, led to demands for reform among the public and in French military circles. The rebuilding of the demoralized armed forces was placed in the hands of the Duc de Choiseul, minister for the army and navy from 1761. A vast reorganization the following year brought standardized regimental organization, and large summer training exercises at brigade and divisional level. Weapons, uniform, and finance were brought to a very high standard, and the new Gribeauval artillery system was introduced in 1765, along with schools of military equitation. However, Choiseul had made many enemies at court and he was dismissed in 1771.

Nonetheless, thanks to these improvements, the performance of the French army in the American War of Independence was creditable, especially given the variety of climate and terrain involved. Choiseul's work was continued from 1775 under King Louis XIV by St. Germain, but he too found resistance to his largely sensible ideas, and was forced to resign in 1777. There followed a period of reinforcement of the privileged position of aristocratic officers.

Biography: Born at Montauban, the son of a general, de Guibert accompanied his father as an aide-de-camp in the Seven Years' War. He instructed himself during long periods of inactivity typical of officers at this time, while his father was assisting de Choiseul with his reforms. Following the Corsican campaign of 1769, de Guibert was promoted to Colonel. From 1772, he lived in Paris and was popular in the literary salons. His first work, *Essai général de tactique,* was published in that year. He had good reason to expect that it would not pass the strict French censorship laws, and so like many other authors, he had his work published in London under an anonymous imprint. The work was a sensational success, and soon ran to further editions, published in Geneva (extracting the sections likely to appeal to a wider audience), and in Liege. A German translation appeared in Dresden in 1774, and an English translation in London in 1781.

The liberal tone of the *Essai* displeased the French court, and although de Guibert was spared punishment because of his youth, and the patronage of Marshal Soubise, his book was banned in France. His success in the fashionable literary salons was guaranteed, but there were plenty of critics. Frederick II of Prussia responded with some reservations, but in good humor, and passed his compliments on via the encyclopedist D'Alembert. This encouraged de Guibert to visit Frederick at Potsdam. On his way back he paid his respects to Voltaire at Ferney, where Voltaire welcomed him cordially. In a letter to Mme De Deffand of November 16, 1773, Voltaire wrote that he detested war, but that he admired De Guibert's system. De Guibert had exhorted Voltaire to continue hating war, but not to confuse this hatred with that of "a science that makes it less deadly."

With the fall of Saint-Germain's ministry in 1777, the supporters of the *ordre profond* took up the charge once again, with Mesnil-Durand leading. Maneuvers held at Vaussieux in 1778 under the orders of Marshal de Broglie to try out the columnar tactics against conventional lines were inconclusive. De Guibert now studied the problems highlighted at these exercises. In his *Defence of the Modern System of War* (1779), he recommended a mixed tactical system, which would combine the benefits of deep and linear formations, dependent on the terrain, troops, and specific circumstances. He argued that the formation should be such that troops could change rapidly from column to line and back again. De Guibert also proposed an expanded role for the cavalry. Equally, he emphasized the importance of battles. Going back on his previous opinions regarding the people in arms, he judged that armies should be made up of professionals who would serve "the interests of the human race."

In his last work, *On the Power of the Public* (published in the year of his death, 1790), De Guibert warned prophetically of the dangers of total war that involved the arming of the people.

Influences: De Guibert was much affected by the campaigns of the French army in the Seven Years' War, and his outlook was molded by debates surrounding the reform of the French army between 1761 and 1771.

The Theory: De Guibert dedicated the *Essai* to his country, and hoped that one day it would return to its former glory and energy. In the *Discours preliminaire*, he criticized the politics of his day, which subordinated military concerns to those of state policy.

He was generally against the "cabinet wars" of the 18th century. These, he felt, were inconclusive and exhausted the state. He looked forward to a time when war would be more decisive. Politics, the art of governing the people, he maintains to be the most interesting of the sciences. It should have for its object the happiness of the nation at home and its respect abroad. At the time, this idea was not covered in any other work. He hoped that one day France would be able to raise a vigorous militia force, better than that of its neighbors, made up of citizens recruited for the defense of their homeland. If France was attacked, it would wreak a terrible revenge.

De Guibert had originally planned a massive new work, which he intended to cover the political and military affairs of France, beginning with an examination of the different European states, before dealing with those of his homeland. Only the military section was ever written, which became the *Essai général de tactique*.

He holds that the science of tactics is made up of two elements: the first simple and limited, the other complex and sublime.

> The second element is, to be frank, the science of generals. It includes all the great parts of war such as movements of armies, orders of march, orders of battle[…] It is everything in a word because it is the art of making the troops act, and all the other parts are secondary things which without it would have no purpose, or would only produce confusion. It is on this second aspect, seen from the wider point of view, where there are absolutely no theoretical texts. (*Essai général de tactique.* Vol. I, pp. 4–5)

The section on elementary tactics offers a summary of debates on the *ordre mince* and the *ordre profonde*. The new tactics of the French infantry allowed them to pass swiftly from line to column and vice versa in good order. The column, ideal for maneuver and attack, is made up of divisions of two companies formed up together. The grenadier and chasseur companies lead and close up the order of march, respectively. However, de Guibert remained skeptical about the much-vaunted shock effect of the column, and was a firm supporter of the *ordre mince*.

Grand tactics, he held, rested first and foremost with the army on march. This aspect for him became most important, and most decisive of all the phases of war. Marshal de Saxe had rightly said, "The whole secret of exercises and of war is in the legs." Frederick the Great made frequent rapid forced marches, he noted, from the Elbe to Silesia, and from Silesia toward the Russians in East Prussia. However, there were still great strides to be made in the art of grand tactics, and in the order of march in particular.

> One must know how to move on from mundane principles, and to this end if this can make the march faster and easier, the army should be separated into several bodies (corps) which come together at a given place, or within striking distance of a predetermined point; […] one must gain in speed what is lost in method, to make speed is the principle and only object of these combinations. (*Essai général de tactique.* Vol II. p. 8)

De Guibert saw clearly the advantage that could be gained from this new divisional maneuver system. The different bodies of troops would follow different routes, but by coordinated movements should be able to be able to form in battle order ready to fight. One part could conduct a flank march, whereas another marched against the enemy's front, all columns converging toward the same objective, "which is to form up in battle order and attack the enemy."

De Guibert reduced Vegetius's (*Epitome of Military Science,* III: 20) seven orders of battle to two: parallel order and oblique order. The first, he argued, is the more natural, the simplest, and the oldest. The second one became used "as mankind became more enlightened." The Greeks and Romans used the oblique order.

Military science was then forgotten, he maintained, and virtually disappeared. Now there was a return to the fighting methods of the Classical Age.

> When military science began to be reborn, we followed the same reasoning as the ancients, and consequently moved away from the parallel order. We sought to maneuver, to turn the enemy's flanks, there were hardly any more battles fought on the whole of the enemy's front, and there were even less as armies became more numerous, and drew up in thinner lines.

The *Essai* closes with *memoranda on the relationship of the science of fortifications, of the knowledge of terrain, of science of provisions, with tactics.* De Guibert reckoned that far too many fortresses had been constructed, and that this had made war more costly in terms of lives and money, and less scientific. There was still a need for fortresses, he said, but fewer of them, and these would be well sited at defiles on the frontiers. "War on the grand scale, the war of campaigns should always be the principle objective."

Application: De Guibert's work was novel in its time for its appreciation of the fundamental relationship between politics and war. There is a distinction between the two parts of the art of war described by others in the age of the Enlightenment. Puységur, Folard, de Saxe, and Frederick II of Prussia, all made a distinction between the simple part and the sublime part (or the greater part), or in other words between the day-to-day routine of army administration and operations, and the higher philosophy of the art of war.

Moreover, de Guibert spoke of the difference between elementary tactics and grand tactics. In the *Defense of the Modern System of War* he called this *la strategique,* or army-level tactics, we would now call this "operational art." The rediscovery of the concept of strategy at the end of the 18th century grew largely from these theoretical writings. The newfound flexibility of armies gave rise to new possibilities, to be carried out at a higher level in the tactics of army groups or even corps-sized formations.

Descendents: During the campaigns of the French Revolutionary Wars the massive increase in the size of the army allowed commanders to practice de Guibert's "march divided, fight united" principle. Hoche, Dumouriez, and Bonaparte all incorporated these principles in the campaigns of 1794 to 1797. During the Napoleonic Wars, the *corps d'armée* system was used extensively by the French and eventually by all European armies.

See also: Bonaparte, Napoleon; Gribeauval, J.

Further Reading
See original works in French.

Toby McLeod

Hay du Chastelet, Paul
(1619–1682?)

Significance: In the 17th century, Paul Hay du Chastelet stands out as an author who considered warfare in the totality, from its legal justification and political purpose ("peace is the final aim of taking arms") down to the basics of recruitment. Like Liddell Hart three centuries later, Hay distinguished between a prudent "Fabian" style of warfare and an offensive "Alexandrian" style.

Context: Hay du Chastelet dedicated his *Treatise on War* to King Louis XIV of France, who would become known not only as the Sun King but also as the King of War, waging wars during 32 years of his 54 years' reign. The *Treatise on War* was published during the preparations for France's war of 1667/1668 with Spain over the Spanish succession and the Habsburgs' possessions north of France, which Louis coveted. The *Treatise* also reflects the upsetting experience of the French civil war of the Fronde (1648–1653).

Biography: Paul Hay, Sieur du Chastelet, probably a native of Rennes in Brittany, was the son of (and is often confused with) the eponymous first secretary of the Académie Française. After his father's death, Paul junior was educated by his uncle, Daniel Hay du Chastelet (1596–1671), also a member of the Académie and the abbot of Chambon. Paul married a descendent of the famous Huguenot captain François de la Noue. Nevertheless, Paul Hay in his publications fervently defended the Catholic point of view. Hay claimed to have had personal experience of warfare.

Influences: Hay du Chastelet was well acquainted with the historians of Antiquity, and stood firmly in the Roman and Catholic just war tradition.

The Theory: Although Hay tried to restrain Louis XIV's lust for war, urging his monarch to fight only for just causes, Hay conceded critically that princes often fought for their interests and glory, but this was not a fact he could approve of. While professing that every detail in war is in God's hand, the *Treatise* paradoxically emphasizes human wisdom, skill, and preparations. Hay identified two styles of warfare: the aggressive, offensive, and impetuous style of Alexander the Great, which he much preferred (including preemptive battle), and the defensive, careful approach of the Roman general Quintus Fabius Maximus, known as *Cunctator* (the hesitator). Classically for his times, Hay gave equal attention to both, and to what should be done in case of victory and in defeat. Hay urged restraint even in victory; defeated civilians and enemy soldiers must be treated well. He thought conquered lands were best pacified by means of good governance. Having lived through the Fronde, Hay showed great concern for the avoidance of insurgencies and civil war, and devised best practice in such cases. The establishment of a just order *postbellum* was central to Hay: "no captain must ever, regardless of what victory he has won, refuse fair conditions to his enemies." Hay also debated problems and opportunities of alliance warfare, mercenaries and other foreign troops, and naval warfare, which he thought of little benefit to France.

Descendents: His *Treatise* was reprinted twice, including a century after its first publication, and was that widely read in France. There is no evidence of any translation into other languages.

Further Reading
For excerpts, see Beatrice Heuser (ed. and trans.), *The Strategy Makers: Thoughts on War and Society from Machiavelli to Clausewitz.* Santa Barbara, CA: Praeger/ABC-CLIO, 2010.

Beatrice Heuser

Herodotus
(ca. 484 BCE–ca. 425 BCE)

Significance: First historian known to have gathered his information systematically, providing a coherent history of the Greco-Persian wars. Herodotus is referred to by historians as the "Father of History."

Context: Herodotus wrote a detailed history of the wars between the Persian Empire and the Greek city-states during the fifth century BCE. The first and larger part of his *Histories* gives an account of Persia's growth and expansionist policies under the Achaemenid dynasty, whereas the second part describes the Persian invasion in Greece, the ensuing battles, and the campaign's ultimate failure.

Biography: Herodotus was born at Halicarnassus in Asia Minor in ca. 484 BCE. His probable involvement in a coup against the Persian tyrant of his native city led to his exile to the island of Samos. Although Herodotus returned to Halicarnassus after some years, he spent most of his early years traveling extensively throughout Greece, the Levant, Egypt, Magna Graecia, and the Black Sea, gathering information for his work. According to tradition, he died at Thurii in ca. 425 BCE.

Influences: Herodotus's first-hand experience of the Persian Empire and its hostility toward Greece most probably led him to the writing of *The Histories*.

The Theory: Herodotus was the first to write a detailed history of the Greco-Persian wars based on information he methodically gathered during his extended travels. When possible, he would interview people involved in major events, such as the Athenian veterans of the Battle of Marathon. Herodotus is our main source about some of the most famous battles such as Marathon, Thermopylae, Plataea, and Salamis.

Application and Descendents: Later ancient historians criticized Herodotus, claiming that he exaggerated and even lied in certain cases. Modern historians, however, praise Herodotus's work, emphasizing on its wealth of geographical and ethnographical information.

Further Reading

Dewald, Carolyn, and John Marincola, eds. *The Cambridge Companion to Herodotus.* Cambridge: Cambridge University Press, 2006.

Ioannis Georganas

Ibn Akhi Hizam, Muhammad Ibn Ya'qub al-Khuttali
(ca. ninth century CE)

Significance: The Abbasid Iraqi army commander Muhammad Ibn Ya'qub Ibn Ghalib Ibn Ali al-Khuttali, known as Ibn Akhi Hizam, was the central figure in Muslim *furusiyya* ("horsemanship" or "chivalry") and wrote the oldest surviving Arabo-Islamic manual on military training and the care of horses. His work thus marked the emergence of Muslim *furusiyya* and determined the content of subsequent *furusiyya* literature.

Context and Biography: Born in Baghdad, where he also died, Ibn Akhi Hizam descended from a distinguished family of *abna'* (literally "sons," meaning the descendents of Arabs who had settled in Khurasan) who served the Abbasid dynasty in Iraq. His uncle, Hizam Ibn Ghalib, was a well-known commander of the Abbasids' Khurasani corps, as well as stable master to the warrior Caliph al-Mu'tasim (833–842 CE). His brother Ya'qub, Ibn Aki Hizam's father, shared the task of supervising al-Mu'tasim's stables, a sophisticated institution with a staff of hundreds. Ya'qub became the chief veterinary surgeon to the Caliph al-Mutawakkil (847–861 CE). Nevertheless, his brother Hizam's fame meant that he was commonly referred to as Akhu Hizam "brother of Hizam"—hence his son's epithet Ibn Akhi Hizam, "the son of the brother of Hizam."

The Theory and Influences: Ibn Akhi Hizam emulated his father and his uncle, joining the Khurasani corps and becoming one of its most prominent commanders. Subsequently, he became stable master to the Caliph al-Mu'tadid (892–902 CE). Ibn Akhi Hizam was an experienced soldier, an expert on horses and a master of *furusiyya* arts; hence, the unmatched importance of his treatise, written for the Caliph al-Mutawakkil.

Commonly entitled *Kitab al-Furusiyya wa-al-Baytara,* "The Book of *Furusiyya* Arts and Veterinary Medicine," the work consisted of two complementary treatises intended as manuals for mounted warriors, army officers, and commanders. The first treatise (hereafter treatise A) is a comprehensive work on horses including equitation, hippology, and farriery. The second treatise (treatise B) mainly deals with the principles of riding and horse mastery, weapons techniques, polo, and hunting. Both were seminal contributions based upon the author's extensive knowledge and practical experience.

Ibn Akhi Hizam's qualities as a *furusiyya* master derived largely from a military and historical process that started with establishment of the Abbasid state in Iraq. *Furusiyya* emerged under the Abbasid Caliphate in Iraq during the second half of the eighth century CE, and flowered during the ninth century. It covered equitation and horse mastery, close combat techniques, archery, hunting, and polo. It also included practical and theoretical knowledge of basic veterinary science, the characteristics of weapons, and the art of war. The scope of *furusiyya* included training, exercises, and games performed on foot, such as wielding arms, archery, boxing, wrestling, and field hockey (*tabtab*).

Furusiyya was subdivided into "upper *furusiyya*" (*al-furusiyya al-'ulwiyya*) or activities on horseback, and "lower *furusiyya*" (*al-furusiyya al-sufliyya*), activities on foot. The overall activities of *furusiyya* were shared by two complementary and intermingling concepts and institutions: noble or civil *furusiyya* (*al-furusiyya al-nabilah* or *al-ahliyyah*) as represented by the Abbasid court and certain elements of civil society, and military *furusiyya* (*al-furusiyya al-harbiyya*) centered upon the training of mounted warriors.

Noble *furusiyya* was a state institution almost from its inception following the founding of Baghdad by the Caliph al-Mansur (754–775 CE). It consisted of training, from childhood, of the male members of the Abbasid family and the sons of notables, in horsemanship, the use of arms, archery, polo, field hockey, and hunting. The Caliph al-Mansur was too old to engage in such activities but he prepared the ground for his heir, al-Mahdi (775–785 CE), and his successors. Al-Mahdi was the first crown prince to be brought up according to the principles of noble *furusiyya*. In 768 CE, the first polo field (*maydan*) in Islam was built adjacent to his palace at al-Rusafa in Baghdad. Al-Mahdi became an archer of repute, skilled with both the long, simple Arab bow and the composite Persian bow. He made hunting into a sophisticated caliphal institution. Al-Mahdi's successors followed his example, and proficiency in *furusiyya* became a prerequisite for the caliphate.

Noble *furusiyya* was a unique blending of Mesopotamian, Arab, and Sassanian cultures within the framework of Islamic civilization and in the Abbasid context. It retained the pre-Islamic Arab concept of the horseman (*faris*) embodying bravery (*shaja'a*), gallantry (*shahama*), manliness (*muruwwa*), and generosity (*sakha'*). The notion of *faris* thus penetrated the Abbasid court *furusiyya*, and the term *furusiyya* is still used in Arabic as a synonym of such virtues, the chivalric aspect of Abbasid noble *furusiyya* surviving even after the institution itself died out.

This ethical dimension was also integrated in military *furusiyya*, which originated within the Abbasids' new army and which became the first professional multiethnic caliphal army in Islam. Meanwhile, the traditional tribal Arab army dwindled rapidly until it was practically extinguished under the Caliph al-Ma'mun (833–842 CE), being officially abolished by his brother and successor al-Mu'tasim. The core of the new army consisted of the nontribal forces recruited in greater Khurasan (now divided between Afghanistan, Iran, Tajikistan, Uzbekistan, and Turkmenistan) during the Abbasid revolution that eventually replaced the Umayyad Caliphate in 750 CE. The majority of those early Khurasani recruits were Arab settlers whose ancestors had come from Iraq during the seventh century CE to control Persia and conquer greater Khurasan. Serving both as cavalry and as infantry, they were good archers, using the powerful Persian or Central Asian composite bow, which neutralized the Umayyad heavy cavalry and secured victory for the Abbasids. The Khurasani recruits introduced the mace and war axe into the caliphal army while still upholding the two most traditional Arab weapons, the lance and sword.

A sophisticated training system epitomized the Abbasid military *furusiyya,* representing an ingenious synthesis of Arab, Persian, Central Asian, and Byzantine military traditions. Its aim was to produce an accomplished and almost unique brand of mounted archers who would be individually more effective than even the Central Asian nomad horse archers, while still being highly proficient with the lance and close combat weapons. Such horsemen were also trained to fight on foot. Furthermore, they were expected to know the basics of veterinary science and be familiar with all weapons, including siege warfare equipment, and the stratagems of war and the art of war. These skills were continuously refined through exercises.

The two treatises of Ibn Akhi Hizam (A and B) come down to us both separately and bearing different titles, and combined as one work are often referred to as his "grand book" (*kitabuhu al-kabir*). Each treatise covers one of the two basic categories of *furusiyya* literature. The first such category includes thematic chapters on equitation, hippology, and farriery; on archery; on the art of war; on arms and war engines; on the chase and polo. The second category includes general *furusiyya* treatises that deal with some or most of the above-mentioned subjects, either in an abridged form or by including portions from the thematic treatises or as entire but small treatises. It also covers the training of the mounted warrior on horseback and on foot.

Treatise A is the oldest preserved Arabic text on horses and their medical treatment. It is also the earliest contribution, probably in any language, in which hippology, riding, training, and veterinary medicine are integrated into one work. Treatise A became the prototype of subsequent treatises. The work is divided into two parts. The core of the first part consists of chapters dealing with the treatment and training of horses, plus a host of chapters dedicated to riding, preceded by remarks on the skills needed by the trainer and the types of horses worth training. The second is devoted to veterinary medicine. All these chapters are largely based upon the author's practical experience.

Ibn Akhi Hizam elaborated upon Abbasid philological works concerning horses, all of which were written in Iraq, especially the work of the Basran philologist Abu 'Ubaydah Ma'mar Ibn al-Muthanna (d. 824 CE) entitled *Kitab al-Khayl* (Book of Horses). This was the most complete philological work on horses, inspiring subsequent treatises whether written by philologists, *furusiyya* masters, or compilers. At one point Ibn Akhi Hizam quotes and disputes the work of a certain Indian named Junna regarding markings and whorls.

In the second part devoted to veterinary medicine, the main reference, besides the author's own experience, was his father Ya'qub. Ibn Akhi Hizam was similarly familiar with earlier Greek and Persian contributions in this field and included several medical prescriptions that he described as belonging to the "ancients." He was, nevertheless, critical of contemporary veterinary medicine. He demanded that veterinary surgeons should be cross-examined before being allowed to practice.

Ibn Akhi Hizam's treatise B served as a model for future general *furusiyya* treatises. These were normally devoted to military *furusiyya,* integrating different disciplines needed to train and educate a mounted warrior.

In his preface, Ibn Akhi Hizam outlined his concept of military *furusiyya* that he suggested, consisted of three fundamentals: horse mastery; proficiency in handling all types of weapons; and bravery. If the first two fundamentals were achieved, the horseman would be technically a perfect mounted warrior, but he would not be a genuine *faris* if he lacked courage. This in turn represented an ethical approach to warfare. He warned that bravery was a conscious act, which meant a wise mixture of daring and caution, good judgment, fear of God, gallantry, patience, endurance, honoring one's duties and obligations, modesty, and the capacity to overcome fear. All these virtues represented the ideal of Abbasid *furusiyya*.

After this introduction, Ibn Akhi Hizam discussed military equitation. It began with an emphasis on riding bareback, not only to teach skills of securing a balanced seat when riding a saddled horse, but also to enable the horseman to fight and survive under all circumstances. He then offers advice concerning horse equipment. This chapter was often either quoted verbatim or simply plagiarized by later treatises, especially those from the Mamluk period.

The core of treatise B lies, however, in the chapters devoted to weapons. These start with the lance, which was considered the most important weapon besides the bow for the training of a mounted warrior. It was also the best means of for testing his aptitude in horsemanship. This chapter remained the standard manual on the subject for many centuries to come. It dealt with the fundamentals of lance training, types of charges and thrusts including, *al-tashdid al-shami aw al-rumi* "the Syrian or Byzantine" couched lance technique, the Khurasani technique, the Daylami or Yemeni technique, and the "modern" Islamic technique known as *al-tashdid al-muhdath*. Then came techniques of lance combat under different circumstances, the technique of lance jousting, and simulated lance combat either by pairs or horsemen or by one lancer facing two or more opponents.

The chapter on swords deals with unique information on the three basic forms of sword used by the Abbasid army. These were the straight, double-edged Arab sword, the single-edged Transoxanian sword called *al-sughdi* ("the Sughdian"), and the "edge and a half" sword called *al-khisrawani* ("the royal Persian"). The last two types represent sabers or proto-sabers with a straight or slightly curved blade. The author gave a set of guidelines on thrusts or strikes, and on the techniques of sword combat on horseback.

Although emphasizing the importance of a shield for the sword-armed man, whether on horse or on foot, Ibn Akhi Hizam made a digression about the different types and functions of shields.

For the sake of thoroughness, the author included in this chapter the essence of a treatise on swords written for the Abbasid Caliph al-Mu'tasim by the celebrated philosopher and chemist Abu Yusuf Ya'qub Ibn Ishaq al-Kindi (800 to ca. 866–873 CE). This treatise is unique in its genre within the group of *furusiyya* thematic "treatises on arms and war engines." It was a remarkable field study, as each type of blade described being known and examined by al-Kindi himself who spent years visiting sword-smiths. This might explain why there was no subsequent attempt to write anything similar. Al-Kindi's work remains undoubtedly the most important source on swords from the entire medieval period. Ibn Akhi Hizam was probably the first *furusiyya* author to make extensive use of it. Nearly all subsequent borrowings from al-Kindi's work by Abbasid and Mamluk *furusiyya* treatises were lifted from this chapter in Ibn Akhi Hizam's treatise B, rather than directly from al-Kindi's treatise.

In his chapter on archery, the author combined his own knowledge with information from his elder contemporary and compatriot Abd al-Rahman Ahmad al-Tabari's *Kitab al-Shamil fi al-Rami* ("Comprehensive Book on Archery"). This chapter deals with types of bows, bowstrings, arrows, thumb rings, training the novice, target shooting, faults and injuries to which the archer was exposed, bracing the bow, shooting at and from a fortress, techniques of shooting from horseback, shooting a lion from horseback, and other subjects.

Treatise B concludes with a chapter on polo (*al-Darb bi al-Sawalija*), which had spread widely across the Muslim world after the Abbasids came to power. Indeed, this "king of games" was being democratized because it had become an integral part of the training of the mounted warrior Ibn Akhi Hizam urged his fellow cavalrymen to constantly play polo. He provided precious information on polo equipment, techniques, and ponies.

Application: During the ninth century, collective and individual lance combats and maneuvers were commonly performed in the *maydans* "hippodromes" of Baghdad and Samarra that were often attended by the Caliph. Ibn Akhi Hizam himself organized and participated in such maneuvers during the caliphate of al-Mu'tadid.

Abbasid *ghulam* (literally "young servant," plural: *ghilman*) took shape during the reign of the Caliph al-Mu'tasim and reached maturity in Baghdad under al-Mu'tadid, in response to the caliphate's need for loyal and efficient elite military units. It was conceived and inspired through the Abbasid noble *furusiyya*. Not surprisingly, the *ghulam's* military training was more rigorous and systematic than that endured by "noble *furusiyya* members" or the Abbasid professional army as a whole. The initially servile status of these *ghilman* (mostly of Turkish origin) ensured their dedication to the training, their obedience to their educators who also taught them literacy and general knowledge, and to the *furusiyya* masters. This largely explains why the *ghilman* were normally affranchised immediately after the completion of the formative training period that might last several years. They then became free, mounted warriors in their respective elite corps and enjoyed numerous privileges.

Descendents: The combined work by Ibn Akhi Hizam, treatises A and B, greatly dominated the hundreds of available *furusiyya* manuals for centuries to come. It became the manual par excellence for *furusiyya* masters, *mamluks,* and *halaqa* troopers (non-*mamluk* professional troops in the Mamluk Sultanate). Indeed, the Mamluk *furusiyya* author and *halaqa* commander Muhammad Ibn Mangli (*q.v.*) warned his fellow troopers and *mamluks* not to consult any other work. Ibn Akhi Hizam deserved the nickname given him by *furusiyya* masters and fellow mounted soldiers, as the *Imam al-Fursan,* "supreme guide of cavalrymen."

The *ghulam* system, which now spread from Iraq to the Abbasid provinces and successor states as far as Spain and India, proved to be long lasting and had a far-reaching impact upon Islamic societies and their neighbors. In most post-Abbasid Middle Eastern societies, the *ghilman* or *mamluks,* as they came to be known, became an integral part of the upper military and administrative class. They sometimes exercised direct rule, as in the cases of the Ghaznavid dynasty of Afghanistan (962–1186 CE) or the Mamluk Sultanate of Egypt and Syria (1250–1517 CE). Thus, the *ghilman* system not only became the finest incarnation of Abbasid *furusiyya* but also the main means of its dissemination.

This dissemination led to the diffusion of the *furusiyya* vital for the education, training, and life-long technical perfection of the mounted warrior. As a result, two main periods of Abbasid *furusiyya* literature can be identified: the first flourishing from the second half of the eighth CE century until the Buwayhid domination of Iraq (945 CE), the second lasting from the mid-12th CE century until the Mongol conquest of Iraq and the destruction of the Abbasid Caliphate in Baghdad (1258 CE). There followed a third significant era of *furusiyya* literature in Syria and Egypt under the Mamluk Sultanate that became the true heir and perpetuator of Abbasid institutions and traditions. However, most of the *furusiyya* treatises produced during this Mamluk period were compilations based upon Abbasid treatises.

It is yet to be determined whether Ibn Akh Hizam's treatise A, which had reached Muslim Spain by at least the 12th century (as attested in the *Kitab al-Filaha* "Book of Agriculture" by the Andalusian agronomist Ibn al 'Aawwam, d. 1185 CE), had any impact upon the evolution of European horsemanship or veterinary medicine. It certainly shaped Muslim horsemanship and veterinary medicine. During the 14th century it was even translated into the Kipchaq Turkish under the title *Kitab Baytarat al-Vazih* "Clear Book on Veterinary Medicine," to be better understood by the Mamluks of Egypt and Syria who had insufficient knowledge of Arabic. There were also Persian and Ottoman Turkish versions of treatise A, although the influence of Ibn Akhi Hizam's treatise A continued until the start of the 20th century when the last important Arabic book on horses appeared, written by Amir Muhammad Pasha Ibn Amir 'Abd al-Qadi al-Jaza'ri (d. 1913) and published in Istanbul in 1907.

Although other Abbasid treatises on polo followed, some of which were more detailed than Ibn Akhi Hizam's chapter, his text was the oldest surviving inclusive document on the subject in any language. All post-Abbasid texts on polo, especially those from the Mamluk period, accepted Abbasid polo rules and "arts" without much further innovation. The Abbasid version of polo spread across the Middle East, subsequently to reach India where polo became popular under the Mughals (1526–1858 CE). From there it was adopted in the 1860s by the British, who spread it worldwide.

See also: Al-Rawandi; Al-Shaybani; Al-Shayzari; Al-Tabari; Baghdadi Manjaniqi, Ya'qūb Ibn Ṣābir; Muhammad; Nizam al-Mulk; Usama Ibn Munqidh

David Nicolle and Shihab al-Sarraf

Kamandaka
(450–550 CE)

Significance: Kamandaka's greatest contribution is to argue that military strategy should always be subordinated to political decision. Unlike other Hindu theorists, Kamandaka introduces the role of riverine navy in conducting land warfare. Kamandaka is important because he expounds the concept of *dharmayuddha* (just war) both in case of internal rebellions and interstate conflicts. Kamandaka focused on restraint on the use of force in both interstate and intra-state affairs. To avoid war, Kamandaka expounds various types of treaties between the sovereign powers, and in *Nitisara,* advances the theory of paternal despotism. He says that the *vijigishu* (the ideal ruler) should behave like a father toward the subjects—the king should, in fact, try to win the subject's "hearts and minds"—and should even try to co-opt some of the rebellious elements. It is therefore necessary that the king should follow the path of righteousness and should use force carefully. At times, says the *Nitisara,* deployment of *dandashakti* (coercive power) is necessary for ensuring *dharma* (rule of law) within the kingdom, but punishment should always be proportional to the crimes committed.

Context: The eclipse of the Kushanas in north India, and of the Satavahanas in Deccan during the third century CE, resulted in political disintegration in the Indian subcontinent. This gave rise to new powers and ruling families, including the Guptas, who established their feudo-federal Gupta Empire in north India under Chandragupta I in 320 CE. By the fifth century CE, the Gupta Empire was disintegrating under both Hunnic invasion and internal rebellions by their feudatories. Kamandaka operated within a political scenario of decentralized Hindu kingdoms with weaker bureaucracies than under the Maurya Empire. Each kingdom was a loose confederation of chieftains over whom the king presided. Hence, Kamandaka's argument that it is essential for a strong ruler to have strong and loyal feudatories.

Biography: Kamandaka came after the Gupta intellectual Kalidasa and was probably a contemporary of the mathematician and astronomer Varahamihira. Kamandaka wrote *Nitisara* between 450 and 550 CE.

Influences: Kamandaka regarded Kautilya as his mentor, and his Nitisara accepts the Kautilyan theory of *mandalas* (circle of states). Kamandaka, like Kautilya, warns his readers that, although the *mandala* is composed of both hostile and friendly powers, all polities are essentially selfish and look after their own interest. Friendliness and hostility toward the *vijigishu* therefore depend on their own perceptions of self-interest. Political alliances are therefore constantly shifting position according to circumstances. Perpetual friendship is impossible in reality, and an intelligent ruler should never put total trust on treaties. Rather, he should use peaceful times in preparing for inevitable times of crisis. After all, assures Kamandaka, in politics nobody can be trusted—not even one's father.

Kamandaka, like Kautilya, warns that internal enemies are more dangerous than external enemies. *Danda* (the state's coercive power) is necessary for both internal and external security, to prevent *matsanya* (the law of fishes in the pond, where the bigger fish swallows the smaller ones). This concept is borrowed from Kautilya. When *matsanya* prevails, *adharma* (unrighteousness) flourishes. In general, the policy of *ahimsa* is to be followed and *danda* is to be used only as a last resort. For maintaining internal security, *danda* should be used only when winning the "hearts and minds" of the subjects fail and punishment of antisocial elements is required.

Kamandaka accepts Kautilya's dictum that in desperate situation, a ruler could follow *kutayuddha* (unjust war). Influential men of the enemy kingdom should be won over by bounties or threats. If they cannot be won over, then they are to be assassinated. Kamandaka also accepts Kautilya's emphasis on the utility of spies, who should be used to spread panic and confusion in the enemy territory.

The principal objective of military campaigns, writes Kamandaka (influenced by Kautilya and Manu) is not the enemy army, but the enemy forts. Siege operation should involve blockading the supply routes to the forts. Kamandaka also follows Kautilya's advice on how to seize the initiative from besiegers.

The Theory: The *Nitisara* argues that the seven interdependent elements of a government are king, ministers, kingdom, castles, treasury, *danda,* and allies. For a ruler trying to be *vijigishu,* the two most important of these seven elements are a solvent treasury and a strong *bala* (army). The principal duty of a king is good governance, which will ensure prosperity in his kingdom. The welfare and protection of his subjects are the twin duties of a ruler. Only a fatalist believes in providence as the cause behind prosperity and adversity; the king requires courage, valor, discipline, and leadership qualities to succeed.

Leaders take recourse to *vigraha* (war) because they are seized with revengefulness and agitated by resentment due to mutual harmful actions. War is also resorted to by one aspiring to elevate his status, that is, aiming at overlordship, or by one suffering from harassment at the hands of his enemies. Other motives include the acquisition of territory, wealth, and allies. Of these three things, territory is most important and allies are least important. Triggers for war may include the abduction of women of the royal family, occupation of forts and capture of territory, the capture of horses and treasures of another king, learned men and soldiers who are enticed away from the kingdom, insulting behavior toward another ruler, usurpation in the kingdom, and interference in the affairs of allies of another kingdom.

Kamandaka assumes that the polities in the international arena are organized in a *mandala*. The sphere round a king consists of 12 other kings of whom four are enemies, four friends, and four neutrals.

The friends of *vijigishu* are of various types. Some kings may be related to the *vijigishu* by blood. Other kings might continue the alliance with the *vijigishu* because such an alliance has lasted for several generations. Many might become allies of the *vijigishu* due to the protection offered to the alliance by the powerful *vijigishu*. The allies are divided into categories of good, bad, and mediocre on the basis of their loyalty and military plus economic strength.

The techniques for avoiding war are *sama* (conciliation), *dana* (gift), and *bheda* (sowing dissension). Somewhat preempting the Prussian philosopher Carl Von Clausewitz, Kamandaka says that politics should occupy the dominant position while a state is conducting war. The *Nitisara* criticizes militarism and considers overdependence on military strength dangerous. Military power should always be subordinated to political judgment.

The principal message of *Nitisara* is to discourage the monarch from launching a war suddenly when pursuing an aggressive strategy. Victory in war is always *anitya* (uncertain), and because war results in mental and physical exhaustion; an intelligent ruler should never indulge in frequent campaigns. The *Nitisara* emphasizes self-restraint: a ruler practicing self-restraint rarely suffers defeat. Fighting with a powerful enemy is never justified ("clouds can never move in a direction opposite to that of the wind"). If attacked by a powerful king, one should not follow the example of snakes (which bite at the slightest provocation) but that of a cane (which bends under pressure but stands straight when the pressure is removed). Even when another of equal strength opposes a king, it is better to make peace rather than rely on the chance of battle. Death and destruction is the essence of war for all the parties. Warfare inevitably results in loss for the monarch and his subjects, and because the principal duty of the king is welfare of his subjects, it is better to make peace than wage war should the enemy demand minimal concessions.

Before starting war, the king should try to avoid hostility through diplomacy and generosity. If necessary, bilateral and multilateral treaties should be signed with other powers. The basic policy should be to follow the law of collective, harmonious existence.

In case of invasion by a stronger enemy, the latter should be won over through diplomatic alliances. The *Nitisara* explains various types of *sandhis* (treaties).

The *Kapalasandhi* is a type of alliance concluded between two powers of equal resources to maintain status quo. *Upaharasandhi* (*upahar* means gifts) involves offers of land, cash, and precious stones. This alliance is further subdivided into two types. When peace is made by ceding territory to a stronger power, it is known as *Aditasandhi*. When peace is made by surrendering mineral and forest resources, it is called *Parikrayasandhi*. *Santanasandhi* (*santana* means children) involves offering the daughter in marriage to the assailant. *Upanyasasandhi* is concluded between two parties for achieving a common purpose, that is, war against a particular polity. A variation of this type of *sandhi* is known as *Samyogasandhi,* which refers to a temporary alliance made between the ruler and his enemy for fighting jointly against a bigger danger. This sort of *sandhi* is necessary, because the *vijigishu* should always avoid a two front war. Finally, *Samgatasandhi* is a long-term alliance between two parties for the purpose of pooling their resources, both in normal times and during emergencies. A treaty that establishes long-term peace between two polities is known as *Kancanasandhi*. A weak ruler signs *Pratikarasandhi* with a strong power. Under the terms of this treaty, the strong power provides military help to the weaker one if the latter is attacked by a third power.

At times, despite alliances, war becomes inevitable. For instance, if the enemy threatens an intimate ally of the *vijigishu,* the latter has no other option except to go for war. Before going to war, an accurate and detailed assessment of the enemy's strength and intention is necessary, and reconnaissance is vital. Similar to Sun Tzu, Kamandaka writes that knowing the enemy assures victory in warfare. For example, detailed information about the river and land routes of the hostile kingdom should be acquired.

Kamandaka suggests that the king should always use his military assets defensively. In case of war, instead of rushing to attack the enemy, the king should form a grand alliance and then absorb or turn the allies of his enemy to slowly strangle the latter. Those allies of the enemy who refuse to be absorbed by the *vijigishu* should be liquidated, thereby indirectly weakening the enemy's strength. However, rapid liquidation of the enemy's allies might concern other members of the *mandala,* who might then unite and attack the *vijigishu*. Hence, the *vijigishu* should move slowly and, instead of totally destroying the enemy allies, should transform them into his dependences. Kamandaka therefore advocates a slow, protracted attritional war or a theory of exhaustion. He elaborates on this indirect strategy: the kingdom of the enemy should be harassed, for example, by destroying its crops.

Kamandaka also describes the characteristics and functions of the *bala*. The term *bala* means an army that was used as a *danda* (coercive instrument) for ensuring good governance. In times of war, the king has to rely on *bala,* which is composed primarily by weapons and soldiers. A ruler whose armed forces are corrupt and ill disciplined is like a kingdom ravaged by famine, and even a brave ruler is let down by cowardly soldiers who desert him in battle. The *bala* should be composed of soldiers whose families have been loyal for generations, and the core of the army should be composed of *Kshatriyas* (the warrior caste). The soldiers' valor and professional skill should be developed, and skillful commanders should be appointed to control them. Soldiers should be equipped with various types of weapons, and different units should specialize in various modes of fighting, for example, with swords or spears. Moreover, the soldiers should be prepared for military service in distant regions over a long period. To ensure loyalty, welfare measures are essential. A covetous or miserly ruler who does not adequately remunerate his men loses their wholehearted support and thus comes to grief, as the enemy can purchase such a ruler's officers and men. So, besides clash of arms, campaigns can be decided by the power of money and political intrigues.

Cooperation between the army and riverine navy is perhaps the most original point of the *Nitisara*. Kamandaka realized that for logistical purposes navy should be used because it was much cheaper and quicker to transport men, animals, and military stores along rivers rather than over land. Kamandaka hints that the river fleets should be used for transporting the army and war materials and also for conducting siege operations around enemy forts located on the riverbanks. At times, Kamandaka also harps on amphibious operations. However, Kamandaka's thrust remains on siege warfare on land and he does not elaborate on the role of a riverine navy in warfare to a great extent.

Whereas Kautilya's suggested force structure for conducting land warfare focuses on cooperation between war chariots, infantry, cavalry, and elephants, Kamandaka suggests a core of elephants, covered with iron armor and protected by infantry. Kamandaka writes that the king should maintain elephant forests for ensuring the supply of war elephants.

The *Nitisara* suggests various sorts of *vhuyas* (army battle formations). Each *vhuya* consists of the following components: *urah* (a detached unit just in front of the center), *kaksa* (flanks), *paksa* (front), *madhya* (center), *prshta* (a unit behind the center), *pratigraha* (reserve in the rear), and finally *koti* (mobile reserve).

The *Achalvhuya* formation consists of infantry in the front, cavalry in the second line, chariots in the third line, and finally elephants in the rear. When the elephants are in the front, cavalry in the second line, chariots in the third line and finally infantry in the fourth line, the formation is called *Aprathihatavhuya*. Shifting elephants to the center, chariots at both the flanks and cavalry on two frontal wings, creates the formation is known as *Madhyavedhivhuya*. When cavalry is in the center, chariots at the two flanks and elephants organized in two wings at the front, the battle formation is called *Antvhidvhuya*. In these two above-mentioned battle formations, infantry is not deployed.

The *Nitisara* categorizes *durgas* (forts) into four types according to their locations: forts on *parvats* (hills); *audakas* (watery forts, built on islands in rivers); *varksams* (forest forts); and desert forts. Desert forts are of two types: *airina* (fort in arid waterless area) and *dhanvana* (fort in sandy desert area). Each of the forts should be surrounded by a moat or ditch, and have ramparts fitted with strong gateways. A fort with sufficient garrison and supplies would be able to withstand a long siege. In addition, the forts should have secret shelters for king and his entourage during enemy siege operations. A king without forts is helpless.

Application: Indian rulers applied Kamandaka's various ideas with different levels of success. For example, Bhaskaravarman, the ruler of Assam around 642 CE, maintained large numbers of elephants and his land army cooperated with his riverine navy, as laid down by Kamandaka. Assam was mostly a forested, roadless terrain with many streams and rivers. The warships, made of logs of wood, were about 70 tons each and a cargo ship used for ferrying soldiers could carry 500 troops. This greatly increased the mobility of Bhaskaravarman's army.

King Devapala of the Pala dynasty in 10th century CE was emblematic of early medieval Hindu rulers who relied mostly on elephants, partly because of Kamandaka's suggestions. He even took the title *hayapati* (lord of elephants). This was adequate as long as the Indian powers were fighting among themselves, but in the long run resulted in their defeats by the Muslims horse archers.

Kamandaka and other Hindu thinkers had certainly neglected the use of cavalry for fast-moving reconnaissance and "hit and run" attacks. At the tactical level, Kamandaka's theory put the clock of art of warfare back: he even continued to emphasize the importance of chariots, though they had become outdated after the Battle of Hydaspes. Kamandaka's conservatism led to him advocating the traditional *chaturangabala* (infantry, cavalry, elephants, and chariots) and neglecting the radical innovations going on the field of cavalry warfare. For example, the Huns introduced wooden saddles, and in the ninth century CE, the Muslims came up with iron stirrups and iron cavalry armor. Hindu failure to counteract mounted archery was particularly damaging after the Muslims introduced bows capable of piercing elephant hide. Besides greater thrust, the Muslim composite bows had greater range than the Hindu bamboo bows.

In the long run, also, fort-based strategic defenses made the Hindu rulers of ancient and early medieval India passive. The Huns during the fifth and sixth centuries CE and the Islamic warlords from ninth century CE onward, repeatedly defeated the Hindu kings because of Hindu inferiority in the mounted branch. For example, Mahmud of Ghazni made 17 successful cavalry raids between 1001 and 1027 CE.

Kamandaka's military strategy of ravaging the enemy territory and avoiding pitched battles, elucidated in the *Nitisara,* met with greater success. The strategy was accepted by the Marathas (Hindu inhabitants of Maharashtra in west India) in response to the *jihad* of Mughal Emperor Aurangzeb (1658–1707 CE). It succeeded partially because the Marathas used light cavalry for harassing the Mughals.

The Marathas used long-distance "guerrilla" warfare, which involved attritional raids for plunder, rather than pitched encounters with the Mughal army. The Marathas realized that they would not be able to successfully meet the numerically superior Mughal heavy cavalry in the open field. Hence, they used "hide and seek" tactics, rapid movement, and bribery. Raiding and counterraiding before the monsoon constituted a principal method of fighting.

The Marathas' basic idea was to prevent concentration of the Mughal forces. To confuse the Mughals, various detachments of Maratha raiding parties operated.

While one detachment conducted deep raids inside Mughal territory, another detachment formed a screen before the Mughal army to prevent it from acquiring intelligence, as well as to reduce its mobility. The third detachment attacked the Mughal line of communications and supply columns. The aim was to choke the enemy's food and water supply and thus force it to surrender without actually fighting it. When the enemy launched counterattacks, the Maratha raiding parties retreated and took advantage of hilly terrain and jungles to slip away. When the enemy retreated, the Marathas advanced. Instead of depending on a large logistical infrastructure, the Maratha cavalry force sustained itself by looting the enemy.

Pillage and plundering of the ports and cities became characteristic features of the Maratha raiding parties.

Maratha raiding strategy could meet with tremendous success. During the Palkhed campaign (1727–1728 CE) against the *Nizam* (a Mughal governor who had become independent of the central government at Delhi) of Hyderabad, *Peshwa* (prime minister of the Maratha State) Baji Rao I avoided pitched battles. Baji Rao I followed mobile harassing tactics with his light cavalry, forcing the *Nizam* to engage in a futile cross-country race with his artillery and heavy cavalry, which wore him out. The *Peshwa's* lighting marches and clever maneuverings eventually forced the *Nizam* into a rugged waterless country, where the *Nizam* was forced to sue for peace. Also, during the first half of the 18th century, the Bengal *Nawabi* included Orissa, West Bengal, Bangladesh, and Bihar. Raghuji Bhonsle (a Maratha chieftain) of Berar sent his cavalry through Orissa into West Bengal in 1743, 1744, and 1745. In 1748, the Marathas invaded Bihar, and in 1750 and 1751, Bengal. In 1751, Alivardi Khan, the *Nawab* of Bengal agreed to cede Orissa to the Marathas.

Descendents: Sukra's work, entitled Sukranitisara, written around the ninth century CE, after the Muslim invasion, places greater importance on the army and unjust war relative to Nitisara, and pays less attention to just rule and using the army as an internal security force.

Sukra gives more weight to waging battles. It is necessary, says Sukra, to enjoy numerical superiority even against weaker enemies: victory becomes certain in case of a three to one superiority over the enemy. Initially, half of the forces should be used for attacking the enemy, but for victory, the king must keep a reserve of up to half his army to be thrown at the critical juncture. Sukra's battle tactics involve launching a holding attack in the front and then sending the principal forces to crush both the wings of the enemy army. Another method involves a tactical retreat to bring the pursuing enemy forces into unfavorable terrain and then launching a sudden counterattack. Sukra notes that an army tired out by marching long distance and in disorder (while the soldiers are recuperating or eating) provides an ideal target for a surprise attack. Instead of an army composed of the feudatories, Sukra demands a well-trained standing army maintained by the central government. This is because complicated battle maneuvers require a trained and efficient army. An efficient army must have a well organized, hierarchical command and should receive weapons from the ruler. For purposes of command, bugles are to be used.

To inculcate discipline, the soldiers are ordered to clean their weapons and armor and maintain their dress properly. Military drill and target practice are emphasized. Undisciplined soldiers are fined. The soldiers' combat strength should be raised by diet, athletic exercise, and wrestling. The king is asked to introduce collective training for the soldiers by encouraging various hunting parties where the soldiers are ordered to kill wild animals in close quarter fight.

Sukra points out a variety of welfare measures for construction and retention of loyalty bonds with the troops. Regular pay is emphasized for ensuring loyalty and morale of the troops. The king should grant extra pay to the soldiers when they are marching. Before the battle, the king should promise rewards and promotions to the military personnel. Another factor for generating morale is to inculcate warlike spirit in the society.

The *Sukranitisara* tell us that infantry followed by cavalry should dominate the army. Unlike Kamandaka, Sukra does not overemphasize the role of elephants in battle. For crossing rivers, mountains, forests, and besieging a fort, Sukra says that combined forces are necessary. Sukra also focuses on the linkages between operational efficiency and logistical sufficiency. Unlike Kamandaka, but like Bana, Sukra gives importance to the draft animals, such as bulls and camels, for logistical purpose. Sukra asserts that logistical back up is needed for an all-arms battle unit to be self-sufficient and capable of detached duties. To prevent indiscipline, the soldiers are not allowed to engage in pillage and plundering. The ruler is advised to open markets inside the camp for distributing supplies to the soldiers.

See also: Bana; Indian Use of Chariots; Kautilya; Manu; Use of Elephants in Indian Warfare

Further Reading

Joshi, P.S., *Chhatrapati Sambhaji*. New Delhi: S. Chand & Company, n.d.

Kantak, M.R., *The First Anglo-Maratha War, 1774–1783: A Military Study of Major Battles*. Bombay: Popular Press, 1993.

The Nitisara by Kamandaki, ed. by Raja Rajendra Lala Mitra, Revised with English tr. Dr. Sisir Kumar Mitra. 2nd ed. Calcutta: The Asiatic Society, 1884.

Sarkar, Jadunath, *House of Shivaji*. 2nd ed. New Delhi: Orient Longman, 1978.

Kaushik Roy

Kant, Immanuel
(1724–1804)

Significance: Kant's views on war, peace, and human history combined a rigorous examination of ethics with the tradition of 18th-century European political theory. His work demonstrates the confident, optimistic quality of late Enlightenment thought. He had a significant impact on later theorists with progressive views of history, including Hegel and Marx.

Context: The currents of 17th- and 18th-century European philosophy form the basis of Kant's ideas. He sought to resolve long-standing disputes on the nature of knowledge and the basis of ethical behavior. Kant's work must also be understood in the context of Newtonian natural law, and the attempt to apply such a view of natural law to human history. Finally, Kant's views on society must be viewed as part of the Enlightenment tradition of political theory.

Biography: Immanuel Kant was born in the Prussian city of Konigsberg in 1724. The son of a harness maker, he was educated at the University of Konigsberg, He joined the faculty of the same institution and remained there for the rest of his life. Although he produced a great body of writing on subjects ranging from astronomy to history, he is best known for his work on epistemology, metaphysics, and ethics.

Influences: Kant's work responded to the philosophical controversies of his day, and so one could say he was influenced by the major currents of 17th- and 18th-century philosophy, even those he ultimately rejected. His views of history and politics drew upon Enlightenment political theory, particularly that of Rousseau. Kant's philosophy of knowledge had a particular relationship to the thought of David Hume. Hume maintained that our knowledge of that world could only come from the experiences of sense. Further, only the actual sense impressions themselves could be said to relate directly to reality. For Hume, the intellectual connections that the human mind makes *between* such impressions—consistency, causation, even the existence of substance itself—are imposed by the mind on sense and must be considered as mere conventions. Such conventions, or "customs," are projected by human thought on nature to lend order to the world.

The Theory: Any discussion of Kant's approach to issues of war and peace must begin with a brief examination of his views on knowledge itself. Kant accepts much of Hume's work: the certainty of mathematics and the importance of sense, for example. However, he attacks Hume's views on convention and custom. For Kant, humans view the world through the prism of human reason and consciousness. They can see it no other way. Thus, such notions as consistency and causation—notions that lend coherence and order to our sense impressions—may be considered as true because they are inherent in the structure of human thought. In other words, because all humanity shares certain fundamental assumptions about nature, those assumptions may be considered valid within the confines of human discourse.

Kant's views on ethics also incorporate this stress on the commonality of human reason. He argues that humanity shares a rational sense of right and wrong, which he terms the "categorical imperative." Emotion and self-interest may cloud this rational understanding of right action. However, a rigorously rational examination of a given situation will result in a shared definition of ethical behavior, based on the common rational basis of human thought. Further, actions may only be considered as truly ethical when they proceed from such a sense of rational obligation.

Ethical actions inspired by emotion or cultural compliance are not truly ethical in a Kantian sense.

The conflict between human emotion and a common rational ethical sense lies at the root of Kant's understanding of warfare and his ultimate expectation of perpetual peace. He maintains that human beings are driven by emotion and self-interest, and that these forces produce the feelings of loyalty and group identity common to tribal and monarchical forms of government. These are the forms of government that most readily resort to warfare as a means of expanding wealth, power, and resources. In addition, warfare results from the human desire to feel superior to others. However, Kant argues that the same forces of self-interest that produce human conflict will ultimately led to its disappearance. As wealth and technology come to determine military power, nations will pursue commercial and economic development as a means of increasing such power. This development will reduce the significance of aristocratic or royal authority and foster the growth of republican institutions, for representative government most effectively marshals the economic resources of a nation. Yet, those same republican institutions will come to question the application of significant national resources to the pursuit of warfare. Further, according to Kant, representative government will allow for the growth of policy based on inherent human reason, as opposed to emotion and self-interest. This will lead to the establishment of a world order based on perpetual peace, as republican governments come to manifest the rational, moral character of humanity.

Kant published his work on perpetual peace in 1795. His ideas on the subject reflect his views on human knowledge and morality, as well as a progressive view of history rooted in Enlightenment notions of natural law and human nature. For Kant, the rise of a rational world order proceeds directly from human nature, as reason replaces emotion as the driving force of society over the course of human history.

Applications: Kant's notion of the progress of world history toward representative government, combined with his ideas on perpetual peace between rational republics, played a significant role in the establishment of 20th-century world institutions. It is important to note that Kant discusses republican government, but does not refer to democracy. In any case, his ideas influenced Woodrow Wilson and the architects of the League of Nations, as well as the Charter of the United Nations. Kant himself did not envision a world order based on institutions; rather, he believed that such an order would proceed from human reason itself.

Descendents: Later theorists of human history and human society owe a significant debt to Kant's ideas. His concept of history as the progressive, predictable unfolding of human nature influenced later German Romantic notions of human society, as well as Hegel's views on ideology and history. Marx's progressive approach to class struggle over time also has a Kantian character. The "whig" interpretation of history, defined in the first half of the 20th century by Butterfield, combines Kantian attitudes with more modern views on the triumph of democracy.

See also: Machiavelli

Further Reading

Flikschuh, Katrin, *Kant and Modern Political Philosophy*. London: Cambridge University Press, 2000.

Kant, Immanuel, "Idea for a Universal History with a Cosmopolitan Purpose." In Reiss, H. S. *Kant. Cambridge Texts in the History of Political Thought*. 2nd ed. Cambridge: Cambridge University Press, 1991.

Kant, Immanuel, *Perpetual Peace*. London: FQ Classics, 1997.

Scruton, Roger, *Kant*. New York: Oxford University Press, 1996.

Wood, Allan, *Kant's Ethical Thought*. London: Cambridge University Press, 1999.

Robert Kiely

Kautilya
(ca. 300 BCE)

Significance: The *Arthashastra,* generally ascribed to Kautilya, is the first known treatise about grand strategy written on the Indian subcontinent, and probably one of the earliest examples in the world of a manual devoted to the strategy of power. A minority group of scholars argue that the *Arthashastra* was a collective effort by several thinkers over a wide period, and it is probable that Kautilya was not the first writer on the science of statecraft. The science of polity developed in India before 600 BCE. Most of these writings were in the verse form, but Kautilya's *Arthashastra* was the first work written in prose. The *Arthashastra* is a pioneering attempt to chalk out a grand theory of warfare, and then to fit it within the "realist" worldview of international politics—that is, in terms of a struggle for survival. Like Machiavelli, Kautilyan philosophy is not moralistic, but empirically examines the dynamics of actual power struggles. It studies human self-interest and aggression to understand political reality. From this perspective, justice and morality appear naïve, utopian and hopeless. In contrast, the *dharmashastras* emphasize that a just ruler should follow righteous policy based on honesty and nonviolence. For Kautilya, diplomatic treaties are mere pieces of paper, to be torn up in accordance with the demands of realpolitik. He maintains that, to avert threats to the state, policies might have to be pursued, which appear ethically repugnant. Questions of morality should never jeopardize the security and independence of the realm.

At the operational level, Kautilya hints at what Carl Von Clausewitz later referred to as the "culminating point of offensive," that is, the point after which the momentum of offence by the aggressor begins to falter. When the invader has frittered away his strength, says Kautilya, the hitherto weak ruler should launch a counteroffensive. However, Kautilya warns against launching a premature counteroffensive, which in his view is equivalent to "entering the flame like a moth."

At the tactical level, Kautilya seems to indicate that the side with bigger battalions would win the day—thereby somewhat preempting Napoleon Bonaparte. To succeed, Kautilya advises, the attacking army must have at least a two to one superiority over the enemy. Victory is said to be certain when the conqueror enjoys an eight to one superiority in infantry and a four to one superiority in cavalry and chariots.

Context: From 400 BCE, large-scale cultivation in the Ganga–Jamuna region had become possible due to intensive use of the iron plough. Increasing agricultural surplus gave rise to huge territorial states that replaced the earlier tribal chiefdoms. Kautilya's *vijigishu* (the ideal ruler and would be conqueror) was the Maurya monarch. In ancient India, the Maurya Empire was the most centralized political entity. However, the state did not yet possess a strict monopoly on the use of organized violence in society, and there was no uniform administration throughout the empire. The Maurya Empire was composed of three units. The core was the Ganga–Jamuna delta, which was administered directly by bureaucrats appointed by the central government. The periphery comprised central and west India. Here, the control of the central government was loose, and many cities and tribes enjoyed internal autonomy. The third layer, or outer rim, included northwest India and the Deccan. The central government enjoyed overlordship over this belt of territory, which functioned as a buffer between the Maurya Empire and foreign powers.

The big empires possessed large cities with fortifications, most of which, like Pataliputra (the imperial capital) were constructed of wood. One of Kautilya's practical recommendations was to dissuade rulers from the use of wood in fortifications, due to timber's propensity to catch fire.

Biography: Kautilya, also known as Chanakya, was an inhabitant of Taxila who lived around 300 BCE. He is associated with Vishnugupta, the principal minister of Chandragupta Maurya (the warlord who established the Maurya Empire in 321 BCE). According to one account, Chanakya aided Chandragupta in defeating the Nanda Empire, which included north India and Kalinga (Orissa).

Influences: The Aryans belonged to the Brahmin and Kshatriya castes. The conquered Dravidians were assigned the rank of Sudras. And the mixed offspring due to union between Sudras and the Aryans were categorized as Vaisyas. The pre-Kautilyan *dharmashastras* (Vedic and Epic religious literature, which occasionally hints at the necessity of good governance by just rulers) advocated a Brahmin or Kshatriya (warrior caste, second in rank in the caste hierarchy coming just after the Brahmins) army. Kautilya warns the ruler against depending on only one social group, as they could be won over by the enemy. The army should be recruited from all the four *varnas* (castes), such as the Brahmins, Kshatriyas, Vaisyas, and Sudras. And when large numbers are required, says Kautilya, recruitment of even the Sudras (lowest caste in the caste hierarchy) is necessary. This is an attempt by Kautilya to integrate all the settled communities inside the subcontinent within an expansive Aryan fold.

The three great Hindu political theorists who preceded Kautilya were Vatavyadhi, Bharadavaja, and Visalaksa. In Vatavyadhi's paradigm, a ruler has only two options before him as regards external relations: peace or war. Kautilya rejects this bipolar compartmentalization. Kautilya also disagrees with Bharadavaja's advice that a weak king must always submit to a stronger king. Similarly, Kautilya challenges the dictum of Visalaksa, that the weak ruler should always fight the strong ruler regardless of the consequences. Kautilya is against a last-ditch stand, which to him reflects false heroism without any strategic gain. Kautilya emphasizes strategic flexibility. He writes that the weak ruler, instead of taking the offensive, should wait for the strong ruler inside forts, which should have adequate supplies of stores and manpower. The king should leave the fort before he is completely cut off by the besieging enemy army and take refuge in another fort. However, Kautilya is not advocating a pure passive defense. He writes that, by taking position within the fort, the weak ruler is temporarily following strategic defense, and should use the breathing space to try and break the alliances of the invader. Simultaneously, the weak ruler must try to form a counteralliance, and should replenish his armed strength. In addition, the weak king should try to incite trouble within the domains of the invading ruler, so that disturbance within his home territory will force the invader to redeploy troops to his own kingdom.

The Theory: The term "artha" means wealth or riches. At times, *artha* also means "purpose," that is, means to bring order. *Artha* also connotes desire for some gain or favor, whereas "shastra" means literature or discourse. *Arthashastra* teaches that strength is power, and that power may be of three kinds: intellectual strength, which provides counsel; a prosperous treasury and a strong army, which provide physical power and valor. The latter is the basis for energetic action. The success resulting from each one is, correspondingly, intellectual, physical, and psychological.

Kautilya writes that states pursue power in the international arena for survival, and that power for power's sake becomes the objective of all the polities operating in the international arena. The *vijigishu* attempts to increase his own power. Augmenting one's own power requires preparing for war. Active hostility is waging war. A king superior to his enemy in power shall attack his neighbor.

The normal state in international affairs is *matsanya*. The term means a state of disorder inside a pond, where small fishes are being eaten by a big fish. Kautilya applies this term to interstate relationships. The big fish represents the *vijigishu* and the small fishes are the weak powers. For Kautilya, the original state of international order is of total anarchy where might is right. The *Arthashastra* preaches the ideal of conquest: the *vijigishu* should be desirous of *digvijaya,* which is defined as control over the subcontinent.

Kautilya says that there are several types of conquest. *Dharmavijayin,* means making conquest for the sake of glory—the ruler is satisfied with mere submission of his enemies. *Lobhavijayin,* by contrast, is defined as making conquest out of greed. In this scheme, land, and money is taken from the conquered people.

Finally, *asuravijayin* involves the killing of the defeated king and the appropriation of his land, money, sons, and wives by the conqueror. Kautilya writes that the *vijigishu* should follow the policy of *dharmavijayin*—otherwise all the members of *mandala* (in this context circle of states within the subcontinent) would combine against him.

Kautilya is pessimistic: his philosophy accepts that internal divisiveness and external aggression are inevitable and interlinked. Troubles in the core might encourage the external powers to threaten the periphery of the state. Again, disaffected subjects may join hands with the ruler's external enemies. To avert these threats, the prime weapon in Kautilya's arsenal is diplomacy. The *dutas* (envoys) implement the diplomatic policies of the ruler, whose maneuverings are centered round the theory of *mandalas*. *Arthashastra* notes that the conqueror imagines the community of states as a wheel. The *vijigishu* is at the hub and his allies, drawn to him by the spokes though separated by intervening territory, are its rim. The enemy becomes vulnerable to harassment and destruction when he is squeezed between the conqueror and his allies.

Kautilya assumes that the enemy's enemy is one's friend. In geographical order, the five types of king directly facing the *vijigishu's* kingdom are listed as: *Ari* (enemy), *Mitra* (friend of the *vijigishu*), *Ari-Mitra* (friend of the enemy), *Mitra-Mitra* (friend of the *vijigishu's* friend), and *Ari-Mitra-Mitra* (friend of the enemy's friend). Rearward in the geographical order are the following: *Parshni-Graha* (rearward enemy), *Akranda* (rearward friend), *Parshni-Graha-Sara* (friend of the enemy in the rear), and *Akranda-Sara* (friend of the friend in the rear). The circle is completed by *Madhyama* (the intermediary or neutral situated close to the *vijigishu* and to the latter's immediate enemy) and *Udasina* (the neutral situated beyond the territory of all those enumerated above and in a position to help or resist the *vijigishu*).

According to Kautilya, internal insecurity is more dangerous than external invasion. An internally insecure polity will never be able to wage war successfully against external enemies. Several types of internal strife might occur. One is the revolt by the ministers or by the army. Even the *purohita* (chief priest) or the crown prince might hatch plots against the ruler. Kautilya prescribes that in cases of treachery, either the leaders of the conspiracies should be won over, or they should be executed. Kautilya also mentions the presence of martial clans inside the kingdoms. They practice agriculture, but in case of necessity might resort to arms. The marriage relations between various martial clans might result in an alliance directed against the ruler. Another source of danger is the *Atavis* (armed jungle tribes). To defuse the danger posed by the *Atavis,* the text prescribes a policy of co-option: the forest chieftains should be granted internal autonomy and in return, the ruler should absorb the armed males of the forest tribes within his own army. Such contingents of the jungle tribe are called *atavi bala*. Kautilya accepts that the combat effectiveness of such troops is quite low: they are interested more in plunder than in combat. Kautilya describes the *atavi bala* within the imperial army as similar to having a snake inside the house. The *bahrikas* (wandering tribes or gypsies) and the *manavas* (criminal tribes) also pose a threat to the state.

To avert general revolt within the society, the ruler should implement *bhedniti,* that is, encouraging mutual hostility and suspicion of the different groups, thereby producing conflict between the various groups. This would enable the ruler to maintain his rule. To prevent the *senapati* (commander in chief) from becoming overpowerful, Kautilya says that the king should balance him by keeping separate military contingents under different commanders.

For maintaining hold over the various groups of rebels, Kautilya emphasizes state surveillance; hence, his focus on the utility of spies. Spies are to be used both for keeping a watch over the state's own territory, and for watching foreign states. This is because the external enemies sponsor the internal rebels. As far as the domestic sphere is concerned, the secret agents should move around in public places to discover whether the common people are loyal to the monarch or not. Kautilya encourages the polity to utilize the other-worldly image of religious mendicants: spies in the guise of ascetics should roam in the cities and the countryside. Kautilya also urges the state to use traders as spies. Because the profession of the merchants takes them to foreign countries, the traders are well suited to function as the eyes and ears of the government for acquiring foreign intelligence.

Kautilya warns the ruler that coercive power of the state should be deployed with care. Unjust or improper use of power might result in *kopa* (revolt of the subjects against the ruler). *Arthashastra* elaborates on different techniques for pacifying insurgency in disturbed areas. The *vijigishu* is advised to win over the people's "hearts and minds," and not to terrorize or economically exploit them. Destruction of the rebellious subjects, says Kautilya, is ruinous in the long run. The conqueror is to adopt the dress, language, and customs of the recently conquered subjects. In addition, respect must be shown to the deities, festivals, and fairs of the conquered people.

Arthashastra demands absolute control by the monarch over the state machinery. The state, in Kautilya's paradigm, consists of the following elements: capital, territory, army, treasury, and ally. A state possesses three types of *shaktis* (power or energy). First, the energy, bravery, and personal drive of the king constitute *utsaha.* Second, the material resources, meaning the treasury, and the army constitute *prabhava.* And finally good counsel and diplomatic alliances constitute *mantra.* Kautilya writes that *prabhavashakti* is more important than *utsahashakti* and *mantrashakti* is more important than the former two.

While fighting, writes Kautilya, the ruler should take care of *desa* (terrain) and *kala* (climate). The interrelationship between *desa, kala,* and *shaktis* generates military power of the state. When the state is forced to conduct regular warfare, the ruler has the option of either conducting positional warfare based on *durgas* (forts), or of offering battles with his army. Kautilya prefers siege warfare. He writes that the capital of the kingdom must be strongly fortified, and that capturing enemy forts is the principal strategic objective in war. In such conflicts, elephants play a vital role.

Instead of structuring the army around the social status of the personnel, Kautilya prescribes wide-ranging military training. Given military training, argues Kautilya, even Vaisyas (commercial caste) could fight as efficiently as the Kshatriyas.

He stresses that, except on holidays, the soldiers must undergo constant training. On a regular basis, the ruler should carry out inspection of the army engaged in training. Kautilya refers to the necessity of drilling the troops and realistic combat training. *Arthashastra* also notes the importance of good horses, which are available in Sindhu (Indus) delta, Kamboja (Gandhara in eastern Afghanistan), and Bahlika (Bactria in Central Asia). Kautilya recommends state factories for manufacturing weapons for the army.

Kautilya emphasizes generalship for winning wars. He writes that before actual fighting, the ruler should assemble the troops and stress the pecuniary aspects of military service. The king should say that he is also a servant of the state like the ordinary soldiers. Besides rhetoric, the king should attempt to raise the morale of the troops just before the onset of battle through the *mantrins* (ministers) and the *purohita* (chief priest). For strengthening combat motivation of the soldiers, the *senapati* should declare rewards for outstanding acts of bravery. In addition, the bards shall tell the soldiers that heaven awaits the valiant and that hell shall be the lot of cowards. By contrast to the role of the hoplite commander, *Arthashastra* says that the general or king should not take his place in the front rank, but should remain with the reserve at a distance of approximately 360 meters behind the main body of troops. The reserve should be used either to reinforce the contingents that have penetrated the enemy line or to parry an enemy counterattack.

Kautilya says that each army should have a secure line of retreat. The site of the battlefield should be such that there must be a forest fort or a mountain fort in the rear where the army could take refuge in case it is defeated. At some distance behind the battlefield, a secure base camp should be set up. This camp should be able to supply provision and reinforcement to the main army confronting the enemy force. Technicians and carpenters are to accompany the army to mend the chariots and the *yantras* (stone-throwing machines). The logistical infrastructure of the army comprises surgeons and physicians with medicines and bandages for treating the wounded soldiers. Women should accompany the army, and they are to provide food and drink.

As regards battle tactics, Kautilya describes various *vyuhas* (battle arrays) depending upon the configuration of the terrain. When the strengths of the two opposing armies are equal, the side making greater use of terrain, time, and soldiers shall win. In general, an army deployed in the battlefield has a center, two flanks, and two wings. At times, the wings have more strength compared to the center. There are different modes of attack; for example, in the "truncheon" formation, the center, flanks, and the wings advance in a straight line.

Kautilya is a proponent of combined-arms tactics. A mounted soldier should be accompanied by six foot soldiers. A chariot or an elephant is to be surrounded by five troopers and 30 foot soldiers. A combined battle group comprises nine chariots, 45 cavalrymen and 270 foot soldiers. Such a battle group has three rows and each row has three chariots. A bigger combined battle group is composed of 315 chariots, 1,575 cavalry, and 10,000 foot soldiers, with 21 chariots in each row. However, at times, pure battle groups composed of only elephants or cavalry are to be deployed. In a pure cavalry, battle group armored horses are placed at the center and unarmored ones at the flanks. In case of a pure infantry battle group, armored infantry is placed at the front and archers at the back.

Like Vegetius's Roman manual, Kautilya's *Arthashastra* details the distance between the soldiers of various arms deployed in the battlefield. The distance between two battle groups is at least 11.25 meters. In the closed order, each infantry soldier equipped with sword or spear is to be separated from the next one in the row by 26.5 centimeters. The distance between two archers in a row should be about 225 centimeters. In the closed order, the distance between two horsemen within the same row is 79.5 centimeters and in open order it becomes 6.75 meters. However, the space between the various types of soldiers could be doubled or trebled depending on the terrain. The main point, writes Kautilya, is to prevent overcrowding.

Kautilya is against "symmetrical" attack: enemy infantry should be attacked by horses, enemy horses by chariots and enemy chariots by elephants. Elephants should be used to break the closed ranks of massed enemy troops. The ruler's best troops should be used to attack the weak or unreliable portions of the enemy's contingents. Against enemy field army, Kautilya prescribes nocturnal raids by special forces.

Application: Asoka the Maurya Emperor (272–32 BCE) followed Kautilya's policy of *lobhavijayin*. In 260 BCE, he attacked Kalinga and annexed it to his empire. The conduct of the campaign was characterized by ruthless cruelty. About 100,000 enemy soldiers were killed and many times that number of noncombatants perished due to the war. In addition, 150,000 people were deported from Kalinga after the campaign and were used to clear wasteland and establish new settlements.

In 374 CE, when the Gupta Emperor Ramgupta was campaigning against the Sakas in Malwa, the latter blocked the passes through which the Gupta army was passing. Ramgupta to extricate his army and save his life agreed to surrender his wife Dhruvadevi to the Saka king. Ramgupta's younger brother Chandra in accordance with Kautilya's policy with special troops conducted a nocturnal raid against the Saka camp and killed the Saka king.

At the level of weaponry, Kautilya discusses weapons that had become obsolete in his time. The Battle of Hydaspes (326 BCE) had already proved the obsolescence of the chariots. Still, Kautilya advocated a *chaturanga* (four limbed) army composed of infantry, cavalry, elephants, and chariots. The Guptas had to fight the Sakas and Huns, who relied on mounted archers. So, the Guptas came up with a cavalry-centric army. Imitating the Central Asian horse nomads, the Guptas introduced mounted archers for skirmishing and armored heavy cavalry for ramming into the enemy force. In 455 CE, at the Battle of Indus, the cavalry-centric Gupta army under Emperor Skandagupta was able to check the Huns. Again, *Arthashastra* emphasizes the use of bows made of bamboo and cane, but, due to the influence of the Sakas, Kushanas, and the Parthians, the Guptas introduced short composite reverse strung bows that were used by the mounted archers. The composite bows were easier to handle and had greater range than the Indian bows.

In the field of siege warfare, Kautilya prescribes use of elephants with front-lets on their trunks as a battering ram against enemy forts. As a reaction, from 500 CE onward, the gates of the Indian forts are covered on the outside with lines of sharp stout iron spikes to prevent the doors from being butted by the elephants.

When the Gupta Empire disintegrated in the second half of sixth century CE, the regional powers followed the mandala policy. During the later half of the sixth century CE, there was rivalry in north India between the Later Gupta kingdom of Magadh and its neighboring power, the Maukharis. There was also tension between the Maukharis and their immediate neighbor, the Pushyabati kingdom. Mahasenagupta (who died in 601 CE) the later Gupta king, made an alliance with the Pushyabati king, Aditya Vardhana, directed against the Maukharis. This fol-lowed the Kautilyan dictum of "the enemy's enemy is my friend."

Descendents: *Panchatantra* is a collection of fables that came into existence around 500 CE under the direction of Vishnusarma. *Panchatantra*, like *Artha-shastra*, accepts that warfare was inevitable. It says that friendship can only be among the equals. Inequality in power between the various polities results in warfare. A soldier who goes to battle does not think about right and wrong. The general message is that the residue of an enemy, such as debt, when united may grow again. So, an enemy should be utterly obliterated. Kamandaka in *Nitisara* (written between fifth and sixth centuries CE) accept that the *vijigishu* should at-tempt to establish political over lordship in the *mandala*. However, compared to Kautilya, Kamandaka gives less stress to immoral policies for establishing politi-cal domination. Banabhatta in Harsacharita composed in the seventh century CE agrees with *Arthashastra* that the best horses are to be found outside India in the regions such as Kamboja and Sindhu. Bana unlike Kautilya also adds that good horses could also be acquired from Persia.

After Kautilya, Manu in *Manusmriti* written around the beginning of Common Era emphasizes the role of forts in warfare. But, Manu unlike Kautilya overem-phasizes the importance of forts and critiques the importance of battles. Manu advocates positional warfare based on a series of forts surrounded by ditches and garrisoned by archers.

From the mid-17th century CE onward, the Marathas (Hindu inhabitants of Maharashtra) became the dominant military power south of River Narmada. The Marathas had left us with no coherent written doctrine of warfare. How-ever, Maratha military theory could be reconstructed from the various letters written by Maratha kings such as Shivaji, Shahu, and the *Peshwas* (hereditary prime ministers). The Maratha military theory was influenced by Kautilya and Manu's focus on the *durgas*. A chain of hill forts protected the base of the

Marathas. From the "protected base" Maratha cavalry parties emerged and conducted raids deep inside the Mughal territory. Kautilya advocates destruction of the countryside. And the Maratha chiefs were votaries of following a scorched earth policy in enemy territories.

See also: Bana; Hindu Tradition of Just and Unjust War; Indian Use of Chariots; Kamandaka; Manu; Use of Elephants in Indian Warfare

Further Reading
Kautilya, *The Arthashastra,* ed., Rearranged, tr. and Introduced by L. N. Rangarajan. New Delhi: Penguin, 1987.
The Kautiliya Arthasastra: A Study, Part 3, ed. and tr. by R. P.Kangle, 2nd ed. Delhi: Motilal Banarasidas, 2000.
Sandhu, Gurcharn Singh, *A Military History of Ancient India.* New Delhi: 2000, Vision Books, pp. 529–30.
Thapar, Romila, *The Mauryas Revisited.* 2nd ed. Kolkata: K. P. Bagchi, 1993.

Kaushik Roy

Khevenhüller, Ludwig Andreas, Graf von Frankenburg zu Aichelburg
(1683–1744)

Significance: Khevenhüller's reputation as a minor 18th-century military theorist is rooted in a regimental manual for cavalry. To the former has sometimes been credited a disproportionate, or at least undocumented influence. This perhaps reflects the curious publishing history of his later *Militarisches Operationen,* a work that surely did not merit bilingual publication.

Biography: In spite of a name that might be taken to imply a minor noble house, Khevenhüller was a well-born member of the Austrian Habsburg service nobility. His maternal grandparents were a Princess Dietrichstein and the famed soldier Raimundo Montecúccoli, and another prominent general, his uncle Count Erculo Montecúccoli encouraged his military intellectual activities at an early date. Khevenhüller rose to the rank of field marshal under Maria Theresa. His distinguished performance in the field during the War of the Polish Succession, the Turkish war of 1737–1739, and during the first years of the War of the Austrian Succession is a matter of record. Less well known is his skillful execution of difficult and unpleasant duties as a military bureaucrat and budget cutter.

Influences: Raimondo Montecúccoli and Eugene of Savoy.

The Theory: Whatever political motives might lie behind it, clearly Khevenhüller's fame as a military intellectual was being driven by some internal factors. With the long-delayed publication of the first and apparently only surviving half of his "Ideen vom Kriege" in 1893/1894, the reason for this became clear. This master-work, whose archival presence in multiple copies testifies to its enduring internal influence, elevates him into the foremost ranks of contemporary military theorists, if not the single greatest author to use this working title, Carl v. Clausewitz. His "Ideen vom Kriege" consists of a first book on general questions of the nature of war, with questions of strategy yoked to policy and moral questions.

Application: His work on cavalry operations were implemented in Habsburg military service. The impact of his broader work on war is unknown.

Further Reading

G. F. M Graf Khevenhüller Observationspunkt für sein Dragoner-regiment. Wein, 1734.

"Ideen vom Kriege," *Mittheilungen des k. und k. Kriegsarchiv* 8–9 (1893–4): 288–441, 318–97. (Note obsolete spelling of "*Mitteilungen*," which may or not be maintained in cataloguing.)

Kurzer Begriff aller militärischen Operationen. Wein, 1756.

von Wurzbach, Constantin, *Biographisches Lexikon des Kaiserthums Oesterreich.* Vienna, 1856–1891.

Erik A. Lund

Le Tellier, Michel and Le Tellier de Louvois, François-Michel
(1603–1685 and 1641–1691)

Significance: Louis XIV's Secretary of War, Michel Le Tellier, started a process of reforming in the French military, and it was left to his son the Marquis de Louvois to totally transform the army. He was a gifted administrator and he welded the small collection of private enterprise armed bands that made up the French army into a thoroughly modern military machine, totally controlled by the authority of the Crown. This new army was orderly, disciplined and loyal to the Sun King.

Context: The French army of the early part of Louis XIV's reign (1643–1715) was mediocre. As late as 1666, the king is recorded as saying that the infantry was "not very good." Discipline was lax, and each regiment's colonel-proprietor organized, armed, clothed and paid his soldiers as he saw fit. This corresponded with the practice of France's European rivals. By the 1670s, however, the French army had become qualitatively and quantitatively better than any other European army, giving the French state an enormous advantage in foreign policy and war. The "new" French army eventually provided the model and terminology for all other European armies of the time.

Biographies: Michel Le Tellier became Secretary of War under Louis XIII in 1643, and was a member of Cardinal Mazarin's Council. During the rebellions of the Frondes (1648–1653) he was in charge of the negotiations with the rebel princes, and was instrumental in the signing of the Peace of Reuil in 1649. During Mazarin's exile he became the Queen's first adviser. Thus Le Tellier became adept at the high intrigue of the court, building a network of clients around him who owed him numerous favors. Foremost among his protégés was the young Jean-Baptiste Colbert, who he introduced to Cardinal Mazarin and who became France's great financial wizard. Le Tellier produced many ordinances and regulations for the management of the army between 1643 and 1666. Although, in practice, not all of them were observed by the assumption of personal rule by Louis XIV in 1661, Colbert's fiscal reforms, and the military finance system of the *ancien regime,* was in place. The reforms were to serve until the revolution of 1789.

In 1660, Michel le Tellier's daughter Madeleine married the Duc d'Aumont, and his family's access to the nobility was assured. In 1667, he was made Chancellor of France and obtained for his son the right to succeed him in the post of Secretary of State for War. Le Tellier was a vehement opponent of the Protestant Huguenots and persuaded Louis XIV to revoke the Edict of Nantes in 1685. The abandoning of this instrument of religious tolerance that ended the French Wars of Religion in 1598, possibly caused great economic disruption as wealthy Huguenots left France for England and Holland. Many talented Protestant officers left France, although many Jacobite Scots and Irish arrived from 1689 onward after the accession of William of Orange to the thrones of England and Scotland. Le Tellier died in 1685. Louis XIV said of him that "nobody was ever a better adviser in every matter of state."

Le Tellier's son, Louvois had shared the post of Secretary of State for War with his father from 1662. By 1672, he was a minister of state in the cabinet of King Louis XIV, and became a rival of Colbert. As superintendent of buildings, arts, and manufacturing, he took charge of the reconstruction and improvement of the palace of Versailles. Le Tellier Senior officially retired from the secretariat in 1677, but Louvois had been the major force for some seven years, even eclipsing the great Turenne as the king's chief military adviser. Louvois dominated the ministry by force of will, traveling extensively to see his master's wishes enacted with the army. The hierarchal system of government *intendants* (military inspectors) that he perfected strictly supervised every aspect of the army's management. He died in office in 1691, probably from overwork, although Voltaire hints that his increasing unpopularity at court may well have led to his murder.

Influences: Michel Le Tellier was a self-effacing and subtle negotiator, very much in the style of Cardinal Mazarin, France's effective ruler during the end of Louis XIII's reign (1642–1643) and the minority of Louis XIV (1643–1661). He was a great innovator and inventor of systems. The son, Louvois, was much more like his master, the king: haughty, imperious, and sometimes brutal.

The Theory: Louvois fought a constant battle against corruption, introducing the offices of war commissioner and army *intendants* to inspect, among other things, the ration strengths. At this time fictitious recruits were frequently enrolled, who never served with the colors, but whose officers continued to draw pay and rations for them. For parades and reviews local derelicts were rounded up to make up the numbers, given a musket and a uniform jacket, rewarded with a day's pay and then sent away. This low-level corruption had been practiced for decades, and was considered a perk of rank. However, when the garrison at Belle-Isle was caught red-handed at this swindle, and its commander severely fined, it was a sign that new standards of financial probity had arrived. Even the war commissioners themselves were not above audit: Commissioner Aubert was caught out in Dunkirk in 1671, dismissed from the service and disappeared without a trace.

Louvois insisted that officers keep up to date with the latest military developments and practices for fear of losing their commissions. Orders and regulations were issued to describe exactly what was expected of officers, and they were obliged to attend regular training exercises where the king himself often turned up to inspect the troops.

The lieutenant colonel of the *Régiment du Roi,* Jean de Martinet, lent his name to a type of strict military disciplinarian, due to the model arrangements that his corps adopted in the field. His example was soon followed, according to the king's wishes, in all parts of the army. Although Martinet was killed in action in 1672, the trend had taken off, and Louvois, with the king's support, pressed on with his reforms.

Louvois also introduced new army ranks that could only be achieved by promotion rather than purchase. After 1661, the ranks of major and lieutenant colonel were only available by promotion, and a new rank of *brigadier* was created to allow talented officers to have a taste of field command, without having to purchase a regiment—a potentially ruinous financial venture.

Improvements in pay and conditions led to better morale in the French army. New uniforms added to a sense of *panache.* This was reflected in the improvement of the performance of the French army, which became the finest and most modern military force of its age.

By January 1678, the size of the army had reached some 280,000, over two-thirds of whom were actively deployed on campaign. Problems of recruitment became acute, especially after the revocation of the Edict of Nantes led to a mass exodus of experienced men, particularly officers. Many fled to Holland, Germany or England where they were enthusiastically received, in view of their up-to-date knowledge and experience. In response, Louvois introduced the militia levy of 1688. Each parish would provide one man, making up a force of nearly 25,000, a handy expedient but one which did not add to the discipline of the army.

Application: Louvois' institution of *dragonnades* to exact punishment on towns for nonpayment of taxes or religious nonconformism, by billeting hordes of licentious soldiery in the homes of respectable bourgeois, attracted opprobrium from his critics, notably the king's mistress, Madame de Maintenon.

Descendents: After Louvois' death in 1691, the later years Louis XIV's reign saw financial collapse in 1709 during the War of the Spanish Succession. No other minister emerged with the organizational skills of Michel Le Tellier or the dynamism and sense of purpose of Louvois.

Further Reading

The magisterial survey of the French army at this period is John Lynn's detailed *Giant of the Grand Siècle. The French Army 1610–1715* (1997). His *Wars of Louis XIV 1667–1714* (1999) gives a good general picture of the conditions of war at the time.

Toby McLeod

Leo VI
(866–912)

Significance: A military manual, usually called the *Tactica* or *Taktika,* attributed to Emperor Leo VI (the Wise), is one of the most comprehensive treatises of strategy and tactics produced in the Byzantine Empire.

Context: In writing his military manual, Emperor Leo VI was not only following a tradition set by previous Byzantine writers, but also one set by a previous emperor, Maurice (r. 582–602), whose *Strategikon* is considered one of the most comprehensive military operations' works of the Middle Ages.

Biography: Although there was some question as to the legitimacy of his birth, Leo VI gained the Byzantine throne in 886 and ruled for the next 26 years, a relatively long time for medieval rulers. He is generally recognized as a good emperor, who improved the economic, religious, and political situation within the empire, and protected and extended its borders against several enemies, including Hungarians, Bulgarians, Russians, Armenians, Arabs, Egyptians, and rebellious Byzantine forces. To facilitate these wars, Leo VI compiled a compendium of effective strategies and tactics for his generals to follow. It, under various titles, is preserved in numerous manuscripts of all or at least part of the text. Leo wrote other political and legal treatises, but his military manual was his most famous work.

Influences: Leo clearly draws material from Classical and Byzantine manuals on strategy and tactics, but much of it also comes from the experiences of his generals. Classical influences include the Romans, Frontinus and Vegetius, and Byzantines, Urbicius, and Syrianus. But, undoubtedly, his greatest source of military information came from his predecessor, Maurice's, *Strategikon.*

The Theory: Leo opens his manual with a discussion of the importance of leadership, first generals and then other officers, their status and decision making. Then follows a long discussion of what an army must do to prepare for engagements: arms and other equipment; drills; punishments; marches; baggage; camps; and other preparations. It is clear that Leo believes that an army's success is determined by its readiness to face the enemy. He concludes his manual with separate sections on battles, sieges, and naval warfare. In this section, he also encourages the study of enemy formations and tactics. Some manuscripts also add sections on Ancient Greek and Roman military practices, and on how generals should react during sieges and how to build fortresses near enemy borders without provoking war.

Application: The number of extant manuscripts of Leo's *Tactica* indicates a popularity that was exceptional among medieval military manuals. They may also suggest an actual application in combat, although conclusive evidence for this cannot be determined from contemporary or near-contemporary sources.

Descendents: Leo's manual ushered in a century of Byzantine military treatises unmatched in number and significance in premodern times, all of which relied, at least in part, on the *Tactica* for material. Several of these were attributed to Leo's imperial successors, Constantine VII and Nikephoros II Phokas, although these, as with Maurice's and Leo's manuals, were likely written by others under imperial patronage.

See also: Maurice (Flavius Mauricius Tiberius Augustus); Vegetius

Further Reading

Dain, A., "Les stratégistes byzantins," *Travaux et mémoires* 2 (1967), 317–392.

Greatrex, Geoffrey, Richard Burgess, and Hugh Elton, "*Urbicius' Epitedeuma*: An Edition, Translation and Commentary," *Byzantinische Zeitschrift* 98 (2005), 35–74.

Haldon, John, *Warfare, State and Society in the Byzantine World, 565–1204*. London: UCL Press, 1999.

Leo VI, *The Taktika of Leo VI*. Ed. and trans. George T. Dennis. Dumbarton Oaks Texts, 12. Washington: Dumbarton Oaks, 2010.

Maurice, *Maurice's Strategikon: Handbook of Byzantine Military Strategy*. Trans. G.T. Dennis. Philadelphia: University of Pennsylvania Press, 1984.

Treadgold, Warren, *Byzantium and Its Army, 284–1081*. Stanford: Stanford University Press, 1995.

Kelly DeVries

Li Ching
(571–649)

Significance: Li Ching's work is the earliest surviving Chinese military writing to provide detailed, concrete and practical guidance on military administration and basic tactics. The contents are comparable to contemporaneous Byzantine military texts.

Context: The T'ang dynasty ruled China from 618 to 907. Under the second T'ang emperor, the warlike T'ai-tsung, the dynasty was at the height of its power and extended Chinese dominion deep into Central Asia.

Biography: Li Ching was one of the most outstanding military leaders of the early T'ang. He directed the campaign that brought the Yangtze Valley under Tang control in 621, and went on to serve T'ai-tsung by leading expeditions beyond China's borders to crush two formidable steppe powers, the eastern Turks (in 629–630) and the Tuyuhun (in 634–635). He also held the offices of minister of war and minister of justice.

Influences: Li Ching's work shows the influence of Sun Tzu's *Art of War* and other ancient Chinese military classics, which it often quotes. It differs from them, however, in that it provides practical, detailed instructions for the management of an army in the field, rather than general principles of war and statecraft. It may not have been the first work of its kind, but it is the earliest whose contents have in large part survived.

The Theory: Li Ching's *Military Methods* has survived in fragmentary form in an eighth-century encyclopedia, the *T'ung-tien* compiled by Tu Yu. The fragments provide detailed prescriptions for the organization, training, and administration of a T'ang expeditionary army of 20,000 men. Their contents cover such topics as formations for battle and march, military law and discipline, the layout of the camp, care of animals, and the treatment of sick and wounded soldiers. Perhaps reflecting the needs of armies campaigning against nomadic opponents, Li Ching devotes special attention to arrangements for pickets, scouts, and patrols, and recommends that an army should deploy for battle in multiple echelons so that some units always remain in formation whereas others disperse in pursuit of the enemy. A surprising lacuna in the *Military Methods* is the absence of any discussion of arrangements for the provisioning of an army on campaign, though this may be more a reflection of the fragmentary nature of the surviving text rather than an omission on the author's part.

Application: Although there are no examples of Chinese generals consciously applying Li Ching's teachings, the details of battles and campaigns mentioned in the T'ang histories are generally consistent with the contents of his manual.

Descendents: Li Ching's *Military Methods* had a substantial impact on later Chinese writing on tactics. Both the *T'ai-pai yin-ching* of Li Ch'üan (probably a mid-eighth century work) and the *Essentials of the Military Classics (Wu-ching tsung-yao)* issued under the Sung dynasty in 1044 include extensive passages borrowed from Li Ching, usually without attribution. Li's writings may also have inspired the *Dialogues of T'ang T'ai-tsung and Li, Duke of Wei*, probably the work of an unidentified scholar in the northern Sung period (960–1126). Li's teachings were not clearly superceded until the Ming general Ch'i Chi-kuang produced his revolutionary manuals for infantry training and tactics in the late 16th century.

See also: Ch'i Chi-kuang; Li Ch'üan; Sun Tzu

Further Reading
Graff, David A., *Medieval Chinese Warfare, 300–900.* London: Routledge, 2002.

David A. Graff

Li Ch'üan
(ca. 760 CE)

Significance: In traditional Chinese astrology, warfare is governed by Venus rather than Mars. Li Ch'üan's *T'ai-pai yin-ching* ("Secret Classic of the Planet Venus") was China's first comprehensive encyclopedia of military knowledge.

Context: In 755, the authority of the Tang dynasty was challenged by the great rebellion of the frontier general An Lu-shan. Although the uprising was quelled in 763, it left the imperial court permanently weakened. This sad situation encouraged scholar officials to take a greater interest in military affairs.

Biography: Li Ch'üan was a scholar who was probably active at the time of the An Lu-shan rebellion and may have held several government offices, including prefect (governor) of Hsien-chou in today's Hopei province. He subsequently lived as a Taoist hermit on Mount Sung (in Honan province).

Influences: Li's work is strongly influenced by the ancient Chinese military classics, above all Sun Tzu's *Art of War* (on which he had once written a commentary). It also borrows heavily from more recent writings such as Li Ching's *Military Methods.* Its last three chapters are informed by the pseudoscientific theory of the five elements and other ancient cosmological and astrological ideas.

The Theory: The contents of the *T'ai-pai yin-ching* range widely. It includes general observations, military regulations, descriptions of weapons (including those used in sieges and naval warfare), diagrams of battle formations, materials dealing with organization, ritual, provisioning, medicine, and even the forms for after-action reports and other sorts of army paperwork. In the opening chapters of the book, Li criticizes the practice of divination and stresses human effort as the key to victory—the sage commander relies on his power of intuition (*shen*) to identify emerging patterns and opportunities.

The last three of Li's ten chapters, however, amount to a handbook of prognostication based on astrology and other pseudoscientific techniques. For example,

"If there is a lunar eclipse when the army sets out, it is inauspicious." This material has led modern Chinese military historians to condemn Li's work as backward and superstitious.

Application: There are no clear examples of the conscious application of Li Ch'üan's theory, but devices described in his book were employed in the warfare of the period (e.g., the "cloud ladder" used against the walls of Feng-t'ien in 783). The ambivalence about divination and astrology seen in the *T'ai-pai yin-ching* was also in evidence elsewhere. For example, in 817 the T'ang general Li Su achieved complete surprise by attacking a rebel force on a day that was considered taboo for combat.

Descendents: The *T'ai-pai yin-ching* was the first in series of increasingly voluminous military encyclopedias with broadly similar contents. These include Hsu Tung's *Hu ch'ien ching* ("Tiger Seal Classic") of 1004, Tseng Kung-liang's *Wu-ching tsung-yao* ("Essentials of the Military Classics") of 1044, Wang Ming-ho's *Teng-t'an pi-chiu* ("What the General Must Know") of 1599, and Mao Yuan-i's *Wu-pei chih* ("Treatise on Military Preparedness") of 1621.

See also: Li Ching; Sun Tzu

Further Reading
Rand, Christopher, "Li Ch'üan and Chinese Military Thought." *Harvard Journal of Asiatic Studies* 39 (1979): 107–37.

David A. Graff

Lindenau, *Feldmarschalleutnant* Karl Friedrich, Graf v.
(1742–1817)

Significance: Participant in the 1790s critique of the methods and views of Frederick the Great as well as the tutor of the Archduke Carl.

Context: Lindenau was an officer in Prussian and Austrian military service. He saw warfare change during the culminating pre–Revolutionary Wars and then the early phases of the Revolutionary and Napoleonic Wars.

Biography: Born into a learned Saxon family, Lindenau joined the Prussian army but fell out with Frederick the Great. He then passed over to Austrian service and saw the peak of his career in the war of intervention over the Dutch Revolution. He is known mainly as Archduke Carl's primary teacher, but Vienna folk tradition remembers him fondly as witty, humane, and tolerant.

Influences: Frederick the Great and Marshal de Saxe.

The Theory: It is supposed that in spite of joining the Romantic critique of Frederick the Great and aligning himself with Montalembert, whose work he translated into German, Lindenau was another mere conservative, geometric systematizer. This may well be true, but it is not obviously based on acquaintance with his work, which appears solidly technical and well reasoned on first impression. He was mostly concerned with the effective deployment of troops in the field, and how to reduce the impact of the Revolutionary Wars.

Descendents: Archduke Carl, Jomini, Scharnhorst, Clausewitz.

Further Reading

Eysturlid, Lee W., *The Formative Influences, Theories and Campaigns of the Archduke Carl of Austria.* Westport, CT: Greenwood, 2000.

Rothenberg, Gunther E., *Napoleon's Great Adversaries: The Archduke Charles and the Austrian Army 1792–1814.* Indiana University Press, Bloomington, 1982.

Erik A. Lund

Lippe, Field Marshal Friedrich Wilhelm Ernst, Graf zu Schaumburg
(1724–1777)

Significance: In an age of dynastic states and armies, Lippe's progressive ideas on universal conscription and advanced education for officers mark him as one of the most important military *philosophes*. He established a paradigm of the citizen army that later Prussian military reformers utilized during the war of liberation against Napoleon. He is one of the few western military thinkers who focused on the morality of war in general and the immorality of offensive war in particular.

Context: Lippe's military thought emerged as a result of his extensive experience in the Seven Years' War and his Classical education. A contemporary of Voltaire and Frederick the Great of Prussia, he drew inspiration from the Enlightenment's desire to reform institutions according to rational precepts. His small county of Schaumburg-Lippe required full, rational mobilization of its military resources to maintain its independence.

Biography: Generally believed to be an illegitimate son of King George I of England, Friedrich Wilhelm Ernst was born in London in 1724 the son of Albrecht Wolfgang, Graf zu Schaumburg-Lippe. He studied in Geneva and Montpelier before entering the British service in 1742 as an officer in the Life Guards. He accompanied his father, a general in Danish service, to France during the War of the Austrian Succession. As a volunteer with the Imperial army, he fought at Dettingen in 1743. In 1748, he became count of Schaumburg-Lippe, a county near Hanover.

Lippe lived in Prussia over the next few years and received a military education from King Frederick II. In 1753 he returned to his capital, Bückeburg, and implemented universal military service. In 1756 he became Major General in the Hanoverian army. During the Seven Years' War, Lippe served with distinction as the artillery commander of allied forces in western Germany.

In 1762, Portugal appointed him commander in chief of an Anglo-Portuguese army hastily organized to defend against a Spanish invasion. His successful defense of Portugal was followed by an extensive reform and reorganization of that country's army. For these efforts the British government gave him the honorary title of field marshal.

Upon his return to Bückeburg in 1764 he established a military academy at Wilhelmstein. His most famous cadet was Gerhard von Scharnhorst. Lippe died in 1777.

Influences: Frederick the Great of Prussia was Lippe's chief teacher of the military art. Classical history and modern enlightened philosophy captivated his intellect. Lippe and Thomas Abbt, one of the foremost Classicists in Germany, developed a lifelong relationship. Lippe knew Voltaire from his Prussian sojourn and developed a long relationship with Johann Gottfried Herder, whom he employed between 1771 and 1776.

The Theory: Lippe's military theory comprises two categories: the theory of defensive war and the establishment of the modern military academy and military state.

His ideas on warfare are found in the unpublished *Mémoires pour servir à l'Art Militaire Défensif.* Lippe was noteworthy in that he condemned all offensive war as immoral and illegal. That is not to say he negated offensive operations. He understood war from the perspective of a small, vulnerable state and believed the only just war was a defensive one. He drew upon his experience in Germany and Portugal and outlined the defensive principles. The army had to occupy "fastened landscapes" or strong points to retard the enemy's progress. Through maneuver, the enemy could be dislodged from your country and routed by militia forces that fought to defend their own land. This last component he drew from his experience in Portugal, where frontier peasant forces drastically curtailed the Spanish invasion. He proposed to garrison borderlands with militia-farmers, not unlike the military border in Croatia.

In numerous other writings, Lippe provided new systems of tactics similar to those espoused by Henry Lloyd and others involved in the French debate over tactics. He wrote extensively on artillery practices and technical reforms, and next to Jean-Baptiste Vaquette de Gribeauval, Lippe stands out as the greatest artillerist of his age.

The military academy at Wilhelmstein was the first of its kind in modern Europe. It taught all the technical branches of war but also provided a liberal and enlightened education that focused on the higher dimensions of warfare. He instructed most of the classes and attracted an international student body. Through the moral improvement of education, he believed one could create competent military officers.

Schaumburg-Lippe was the quintessential military state, and it was Lippe's belief in "people's army" and "people's war" that mark his thought as a landmark break with the Old Order. He argued that universal conscription into what he called a *Landmiliz* was the most rational, efficient, and practical form of military organization to serve national policy and facilitate pure defensive war.

Application: Lippe, as count of Schaumburg-Lippe, implemented universal military service and established a military academy to teach the higher art of war to military officers across Europe. The expense of such a system led to drastic budget cuts after his death. Nevertheless, his system maintained his county's independence until the Napoleonic era, when Hanover permanently annexed it.

Descendents: Lippe influenced contemporaries and future military thinkers in the German-speaking world. General Henry Lloyd adopted many of his ideas pertaining to military recruitment, training, and organization. Lippe's concerns with a people's army, conscription, and military education affected Scharnhorst, Gneisenau, and Clausewitz, and became paramount during the war of liberation against Napoleonic France. He was less well known outside of Germany.

See also: Clausewitz, C.; Lloyd, H.; Scharnhorst and Gneisenau

Further Reading

Ochwadt, Curd, ed., *Graf zu Schaumburg-Lippe: Schriften und Briefe.* 3 vols. Frankfurt am Main: Vittorio Klostermann, 1976–1983.
Savory, Reginald, *His Britannic Majesty's Army in Germany during the Seven Years' War.* Oxford: Clarendon Press, 1966.

Patrick J. Speelman

Lipsius, Justus
(October 18, 1547 to March 23, 1606)

Significance: Lipsius blended Roman stoicism and the Roman republican emphasis on training, discipline and citizen service.

Context: Lipsius's works on political and military topics were published and widely circulated during the Eighty Years' War and after.

Biography: Born in Brabant in 1547, Lipsius received an outstanding university education and immediately entered academic life. He published his first serious work at the age of 20. He would hold positions at several universities as a lecturer. In 1583 and 1584, he was the professor of Maurice of Orange, the future commander and reformer of Dutch forces. He continued to teach and publish until his death at Leuven in 1606.

Influences: Lipsius was most influenced by the combination of the Classical Stoics, especially Seneca, by Tacitus, and by Christianity.

The Theory: To achieve victory a commander must insure that his troops are thoroughly trained and maintain rigid discipline. Wherever possible, troops must be drawn from the indigenous population.

Application: Lipsius's theories on war appear throughout his lectures and writings. He influenced all the Dutch commanders of the Eighty Years' War. When Lipsius published his *Militia Romana,* the Dutch state's general immediately had a copy sent to Maurice of Orange. His theory of discipline and soldierly virtue were widely popular and influenced the concept of military service and command for the next 200 years.

Descendents: Maurice and William of Nassau, Montecúccoli, Archduke Carl

Further Reading

Oestreich, Gerhard, *Neostoicism and the Early Modern State.* New York: Cambridge University Press, 1982.

Lee W. Eysturlid

Lloyd, Major General Henry Humphrey Evans
(ca. 1729–1783)

Significance: General Lloyd was the first British military theorist and a progenitor of the "principles of war." Symbolic of military philosophy in the age of the Enlightenment, his many works on history, politics, and economics make him a precursor to 19th-century military theory personified by Jomini and Clausewitz. As an enlightened *philosophe* and reformer, he joined the effort to revitalize tactics, which would culminate in the methods of the armies of the French Revolution and Napoleonic eras. He is arguably the father of military sociology and was one of the first theorists to articulate the complex relationship between war, state, and society.

Context: Lloyd wrote during the Enlightenment and his writings exhibit many of the values and assumptions of that cultural movement. As a military *philosophe* he approached the study of war with an eye toward reform and perfecting the military art. He based his theory on the study of the wars of contemporary Europe, most notably the Seven Years' War (1756–1763).

Biography: Mystery and obscurity surround Lloyd's early life. He was born in Wales in the county of Merionethshire in 1729. The son of the Reverend John Lloyd, he attended Jesus College, Oxford, but did not take a degree. His father's premature death undermined Henry's future. Inheritance laws provided his stepfather with the family's estates and the prospect as a lawyer's apprentice provided little hope for future gain. The young man left Britain for the continent.

Deep in debt, Lloyd fled Berlin after an ill-fated affair. Venetian Jesuits rescued him, paid his debts, and provided further education for a clerical career. He ventured to Spain and served as secretary to the Marquis de la Minas. Here he was first introduced to military education and engineering. In 1745, Scottish Jacobites under Lord John Drummond discovered him in northeastern France and hired him as a tutor for his sons. Lloyd joined the Jacobite cause and served as a volunteer under Marshal Saxe at the Battle of Fontenoy (1745). Afterward he escorted Bonnie Prince Charles's expedition to Scotland and served as a liaison between the Young Pretender's army and Welsh supporters. British authorities, using the general warrant, arrested him in southern England. Placed under house arrest in London, he escaped the Jacobite slaughter at Culloden. The Drummond family rescued him from incarceration and the Jacobites escaped back to France. Lloyd and the younger John Drummond joined Lowendahl's army that besieged the Dutch fortress of Bergen-op-Zoom (1747).

The interwar period, 1748–1756, proved difficult for Lloyd's career prospects. According to Drummond, he returned to Prussia but rejoined the French service at the outbreak of the Seven Years' War (1756–1763). The government sent him to southern England to survey prospective invasion sites. Lloyd, who traveled incognito as a merchant, returned with a troubling assessment: any invasion was doomed to failure. Wishing to return to battle, he joined the Austrian army in 1758, and he became a lieutenant in Franz Moritz, Graf von Lacy's General Quartermaster Corps. He experienced the myriad campaigns in Central Europe, being present at both the battles of Hochkrich (1758) and Maxen (1759). Lloyd was promoted to captain in the light infantry, but he resigned his commission in early 1761, promising not to offer his services to the Prussians.

Lloyd briefly joined the court of Prince Xavier of Saxony. In 1761, Prince Ferdinand of Brunswick recruited Lloyd into his service as his general adjutant. After the war Lloyd found himself unemployed and with few prospects. The elector of Cologne rewarded him with the honorary commission of major general, a title that included no pension.

General Lloyd tried to gain employment in Portugal under the Graf zu Schaumburg-Lippe, a famous soldier and military reformer; but the Portuguese leadership rejected his application. Afterward he traveled to Italy and for some time resided with his close friend and Italian *philosophe,* Pietro Verri. He and Verri had served together in the Austrian army and shared common philosophic pursuits. By now, Lloyd had become an enlightened *philosophe* and an enemy of superstition, the Church, and the Bourbon cause. In 1766, his critical analysis of Frederick the Great's campaigns was published anonymously as *History of the Late War in Germany*. Lloyd next focused on economics, politics, arguing with priests, and spying for the British government. In 1768, he was arrested on route to support Pasquale Paoli's rebellion against French administration of Corsica.

In 1770, Lloyd returned to London upon the death of his patron, Lord Granby. He returned to Italy with a wife, Mary Garnett. Lloyd published the anonymous *Essay on the English Constitution* (1770) in support of John Wilkes. The following year he published the anonymous *An Essay on the Theory of Money,* which stands as an early form of liberal economics and forerunner of the quantity theory of exchange.

In 1772, Lloyd joined the Russian army with the rank of major general. It seems he became a favorite of Catherine the Great, and even planned a war against China over the disputed eastern frontier. In 1774, he and General Rumiantsev planned the final operations of the Russo-Turkish War (1768–1774). Lloyd, accompanied by a group of British observers that included Henry Clinton, bottled up the Turks at the fortress of Silistria as the main Russian army struck at Shumla. This ended the war and Lloyd's Russian adventure. Denied military honors, he abruptly quit Russian service. No doubt, the death of his wife made him tarry to England.

Lloyd resumed his military writings. In 1779, he wrote a controversial pamphlet, *Rhapsody on the Present System of French Politics; on the Projected Invasion and the Means to Defeat It*. With a Franco-Spanish invasion looming, Lloyd used his pen to assure Britain that the invasion would fail if certain precautions were taken in Portsmouth and Plymouth. His veiled denunciation of British colonial policy in general, and of Lord George Germain and Jeffrey Amherst in particular, that led to governmental suppression of the pamphlet. Lloyd's attempt to gain command of American loyalist forces was ignored and he retired to the Austrian Netherlands to continue his intellectual pursuits.

Lloyd's magnum opus, *Continuation of the History of the Late War,* was published in 1781, with a second narrative volume of the war already in manuscript form. He next determined to write a history of the war in Westphalia and Portugal. In the summer 1783 he died in Huy. British agents absconded with his papers and Catholic fanatics exhumed and mutilated his body and dumped it on the roadside. The second volume of his narrative history of the Seven Years' War was published from his manuscripts in 1790.

Influences: Classical writers such as Caesar and Arrian provided a solid grounding for Lloyd's military thinking. The 17th-century Habsburg general, Raimondo Montecúccoli, as well as such contemporaries as Marshals Saxe and Lacy, and the Count of Schaumburg-Lippe proved pivotal to his intellectual development. The major thinkers of the Enlightenment, from Voltaire to Hume, exerted great sway over his critical analysis of economics, society, and warfare.

The Theory: Lloyd's theory is not altogether systematic and must be examined within four main categories.

First, he conceived of the "principles of war," which he extrapolated from his military experience as an Austrian staff officer during the Seven Years' War. History provided lessons for military conduct only if an officer took the time to study recent experience by analyzing the military campaigns, reading and comparing primary descriptions of battles, and visiting actual battlefields, to reenact the engagement in their mind's eye. The principles of war are found in his two volumes on the Seven Years' War in Germany.

The principles of maneuver and marching flow through his historical analysis of Frederick the Great's campaigns. Mathematics and the understanding of space and time necessarily imbued the officer with the tools to outmaneuver his enemy. For the army that marched best, must certainly win. Lloyd heaped praise on Frederick's ability to march and orchestrate maneuvers on and off the battlefield.

Positional warfare also came under the guidelines or principles. The "key point" or "strong point" was the cardinal attribute of any position. If one understood key points, then the success of actions and engagements was assured. Knowledge of the terrain and country enabled the commander to better understand the nature of key points.

Lloyd, though an engineer by training, did not advocate sieges, as they were slow, expensive, and detrimental to an army's morale. He emphasized offensive field operations, where prudence, the initiative, and a basic understanding of time and space relations were the core principles. He especially highlighted the "velocity" of an army, which when combined with wholesale pursuit, could achieve tactical victory. For Lloyd the offensive required daring leadership, as "time was everything in war." The battle of Zornsdorf directly influenced these offensive principles.

Similar principles animated defensive warfare, where prudence was the chief characteristic. Fighting battles may be necessary but in the main, they had to be avoided, as they were risky ventures when you were weaker than your opponent was. In retreat, one had to divide your forces into as many large bodies of troops as possible so the enemy could not pursue you. Frederick's defeat at Kolin informed Lloyd's outlook on the rules of defensive war. Lloyd's caution contrasted greatly with the sense of audacity in his principles for the offensive.

> Modern principles of war emanated from his analysis. Lloyd considered a well-defined "objective" necessary for military victory: it was folly to engage in operations without a clearly defined goal. According to Lloyd, the inability of the Austrians to define objectives and pursue them with vigor was the main cause of their defeat.

Lloyd clearly defined the principle of "mass," though he criticized those who believed superior numbers guaranteed victory. A few brave troops aptly led could defeat larger forces, and numbers meant nothing if commanded by ignorant, incompetent men. In fact, too many soldiers might actually lead to the disintegration of unity of purpose and render an army unmanageable.

The battle of Leuthen offered many lessons from which Lloyd posited a principle later called "economy of force." Frederick had brought more men into the action at the decisive point and therefore won a historic victory. Lloyd deduced that any general who could bring more men into action than the enemy at the decisive point would normally win the battle.

From the battle of Maxen, Lloyd deduced the principle of outflanking attacks. No army, he concluded, could keep the battlefield if it was pinned down by one force and then attacked in the flank by another. However, caution was necessary even here. Lloyd warned that anything was possible in war and a good general must understand all contingencies so they may not be deceived or caught unprepared. Lloyd also castigated Frederick the Great's missteps and criticized that commander's penchant for repeatedly trying to replicate the victory of Leuthen. Repetition of tactics (in this case flank attacks) only made one's generalship predictable.

Next, Lloyd engaged in the great debate on tactical forms, which dominated military literature of the era. In this endeavor, he stood as a military reformer.

An advocate of bold offensive operations, he suggested tactical reforms that he called his "new system." It is found in his work on British coastal defense, but is elaborated upon in his philosophy of war in *Continuation of the History of the Late War in Germany*. Lloyd believed modern weaponry had made the battlefield an indecisive affair. Armies could approach one another, but the firepower of muskets and artillery never allowed them to close to a decisive melee encounter. Therefore, his new system of tactics emphasized the use of "lances" or pikes in shallow column formation supported by firearms and cavalry. This line of divisions comprised battalions of five companies each. The line would be four deep but not contiguous. The breaks in the line demarcated the battalions, which he believed would allow for more flexibility on the battlefield. Light infantry, cavalry, and artillery protected the flanks of these battalions. The goal was to approach an enemy arrayed in traditional line formation and outflank it on the battlefield, thereby pinning it down and allowing for a mass charge with lance. The light infantry would screen the advancing battalions and provide a modicum of protection before the melee. The turn from firepower to a reliance on close combat, Lloyd believed, would return decision to the battlefield. His system, he believed, represented an army that embodied the virtues of strength, agility, and universality. However, he never addresses the problem of stalemate if the opposing armies were arrayed in like manner.

Third, Lloyd theorized about the interconnected relation between war, state, and society, and the underlying psychology of military institutions. Following Montesquieu, he analyzed the military systems of monarchies, republics, and despotisms in the *Continuation*. His analysis also criticized absolutism. Contemporary monarchies approached despotism and threatened the well-being of the state, and too many short wars were fought on royal caprice. Republics were best suited for defensive wars; as they tended to rely upon militia forces rather than long-term professionals, they rarely were motivated to go to war unless fighting for their homeland. Lloyd saw the Roman Republic as an ideal form that synthesized aristocratic military values with that of patriotic citizens.

> Lloyd went beyond simple political analysis. He believed that psychology could unlock the potential for war making as well. Commanders had to understand how to motivate and imbue their soldiers with enthusiasm in order to better control it and achieve victory. He criticized the harsh methods of discipline in his own day, even though admitting the fear of pain was a good motivating tool. Instead, officers must develop firm relationships with their men, toil with them, and encourage them, rather than simply commanding and directing. An army, he argued, was like an unruly sea. It had to be understood and navigated, but it could never be totally controlled by will alone. This focus on the socio-political and psychological underpinnings of military institutions and warfare make Lloyd a pioneer of military sociology.

Last, Lloyd developed the study of operations and coined the term "lines of operation" to better understand the nature of military campaigns. Conceiving of campaigns as planned operations with distinct objectives and phases, Lloyd stands as a pioneer in campaign analysis and the operational art. The lines of operations were simply lines upon which an army acted toward a defined objective. He first uses the term in his pamphlet on British defense and later elaborates more fully in the *Continuation*. Lloyd drew his inspiration for this analysis from Frederick the Great's use of interior lines of operation, because he was able to keep his enemies' armies from uniting so he could fight them in turn.

Application: Lloyd died six years before the French Revolution and was a well-known military theorist throughout the era. His writings, translated into French, German, Italian, and Russian, were standard readings for officers in Britain and elsewhere. His analysis of British defense saw six editions during the Napoleonic Wars. However, the New Tactical system was never utilized. Guibert offered a compromise synthesis that took into account the strengths of the column and line, but the Napoleonic era rendered much of 18th-century theory obsolete. Lloyd's concept of "lines of operations," his discernment of principles of war, and emphasis on the sociological dimension of military theory comprised his enduring legacy.

Descendents: Lloyd's conceptualization of war as a phenomenon interrelated with society, economics, and politics, makes him the forerunner, if not inspiration for Jomini and Clausewitz. Jomini based much of his analysis of Frederick the Great's campaigns on Lloyd's histories, and defended the Welshman from posthumous attacks by the Prussian Tempelhof, who excoriated Lloyd's criticism of Frederick. The 20th-century Soviet general Alexander Svechin, in his attempt to infuse the Red army with a theoretical basis, based his ideas on the traditional Russian appreciation of Lloyd's operational ideas.

See also: Jomini; Lippe, Friedrich Wilhelm Ernst; Saxe, M.

Further Reading

Gat, Azar, *The Origins of Military Thought from the Enlightenment to Clausewitz.* New York: Oxford University Press, 1989.

Speelman, Patrick J., *Henry Lloyd and the Military Enlightenment of Eighteenth-Century Europe.* Westport: Greenwood Press, 2002.

Speelman, Patrick J., ed., *War, Society and Enlightenment: The Works of General Lloyd.* Leiden: Brill Academic Publishers, 2005.

Patrick J. Speelman

Loque, Bertrand de (aka François de Saillans)
(b. between ca. 1540–1550, d. after 1600)

Significance: Loque wrote in favor of a prince's right to support subjects of another prince against him or her, if the latter suppressed the true faith (by Loque's definition, Protestantism)—a notion foreshadowing today's concept of the responsibility to protect.

Context: The French Wars of Religion form the background to Loque's work; they were seen by contemporaries as turning on the question of whether subjects have the right to rise up against their prince, if the latter prevents them from practicing their faith. This links up with the question of whether subjects can have the right to rise up against their sovereign, if he or she is a tyrant. The treatise on war was dedicated to the newly instated, then still Protestant, King Henry IV of France.

Biography: François de Saillans was born in Valence, France, as the son of a Catholic baron and crown official. De Saillans converted to Protestantism, influenced by his uncle, a professor of the University at Valence. He took part in a Protestant uprising in 1561, which clashed with forces led by his own father, who disinherited him. He fled to Geneva to study Protestant theology, and then disappears from the records. A decade later, an otherwise enigmatic figure going by the name of Bertrand de Loque was active as a Protestant minister and theologian in Aquitaine. He was identified by one of his Jesuit adversaries as François de Saillans. Loque's other writings concern Protestant theology, and he was called upon to defend the Protestant position in disputes.

Influences: Although a Huguenot, Loque nevertheless stands firmly in the Ciceronian–Augustinian tradition of seeing war as just if commanded by God and fulfilling the classical criteria. Loque, like other French authors of his period referred to as the *Politiques,* developed an early form of what is now called the responsibility to protect, the right of one prince (government) to intervene in another prince's (government's) realm to protect subjects from tyranny.

The Theory: The Protestant clergyman and theologian Loque rejected the views of other Protestant schools that all war is an *absolute* evil. To be just, however, a war has to be prosecuted with strict discipline, and with all possible clemency toward vanquished populations and soldiers. Loque interestingly explored the duties of a prince toward his subjects, hinting at their right to stage an insurgency against a tyrant, that is, a prince who ruled badly. He denied the right of princes to use force against heretical subjects except in extreme cases. Like Clausewitz long after him, Loque underscored the need for a good understanding of one's own war aims prior to going to war.

Further Reading

For excerpts, see Beatrice Heuser (ed. and trans.), *The Strategy Makers: Thoughts on War and Society from Machiavelli to Clausewitz.* Santa Barbara, CA: Praeger/ABC-CLIO, 2010.

Beatrice Heuser

Machiavelli, Niccolò di Bernardo dei
(1469–1527)

Significance: Machiavelli's *Art of War* is considered the first "modern" military treatise and transmitted the arguments of ancient Greek and Roman writers regarding militia forces, to Renaissance Europe.

Context: Machiavelli's ideas were conditioned by the political and military turmoil in Florence and the other Italian city-states in the late 15th to early 16th centuries.

Biography: The most influential political and military theorist of the Renaissance, Niccolò Machiavelli was born into an impoverished noble family in Florence on May 3, 1469. He served the Florentine Republic as a bureaucrat and diplomat (1498–1512), and as chancellor and secretary of the Ten of Liberty and Peace, he was much involved in military affairs. His public career ended with imprisonment and torture when the Medici returned to power in Florence in 1512. He subsequently retired to his country estate and died in Florence on June 21, 1527.

Influences: Machiavelli borrowed heavily from Vegetius and other Classical Greek and Roman military writers and historians, and he was also influenced by events in his own time.

The Theory: Machiavelli is best known for his works on history and politics (*The Discourses* and *The Prince*), in which he stressed the inseparable nature of political and military matters and argued that politics had a morality of its own. He also published, in 1521, a treatise entitled *Dell'arte della guerra* (*The Art of War*) in which he argued for a return to ancient Roman military virtues. He proposed to revive the power of the Florentine city-state by replacing the ineffectual and uncommitted *condottieri* (mercenaries) with an army of citizen militiamen who had a personal stake in the outcomes of battles. He argued that a disciplined and well-trained militia would defend republicanism and liberty against tyranny, would be a means for instilling respect for authority, have a sense of common purpose, and would cost less than a standing army of mercenaries. He also stressed the value of proper training, the primacy of infantry (with cavalry in a supporting role), and the minimal value on artillery.

Application: Machiavelli played a major role in the promulgation of the Florentine *Ordinanza* of December 6, 1506, which established compulsory militia service for Florentine men between the ages of 18 and 30. This freed Florence from reliance on mercenaries. In 1508–1509, 2,000 militiamen took part in the siege of Pisa and enabled the Florentines to maintain the siege through the winter, thereby starving the Pisans into surrender. However, when put to the test against the experienced Spanish troops of the Holy Roman emperor at the siege of Prato in 1512, the Florentine militia failed.

Descendents: Machiavelli was responsible for the Renaissance revival of interest in classical military knowledge and its application to the problems of modern military affairs. His arguments for militia forces were still being cited in the United States in connection National Guard reform as late as 1903.

See also: Vegetius

Further Reading
Machiavelli, Niccolò, *Art of War.* Translated by Christopher Lynch. Chicago: University of Chicago Press, 2003.

Machiavelli, Niccolò, *The Art of War.* Translated by Ellis Farnsworth. Revised edition by Neal Wood. New York: Da Capo Press, 2001.

Ridolfi, Roberto, *The Life of Niccolò Machiavelli.* Translated by Cecil Grayson. London: Routledge and Kegan Paul/Chicago: The University of Chicago Press, 1963.

Charles R. Shrader

Maizeroy, Brigadier General Paul Gédéon Joly de
(1719–1780)

Significance: Maizeroy contributed to the French military debates that resulted in Guibert's new tactical system of 1772. He resurrected the concept of "strategy," the first modern thinker to use the term, and began to shift attention toward the study of the conduct of operations.

Context: Following France's defeat in the Seven Years' War, theorists focused on army reform and experimented with new tactical models. This effort expressed the Enlightenment's concern with universal principles.

Biography: Born in 1719, Maizeroy fought in the French army under Marshal Saxe during the War of Austrian Succession (1740–1748). In the Seven Years' War (1756–1763) he achieved the rank of lieutenant colonel. His most famous work is *Cours de tactique, théoretique, practique, et historique* (1766). Another volume, *Theorie de la guerre* (1777), followed a decade later. Maizeroy died in 1780, as a brigadier general.

Influences: Ancient Greek and Roman military forms exerted the greatest influence on Maizeroy's thinking. The ideas of Chevalier de Folard, Baron de Mesnil-Durand and the Marshal de Saxe informed his theory.

The Theory: Maizeroy created a universal theory of tactics and strategy. His tactical ideas are found in *Cours de tactique, théoretique, practique, et historique* (1766). An admirer of the Roman Legion, Maizeroy advocated columnar organization and combat doctrine. He devised the "cohort," a basic tactical formation of 640 soldiers, armed with musket and bayonet, drawn up in a front eighty men wide and eight ranks deep. The goal was to charge the enemy and initiate shock combat, rather than rely upon firepower. These advancing cohorts would be flanked by skirmishers and supported by cavalry.

Maizeroy revived the term "strategy" in *Theorie de la guerre* (1777), basing it upon the sixth-century work, *Strategicon,* attributed to the Byzantine Emperor Maurice. By shifting attention to the conduct of operations, Maizeroy altered the trajectory of military philosophy. He believed that strategy could be understood through universal principles, which he called the "military dialectic."

Application: Advocates of Maizeroy's *l'ordre profound* could point to few modern successes. The ill-fated British column at Fontenoy (1745) undermined his arguments, and the early French Revolutionary armies, which fought in depth rather than in linear formation, did so due to inadequate training and discipline. His denigration of firepower, including artillery, made his tactical ideas irrelevant by the end of the Napoleonic era.

Descendents: The emphasis on shock over firepower was a common theme in the late 1700s. Maizeroy's shallow formations made his system more moderate than Folard's, but the Comte de Guibert's combination of columns for movement and linear formations for fighting reflect the final synthesis of this debate.

See also: Folard; Guibert, J.; Saxe, M.

Further Reading
Gat, Azar, *The Origins of Military Thought from the Enlightenment to Clausewitz.* New York: Oxford University Press, 1989.

Patrick J. Speelman

Majorovich, Andrea
(fl. 1750?)

Significance and Theory: Majorovich reached at least colonel's rank in the Venetian army. He was an engineer, but is remembered (to the extent that he is remembered at all), for his "Art of War, Reduced to Scientific Principles" ("Del'Arte della guerra"), a manuscript on the art of war originally deposited in the military archives of Venice but now held as folio 7/22 in the Kriegswissenschaftlichen Memoiren collection of the Kriegsarchiv Staatsarchiv in Vienna. Like other still-unpublished Venetian military theorists, Majorovich takes amphibious operations as normative and integrates the loading, transport, and assault/landing phase into the basic theory of military operations.

See also: Folard; Feuquières; Frederick II ("the Great"); Picq; Saxe, M.

Erik A. Lund

Manu
(ca. 100 BCE)

Significance: Manu was the first Hindu theoretician to treat law in a systematic manner. Manu collected a large number of laws and provided detailed explanations justifying them. This compilation is known as *Manusmriti* or *Manusamhita* or *The Laws of Manu,* and was composed at the beginning of the Common Era or slightly earlier. Manu's codes represent an attempt by Hindu philosophy to harmonize the Asokan world-view with the legacies of Kautilya.

Hindu philosophy features a bipolar division between *dharma* (right) and *adharma* (wrong). The laws of Manu discern this bipolarity in every aspect of human life, including politics: *Manusmriti* addresses the questions of statecraft, the proper way for a ruler to rule and to punish transgressors in the realm. Because Manu belonged to the *dharmashastra* writing tradition, he occasionally considers himself as the moral teacher even while dealing with *rajadharmas* (duties of a king for good governance). As if preempting the western Enlightenment's quest for the search of laws with universal validity, *Manusmriti* asserts that it aims to establish a science of eternal political principles.

Context: To an extent, *Manusmriti* was the Brahmin reaction against the rise of heterodox sects such as Buddhism and Jainism. After the collapse of the Maurya Empire during the early second century BCE, multiple regional powers emerged in India. The Mauryas were primarily replaced by the Sungas, a Brahmin family that patronized Brahmanism. The Sungas responded to Asoka's patronage of Buddhism by discriminating against Buddhists. The Sungas were able to establish their sway only in north India, but were replaced in 112 BCE by another Brahmin dynasty, the Kanvas.

Manu's military thoughts were shaped by the way recent or contemporary powers had structured their forces. For example, Kharavela, the expansionist ruler of Kalinga (Orissa) around the mid-second century BCE, possessed an army was composed of elephants, infantry, and chariots. In Manu's military world view, elephants and chariots get prominence.

Biography: Although we can use circumstantial evidence to estimate the periods when Manu was active, we have no information about Manu's private life. Most of the ancient Indian texts mask their true authorship to bolster their claims to be transcendentally based and representing absolute truth. Western military tracts lie within the school of western philosophy, rooted in Classical Greek thought. Greek *philosophia* generates ceaseless inquiry and search aiming at wisdom. By contrast, Indian *darsana* is systematic elaboration of truth, or an aspect of it, which has already been grasped. It is not the search for truth but exposition of it, intellectual vindication, conceptual fixation, and classification of what has been received. In *philosophia,* the individual thinker, captivated by the love of wisdom, plays the decisive role. But, in *darsana,* the individual thinker, great or small, plays a subordinate role. He does not found a system but carries its explication forward. So, whereas we have detailed information about the western military theoreticians such as Tacitus, Livy, Xenophon, etc., our information regarding the Indian *acharyas* (theoreticians/teachers/preachers) such as Manu is minimal.

Another characteristic regarding the literature of ancient India (such as *Manusmriti*), which reduces their historical value, are their claims to be based on the teachings of mythical sages. Authors tend to eliminate references to actual events or persons.

Influences: Ancient India's Sanskrit literature includes a genre of *niti* writings. *Niti* means righteousness, moral conduct, and morality. It could also be translated as the science of moral philosophy. To an extent, *niti* is a set of directions for civilized human conduct. *Niti* also means policy, prudence, wisdom, and right course of action and it highlights statesmanship and political wisdom. One aspect of *niti* discusses military policy, the direction and management of a polity's military assets. The *niti* literary tradition partly shaped *Manusmriti*.

Manu followed Kautilya's grand strategic thought by granting importance to coalition warfare. *Manusmriti,* following *Arthashastra,* argues that diplomacy, rather than warfare, should take the preeminent role in the formulation of grand strategic policy. While discussing military operations, Manu, like Kautilya, emphasizes the role of forts rather than pitched battles. Therefore, instead of a battle-centric strategy, Manu proposes an attritional strategy, with forts, rather than the enemy's army, constituting the prime objectives of warfare. For conducting siege warfare, *Manusmriti,* like *Arthashastra,* focuses on the role of spies and alliances.

Manu's preference for forts in warfare was due to the spread of walled towns in India from fourth century BCE. During Alexander's invasion of India, battlements and ramparts were common in the Indian forts. For example, Pataliputra, the capital of the Maurya Empire, had a wall with 64 gates and 570 towers surrounding the city. The palisade had loopholes for archers and outside the wall was a ditch filled with water from the River Son. The Andhras (Satavahanas), who emerged as the dominant power in central and south India after the Maurya Empire, depended on 30 walled towns inside their kingdom.

Manu uses the word *dharma* frequently. In the *Rig Veda,* no moral sense is attached to *dharma,* which merely signifies "upholder" or "supporter." In the *Yajur Veda, dharma* means "firm" or "imperturbable." During the Vedic era (1500–500 BCE), moral content was reserved for the word *rita,* the violation of which demanded of the sinner penitence and prayer to the god Varuna. *Rita* stands for order, a regulating principle that runs through all creation. Gradually the moral sense of *rita* was incorporated in *dharma.* The *Bhagavad Gita* says that a king, a *kshatriya* (member of the warrior caste) by vocation, should fulfill his *dharma* by indulging in righteous war, and by ensuring that each member of his kingdom or society could perform their duty properly.

Manu's emphasis on *dharmayuddha* was shaped by the Epic and *Puranic* literature, which came into existence between the fifth and first century BCE. The laws of war, as enunciated in the Epic and *Puranic* literature, distinguish sharply between combatants and noncombatants. Under no circumstances are noncombatants to be harmed. Further, unarmed enemy soldiers are not to be attacked, nor is a fleeing enemy to be annihilated.

The Theory: *Manusmriti* gives the state the supreme role in human affairs. The rod (*danda*) represents the coercive dimension of the state. *Danda* also means the science of government. At times, Manu equates *danda* with the king. He writes that the king should be "manly"—he should be knowledgeable in *dharma, artha* (financial power), and *kama* (sexual prowess). A king properly wielding *danda* prospers, but a sensual king, who follows unfair and base policies, perishes due to *adharma.*

The word *dharma* is derived from the word *dhri* (to sustain or uphold). *Dharma* is natural law for inanimate objects and natural phenomena, as well as an ethical and social standard of behavior. *Dharma* and truth are interchangeable concepts. In the context of political science, *dharma* means *rajadharma* (a code of kingly duties for the ruler). By following *dharma,* even a weak ruler could become strong. For Manu, *dharma* means an inherent law of the universe, inviolate and fixed. However, he also equated it with man-made laws. So, *dharma* represents truth both at the mundane level of reality, and in the sphere of metaphysics. In *Manusmriti,* *dharma* appears both in the sense of righteousness and in the particular sense of social rules and court laws. The ethical content of *dharma* includes *dhriti* (steadfastness), *kshama* (patience), *dama* (self-control), *asteya* (honesty), *saucham* (purity), and *dhi* (wisdom).

One aspect of *dharma* is security for the ruler and his domain. *Danda* should be used, writes Manu, to implement *dharma,* which means keeping the four castes within the kingdom and the neighboring kingdoms within their proper place. The policy of using *danda* is also called *dandaniti,* which for Manu is equivalent with *rajniti* (governance). The king is the protector of *dharma.* As regards a kingdom's internal security, *Manusmriti* says that the rod alone chastises all the subjects, protects them, and stays awake while they sleep. Wise men know that justice is the rod. Manu warns the ruler about judicious use of force. Deployment of too much or too little force is dangerous. Properly wielded, with due consideration, it makes all the subjects happy; but inflicted without due regard, it destroys everything. When *artha* and *kama* go against *dharma,* the former two should be abandoned by the king.

Manu designates the state as having six parts: king, ministers, territory, forts, treasury, and finally the army. In Manu's framework of *rashtraniti* (state's policies), the army occupies the lowest place. Combat occupies a peripheral position within grand strategy. He asserts that the king should try to conquer his enemies by conciliation, bribery, and dissension, rather than by battles. Because neither of the two powers engaging in battle can be confident of victory, the king should avoid war. The king should prevent his ally from slipping away and joining the enemy side. The diplomats' job is to disorganize the enemy alliance and to shore up an alliance against the invaders. But, despite the best intention of a righteous ruler, war might still occur. *Manusmriti* notes *yuddha dharma samatanah* ("war is the eternal law of the kings").

Unlike Kautilya's recommendation of *kutayuddha* (unjust war), Manu suggests *dharmayuddha* (just war). *Dharmayuddha* is to be waged by the *kshatriyas* (warrior caste), because *dharma* is the *kshatra* (duty) of a *kshatriya.* In contrast to Kautilya, Manu is against recruiting all the four castes into the army. Following *Arthashastra, Manusmriti* notes that *dharma* should be implemented by *chaturangabala,* which is the four-limbed army composed of *patti* (infantry), *hastis* (elephants), *asvas* (cavalry), and *rathas* (chariots). Whereas Kautilya gives equal importance to the four components of the army, Manu gives the least importance to the *asvas.* In doing so, Manu ignores the military significance of the Central Asian horse trade, on which the survival of the Hindu polities against the onslaught of Central Asian steppe nomads would eventually depend. The nomads are designated in *Manusmriti* as *mlechchas* (impure outsiders).

If at all battles become necessary, then the king, writes Manu, should fight with horses and chariots on a level ground. Manu, instead of advocating an aggressive war for complete destruction of the enemy by all means, preaches a sort of ceremonial war. He critiques *yana* (preparing for attack without declaring war). He is also against the use of new deadly weapons, despising the horse archery intro-duced by the "unclean foreigners," that is, the Parthians. Manu is also against the use of deception, treachery, and surprise in battle. Worse, Manu is against attack-ing the retreating enemy. *Manusmriti* warns the king that while waging war, his soldiers should not kill the hostile troops with weapons that are concealed, barbed, or smeared with poison or whose points blaze with fire. A righteous warrior should not kill anyone who folds his hands in supplication and asking for mercy, or any-one who surrenders. Nor should the righteous king attack enemy soldiers without armor, or without weapons, or whose weapons are broken. Further, any enemy sol-dier who is asleep or engaged in combat with someone else should not be attacked. Any hostile military personnel who are badly wounded should also be allowed to leave the field. For Manu, war, both at the strategic and tactical levels, becomes a sort of royal sport. Tactics are reduced to a duel among equals.

Manu prefers siege warfare over battles, and he is less idealistic as regards sieges. He lays down a cautious policy for taking the enemy's forts. When the king has besieged the enemy, he should harass the latter's kingdom, and spoil the fodder, food, water, and fuel. The king should break water tanks, ramparts, and ditches, but also try to win over the important persons of the enemy kingdom.

A city ought to be protected by a fort. Manu discusses various types of forts: fort with desert on all sides, fort with water all around, fort with brick rampart, fort inside a forest, and fort on a hill. He considers the hill fort as the best. Forts are important because they allow the defender to oppose a numerically superior enemy and also function as bases. They also allow a defeated army to recuperate before launching a counterattack. The forts should be guarded with both man-made and natural obstacles—the most important man-made obstacle is the rampart. Even a marching field army should resemble a fort surrounded by elephants and infantry. Foot archers are Manu's favorite defensive weap-ons against a besieging army. One bowman on the rampart could deal with 100 besiegers.

As mentioned above, Manu does not realistically assess the threat to India by foreigners. These threats are mentioned, for example, in Patanjali's text on gram-mar, titled *Mahabhashya,* which was written around the second century BCE, and the *Gargi Smahita.* In the event, the Indo-Greek, Scythian, and Parthian forces, centered round cavaliers with chain-mail armor and equipped with bows and lances, outclassed the *chaturangabala.* Manu's ritualistic symmetrical positional warfare was certainly no match against them. Manu neglects the foreign powers (*Yavanas*) because they belong outside the caste boundaries, and instead portrays an idealistic *mandala* (circle of kingdoms) composed only of Hindu kings fol-lowing righteous policy and "humane warfare." Nothing could be more detached from reality.

Application: The tactical effectiveness of the Hindu armies in the post-Maurya age was reduced due to the concept of just war that *Manusmriti* emphasized, par-ticularly when facing the steppe nomads. Language gives a clue to the nature of the enemy: the Sanskrit ethnonym for the Central Asian people who destroyed the Bactrian Greeks and who were called Sakas in Iran is *Shakas*. The Iranian *sak* means to go, flow or run, and hence Saka means "running swift." The Saka army was mostly composed of horsemen who used boots for the cavaliers, saddles, bridles, compound bows, and stirrups made of rope.

The Sakas originally inhabited the region around Rivers Oxus and Jaxartes. However, they were pushed south by the Yueh-Chih (known as Kushanas in India), and *en route* destroyed the Greek kingdom of Bactria. Saka rule eventually included the Indus plain and Mathura. However, the Sakas themselves came under pressure from the Kushanas around the mid-first century CE, and the Sakas became feudatories of the Kushanas. By this time, the Kushanas were pushed south by the Hsung-nu (Huns). The greatest Kushana ruler Kanishka (78–144 CE) ruled over a considerable portion of north and central India. After Kanishka's death, the Kushanas themselves came under pressure from the Parthians: Mithradates II established Parthian power in India around first century BCE. No Indian ruler was able to defeat the Parthians, and only the Persians saved India when in 226 CE, Ardashir overthrew the Parthians and established Sassanian power in Iran. The Kushana kings became subordinated to the Sassanians. The Kushanas in turn pushed the Sakas into Kathiwad Peninsula in Gujarat and Malwa in central India. Here they continued to rule until Chandragupta, the Hindu Gupta Emperor (375–415 CE) extirpated the last Saka ruler Rudrasimha III. When the Huns invaded India around mid-fifth century CE, the Guptas were able to check them along the Indus.

The Guptas' were finally able to beat the non-Hindu invaders because the Gupta military had been reorganized around mobility. The idea of entrenched force following a strategic defense, as suggested by Manu, was replaced by the theory of mobile aggressive warfare. The Guptas even copied horse archery from the Parthians. Kalidasa's *Raghuvamsa*, written in the fifth century CE, notes that each Gupta horseman was equipped with a coat of mail going down to knees, a long lance, bow, and a quiver of arrows. The cavalry marched in well-ordered close formations. This practice died out after the disintegration of the Gupta Empire in 550 CE. In the post-Gupta era, the Hindu armies went back to the traditional *chaturanga* system as emphasized by Manu. The *Siva Dhanurveda* (a manual dealing with training for archery), written a few centuries after *Manusmriti,* is silent on the issue of horse archery.

Manu's influence on Hindu fortifications was significant. For example Delhi, the capital of Prithviraja (a Rajput chieftain who ruled in twelfth century CE), was turned into a fort. It had a wall of 4.5 miles in length with nine gates and several bastions. The Marathas (inhabitants of Maharashtra in West India) and the Rajputs accepted Manu's theory regarding hill forts. The Rajput forts of Mandu and Ranthambhor were constructed on the summits of hills. By the mid-seventeenth century CE, most important Maratha forts were constructed on hilltops.

Descendents: Bhartrihari's Sanskrit work, *Atha Nitishatakam,* written in first century CE, throws light on the polity and on human behavior both in the private and public spheres. This work criticizes the selfishness and greed, and criticizes the temptations of money and lust. Bhartrihari emphasizes that those who do not tread the path of *dharma,* are burdens on this mortal world. Like *Manusmriti,* the *Atha Nitishatakam* advocates *dharmayuddha.* Bhartrihari claims that it is the duty of warriors to be *yudhi vikramah* (chivalrous) while combating the enemy. The men who are truthful and glorious prefer to lay down their lives than to renege on their promises and surrender their ideals. Good conduct and unblemished moral character are required from both the warriors and the kings.

Like *Manusmriti, Atha Nitishatakam* declares that a king's duty concerns the power to rule and make others obey, and it throws light on good governance. The king should take care of the public and ought to be forgiving. Both in Manu and Bhartirhari's scheme, armed forces occupy a secondary position. The king's power depends on his horses and elephants.

In *Atha Nitishatakam,* as in *Manusmriti,* there is constant tension between the role of human agency and the part played by *daiva* (chance/Providence) in shaping history. At one point, Bhartrihari writes that luck decides everything: human agency is reduced to a negligible factor. Elsewhere, he asserts that just as the sun illuminates the whole world with its powerful rays, a warrior, by dint of his valor, can conquer the enemies. He continues that in such a case, the role of luck is transitory. Like Manu, he believes in the *karma* theory.

The *Atha Nitishatakam* offers two modifications of *Manusmriti.* Bhartrihari comments on the necessity at times of asymmetric responses on the battlefield. For controlling elephants in the battlefields, he refers to the use of *ankushenas* (hooked hammers) by the *mahouts* (elephant drivers).

Manu's focus on good governance also influenced the evolution of Kamandaka's theory of paternalist despotism around sixth century CE, and to an extent Narayana's *Hitopadesa,* which was composed between 800 and 950 CE. One chapter of *Hitopadesa* deals with *vigraha* (war). The king's primary duty is to protect the people and then to increase their prosperity. This in turn makes hostility with other kings inevitable. Unlike Manu, Narayana says that when two sides deploy same amount of military power then the side using cunning could get inside the citadel of the enemy. Pragmatic power politics, rather than emotion should shape the search for allies. During battle, the soldiers should be brave and bold.

Manu does not pay any attention to the importance of sea power. However, numismatic evidence points to the fact that the Satavahana rulers like Pulumayi and Yajnasri maintained a sea-going fleet composed of two-mast sailing ships. The Satavahanas, who derived much income from custom duties levied on the Indo-Roman trade carried out between the Roman province of Egypt and the West Indian ports, were aware of the importance of controlling sea routes and coastal lanes.

See also: Hindu Tradition of Just and Unjust War; Indian Use of Chariots; Kamandaka; Kautilya

Further Reading
The Laws of Manu, With an Introduction and Notes, tr. by Wendy Doniger with Brian K. Smith, New Delhi: Penguin, 1991.

Majumdar, Bimal, Kanti, *The Military System of Ancient India.* Calcutta: Firma K. L. Mu-
    kopadhyay, 1960.
Majumdar, R. C., *Ancient India.* 8th ed. New Delhi: Motilal Banarasidas, 1994.
Thapar, Romila, *The Penguin History of Early India from the Origins to 1300 CE.* New
    Delhi: Penguin, 2003.

Kaushik Roy

Marlborough, John Churchill, Duke of
(1650–1722)

Significance: Marlborough's career as captain general of British land forces and
leader of the European coalition against Louis XIV during the War of the Spanish
Succession (1702–1713) became a model for those who sought decisive victories
during the "classical" age of 18th-century European warfare.

Context: Marlborough was a leading figure in the European wars of the early 18th
century.

Biography: Marlborough became a page to the Duke of York (later James II) and
in 1667 joined the guards. He served in the Third Dutch War under the Duke of
Monmouth and Turenne. He was promoted to colonel in the British army in 1678,
and defected to William of Orange in 1688. He became lieutenant general and the
Earl of Marlborough in 1689, and in 1702, assumed virtual control of the British
army as captain general. After a series of brilliant campaigns, he died in 1722.

Influences: Marlborough served under Turenne during the Third Dutch War, and
later prospered in partnership with Prince Eugene of Savoy.

The Theory: Although one may pursue his ideas through his voluminous published correspondence, Marlborough wrote no treatises on military theory. He
achieved his triumphs by bold maneuvers and the perfection of tactical developments such as platoon fire and an inspired use of combined arms. Marlborough's
skillful use of firepower freed the British army from the debates over shock versus
fire that were central to much 18th-century controversy, particularly in France. The
awesome reputation of the 18th-century British infantry rested on the foundation
laid by Marlborough.

   As leader of a great coalition, Marlborough demonstrated genius as a maker
of grand strategy. Although his campaigns were centered in Flanders, he saw the
war as a whole; thus his 1704 campaign in Germany. In addition, he was prepared to divert resources from Flanders to support allied interests in Italy, Spain,
and the Mediterranean. He understood the value of sea power and worked tire-
lessly to harness a coalition of powers with divergent and sometimes conflicting
interests. He was a master of personal diplomacy and achieved one of history's

great partnerships with the Austrian general, Prince Eugene of Savoy. His Achilles heel was the shifting British political scene that eventually undid much of his achievement.

Application: Marlborough was a great battle commander, winning celebrated victories over French armies at Blenheim in Germany (1704) and in Flanders at Ramillies (1706), Oudenarde (1708), and Malplaquet (1709).

Descendents: A veteran of Marlborough's army, Humphrey Bland, attempted to distill his experience in his *A Treatise of Military Discipline*. It ran through many editions in the 18th century, and in this way, Marlborough continued to influence practice. However, Bland focused on the "nuts and bolts" rather than military theory. Many of Marlborough's biographers agree that his greatest long-term influence was upon his descendent, Sir Winston Churchill, whose experience in writing Marlborough's biography in the 1930s helped prepare him for the challenges of the 1940s.

See also: Crissé; De Ligne; Maizeroy; Puységur

Further Reading
Chandler, David, *Marlborough as a Military Commander*. London: Scribner, 1973.

Armstrong Starkey

Masashige, Kusunoki
(1294–1336)

Significance: Masashige's loyalty to Emperor Go-Daigo was held as an example of the loyalty to the Japanese emperor that was expected of all members of the new Japanese military in the years preceding World War II.

Biography: Although little is known about Masashige's early years, he was a small landowner during the reign of the Emperor Go-Daigo in the early 14th century. Having declared his loyalty to the emperor when the Hojo family attempted to usurp power from him, Masashige committed himself and his life to the emperor's defense. He conducted a brilliant campaign against the Hojo from approximately 1334 until his death in 1336.

Influences: Although Masashige did not introduce a particular theory of warfare or any unique philosophy of war, he did provide an example of unswerving loyalty that would serve, for better or worse, as a rallying point for the nascent Japanese military in the years of the Meiji restoration. In addition, he provides an example of brilliant defensive tactics that succeeded in thwarting the Hojo at the battle of Chihaya.

The Theory: Masashige, having declared his allegiance to the emperor when many other samurai openly declared their allegiance to the families such as the Hojo, which sought to usurp the emperor's power, as well as the power of competing families, committed himself to a Fabian strategy of preventing the defeat of his small force. His conduct in battle was marked by tactical brilliance and the ability to sustain the morale of those who had also committed themselves to maintaining and eventually restoring Emperor Go-Daigo's power. At the siege of Chihaya, an action in which Masashige's small force was surrounded by the Hojo, numerous ruses and surprise maneuvers such as the use of rolling rocks and logs against oncoming forces helped not only to cause casualties among the enemy but also to sustain the morale of his own men. Having succeeded in resisting long enough for Go-Daigo to return to power, peace was short lived due to infighting in the ranks of the loyalists. In 1336, still trying to defend the emperor, Masashige was forced to commit suicide as his forces had been surrounded and defeated at the battle of Masatsura.

Application and Descendents: Following the Meiji Restoration in 1868, the Japanese government sought to create an army and navy along western lines. Needing to provide some model of loyalty to the emperor, which at this time was Emperor Meiji, the leadership looked to Masashige as the finest example of loyalty against great odds that could be found among the samurai of feudal Japan. Unfortunately, Masashige's name is now occasionally associated with the kamikaze and other fanatical elements of the Japanese military of World War II. However, a large statue of Masashige stands today in Tokyo, very close to the emperor's palace.

Jeffrey M. Shaw

Maurice of Nassau, Prince of Orange, Stadtholder of Holland
(1567–1625)

Significance: Maurice of Nassau was responsible for the development of more maneuverable infantry formations, combining the shock action and firepower of pikemen and musketeers into battalions. These units of about 550 men each would be drawn up 10 ranks deep in checkerboard formation on the battlefield, each one supporting its neighbors. This gave the Dutch great tactical flexibility, and a significant advantage over their opponents, the redoubtable Spanish army of Flanders. The Spanish fielded large *tercios* of several thousand men each, walking castles of muskets and pikes, hard to shift, but unwieldy. Maurice's reforms provided the tactical model for practically all the armies of Protestant states of Europe the 17th century, especially the Swedish army of Gustavus Adolphus, its German allies, and the Royalist and Parliamentarian armies of the English Civil War.

Maurice was also responsible for the regularization of the conduct of siege operations. Mercenary soldiers of the 16th century generally hated digging, and local peasantry proved unwilling conscript labor. Improved pay and conditions, introduced by Maurice, improved the Dutch army's enthusiasm for the backbreaking work of siege engineering, which was less risky than open battle. Maurice created a corps of engineer officers, the *commies van der fortificatien,* supervised by the *ingenieurs* (engineers) and *controlleurs* (inspectors). At the head of this professional body, as quartermaster general, was Simon Stevin, who had been Maurice's instructor in mathematics and fortification at Leyden University. Here Maurice endowed a chair in surveying and fortification in 1600.

Context: The Dutch army was created from virtually nothing in 1568 at the beginning of the long Eighty Years' War against the Spanish, then rulers of the Low Countries. Without a workable military force, the new Dutch Republic would have been rapidly extinguished. However, a large army was out of the question: the republic had a relatively small population, and the Dutch seafaring tradition attracted many who would otherwise be suitable recruits. The army came to consist primarily of foreigners, either mercenaries or Protestant coreligionists. These found service in the Dutch cause agreeable, because they paid promptly and all year round, and not just for the campaign season. With a professional, disciplined army at his disposal, Maurice found it easier to introduce his new ideas.

Biography: Maurice succeeded his father William the Silent in 1584, after the latter's assassination. He had received a first-class education at the University of Leyden. With his brother and cousin, William Louis and John of Nassau, he declared the Dutch Republic's independence from Spain. He became stadtholder of Holland and Zeeland in 1585, and captain general of the Dutch army in 1587, replacing the unsuccessful English commander Robert Dudley, Earl of Leicester.

Maurice's opportunity to dislodge the Spanish occupiers of his homeland came in 1589. The Duke of Parma had pushed the Dutch back to their strongholds in the northern provinces of Holland and Zeeland, where the low lying, marshy terrain was well suited to defense. However, the calamitous 1588 Armada campaign had weakened Spain's military strength, and when Parma was sent to France to fight the future King Henry IV, Henry of Navarre, Maurice attacked and captured Breda on March 4, 1590.

Maurice's plan now was to strengthen the southern borders of the central redoubt of the republic, Holland and Zeeland, and to isolate the Catholic supporters of the Spanish in the north around Groningen. He could shift forces rapidly using interior lines, before the Spanish, working around the outside perimeter, had time to react. Also, fully half of the Spanish army of Flanders was in France, and what few forces remained could not muster a credible relieving field army for fear of leaving key garrisons denuded of troops. Maurice pressed on into Brabant, and several important towns fell into his hands in the course of a single summer's campaigning. However, Nijmegen held out, and Maurice had to be content with building a large fortress, the Knodsenburg, to prevent any sallies by the garrison across the Waal and into Holland.

The year 1591 saw a triple offensive by Maurice, initially on the River Ijssel to the north and east of the "redoubt" of Holland and Zeeland. On May 27, a pontoon bridge was constructed to an island facing Zutphen, where Dutch sailors set up a battery. The garrison surrendered three days later. One of the few remaining avenues into Holland was thereby sealed off. Isolated from any support, Deventer fell after a whirlwind bombardment on June 11. The lower Ijssel was now in Dutch hands, and once the captured fortresses were expertly strengthened it would be extremely difficult for the Spanish to recapture.

Parma was now forced to leave France, and deployed in front of the Knodsenburg fortresses outside Nijmegen. Maurice refused to be drawn out, and waited until an irate King Phillip II ordered Parma back to France on July 24, leaving a skeleton force of 9,000 to defend the whole of Flanders and Brabant. Responding to this new opportunity, Maurice mounted a second rapid and audacious strike on the Flanders coast at Hulst, which he took on September 24. This threatened the wealthy town of Antwerp a mere 16 miles away. The third offensive saw Maurice reembarking the army, landing at Dordrecht, and marching overland to Nijmegen, which he duly captured October 21. He was only 24 years old.

The following year saw Maurice's efforts directed at the Catholic provinces in the northeast. On May 28, 1592, he surrounded Steenwijk, which barred his route north into Friesland. A huge mine was detonated on June 24, and the starving garrison surrendered on July 4. Mining would not be possible, though, at the next of Maurice's objectives, the great five-bastioned fortress of Coevarden, which lay deep in marshy terrain. Maurice's engineers sapped forward in a covered trench and the garrison surrendered on September 12. An emergency in the southern United Provinces prevented the final reduction of the northeast, when in 1593 Maurice was forced to tackle the fortress of Geertruydenburg, on the coast north of Breda. Here, more than in any previous siege, was the power of the spade demonstrated—four massive encircling forts were constructed by the besiegers, strongly posted with cannon and musketeers, and although the Spanish under Mansfield hovered outside, they could see no way in to relieve the town without risking substantial losses—something that they could ill afford. In June, the fortress surrendered. William, Maurice's brother called it a "second Alesia," a reference to Caesar's Gallic War that no doubt pleased Prince Maurice, the classical scholar, greatly.

Now Maurice again besieged Groningen, scene of a fierce artillery duel between Spanish and Dutch gunners. The issue was never in doubt and the fortress capitulated on July 22. Maurice thereafter avoided open battle with the Spanish, and after the Duke of Parma's death in 1592, faced a number of distinctly second-rate Spanish generals.

The new Spanish governor of the Netherlands, Archduke Albert, was drawn off to fight in Artois in 1597, and after a lengthy period of consolidation and recruitment, Maurice mounted another offensive, profiting from his enemy's distraction by the French Wars of Religion. He seized Rijnberk and seven other fortresses on the Rhine, creating a buffer zone closing "the fence of the Netherlands."

In 1597, Maurice won a significant victory over de Rie, Count of Varas, at Turnhout. Varas's force consisted of the Spanish native *tercio* of Naples commanded by the Marquis of Treviso, a couple of Walloon regiments, those of La Barlette and Hachicourt, Sulz's German regiment, and two cavalry units, one of heavy lancers and one of light *herreruelos* (mounted harquebusiers). The total Spanish force amounted to 5,000, with their nearest support ensconced in Antwerp. All seemed propitious for Maurice to defeat the isolated Spanish army with a force of 6,000 infantry and 800 pistol-armed cavalry. Advised of his approach, Varas evacuated Turnhout, which lacked fortifications, heading for Herenthals. However, the roads were mired and his progress was slow. At daybreak Varas was strung out in line of march on the moorland of Thiel, his entrance and exit from the heath constrained by narrow roads, flanked by ditches on either side. Whereas the Spanish could well have deployed for action on encountering Maurice's advance guard shortly after dawn, they seemed keen to make their escape. Maurice pressed on to the attack with only his cavalry, breaking the Spanish horse. The Dutch horse then rode on to the disorderly Spanish foot, and forced them to surrender. A combined attack of horse and foot on the Neapolitan *tercio* shattered them. The two Walloon regiments suffered a similar fate. Thirty-eight infantry standards were taken. Varas's army had been completely routed and Maurice's victory gave him undisputed control over the vital eastern provinces. The Dutch killed 2,000 and captured 500 Spanish, for the loss of only around 100 men.

However, a truce between France and Spain on May 2, 1598, and the end of the French conflict allowed the Spanish to concentrate on the Low Countries. They immediately recaptured Rijnberk, but then got bogged down on the southern frontier among the waterways. They contented themselves in building a fortified base at Fort St. Andries at the confluence of the Waal and Maas Rivers, 10 miles north of s'Hertogenbosch, before the army mutinied, allowing Maurice to besiege the place in the spring of 1600. Fort St. Andries surrendered in May after a substantial bribe was offered and accepted.

The new spirit of confidence gained led Maurice to perhaps his greatest gamble at Nieuport in July 1600. Seizing the opportunity offered by a collapse in Spanish finances, and the resulting mutiny of unpaid mercenaries, Maurice used Dutch command of the seas to land at Nieuport, a port being used as a base by privateers preying on Dutch shipping. The Spanish army of Flanders now rallied under Archduke Albert to face the Dutch, placing themselves across Maurice's lines of communication between Ostend and Nieuport, which was by now under siege. The Dutch army under Maurice tried to break out for Ostend, but the vanguard was routed. The Spanish infantry bludgeoned their way through the Dutch center held by English regiments. However, hard fighting in the heat and the heavy going of the sand dunes left them disorganized and tired, just as the Dutch cavalry, having chased off their opposite numbers, slammed into them from the flank. The Dutch reserve infantry completed the rout. Maurice's path to Ostend and safety was clear, and the army was evacuated in early August.

Archduke Albert resolved to do something about the enclave of Ostend that threatened his grip on Flanders. This was a tough nut to crack—it had a double ring of stout defenses and could be easily resupplied by sea. Equally, it was protected by tidal creeks to the east and west. Siege guns had be dragged along the coastal dunes, because the land to the south was sodden. On July 5, 1601, 12,000 Spanish arrived. By January, after months of siege and violent bombardment, the attackers were suffering greatly from the cold and wet conditions. A costly and unsuccessful assault on January 7–8, 1602, did nothing to alleviate their suffering. The siege of Ostend now assumed epic proportions, dragging on in a grisly routine through 1602 and most of 1603. The whole of Europe held its breath. The Pope even sent a military engineer, Pompeio Targone. In late 1603, another Italian "expert," Ambrogio Spinola, arrived. Despite his total lack of military experience, Spinola had learned much of the art of war from patient and lengthy study, and was able to provide not only considerable financial support, but also positive and firm leadership. Under Spinola's direction the Spanish built causeways across the western tidal creek and captured several outer bastions. The Dutch were duly forced to abandon the outer defenses and retreat to the inner fortification, hastily rebuilt and strengthened. Storms in August collapsed these ramparts and the Dutch were forced to seek terms, surrendering on September 20. The siege had lasted nearly three years and four months, and cost the Spanish an estimated 40,000 lives, at the expense of which they had removed the last Dutch foothold in the south.

To try to relieve pressure on Ostend, Maurice had captured Rijnberk in 1601, Grave in 1602, and mounted an unsuccessful siege of s'Hertogenbosch in 1603, but all was in vain—the siege of Ostend continued. A small compensation was found in the capture of Sluis on August 19, 1604.

The Spanish renewed the offensive in the east during 1605 and 1606, under the dynamic and able Spinola. After initially threatening Sluis in 1605, he swung abruptly east, crossing the Rhine at Kaiserswörth with 15,000 troops and swiftly reduced Oldenzaal and Lingen, completely outfoxing Maurice. The Spanish captured Grol on August 14, 1606, threatening the provinces of Overijssel and Gelderland, but Spinola was prevented from further exploitation by unusually wet weather.

Despite an unbroken string of victories against Maurice, Spinola argued for a peace treaty, recognizing that the Spanish treasury was nearly empty. A 12-year truce was signed in 1608, giving de facto recognition to the Dutch state. Maurice disagreed with the "peace party" in the States General that had negotiated the truce, and feared a renewed Spanish offensive. A quarrel between the Protestant sects of Calvinists and Arminians added much rancor to the debate. Eventually, Maurice got his way, and the leader of his enemies, his former mentor and sponsor,

Johan van Oldenbarnveldt, was tried for treason in dubious legal circumstances, and executed.

The truce with the Spanish lasted until 1621, when, thanks to Maurice's machinations, and the ambition of Philip IV of Spain and his first minister Olivares, the United Provinces became sucked into the Thirty Years' War. Spinola had kept his mercenary army together, and Maurice had no more success against him now than he had before the truce. He was unable to emerge from the defensive zone to link up with the French further south. Spinola took Jülich in 1622, then turned on Bergen-op-Zoom in the west of Brabant, but was forced to raise the siege through lack of funds and an approaching Dutch relieving force.

After a period of rest and recruitment, Spinola laid siege to Breda in August 1624. He planned to isolate and starve the town while seeking to engage and destroy any relieving force. Maurice died on August 28, 1625, while the siege was still underway, to the very end enquiring as to the fate of the town. The fall of Breda on June 15, Maurice's home and first conquest, was a bitter blow to the Dutch, but Spinola fell foul of jealous rivals at the Spanish court who blocked supplies to his army and eventually sent him back to his native Italy, broken and disillusioned.

In his 58 years, Maurice had captured 38 towns and 45 fortresses by siege, and a further 5 towns and 10 forts by surprise. He had relieved 12 sieges, and won two major field engagements against the mighty Spanish army of Flanders.

Influences: Like many other military thinkers of this period, from Machiavelli onward, Maurice was inspired by Classical military writers such as Vegetius, Frontinus, and Leo. He took the system of drill and maneuver directly from Aelian (Aelianus Tacticus), the Greek military writer of the second century, who lived in Rome. He even recommended that his officers learn Latin, and equipped an experimental company in Roman fashion complete with spear, shield, and sword. More conventionally, he borrowed the Roman practice of orderly military camps, regular realistic battle training, and a basic tactical unit analogous to the Imperial Roman cohort of about 500 troops.

The Dutchman Justus Lipsius (1547–1606) produced a definitive five-volume illustrated treatise on Roman military customs *De Militia Romana* in 1595, and Maurice learned much from him as his pupil at Leyden University. Lipsius followed this by a treatise on ancient siege warfare, the *Poliorceticon,* which was published in 1596, and was inspired by Maurice's capture of Deventer. The pupil had become the master.

For Lipsius it was not just a question of slavishly copying the Roman model of warfare. He wanted, like them, to develop a scientific approach to the art of war, and of military organization. He did not see war as an act of uncontrolled violence, but the measured application of armed force, under the command of a competent and legitimate authority, serving the interests of the state. Lipsius called for a complete reform of existing military systems, and although he recognized that he was only an amateur himself, he stressed that the Classical historians such as Polybius, from whom he drew inspiration, were "the real teachers of the art of war." He stressed the role of infantry over that of the cavalry in major campaigns, pointing out that these were easier to raise and maintain. Generally, he said, it was better to fight with a small well-trained force, than a large army of poorly trained troops. He was against the employment of mercenaries too, preaching the merits of a truly national army composed of professional standing troops, reinforced by reservists in time of emergency. To keep order and discipline, he recommended regular training, severe regulations, self-control, and obedience.

The Theory: Maurice's Dutch battalions would ideally draw up in the field 10 ranks deep. A body of 220 pike men would be flanked by two "sleeves" of shot, each of 135 mixed harquebusiers and musketeers, with a "forlorn hope" of 60 skirmishing shot out in front. Proportionally, the Dutch regiments consisted of more officers and junior leaders (modern noncomissioned officers or NCOs) then their opponents, to maintain order and discipline while maneuvering.

In 1594, William-Louis of Nassau had written to his cousin Maurice, suggesting salvo fire, or volley fire by ranks, a tactic that he had discovered in his reading of Aelian. Following the practice of the ancients, he proposed that each rank of shot would discharge its weapons at once, and then smartly retire to the rear while reloading. By this method he assumed that a continuous rolling fire could be kept up. Although it is difficult to see how this method of fire by countermarching (called "extraduction" or going forward, and "introduction" when going backward) could be maintained for long in a real battle, the discipline of practicing this evolution would have produced a coordination, smartness, and precision in drill that would have given the Dutch infantry a considerable edge in any roughly equal contest with their opponents.

Maurice's methods of siege warfare involved extensive and complicated digging of saps, parallels, and supporting square forts used as refuges in case of attack. In any siege he built trench lines of circumvallation facing the surrounding countryside and contravallation facing the besieged town, following the ancient Roman model. Thus protected from interference, the workmen would operate from one of the forts, digging a zigzag trench toward the enemy defenses, supported all the while by massed cannon firing from a *batterie royale* placed on some convenient high ground nearby within 200 yards of the enemy parapet. When the trench or sap got near enough to the enemy defenses an assault would be mounted, but first the defenders would be offered the chance to surrender with honor to prevent the unnecessary effusion of blood during and after the storming. In 1588, a new invention, the mortar, was used for the first time. It consisted of a stubby-barreled artillery piece that lobbed large fused bombs high into the air, and into the interior of the opposing fortress or town, where they exploded, causing fires and confusion.

His system of fortification involved the use of earthen ramparts and wet ditches, ideally suited to the low-lying terrain of the Netherlands and easily built with intensive labor and low cost. Initially, these low-profile fortifications were added to existing medieval defensive structures, but by the 1570s they incorporated out-works such as detached bastions and ravelins. Eventually, these came to be revet-ted with masonry, and formed the model of the permanent fortifications of the later 17th century.

The basis of Maurice's system of defense was a stout earthen bank defended by sharpened stakes and a wooden palisade that fell into a broad ditch, protected by another bank well within musket range. This double row of fortifications was usually arranged in the shape of a multipointed star, which allowed the defenders to give enfilading fire on any threatened portion of the perimeter. These complex earthworks, frequently defended by further outer triangular hornworks and demi-lunes, offered an unrivalled defense in depth. They were also comparatively cheap to build when compared to their Italian counterparts, which required large quanti-ties of masonry to complete.

Maurice was also adept at constructing temporary outposts called *Schanzen* (sconces), literally "lairs," such as those built along the Waal and Maas in 1599, and improved in 1605–1606, which consisted of signal bonfires to warn of any Spanish sally from s'Hertogenbosch.

Application: Although Maurice's battalions were nominally 550 strong, in prac-tice their strength varied: at a review in 1592 they were anything from 750 to 1,030. In the same way, infantry companies were normally about 120 strong, as opposed to the ideal 150. Maurice is widely supposed to have increased the ratio of pikes to shot, but in fact it remained at about a two to three ratio, not much different from the 1580s, that is, before he assumed command. A wide variety of firearms of various sizes remained in use, at least until the 1620s when the musket became the standard weapon, with 10 or 12 shot to the pound.

Maurice's reforms made the Dutch rebels into a dangerous threat to the veteran Spanish forces. It allowed them, with help from Protestant allies such as England, not only to resist the Spanish onslaught, but to also mount serious and convincing counteroffensives.

Nonetheless, these new techniques introduced by Maurice were more evolu-tionary than revolutionary. Dogma was always secondary to pragmatism, espe-cially given the difficult conditions of war in the Low Countries. Even the Spanish *tercios* could, when necessary, reduce their numbers and increase their frontage, by thinning the depth of the formation, in response to recruitment shortages, or to bring more firearms to bear in a given tactical scenario.

Both Dutch and Spanish engineers developed new techniques in fortress war-fare, and Maurice copied many of his ideas from Parma's complex siege works of the 1580s, taking them even further. In turn, assisted by turncoat rebel engineers, the Spanish used many of Maurice's innovations.

From 1621 neither side showed the same determination and military innova-tion slowed down, especially after Maurice's death in 1625. The existence of the United Provinces was never threatened in the second phase of the Eighty Years' War, nor did they try to launch any major foray from the "redoubt" of Holland

and Zeeland. The war became a series of long and predictable sieges on the Maas–Waal River line.

Descendents: The Dutch wars provided a training ground for the commanders of the Thirty Years' War and the English Civil War. Training manuals were published in the Netherlands and widely sold across Europe by military entrepreneurs such as Jacob de Gheyn.

The Dutch reforms of Maurice of Nassau were continued and developed in the 1620s by Gustavus II Adolphus of Sweden, who was greatly inspired by Maurice's innovations. In the Swedish infantry firepower and offensive action were emphasized, and the Swedes improved considerably on Maurice's system by organizing the infantry in flexible, balanced brigades, which could take on and beat the Imperial *tercios*. Gustavus also added regimental guns to the brigades to boost their firepower, reducing the depth of the line from Maurice's original ten men to six or five, and even in some cases, three ranks deep. By combining tight fire discipline and salvo fire by multiple ranks, followed up by a brisk pike assault, the initial impact of the Swedish brigade formation could be decisive. Having said that, all this depended on intensive training, high motivation and good quality recruits, and these became rarer as the Thirty Years' War dragged on after the death of Gustavus at Lützen in 1632. The later Swedish armies, largely made up of inferior German mercenaries, could not match the élan and discipline of native-born Swedish regiments, and the effectiveness of the Swedish infantry never again reached the heights of its prowess in 1631 and 1632.

In fortress warfare, more than in any other sphere, Maurice's innovations were borrowed and improved on, even as he was not above adopting the novelties and developments of his enemies. Although being cheap, the Dutch earthen defenses required large numbers of troops to man effectively, and were easily demolished by nifty spade work, or turned against their owners, when the attackers dug their own positions into them. The wet ditches often prevented the reinforcement of isolated detachments in the outer works, and provided no obstacle at all when they froze over in the harsh winters of the late 16th and early 17th centuries. Given enough time, moreover, a sustained artillery bombardment would reduce these earthworks into mud, unless the defender was constantly engaged in repair—not always possible under the attentions of enemy cannon and musketeers. "The Dutch system" was really a series of elaborate field works, without permanent stone reinforcement.

See also: Coehoorn, Menno Van; Frontinus; Gustavus II Adolphus; Vegetius

Further Reading

The historical literature of the long Dutch fight for independence, and the part played therein by Maurice of Nassau is rich and varied. As a primer, the great Dutch historian Pieter Geyl's *The Revolt of the Netherlands* (1932 and many reprints) is a must. Geoffrey Parker's magisterial *The Dutch Revolt* (1977) is an object lesson in the writing of history. Christopher Duffy is an invaluable aid in understanding the nature of 16th-century positional warfare, and no serious student of sieges should be without a copy of *Siege Warfare* (1979). George Gush's *Renaissance Armies* (1975 and 1978) is an old favorite. For a comprehensive treatment, Sir Charles Oman's *The History of the Art of War in the Sixteenth Century* (1937), belies its age by its scholarly and comprehensive discussion of the topic. For scholars preparing for examination, Peter Limm's *The Dutch Revolt* (1989) is lively and engaging, and neatly encapsulates all the key historical debates. More recently, Thomas Arnold's *The Renaissance at War* (2001) is a visual treat, with its great illustrations and informative text.

Toby McLeod

Molyneux, Sir Thomas More, First Baronet
(1724–1776)

Significance: Thomas Molyneux was a pioneer of amphibious warfare. His work, *Conjunct Expeditions* (1759), was the first to use the term "amphibious operations" and highlighted many of the challenges in executing combined operations. Conjunct expeditions that have been carried on jointly by the fleet and army, with a commentary on a littoral war was the first history of amphibious operations in British military writing. Molyneux concluded that British military practice for amphibious operations was lacking in the areas of ideal command arrangements, an appreciation of the value of surprise and strategic deception, and the conduct of landing operations.

Context: Thomas Molyneux's work on combined operations was published at the height of the Seven Years' War after a series of unsuccessful British amphibious operations against French coastal targets, Rochefort, St. Malo, and Cherbourg.

Biography: Molyneux served in the British army and retired as a lieutenant in the Foot Guards Regiment before representing Haslemere in the House of Commons in 1759. He died in October 1776.

Influences: Molyneux was one of the first writers to examine amphibious operations as a separate form of warfare and as such had little theoretical framework within which to operate.

The Theory: In *Conjunct Expeditions,* Molyneux examined 68 joint army–navy operations conducted by England or against England since the reign of Elizabeth I. He divided these operations into major and minor operations and showed that 27 major and 11 minor operations had "miscarried," and 7 major and 23 minor operations had succeeded. Based on this evidence, Molyneux identified several specific challenges to conducting successful combined operations. Many naval and military commanders lacked experience with their counterpart and the capabilities of the partner force. He also criticized the landing boats currently used by the Royal Navy, arguing that they were too crowded. He stressed the difficulty of reembarking the landing force even when this portion of the operation was unopposed. Many of Molyneux's recommendations were made regarding the conduct of amphibious raids against specific targets.

A necessary condition for successful amphibious operations, according to Molyneux, was local naval superiority to provide naval gunfire support and to protect the landing force from naval attack. He also argued that the troops being landed should be organized so the soldiers would be ready for combat immediately after landing. He viewed combined operations as a necessary component of national defense, stating in *Conjunct Expeditions* that "The fleet and army, acting in consort, seem to be the natural bulwark of these kingdoms."

Application: Molyneux's ideas about amphibious warfare were not adopted in entirety by the British military apparatus. However, his conclusions were successfully employed by General James Wolfe in the capture of Quebec in September 1759. Many of his principles regarding unity of purpose and command were adopted during amphibious operations in World War II.

Descendents: Molyneux's focus on combined operations were further developed by British naval historian Philip Colomb and U.S. marine Earl Ellis.

See also: Colomb, P.; Ellis, "Pete"

Further Reading

Roger Beaumont's *Joint Military Operations: A Short History* (1993) places Molyneux in the context of other theorists on amphibious warfare. A. D. Harvey's *Collision of Empires: Britain in Three World Wars, 1793–1945* (1992) provides coverage of Molyneux in the context of the Seven Years' War.

Corbin Williamson

Montecúccoli, Raimondo Count of, Prince of the Empire, Duke of Melfi
(1608–1680)

Significance: This prolific author, theorist, and military commander bridged two prominent trends of the mid-1600s, the emergence of the scientific community and an institutional military. He was widely read and studied by such prominent 18th-century commanders as Frederick the Great and Napoleon, and in the Whig interpretation of the history of military theory is the most prominent exponent of "maneuver" over "battle."

Context: A junior commander during the later stages of the Thirty Years' War, Montecúccoli came to prominence in Emperor Leopold I's revanchist wars of the 1650s and 1660s. He was commander in chief during the Polish war that restored the pro-Habsburg status quo in Poland. He then became President of the Court War Council, taking the field to defeat a major Turkish incursion at the Battle of Szventgótthard. The subsequent campaign was less successful, and he retired as President of the Court War Council to produce a defense of his actions. At this point he would have been remembered for guiding the Court War Council into the modern era of bureaucratization, if only because it was once the exemplar of the allegedly paralytic Austro-Hungarian state bureaucracy. However, he was recalled to the field when Louis XIV launched a blitzkrieg invasion of the United Nether-lands in 1672. In the years 1672–1674, Turenne and Montecúccoli engaged in a series of campaigns along the Rhine that were widely studied by military histo-rians of the next century. The details of these campaigns emphasize marches and countermarches, the placement of bridges, supply depots, and defensive lines. In late writings, Montecúccoli speaks of 50,000 men as the largest feasible field army, and Clausewitz's discussion of these campaigns appears in book 6, chapter 30, "Campaigns Where a Decision is Not the Objective." In short, the old general is no more than a "cunctator," or delayer. This is the very stereotype of the old politician applied to a general. The politician aims to delay a potentially dangerous decision until time has made it obsolete; the general to avoid a battle whose outcome might be too disastrous. To 19th-century writers, this was the definition of loss of nerve and lack of energy. However, Montecúccoli's campaigns aimed to distract Louis from finishing off the Netherlands, and were entirely successful at this.

Biography: Born into a family with close connections with the Dukes of Modena, Montecúccoli's rise to prominence coincided with that of even more prominent Modenese clients such as the Capraras, and to Pope Pius II, whose election as pon-tiff in 1672 coincides with Montecúccoli's return to command. During the Thirty Years' War, it was not uncommon for junior officers such as Montecúccoli to be taken prisoner and held for ransom, and it was in one of these periods of forced inactivity that the young Italian's best known theoretical works on the art of war originate. Fortunately, military success and the timely death of a brother combined to pluck the Modenese from obscurity at just the right time. He married into the prominent Czech Aulic house of Dietrichstein, built an impressive manor house, and fathered four children in the 1650s. Although his direct line became extinct with the death of his son, Herculo (a minor military theorist in his own right), his daughters married well. He is the direct ancestor of Field Marshal Khevenhül-ler among others, who thus had German, Czech, and Italian grandparents. Other Montecúccolis, of genealogically imprecise origins, were still prominent in the service of the Habsburg state in 1866, when Admiral Montecúccoli won the Battle of Lissa.

Influences: Vegetius, Julius Caesar, Justus Lipsius, Giorgio Basta.

The Theory: Montecúccoli is known in his published works for espousing an axiomatic and "geometric" theory of military operations. However, the conceit is not pushed very far. We find nothing like the absurd lengths found in later writers. On the contrary, "geometric" axioms soon turn into aphorisms, leaving the full rigors of the geometric approach, so famously criticized by Clausewitz (5:15), to others. Because Montecúccoli appears in Clausewitz as the great exemplar of the idea of war as maneuver (6:30), and so do the later geometric theorists, it is very tempting to conflate the critiques of 5:15 and 6:30 and see Montecúccoli as a "geometrician." We can also get there by talking about discipline. This is very important to the Roman authorities and to Lipsius, and of course disciplined troops often form "geometric" shapes like squares. Excessive discipline appears alongside "limited" theories of war as the great weakness of 18th-century military practice.

It should be clear, though, that this just reduces Montecúccoli to the straw man of an argument that appears to be about the history of military theory but really goes to the concerns of 19th-century Whig politics. Montecúccoli was *not* a straw man. He was a highly successful commander. Was it just that military theory has no bearing on military success, so that one can be a silly and febrile theorist and a highly successful practitioner? This would be a very discouraging conclusion.

It also seems to be wrong. In the first instance, it is anachronistic and presumptuous to impose cut-and-dried distinctions between "battle" and "maneuver." This is how we think about things today. It is clearly not the way Montecúccoli attacked military theory. It also conflates the bored young officer with the seasoned old soldier. We can get around this to an extent by focusing, as Gunther Rothenburg does, on the late apologia, "Della guerra col Turco," but it seems more promising to ask ourselves just where the geometric theorizing is taking us.

Monteuccoli's efforts may not take him very far, but that is not necessarily the case for the reader. There is an obvious correlation with the by now centuries-old revival of Neoplatonism. Although often a serious philosophical enterprise, Neoplatonism is often at its heart an attack on authority resting on Aristotelian modes of analysis. Because much authority, and notably religious authority, had built its position on Aristotle, going back to Plato could be a highly productive political strategy. Notable scientific thinkers and theologians such as Copernicus, Galileo, and Justus Lipsius are very emphatically anti-Aristotelian and, less explicitly, Neoplatonic. As with Montecúccoli, we do not necessarily have to carry this argument further into the subtleties of academic philosophy. These contestants might have been great minds, but they were rejecting Aristotle and embracing Plato with very little serious understanding of either. Montecúccoli's attempt to understand war as an ideal species, rather like the perfect right triangle, is just one more example of a common variety of *jeu d'esprit* that begins by misunderstanding Aristotle, moves on to bowdlerizing Plato, and only then finds serious footing and productive grounds to work in new fields. We are not going to get an extended discussion of ideal forms, teleology, form, substance, and agency in Montecúccoli, any more than anywhere else. Was this as obvious to Montecúccoli as it is to us? It is tempting to think so. There is certainly little evidence that this was more than a half-hearted essay, that what he was doing was no more than nailing some very conventional colors to the mast before moving on.

It is here that the Clausewitzian critique (and it is more to be associated with authors who take up the Clausewitzian cudgels, such as Max Jähns then with the great Prussian himself) is actually quite helpful. For any young theorist, being a successful general and administrator is just precisely grounds for criticism. Montecúccoli speaks for "old Europe"—not because he died old, or because he was a famous old man, but because he is philosophically *old*. We attribute caution, subtlety and a taste for limits because these are the weaknesses of age. When we look at Montecúccoli's aphorisms, the case is made even more clearly.

The wise old general talks of delay and caution, money, maneuvers, lines of communication, and bases of operation because he was a successful general. Yet he is also conscious of the one resource that he has to conserve. Montecúccoli was hardly the first military thinker to impress people with the clever line about there being "three things needful in war: gold, gold, and gold," but his campaigns show how seriously he took it. However, this is not just a clever comment. It is also a line in the sand, a place where the greatest political theorist of the age drew a fundamental divide between himself and all that came before. Niccolò Machavelli inverts the formula, saying that soldiers can always get you gold. *Now* we see Montecúccoli as a conservative. Machiavelli may be famous as a political cynic here, but this strand of policy derives from his idealism. Machiavelli's perfect state is poor but militant. Its republican constitution is based on universal military service, and the practice of arms is the necessary foundation of a virtuous citizenry. Lipsius uses much the same language in his encomiums to the Princes of Nassau, and for all his admiration of Lipsius, Montecúccoli refutes it plainly. In real states, money does come first. Idealism is not a substitute. Administration comes before morale. Old men understand politics.

To an extent, this is speculation. We are building a picture of Montecúccoli that his extant writings just will not support. We very badly need to see the many unpublished manuscripts that have been talked about for more than a century. A good intellectual biography of Montecúccoli would be welcome, as would be a full scale publication of his papers. Unfortunately, he belongs in a very long list of influential Italians and Austrians who have not been served in this way. Until that day comes, we have a disjuncture between the successful man of action and the straw man of theory.

Descendents: Khevenhüller, Frederick the Great, Napoleon, Archduke Charles of Austria.

See also: Basta; Folard; Khevenhüller; Lindenau; Maizeroy; Picq; Saxe, M.

Further Reading
Barker, Thomas Mack, *The Military Intellectual and Battle: Montecuccoli and the Thirty Years War.* Albany: State University of New York Press, 1974.

Montecúccoli, R., *Aforismi dell'arte bellico.* Milan: Fratelli Fabbri, 1973.

Montecúccoli, R., "Concerning Battle." Trans. Thomas Mack Barker. In *The Military Intellectual and Battle: Montecúccoli and the Thirty Years War,* by Thomas Mack Barker. 73–173. Albany: State University of New York Press, 1974.

Rothenburg, Gunther, "Maurice of Nassau, Gustavus Adolphus, Raimundo Montecuccoli, and the 'Military Revolution' in the Seventeenth Century." In *Makers of Modern Strategy from Machiavelli to the Nuclear Age,* ed. Peter Paret, 32–64. Princeton, NJ: Princeton University Press, 1986.

Erik A. Lund

Mubarakshah, Fakhr-i Mudabbir
(ca. 1150–1224 CE)

Significance: Mubarakshah dedidated his *Adab al-harb wa'l-shaja'ah* to Iltutmish Shams al-Din, the *Mamluk* Sultan of Delhi (1211–1236 CE). Written in Persian, it was a treatise on statecraft in the Persian tradition of "Mirrors for Princes."

Context and Biography: His full name was Fakhr al-Din Muhammad Ibn Mansur Mubarakshah al-Qurashi. Born around 1150 CE, probably in Ghazna, modern Afghanistan, Mubarakshah experienced the conquest of the Ghaznawid dynasty by the Ghurids in 1186 CE. After studying in Lahore, and producing a book of genealogical tables from the Prophet Muhammad onward, he joined the court circle of the first Turkish *Mamluk* or "slave king" of northern India, Qutb al-Din Aybak (1206–1210 CE). He died around 1224 CE.

Influences and Theory: His substantial, if rather idealised discussion of warfare includes sections on tactics, troop organization, various weapons, and sieges. The book also deals with historical anecdotes as object lessons, many relating to military matters in the poorly recorded eastern Islamic world.

Some military chapters of the *Adab al-harb wa'l-shaja'ah* are based upon Abbasid military theory developed during the 8th to 10th centuries CE, including section on "How to arrange an army firmly and to maintain that (arrangement)," and on "How to bring the army to a halt and the place to do this." Other sections reflect more recent Indo-Islamic, Indian, and Turkish military ideas, otherwise lost aspects of earlier military practice, plus plans of such arrays and exercises in the tradition of Islamic *furusiyya* military training manuals.

The plans include "The battle layout of the Turks when the *Khaqan* (senior ruler) is present," perhaps based on the Central Asian Kara-Khitai (early 12th to early 13th centuries CE) and mirroring Chinese tactics against Central Asian nomads. "The battle plan of the Persian *Padishahs*" was probably based upon pre-Islamic Sassanian practice. "The battle array of the Rumi which Alexander (the Great) used to defeat Darius" might be based upon perceived Greco-Roman and Byzantine military tradition, and "The battle array of the kings of Himyar

(Yemen)" seems to be a survival of pre-Islamic Arabian concepts. "The battle array of the Indians that was originated by Garshasp" reflects the military practice of Hindu India prior to the Islamic conquests.

Sections that focus on military practice in the eastern provinces of the Islamic world, including northern India, highlight cavalry maneuvers and unit training, and others deal with various weapons. The somewhat archaic archery terminology in the *Adab al-Harb* may reflect the survival of pre-Turkish, Persian, or Arab styles of archery in these eastern Islamic regions. There is also information on indigenous Indian archery. The attention that Mubarakshah paid to infantry might result from the old-fashioned character of his work but could reflect the continuing importance of infantry in Indian warfare.

Application and Descendents: Mubarakshah's *Adab al-harb* probably soon became an outdated literary curiosity.

See also: Al-Rawandi; Naṣûḥ bin Karagöz, called Matrakçı, Matrâqî, Silâḥî, etc.; Sirhindi, A.; Timur, Amir (or Tamerlane or Timur the Lame); Usama Ibn Munqidh

David Nicolle

Muhammad Ibn Abdallah
(570–632 CE)

Significance: Most of the literature concerning Muhammad addresses his role as a great seer who founded the religion of Islam, his achievements as a social revolutionary, or his abilities as a statesman and administrator who created new institutions to govern the peoples of Arabia. But Muhammad was also a great strategist, political and military theorist, and a successful troop commander. In the space of a single decade he fought eight major battles, and led 18 raids. He also planned 38 other military operations where others were in command but operating under his orders and strategic direction. He was wounded twice, suffered defeats, and twice had his positions overrun by superior forces before rallying his troops to victory. Muhammad had no military training before commanding an army. Yet, he became an excellent field commander and tactician and an even more astute political and military theorist and strategist. In his thinking and application of force Muhammad was a combination of Clausewitz and Machiavelli, who always employed force in the service of political goals. He was an astute grand strategist whose use of nonmilitary methods (alliance building, political assassination, bribery, religious appeals, mercy, and calculated butchery) was always aimed at strengthening his strategic position.

Muhammad's contributions to warfare as a military theorist are found in three areas: First, he created and led history's first successful insurgency, bringing into being the structure and methodology of insurgent warfare that has been imitated by almost all successful insurgencies that followed. Second, he introduced a new type of Arab warfare, reforming the Arab armies and bringing into being a completely new kind of military force, one that made possible the Arab conquests. Third, Muhammad was the inventor of ideological warfare, creating a new moral justification for war (*jihad*) that has often served as the ideological basis for Muslim wars and insurgencies ever since.

Context: Within Arabia itself, the traditional religion of idol worship never produced a sacerdotal class and state institutions that might have defended the old religion against the challenge of Islam. Had there been some form of religious institutional resistance as was faced by the heretical Christian sects of the imperial realms of Byzantium and Persia, it is unlikely that Islam would have succeeded with Arabia. Moreover, the inability of religious sects outside Arabia to project their influence and oppose Muhammad further facilitated the success of Islam. The religious persecutions and sectarian strife within both Byzantium and Persia, sometimes against their own Arab allies, made it impossible for the imperial powers to project force against the new creed of Islam in Arabia permitting Muhammad a free hand to begin his insurgency and establish the new religion free from outside interference.

At the same time the tribal social order characteristic of Arabian society from time immemorial was breaking down under the impact of commercialism, weakening its ability to protect its members from violence, slavery, and exploitation and destroying the traditional basis of status and obligation. It was no accident that many of Muhammad's early followers were those who had been dispossessed or oppressed by the new conditions. When Muhammad preached the need for a new community, the *ummah* or community of believers, as the basis for a new society, his preaching fell on receptive ears. The social unrest within Arabia during Muhammad's lifetime provided the opportunity for Muhammad to quickly become an influential figure, something that would never have happened in the normal course of tribal custom had the wariness and fear of continual warfare not been so overpowering.

The emphasis placed here on the larger forces shaping Arabia at the time of Muhammad's insurgency ought not to be taken to suggest that his success was inevitable or that anyone but Muhammad could have achieved it. Muhammad's brilliance lay in recognizing these forces and utilizing them to his advantage. Muhammad was no accidental prophet. He was a brilliant revolutionary fighter who understood the nature of the environment in which he fought and used it to his advantage.

Biography: Muhammad Ibn Abdallah was born on August 20, 570, in Mecca. He was an orphan raised by his grandfather and uncle. Muhammad worked as a caravaneer, and, when he was 25, married a wealthy widow, establishing himself by running her business of organizing caravans. We have no accurate information concerning Muhammad's life between 595 and 610, the year he received his first revelation. He spent the following years attracting converts to the new religion of

Islam until moving to Medina in 622. Over the next decade, Muhammad conducted a guerrilla campaign against Mecca and the other towns that opposed him, before finally defeating them in a series of conventional battles. Muhammad died in 632.

Theories:

Insurgency

Muhammad was not a conventional field general. He was, instead, a new type of warrior, a fiery religious revolutionary and guerrilla leader. He created and led the first genuine national insurgency in Antiquity that is comprehensible in modern terms. Muhammad's goal was the replacement of the existing Arabian social order with a new one based upon a radically different ideological view of the world. To achieve this, Muhammad created the methodology now recognized by modern theorists as characteristic of a successful insurgency. If these characteristics are employed as theoretical categories of analysis, it is clear that Muhammad's successful campaign to spread Islam throughout Arabia fulfilled each of the analytical criteria.

Charismatic Leader: The first requirement for an insurgency is a determined leader whose followers regard him as special in some way and worthy of their following him. In Muhammad's case, his own charismatic personality was enhanced by his deeply held belief that he was indeed God's Messenger, and that to follow Muhammad was to obey the dictates of God himself.

Messianic Ideology: Insurgencies require a messianic ideology, one that espouses a coherent creed or plan to replace the existing social, political, and economic order, usually seen as unjust, with a new order that is better, more just, or ordained by history or even God himself. Muhammad used the religious creed of Islam to challenge traditional Arab social institutions and values as oppressive, unholy, and worthy of replacement. To this end he created the *ummah* or community of believers, God's community on earth, to serve as a messianic replacement for the clans and tribes that were the basis of traditional Arab society.

Revolutionary Cadre: Successful insurgencies require a disciplined cadre of true believers to do the work of organizing and recruiting new members. Muhammad's revolutionary cadre consisted of the small group of original converts he attracted in Mecca and took with him to Medina. These were the *muhajirun* or emigrants. The first converts among the clans of Medina, the *ansar* or Helpers, also filled the ranks of the cadre. Within this revolutionary cadre was an inner circle of talented men who advised Muhammad and saw to it that his directives were carried out.

Secure Operational Base: Once Muhammad had created his cadre of revolutionaries, he established a base at Medina, from which to undertake military operations against his adversaries. These operations initially took the form of ambushes and raids aimed at isolating Mecca, the enemy's main city, and towns that opposed him. Medina was strategically located in that it was a short distance from the main caravan route from Mecca to Syria that constituted the economic lifeline of Mecca, and was also sufficiently distant from Mecca to permit Muhammad a relatively free hand in his efforts to convert the Bedouin clans living along the caravan route. Muhammad understood that conversions and political alliances with the Bedouins, not military engagements with the Meccans, were the keys to success.

Armed Force: Insurgencies require an armed force and the manpower to sustain them. It was from the original small cadre of guerrillas that the larger conventional army grew. This conventional force ultimately permitted the insurgency to engage its enemies in set-piece battles when the time and political conditions were right. Muhammad may have been the first commander in history to conceive of the doctrine of "people's war, people's army," a military struggle in which the entire society (*ummah*) takes part. He established the idea among his followers that God had commandeered all Muslims' purposes and property for His efforts and that all Muslims had a responsibility to fight for the faith. The attraction of the ideology of Islam more than anything else produced the manpower that permitted Muhammad's small revolutionary cadre to grow into a conventional armed force capable of large-scale engagements.

Weapons Supply: Like all insurgent armies, Muhammad's forces initially acquired weapons by stripping them from prisoners and the enemy dead. Weapons, helmets, and armor were expensive items in relatively impoverished Arabia, and the early Muslim converts, drawn mostly from among the poor, orphaned, widowed, and otherwise socially marginal, could ill afford them. At the battle of Badr, the first major engagement with an enemy army, the dead were stripped of their swords and other military equipment, establishing a practice that became common. Muhammad also established the practice of requiring prisoners to provide weapons and equipment instead of money to purchase their freedom. His ability to obtain sufficient weapons and equipment gave Muhammad an important political advantage. Many of the insurgency's converts came from the poorest elements of the Bedouin clans, people too impoverished to afford weapons and armor. Muhammad supplied these converts with expensive military equipment, immediately raising their status within the clan and guaranteeing their loyalty to him, if not always to the creed of Islam. In negotiations with Bedouin chiefs, Muhammad frequently made them gifts of expensive weaponry. Several pagan clans were won over to Muhammad's insurgency in this manner, although they did not convert to Islam.

Popular Support: An insurgency must also be able to sustain the popular base that supports the fighting elements. To accomplish this, Muhammad changed the ancient customs regarding the sharing of booty taken in raids. The chief of a clan or tribe traditionally took one-fourth of the booty for himself. Muhammad decreed that he receive only one-fifth, and even this he took not for himself but in the name of the *ummah*. Under the old ways, individuals kept whatever booty they had captured. Muhammad required that all booty be turned in to the common pool where it was shared equally among all combatants who had participated in the raid. Most importantly, Muhammad established that the first claimants on the booty that had been taken in the name of the *ummah* were the poor and the widows and orphans of the soldiers killed in battle. He also used the promise of a larger share of booty to strike alliances with Bedouin clans, some of whom remained both loyal and pagan to the end fighting for loot instead of Islam. Muhammad's later military successes against towns, oases, and caravans provided an important source of wealth to supply the insurgent popular base with the necessities of life.

Political Police: The leader of an insurgency must take great care to guard his power from challenges, including those that come from within the movement itself. Like other insurgent leaders who followed, Muhammad surrounded himself with a loyal group of men who acted as his bodyguard and carried out his orders without question. The *suffah* comprised a small cadre who lived in the mosque next to Muhammad's house. Recruited from among the most pious, enthusiastic, and fanatical followers, they were generally from impoverished backgrounds with no other way to make a living. The members of the *suffah* spent their time studying Islam and leading a life of spiritual avocation. They were devoted to Muhammad and served not only as his life guard but also as a secret police that could be called upon at a moment's notice to carry out whatever task Muhammad set for them. These tasks included assassination and terror.

Intelligence: No insurgency can survive without an effective intelligence apparatus. As the Muslim insurgency grew, Muhammad's intelligence service became more organized and sophisticated, using agents-in-place, commercial spies, debriefing of prisoners, combat patrols, and reconnaissance in force as methods of intelligence collection. Muhammad seems also to have possessed a detailed knowledge of clan loyalties and politics within the insurgency's area of operations and used this knowledge to good effect when negotiating alliances with the Bedouins. Muhammad often conducted an advance reconnaissance of the battlefields upon which he fought, and only once in 10 years of military operations was he taken by surprise. We have no knowledge of how Muhammad's intelligence service was organized. That it was part of the *suffah,* however, is a reasonable guess.

Propaganda: Insurgencies succeed or fail to the degree that they are able to win the allegiance of the great numbers of the uncommitted, and their support for the insurgency's goals. Muhammad understood the role of propaganda in the struggle for the minds of the uncommitted and went to great lengths to make his message public and widely known. In an Arab society that was largely illiterate, the poet served as the major conveyor of political propaganda. Muhammad hired the best poets money could buy to sing his praises and denigrate his opponents. He publicly issued proclamations regarding the revelations he received as the Messenger of God, and remained always in public view to keep the vision of the new order and the promise of a heavenly paradise constantly before his followers and those he hoped to convert. He sent "missionaries" to other clans and tribes to instruct the pagans in the new faith, sometimes teaching the pagans to read and write in the process. Muhammad understood that the conflict was between the existing social order and its manifest injustices and his vision of the future, and he surpassed his adversaries in spreading his vision to win the struggle for the hearts and minds of the Arab population.

Terror: The use of terror seems to be an indispensable element of a successful insurgency and no less so in Muhammad's case. Muhammad used terror in two basic ways.

First, he utilized terror to keep discipline among his followers by making public examples of traitors or backsliders. Muhammad also ordered the assassination of some of his political enemies, including poets and singers who had publicly ridiculed him. When his armies marched into Mecca, Muhammad's police set about hunting down a list of old enemies marked for execution.

Second, he used terror to strike fear into the minds of his enemies on a large scale. In the case of the Jewish tribes of Medina, Muhammad seems to have ordered the death of the entire Beni Qaynuqa tribe and the selling of their women and children into slavery before being talked out of it by the chief of one of his allies. On another occasion, again against a Jewish tribe of Medina, he ordered all the tribe's adult males, some 900, beheaded in a city square, the women and children sold into slavery, and their property distributed among his Muslim followers. Shortly after the conquest of Mecca Muhammad declared "war to the knife" against all those who remained idolaters, instructing his followers to kill any pagans they encountered on the spot. Such public displays of ruthlessness and brutality strengthened Muhammad's hand when dealing with opponents and allies.

When examined against the criteria that modern analysts use to characterize an insurgency, Muhammad's military campaign to establish Islam in Arabia seems to qualify in all respects.

The insurgency came to an end when Muhammad marched into Mecca at the head of an army of 10,000 organized along conventional lines. These armies were used by Muhammad's successor, Abu-Bakr, to undertake a war of religious conversion (*riddah*) (632–634 CE) against the remaining pagan tribes of Arabia. Shortly thereafter, Abu-Bakr launched the wars of Arab conquest against the Byzantines and Persians. It was during these wars that Muhammad's military reforms of Arab armies were most manifest.

Military Reforms

The conduct of war usually reflects a society's values at least as much as the capabilities of its military technologies. Being a good warrior had always been a central virtue in the Arab idea of what constituted a good man. This warrior ethos was expressed in the Arabic terms *muruah* and *ird*. *Ird* is understood as honor, and honor was closely tied to the obligations to avenge any wrong done to a man personally, to any others to whom he had extended his protection, or to his clan. *Muruah* literally means "virility" or "manhood." The Arab warrior's courage and honor were most commonly demonstrated by his performance in the *ghazw* or raid, in which a group of Bedouins would attack another clan to steal their flocks, camels, or women. This was not "war" in any real sense of the word, because the object of the raid was to steal and not kill. Arab "armies" were collections of individual warriors fighting for their own honor and opportunity to acquire loot. In this regard, they were not unlike the gatherings of warrior knights that comprised the armies of medieval Europe. The Arab "wars" of the pre-Islamic period were never fought for what we would call today strategic objectives. These "battles" were tactical engagements only, and no attempt was made to achieve strategic victory.

The Arab relied solely upon his kin, clan, and tribe to protect him. In Arab warfare, other than the blood feud, there were rules of chivalry in which one's opponent possessed equal moral standing and worth. A warrior did not slay the wounded or kill cruelly or unnecessarily. The Arab tradition of ransoming prisoners also limited the killing. The result of these values was that Arab warfare in the pre-Islamic era was limited in scope, scale, frequency, and brutality. The blood feud, by contrast, knew no such rules or limitations. No restrictions were placed upon how and when a man might be killed; in his sleep, by treachery, poison, or betrayal. In a blood feud no moral standing was granted one's enemy, and torture, cruelty, and brutality were often the result.

Muhammad changed the traditional moral basis of Arab warfare, removing the traditional restraints on killing, and bringing to Arabia a truly modern method and moral perception of war. His objective was to destroy the old Arab social order based on clan and kin and replace it with a new type of society, the *ummah,* comprising a community of believers. The model for the new community was not the clan per se, but the clan as it operated when engaged in a blood feud. Any rules of ethical behavior applied only to the community of believers; those outside the *ummah* were held to possess no moral standing and could be killed or enslaved without moral consequences. Whereas the blood feud had proposed a life taken for a life lost and never more than that, Muhammad redefined moral killing as a life taken for political or religious purposes. The new moral basis of war led to a more violent form of warfare—political ideological warfare—conducted on a larger scale with ever-increasing casualties and consuming far more innocents than before.

Muhammad was first and foremost a religious revolutionary, the commander of an insurgency that had yet to create a military force that could bring his new social order into being. If he was to achieve his end of creating a new society governed by new ethical precepts, the old rules of war had to be changed because they were ineffective in achieving the revolutionary goals that Muhammad had set for himself. Muhammad's successful transformation of Arab warfare marks him as one of the great military reformers of the ancient world. And it was Muhammad who reformed Arab warfare and fashioned the military instrument his successors used to establish the great empire of Islam.

Social Composition: Muhammad changed the social composition of Arab armies from a collection of clans, tribes, and blood kin loyal only to themselves into a national army loyal to a national social entity, the *ummah.* Loyalty to the *ummah* permitted the national army to unify the two traditional combat arms of infantry and cavalry into a genuine combined-arms force. Each of these two combat arms drew their soldiers from different socioeconomic backgrounds, town dwellers and Bedouins, and each possessed only limited experience in fighting alongside the other. Bound by clan loyalties and living in settlements, Arab infantry was steadfast and cohesive and could usually be relied upon to hold its ground, especially in the defense. Arab cavalry, on the other hand, was unreliable in a fight against infantry, often breaking off the fight to escape damage to their precious mounts or to make off with whatever booty they had seized. Bedouin cavalry was, however, proficient at the surprise attack, protecting the flanks, and pursuing fleeing infantry.

Muhammad was the first commander of an Arab army to successfully join both combat arms into a national Arab army and to use them in concert in battle. This was more than a mere technical reform. The ability to combine both combat arms was the result of Muhammad's creation of a new type of community that made it possible to submerge the clan and blood loyalties of traditional Arab society into the larger religious community of believers, and combine the two primary elements of traditional Arab society, town dwellers and Bedouin tribes, into a single Arab national identity.

Unity of Command: Before Muhammad, Arab military contingents fought under the command of their own clan or tribal leaders, sometimes assembled in coalition with other clans or tribes. Although the authority of these clan chiefs was recognized by their own clan, every clan chief considered himself the equal of any other with the result that there was no overall commander whose authority could compel the obedience or tactical direction of the army as a whole. Clan warriors fought for their own interests, often only for loot, and did not feel obligated to pursue the larger objectives of the army as a whole. To correct these deficiencies, Muhammad established a unified command for his armies. Command of the army was centered in the hands of Muhammad himself. As commander in chief, Muhammad established the principle of unified command by appointing a single commander with overall authority to carry out military operations. All commanders were appointed by him and operated under his authority. The establishment of a unified military command gave Muhammad's armies greater reliability in planning and in battle. Unified command also permitted a greater degree of coordination among the various combat elements of the army and the use of more sophisticated tactical designs that could be implemented with more certainty, thereby greatly increasing the army's combat power. For the first time, Arab forces became an instrument of their commander's tactical will.

Combat Unit Cohesion: The moral basis of traditional Arab warfare placed an emphasis on the courageous performance of individual warriors in battle. One consequence was that Arab armies and the clan units within them did not usually reflect a high degree of combat unit cohesion. Muhammad's armies, by contrast, were highly cohesive. Muhammad did not just strengthen the blood and kin ties of the traditional Arab clan. He went far beyond that in creating the *ummah* as a higher locus of the soldier's loyalty, which transcended the clan. Religion turned out to be a greater source of unit cohesion than blood and clan ties, the obligations of faith replacing and overriding the obligations of tradition and even family. Muhammad's soldiers quickly gained a reputation for discipline and ferocity in battle, soldiers who cared for each other as brothers—which, under the precepts of Islam, they were.

Motivation: Muhammad's armies demonstrated a higher degree of military motivation than traditional Arab armies, and Muhammad raised the status of the warrior even above what it had been traditionally. The booty garnered from raids was distributed fairly to all combatants in the name of the *ummah*. Muhammad's soldiers were actually paid better than Persian or Byzantine soldiers.

But better pay was only a small part of the motivation of the soldiers of Islam. The idea of a soldier motivated by religion in the certainty that he was doing God's work on earth seems to have been one of Muhammad's most important military innovations. No army before Muhammad ever placed religion at the center of military motivation and defined the soldier primarily as an instrument of God's will on earth. The result, often still seen in Islamic societies, was a soldier who enjoyed much higher social status and respect than soldiers in armies of the west. A central part of the motivation of the Islamic soldier was the teaching of his faith that death was not something to be feared, but to be sought. Muhammad's pronouncement that those killed in battle would be welcomed immediately into a paradise of pleasure and eternal life because they died fulfilling the command of God was a powerful inducement to perform well on the field of battle and produced a far more dedicated soldier than Arab armies had ever witnessed before.

Strategic War: Arab warfare prior to Muhammad's reforms involved clans and tribes fighting for honor or loot. There was no sense of strategic war in which long-term, grand-scale strategic objectives were sought and toward which the tactical application of force was directed. Muhammad was the first to introduce the notion of war for strategic goals to the Arabs. Muhammad's ultimate goal, the transformation of Arab society through the spread of a new religion, was strategic in concept. Although Muhammad began as an insurgent, he was always Clausewitzian in his thinking, in that the use of force was not an end in itself but a tactical or operational means to the achievement of strategic objectives. Muhammad was the first Arab commander to use military force within a strategic context. Had he not introduced this new way of thinking to Arab warfare, the use of later Arab armies to forge a world empire would not only have been impossible; it would also have been unthinkable.

Experienced Combat Officer Corps: As commander in chief, Muhammad sought to identify and develop good officers wherever he found them. Young men were appointed to carry out small-scale raids to give them combat experience. He sometimes selected an officer from a town to command a Bedouin raid to broaden his experience in the use of cavalry. He frequently appointed the best officers of his former enemies to positions of command once they had accepted Islam. Muhammad always selected his military commanders on the basis of their proven experience and ability, and never for their asceticism or religious devotion. He was the first to institutionalize military excellence in the development of an Arab officer corps of professional quality. It was from Muhammad's corps of trained and experienced field commanders that generals such as Khalid al-Walid (the Sword of Allah) and Amr Ibn al Aasi came to command the armies of the later Arab conquests.

Training and Discipline: We have only scant references to how Muhammad trained his soldiers; that he did so is almost a certainty. There are clear references to required training in swimming, running, and wrestling. References in various texts suggest that Muhammad trained these units in rank and drill, sometimes personally formed them up and addressed them before a battle, and deployed them to fight in disciplined units, not as individuals as had been the common practice. These disciplined "artificial clan" units could then be trained to use a wider array of tactical designs than was heretofore possible. Although Arab fathers continued to train their sons in warfare long after Muhammad's death, the armies of the Arab conquests and later those of the Arab empire instituted formal military training for recruits.

Logistics and Force Projection: Muhammad seems to have had the caravaneer's concern for logistics and planning, an expertise that permitted him to project force and carry out operations over long distances across inhospitable terrain. Muhammad had been an organizer of caravans for 25 years before he began his insurgency. Planning a caravan required extensive attention to detail and knowledge of routes, rates of march, distances between stops, water and feeding of animals, location of wells, weather, places of ambush, etc.—knowledge that served him well as a military commander. Unlike some other armies that he fought, Muhammad never seems to have had to change or abandon his plans due to logistical difficulties. Muhammad's armies could project force over hundreds of miles. By traditional Arab standards, Muhammad's ability to project military forces of substantial size over these distances was nothing short of astounding. Without this capability, the Arab conquest that followed Muhammad's death would have been impossible.

Muhammad revolutionized the conduct of Arab warfare in ways that made possible the transformation of Arab armies from entities fit only for tactical engagements into armies capable of waging war on a strategic level where they could engage and defeat the major armies of their day. This military transformation was preceded by a revolution in the manner in which Arabs thought about war. The old chivalric code that limited the bloodletting was abandoned by Muhammad and replaced with an ethos less conducive to restraint in war, the blood feud. Extending the ethos of the blood feud beyond the ties of kin and blood to include members of the new community of Muslim believers inevitably worked to make Arab warfare more encompassing and bloody than it had been.

Once established in their new lands in the Byzantine and Persian empires, the Arabs attempted to remain ethnically homogenous and a religious society apart from the conquered infidels. But their numbers were small, and the attempt to sustain an Arab identity apart from the infidels was bound to fail in the long run on the grounds of numbers and conversions. With gradual assimilation and widespread conversion the old Arab citizen armies gradually gave way to professional armies manned largely by non-Arab Muslims. By the middle of the ninth century CE the old Arab empire had ceased to exist, and with it the Arab "army of God" that Muhammad had fashioned also disappeared.

Ideology and Jihad

Muhammad founded the first Islamic political community in Medina in 622. From then on, Islam was not only a religion to be preached, but also a social–political order to be imposed, when necessary by force. Thus, in the years following Muhammad's death, Islamic scholars developed an account of the Islamic law of war. This body of law, essentially complete by 850 and still regarded as binding by many Sunni Muslims, amounts to a comprehensive imperialist ideology giving divine sanction for the subjugation and permanent subordination of non-Muslims.

Revelations on War: Like all Islamic law, the law of war rests ultimately on two foundations: the example and teaching of Muhammad (the *sunnah*) and the uncreated, literal, infallible word of God (the *Koran*). Because the *Koran* is not organized chronologically and often appears inconsistent, its interpretation depends heavily on biographical accounts of Muhammad's life and teachings (the *sira* and *hadith*).

The earliest extant biography of Muhammad, that of Ibn Ishaq (d. 768), asserts that divine revelations to Muhammad regarding warfare went through three stages. First, when Muhammad was still in Mecca, God forbade the Muslims to fight. Second, after the migration to Medina (*hijra*) in 622, God gave permission to the Muslims to fight against the Meccans, who had wrongly driven Muhammad and his followers from their homes (see Koran 22:39–41). Third, after the Muslim conquest of Mecca in 630, God commanded the Muslims to wage war unconditionally against all non-Muslims until all people live under God's law (see Koran 2:216–7, 9:5, and 9:29). The aggressive, violent verses of *sura* 9, the last portion of the Koran to be revealed, are known as the "sword verses" and are considered by classical exegetes to have abrogated the more peaceful verses revealed to Muhammad at earlier stages of his career.

Jihad: At the heart of the Islamic law of war is the concept of *jihad.* This is the verbal noun of the Arabic verb *jahada,* meaning "to endeavor, to strive, to struggle." *Jihad* can refer generically to any worthy endeavor, but in Islamic law it means primarily armed struggle for Islam against infidels and apostates. The central part of the doctrine of jihad is that the Islamic community (*ummah*) as a whole, under the leadership of the *caliph* (successor to Muhammad as leader of the Muslims), has the duty to expand Islamic rule, ultimately until the whole world is governed by Islamic law. Expansionist *jihad* is thus a collective duty of all Muslims, which means that if a sufficient number take part in it, the whole community has fulfilled its obligation; if not, the sin falls on all Muslims.

When the initial wave of Islamic conquests had subsided in the eighth century, Islamic jurists taught that the *caliph* had to raid enemy territory at least once a year to keep the idea of *jihad* alive. Land occupied by Muslims is known as the *dar al-Islam,* or the "land of Islam," whereas all other territory is known as the *dar al-harb,* "the land of war." Islamic law posits the inalienability of Islamic territory: if infidels attack the *dar al-Islam,* it becomes the individual duty of all able-bodied Muslims in the area to resist and of other Muslims to assist them. Thus *jihad* can be defensive as well as offensive.

Rules of Jihad: Before waging expansionist *jihad,* the Muslim commander must invite the neighboring infidels to convert to Islam. If they refuse, he must invite them to accept Islamic rule and to pay a special poll tax (the *jizya,* called for by the Koran 9:29), symbolizing their subordination to the Islamic state. If they refuse both options, they must be attacked. In the waging of war, all adult, able-bodied, unbelieving males may be targeted, except for slaves and monks. Women and children may not be targeted directly, unless they act as combatants (and this can mean aiding the enemy by propaganda or spying). However, based on the example set by Muhammad, enemy towns may be starved by siege, catapults may be used even if they cause damage indiscriminately, and it is permissible to kill women in night raids when Muslim fighters cannot easily distinguish them from men. Some Islamic jurists also permit wholesale destruction of enemy towns by fire or flood and destruction of orchards. Islamic law prohibits mutilation of the dead and torture of captives (although the definition of torture is problematic, because Muhammad's example is normative, and he imposed many punishments that would certainly qualify as torture today). All moral limits on the waging of war may be set aside in cases of necessity, under the juristic principle that "necessity excuses one from any rule whatever." Following Muhammad's own practice, the victorious Muslim commander may seize as booty the lands and possessions of the vanquished foe, retaining one-fifth for the Islamic state and distributing the rest among his fighters. He may also execute, enslave, ransom, or release subjugated non-Muslim men, depending on what is in the best interest of the Muslims. Captured women and children may not be killed, but may be enslaved, and Muslim men may have sexual relations with female slaves acquired by *jihad,* any previous marriage of such women being annulled by their capture.

Until the entire world is governed under Islamic law, a state of permanent war exists between the Islamic state and lands governed by infidels. Muslim rulers may enter into peace treaties with their infidel neighbors, but these are temporary truces that may last no more than 10 years (according to the precedent set by Muhammad in the Treaty of Hudabiyya in 628) and such truces may be broken whenever it is in the interest of the Muslim side to do so. A non-Muslim who is not protected by a treaty is called a *harbi,* meaning "one who is in a state of war." The life and property of a *harbi* are completely unprotected by law unless he has been given a temporary safe-conduct (*aman*) by an adult Muslim or has accepted status as a *dhimmi* (see below).

Shiite Doctrine: The above summary focuses on the classical Sunni doctrine of *jihad.* Shiites (10–15% of Muslims) subscribe to a somewhat different doctrine, believing that expansionist *jihad* can only be waged under the rightful leader of the Muslim community, whom they call the *imam.* Twelver Shiites believe that the last *imam* went into occultation, or hiding, in 874 and that the collective duty to wage expansionist jihad is suspended until his return in the apocalyptic future. Shiite scholars do, however, affirm a duty to wage defensive *jihad* against infidel invaders.

Treatment of Conquered Non-Muslims: One final aspect of the classical Islamic doctrine of *jihad* pertains to the treatment of subjugated non-Muslims whom the *caliph* chooses not to kill or enslave. Non-Muslims whose religion rests on a scripture revealed before the time of Muhammad (called "scriptuaries" or "people of the book," e.g., Jews, Christians, and Zoroastrians) are allowed to practice their religions under certain conditions (except in Arabia, where Muhammad dictated that no faith but Islam shall be allowed). Such non-Muslim subjects of the Islamic state are called *dhimmis,* and the treaty of surrender under which they live is called the *dhimma.* The conditions imposed on *dhimmis* by Islamic law serve three purposes: first, to keep political power in the hands of Muslims; second, to reserve the public space of society, and the right to proselytize, for Islam alone; and third, to remind *dhimmis* of their humbled condition and the superiority of Islam.

Dhimmis had to pay an annual poll-tax (*jizya*), which often was an onerous financial obligation exacted in a humiliating manner; they had to pay land tax or rent on their land (*kharaj*), because ownership passed to the Islamic *ummah* upon conquest; they could not build any new churches or synagogues or repair existing ones; they could not practice their religion in public (no ringing of bells or blowing of the *shofar*); they could not bear arms; they could not hold government jobs above the menial level; they had to wear special clothing to distinguish themselves from Muslims; they had to show public deference to Muslims, for example, by not passing them on roadways; they could only ride donkeys, not horses, and they had to ride sidesaddle, like women; their houses and graves had to be lower than those of Muslims; they could not proselytize or discuss Islam or the Koran or insult Muhammad; they could not offer aid of any sort to enemies of the Islamic state; *dhimmi* men could not marry Muslim women or own Muslim slaves; a *dhimmi's* word did not count in legal matters against that of a Muslim. When a *dhimmi* violated the conditions of this pact, the *caliph* could choose between the same four options available to him in connection with prisoners of war: execution, enslavement, ransom, or release. Otherwise, the *caliph* had the duty to protect the *dhimmis* and their property.

For other non-Muslims, classical Islamic law has no tolerance at all: apostates from Islam, pagans, atheists, agnostics, and "pseudo-scriptuaries," that is, members of cults that have appeared since Muhammad's day, for example, Sikhs, Bahais, Mormons, and Qadianis (aka Ahmadis). These groups all have the option of conversion to Islam or death. (However, the Sunni Hanafi school is somewhat less intolerant, because it would accept the *jizya* from all non-Muslims except apostates from Islam and Arab idolaters.)

Descendents: There was no major modification of the Koran's military theory before the 19th century. Beginning in the 19th century, Sunni Islamic modernists began to modify the classical law of war. The Indian Muslim thinker Sayyid Ahmad Khan (1817–1898) argued that *jihad* was obligatory for Muslims only when they were prevented from exercising their faith, thus restricting *jihad* to a defensive purpose. The Egyptian Mahmud Shaltut, who taught at Egypt's prestigious Al-Azhar University in the mid-20th century, likewise reinterpreted the Koran to restrict *jihad* to a defensive end, which is probably the majority view among Sunnis today. On the other hand, conservative Sunnis, such as the Wahhabis of Arabia, still adhere to the traditional doctrine, as did Islamic radicals such as the Egyptian Sayyid Qutb (d. 1966) and the Pakistani Abu Ala al-Mawdudi (1903–1979).

See also: Al-Shaybani; Baghdadi Manjaniqi, Yaʿqūb Ibn Ṣābir; Ibn Akhi Hizam, Muhammad Ibn Yaʾqub al-Khuttali

Further Reading

Bostom, Andrew, *The Legacy of Jihad: Islamic Holy War and the Fate of Non-Muslims.* Amherst, NY: Prometheus Books, 2005.

Cook, David, *Understanding Jihad.* Berkeley: University of California Press, 2005.

Gabriel, Richard A., *Warrior Prophet: The Military Biography of Muhammad, Islam's First Great General.* Norman: University of Oklahoma Press, 2006.

Hamidullah, Muhammad, *Battlefields of the Prophet.* Paris: Revue de Etudes Islamiques, 1939.

Ibn Ishaq, *The Life of Muhammad,* trans. A. Guillaume, *The Life of Muhammad: A Translation of Ibn Ishaq.* Karachi: Oxford University Press, 1967.

Peters, Rudolph, *Jihad in Classical and Modern Islam: A Reader.* Princeton: Marcus Wiener Publishers, 1996.

Rodinson, Maxime, *Muhammad.* New York: The New Press, 2002.

Watt, W. Montgomery, *Muhammad at Medina.* London: Oxford University Press, 1956.

Richard A. Gabriel and Joseph S. Spoerl

Naṣûḥ bin Karagöz, called Matrakçı, Matrâqî, Silâḥî, etc.
(ca. 1495?–ca. 1565?)

Significance: Indigenous Ottoman martial art.

Context: In the early 16th century, the Ottoman Empire possessed probably the most powerful and disciplined army in the world, combining artillery, infantry, and cavalry. Their artillery routed their most powerful neighbors, the rising Safavids in Iran and Azerbaijan and the long-famed military power of the Mamlûk state in Syria and Egypt. Both abjured the use of firearms as unfitting for warriors, whereas the Ottomans were early and effective adopters. The janissary corps formed the elite of the Ottoman infantry.

Biography: Naṣûḥ Karagöz may have been born in Bosnia at the end of the 15th century. He was brought to the palace school in Istanbul as a child, likely through the *devşirme* levy of boys, where he distinguished himself early. The contemporary historian 'Âşıḳ Çelebi relates that Naṣûḥ was the prize pupil of the best teacher at the palace school.

In 1517, likely upon the Ottoman conquest of the Mamlûk Sultanate, he presented Selim I with a treatise on administrative mathematics, which later became his most copied work. Naṣûḥ may well have stayed in conquered Cairo with the early Ottoman administration. At some time before 1522, the Ottoman governor, a former Mamlûk official, is said to have presented him with a certificate certifying his supremacy in the martial arts, for which the Mamlûks were famed. His prowess, indeed supremacy, in martial arts is confirmed by numerous sources.

Around this time, Naṣûḥ translated the world history of Ṭabarī (d. 923) from Arabic to Ottoman Turkish, only then being created as a literary language. Naṣûḥ added to it throughout his life in Ottoman, placing the Ottoman dynasty at the center of cosmic history. Sections of his uncompiled history are narratives of individual Ottoman campaigns, for example, his *Beyân-ı Menâzil-i Sefer-i 'Irâḵeyn-i Sultan Süleyman Khan* (*Collection of Stopping Places of the Campaign of the Two Iraqs of Sultan Suleyman Khan*, 1537), three of which are decorated with masterful miniatures by Naṣûḥ himself. In addition, we fortuitously possess a copy of an apparently unique document: a 1530 imperial decree by Süleyman I (r. 1520–1566) praising Naṣûḥ's martial skills and chartering him to write a book on skills of arms, which he completed in 1533.

In this decree, as elsewhere, he is referred to as Naṣûḥ-ı Silâhî, Naṣûḥ, the man-at-arms. Another sobriquet he bears is al-Matrâqî; hence, his most widely known appellation, in modern Turkish "Matrakçı Nasuh." Both these names mean "one who does *matraḵ*." *Matraḵ* was a martial art Naṣûḥ invented, akin to kendō, with some 160 different skills to be mastered, and scored by striking the opponent's head with a *matraḵ*, a padded staff or club. Other than some miniatures depicting *matrakçı*s drilling as a public entertainment, we know fairly little about the art. It seems to be the sole original hand-to-hand combat art to have originated in the early modern Islamic world.

Naṣûḥ died sometime after 1560, though the exact date is unknown.

Influences: Mamlûk military training exercises.

The Theory: As mentioned above, the details of *matraḵ* remain obscure and merit investigation.

Application: Increasing effectiveness of close-quarter combat.

Descendents: Unknown. A revived form of *matraḵ* is practiced in Turkey today, but how closely it resembles the original is an open question.

William J. Walsh

Onasander (Onasandros, Onesandros, Onosandros), Philosopher

Significance: Onasander's General is among the most influential military treatises of Antiquity. It remained very popular at least until the Renaissance and was found useful even during the 18th century by the great Maurice de Saxe.

Context: By about mid-first century AD Romans had achieved a preeminent position in Europe and Mediterranean. The treatise was written as a reflection of the reasons why this had come about.

Biography: Onasander is usually considered to have been a philosopher/military theorist who lived during the first century AD. He wrote two treatises, a military work and a commentary upon Plato's Republic (not extant).

Influences: The principal sources of inspiration for Onasander were the successive generations of Roman generals who had conquered the known world as well as Greek history and military theory. Onasander dedicated his military treatise to Quintus Veranius (a consul in AD 49 and governor of Britain in ca. AD 58/59), which suggests that he wrote the book to gain Veranius's goodwill.

The Theory: Onasander's General (*Strategikos, Strategicus*) emphasizes the role of the general and his personal qualities in war. The treatise presents a summary of the principles of Roman generalship as interpreted by Onasander.

The treatise consists of 42 arbitrary chapters, which include the following general themes: (1) the choice of a general; (2) preliminary considerations (council of war, cause of war, divine help); (3) marching (hollow square, reconnoitering, logistics), fortified camp, and training; (4) things to do the day before the battle; (5) things to do during the battle; (6) things to do after the battle; and (7) siege warfare (techniques and equipment). The treatise lists the various combat maneuvers (wheeling; passing through files; forming two-fronted formation; forming a column, etc.) that the individuals and different-sized units and battle lines were required to be able to perform in all types of weathers and terrains. Onasander's list of battle formations (the battle line with reserves; tripartite line with advanced flanks; crescent; oblique; use of terrain) is essentially the same as in the military treatises of Frontinus and Vegetius.

The general was required to pick and choose the best tactics to the situation and this could also include the use of ruses and stratagems. Onasander's treatise emphasizes the importance of general's role throughout the campaign and stresses his ability to use the maneuvers, formations, and in particular his ability to lead the men. The manual also stresses the importance of the morale and the adjustment of the tactics to the circumstances.

Application: Onasander's instructions are so general in nature that most of his precepts, such as, for example, the use of ambushes and the spreading of disinformation, were and are continually used in one form or another in warfare. The popularity of Onasander's text suggests that his manual has had both direct and indirect influence upon many military commanders.

Descendents: Onasander's General retained its popularity up to Renaissance and beyond. It was used as a source by Maurice, Leo the Wise, and Ouranos. The universal nature of Onasander's guidelines means that some of its instructions remain useful even today.

See also: Frontinus; Leo VI; Maurice (Flavius Mauricius Tiberius Augustus); Vegetius

Further Reading
Campbell, Brian, *Greek and Roman Military Writers: Selected Readings.* London: Routledge Classical Translations, 2004.

Ilkka Syvänne

Pepys, Samuel
(1633–1703)

Significance: Pepys provided standardization and accountability for the English navy at a crucial point in the evolving balance of naval power in Western Europe in the late 17th century.

Context: Pepys inherited a naval establishment suffering corruption and inefficiency.

Biography: Samuel Pepys was born in 1633 in London. Despite a modest family background, he was educated at St. Paul's School in London and Magdalene College, Cambridge. As a secretary to Sir Edward Montagu, he was introduced to government service. Montagu became commander of the fleet during the Restoration and arranged for Pepys to be appointed clerk of the king's ships. Later Pepys served as survey general of the victualing service (1665) and secretary of the admiralty (1672).

Pepys worked to improve the structure and operations of what became the Royal Navy. Despite a lack of experience in maritime affairs, he proved a skilled administrator and established standards for procurement, training, discipline, and general administration.

Pepys died in London in 1703.

Influences: Pepys became skilled at political intrigue from his association with Montague and his emphasis on efficiency may have been shaped by the military reforms under Cromwell.

The Theory: Pepys introduced concepts of professionalism, accountability, and efficiency to the administration of the English navy. He stressed the need for oversight and for placing people with proven capabilities in positions of responsibility.

Application: Pepys established the need for standards in government service in general and at the admiralty specifically.

Descendents: Virtually every administrator in British government service was affected by Pepys's standards and example.

See also: Mahan, Alfred Thayer; Marlborough, Duke of

Further Reading
Bryant, Arthur, *Pepys—The Saviour of the Navy 1683–1689.* London: Collins, 1948.
Pepys, Samuel, *Samuel Pepys's Naval Minutes,* edited by J. R. Tanner. London: Printed for the Navy Records Society, 1926.

Joe Caddell

Pizan (or Pisan), Christine de
(1363–ca. 1430)

Significance: Christine de Pisan's *Le livre des fais d'armes et de chevalerie* (The Book of Deeds of Arms and of Chivalry), written ca. 1410, is rare because it is a manual of the art of warfare at a time when few of these were being written—although more appeared in 15th-century Europe than at any time since the Roman Empire—but it is unique, for any time, in that it was written by a woman. Her manual draws much from Classical Roman treatises, primarily Frontinus and Vegetius, and the medieval *Arbre de Batailles,* by Honoré Bouvet, but also shows an awareness of the latest military technological innovations and chivalric discussions.

Context: By the time Christine de Pisan wrote her military treatise, the Hundred Years' War had been fought for more than 70 years. English successes had slowed, with France regaining much lost land during the reign of Charles V (r. 1364–1380). But his successor, Charles VI (r. 1380–1422) had proven mentally unstable, with two factions—the Burgundians and the Armagnacs—vying for control of his virtually absent throne. In 1407, the head of the Burgundian faction, Duke John the Fearless, had the head of the Armagnac faction, Duke Louis d'Orléans, assassinated in Paris. What had previously been relatively nonviolent became open warfare, which John the Fearless dominated, until his own assassination in 1419. Although it is not known if Christine wrote her military manual at the behest of John the Fearless, she clearly planned to use it to gain further patronage for the very rich Burgundian duke.

Biography: Despite her surname, Christine was born in Venice in 1363, although she spent most of her childhood and adult life in Paris, her father, Thomas de Pizan, serving as court astrologer, alchemist, and physician for

King Charles V. Married to Etienne du Chastel, a court secretary, at a young age, Christine was widowed after 10 years, forcing her to seek an alternative means to support her three children. She began writing, ballads, poems, and books, ultimately publishing more than 300 ballads and poems, and 41 books before her death ca. 1430. Interestingly, her last work, *Ditié de Jehanne d'Arc,* was written as a defense for yet another woman who had taken on a nontraditional gender role, Joan of Arc, although Christine did not live to see the latter burned.

Influences: Although many more military manuals were written during the last two medieval centuries (the 14th and 15th) than during the previous millennium, Christine's major influences were two Ancient Romans, Sextus Julius Frontinus and Publius Flavius Vegetius Renatus. She also used the work of the near contemporary and very popular French writer, Honoré Bouvet.

The Theory: As clear in the title of her manual, Christine's intent is not only in discussing strategy and tactics. She begins her work with discussions on justifications of war, which incorporated both theological and legal definitions, and leadership, which, she determines, should not be a ruler. She also addresses the issues of raising, training, and using an army. It is here where Christine places her battlefield tactical advice. Section II discusses siege warfare, including the military technology and personnel needed for an effective siege (it is here where she initially mentions gunpowder weapons). The final three sections focus on various questions of chivalry and the "laws of war": the treatment of combatants and noncombatants by a victorious army; the granting of safe conduct; letters of marque; and judicial combats.

Application: It is not known how John the Fearless received the text, or even whether he did receive it. Modern translators, Charity Cannon and Sumner Willard, claim that John's protégé, Count Louis de Guyenne, and Arthur de Richemont, a French general and royal military advisor, were influenced by the manual, but there is little evidence to substantiate this.

Descendents: Jean de Bueil's *Le Jouvencel,* written ca. 1465–1470, draws much from Christine's manual; otherwise it appears to have had little influence on other 15th-century military manuals.

See also: Tartaglia (The Stammerer) (aka Niccolò Fontana)

Further Reading
Hall, Bert S., "'So Notable Ordynaunce': Christine de Pizan, Firearms, and Siegecraft in a Time of Transition." In: *Cultuurhistorische Caleidoscoop aangeboden aan Prof. Dr. Willy L. Braekman.* Ghent: Stichting Mens en Kultuur, 1992, pp. 219–40.

Le Saux, Françoise, "War and Knighthood in Christine de Pizan's *Livre des faits d'armes et de chevallerie.*" In: *Writing War: Medieval Literary Responses to Warfare.* Ed. Corinne Saunders, Françoise Le Saulx, and Neil Thomas. Cambridge: D.S. Brewer, 2004, pp. 93–106.

Pisan, Christine de, *The Book of Deeds of Arms and of Chivalry.* Ed. Charity Cannon Willard. Trans. Sumner Willard. State College: Pennsylvania State University Press, 1999.

Pisan, Christine de, *The Book of Fayettes of Armes and of Chyvalrye.* Trans. William Caxton. Early English Text Society. 2nd ed. London: Humphrey Milford, University of Oxford Press, 1937.

Soret, David, "Le syndrome de Mars: La guerre selon Christine de Pizan," *Cahiers d'histoire* 40 (1995), 97–113.

Willard, Charity Cannon, "Christine de Pizan on Chivalry." In: *The Study of Chivalry: Resources and Approaches.* Ed. H. Chickering and T.H. Seiler. Kalamazoo, 1988, pp. 511–28.

Kelly DeVries

Polybius
(ca. 200 BCE–ca. 118 BCE)

Significance: Polybius's *Histories* (or *World History*) provides a thorough description of the rise of Rome, its conflict with the Greek city-states, the Macedonian kingdom and Carthage.

Context: Polybius wrote a detailed history of the Macedonian and Punic Wars.

Biography: Polybius was born to a noble family in the city of Megalopolis, Greece in ca. 200 BCE. His family's political power led to his appointment as a cavalry commander of the Achaean League in 170/169 BCE. After the end of the war between Rome and the kingdom of Macedonia, the Romans demanded the extradition of about a thousand Achaeans of suspected loyalty. Polybius was among the hostages who were transferred to Italy. There he befriended Scipio Africanus whom he followed in some of his expeditions, acting as his political and military advisor. Polybius was an eyewitness of the siege and destruction of Carthage by Scipio. According to tradition, Polybius died, at the age of 82, of a fall from his horse.

Influences: His friendship to Scipio Africanus and other prominent Romans offered him with an in-depth knowledge of Rome's politics, military infrastructure, and tactics.

The Theory: Polybius is one of the first historians to attempt to present history as a sequence of causes and effects, based upon a careful examination of tradition and critical reasoning. Polybius focused not only on his personal observations but also always strived to interview eyewitnesses and actors, such as war veterans, to clarify details of the events he was writing about.

Application and Descendents: Polybius is quoted extensively by later historians such as Strabo and Athenaeus. He is also mentioned by Cicero and heavily used for information by Diodorus, Livy, Plutarch, and Arrian. The latter in particular, speaks of Polybius with great respect, with reference to his excellence as an authority on military affairs.

See also: Frontinus; Onasander (Onasandros, Onesandros, Onosandros), Philosopher

Further Reading
Walbank, Frank, *Polybius, Rome and the Hellenistic Word: Essays and Reflections.* Cambridge: Cambridge University Press, 2002.

Ioannis Georganas

Saxe, Marshal General of France, Comte Herman-Maurice de
(1696–1750)

Significance: Maurice de Saxe was the single most successful French commander of the first half of the 18th century. Theoretician and practitioner of war, he introduced many innovations, notably the all-arms legion formation that included regular light infantry and cavalry.

Context: The armies of Louis XIV had, on the whole, performed poorly in the War of the Spanish Succession (1701–1715). Despite signal victories at Denain under Marshal Villars (1712) and Alamanza under the English renegade Duke of Berwick (1707), they had been repeatedly beaten in open battle. This called for a reassessment and a new model of conducting military business, based on the science and rationalism of the European Enlightenment.

Biography: The illegitimate son of the Elector Frederick-Augustus "the Strong," who was simultaneously elector of Saxony and king of Poland, Herman-Maurice, Comte de Saxe, was born at Goslar in the Harz region of Saxony on October 28, 1696. At the tender age of 12 he had his first taste of military life while under the tutelage of the Count of Schulenburg and Frederick of Württemburg. He fought as an ensign of infantry at the siege of Lille, on the side of Allied armies under Marlborough and Prince Eugene of Savoy, who were trying to take the French-held town. In 1711, he was formally recognized by his father, and was made Count of Saxony (Comte de Saxe) and took command of the Saxon Beust cuirassier regiment. He fought against the Swedes under Magnus Stenbock at Gadebusch on

December 20, 1712, where his regiment suffered heavy losses in a severe defeat of the combined Danish and Saxon army. This disaster taught him valuable lessons regarding discipline and the chain of command: his regiment had fallen apart in the retreat, and he was forced to march for four days with the servants in the baggage train as a punishment.

The young Maurice was married at age 15 to the rich Saxon heiress Johann-Victoria von Loeben, in an attempt by his father to curb his precocious and rakish ways.

The end of the Great Northern War in 1716 brought the disbandment of a number of regiments, including Maurice's cuirassiers. Maurice was unhappy about being demobbed and complained to his father, who threatened to have him imprisoned. He retired to his estates to sulk, and in 1721 obtained an annulment of his marriage. His father now suggested that he seek employment in the French service. He spent every penny of his fortune in purchasing the colonelcy of the Sparre Infantry Regiment, which he rechristened de Saxe. The lack of action bored him, and in 1725 he left for Warsaw to pursue his putative claim to the Duchy of Courland in the Baltic region. With the support of his lover and fiancée, the Dowager Duchess Anna Ivanovna, the future Czarina, he duly received the ducal crown, but the Polish diet refused to recognize his claim. In any case, his father annexed the territory, causing a succession crisis, and without an army, and now not even the support of the Duchess (who he had abandoned for a chambermaid), he was forced to flee to Paris in 1727, pursued by Russian soldiers.

This was the low point in his life. His mother died shortly thereafter, and he lost his mistress, the actress Adrienne Lecouvreur. These sad events were shortly followed by the death of his father. Dispirited and broke, forgotten by high society since the Courland adventure, he threw himself into a febrile period of study and writing. At the age of 36, he wrote down his thoughts on the art of war in a work entitled *Mes Rêveries*. These were not for public consumption, but intended only as a memorial to his father and for the enlightenment of his military associates. He produced a second manuscript in 1740, bequeathed to the Count of Frisia, which was published years after his death in 1756 in The Hague by de Bonneville.

The War of the Polish Succession saw de Saxe reappear on the international stage. The French-sponsored Stanislas Leszczynski was elected king of Poland by the Diet of Nobles on September 12, 1733, and on October 5 his opponents put forward Frederick Augustus of Saxony, Maurice's half brother, as a rival claimant. De Saxe served under Berwick on the French side, and soon gained glory, coming to the attention of the influential Duc de Noailles. In August 1734, he was promoted to lieutenant general and his illustrious career truly began. Although peace was signed in 1735 in favor of the claim of Frederick Augustus, Maurice de Saxe was now one of the foremost of France's military commanders.

At the outbreak of the War of the Austrian Succession (1740–1748), Maurice was sent to join French volunteers fighting on the side of the Bavarians against Austria. He crossed the Rhine at the head of a division of cavalry in August of

1741. On the night of November 25–26, 1741, a body of French grenadiers under his command took the fortifications of Prague by assault. Maurice was the author of this *coup de main,* taking his inspiration from the work of the fire-eating military thinker, the Chevalier de Folard. De Saxe wrote to him immediately to inform him of his great success.

The campaign in Bohemia disillusioned him greatly. The majority of soldiers and officers, he felt, did not have the necessary qualities for aggressive fighting in de Folard's much-vaunted columns. Nevertheless, de Folard inspired de Saxe to read military writers, especially the ancient texts. This study was added to experience, which made him one of the most remarkable captains of the 18th century, the only one of his contemporaries never to have been beaten—unlike Prince Eugene of Savoy, or Frederick II "the Great" of Prussia.

Maurice de Saxe proved the worth of his *Rêveries* when, as Marshal of France, he became commander in chief of the army of Flanders in 1744. He showed himself first and foremost as a master of maneuver. With his light troops and hussars, and the elite *Arquebusiers de Grassin,* and *Voluntaires de Saxe,* he carried on *la petite guerre* of raids and skirmishes, causing great alarm in the Allied ranks and finally preventing them from moving. He then channeled them in the direction he wanted. When, in 1745, the Hanoverian Duke of Cumberland decided to relieve the French siege of Tournai, de Saxe blocked his route on a piece of ground of his own choosing, a defensive position around the village of Fontenoy, itself strongly fortified. The resulting battle was a resounding victory for Louis XV's army, watched by the king himself. The battle ensured de Saxe's place among the great commanders.

After Fontenoy, Ghent, Antwerp, Namur, Mons, and Brussels all fell into French hands. The best part of the Hanoverian-British army was then withdrawn to face the Jacobite rising under Prince Charles Edward Stuart in Scotland—at one point it was rumored de Saxe himself would lead a French expeditionary corps. De Saxe won another major victory against the Allied armies, deprived of British support, at Raucoux (Rocourt) in 1746. Even after the Jacobite emergency was over, he was able to convincingly defeat the combined British and Allied force at Lauffedlt in 1747. Here, at last, he was able to exploit the abilities of the French infantry by using dense attack columns.

In recognition of his talents, Maurice de Saxe was created Marshal General of France, an honor that had only been previously bestowed on Turenne and Villars. His final campaign, in 1748, captured Maastricht, after which, plagued by dropsy, he retired to his chateau at Chambord, attended by his menagerie, his regiment, and various mistresses. He died of a "putrid fever" on November 30, 1750.

Influences: De Saxe was inspired by the writings and exploits of the Chevalier de Folard. He had also learned much from his service with the Austrian commander Prince Eugene of Savoy. Before writing *Mes Rêveries,* he read widely, especially Puységur's *La Science du chef d'armée,* Onasander's *Strategikos,* and Vegetius's *Epitome of Military Science.*

The Theory: The *Rêveries* starts: "War is a science hidden in shadow, where one walks with an uncertain step in the darkness: routine and prejudices are its basis, a natural result of ignorance. All sciences have principles and rules, war has hardly any."

De Saxe discusses the finer details concerning the raising of troops, clothing them, paying them, training them, and forming them for battle. He also raises the question of military service. He envisaged universal military service for a period of five years, the minimum time needed to train the soldier. Prefiguring the French *philosophes* of the second half of the century, he criticized contemporary society, which he saw made up of oppressors and oppressed. Nowhere was this situation worse, he thought, than in the army.

De Saxe looked at military dress and suggested a "Roman" helmet in place of the tricorn; indeed his personal guards wore a fanciful comic-opera classical outfit. He also looked at the military boot and the commissariat. He saw cadenced marching as a solution to the difficulty of battalion drill maneuvers in close order. This had been practiced by the Romans, but supposedly forgotten when their empire fell. De Saxe also followed his mentor Folard in downplaying the effect of firepower:

> Gunpowder is not as frightening as it is thought. Few people in battles are killed fair and square from the front, I have seen entire volleys kill only four men, and I have never seen enough damage caused to prevent an advance in order to inflict revenge with firm thrusts of the bayonet, and muskets fired at point blank range. (*Mes Rêveries* pp. 29–30)

Infantry fire, he felt, should be reserved for those occasions when a charge into hand-to-hand combat was impractical, such as when assaulting buildings or fortifications, and should be delivered at will, each soldier firing as he was ready, without the need for orders.

Fascinated, like many others, by the Roman legions, he designed a new formation that closely integrated infantry and cavalry. This latter-day legion of around 3,500 men, would be organized into four regiments, each made up of four centuries of 184 men apiece, with a further half legion each of light infantry and cavalry. In his system, the centuries would form up four ranks deep, the two rear ranks being armed with half pikes as well as their musket. The use of light infantry predated the *voltigeurs* of the Revolutionary and Napoleonic Wars. They were to be dispersed about 60 to 120 meters in front of the main body, from where they would cover the advance, and would open fire at will on the enemy at 200 yards. The cavalry would support the light troops and pursue a beaten enemy. The regiment would also have its own artillery pieces, ironically called *amusettes* (loosely translated as "ticklers") in size half way between a light three-pound regimental gun and a wall gun, or heavy musket. Pikes would be retained. An army, he opined, should not exceed a total strength of 50,000.

De Saxe greatly respected Folard, but could not agree with him regarding the use of the column. He believed that such a formation would be hard to maneuver, and that the ranks would become mixed up. The depth of ranks would not increase the shock effect: the men in the rear ranks would not be able to push against those in the front ranks, as this would only shove them onto the enemy's bayonets. Instead, he advocated a formation suited to the type of fighting undertaken. If a column was called for it would be made up two battalions four ranks deep, one behind the other.

In battle, de Saxe maintains, one should take care that all arms were able to support one another. Rather than placing all the infantry in the center and the cavalry on the wings, small bodies of horse would be deployed in the second line in the center, and in the front on the wings, supported by infantry squares (*Mes Rêveries* pp. 81–90). In this, he harks back to the writings of the Imperial general Raimundo Montecúccoli (1609–1680).

The second part of the book tackles higher strategy. De Saxe is critical of reliance on fortified towns, apart from a few well-chosen ones. Rather, he says, a country could be defended with a few well-sited forts purely for military use, without the necessity of sheltering a civilian population. A model fort is shown, supported by a series of outworks at a distance of 2,000 paces.

As far as different ways of fighting are concerned, he draws lessons from the battle of Malplaquet, where he was allegedly present with Prince Eugene's army. Instead of building traditional lines of trenches, he says that the French should have built redoubts. This arrangement would have helped encourage the "natural" aggression of the French soldier in easily allowing counterattacks, and would also have made withdrawal easier (*Mes Rêveries* pp. 177–179).

> When ten enemy jump into a trench, everyone around them will flee and whole battalions will abandon it. If they see a troop of cavalry ride into it half a mile away, everyone will fly […] Men are easily upset when something happens that they do not expect: this rule is general in war, it decides all battles and skirmishes. (*Mes Rêveries* p. 181)

Rather than forming battalions four deep at the parapet of the trench, only one rank should be placed there. The others would be formed up 30 paces away, ready to charge the enemy, as soon as they occupy the fortification. Better still, de Saxe says, strong self-contained redoubts should be built, with all-round defense, such as the ones that brought victory to the Russians over the Swedes at Poltava in 1709.

The *Rêveries* ends with a section entitled "The qualities expected of the army commander." In the higher arts of war, de Saxe takes Prince Eugene as his ideal. Above all, he says, the army commander should retain freedom of judgment, without interference from politicians or ministers. A skillful general could make war his whole life long, without ever offering battle.

> Frequent small battles will be necessary to wear down the enemy little by little so to speak, after which he will be obliged to retire … I do not mean that when one comes across the opportunity to crush the enemy, that one should not attack him, or profit

from the wrong steps he may take, but I do mean that war can be made without leaving anything to chance, and this is the high point of the perfection of the general's skill. However having offered battle you must know how to gain by victory, and above all not to content oneself with merely winning the field as is the usual custom. (*Mes Rêveries* p. 215)

Application: Despite his progressive vision, de Saxe's work included some apparently archaic ideas when it appeared posthumously in 1756, like the use of the pike and shield, and full armor for the cavalry. However, *Mes Rêveries* were written in 1732, when musketry seemed rather ineffective in most European armies. That said, de Saxe's writings, and indeed his reputation, certainly influenced French commanders in the Seven Years' War (1757–1763). However, despite initially encouraging performances against the Hanoverian-British army (under the now infamous "Butcher" Cumberland) by the Ducs de Broglie and de Chevert at Hastenbeck in July 1757 (incidentally using a columnar attack formation), the defeats of Rossbach (1757) and Minden (1759) cast a pall over the French army's reputation, and led to a great deal of soul-searching among senior military personnel, such as de Guibert.

Descendents: For many de Saxe was the ideal French commander (despite being born in Germany). His spirit, dash, and vigor inspired many later military theorists, especially de Guibert.

See also: Folard; Guibert, J.

Further Reading

The best accounts of Maurice's major campaigns are to be found in M. S. Anderson's *The War of the Austrian Succession* (1995) and Reed Browning's 1993 work of the same name. The best biography is Jean-Pierre Bois's *Maurice de Saxe* (1992), at present only available in French. A livelier, but older biography in English is Jon Manchip White's *Marshal of France: The Life and Times of Maurice, Comte de Saxe* (1962). The full text of *Mes Rêveries* is widely available via the Internet.

Toby McLeod

Sertorius, Quintus

Significance: Sertorius showed that it was possible to defeat the famed Roman legions with a ragtag army by using guerrilla warfare and stratagems.

Context: Sertorius's revolt in Spain was a continuation of the internal upheavals that had been taking place since the 130s BC, and which had caused the first Roman Civil War that had ended in the victory of the *optimates* and Sulla.

Biography: Sertorius was born at Nussa in ca. 125 BC, and was therefore a "new man." He gained military experience in the wars against the Cimbri and Teutones, in Spain, in the Social War, and First Civil War. Sertorius had sided with the *populares,* and he had to flee from Rome in late 83 BC. Sertorius continued to fight and from 80 BC onward he led a skillful guerrilla campaign against the Sullans in Spain until Perperna, his subordinate, assassinated him in 72 BC.

Influences: Sertorius learned his trade mainly under Marius, but to this he added his own personal ingenuity and inventiveness in the waging of guerrilla war that surpassed his mentor's achievements in these fields.

The Theory: To Sertorius, the war he waged in Spain was always part of the ongoing Roman civil war. His aim was to present himself and his supporters as the only legitimate government of Rome and thereby raise a revolution against the Sullans. However, Sertorius did not forget the interests of the native Lusitanians and Spaniards. He waged war for the hearts and minds of the locals and local aristocracies successfully by treating them well, and he made the bond between the superstitious Spaniards and himself stronger by claiming to possess supernatural foresight. Sertorius also discerned the right balance between the employment of force and clemency.

Sertorius knew the weaknesses of the Roman military system, and how to exploit those. The use of several commanders/governors enabled Sertorius to defeat the different commanders separately. Sertorius proved that the Roman commanders were also gullible and could be defeated through the use of ambushes and stratagems. Sertorius demonstrated that the cumbersome legions were impotent when opposed by lightly equipped forces in the mountainous terrain. If the Romans attacked, Sertorius fled, and if they stayed in place, he harassed them. Sertorius showed that the Roman supply network was wholly inadequate to cope with his strategy, which also included the use of pirates to cut off naval supply routes.

Application: Sertorius was the foremost practitioner of his own art in Antiquity. For example, Sertorius was once able to fool Pompey the Great into thinking that he was trapping Sertorius between himself and the city of Lauron although in truth it was Sertorius who was trapping Pompey between his two armies. One of Sertorius's battle formations, the posting of flexible auxiliary infantry cohorts in front of the Roman cohorts, which he had copied from Marius, also became one of the standard Roman battle formations, a prime example of which is the Battle of Mons Graupius in 83/84 AD.

Descendents: Sertorius's greatest exploits were preserved in the collections of military stratagems (Frontinus, Polyaenus), and Plutarch's biography, which have served as sources of inspiration for generations of commanders. The general principles of Sertorius's guerrilla war are still valid.

See also: Frontinus; Marius

Further Reading

Konrad, C.F., *Plutarch's Sertorius: A Historical Commentary.* New York: University of North Carolina Press, 2004.

Ilkka Syvänne

Shang Yang
(d. 338 BCE)

Context: Shang Yang (d. 338 BCE) was one of the most important statesmen and political theorists in world history. The policies he instituted led directly to the Qin conquest, which unified China for the first time in 221 BCE.

Biography: Gongsun Yang, usually called Shang Yang, or Lord Shang, was born into a family with distant connections to the early Zhou dynasty. His enjoyed sufficient education and social standing to obtain a government position in the kingdom of Wei. He left Wei for a position in the Qin kingdom under Duke Xiao. In that position, he instituted policies that vastly increased Qin's power. These policies alienated the Qin aristocracy and the heir apparent, and when Duke Xiao died, Shang Yang was executed, reportedly torn apart between four chariots.

The Theory and Application: Shang Yang's policies for developing the power of the Qin kingdom would today fall under the rubric of "grand strategy," that is, an all-encompassing plan designed to harness the entire resources of a state for military purposes. At root, he believed that all human actions could be controlled by rewards and punishments, and that the rigid enforcement of this system would maximize the ruler's power. The system of laws and regulations should be applied universally, without regard for birth, class, or relationship to the ruler.

The Qin kingdom was comparatively poor in the fourth century BCE, a time of relentless interstate conflict in East Asia. Shang Yang sought to increase agricultural production, attract migrants, and improve military performance. But rather than institute a series of unrelated measures to achieve these ends, as other states at the time were doing, he established a complete reform of government and society based upon a few simple principles. These reforms attached individual subjects directly to the central state, bypassing and undermining the aristocrats, large lineages, and feudal institutions. This approach was extremely disruptive of not only the social order, but also the political order as well. It was also enormously effective in increasing the Qin kingdom's power to the point where it could undertake and succeed in a campaign to conquer all of the surrounding Chinese kingdoms.

Shang Yang did not leave a set of writings (extant works attributed to him are later forgeries) by which to judge him, but the significance of his policies prompted many thinkers to comment on him either directly or indirectly. We know from

Han Feizi, a later legalist, that Shang Yang proceeded from the two principles of establishing the law (*dingfa*) and treating the people as one (*yimin*). In practice this meant applying a strict set of laws equally throughout the populace. These were radical ideas in the fourth century BCE and the interpretation of their moral content has been debated ever since. Shang Yang's precepts were anathema to the Confucian school of thought, though the fact that Shang ordered Confucian texts burnt to diminish Confucian influence in Qin may indicate that the contempt went both ways. Ironically, both Confucians and Shang Yang sought a meritocratic society. For Confucians, this would be based upon rewarding morality, and for Shang Yang, tangible service to the state in the form of military accomplishment or agricultural production.

To improve law and order, Shang Yang made individuals who knew of a crime but did not report it subject to punishment equal to that of the perpetrator. This principle, like so many others of Shang Yang's, would persist in one form or another up to the present day. The idea of mutual responsibility among household or community members, resulting in mutual surveillance, was an efficient way to police society. It directly clashed with the Confucian value of placing family before all else. Mutual responsibility also removed any hierarchical authority outside of the government itself, preventing an individual from having any ties of loyalty that transcended his or her relationship to the state. Not only was no one above the law, everyone was required to enforce it. The state became all encompassing, and its authority absolute.

Shang Yang used land reform to increase production, improve military performance, and undermine the nobility. Rather than allow the nobility to control land and distribute it as they saw fit, Shang Yang used land as a reward for military service. Success in battle not only resulted in being awarded more land, it also brought higher military rank. It was therefore possible for a militarily successful individual to climb to a high status accompanied by landed wealth solely through service to the state. Nobles who lacked military accomplishments found their powers within the military and the economy greatly diminished, with a concomitant loss of power within society as a whole. The sole route to status and wealth was through service to the government.

The importance of military accomplishment in Shang Yang's system was tied to the Qin state's expansionistic agenda. This allowed the ambitious to risk their lives in the pursuit of Qin goals, but was deeply flawed in two ways. First, it was only a functional system during a period of expansion and intense military activity. Once peace was established, the military route would no longer provide enough rewards to satisfy the ambitious. Second, in almost exclusively rewarding those who were capable soldiers and generals in a time of constant campaigning, the state created a large number of high-ranking officers who were only skilled in warfare. Lacking any other profession or orientation, they were a burden and threat to the state.

Despite these larger drawbacks, Shang Yang's policies were extremely successful in the short and medium term. Qin armies proceeded to conquer the surrounding states, culminating in the unification of China under Qin rule in 221

BCE. This took over a century to accomplish, demonstrating that although legalist policies provided the Qin with an advantage over the other states, its opponents were formidable. The vagaries of war did not always favor the Qin, and its own acceptance of legalist policies waxed and waned. Qin rulers tended to prefer a system that enhanced their own power at the expense of the aristocracy and other powerful groups. Shang Yang's policies set Qin on the road to centralization and an absolutist state. Other states were not unaware of Qin practice, and many carried out some form of parts of Shang Yang's program, but the most truly centralized state won out over a century of conflict. It was, in a sense, a Darwinian contest of government policies.

Descendents: The success and persistence of Shang Yang's policies lay in the logic of his fundamental principles. Tying every subject directly to the state, and thus the ruler, was not only extremely attractive to the ruler but also ideologically compelling. It reinforced the preexisting concept of the ruler as son of heaven, the man who possessed the mandate of heaven, and was the interface between heaven and earth. In this sense, the legalist paradigm for secular power mirrored the Confucian, or at least, originally, Zhou dynasty, spiritual position of the unified ruler. When the Qin finally unified China, the ruler, now emperor, became spiritual and temporal head of all under heaven.

Conversely, the strength of Shang Yang's system and the institutional framework that grew out of it overwhelmed the person of the ruler. The supreme ruler was the linchpin that held the system together, but he was not really free to act as he thought fit. A bureaucracy and government oriented toward war and conquest tended to follow that course regardless of the ruler's own interests. The value of the system lay in its impartial rewarding of merit regardless of a person's origin. Officials were supposed to mechanically administer the rules. Although the ruler could change the rules as he saw fit, he was surrounded by officials and servitors selected by the existing system. The men around him embodied the system, and were not trained to question it.

The conflict with Confucianism would continue to be played out for the rest of imperial Chinese history. Legalism, as Shang Yang's doctrines and those of his successors would come to be known, underlay the institutions of the large imperial governments that controlled China in succession for over two millennia. This was necessary to establish and run a sprawling bureaucracy, and to manage the tens of thousands of functionaries that comprised the government. Yet at the same time it was equally important to cloak that rigid, amoral system of laws and regulations with a morally and ideologically compelling shroud of Confucianism.

Legalism was necessary and effective, but intellectually repugnant to the Chinese elite. Shang Yang's policies ran counter to elite privilege from the very beginning, rendering all subjects directly accountable to the state on an equal footing. Moreover, legalism was predicated on the notion of a completely centralized, top-down system whereby a ruler established fixed laws that his officials applied without interpretation. This obviated the need to appoint only moral men to positions of authority because officials had no personal discretion in applying laws. Although Confucians might object to such a system on moral and intellectual grounds, there were more pragmatic reasons for believing that a purely rules-based system would work. Many criminal cases required considerable discretion on the part of the official to determine which rules applied. Legalist practice also prevented an official from taking account of extenuating circumstances that might justify certain nominally illegal but morally acceptable actions.

Shang Yang's laws were not an expression of a particular morality, but of the needs of the ruler's power and authority. This power had no goal beyond the absolute empowerment of the ruler. By themselves, Shang Yang's policies created a powerful, centralized state that was inherently unstable. The concentration of power in the ruler made the government dependent upon his competence, and disenfranchised a broad swath of the elite, without simultaneously creating a large constituency of government supporters. The ruler held immense power, but in holding it nearly exclusively, he had to exercise it constantly and well to hold his government together. Without customary or moral restraints on behavior, only laws, the ruler's authority rested on the actual exercise of force.

Shang Yang's policies were all, ultimately, directed toward waging war. The power of the state, and the power of the ruler over that state, was demonstrated through conquest. Legitimacy in the legalist system was the result of proven power and authority, and the best proof was a centralized, unified government achieved through success in war. The imperial Chinese state was therefore a military machine without any foreseeable constraint, whether legal, moral, or functional. In Shang Yang's time, the possibility of conquering all of the Chinese states and exerting real, temporal authority using a centralized bureaucratic institution throughout the resulting territory was only theoretical. Yet it was a theory of government and war that laid the foundation for two millennia of Chinese empire. The Chinese empire was necessarily born out of war, and repeatedly recreated by war. And it was Shang Yang who first understood that necessity, and created a state apparatus to carry it out. Although his policies were downplayed by subsequent dynasties, they formed the legal framework for all of the major imperial governments in Chinese history.

See also: Kautilya; Li Ching; Li Ch'üan; Muhammad; Sima Qian; Sun Tzu

Peter Lorge

Sima Qian
(?145–?86 BCE)

Significance: Sima Qian remains one of the most important historians in Chinese history. His major work, *The Records of the Grand Historian (Shiji)*, established the format for all subsequent official histories. His prose style became a model for later writers in all areas.

Context: Sima Qian was a court official during the height of the Han dynasty (206 BCE to 220 CE), and served under one its most martial and expansionary emperors, Han Wudi. His position gave him access to the imperial library and its records.

Biography: Sima Qian (?145–?86 BCE) succeeded his father, Sima Tan (d. 110 BCE), in the office of grand historian, a post that also included astrologic responsibilities. His father began the work of history that would make Sima Qian famous, and it was filial responsibility that drove Sima Qian to complete it, enduring great suffering in the process. For example, he defended the character of a general reported to have surrendered to the enemy. When the report turned out to be true, Sima was sentenced to castration, which he underwent rather than take the socially expected route of suicide, so that he could finish the history.

Sima Qian was not explicitly or intentionally a thinker on war, but *The Records of the Grand Historian* nonetheless expresses a consistent viewpoint with respect to war in history. Also, Sima Qian's biographies of Sunzi (Sun Tzu) and Wuzi codified the fame of these two military thinkers, and gave them a human face apart from their writings. His reputation was cemented, however, by *The Records of the Grand Historian,* which became one of the foundation stones of Chinese history.

Perhaps because of his service at court, or because of the need to create an engaging narrative, Sima portrayed war in terms of personalities. He was aware of the significance of decisions by individual leaders, and the shaping of decisions by leaders' personal characteristics. As such, events were determined by the interactions of individual leaders rather than the larger sweep of history. Even extraordinary generals made serious mistakes, and no particular personality was ideal. In one instance, he compared two successful generals, one careless of discipline and camp craft, the other punctilious. The soldiers loved the careless general, yet his methods had serious drawbacks. Both generals succeeded in their own ways, however.

Sima was profoundly ambivalent about war, while accepting that it was inevitable in an empire that abutted powerful steppe confederations and occasionally suffered political fragmentation. His narrative never discusses the larger scope of campaigns, only the individual battles. Sima suggested that war was a highly contingent pursuit where cleverness and bravery mixed with luck and mistakes to produce unpredictable outcomes. Individual heroics could be decisive, or they could lead to disaster.

The narrative of *The Records of the Grand Historian* was influenced by the unification of the many disparate Chinese kingdoms under the Qin dynasty in 221 BCE. Sima does not indicate whether or not he considered the Qin conquest a positive change from the incessant warfare of the earlier spring and autumn period (722–481 BCE) and warring states period (481 or 403–221 BCE). His perspective does seem to match earlier records, though, in considering the earlier wars as powered by rulers of individual kingdoms or their ministers, driven not by rational calculations of cost and benefit, but by the desire for wealth and glory.

As the spring and autumn period aristocracy gave way to a rising professional class of generals, rational, or at least competent, military advice became available. This was best exemplified in the lives of Sun Wu (Sunzi) and Wu Qi. Sunzi's competence in forming even a group of palace women into an organized military unit, at the court of Helu, king of Wu (r. 514–496 BCE), demonstrated what a professional could do, but also the costs of employing such a man—Sunzi executed the king's two favorites despite the king's objections to achieve complete obedience. Effectiveness in war therefore required an extremely rigid enforcement of discipline that superceded the ruler's own power.

Similarly, Sima used the life of Wu Qi to illustrate, on the one hand, the capabilities of a professional general and, on the other, how personality flaws ultimately destroy an ambitious man. Wu Qi was undefeated as a general, but arrogant, avaricious, lecherous, and ruthless. His harsh discipline and unyielding application of efficient government as prime minister of Chu dramatically enhanced the power of Chu, but also aroused the animosity of members of the disenfranchised Chu aristocracy. These aristocrats later killed Wu Qi.

Sima Qian offered a rather mixed message on war. Field generals required not only bravery and cunning, but also luck. Misfortune could always strike. Even great strategists could be brought down by their own personality flaws. Professional competence in warfare often clashed with entrenched political interests. Ultimately then, Sima Qian argued that the inevitability of war required the maintenance of good generals, who could be as much of a threat to the enemy as to themselves.

See also: Ch'i Chi-kuang; Li Ching; Li Ch'üan; Shang Yang; Sun Tzu

Peter Lorge

Sirhindi, Abdullah
(ca. 15th century CE; writing about 12th century CE)

Significance: In the 12th century CE, the Indian subcontinent's Rajput polities were replaced by the centralized Delhi Sultanate, which persisted until the 16th century. The *Tarikh-i-Mubarakshahi* of Abdullah Sirhindi narrates the foundation of the Delhi Sultanate by Muhammad Ghori (also known as Muhammad bin Sam or Shihabuddin Ghori) and his descendents between 1192 and 1448. Sirhindi describes the battles of Muhammad Ghori and how, due to the large-scale use of Central Asian horses, Ghori greatly increased the tempo of battle in the Indian subcontinent and defeated the Rajput confederacy.

Context: Islamic civilization came to Central Asia when the Arab armies entered Khorasan in the eighth century CE. In 750, the Umayid Caliphate was replaced by the Abbasid Caliphate. The Abbasids, instead of recruiting Arabs (who tended to be supporters of the Umayids), inducted nomadic, Islamic Central Asian Turks

(Tatars or Turkomans) into their armies. On the vast, semiarid plains of the Eurasian steppe, which extended from Chinese Turkestan to South Russia, only cavalry could really dominate, and Turkish mounted archers were more effective under these conditions than the Arabian lance-bearing cavalry. The steppes produced the best horses in Eurasia. The nomads depended on the horses for game hunting and transportation, and became skilled in archery. In times of need, the nomads could drink blood from their mounts, and horsemeat was considered a delicacy.

The Turks who had accepted Islam carved out principalities when the Abbasid Caliphate disintegrated. The Ghaznavid Sultanate, comprising eastern Iran and Afghanistan, was one such principality. Mahmud Ghazni invaded India 17 times, but his successors proved to be weak. Muhammad Ghori, another Turkish chieftain, overthrew the Ghaznavid Empire in 1174 and controlled Afghanistan. Ghori decided to conquer Hind, which brought him in conflict with the Chauhan clan of Rajputs, who had made themselves masters of Delhi in the 11th century. Prithviraj III Chauhan (also known as Rai Pithora) the ruler of Ajmir from 1179 to 1192, tried unsuccessfully to stem the tide of Turkish conquest. Ghori's victories allowed the formation of the Delhi Sultanate in India.

Biography: Abdullah Sirhindi, the author of *Tarikh-i-Mubarakshahi* lived in Delhi around the late 15th century when the Sayyid dynasty (1414–1451) was ruling the Delhi Sultanate.

Influences: Under the Delhi Sultanate, Persian culture was dominant. Sirhindi falls within the medieval Persian tradition of history writing, in which history was considered to be a biography of kings and dynasties. The writing of political and military histories was undertaken by political chroniclers or court historians who had intimate contact with the ruling class. Sirhindi emphasizes the political glory of his royal patron. The conduct of the monarch represents the highest human activity, and the court and camp are the most important institutions worth studying. By contrast, Arab scholars looked down upon the idea of dedicating their works to rulers and nobles. The objective of the Persian historians such as Sirhindi was to exaggerate the military achievements of their patrons. Yet when the historian is recording an event, he refers to reliable individual witnesses and sources. Sirhindi also used the *Fath Namas* (military dispatches) issued by the sultans after the conclusion of their campaigns.

Sirhindi was particularly influenced by Rashid Vatvat (1114–1177), who was a scholar in the court of Khwarazm Emperor Shah Atsiz. In *Hadaiq-us-Sihr,* Rashid describes Atsiz's campaigns. Sirhindi was probably also inspired by Hasan Nizami's military history, *Taj-ul-Maathir,* which was completed in the 13th century. Hasan Nizami notes the armor-piercing qualities of the crossbow and the protection offered by chain armor as important factors in ensuring Muslim victory over the Hindu Rajputs. For close quarter combat, the Muslim cavaliers used iron maces, battleaxes, daggers, and javelins, whereas the Hindus depended on spears and lances. He also writes that the Delhi Sultanate's cavalry forces, equipped with horseshoes, had an edge over the unshod cavalry forces of the Rajputs.

The Theory: The Muslim invaders of India combined mounted archery of the Central Asian Turks with Arab tactics of cavalry charging with lances. Ghori introduced a unique combination of light and heavy cavalry tactics to Indian warfare. The light cavalry of unarmored horse archers were to implement swarming or harassing tactics by attacking the flanks and rear of the enemy. And the heavy cavalry (both the cavaliers and their mounts were covered with armor) functioned as a battering ram. The use of heavy cavalry as a battering ram was adopted from the technique used by the Arab general Muhammad Qasim. Ghori planned that while the horse archers were to conduct swarming harassing attacks around a Hindu force, the armored cavalry equipped with lances would complete the victory by charging at the tired enemy. In 1192, Ghori divided his army into five groups. Four groups comprising horse archers were ordered to attack the Rajputs by turns. The fifth group consisted of armored cavalry was kept as a reserve under direct control of Muhammad Ghori. Ghori's light cavalry launched surprise attack and simultaneous attacks from different directions. Thanks to the mobility of the Central Asian mounts, the Turks could easily and effectively mount battlefield attacks at whatever point they wanted. Speed enabled the Turks to surprise their Hindu opponents, and combined with surprise produced a lethal multiplier effect. This paralyzed the Hindu armies. One Turkish cavalry army was able to cover 45 miles in one night.

The Rajputs, despite frequently enjoying numerical superiority, were repeatedly defeated by the Turks' superior techniques. They had no answer to Ghori's composite swarming and shock tactics of the cavalry. Indeed, the contingents supplied by the feudatory Rajput chiefs to their political overlord were neither disciplined nor trained, and Ghori's techniques fractured the cohesion of the Rajput armies. Due to unavailability of good horses, the Rajput chiefs suffered both from strategic and tactical disadvantages. The Rajputs could neither conduct rapid raids like those of the Turks nor counter them. The Hindu armies were overdependent on the elephants. The elephant-centric armies of the Hindus were slow and incapable of long-distance operational strikes. The Hindu armies also could not move during summer, as the elephants could not endure thirst. In the rapidly fluctuating scenarios in the battlefield, the ponderous elephant-oriented Hindu armies were incapable of showing flexibility by changing fronts and launching quick counterattacks.

Around 1175, Muhammad Ghori invaded India from Afghanistan and conquered Sind and western Punjab. The Rajputs mobilized in response. The result was the First Battle of Tarain in 1191 between Muhammad Ghori and the Rajput Confederacy led by Prithviraj Chauhan. The battleground, Tarain (or Tararoi) was a small village by the river Sarsuti, about eighty miles from Delhi.

Whereas Muhammad depended mostly on cavalry, the Rajputs relied upon horses and elephants. The Muslim army was divided into four groups: right, left, center, and the vanguard, and Muhammad Ghori personally commanded the center. The Rajputs deployed 100,000 cavalry and opened the battle with a frontal cavalry charge. Due to their numerical superiority, the Rajputs cut off Ghori's center from his wings. Ghori's vanguard, composed of Khalji and Afghan troopers, melted away, and the cavaliers at Ghori's center were afraid that they might be cut off. To inspire the men, Ghori charged toward Govind Rai, the ruler of Delhi. He threw a lance that broke Rai's teeth but Govind Rai threw a spear, which seriously wounded Muhammad. The Muslim soldiers at Ghori's center, believing that the sultan was dead, initially faltered, but seeing that Ghori was merely wounded, they regained heart. They broke through the surrounding Rajput cavalry and Ghori's wings joined up. However, because Ghori was seriously wounded, the Ghorid army carried out a fighting withdrawal.

Probably influenced by the idea of *dharmayuddha,* Prithviraj did not pursue the retreating foe. Instead, he halted his troops and besieged the fort of Sirhind.

Ghori met Prithviraj again at Tarain in 1192. Ghori's standing army numbered 120,000 troops, but due to the threat posed to Khorasan by the Khwarazm Empire, Ghori was able to bring only 40,000 cavalry to India. Prithviraj collected a numerically superior force. However, the combined Rajput force was an inchoate, loose conglomeration of contingents brought by 150 chiefs. They were neither equipped uniformly nor had collective training.

The battle started at sunrise and continued till sunset. When the Rajput elephants and horses attacked the horse archers, the latter conducted a tactical retreat. When the Rajput forces stopped, the horse archers attacked them. This sort of successive attack, retreat and counter-attack by the four groups of Ghorid Army wore out the Rajputs. On Muhammad's side, when one group of horse archers tired, another group took up the task. At day's end, the issue was decided by the charge of Ghori's reserve comprising of 12,000 horsemen covered with chain mail armor, helmets and equipped with lances. Sirhindi writes that about 100,000 Hindus, including Govind Rai, lost their lives. Prithviraj fled from the battlefield, but was captured and executed.

The figures for the Rajput armies in the two battles of Tarain are difficult to accept. Sirhindi deliberately exaggerates the number of Rajput host to cast the Islamic warriors in a heroic light. Probably, they refer to the potential number of force that could theoretically be mobilized by all the Rajput chiefs, rather than the actual number brought by them in the battlefield.

Ghori also used the *mamluk* institution for inducting the Turkish-mounted archers in the army. From the ninth century CE onward, *mamluks* or *ghulams* constituted the core of the Islamic armies from the Indus to Egypt. The term *mamluk* meant "slave," but the term had a different meaning from the western understanding. Poor Turkish boys were sold by their parents to the merchants, who supplied them to *amirs* (chiefs). They became the *amirs'* retainers, and received military training and education. Occasionally these slave soldiers enjoyed more power and prestige than the *amirs'* natural sons. Under the *amirs,* the *mamluks* reached top positions in the army and after the death of their patrons even succeeded to their offices and in some cases their thrones. Usually, the *mamluks* provided the *amirs* with a highly effective officer corps.

Application: The combination of swarming and ramming tactics by the Delhi Sultanate's cavalry proved adequate in repelling the Mongol invasions commencing in the late 13th century. In 1296, Targhi's force of 20,000 Mongol cavalry was routed by Alauddin Khalji's army. The Delhi Sultanate also exploited internal divisions within the Mongol Empire after 1270. During the 13th century, the Central Asian Khanate attacked the Delhi Sultanate, but the Ilkhans of Persia observed benevolent neutrality toward the sultanate. The situation changed when Amir Timur replaced the Chaghtai Mongol Khanate in Central Asia.

> The techniques of surprise raids by cavalry, swarming tactics by light cavalry, and the use of heavy cavalry as a battering ram were used by Sher Khan, who founded the short-lived Suri Empire in north India. In 1534, the Battle of Surajgarha was fought between Sher Khan and Ibrahim Khan the general of Husain Shahi Bengal Sultanate. Ibrahim deployed his army, comprising of elephants, cavalry, infantry and artillery, in a single line. The core of Sher Khan's army was cavalry. Like Muhammad Ghori, Sher used light cavalry (unarmored horse archers) for harassing the enemy. At dawn, the horse archers advanced and after firing a volley of arrows turned back. Then they advanced again, and the continuous discharge of arrows demoralized Ibrahim's soldiers. At midday, Ibrahim was forced to advance against the horse archers, leaving the protection of his artillery. Sher then used a contingent of 5,000 heavy lancers, which he had posted behind a hill, to launch a sudden frontal cavalry charge against Ibrahim's tired soldiers. Sher's victory was complete and he conquered Bengal.

Descendents: Srivara wrote Zaina Rajatarangini during the late 15th century in the context of Sultanate of Kashmir, which remained independent of the Delhi Sultanate. Srivara, like Sirhindi, maintains that horse archers should be combined with a "ram" of lance-bearing heavy cavalry. In Sirhindi's paradigm, the light horse archers remain unarmored, but Srivara argues for giving armor to the horse archers, thus making them heavy cavalry. This reduced speed but gave greater protection to both the mounts and bowmen. Srivara, instead of merely focusing on cavalry, also discusses gunpowder and infantry. Sirhindi gives no importance to infantry. Srivara notes that along with cavalry, disciplined infantry is necessary for winning battles. Srivara focuses on the cooperation between infantry equipped with heavy spears and cavalry. He mentions that the state employed artisans for manufacturing cannonballs and both field guns and siege artillery.

See also: Hindu Tradition of Just and Unjust War; Use of Elephants in Indian Warfare

Further Reading
Bhakari, S. K., *Indian Warfare: An Appraisal of Strategy and Tactics of War in Early Medieval Period.* New Delhi: Munshiram Manoharlal, 1981.

Nizami, Khaliq, Ahmad, *On History and Historians of Medieval India.* New Delhi: Munshiram Manoharlal Publishers Ltd., 1983.

The Tarikh-i-Mubarakshahi, by Yahiya Bin Ahmad Bin Abdullah Sirhindi, tr. into English from the Original Persian with Textual Notes and Index by H. Beveridge. 3rd ed. New Delhi: D. K. Publishers, 1996.

Kaushik Roy

Sun Tzu
(ca. 500 BCE–300 BCE)

Significance: The 13 chapters of *The Art of War* deal with perhaps the earliest comprehensive theory of conflict, and certainly one of the most profound. It has had a tremendous influence on later military thought and practice in East Asia, and today its lessons are studied by both soldiers and civilians in all regions of the world. Sun Tzu presents his theory in the form of discrete nuggets of wisdom, giving us his conclusions while omitting the process of reasoning by which he arrived at them. This book was written more than 2,000 years before Clausewitz's *On War,* at a much earlier point in the development of civilization and literacy. Thus, it is all the more remarkable that when the scattered, aphoristic sayings of Sun Tzu are considered together they amount to a comprehensive and largely coherent theory of war, including both tools of analysis and recommendations for action. Although the author's attention is most often directed at the operational level, his observations cover the whole range from minor tactics to grand strategy. Where Clausewitz's concern is with the commander in the field after war has been declared, Sun Tzu treats diplomacy and war as a single field of activity. *The Art of War* covers not just operations, but also discusses intelligence, logistics, leadership, and the influences of terrain and psychology (which are often considered in relation to one another). The text includes a rational calculus for making decisions regarding war and peace (and predicting victory and defeat) that resembles today's net assessment. It places great emphasis on accurate intelligence, gathered by means both of spies and of direct observations of signals and indicators coming from the enemy camp, as the key to victory. The use of deception is also strongly advocated, and intelligence is essential both for carrying out effective deception operations against the enemy and for recognizing their own efforts at deception for what they are—enabling one to distinguish between an opportunity and a trap. Perhaps reflecting an incipient military professionalism as well as the absence of real-time communications, Sun Tzu is also strongly in favor of the command autonomy of the general in the field.

With regard to war as a process or sequence of actions, Sun Tzu seems to envisage a conflict beginning with rational calculations of gain or loss and prediction of victory or defeat. Once the conflict is underway, *The Art of War* presents a hierarchy of targets, prioritizing those that are more likely to lead to victory in a less costly and destructive way (attacking the enemy's plans) over those that are likely to lead to result in high casualties (assaulting fortified positions). This is in keeping with the overall preference of the text for attacking the enemy's vulnerabilities and avoiding their strengths. If the enemy is at first superior, a decisive confrontation is to be avoided until the odds have changed or an opportunity presents itself. That opportunity is not to be passively awaited, but is actively shaped by means of deception and maneuver that forces the enemy to react so that their weak points are exposed and one is able to concentrate overwhelming force against a fraction of the enemy's force: "Thus it is that in war the victorious strategist only seeks battle after victory has been won, whereas he who is destined to defeat first fights and afterward looks for victory" (Sun Tzu, tr. Giles 1910, 30).

Context: *The Art of War* was written during a time of transition in Chinese history. Rulers were consolidating and centralizing their authority, and the larger and more powerful states were invading and annexing their weaker neighbors, a process that left only seven major powers standing by the middle of the third century BCE. Driven by the increasingly ruthless interstate competition, the character of warfare was also changing. During the time known as the spring and autumn period (722–481 BCE) battlefields were dominated by chariot-riding noblemen who indulged in what might be termed chivalrous behavior and often seemed to regard war as a sporting event rather than a tool of state policy. The warring states period that followed, lasting from about 450 BCE to the unification of China by the state of Ch'in in 221 BCE, was radically different. War was serious business, and huge armies composed mainly of infantry conscripted from the farming population were subjected to harsh discipline and drilled to maneuver in response to their generals' commands.

The exact date when *The Art of War* was written (or compiled) is highly uncertain. Those who accept the biographical information about Sun Tzu found in traditional Chinese sources believe that the book dates from about 500 BCE. Other scholars, such as Samuel B. Griffith, have argued for a later date based on the military technology mentioned in the book. They prefer to place *The Art of War* in the second half of the fourth century BCE because it mentions the crossbow (not attested before about 350 BCE) but not cavalry (which did not come into use in China until shortly before 300 BCE). Traditionalists counter that mention of the crossbow might be a later insertion. This debate has yet to be resolved, though an increasingly popular view is that the book took shape gradually over time, perhaps being assembled by Sun Tzu's disciples during the fifth century BCE. The earliest extant copy, written on bamboo strips and unearthed by Chinese archaeologists from a second century BCE tomb at Lin-i, Shantung province, in the early 1970s, demonstrates not only that the 13 chapters of *The Art of War* were substantially the same as today, but also that there then existed numerous additional and possibly apocryphal chapters, which were subsequently lost. Sun Tzu's theories are not mentioned in other Chinese texts before about the middle of the third century BCE.

The ideas presented in *The Art of War* are more in keeping with the values and practices of the warring states than those of the spring and autumn period. This can be seen in the opening lines of the first chapter of the text, which declares, "The art of war is of vital importance to the State. It is a matter of life and death, a road either to safety or to ruin" (Sun Tzu, tr. Giles 1910, 1). The imprint of the warring states can also be seen in chapter 7, where we are told that "gongs and drums, banners and flags" are to be used to organize large masses of men into a single body, responsive to a single command, so that "it is impossible either for the brave to advance alone, or for the cowardly to retreat alone" (Sun Tzu, tr. Giles 1910, 64). This is in sharp contrast to the ways of the spring and autumn period, when hotheaded warriors might charge the enemy line by themselves to show off their bravery.

Biography: Almost all the information we have regarding the author of *The Art of War* comes from only two sources, the *Historical Records* (*Shih-chi*) completed by the Han-dynasty historian Ssu-ma Ch'ien about 100 BCE and the *Spring and Autumn Annals of Wu and Yue* (*Wu Yueh ch'un-ch'iu*), an even later work written by Chao Yeh shortly before 100 CE. Unfortunately, both sources include elements of fiction and are less than completely reliable guides to the distant past. According to these early histories, the real name of Sun Tzu (or Master Sun) was Sun Wu, and he was a brilliant strategist and military commander who came from the state of Ch'i (in what is now Shantung province), entered the service of the ruler of the southern state of Wu (near the mouth of the Yangtze River), and helped to lead Wu's armies to victory over the powerful neighboring kingdom of Ch'u in 506 BCE. This story is not, however, corroborated by other early sources such as the *Tso chuan* (*Tradition of Tso*), which covers the military history of this period in some detail, and it deals with elements with a strongly fictional flavor (such as the famous parable of Sun Tzu training the king of Wu's concubines to maneuver in military formation). Even if all of this material is substantially correct and the Sun Wu mentioned by Ssu-ma Ch'ien and Chao Yeh was indeed the author of the 13 chapters of *The Art of War,* he remains a very shadowy figure. And if, as there is reason to believe, *The Art of War* was written at a later date, we know nothing at all about its author except that he was probably an experienced military commander who chose to attribute his own ideas to a famous general of earlier times to invest them with greater credibility.

Influences: *The Art of War* must be located near the beginning of the Chinese tradition of prescriptive writing about war and strategy, but it was not without antecedents. In chapter 7, Sun Tzu actually quotes an earlier text, *The Book of Military Administration* (*Chun cheng*), regarding the need for signals such as drums and flags to control the movements of masses of troops. Unfortunately, nothing else is known of this work and it has not survived to the present day. Among the extant Chinese military treatises, the only one with substantial contents that likely antedate *The Art of War* is the *Ssu-ma Fa* (*Methods of the Minister of War*), a work traditionally attributed to a sixth century BCE general and statesman named T'ien

Jang-chü. The contents and recommendations of the *Ssu-ma Fa* differ considerably from those of *The Art of War,* with an emphasis on ritual propriety rather than deception and maneuver. The book appears to reflect the thinking of an earlier, more rules-obsessed period of Chinese history. We may speculate that *The Art of War* represents a reaction against earlier approaches to war rather than a continuation of the ways of the past.

Although *The Art of War* does not appear to be deeply grounded in an earlier Chinese literature on the conduct of war, it is clearly informed by other, roughly contemporary theories not specifically military in character. Mention of the alternation of *yin* and *yang* and the five notes, five colors, and five flavors either anticipates or reflects the thinking of the school of the five elements (or five agents, *wu hsing*) that sought to identify a master pattern underlying all the varied phenomena of experience (flavors, colors, seasons, directions, organs, emotions, etc.) and manipulate the sympathetic resonances thought to exist within and between the various categories. The idea of *shih,* or "situational advantage" (to be discussed in more detail below) resembles the thinking of the legalist philosopher Shen Tao (ca. 350–275 BCE), who argued that political power was more a function of an individual's position within an organizational structure than of any inherent qualities of that individual. An even stronger philosophical influence evident in *The Art of War* is of that of ideas that later came to be labeled as Taoist, especially those ideas presented in the *Tao Te Ching* (conventionally attributed to the sixth century BCE philosopher Lao Tzu, a figure no less shadowy than Sun Tzu himself, but probably dating from a somewhat later period). The *Tao Te Ching* and *The Art of War* both identify water as a powerful force worthy of emulation, both point to the efficacy of dealing with problems while they are still incipient rather than fully apparent, and both share a negative assessment of war as a wasteful and destructive activity. The moralism characteristic of the school of Confucius (556–479 BCE) is not in evidence in *The Art of War*—with the possible exception of the first chapter, where one of the five basic categories of analysis for predicting victory or defeat is the moral quality of government.

The Theory: Above all else, *The Art of War* advocates a coldly rational approach to both the conduct of war and decisions regarding war and peace. War is understood to be an extremely hazardous activity that not only carries a high cost in human life but may also lead to the destruction of the state itself. Therefore decisions must not be influenced by anger or other emotions, which easily lead to errors, but are to be reached instead by a painstaking process of calculating the relative strengths and weaknesses of the two sides. This involves five categories of comparison: (1) the moral quality of government in the opposing states, (2) the ways in which climate and weather work to the advantage or disadvantage of the two sides, (3) the impact of the terrain on the fortunes of the two sides, (4) the qualities of the opposing generals, and (5) the relative effectiveness of the organization, laws, and administrative systems of the two sides. On the basis of these calculations, we are told, it is possible to predict victory and defeat and thus avoid losing wars by fighting only when victory is assured. (By the same token, once a war is underway, commanders in the field are to escape defeat by avoiding battle with stronger enemy forces.) These calculations can deliver the desired result only if they are made on the basis of complete and accurate information regarding both one's own forces and those of the enemy. Hence, the tremendous emphasis that Sun Tzu places on intelligence gathering.

Spies, in Sun Tzu's view, are by far the most efficacious means of gathering information about the enemy, and the last of the 13 chapters of *The Art of War* is devoted entirely to examination of the different types of spies and the ways in which they are put to use. They include not only "surviving spies" (who bring back information from the enemy camp) and double agents, but also "doomed spies" who may be used to spread disinformation. While extolling the value of intelligence gathered by human agents, Sun Tzu adamantly rejects another form of intelligence gathering that was widespread in the ancient Chinese world, namely, the use of various forms of divination to acquire foreknowledge from the spirit world.

One of the reasons that war is not to be undertaken lightly is its damaging effect on the economy. The second chapter of *The Art of War* explores this effect and offers recommendations for waging war and directing campaigns in such a way as to minimize its impact. Sun Tzu points to the costs of raising an army and maintaining it in the field, observing that no state has ever benefited from protracted warfare. The ideal is thus to defeat the enemy quickly, without having to call up reinforcements or resupply the army in the field repeatedly. Noting the high cost of transporting grain over long distances, Sun Tzu recommends that the army should feed itself with provisions captured from the enemy.

A recurring theme in *The Art of War* is the desirability of winning at the least possible cost and effort, minimizing the bloodshed and destruction associated with victory and ideally even subduing the enemy's forces without fighting. The general is advised to prepare the ground for victory by upsetting the enemy's plans, so that the decisive encounter when it comes is one-sided rather than hotly contested. More direct and costly approaches, such as storming walled cities, are presented as distinctly inferior. The ideal is not simply to minimize one's own losses, but to minimize the enemy's losses as well. It is better to preserve the enemy's military units and cities rather than destroying them, the assumption being that once taken intact they can be incorporated into one's own army and state. Some analysts, most notably Alastair I. Johnston, have argued strenuously that this apparent advocacy of nonviolent or minimally violent victory is contradicted by other passages in *The Art of War* that presuppose the actual clash of arms, and probably represents an ideal rather than a practical goal attainable under most real-world conditions.

The Art of War also places great emphasis on the role of the general in bringing about victory. With justification, it has been said to represent the views of an emerging class of military specialists in warring states China who were seeking to enhance their own authority and maximize their professional autonomy. Sun Tzu attributes awesome power and effectiveness to the general who practices the art of war in accordance with the book's teachings. For example, "the leader of armies is the arbiter of the people's fate, the man on whom it depends whether the nation shall be in peace or in peril" (Sun Tzu, tr. Giles 1910, 16). He is also said to hold the enemy's fate in his hands. The skillful general is a virtual sage who is able to perceive the patterns underlying the apparent chaos of armed conflict and then act on them to achieve certain victory. The personal qualities of the general are of great importance: he must have no character flaws or emotional weaknesses—such as being easily angered—that can be exploited by the enemy to encompass his down-fall. Once a ruler has found the right sort of general, the worst thing he can do is hobble his man by trying to micromanage field operations from the distant capital. When the army is on campaign, the authority of the general must be supreme; there are commands from the ruler that should not be obeyed.

When he deals with the general's maneuvering of his army in the field, Sun Tzu employs a technical vocabulary that requires careful elucidation. Among the key terms are *hsing* (shape or form), *hsu* and *shih* (weak points and strong points), *cheng* and *ch'i* (the straightforward and the tricky), *shih* (situational power), and *ch'i* (spirit or morale).

Hsing has been translated into English as "dispositions," "deployment of forces," and "configuration." The basic meaning of *hsing* is shape or form. It is the configuration, disposition, or deployment of a military force that, if observed by the enemy, is likely to reveal one's own intended plan of action. Hence, it is necessary to conceal one's own form to the greatest extent possible—either giving the impression of formlessness or projecting a false form to deceive the enemy. The other side of the coin is that one should not only do everything pos-sible to discover the enemy's true form, but also take active measures to impose a form on the enemy that opens up weak points and exposes them to attack and defeat (e.g., by offering some sort of bait or leaking false intelligence). Like many words in classical Chinese, *hsing* can function as either a noun or a verb depend-ing on where it is placed in a sentence. When functioning as a verb, it means "to shape" the enemy.

Knowing the enemy's form allows us to identify their strong points and weak points. "Strong points" and "weak points" are Lionel Giles's translation of two paired concepts that are of great importance in *The Art of War, shih,* and *hsu*. These can designate something very concrete, for example, strongly fortified positions on the one hand and gaps in the enemy line on the other. Or they can be used in a more abstract and metaphorical sense, where *hsu* might apply to low morale on the home front or a lack of will in the political leadership. Sun Tzu recommends that all attacks be aimed so as to target the enemy's weak points and avoid confronting their strong points. His is a strategy of pitting strength against weakness—not, as was so often the case in western military history, pitting strength against strength. Hence, Sun Tzu says that the army should be like water, flowing around the rocks (or strong points) and through the gaps in the enemy's defense.

Another paired set of concepts that appears in *The Art of War* is *cheng* and *ch'i*, translated by Giles as "direct" and "indirect" methods of maneuver. These terms, perhaps more than any others, have bedeviled translators of *The Art of War*. They have been variously rendered as "orthodox"/"unorthodox," "regular"/"irregular," and "straightforward"/"tricky." None of these translations captures the full meaning of the terms. *Cheng* refers to a straightforward approach that is more or less expected by the enemy, whereas *ch'i* refers to a crafty, unexpected maneuver intended to take one's opponent by surprise. To provide concrete examples from the basically linear battle tactics of ancient, medieval, and early modern times, a *cheng* effort might be a frontal assault directed against the center of the enemy line, whereas a *ch'i* maneuver might take the form of an ambush or a strike against the enemy flanks or rear. Of course, like all of the key ideas in *The Art of War*, these concepts can be adjusted to apply to the level of strategy or grand strategy, as well as that of tactics. It is also important to bear in mind that *cheng* and *ch'i* have more to do with *perceptions* and *expectations* than with physical formations. If the enemy is expecting to be hit in the flank or rear, then a frontal attack might be a *ch'i* maneuver. And *cheng* and *ch'i* can transform into one another quite easily, as when, for example, a *ch'i* maneuver anticipated and blocked by the enemy becomes a *cheng* effort. Sun Tzu's advice is to engage with *cheng* and then win with *ch'i*. It would seem that the *cheng* effort is supposed to pin the enemy, distract his attention, and set him up for a devastating and unexpected *ch'i* maneuver that will decide the outcome of the conflict.

Another key concept for Sun Tzu, and one that is truly central to understanding how to achieve victory, is *shih* (this is a different character from that for "weak point"). The same term appears in some of the writings of the legalist school of ancient Chinese political philosophy, where it designates the power that derives from occupying a particular position in an institutional structure—the prime minister has power because he occupies that particular office, not because he is especially clever or muscular. Similarly, *The Art of War* uses *shih* to refer to the power that comes from being in a particular situation or occupying a certain position. This could be an advantageous topographical location, or it could be a set of moral or psychological conditions that act as a force multiplier. Sun Tzu uses various metaphors to illustrate this concept, including boulders on a mountaintop, water pent up behind a high dam, and the fully drawn bow of an armed crossbow—just waiting for the trigger to be released at the right moment.

Ch'i is a second term that is not to be confused with another word of the same Romanized spelling and similar pronunciation (that is, *ch'i* as "indirect"). This *ch'i* has often been rendered it into English as "spirit" or "morale," but some have refused to translate it at all. This squeamishness is because *ch'i* is actually a key term in ancient Chinese scientific (or pseudoscientific) thought, where it refers to the fluid substrate that underlies both matter and emotions and links humans to the physical environment around them. Water vapor in the form of clouds or steam was thought to be a visible manifestation of *ch'i*. For Sun Tzu, *ch'i* was something that could be observed, understood, and manipulated to achieve victory. For example, "a soldier's spirit (*ch'i*) is keenest in the morning; by noonday it has begun to flag; and in the evening his mind is bent only on returning to camp. A clever general therefore avoids an army when its spirit is keen, but attacks it when it is sluggish and inclined to return. This is the art of managing *ch'i*" (Sun Tzu, tr. Giles 1910, 66–67, modified).

This passage is one among many that point to the central place of psychological considerations in *The Art of War*. The ancient text repeatedly emphasizes the need to understand and control or manipulate mental/emotional states—both those of one's own troops and those of the enemy—to avoid defeat and achieve victory. Repeatedly, a particular situation is understood to elicit a specific emotional and behavioral response. Perhaps the most famous example is Sun Tzu's admonition not to interfere with an army returning home, and to leave an outlet rather than surrounding an army completely. "Do not press a desperate foe too hard" (Sun Tzu, tr. Giles 1910, 68–69). The implicit understanding, made explicit by Sun Tzu's commentators, is that a cornered enemy will fight with a primal savagery born of desperation and thus be dangerous to confront.

Psychology also comes to the fore in Sun Tzu's discussion of different terrains, a subject that receives considerable attention in *The Art of War*. Sometimes the significance of ground is seen only in terms of physical factors (as with the danger of being drawn into precipitous terrain where one can be easily ambushed), but often ground is classified and labeled according to psychological rather than topographical criteria. This is especially true in chapter 11 ("The Nine Situations"). The first of these situations, "dispersive ground" (*san ti*), is so called because soldiers are fighting in their home territory and thus (as Giles explains it), "being near to their homes and anxious to see their wives and children, are likely to seize the opportunity afforded by a battle and scatter in every direction" (Giles 1910, 114). Sun Tzu advises against battle on dispersive ground. At the other extreme, in terms of psychological effect, is what Giles translates as "desperate ground." The Chinese, *ssu ti*, literally means "dead ground," "deadly ground," or "fatal ground"; General Griffith translated it as "death ground." It is defined as "Ground on which we can only be saved from destruction by fighting at once" (Sun Tzu, tr. Giles 1910, 117). Such situations are not necessarily to be avoided, but actually offer potential advantage. In the same chapter Sun Tzu goes on to offer the following advice: "Throw your soldiers into positions where there is no escape, and they will prefer death to flight. If they will face death, there is nothing they may not achieve. Officers and men alike will put forth their uttermost strength." He continues, "Soldiers when in desperate straits lose the sense of fear. If there is no place of refuge, they will stand firm. . . . If there is no help for it, they will fight hard." And he comes back to the same idea near the end of the chapter: "Place your army in deadly peril, and it will survive, plunge it into desperate straits, and it will come off in safety. For it is precisely when a force has fallen into harm's way that it is capable of striking a blow for victory" (Sun Tzu, tr. Giles 1910, 125, 143–5).

This is the most clearly spelled-out example of one of the key concepts in *The Art of War* that a general can most effectively motivate his soldiers not by haranguing them and making demands, but by placing them in an objective situation that triggers the desired state of mind and behavioral response: "without waiting to be asked, they will do your will; without restrictions, they will be faithful; without giving orders, they can be trusted" (Sun Tzu, tr. Giles 1910, 126). It may also be considered as a concrete example of the application of *shih* (situational power) to achieve victory, as soldiers are placed in a situation that induces a psychological dynamic that acts as a tremendous force multiplier. Sun Tzu's discussion of "deadly ground" resonates with some of the key passages on *shih* in chapter 5: "The clever combatant looks to the effect of combined energy, and does not require too much from individuals. . . . When he utilizes combined energy, his fighting men become as it were like unto rolling logs or stones. For it is the nature of a log or stone to remain motionless on level ground, and to move when on a slope" (Sun Tzu, tr. Giles 1910, 41).

Before leaving the subject of psychology in *The Art of War,* it is important to note that its application is not limited to one's own troops and those of the enemy, but also extends to the mind of the general himself and the mind of his opponent. Sun Tzu advises both generals and rulers not to make military decisions on the basis of anger and other emotions, but according to a cold, rational calculus of anticipated gain or loss. Anger, along with several other emotions, is cited as one of the several faults of the general that is likely to bring about defeat. Conversely, efforts should be made to arouse just such feelings in one's opponent, so that he will make costly errors of judgment. Sun Tzu's advice to offer baits to the enemy to shape them to one's own advantage, and to force them to rush to defend that which they hold dear, also consists of a strong psychological component—the basic idea is to move the enemy, to set them up for defeat, by understanding their hopes, desires, and fears and then playing upon them to elicit the desired response. To a very considerable extent the tremendous emphasis given to intelligence and deception in *The Art of War* ultimately boils down to a mental contest between the two commanders, with the road to victory running through the misperceptions planted in the mind of one's opponent.

Despite the subtlety and sophistication of *The Art of War,* it is possible to question Sun Tzu's theory on some points. More than once we are told that if intelligence is gathered properly and analysis performed correctly, the outcome of any conflict is entirely predictable. In the first chapter, we are introduced to five analytical factors beginning with the "moral law," and Sun Tzu goes on to say, "These five heads should be familiar to every general: he who knows them will be victorious; he who knows them not will fail." At the end of the same chapter he claims, "I can foresee who will win or lose." And of course, "If you know the enemy and know yourself, you need not fear the result of a hundred battles" (Sun Tzu, tr. Giles 1910, 3, 8 modified, 24–25). This is a rather extreme claim, and one of the points where Sun Tzu's understanding of war differs quite dramatically from that of Clausewitz (who, although an advocate of rational calculation, was much more skeptical about the possibility of achieving certainty in war). Here Sun Tzu's claims regarding the super-competence of the general and particularly his ability to achieve absolute certainty through rational calculation would seem to be an instance of the rhetorical overkill encouraged by the competition of the so-called "Hundred Schools" of thought in ancient China. Certainly, it accords less well with what we know of the reality of warfare over most of recorded history (in both China and the West) than do Clausewitz's views on the subject.

Sun Tzu's emphasis on the sage-like qualities of the general is to a great extent justified by the depth and complexity of *The Art of War* and the frequent ambiguities and even contradictions that are found in the text. This is not a cookbook that provides the recipe for certain victory in several obvious, clear-cut steps; on the contrary, it requires something akin to genius to identify those portions of the text that are most directly relevant to a particular real-world military situation and then adapt and apply them successfully. The annals of Chinese military history are filled with stories of generals who thought they understood *The Art of War* going down to defeat because they failed to identify those aspects of Sun Tzu's teaching that were most salient to the immediate situation (as opposed to those that were relatively trivial).

With regard to any given real-world military situation, a number of different principles and recommendations from *The Art of War* may be found to apply—with some of them actually giving contradictory indications of the strategy to be followed. One of the best-known pearls of wisdom in *The Art of War* is that "There is no instance of a country having benefited from prolonged warfare" (Sun Tzu, tr. Giles 1910, 12). And in the 20th century, no East Asian political or military leader was more renowned as a student and practitioner of Sun Tzu's teachings than the late Mao Tse-Tung. Yet the title of one of Chairman Mao's most important military writings is *On Protracted War,* and Mao in fact waged protracted war for many years against Chiang Kai-shek's Nationalist government and against the Japanese invaders of China in the 1930s and 1940s. The Chinese Communist leader interpreted Sun Tzu's dictum on prolonged warfare in light of other passages in *The Art of War* that urged one to wait for the right opportunity, and in light of the overall real-world situation that he faced.

Ever since the middle of the third century BCE, Confucian thinkers have faulted Sun Tzu for his emphasis on deception and trickery. In his "Debating War" chapter, the philosopher Hsun Tzu attacked the ideas of the "Lord of Lin-wu" (apparently a surrogate for the author of *The Art of War*), maintaining that a virtuous ruler fighting a righteous war with the support of his people would necessarily triumph without any need to resort to underhanded schemes. Modern, western theorists such as Michael I. Handel have pointed to a different problem arising from Sun Tzu's emphasis on intelligence and deception: "Paradoxically, Sun Tzu's recommendation that deception be used whenever possible in essence contradicts his basic assumption that accurate intelligence can be gathered and used effectively" (Handel 1996, 146). Put another way, when two skilled practitioners of the Sunzian "art of war" match wits with one another, there arises the paradox of the unstoppable force encountering the immovable object.

Another weakness of *The Art of War,* especially in view of the claims that are made regarding the timelessness and universal validity of Sun Tzu's teachings, is that many of its recommendations are based on unarticulated assumptions specific to its time and place of origin. It is easy enough for modern readers to set aside the obviously antiquated elements of *The Art of War*—for example, that high dust clouds rising straight up betoken the arrival of chariots, whereas dust clouds low and spread out herald the approach of infantry—and abstract the general principle (in this case, that different sorts of signs signal the approach of different sorts of forces). It is much harder to recognize that many of Sun Tzu's psychological assumptions are rooted in the culture, society, and institutions of ancient China and may not necessarily hold true in other times and places. We should recall that Sun Tzu suggests that armies campaigning within their home countries are likely to disperse rather than fight, and that he repeatedly extols the advantages to be gained from placing soldiers in desperate situations where retreat is impossible. Such passages must be understood in light of conditions of the warring states period, when mass armies were made of poorly motivated peasant conscripts and ideological motivators such as modern nationalism were entirely absent.

Application: The earliest recorded example of the deliberate application of Sun Tzu's teachings in battle comes from 205 BCE, during the wars that led to the establishment of the Han dynasty, when a Han column under Han Hsin was confronted by the army of the state of Chao near the mouth of the Ching-hsing Pass. Despite the fact that he was commanding a relatively weak force, Han Hsin led his men out to challenge the strong deployment of the Chao army—even going so far as to line up his men with their backs to a river so that there was no hope of escape. This desperate position was actually the key to victory, spurring his otherwise indifferent soldiers on to heroic efforts. After the battle, Han Hsin paraphrased *The Art of War* to explain the victory to his subordinates: "Put your army into a desperate situation and it will come away safely; place it in peril and it will survive."

Sun Tzu's teachings continued to be the stock in trade of military commanders throughout the long history of imperial China. Li Shih-min (600–649), the second emperor of the T'ang dynasty and a key field commander in the civil wars that marked the transition to T'ang rule, employed the same winning formula in almost all of his campaigns during the years from 618 to 622. These included the Ch'ien-shui-yuan campaign against Hsueh Jen-kao (618), the He-tung campaign against Sung Chin-kang (619–620), and the encirclement of Loyang that culminated in the defeat and capture of Tou Chien-te at the decisive battle of the Hu-lao Pass (621). Occupying a strongly fortified camp, he would refuse to come out for a decisive engagement until his opponent had weakened or had made a mistake that gave him the opening he needed. As soon as the opportunity presented itself, he would strike immediately and with all of his strength. Li Shih-min is thought to have been thoroughly familiar with *The Art of War,* and his method certainly echoes Sun Tzu's recommendation that one make oneself impossible to defeat while awaiting the opportunity when it would be possible to defeat the enemy. Needless to say, the Tang leader did not passively wait for his chance but took active measures to bring about a shift in the balance of forces by raiding overextended supply lines or making feints and offering baits to lure his opponent into an unfavorable situation. These actions, too, were entirely in keeping with Sun Tzu's injunction that one should take steps to shape the enemy, and should only join battle when victory is assured. Once Li Shih-min committed his army to a decisive engagement, his maneuvers on the battlefield also followed Sun Tzu's dictum regarding the proper use of *cheng* and *ch'i* forces. As at Chieh-chou in 620 and at Loyang in 621, he would typically pin or distract his opponent by engaging him frontally with infantry units, then finish the engagement with a lightning cavalry thrust against flanks, rear, or whatever weak point had appeared in the enemy battle line.

Sun Tzu's ideal of winning without fighting was also occasionally realized in practice. For example, it has been plausibly suggested that the vast size of the armadas that the Ming admiral Cheng Ho led to Southeast Asia and the Indian Ocean in the early 15th century, involving hundreds of ships and tens of thousands of military personnel, was a deliberate attempt to awe local potentates into submission by a display of overwhelming force. If so, the strategy was largely successful, as Cheng Ho's soldiers found it necessary to bloody their swords only three times in the course of seven long voyages between 1405 and 1433. Winning without fighting, or at least with minimal fighting, could be achieved in China's recurrent civil wars through bribery and deal-making. Repeatedly, internal conflicts in China involved a "bandwagoning" process that saw generals defecting from one side to the other when the incentives were right. During the Northern expedition of 1926–1928, when the armed forces of the Chinese Nationalist Party (KMT) drove north from Canton in an effort to defeat the warlords and reunify the country, success was achieved largely by making deals with various warlords—leaving them in command of their old troops and territories and accepting them into the KMT. The Chinese Civil War of 1946–1949 saw the defection of very substantial formations from the Nationalists to the victorious Communists; these units were then incorporated into the Communists' People's Liberation Army (PLA) and redeployed against their erstwhile comrades. All of this was, of course, entirely in keeping with Sun Tzu's recommendation that enemy units should be taken intact and used to strengthen one's own forces.

The operational plans of the Chinese Communists also showed the imprint of *The Art of War*. An early example was the defeat of Chiang Kai-shek's First Encirclement Campaign against the Kiangsi Soviet Republic in 1930. Rather than confronting the advancing Nationalist columns head-on, the Communists leaders Mao Tse-Tung and Chu Te withdrew to concentrate their numerically inferior forces and lure their opponents on a reckless pursuit into unfamiliar territory. Communist units employed a variety of ruses to deceive their Nationalist pursuers, leaving hot meals half eaten and deliberately abandoning equipment by the wayside. The concentrated Communist forces ambushed and destroyed the overconfident 18th Division of the Nationalist army, and then turned to shatter the 50th Division. The Communists' conduct of the campaign was entirely in keeping with

Sun Tzu's teaching regarding deception, speed, maneuver, and the concentration of one's entire strength against a fraction of the enemy's. Nearly two decades later, the influence of Sun Tzu was apparent during the Huai Hai Campaign, the climactic engagement of the Chinese Civil War. Between early November 1948 and mid-January 1949, Communist forces led by Su Yü and Liu Po-ch'eng used their superior mobility to encircle one Nationalist army after another in the vicinity of Hsu-chou, forcing other Nationalist units to respond and expose themselves to encirclement and destruction in turn. The cascading Communist victory, which eventually encompassed the elimination of five Nationalist armies totaling some 500,000 men, is a classic example of the application of Sun Tzu's notion of "moving the enemy."

Descendents: It is no exaggeration to say that Sun Tzu's *Art of War* has left its mark on virtually all subsequent Chinese military writings. Although many military treatises would appear after *The Art of War,* none would have the same profundity and far-reaching impact and almost all would show the influence of Sun Tzu's ideas, in many cases incorporating direct quotes from the ancient classic. More than any other work, *The Art of War* came to be regarded by the Chinese as their single most profound and comprehensive statement on conduct of war.

The influence of *The Art of War* is already apparent in the *Liu T'ao,* a work probably dating from the third century BCE, which quotes or paraphrases Sun Tzu several times (though without attribution) on such matters as the value of the general to the state, the need to present a facade to the enemy that is the opposite of one's true condition, the desirability of striking suddenly and unexpectedly. The *Liu T'ao* also echoes *The Art of War* by pointing out that war is the greatest affair of the state, the road to survival or destruction. Sun Tzu's influence can also be seen in the *Military Methods* of Sun Pin, a work of roughly the same date as the *Liu T'ao* that disappeared from circulation after the Han dynasty and was then rediscovered by archaeologists in 1972 in the same Han tomb at Lin-i, Shantung. The tomb yielded the earliest extant copy of *The Art of War.* Sun Pin, himself a shadowy figure whose story most likely includes some fictional elements, was reputedly a descendent of Sun Tzu, and the work that bears his name develops many of the ideas broached in *The Art of War.* Key concepts such as "situational advantage" (*shih*) are discussed at length, as are the positive characteristics of the general that lead to victory and the negative characteristics that bring about defeat. A much later example of the influence of Sun Tzu is the *Dialogues of Li, Duke of Wei,* a book that purports to be a dialogue between T'ang T'ai-tsung (Li Shih-min, the second T'ang emperor) and one of his generals, Li Ching, but was probably actually the work of an unknown author writing several hundred years later in the five dynasties (907–960) or northern Sung (960–1126). The *Dialogues* is in fact an extended exploration of the concepts of *ch'i* and *cheng* that were first introduced in *The Art of War.*

In the late 11th century, during the northern Sung period, *The Art of War* was brought together by imperial command with six other military classics, including the *Liu T'ao* and the *Dialogues,* to form the *Seven Military Classics* collection intended to serve as the basic curriculum for men preparing for examinations that would qualify them for military rank and office. These works, and especially *The Art of War,* remained at the core of the military examinations in the Ming (1368–1644) and Ch'ing dynasties (1644–1912). After Chinese military writing took an encyclopedic turn beginning with the work of Li Ch'üan in the eighth century, *The Art of War* was also incorporated in its entirety into several massive military encyclopedias such as the *Wu-pei chih* compiled by Mao Yuan-i near the end of the Ming period.

Given the ambiguity of many of the passages in *The Art of War,* a substantial tradition of commentary developed around the core text as Chinese scholars undertook to offer explanation, interpretation, and historical examples. Eleven commentaries on Sun Tzu, ranging in from the second century CE to the time of the southern Sung dynasty (CE 1126–1279) have been especially influential in shaping modern understanding of the text. The earliest and most important of these commentaries was written by Ts'ao Ts'ao (CE 155–220), himself an outstanding general and statesman who dominated the Eastern Han court in its final years. (It took the archaeological discovery at Lin-i to lay to rest the suspicion that the extant 13 chapters of *The Art of War* might have been the product of Ts'ao Ts'ao's editorial work.) Other commentators were "Mr. Meng" (a scholar of uncertain date who may have lived in either the third century CE or the sixth); Li Ch'üan, the author of an eighth-century military encyclopedia, the *T'ai-pai yin-ching;* Tu Yu (735–812), who included extensive quotations from and comments on *The Art of War* in the military section of his encyclopedic history of the development of Chinese institutions, the *T'ung-tien;* Tu Mu (803–852), the famous poet and grandson of Tu Yu; Ch'en Hao (probably T'ang dynasty, dates uncertain); Chia Lin, a strategist of the late eighth century; and Mei Yao-ch'en (1002–1060), another poet; and three more Song scholars (Wang Hsi, Ho Yen-hsi, and Chang Yu) round out the list of 11.

In 20th-century China, the influence of *The Art of War* was especially marked in the military thought of the Chinese Communist leader Mao Tse-Tung (1893–1976). Mao's military writings of the Yenan period (1936–1946) are littered with quotations and concepts borrowed from the ancient military classic. In *Problems of Strategy in China's Revolutionary War* (1936), for example, Mao quotes Sun Tzu with regard to the projection of false appearances, the concentration of one's own forces against those of the enemy, and the value of careful study and analysis. He explains his policy of "strategic retreat" in Sunzian terms as "a planned strategic step taken by an inferior force for the purpose of conserving its strength and biding its time to defeat the enemy, when it finds itself confronted with a superior force whose offensive it is unable to smash quickly." And Mao is also at pains to point out that his own advocacy of protracted war against more powerful foes does not directly contradict Sun Tzu's preference for quick decision, but simply reflects the need to wait for the right conditions to achieve the desired result. *The Art of War* continues to shape the thinking of both military professionals and the general public in the People's Republic of China. New editions of Sun Tzu's work, including translations from the original classical Chinese into the more colloquial modern Chinese idiom, are constantly appearing in print, with many of them issued by publishing houses controlled by the armed forces.

Until quite recent times, knowledge of *The Art of War* outside of China itself was limited to East Asian countries within the sphere of Chinese cultural influence, especially those whose elites had adopted Chinese characters as their primary writing system. Sun Tzu's work was known in Japan by about 700 CE, but given the individualistic behavior of the samurai in battle, we may question how much influence it had on actual military practice before the 16th century, when the disciplined large-scale armies presupposed by Sun Tzu finally became the norm for the contending territorial lords (*daimyo*). *The Art of War* was studied by the modern Japanese military in the first half of the 20th century, and surely contributed to the penchant for surprise, speed, and maneuver (as demonstrated, for example, in the Malayan campaign of 1941–1942).

Sun Tzu was first brought to the attention of western readers through the French translation of the Jesuit missionary J.J.M. Amiot (Paris, 1772). It is sometimes asserted that this edition was read by the young Napoleon Bonaparte and influenced his approach to the conduct of war, though positive evidence for this would seem to be entirely lacking. The influence of Sun Tzu on western military thought becomes clear only in the 20th century. The first competent English translation, that of Lionel Giles (1910), was brought to the attention of the influential British military theorist Basil H. Liddell Hart in 1927. Liddell Hart would later characterize Sun Tzu's ideas as "the concentrated essence of wisdom on the conduct of war" (Griffith 1963, v). Sun Tzu's emphases on attacking weakness and winning without fighting seemed to offer an alternative to the bloody frontal attacks of World War I and contributed to Liddell Hart's formulation of the concept of the "indirect approach" (which is, not coincidentally, the way that Giles had chosen to translate *ch'i*). A later translation by Brigadier General Samuel B. Griffith, United States Marine Corps (USMC), helped to bring *The Art of War* to the attention of the U.S. military. By the early years of the 21st century Sun Tzu's ideas were invoked in various field manuals issued by the U.S. armed forces and were an object of study at military academies and staff colleges throughout the world. *The Art of War* has also attracted a large nonprofessional readership in many countries, and numerous books have appeared in recent years that seek to apply Sun Tzu's teaching to business, management, and virtually every other sphere of human experience that involves strife and competition.

See also: Li Ching; Li Ch'üan; Liddell Hart; Mao Tse-Tung

Further Reading

Handel, Michael I., *Masters of War: Classical Strategic Thought.* 2nd ed. London: Frank Cass, 1996.

Johnston, Alastair Iain, *Cultural Realism: Strategic Culture and Grand Strategy in Chinese History.* Princeton, NJ: Princeton University Press, 1995.

Meyer, Andrew, and Andrew Wilson. "Sunzi Bingfa as History and Theory." In Bradford
    A. Lee, ed. *Strategic Logic and Political Rationality: Essays in Honor of Michael I.
    Handel.* London: Frank Cass, 2003, pp. 99–118.

O'Dowd, Edward, and Arthur Waldron. "Sun Tzu for Strategists." *Comparative Strategy*
    10 (1991): 25–36.

Sawyer, Ralph D., *The Seven Military Classics of Ancient China.* Boulder, Colorado: West-
    view Press, 1993.

Ssu-ma Ch'ien, *The Grand Scribe's Records,* vol. 7: *The Memoirs of Pre-Han China.* Trans.
    William H. Nienhauser. Bloomington: Indiana University Press, 1994.

Sun Pin, *Sun Pin: The Art of Warfare.* Trans. D.C. Lau and Roger T. Ames. New York:
    Ballantine Books, 1996.

Sun Tzu, *The Art of War.* Trans. Samuel B. Griffith. Oxford and New York: Oxford Uni-
    versity Press, 1963.

Sun Tzu, *Sun Tzu on the Art of War.* Trans. Lionel Giles. London: Luzac and Company,
    1910.

David A. Graff

Thucydides, Son of Oloros, Strategos
(ca. 460–ca. 400 BCE)

Significance: The historian of the Peloponnesian War introduced a fact-oriented depiction of war. He analyses power rivalry, and emphasizes the interplay between rationality and irrationality.

Context: After Greece repelled the Persian invasion, monarchical Sparta and democratic Athens vied for hegemony. Between 431 and 404 BCE, the contest erupted into war. Thucydides was the first to depict the events as a cohesive era (*syngraphē*). The warfare was increasingly ideological, and involved quick strategic changes, unusual brutality, and exhaustion of resources.

Biography: Thucydides probably came for a rich Thracian family that immigrated to Athens. He identified with Athens, if with critical overtones. Eventually, the Athenian *ecclesia* elected him "strategos" (highest officer rank, comparable to general), but he suffered banishment for failure and, like Herodotus, spent the rest of the war with Sparta as an independent observer. From this material emerged his *(History of the) Peloponnesian War.*

Influences: In spite of early philosophy's interest in war and its symbolism (Heraclitus: "War is the father and king of all."), Homer's epics dominated the perception of wars before Thucydides. Even Herodotus limits himself to poem-like lists, and uses myths and divine wrath to explain motives and events. He saw politicians not as individuals, but as representatives of general traits. Thucydides considers Herodotus as gullible and superficial, yet he inherited his predecessor's methodology: the collection of testimonies and personal impressions (see 1, 22), and the aspiration to render the facts credibly, instructively, and aesthetically.

The Theory: Thucydides composed numerous speeches, based on real speeches and events, to represent the strategies and tactical considerations of the belligerents. Although he avoids direct judgments, he favored the Periclean strategy for the Athenians (a land defense with naval supply lines and offensive marine expeditions against Spartan allies) (1, 141–145).

Thucydides was the first in the western tradition to differentiate between a publicly avowed reason for a war (*aitia*), and the actual cause (*prophasis*) (1, 23, 5–6). However, he also indulges in propaganda, claiming moral and cultural superiority for Athens (1, 73–79 and the funeral oration of Pericles, book 2).

Thucydides describes changing policies and actors and deplores strategic offensives of no more than psychological value—such as the effort to conquer Sicily (2, 65). He observes radicalization and violence that prepares the way for the "Pathology of War" (3, 82–84): an ideological war between two parties with different types of government resulting in fanaticism, the persecution of internal sceptics, and the attempt to export political revolution. Civic virtues are reevaluated and inverted, and the negative drives that Thucydides considers dominant in humankind take precedence: fear, ambition, recklessness, greed, and a zest for crimes. Savage or evil actors gain the advantage. The pestilence that rages without warning and is no respecter of persons symbolizes irrational behavior. Thucydides hopes to "immunize" his readers through his information (2, 47–54). He fails to explain, however, why far-sighted politicians such as Pericles start wars. He does mention, though, that leaders sometimes prevent peace for purely selfish reasons (5, 16. 26).

The Melian Dialogue (5, 84–116) is even more pessimistic. In a fictitious exchange between neutral Melos and Athenian messengers, who want to secure the island, the Athenians dismiss Greek values—ancestry, laws and treaties, respect for the Gods—as irrelevant: "The strong do what they can while the weak suffer what they must" (5, 89). In fact, "for of the gods we assume and of men we know that the whole of their nature urges them to rule wherever they may" (5, 105). Those who avoid political amorality are "unreasonable" (5, 111) and deserve death. Melos surrenders and is depopulated.

It is unclear how far Thucydides identifies with this logic. However, he then describes the unprovoked Athenian attempt to conquer Sicily—an effort fuelled by pride, greed, and a yearning for adventures (6, 24; 30–32). Unnecessary risks, arrogance, problems with supplies, and inept leaders destroy the expedition (7, 87).

Application: Thucydides was fundamental to all of later European (military) history. His assumption of the immutability of human nature allowed predictions of military actions and guided strategy.

Descendents: Thucydides influenced later Greek historiography. His conservatism and pessimism also made him the model for Tacitus. Machiavelli used him to waive moral restrictions on policy and warfare. Morgenthau saw Thycidides as the father of political realism. Mahan focused on his naval doctrine. Thucydides's speech on the fallen (2, 25–46) has become the parent text of countless rhetorical efforts in times of war (Churchill) as well as for the praise of (modern) democracy. The Melian Dialogue still inspires antiwar campaigns.

See also: Machiavelli

Further Reading
Cawkwell, G., *Thucydides and the Peloponnesian War.* London: Routledge, 1997.
Price, J. J., *Thucydides and Internal War.* Cambridge: Cambridge University Press, 2001.

Dietmar Herz

Timur, Amir (or Tamerlane or Timur the Lame)
(April 8, 1336 CE to February 14, 1405 CE)

Significance: Amir Timur's autobiography, entitled *Malfuzat-i-Timuri,* describes the battles he fought against the Delhi Sultanate. Some scholars doubt the authenticity of Timur's autobiography, but whether Timur wrote it himself or not, the book gives some idea of contemporary war. At the strategic level, Timur implemented deep-penetration attack by fast moving cavalry and at the tactical level, he created the *taulqama* charge. The Delhi Sultanate never recovered from its defeat by Timur. Its fragmentation enabled Babur to invade India in the first half of the 16th century CE.

Context: After the death of Firuz Tughluq in 1388, the Delhi Sultanate weakened. South and central India had already been lost before Firuz's accession to the throne in 1351, but now the Delhi Sultanate's hold over north India started collapsing. In 1394, an independent kingdom emerged at Jaunpur, which threatened the sultanate's control of the Ganga–Jamuna *doab* (the fertile region in north India between Rivers Ganga and Jamuna). Malwa and Gujarat, the two provinces of the sultanate, became independent of Delhi's control. After the death of Firuz, the *iqtas* (military governorships) became hereditary. Firuz's army numbered 90,000 cavalry and 480 elephants, but after his death, the size of the Delhi Sultanate army also shrunk.

Between 1382 and 1405, Timur rampaged with his army across Eurasia, operating in places as far apart as Moscow, Tien Shan Mountain and Anatolia. Timur considered attacking either China or India, and finally took the decision to attack India, even though his *maliks* (military chiefs) disliked operating in the region's hot climate. Timur argued forcefully that this expedition would be a *jihad* (holy war) directed against the infidels (Hindus) of Hindustan. In reality, Timur was interested in acquiring riches from the weak Delhi Sultanate.

In December 1398, Timur led a plundering expedition into the heart of north India against the Delhi Sultanate. When Timur arrived at the scene, the fate of the sultanate's Tughluq dynasty was sealed. After Timur's departure, the Tughluq dynasty was replaced by the Sayyid dynasty.

Biography: Timur's family belonged to the Gorgan branch of the Turko-Mongol Barlas tribe. Timur's father Amir Turghay was the governor of Kash in Transoxiana. Timur was born near Samarkhand, probably in 1320. In 1336, Timur was wounded by an arrow and became permanently lame. In 1370, he became the ruler of Balkh. Between 1392 and 1397, Timur took the regions around the Caspian Sea, which included Fars, Armenia, Georgia, Mesopotamia, and South Russia, from the Golden Horde Mongols. Timur was not interested in establishing a centralized administrative fabric over these territories. Each victory raised his prestige and he gathered booty for his army from the treasuries of the defeated kingdoms. The most important tax from the newly subjugated areas was *mal-i-aman* (ransom money). It was actually tribute from the defeated people.

In 1628, Abu Talib Husaini, a historian in the court of *Padshah* Shah Jahan, translated *Tuzuk-i-Timuri,* originally written in Turki, into Persian as *Malfuzat-i-Timuri.* Timur's autobiography recorded his life story from the ages of 7 to 74.

Influences: Timur's military system was a product of the Turko-Mongol culture. Like Chingiz Khan's Mongol army, Timur's army was organized on the basis of *tumens* (divisions). The theoretical strength of each *tumen* was 10,000 soldiers, and Timur had more than 13 *tumens.* The troops were equipped by the *amirs* who led them. The officers in charge of conscription (*tovachis*) were charged with overseeing the *amirs* and the governors of the provinces who were under the obligation of supplying the required number of soldiers with proper equipment. Each of his *tumen* was further subdivided into *kushunats* (regiments of 1,000 soldiers) and each *kushunat* had a separate commander.

The Ilkhanid Mongol Empire of Persia resorted to *cherik* (conscription or military levy). Conscription was calculated at one soldier for every nine households for the settled population, whereas among the nomads all adult males were expected to serve. Timur adopted this *cherik* system. His *cherik* troops were commanded by the *darughas* who were appointed in the cities and towns of conquered regions. In Timur's military system, the office of commander in chief was known as *amir-ul-umara.* Cheku Barlas, who also commanded the Qaraunas (a particular Turkik tribe favored by Timur) troops, held this office. Below him came the *amirs* and below them were the *bahadurs.*

The Theory: Timur's *institutes* laid down an order of battle based on Central Asian practices, and followed for battlefield deployment by the Mughal army from the mid-16th century. The army was divided into a vanguard, right wing, left wing, center, and rear guard. The rear guard was used as a tactical reserve either for supporting the wings or for delivering an outflanking charge. The center was the strongest contingent and was flanked by two detachments both at the right and left sides. Special contingents of horse archers for outmaneuvering and outflanking the enemy's flanks and rear were stationed both at the right and left wings. They were known as *taulqama* (turning) parties. In addition there was the *Qarawal* (scouts and skirmishers). It was a mobile force posted in front of the van. The *Qarawal* conducted limited advance and tactical withdrawal to confuse the enemy.

Timur also developed a self-contained advance guard, which functioned as a deep-penetration force designed to harass the enemy and evaluate enemy resistance. Timur's main army advanced behind his dedicated deep-penetration force.

Tactically, he developed the *taulqama* technique, which involved simultaneous attacks on the enemy's flank and the rear with horse archers.

Application: Before attacking India, Timur took pains in accumulating information regarding the physical geography of the subcontinent and the military strength of his adversary. Timur noted that a successful campaign against the Delhi Sultanate would require crossing the big rivers such as Indus and Ganges. He observed that these rivers could only be crossed with bridges made of boats. Beyond these barriers, the military strength of the Delhi Sultanate was centered on the elephants clad in mail armor. These elephants were trained to lift riders from horses with their trunks, throwing them to the ground and crushing them. Timur concluded that 100,000 Tatar horsemen would be adequate for defeating the sultanate.

In late 1396, Timur's grandson Pir Muhammad captured Uch and Dipalpur in Punjab with the advance guard. Next, Pir Muhammad laid siege to Multan. In March 1398, Timur started with the main body from Samarkhand. In September 1398, Timur crossed the Indus. Pir Muhammad and Timur joined their forces at Multan, and advanced on Delhi. Outside Delhi, Sultan Mahmud Shah deployed 10,000 cavalry (of them 4,000 armored), 40,000 infantry, and 125 armored elephants. Timur's army was divided into right and left wings, center, advance guard, and the reserve. Timur himself commanded the center.

While Timur's advance guard attacked the front of the sultanate army, mounted archers from the right and left wings launched a *taulqama* charge. As a result, the left and right wings of the sultanate army disintegrated. Meanwhile, the Indian center was advancing against Timur's center with elephants. Atop these elephants were big *howdahs* from which the sharpshooters flung fireworks on Timur's troops. Timur placed some camels loaded with dry grass in front of the elephants and then set the dry grass on fire, scaring and turning the elephants. Timur strengthened his own center with the royal guards drawn from the reserve and his horse archers shot at the *mahouts* (drivers) of the elephants. As the sultanate army disintegrated, Mahmud fled and Timur entered Delhi. For three days, his soldiers sacked Delhi and massacred both Hindus and Muslims. Timur then rampaged east of Delhi in the direction of Meerut. When he left India on March 3, 1399, Timur took with him large number of artisans, masons, and builders from India to rebuild Samarkhand.

Descendents: After defeat at the Battle of Delhi (October 7, 1556) at the hand of Hindu warlord Hemu, the Mughals revamped their battle order. The Mughals came up with *harawal-i-manqula,* a fast-moving contingent that operated as the long-distance advance guard. The best soldiers were put in it and it was sent for deep strikes inside enemy territory. This was clearly based on Timur's advance guard. A deep-penetration raid by the *harawal-i-manqula* was able to capture Hemu's artillery just before the Second Battle of Panipat in 1556. The Mughals also used Timur's system of subdividing his army into a vanguard, right wing, left wing, center, and rear guard.

Timur's autobiography encouraged his distant descendents such as Zahiruddin Babur and Jahangir to write their own autobiographies.

See also: Babur; Fazl, Abul

Further Reading

The History of India as Told by Its Own Historians: The Muhammadan Period, ed. From the Posthumous Papers of H. M. Elliot, by John Dawson, vol. 3. 4th ed. New Delhi: D. K. Publishers, 2001.

Manz, Beatrice, Forbes, *The Rise and Rule of Tamerlane.* 3rd ed. Canto: Cambridge, 1999.

Kaushik Roy

Tran Hung Dao
(1228?-1300)

Significance and Biography: Tran Hung Dao was a prince of the Tran dynasty. Between 1285 and 1288, he commanded the Vietnamese army in its successful resistance against two Mongol invasions by the Yuan dynasty. He relied on three strategies that have characterized Vietnamese resistance to foreign invasions: mobilizing the nation through appeal to patriotic sentiments, choosing ground to fight on that neutralized the enemy's strengths, and wearing opponents down through guerilla warfare.

The Theory: He is presumed to have written the famous 1285 proclamation, *A Call to the Officers and Soldiers of the Army,* for distribution to the army. It urges resistance by dramatically contrasting life under foreign rule with that of indigenous rule, and praising examples of loyal subjects and devoted soldiers in times of adversity. The second work attributed to Tran Hung Dao is an instruction manual entitled *The Essentials of the Military Arts,* which drew on Chinese classics familiar to the Viet literate elite and Viet historical tactics.

Application: The strategies advocated in this book worked against the Mongols. Battle on open plains was avoided where possible in preference for fighting in rugged and forested terrain or on the water where the Mongol strength in cavalry was negated. In 1285, the Tran kingdom of Dai-Viet (modern North Vietnam) refused the Mongol Yuan army transit through their territory to attack Champa. This led to a Mongol invasion under crown prince Toghan. Rather than risk total defeat by head-on resistance, Tran Hung Dao concentrated on moving the court around the country to evade Mongol capture and denying supplies to their pursuers by burning crops. After the Mongols were worn down by tropical diseases and overextended supply lines, Tran Hung Dao went onto the offensive, seeking battles on or near water to counter the Mongol cavalry. After a Mongol army was ambushed and defeated in the south, the Mongols withdrew to China.

Prince Toghan invaded again in 1287 by land and sea. The Mongols easily defeated Dai Viet forces stationed along the border and advanced on the Tran capital Thang Long (i.e., Hanoi). The Viet did not contest the capital, but rather struck at the Mongols' exposed communications. The remnants of the defeated border force ambushed and captured the Mongol supply fleet, and Tran Hung Dao's main army recaptured territory in the Mongol rear. As the Mongols advanced south, they gained two victories on land, but were defeated at sea. Constant Viet guerilla warfare caused Mongol casualties to mount. Eventually, Toghan decided to withdraw. He successfully led the land force back to China after fending off an ambush and then dividing the army to complicate pursuit. Meanwhile, Tran Hung Dao totally destroyed the Mongol fleet after using a faked retreat by small vessels to lure the Mongols into a trap set in the Bach Dang River, a branch of the Red River Delta. For months beforehand, Tran Hung Dao had planted huge steel-tipped wooden stakes below the high tide mark. As the tide receded, the Mongol fleet was embedded on the stakes and wiped out.

Prince Hung Dao was never defeated in battle and remains one of only two commanders ever to defeat the Mongols. Although the invasions failed, the threat of renewed Mongol invasion only ended when Viet rulers sent a tribute-bearing embassy to Peking to reaffirm their submission to the Yuan emperor.

See also: Giap, Vo Nguyen; Southeast Asian Naval Warfare; Sun Tzu; Thai Military Culture (Ramathibodi II)

Further Reading

Nguyen Khac Vien, *Vietnam: A Long History.* Hanoi: Foreign Languages Publishing House, 1987.

Truong Buu Lam, *Patterns of Vietnamese Response to Foreign Intervention: 1858–1900.* Detriot, MI: Monograph Series No. 11, Southeast Asia Studies, Yale University, 1967.

Paul D'Arcy

Usama Ibn Munqidh
(1095–ca. 1185 CE)

Significance: Usama Ibn Murshid Ibn 'Ali Ibn Munqidh is one of the best known medieval Arab-Islamic writers on military matters, though none of his works were intended as military or political manuals.

Context: Usama was a member of the Banu Munqidh Arab clan, which was itself of Bedouin origin and formed part of the Banu Kinana tribe of the Banu Kalb tribal confederation. The Banu Munqidh was prominent in Syria and to a lesser extent Egypt in the 11th and 12th centuries, also ruling a tiny principality centered upon the central Syrian town of Shayzar from 1081 to 1157 CE. Most of its leading members were then wiped out in an earthquake.

Biography: Usama Ibn Murshid was born in 1095 CE, into a ruling family whose military power rested upon their numerous kinsmen, related Arab clans and the urban population of Shayzar. Having been absent from Shayzar at the time of the earthquake, Usama Ibn Munqidh went on to serve various dynasties as a soldier, officer, and diplomat, occasionally getting involved in the tangled politics of the time. Usama was, however, retired and elderly when he was summoned to join Saladin's entourage in 1174 CE. Several years later he fell from favor and was virtually exiled to Hisn Kayfa, overlooking the River Tigris in what is now southeastern Turkey. It was here that he completed most of his poetry and prose.

Influences: The Banu Munqidh enlisted small numbers of Kurdish or other mercenaries and slave-recruited Turkish *mamluk* élite soldiers. Their foes ranged from fellow Muslims, invading Christian Crusaders and Byzantines, to Isma'ili Shi'a Muslim "hashishin" or "assassins."

The Theory: Usamah Ibn Munqidh's most famous book, *Kitab al-I'tibar* "The Book of Learning by Example," is sometimes described as his memoirs but the main purpose of its anecdotes was to illustrate the inevitability of fate. With perhaps one exception, the military anecdotes were not intended as military instruction, though most are found in a section entitled "Wonders of Warfare against Muslims and Franks." Others were included in the lost first chapters of the *Kitab al-I'tibar,* a few lines of which survive as quotations by later writers. Comparable military anecdotes were included in Usama's *Lubab al-Adab* or "Kernels of Refinement" and *Kitab al-'Asa* or "Book of the Staff."

Application and Descendents: According to some sources Saladin often consulted the old warrior on matters of warfare and gentlemanly conduct. Usama Ibn Munqidh's subsequent impact within his own cultural context was that of a superb writer, famous for his style and skill in verse and prose, rather than for the contents of his works, military or otherwise.

See also: Al-Shaybani; Al-Tarsusi, Mardi bin Ali; Baghdadi Manjaniqi, Ya'qūb Ibn Ṣābir; Ibn Akhi Hizam, Muhammad Ibn Ya'qub al-Khuttali

David Nicolle and Shihab al-Sarraf

Valturio, Roberto
(1405–1475)

Significance: Art influenced all forms of intellectual discourse in Renaissance Europe, including the depiction of military technology. Several men, described by modern historians as "courtly engineers," utilized the innovations in art to depict military technology, sometimes simply as an intellectual exercise and sometimes to gain employment. Among these depictions are "state-of-the-art" military technology, including gunpowder weapons, although, as often, fantastical weapons are displayed. Perhaps the most popular of these courtly engineers was the Italian, Roberto Valturio. His work, *De re militari* (Concerning Military Matters), composed in 1455, was copied at least 22 times as a manuscript and was printed both in Latin and Italian before 1500.

Context: By the time Valturio wrote *De re militari,* gunpowder weapons had been used in European conflict for more than a century. However, to many they remained a poorly understood novelty, even as military engineers were making rapid improvements in the chemistry of the gunpowder and metallurgy of the actual weapons. Rulers and generals knew that for their armies to be successful they needed to keep up with these innovations and to, if possible, foresee future developments in technology to wage their own wars and defend against others. These included personal arms and armor (including hand-held gunpowder weapons), artillery and other siege weapons, fortifications, ships, and logistical technologies.

Biography: Valturio was born in Rimini in 1405, the son of Cicco di Jacopo de' Valturii, where he lived until 1438, when he moved to Rome. In Rimini he was well educated, especially in Greek and Latin. This undoubtedly prepared him to serve as apostolic secretary to Pope Eugene IV, a position he filled until sometime around the pope's death in 1447. He returned to Rimini and entered the employment of its *podestà,* Sigismondo Pandolfo Malatesta, as his private secretary. Although it appears that Valturio had no specific military responsibilities before, sometime between 1455 and 1460 he wrote the *Elenchus et index rerum militaria* (A List and Index of Military Matters), apparently at Sigismondo's behest. Known from the very beginning as *De re militari,* a title borrowed from Vegetius's famous late Roman work, it became immediately popular. Copies of the manuscript were sent to Louis XI, king of France, Francesco Sforza, Duke of Milan, and Lorenzo de' Medici, leader of Florence. It also became the first courtly engineering manual to be published, in 1472 in Latin, with an Italian translation following in 1483. A French version was printed in 1532. Undoubtedly, Valturio knew of this success when he died in 1475, still associated with the Malatesta court in Rimini.

Influences: Valturio seems to have known of and had access to the courtly engineering works of Guido da Vigevano, Conrad Kyeser, and Taccola, as their influences can be seen in a number of the *De re militari's* illustrations. How these books were acquired has not been determined, although they may have been in Malatesta's library, which was renowned for the number and quality of its books.

The Theory: Heavily illustrated, Valturio's colorful drawings appeared as 82 woodcuts in the published work, attributed to Veronese artist, Matteo de' Pasti. It is for these drawings, more than for the text, that this book is valuable. In an age when military technology was rapidly changing, the works of courtly engineers were important in tracking and publicizing innovations. Valturio accurately depicts many new technologies, as well as some older ones. However, like other courtly engineers, he also sometimes ventures into the fantastical, depicting machines that could not possibly have been constructed.

Application: That Malatesta sent copies of this text to several other important European leaders suggests that he was very impressed with Valturio's work. But, it cannot be ascertained whether he, or any of the others who possessed the *De re militari,* built Valturio's machines or put into practice any of his other military ideas.

Descendents: The *De re militari* became very influential in Europe during the late 15th and early 16th century, perhaps the most influential of any courtly engineering text. Among others, Leonardo da Vinci used it in compiling his notebooks of drawings on military technology, and Machiavelli used it in composing his military manual, *Dell'arte della Guerra* (The Art of War), which appeared in 1520.

See also: il Taccola; Kyeser, Conrad; Machiavelli; Martini, Francesco di Giorgio; Vinci, Leonardo da

Further Reading
Gille, Bertrand, *Les ingénieurs de la Renaissance.* Paris: Hermann, 1964.
Rodakiewicz, E., "The *editio princeps* of Valturio's *De re militari* in Relation to the Dresden and Munich mss.," *Maso Finiguerra,* 5 (1940), 14–82.
Valturio, Roberto, *Elenchus et index rerum militarium (De re militari).* Verona, 1472 [with several later Latin editions and translations following].

Kelly DeVries

Yi Sunshin
(1545–1598)

Context: The *Imjin Waeran War* between Korea and Japan (1592–1598).

Significance: Yi Sunshin designed and developed the first armored warship at the end of the 16th century.

Biography: From 1592, Yi Sunshin, "naval commander of the three provinces" turned the few Korean ships into an efficient military tool based on the use of artillery and maneuver. He designed the first modern armored warship.

Influences: Unknown.

The Theory: The "turtle-ship" was made in the shape of a turtle, with a dragon-shaped forehead able to made smoke, heavy guns, and armored desk. The turtle-ship

was impossible to aboard from another ship because his roof was closed and protected by sharpened heads. Turtle had both a little sail, and oars, allowing the ship
to engage his opponents.

Application and Descendents: The turtle-ships were used mainly as the spearhead
of the Korean squadrons, to make the main shock against the Japanese vessels.
Though used in the 16th century, some scholars wanted to build again turtle-ships
to repel foreign invasions in the second half of the 19th century (1866–1871).

Further Reading

Nanjung ilgi. War Diary of Admiral Yi Sun-Sin, transl. by Ha Tae-hung; ed. by Sohn Pow-
key. Seoul: Yonsei Univ. Press, 1977.

Laurent Quisefit

II

Politics and Grand
Strategic Theory

The writers in this section were attempting to create works that would allow for the combination of political goals with the strategic possibilities of the military force available. This again does not preclude mentioning tactical necessities, but the focus remains more that of the "operation" of armies, as seen in the work of **Cauis Mauris.**

Barrin, Rolland-Michel, Marquis de La Galissonière
(1693–1756)

Significance: La Galissonière's persuasive argument for defending France's American empire against British and Anglo-American expansion was the rationale behind the Marquis de Duquesne's seizure of the Forks of the Ohio. This, in turn, became the cause of the French and Indian War.

Context: In the aftermath of the War of the Austrian Succession, the French crown was undecided as to the wisdom of holding on to its North American empire. New France had never been particularly profitable and the expense of defending it had become a drain on the treasury. Britain's naval supremacy and the spectacular population growth of its American colonies, moreover, had convinced many that the fate of Canada and Louisiana was a foregone conclusion. La Galissonière's "Memoir" challenged this and set Britain and France on a collision course in North America.

Biography: Born in 1693 to an important naval family, Galissonière became a midshipman in 1710 and reached the rank of captain in 1738. During the War of the Austrian Succession, he commanded several ships and superintended coastal defenses. In 1747, La Galissonière was made "commandant general" or acting governor of New France. He arrived in Quebec knowing little about the country, but immediately set out to learn what he could. What he discovered was not encouraging: Nearly bankrupt from three years of war, the colony was under a virtual blockade by the British fleet. Worse, it was clear that the Americans intended to push the French out of Canada entirely. Galissonière, nevertheless, set out to strengthen the embattled colony. He sent a steady stream of requests to Paris for troops, munitions, and funds. France was in dire financial straits as well just then, and the minister of marine turned these down. He had little enough for the navy, let alone support Canada. Galissonière did what he could but, faced with official indifference, he asked for a replacement in 1749. His concern for the colony, however, remained and, in December 1750, he made his case for holding France's North American empire.

The Theory: La Galissonière began with the assertion that the honor of France and the preservation of the Catholic religion required it. He continued with more practical arguments: New France, he said would inevitably become a valuable region, "an immense country, a numerous people, fertile lands, forests of mulberry trees, mines already discovered, etc." Even if it did not, he continued, "We ask if a country can be abandoned, no matter how bad it may be, or what the amount of expense necessary to sustain it, when by its position it affords a great advantage over its neighbors." Canada, he wrote, "constitutes . . . the strongest barrier that can be opposed to the ambition of the English. . . . it alone is in a position to wage war against them in all [Britain's] possessions on the Continent of America; . . . whose power is daily increasing, and which, if means be not found to prevent it, will soon absorb not only all the Colonies located in the neighboring islands of the Tropic, but even all those of the Continent of America." France, with its wealth committed to its vast land army, could never match British sea power. Given this, Canada was the only barrier to British expansion. If it was removed from the equation, North America, Mexico, and the French Caribbean would inevitably fall and, with them, the balance of power in Europe as well.

Application: It was not a particularly new argument, but it became French policy in the early 1750s. Based upon La Galissonière's warning, the French would build Forts Presque Ile, Le Boeuf, and Duquesne to bar Anglo-American expansion into the Ohio Valley. The British would counter with General Edward Braddock's expedition, triggering the Seven Years' War and the beginning of the Age of Revolution.

Further Reading

Eccles, William J., *The Canadian Frontier, 1534–1760.* Albuquerque: University of New Mexico Press, 1983.

Groulx, Lionel, *Roland-Michel Barrin de la Galissonniere: 1693–1756.* Toronto: University of Toronto Press, 1970.

White, Richard, *The Middle Ground: Indians, Empires, and Republics in the Great Lakes Region, 1650–1815.* Cambridge: Cambridge University Press, 1991.

Claiborne Skinner

Caesar, Gaius Julius
(100–44 BC)

Significance: Caesar was one of the great practitioners of Roman style warfare, and made original, if illegal, use of Roman arms in the conquest of Gaul.

Context: His *Commentaries* on the Gallic Wars and the Roman Civil Wars set the standard for writing about military operations as well as self-promotion.

Biography: After Alexander the Great, Julius Caesar was perhaps the greatest of all the ancient Western military commanders and rulers. Coming from a privileged youth he immediately began a long and well-known military career, serving first under Marius and Sulla. Later he had independent commands as consul in Gaul, which he conquered with ruthless efficiency. His quest for power brought him into conflict with Rome's other leading citizen, Pompey, which resulted in a protracted civil war. The winner, Caesar quickly made himself dictator and set the stage for the end of the republic. Having frightened the old Senatorial elite with his power, he was assassinated in 44 BC.

Influences: Caesar was a product of the Roman military reforms of Gaius Marius and the Roman emphasis on political honor as derived from military success.

The Theory: Although Caesar does not forward any specific tactical or strategic formulas, his *Commentaries* reflect the brilliance of mind of a general that made dynamic use of the Roman military machine.

Application: In both the Gallic and Civil War campaigns the reader sees Caesar as the practitioner of maneuver warfare, maximizing the marching and fighting abilities of his legions. He can also be seen as the advocate of what might be called "total war," engaging his enemies with ruthlessness.

Descendents: The *Commentaries* influence the rest of the Roman ancient world and readers in the Western world to the present.

See also: Constantine, "the Great" (Flavius Valerius Aurelius Constantinus Augustus)

Further Reading
Fuller, J.F.C., *Julius Caesar: Man, Soldier, and Tyrant.* New Brunswick, NJ: Rutgers University Press, 1965.
Grant, Michael, *Julius Caesar.* New York: McGraw-Hill, 1969.

John Serrati

Carnot, Comte Lazare Nicolas Marguerite
(1753–1823)

Significance: As the military expert of the Committee of Public Safety, Carnot organized the 14 armies of the French Republic against the invading forces of the First Coalition in 1793. The recruitment was based on universal conscription (*levée en masse*), which enabled the French to build up mass armies. In operational terms, Carnot supported the annihilation of the opposing armies. His organizational skills awarded him the honorary title *Organisateur de la Victoire* (Organizer of the Victory).

Biography: Descending from the French gentry, Carnot entered the army as an officer in the engineer corps. After 1789, he became fascinated by the new political ideas and made a quick career. In 1793, he was appointed military expert of the Committee of Public Safety. He opposed the most radical movements under Robespierre and also remained reserved toward Napoleon. Only in the latter days of Napoleon's reign was Carnot entrusted with a military command, and he became minister of the interior during the Hundred Days reign. The Restoration exiled him after 1815. His ashes were transferred to the Panthéon in 1889.

Influences: Carnot was influenced by the ideas of the French Revolution on citizenship, and by the rich military tradition of 18th-century France.

The Theory: The total destruction of the enemy was pivotal in Carnot's military thinking. A mass mobilization of the male population as well as quick and decisive military victories would lead to success. He advised the French commanders to reduce the manning of fortresses and use the saved men for active operations (economy of force). In battle, the probing attacks on a broad front (deception) were followed by forceful attacks (surprise and concentration of force) and should allow the French armies to encircle the enemy with a swift pincer movement (speed and momentum). The routed opponent had to be pursued relentlessly. According to Carnot, this approach would bring the annihilation of the enemy.

Application: Carnot's operational theory proved successful in Belgium in 1794 and partly in Germany in 1796. However, these exploits were somewhat flawed by Carnot himself as he often counteracted his own principles. For example, he tried to influence directly the decisions of his generals from Paris although in theory he advocated freedom of action for subordinates. Furthermore, he violated his principle of concentration of force by deploying two separate armies in the campaigns, always eager to encircle the enemy by a pincer movement.

Descendents: Carnot laid the organizational foundations for mass armies on which Napoleon could build his later victories. He emphasized the role of science in modern warfare and was responsible for the foundation of the *polytechniques.*

See also: Bonaparte, Napoleon; Clausewitz, C.; Frederick II ("the Great"); Guibert, J.; Jomini; Le Tellier; Picq

Further Reading

Reinhard, Marcel, *Le Grand Carnot: Lazare Carnot. 1753–1823.* Paris: Hachette, 1994.

Telp, Claus, *The Evolution of Operational Art. 1740–1813.* London and New York: Frank Cass 2005.

Peter Lieb

Constantine, "the Great" (Flavius Valerius Aurelius Constantinus Augustus)
(272–327 AD)

Significance: Although best known for his involvement with Christianity, Constantine was the foremost general of the late Roman era.

Context: Constantine's leadership was critical in the unification of Rome under a single leader and in the defeat of several barbarian invasions.

Biography: Constantine was born in Naissus, or present-day Serbia, and served as an officer in the Roman army and then as governor of Dalmatia. He engaged in a series of civil wars within the empire, out of which he emerged victorious. Constantine reorganized and reformed much of the empire, revitalizing it. After his defeat of his internal enemies Constantine campaigned against northern enemies and Dacia. He died in 327 while on campaign.

Influences: Constantine stands at the end of a long line of Roman commanders that were the consummate practitioners of the Roman system, including Julius Caesar and Diocletian.

The Theory: Although not the creator of any particular military theory, Constantine was brilliant in his use of the late-Roman imperial army. In this sense his use of ruthless violence might be seen as the ancient equivalent of "total war."

Application: Constantine applied his concept of military force in the northern reaches of the late Roman Empire in his campaigns between 332 and 337.

Descendents: All of the late Roman and Byzantine emperors looked to emulate his military abilities as a commander and organizer.

Further Reading

Cameron, Averil, *The Later Roman Empire: AD 284–430.* London: Fontana Press, 1993.

James, Elizabeth, and English Stephen, *Constantine the Great General: A Military Biography.* Barnsley, UK: Pen and Sword, 2012.

John Serrati

Dubois, Pierre
(ca. 1255–post 1321)

Significance: Calls to Crusade were frequent in the years following 1291 and the fall of Acre, the last city in the Holy Land occupied by European Christians. Among these, Pierre Dubois, an advisor to French King Philip IV (the Fair) and English King Edward I provided not only a call to Crusade, but, in his *De recuperatione terrae sanctae* (*The Recovery of the Holy Land*), written ca. 1306, also provided a strategic analysis of how the Holy Land might be recovered by a unified Christian campaign.

Context: After almost two centuries of European Christian occupation of at least part of the Syrian and Palestinian coast—known to contemporaries as the Holy Land—in 1291, the last outpost, Acre, fell to Mamluk attackers. The defenders of the city, largely soldiers from the monastic military orders, the Hospitallers and Templars, fought valiantly, but their numbers were insufficient to withstand the persistent assaults of their Muslim enemies. The defeat shocked all of Europe, eliciting calls to return to the Holy Land with a large and well-armed military to reoccupy those lands that had been lost. Pierre Dubois added his voice to these with two works written in the first decade of the 13th century.

Biography: Pierre Dubois was born in Normandy around 1255, although the date and place are not confirmed in any of his writings. He is associated with Coutances later in his political and educational career, as the city's representative at the *states-general* and as *bailli* and procurator of its university; consequently this city is often given as his birthplace. He was educated at the University of Paris, the most prestigious educational institution in the Europe of the time. Later he was an advisor to both the French and English kings, during which time he was an ardent defender of royal power, especially in disputes with the Church, writing treatises against both Pope Boniface VIII (1304) and the Templars (1308).

His first work calling for a new Crusade, *Summaria, brevis et compendiosa doctrina felicis expeditionis et abbreviationis guerrarum et litium regni Francorum* (A Concise and Comprehensive Theory for a Successful and Short Military and

Legal Expedition for the King of France), was written in 1300, but its impact seems to have been insignificant. A much more important call to Crusade, *De recuperatione terrae sanctae,* was written approximately five years later while under the patronage of King Edward I of England. Most historians, however, believe that it was the French king whom Dubois intended to lead the Crusade.

Influences: Pierre Dubois does not cite any military influences for his work. Among his nonmilitary influences were scholastic philosophers, Thomas Aquinas and Siger of Brabant, who were teaching at the University of Paris during Dubois's stay. He also was influenced by the works of Roger Bacon, an Oxford Franciscan friar whose works were known throughout Europe. Bacon wrote about warfare, including providing the earliest known European recipes for gunpowder, but these are not referred to by Dubois.

The Theory: Although writing less than two decades after the fall of the Holy Land, Dubois does not blame the loss on any specific failing by Christian forces— although in his later treatise justifying the arrest of the Templars, *Quaedam proposita papae a rege super facto Templariorum* (Certain Propositions to the Pope from the King Concerning the Deeds of the Templars), he mentions that they failed at Acre. It is clear, however, that he believes a new Crusade, led by the French, but with English assistance, would be able to recapture the lost lands. Before launching the campaign, certain goals needed to be met. First, there needed to be peace in Europe, hence, Dubois's appeal to both the English and French kings, who had been at war in the 1290s. Second, the monastic military orders needed to be united, with vows renewed and new leaders chosen. Third, the French king needed to enforce military recruitment obligations on all his lords, and, if needed, to seize ecclesiastical properties to fund the Crusade. Dubois then outlines how these resources might be used to reconquer the Holy Land.

Application: Philip IV and Edward I ignored Dubois's call to Crusade, just as they ignored several other such calls made during their reign. Both would claim that rebellions among their subjects, the Flemings for the French and the Scots for the English, kept them from mounting expeditions into the Middle East, although both also taxed the churches in their kingdoms, ostensibly to mount these campaigns. Within a year of Dubois's treatise, Philip had also begun to imprison French Templars, seizing their lands and possessions. Dubois wrote the justification for these arrests. The urgency for a Crusade to regain the Holy Land faded.

Descendents: Although several more calls to Crusade were made throughout the next two centuries, none seem to have been influenced by Pierre Dubois's treatises. By the middle of the 14th century, Ottoman successes in the Eastern Mediterranean also redirected Christian efforts against Muslims there rather than in the Holy Land.

Further Reading

Dubois, Pierre, *Summaria brevis et compendiosa doctrina felicis expedicionis et abreviacionis guerrarum ac litium regni Francorum (nach dem Cod. Lat. NR. 6222 C der Bibliothèque Nationale zu Paris)*. Ed. Hellmut Kämpf. Veroffentlichungen der Forschungsinstitute an der Universität Leipzig, Institut für Kultur- und Universalgeschichte. Quellen zur Geistegechichte des Mittelalters und der Renaissance, 4. Leipzig and Berlin: B. G. Teubner, 1936.

Dubois, Pierre, *The Recovery of the Holy Land*. Trans. Walther I. Brandt. New York: Columbia University Press, 1956.

Housley, Norman, *The Later Crusades, 1274–1580: From Lyons to Alcazar*. Oxford: Oxford University Press, 1992.

Schein, Sylvia, "Philip IV and the Crusade: A Reconsideration." In: *Crusade and Settlement*. ed. P. W. Edbury. Cardiff, 1985, pp. 121–26.

Kelly DeVries

Fabius Maximus Verrucosus Cunctator, Quintus, Dictator
(ca. 285–203 BCE)

Significance: Known for employing a strategy of attrition against an invading enemy, holding off from serious engagements, while gradually reducing the enemy's supplies and numbers through brief skirmishes.

Context: Hannibal's invasion of Italy during the Second Punic War (218–202 BCE).

Biography: Chosen dictator of the Roman Republic after the disastrous battles of Trebbia River and Lake Thrasimene in 218 and 217 BCE, Fabius was given the task of preventing Hannibal from destroying Rome in mid-217.

The Theory: The immediate predecessors of Fabius sought to bring the Italian invasion of Hannibal to an end through decisive battles, only to fall victim to Hannibal's strategic gifts and talent for subterfuge. Fabius, however, recognized that Hannibal was an invader in a land foreign to him, one so far removed from his home territory that reinforcement and, importantly, resupply would be practically impossible. Instead, Hannibal was forced to rely on what could be gotten from seizure from Rome's Italian allies or from the voluntary contribution of the Italians he encountered. The former could only yield so much (especially as Hannibal deliberately ravaged the territory of Italians still friendly to Rome in an attempt to draw the Romans into battle). The latter, too, was limited in what the land could provide, and all the more in light of the fact that Hannibal's erstwhile confederates were of fickle temperament and stuck by him only as long as he kept defeating the Romans.

By contrast, Roman territory (as opposed to that of their allies) was generally untouched during the war, leaving their ability to resupply unaffected, and although the actions of 218 and the early part of 217 had destroyed two armies, Rome still enjoyed a numerical advantage. By maintaining his army and positioning it between Hannibal and Roman territory but avoiding a major battle, Fabius hoped to blunt Hannibal's momentum acquired from his earlier victories over the Romans and, more importantly, to force him to consume his supplies without making progress toward his aim of defeating Rome and tax the patience of Hannibal's Italian associates.

Application: Livy, the major Roman source on the Second Punic War, reports that this strategy of delay had the desired effect, and had it been continued after Fabius was forced to lay aside his dictatorship; Livy suggests Hannibal would have been defeated through inaction before the end of 216. However, the principal weakness of this strategy is that it also wore down the patience of the Romans themselves, who grew exasperated by the prolongation of the war. This eagerness for decisive action led one of consuls of 216, Caius Terentius Varro, to offer battle at Cannae, resulting in the worst military defeat of the Roman Republic. Afterward, the Romans returned to this strategy of delay (now often called a "Fabian strategy"), although not in its purest form. Instead, delay was used to weaken Hannibal only up to that point where it seemed a decisive, killing blow would be effective.

Later commanders who have attempted to use "Fabian" maneuvers include the Russian high command during Napoleon's invasion of 1812, and Sam Houston during the so-called "Runaway Scrape" in the Texan Revolution of 1836. Both, however, have had to contend with the fact that such a strategy is generally unpopular with the civilian population (especially when combined with "scorched earth" tactics, as was the case in 1812), such that both were eventually compelled to give battle.

See also: Hannibal

Seth Lyons Kendall

Marius, Caius
(consul 107, 104, 103, 102, 101, 100, 86 BCE) (157–86 BCE)

Significance: Although a superb field commander justly renowned for his many victories in combat, as a theorist Caius Marius is notable for being the first known Roman to refuse to be bound by the traditional rules for the recruitment of the Roman army. Before Marius, Rome's legions tended to consist wholly of men who (1) met a minimum property qualification, making them eligible for service, and (2) were mustered by draft from the pool of available men. As a consequence of this rule, Rome deprived itself of the greatest part of its manpower for military use (as those too poor to meet this property qualification heavily outnumbered those who could). At the same time, it forced the remaining smaller segment of the population into greater and greater military burdens. By the time Marius became consul, service in the legions was so unpopular that it became difficult to enlist men, and those magistrates who attempted to do so faced an unpopularity that threatened to cripple their political careers. However, as the consul of the republic in 107 BCE and therefore tasked with both fighting a war and gathering men for it, Marius was able to sidestep both the impediments to recruiting and odium attached to it by stepping beyond the traditional method of mustering his troops. Instead of conscripting those men whose property rating rendered them liable for duty, Marius threw open membership in his army to any who were both able-bodied and able to serve, no matter what their level of wealth. By this means he filled up his legions with volunteers with almost no effort, an example soon followed by all generals who succeeded him.

Context: Although Marius would become a successful general in service to Rome for over 20 years, his reform of recruitment took place in the year 107. In this year he was elected consul for the first time and given the responsibility for winning the Jugurthine War. This came at the end of a century, which had begun with Italy recovering from the ravages of Hannibal, and had seen numerous foreign wars and the acquisition of territory, requiring huge numbers of men for front line and garrison duty overseas, often for lengthy periods. The unpleasantness of these assignments greatly diminished the willingness of those bound to military service to submit to the draft, just as the decline in economic prosperity caused by Hannibal's destruction and the massive numbers killed during the Second Punic War and later conflicts had greatly diminished the numbers of men able to do so. Contemporary sources have noted the doubt shared by some as to Rome's capacity to maintain its empire under such conditions.

Biography: Caius Marius was born in the year 157 BCE near the town of Arpinum, a town in central Italy, which the historian Livy states had fallen under Roman sway by at least the fourth century and whose inhabitants had been given Roman citizenship in 188. As full Roman citizens, Arpinates were entitled both to hold and run for office in Rome. However, due to their recent acquisition of their citizenship, such men would be definition be *novi homines* ("new men"; i.e., not part of the Roman political establishment) upon whom Rome's ruling class looked with suspicion and contempt and for whom the people could not generally be persuaded to vote. Arpinates were also held to military service—at least, those who met the minimum property qualifications would be (more below)—and thus Marius found himself in the army in 134, fighting in Spain. During this campaign Marius was on the staff of consul Publius Cornelius Scipio Aemilianus, the conqueror of Carthage, who praised the younger man's military gifts.

Perhaps inspired by that great captain's plaudits, Marius decided to run for various political offices in the capital, because election high offices brought with them military commands. However, he found the going rough due to his *novitas* ("newness"). A few low-level defeats and alleged electoral irregularities impeded his progress, with the only bright spot coming in the form of a minor command in Spain during which, according to Plutarch, he successfully cleared his province of pirates. By 109, his quest for the consulate—Rome's highest office—had stalled. However, in that year his military abilities and few connections led to his appointment as *legatus* (a high-ranking subordinate commander) to the consul Quintus Caecilius Metellus, who was being sent to Africa to replace the generals who were proving unsuccessful in the war against Jugurtha. The historian Sallust, the main authority on the so-called "Jugurthine War," makes it clear that Marius was functionally second-in-command to Metellus. His success in this capacity soon made him famous in Rome.

Sensing that his star was on the rise, Marius managed to return to Rome to run for the consulate late in 108. In spite of the strenuous opposition of Metellus and the equal disapprobation of the senate, Marius was both elected consul and given the assignment of replacing Metellus in Africa. As was his right, Marius asked the senate for funds for, and permission to recruit, reinforcements for the army in Africa. The senate allowed both, in the hopes that his attempt to hold the *dilectus* ("draft") would destroy his great popularity among the common people (more below). However, Marius was able to sidestep this pitfall by means of an innovation: instead of drafting those eligible to fight, Marius called for volunteers from the entire populace no matter what their property rating, using the funds he had already been voted to equip and supply them. Sallust notes that by this measure Marius gathered a much greater number of men then anyone could have predicted, and took them to Africa in 107.

Like Metellus before him, Marius accumulated a number of victories over Jugurtha, but found it slightly more difficult to conclude the war than he had anticipated. Nevertheless, he was retained as *proconsul* (a consul whose office has expired but who is given, or allowed to finish, a military command) for the next two years. In 105, Marius was able to use the talents of his subordinate Lucius Cornelius Sulla to spring a trap for Jugurtha and capture him. This ended the war, though later on Sulla would attempt to arrogate to himself sole credit for the victory, driving a wedge between the two men that later became a bitter enmity. In the meantime, Marius was not allowed much time to bask in his glory: an incursion of Germanic peoples called the Cimbri and Teutones into territory occupied by Rome's allies proved to be a significant threat, culminating in a disaster for Roman arms at the battle of Arausio in 105. The widespread this defeat caused in Rome is attested by Sallust, and in their terror the people apparently turned in desperation to a proven commander. Thus, Marius was elected consul a second time by them for the year 104, even though he had not sought the office (nor even been in Italy to run for it). Marius was given the task of repelling the Germanic threat.

To meet this challenge, the antiquarian Aulus Gellius affirms that he acquired reinforcements in the same way that he had gotten then for the Jugurthine War: by calling for volunteers from across the economic spectrum. Bolstered by these

forces, to whose training and weaponry he made some minor but important alterations, Marius proceeded to wage a cautious war against the Teutones and Cimbri.
For almost the entirety of his second consulate, Marius waited and trained his men
in his new system while the enemy briefly waged war elsewhere. In the meantime,
the Roman people reelected him consul for a third and fourth time so that he might
continue his campaign without threat of being superseded by a new consul-elect
(a proconsul could always be relieved in the field by a consul then in office). In
102, he defeated the Teutones in two battles near Aquae Sextiae. Elected consul a
fifth time, Marius completed his destruction of the Germanic threat by defeating
the Cimbri at Vercellae. As reward for these actions, Marius was made consul a
sixth time, during which he put down a revolt in Rome itself.

Over the next 10 years Marius was out of office, during which he found his
political duties as a member of the senate irksome. Apparently, Marius began to
long for another command, and according to the biographer Plutarch, he seems to
have tried to provoke Mithridates, king of Pontus, into a war, which Marius could
then be tapped to lead against him. Such actions put him on a collision course with
Sulla, his one-time friend and subordinate and now bitter enemy, who also sought
such a war so that he himself could be given the command as consul. The two also
quarreled over Sulla's repeated claims that he alone deserved credit for the end of
the Jugurthine War, but their animosity was forced to be suspended when a confederacy of Rome's Italian Allies rose against the commonwealth in late 91. When the
spring campaigns began the next year, Marius found himself in the field again as
legatus to consul Publius Rutilius Lupus. In mid-90 Lupus disregarded the advice
of Marius and attacked the enemy near the River Tolenus, a battle in which he was
killed in ambush. Marius was left to rescue whatever the army he could extricate
from the trap and to keep the Italians from marching on Rome directly through the
avenue left open by the attack of the consul. Marius was able to accomplish both
of these objectives, and toward the fall of 90 he managed to defeat the Italians in
a great battle in southern Italy.

Marius was not given a command in the next year, for which his enemies in the
senate were probably responsible. Marius himself claimed that poor health kept
him out of action, yet by 88 he was in sufficient shape that he could take part in
vigorous military training exercises with the youths of Rome on the Campus Mar-
tius. These were conducted, according to Plutarch, to show the people of Rome
that Marius was fit to lead a campaign against Mithridates, which the senate had
declared in the previous year. Here, again, he ran afoul of the ambitions of Sulla,
who was the consul for 88 and had already been assigned to the eastern command.
Marius seemed to get the better of his former lieutenant by using the last of his
political resources to get the command transferred to himself. However, Sulla had
other ideas: as a serving consul in 88 mopping up the last remnants of the war with
the Allies, he, unlike Marius, already had men directly under his control. These
he led against the government in Rome, an action unprecedented in Roman history. Marius scraped together some men to try and stop him, but was ultimately
defeated and driven from the city. This left Sulla to occupy the capital, and he

swiftly reversed the change of command; for good measure he also had Marius declared an outlaw, one to be killed on sight.

After a series of hair-raising adventures evading the men Sulla sent after him, Marius was able to escape Italy to Africa. There he was able to gain some supporters for his own planned march on Rome. He soon found an ally in Lucius Cornelius Cinna, consul of 87 who was also driven from Rome as a result of urban violence. Together the two men raised an army and led it against the other consul of 87, Gnaeus Octavius. After a series of successful battles largely orchestrated by Marius, Octavius was defeated and killed. Cinna promptly returned to Rome and reversed the sentence of outlawry passed against himself and Marius. The latter proceeded to indulge himself in revenge against his many enemies in the senate, of whom several were put to death by his command. Marius was elected consul along with Cinna for 86, but died in January of that year.

The Theory: Although Marius enjoyed many victories as a general, which were of lasting import for Rome, his greatest influence on the Roman military stemmed from two sources. One was his alterations to Roman training and equipment, which were adopted by all subsequent Roman commanders. Of more profound significance, however, was his innovation regarding the way soldiers were raised for the legions, one employing unorthodox means to produce a larger and more enthusiastic army than Rome had seen for some time. Because complete understanding of this new method can only be understood by contrasting it with the previous manner of recruitment, this will be explained below.

For most of Rome's history the commonwealth had relied upon what was in theory supposed to be a citizen militia, one whose soldiers were capable of furnishing their own arms, equipment, and provender. Adoption of this policy was motivated by social and, presumably, economic concerns; economic, in that men serving at their own expense did not require those expenses to be met by the state; social, in the sense that those capable of meeting those not insignificant costs would almost have be men of property, and as such more invested in the welfare of their country (and thus less likely to betray it through cowardice in the form of desertion, or cupidity in the form of bribery) than the poor. Determination of who would be eligible for military service was came from a property rating taken during the census, and from the pool of those deemed capable of serving (known as *assidui*) men were chosen for a particular military campaign through a draft (*dilectus*).

Although this system may have worked well during the early days of the republic, as time went on, increasing number modifications would have to be made to it to compensate for problems that began to emerge. In the first place, as the territory under Rome's power grew and the number of the commonwealth's enemies multiplied, wars began to take longer and longer to conclude. Because Rome's soldiers were not professionals but (in many cases) small farmers called into service as needed, extended operations on the field put their farms and therefore their livelihoods in jeopardy. To counter this difficulty, the state began to offer compensation (*stipendium*) to its soldiers; the men could theoretically send this money home, allowing their families to hire laborers (or purchase slaves) to do the work they themselves could not perform while away under the standards. The money for these *stipendia* were raised through taxation (*tributum*). Additionally, extended operations proved too lengthy to allow any of the men to carry enough food for the duration. This required that the Roman state also provide meals for its soldiers, though the costs of these were deducted from the soldiers' *stipendia*. Finally, at some point the sources make it clear that the government also supplied weapons for its legionaries (perhaps to ensure a uniformity of equipment and reduce the potential chaos caused by varying quality of weapons among the men, or to ease the transition between the old hoplite equipment and the new kinds of arms demanded by the maniple when that formation was adopted by the army in the late fourth century). The cost of this equipment was also deducted from the *stipendium*.

Because of these alterations, by the late second century, Rome no longer truly derived its fighting men from such citizen soldiers who supplied their own materiel. Rather, its soldiers were paid, and given food and weapons by the army itself (indeed, by the 120s BCE even the deductions for food and weapons were theoretically no longer collected). Nevertheless, although the economic reasons for it evaporated, Rome's soldiers were still selected in the same manner as earlier: eligibility for military service was still dependent on property rating (even though the minimum amount of property to qualify for service was reduced several times), and actual service in the legions was determined by the *dilectus*. This functionally excluded what was almost certainly the vast majority of Rome's able-bodied men, those too poor to be given the status of *assidui* even after the reduction in the minimum property rating. Such men were variously called *proletarii* (whose name comes from the fact that the only thing they contributed to the state were *proles,* or offspring) or *capite censi* (derived from the fact that only their heads were counted on the census). Although on occasion even these men could be pressed into service, such occurrences were rare and almost always in the case of a *tumultus,* a crisis that directly threatened the city itself. More importantly, it does not seem that these men were encouraged or even allowed to volunteer for military service of their own accord. The sources do mention a few occasions on which volunteers were solicited, but in these instances it is not entirely clear whether those who stepped forward belonged to the *proletarii* or whether they, too, were undrafted *assidui*.

The consequence of this tradition was that the burden of military service fell heavily on the *assidui,* a burden that became even more weighty over the second century. This was due in part to the lasting effects of Rome's war with Hannibal, which had involved enormous losses and ravaged territory. Rome's territorial expansion also led to a broadening of potential enemies and thus to an increase in foreign wars, whose conduct and aftermath led to additional demands for combat troops and garrisons (which were not infrequently extremely hazardous or unpopular assignments). As a result, Rome's consuls, who were tasked with raising the armies for the various military actions they were to lead, progressively began to find holding the *dilectus* troublesome: at least four times in the 50 years before the year 107 popular outcry had caused tribunes to disrupt the levy.

These difficulties would be confronted by Marius upon his election to consul in the year 107, with the mandate for finishing the war then being prosecuted in Africa against Jugurtha (see above). As was mentioned earlier, the senate—although taking a grim view of his election—did not refuse Marius his request to raise reinforcements for the army then in Africa, nor the funds for payment, weapons, and supplies for the same. Indeed, the senate had hoped that Marius would conduct the levy, and that the unpopularity that had come to be attendant on it would serve to ruin him politically. Marius would disappoint them, however, by not calling for a *dilectus*. Instead, he resorted to *evocatio* (a call for volunteers). According to Sallust, the majority of those to answer the call were *capite censi*. Using the money, weapons, and supplies voted to him, which was usually destined for *assidui* and distributing them to his volunteers, Marius led his men—in numbers greater than anyone had expected—to Africa and brought the Jugurthine War to a successful conclusion.

Application: The ancient sources do not indicate whether or not Marius had intended a thoroughgoing reform of Rome's policy for raising soldiers in his call for volunteers. It is quite probable that he had not, but had turned to volunteers merely as a temporary expedient designed to overcome the particular challenge he faced in 107. Yet even if a comprehensive overhaul was his aim, he did not accomplish one in the strictest sense: Romans would still be classified by property in the census after 107, and those designated as *assidui* would be liable for conscription well into the late republic. Nevertheless, the success of his innovation could not be denied, and Marius himself would return to it in his wars against the Teutones and Cimbri as described above.

The surviving classical sources that wrote about Marius are generally hostile to him, and even those sympathetic to the man often take a dim view of his *evocatio*. Although even the earliest of them were composed almost a half a century later, it is reasonably certain that their hostility mirrors that of the senate in 107. Their objection centers around the fact that, as so many of the new volunteers were poor, they would owe less devotion to the state than to the commander who gave them employment, pay, and the opportunities for enrichment by means of enemy spoil (among other emoluments). This would seem to be justified based on the events of 88, when Sulla used men raised in this manner to march on Rome, and by the subsequent repetitions of this action during the long period of civil war that wracked the commonwealth between 87 and 27 BCE, in which armies more loyal to their general than to their country followed the one against the other. In spite of the danger, however, the *evocatio* gradually became established practice followed by most commanders after Marius, and the manpower raised by this measure helped defend the Roman state from threats internal and external for the next five centuries. It can be argued that all subsequent volunteer armies, whether consciously following the example of Marius or otherwise, recruit their numbers in much the same manner as he did.

Further Reading

Carney, Thomas, *A Biography of C. Marius.* Chicago: Argonaut, 1970.

Gabba, Emilio, *Republican Rome, the Army and the Allies* (P. J. Cuff, translator). Berkeley: University of California Press, 1976.

Gargola, Daniel, "Aulus Gellius and the Property Qualifications of the Proletarii and the Capite Censi." *Classical Philology* 84 (1989): 231–234.

Seth Lyons Kendall

Mendoza, Don Bernardino de

(1540–1604)

Significance: Spain is usually identified with the *leyenda negra* of terrible oppression of its own subjects, both in the Spanish-ruled Netherlands and in the American colonies, especially if they were branded as rebels. The work of Mendoza, however, like that of Sancho de Londoño and Francisco de Vitoria, shows that the strategies of brutal repression were seen with disgust among some Spanish intellectuals. They urged an alternative strategy counterinsurgency, in which good governance would serve to win the support of the population and the isolation of rebel leaders. Moreover, Mendoza made the case that a prince might feel morally obliged to come to the aid of oppressed subjects of a tyrant, an early articulation of what today is referred to the responsibility to protect. Finally, Mendoza's writing marks the beginning of a new trend that would see its culmination around the time of the French Revolution and with Clausewitz, in that Mendoza rejected a slavish adherence to the opinions of the Ancients, instead emphasizing the changes brought on by new military technology, especially gunpowder.

Context: Mendoza's work appeared during a wave of publications sparked by the interconnected Spanish–Dutch–English–French wars. The Duke of Alba had been put in charge of the counterinsurgency operations against the uprising of the Calvinist Dutch nobility against the rule of King Philip II of Spain, of which Mendoza thus was to obtain firsthand experiences. Mendoza published the *Theory and Practice of War* in 1594. The book was dedicated to the crown prince, the future Philip III of Spain.

Biography: Don Bernardino de Mendoza was born around 1540, probably in his family's hometown of Guadalajara, to a Spanish noble family that traced its ancestry to the 12th century. His father was the Count of Coruña and Viscount of

Torija, and on his mother's side there was a famous cardinal, but Don Bernardino as the 10th of nineteen siblings had to earn his living. He obtained his schooling in Alcalá, and in his mid-teens, obtained diplomas in arts and philosophy, and was then elected a member of the Colegio Major de San Ildefonso of Alcalá. He read Latin, Greek, French, English, and Italian besides his Castilian mother tongue. He entered the king's service in 1560 as an officer, and proceeded to fight in the Spanish expeditions around the Western Mediterranean. He fought under the infamous Duke of Alba, first accompanying him to Italy in 1567 and then during his campaigns in Flanders, seeing action at Mons, Nijmegen, Haarlem, and Mook. In 1591, he published remarkably impartial *Commentaries . . . on the Wars in the Netherlands, 1567–1577.*

Three of Don Bernardino's siblings rose to places of great influence at court, including one other ambassador and later Viceroy of New Spain, one chamberlain, and a sister who became the teacher of the princes. This, and enduring contacts with other graduates of San Ildefonso, helped his career. Mendoza was knighted in 1576 and joined the prestigious Order of St. James, and henceforth worked only as a diplomat. After an earlier mission to Pope Pius V to secure his support for Alba's campaign, he was in 1578 dispatched as full ambassador to the Court of St. James in London.

In the 16th century, diplomats often combined the roles of government representatives, intelligence agents, and subversive agitators. In London, Mendoza meddled vigorously with politics, becoming a central agent in the captive Mary Queen of Scots' attempts to oust her cousin Elizabeth I from the English throne. His activities were discovered, and Mendoza's accreditation was revoked in 1584 and he was sent packing; Mary Queen of Scots was executed for treason and conspiracy against the monarch in 1587.

Mendoza's next mission was to Navarre, to persuade the Protestant Bourbon King Henri to join Philip II of Spain in a war against Catholic King Henry III of France. When it came to the Valois-Habsburg rivalry, religion gave way to dynastic rivalry. It does not lack poignancy that Mendoza was subsequently accredited as ambassador to Henry III. From a distance, he was still involved in the plot that would lead to Mary Queen of Scots' execution, and he supported the formation of the Catholic League by the Duke of Guise, Mary Stuart's maternal cousin, who was murdered in 1589. Mendoza continued to lend his support to one faction of the League. Mendoza's mission ended in 1590 or 1591 with the death of Henri III, and Mendoza returned to Madrid, afflicted by poor eyesight.

Whereas earlier biographers claimed that Mendoza was married and had a daughter, most recent literature suggests he was never married. Despite his progressive blindness, Mendoza started lecturing on military matters at the Academy of Mathematics in Madrid shortly after the publication of his *Theory and Practice of War.* With revenues from estates granted to him with by the crown, he bought a house next to the Monastery of Saint Anne in Madrid, which upon his death in 1604, he left to the Monastery, which thereafter would be rededicated to Saint

Bernhard, Bernardino's namesake. This led to an alternative earlier interpretation that he died in poverty in an almshouse belonging to the Monastery of San Bernardo. He was buried in the church of Torija.

The Theory: Mendoza stressed diplomats' need for military experience, which is precisely what makes his and a few other books on war through the centuries stand out from the mass of their competitors: Mendoza was one of those rare men who combined experiences of both, with added erudition.

The work contains sections on the dangers of starting a war if one has insufficient money to pay the troops throughout it, a problem common to all states of Europe at the time. Apart from the standard passages on the virtues needed in a good general or captain, in good officers, and good soldiers, there are equally standard passages tactical dimensions of warfare: on camps and fortifications, on sieges, on the best configuration for ground forces in battle and on the march, and on naval warfare (with a particular focus on sieges of ports). The most remarkable features of this work include its insistence on leniency in counterinsurgency campaigns, such as the one that Spain was engaged in the Netherlands during the time of Mendoza's writing. Mendoza clearly did not approve of Alba's harsh rule, which is reflected in his views on how to handle rebels or insurgents.

Mendoza, like the French *Politiques,* articulated the obligation to intervene on behalf of another prince's oppressed populations (in UN terminology, the responsibility to protect). He sided with the latter faction in the long-standing debate on whether the offensive or defense are preferable, famously noting that "one should go to battle with a leaden foot," and detailing the advantages of fighting, defensively, only in one's own country. Mendoza noted that a superiority of forces over those of the enemy is needed for an attack, compared with smaller numbers for defense, and opined that aggression is more dangerous than defense. We find echoes of medieval thinking in Mendoza's emphasis on God's role in war, and on the regnal/feudal spirit in which the vassals should feel to sacrifice service and their own goods and persons for the king's cause, in return for protection of honor. He argued that alliances must be honored, but he also pondered the benefits of neutrality and of balance-of-power politics. In a Machiavellian vein, Mendoza argued that desire for conquest is a natural human craving and acceptable in a king. Mendoza preferred native soldiers to mercenaries, but recognized the advantages of role specialization among different national contingents, common in his age.

Influences: In an age where intellectuals still preferred Latin to the vernacular, Mendoza, choosing to write in his native Castilian Spanish to secure a wider readership among soldiers, nevertheless applied sentence structures of paragraph length that are commonly found in classical Latin texts, making the work difficult to ingest, especially in the absence of any division into chapters.

Some of Mendoza's arguments resemble those of Justus Lipsius—one of the political philosophers who inspired the Dutch rebels—made in Lipsius's fifth book of his *Politicorum sive civilis doctrina,* a work that Mendoza later translated into Castilian. Mendoza was not alone in echoing Machiavelli's negative views on mercenaries, but Mendoza argued his case in a more balanced fashion. Mendoza's implicit criticism of the brutal strategy of repression of the Duke of Alba tallies with that made by Luis Valle de la Cerda in 1583. Like Christine de Pizan and Machiavelli, Mendoza thought it "very dangerous to employ force against your own subjects," and saw rebellion as a function of poor governance, not of wickedness of the rebel subjects. Jensen has argued that Mendoza was influenced by the French *Politiques,* writers during the French Wars of Religion, who argued that a prince had a responsibility to intervene to protect another prince's subjects against tyranny.

Descendents: Mendoza was sufficiently widely known to engender a considerable degree of interest in his work on war abroad. It was translated in his lifetime into French, English, and German. Mendoza's work influenced that of Santa Cruz de Marcenado, writing almost a century and a half later, but the difficult style of his writing soon made it unreadable to later generations.

Further Reading

Agrela, José Miguel Cabañas, *Don Bernardino de Mendoza: un escritor-soldado al servicio de la Monarquía católica, 1540–1604.* Madrid: Torrejón de Ardoz, 2001.

Herrero Casado, A., "Bernardino de Mendoza," *Torre de los Lujanes* Vol. 9 No. 13 (1989), pp. 30–45, also available on http://www.aache.com/doc/bernardino.htm.

Jensen, De Lamar, *Diplomacy and Dogmatism: Bernardino de Mendoza and the French Catholic League.* Cambridge, MA: Harvard University Press, 1964.

For excerpts, see Beatrice Heuser (ed. and trans.), *The Strategy Makers: Thoughts on War and Society from Machiavelli to Clausewitz.* Santa Barbara: Praeger/ABC-CLIO, 2010.

Beatrice Heuser

Nizam al-Mulk, Abu 'Ali al-Hasan Ibn 'Ali
(ca. 1018–1092)

Significance: Abu 'Ali al-Hasan Ibn 'Ali Nizam al-Mulk wrote on general military theory.

Context: Abu 'Ali al-Hasan was one of the most important political figures in the 11th century CE Middle East.

Biography: Born in around 1018–1020 CE in modern-day Iran, he probably studied Islamic law of the Shafi'i school at Nishapur. His family shifted their allegiance from the Ghaznavid dynasty (977–1186 CE) to the increasingly power-ful Seljuq Turks. He entered prince Muhammad Alp Arslan's service around 1055 CE. He was soon appointed a *wazir* or minister and was given the name *Nizam al-Mulk,* "Good Order of the State."

After Alp Arslan was became sultan in 1063 CE, Nizam al-Mulk became se-nior *wazir* of the entire Great Seljuq state, thereafter accompanying the sultan on numerous campaigns and leading several expeditions himself. As senior *wazir* under Alp Arslan (1063–1073 CE) and Malik Shah (1073–1092 CE), he had to maintain a large tribal army. He abandoned the old 'Abbasid tax-farming sys-tem in favor of an *'iqta* system of fiefs whereby military governors supported themselves and their troops with local revenues. He sent nomadic Turcomans on campaigns beyond Seljuq territory. Local rulers, whether Sunni or Shi'a Muslim or Christian, were often left in place as vassals. Good relations were established with the 'Abbasid Caliphs in Baghdad.

In 1086, CE Sultan Malik Shah asked Nizam al-Mulk to write what became his *Siyasat namah* or "Book of Government," which he completed revising in 1091 or 1092 CE shortly before he was assassinated.

Influences: The *Siyasat Namah* was a book of instruction in the Persian literary tradition of "mirrors for princes." As a believer in awe-inspiring state power to forestall and crush dissent, Nizam al-Mulk sought to combine Iranian traditions of absolute monarchy with Islamic concepts of social justice.

The Theory: Many of the strategic and military chapters in the *Siyasat Namah* are theoretical, though several chapters added shortly before his assassination focused upon current threats to the Seljuq state.

The *Siyasat Namah* argued in favor of having varied ethnic units at court, with competition being encouraged between them. The author also presented an ideal-ized training schedule for élite troops.

The 13 specifically military chapters were: concerning intelligence agents and reporters; on sending spies; concerning "solitaries" (élite guards), their equipment and administration; on the provision and use of jeweled weapons (by palace guard units); on keeping fodder ready (for the horses); on settling the payments of the army; on having troops of various "peoples"; on taking hostages; on keeping Turcomans (nomadic tribal Turks) in service; concern-ing the training of pages in the palace; concerning the requests and petitions of soldiers, servants and retainers; on preparing arms and equipment for wars and expeditions; and concerning commanders of the guard, mace bearers and instruments of punishment.

Application and Descendents: Unlike most other Persian military writing of this period, Nizam al-Mulk's *Siyasat Namah* continued to be used as a training manual for Persian, Ottoman Turkish, and Moghul Indian officials for many centuries.

See also: Al-Rawandi; Mubarakshah, Fakhr-i Mudabbir; Naṣûḥ bin Karagöz, called Matrakçı, Matrâqî, Silâḥî, etc.; Sirhindi A.; Timur, Amir (or Tamerlane or Timur the Lame); Usama Ibn Munqidh

David Nicolle

Rühle von Lilienstern, August
(1780–1847)

Significance: Several years before Clausewitz, Rühle was among the first to draw lessons from the cataclysmic experience of the Napoleonic Wars. Rühle's work, eclipsed by Clausewitz's, is nonetheless of lasting relevance and merits rediscovery, as it points the reader in crucial directions that Clausewitz failed to explore. These include the role of war as the settlement of large-scale disputes where no supreme court exists, pointing to the glaring need for such an institution, and the complex relationship between small war and major war. Rühle, with his recognition that warfare is a dynamic interaction of two sides, recognized that it is impossible to study war satisfactorily through any primitive one-variable-one-dependent-variable interpretation. Rühle produced pioneering thoughts about coercion, morale, and the relationship of space and time in warfare.

Context: The background to Rühle's writings is the Napoleonic Wars to which he bore personal witness from 1806 until 1815 both on the side of France's enemies and on that of her allies. Rühle wrote, first, a polemic (*On War*), when the threat of Napoleon was not entirely banished, as his comeback in 1815 would show, and then, after Waterloo, a two-volume field manual for Prussian soldiers.

Biography: (Johann Jacob Otto) August Rühle von Lilienstern was born in Berlin on April 16, 1780, to a Hessian father, who was a lieutenant in the service of the Prussian monarchy, and to a Pommeranian mother. At the age of 13, August joined the cadet corps in Berlin, and toward the end of 1795, the *Garde* Regiment in Potsdam. In 1801, he enrolled with Colonel Scharnhorst's Academy for Officers in Berlin. He was in the same promotion as Carl von Clausewitz, and the two young men competing for the top marks in their year. The curriculum included mathematics, natural sciences, philosophy, politics, and music, as well as military sciences. Another teacher, Massenbach, became Rühle's patron, and assured his admission to the newly formed General Quarter Master's Staff in 1804. Under Massenbach's command, in the Headquarters of Prince Hohenlohe-Ingelfingen, Rühle participated in the campaign of 1806, losing his position after the Prussian defeat of Jena and Auerstedt.

Repairing to Saxony, he wrote an eyewitness account of that campaign, which he brought to the attention of Duke Charles Augustus of Saxe-Weimar, who in turn hired Rühle as tutor to his second son, Prince Bernhard. Both Rühle and Prince

Bernhard sought to make the best of this, Rühle devoting his time to his research and writing, and especially the editorship of a journal *Pallas* devoted to political and military matters, while the prince led a wild life. Rühle, too, socialized widely, which acquainted him with his future wife, a widowed daughter of a general, and several leading German intellectuals. When Prince Bernhard was dispatched with a Saxon contingent to fight alongside Napoleon's armies against Austria, Rühle with the rank of Colonel accompanied him, keeping the war diary. Rühle also published an eyewitness account of the campaigns of 1809.

With Prince Bernhard no longer in need of tuition, Rühle was dismissed in 1811, and unsuccessfully tried his hand at farming, using up his small fortune. In 1813, he therefore volunteered to join the Prussian army, to fight, this time *against* the French, in Blücher's general staff. He wrote a *Military Cathechism* or handbook, and worked closely with Scharnhorst, Gneisenau, and Müffling, until a throat disease forced him to take prolonged sick leave. In 1813, he produced his short treatise criticizing Kant's *Eternal Peace,* originally headed *An Apology of War,* which he republished one year later under the title *Vom Kriege* (On War), which inspired Clausewitz's choice of title for his own more famous work.

In September 1813, Rühle rejoined Blücher's headquarters. He coordinated the Allies' operations before the great Battle of Leipzig (the "Battle of Nations"), gaining admiration for his successful shuttle diplomacy between Bülow, Bubna, and Tauentzien. After Leipzig, Rühle was promoted as lieutenant colonel and commissar general for military procurement and recruitment, working from Frankfurt am Main. Given the diversity of the German states, his activities were of varying success. Rühle was then charged with reorganizing the armed forces, and for this purpose was present at the Vienna Congress. After a brief secondment as colonel to Aachen (Aix la Chapelle) to the General von Dobschütz to organize a militia, he returned to Berlin, assuming a variety of duties, including Chief of the Section for War History of the newly formed Grosser Generalstab, from 1821 chief of the Supreme General Staff itself under Lieutenant General von Müffling. In 1817/1818, he published a *Handbuch für den Offizier* (handbook or field manual) in two volumes, and acted as editor of another military journal, besides writing prolifically.

Having been promoted as lieutenant general in 1835, he, in 1837, became Clausewitz's second successor as director of the *Allgemeine Kriegsschule* (which later became the *Kriegsakademie*), and finally became inspector general for military education and director of the officers' exams board. He was a member of commissions devoted to education, military justice, and the development of the railway system. In 1839, he received an honorary doctorate from the University of Kiel. He died aged 67 on July 1, 1847, in Salzburg on the way back from a spa where he had hoped to find relief from his recurrent throat ailment.

Influences: Rühle's pamphlet *On War* was a polemic directed against Immanuel Kant's *On Eternal Peace*. Rühle was influenced by the ultranationalist political philosopher Johann Gottlieb Fichte.

The Theory: Coming straight out of the shattering experience of the Napoleonic Wars, in which Prussia had eventually fared especially badly because it had endeavored to stay out of the fray, Rühle in his pamphlet *On War* wrote in defense of war, scoffing at all those who refused to acknowledge the necessity of war in the hope of saving their own skin. He acknowledged that "war is the way and means to settle the conflicts of peoples by means of fortune and the use of arms," it is a "violent endeavor of states to seek peace or a legal convention." The recognition that war can be necessitated by the failure to achieve a negotiated settlement to a conflict by peaceful means, and by the absence of a mutually recognized supra-state court of justice was in itself not new; it went back to great thinkers such as Christine de Pizan. In Rühle's age, however, few writers cared to recognize this. This idea points to the principal way to avoid war, namely by settling conflicts in an international court of justice, the absence of which he acknowledged here and in his *Handbooks* as chief reason for going to war. Rühle's reflections on the purpose of war, which in their complexity thus go far beyond Clausewitz's simple idea that one's aim in war is to impose one's will upon the enemy. Rühle's great insight in his *Handbooks,* which strategists of the following century and a half ignored with terrible effects, is that military victory is by no means the one and only aim of all warfare. Rühle acknowledged that the aim *should* be peace—as all the European thinkers of previous centuries had done. But he also stressed that for many, it was not, and that state leaders (like Napoleon) might well see it in their interest to perpetuate war to satisfy their own ambitions. Where Clausewitz dodged such considerations by claiming that they exceeded the limits of his work, Rühle examined closely the political and other aims that might be pursued by war. He was perhaps the first to articulate that world opinion—the international community—is a judge of states' actions. Even the greatest military victory might be disadvantageous if it mobilizes international opinion against you.

In his *Handbooks,* he examined conflicts on all levels, from the primary level of the duel over gang warfare all the way up to full-scale interstate war, emphasizing the commonality of all these forms of violent clashes. He recognized that war is a dynamic interaction of two parties: neither side retains the same configuration of forces, or can adhere to an unalterable strategy or even tactics throughout. Both must constantly adapt their behavior to the enemy's, whom they seek to harm. The two parties in warfare are thus mutually dependent, mutually influencing variables.

Rühle also very interestingly explored small war, not from the point of view of the counterinsurgent or even the partisan leader, as all authors before him had done, but from the point of view of a side that might stand to benefit from it. He also considered the conduct of small wars alongside or within major wars. He explored coercion—usually thought to be a mid-20th century discovery—and presented an anatomy of courage and morale long before Charles Ardant du Picq. He explored the implications of gaining or sacrificing time and space, and the trade-off it might imply, particularly in the context of windows of opportunity—long before such a term was coined.

Descendents: Rühle's pamphlet *On War* and his *Handbooks* not only lent the title but also key concepts to Carl von Clausewitz more famous work, nowhere acknowledged by the latter. Above all, these concepts, which Clausewitz made his own, included the idea of war as a duel, the realization that it is a dynamic interaction of two contestants, and the emphasis on war as a tool of politics.

Further Reading

Langendorf, Jean-Jacques, *Rühle von Lilienstern oder die romantische Einheit des Krieges.* Vienna: Karolinger, 1984.

Sauzin, Louis, *Rühle von Lilienstern et son Apologie de la Guerre.* Paris: Nizet & Bastard, 1937.

For excerpts, see Heuser, Beatrice (ed. and trans.), *The Strategy Makers: Thoughts on War and Society from Machiavelli to Clausewitz.* Santa Barbara, CA: Praeger/ABC-CLIO, 2010.

Beatrice Heuser

Santa Cruz de Marcenado
(1684–1732)

Significance: Santa Cruz wrote the most comprehensive early treatment of the subject of counterinsurgency. It follows the general tenor of writings on this subject since Machiavelli, all of which urge clemency and the need to win the hearts and minds of the local populations, rather than trying to subdue them through terror. Nevertheless, Santa Cruz's humanist discussion of counterinsurgency is the most sophisticated and extensive treatment of this subject prior to the 19th century, when European writers' approaches to counterinsurgency and colonial warfare changed fundamentally, and to the worse.

Context: Santa Cruz took part in the War of the Spanish Succession (1701–1714), which was effectively both a civil war and an interstate war, and in Spanish colonial wars, which would eventually cost him his life. He also took part as diplomat in the Franco-Spanish peace conferences of the 1720s.

Biography: Don Alvaro Navia-Oroso y Vigil was born on December 19, 1684, in Santa María de Vega in Asturia in Spain, the only son of an aristocratic family, from whom he would inherit the title of third Marques Santa Cruz de Marcenado and Viscount of Puerto. He studied grammar, rhetoric, and philosophy in the monastery Santo Domingo in Oviedo; at the age of 18, he matriculated at the University of Oviedo, but left after only a year to pursue a military career. Already in his teens, he had been put in command of the local militia, and in 1701, at the outbreak of the War of the Spanish Succession, he joined the Bourbon forces, fighting at Valencia, and bravely, but unsuccessfully, defending Cuidad Rodrigo (1706), and more successfully Tortosa (1709), each time standing out for bravery.

The new Bourbon King Philip V of Spain sought to increase his country's influence and security in the Western Mediterranean. Two years after the end of the Spanish War of Succession in 1713, Don Alvaro was sent to Ceuta, a Spanish-occupied territory of North Africa, as inspector of the Spanish forces. As high-ranking officer, Don Alvaro in 1718 took command of the Spanish forces in Sardinia. Around this time, he had succeeded to the title of Marques and was inspector of the Spanish forces both in Sardinia and Sicily, and governor of Cagliari. This marked the change of his career from officer to diplomat. From 1722 to 1727, he was sent as Spanish ambassador to Turin, capital of the kingdom of Victor Amadeus II (1666–1732), who ruled both Savoy and the newly created kingdom of Sardinia. Santa Cruz's house in Turin became a cultural center. Here he began to write his 11-volume work on war, the *Military Reflections* (*Reflexiones Militares*) but also a work on economics. He planned to write an encyclopedia in Spanish, a never-completed *Diccionario universal.* Santa Cruz negotiated the accession of Victor Amadeus to the Treaty of Hanover.

The peace settlement of the Spanish War of Succession broke down in 1726. When diplomatic negotiations were resumed in 1727, Santa Cruz was dispatched to participate in the peace conference that took place in Soissons and Paris until 1731. He spent his fortune on keeping up his ambassadorial residence in Paris, with all obligations of entertainment, and left his family considerable debts. During this time, he published the final volume of his *Military Reflections.*

Santa Cruz seemed to have reached the peak of his career when in 1731 he was tipped off as the next Spanish war minister. But a rival faction at the court of Philip V prevented his appointment. Instead, Santa Cruz was once again sent to Ceuta, this time with the remit to reconquer Oran, which had been captured by Ottoman forces in 1708. It was ruled by Mustafa Buk el Ağa, from whom Santa Cruz succeeded in recapturing the deserted town in mid-1732. The Turks refused to admit defeat, and harassed the Spanish garrisons in the area. On November 21, 1732, Santa Cruz led his soldiers on a sortie from Oran to confront superior Ottoman forces in open battle. The latter, numbering about 50,000, led the Spaniards into an ambush. Although the bulk of the Spanish soldiers got away, Santa Cruz, hit by bullets in the thigh and then mortally, in the chest, was pulled down from his horse and cut to pieces. His head was later exhibited in Argel as trophy; no remains were left for burial.

Santa Cruz had married three times, leaving six sons and two daughters, and all but one of his younger sons followed him in a military career. Santa Cruz de Marcenado was celebrated as a hero in Spain, as Oran remained a Spanish possession until the late 18th century, when it was destroyed by an earthquake.

Influences: Santa Cruz's library contained many Classical authors such as Caesar, Vegetius, and Leo VI, besides Machiavelli's *Art of War* and the works of Mendoza, Montecúccoli, Folard, Feuquières, Allain Manesson Mallet, Blaise de Montluc, the Chevalier de la Valière, William of Nassau, and also Justus Lipsius. Santa Cruz's work follows a classical pattern of military handbooks since Vegetius.

The Theory: Santa Cruz's education had conditioned him to use the approach of theological and legal scholars. In his *Reflections,* he deduced general statements from a great multitude of detailed examples derived from Classical authors, the Hebrew Bible, and more recent historical events, as well as from other authors on war. The 11 volumes thus make heavy reading. They cover warfare on all levels, from the skills necessary for the general, the legal issue of when to choose war and when to choose peace (*ius ad bellum*), the strategic question of with whom and when to form alliances, preparations for war, the beginning of war, to the tactical issues of how to organize camps, marches, whom to use as spies, and how to deal with insurgencies ("rebellions"). They include the strategic question of whether to choose an offensive war and how to hold on to conquered territories, or a defensive war; and the tactical question of when to give battle and when to avoid it, how to prepare for battle and the results for both sides, developments in battle, its outcome for either side, the political question of how to behave after a battle is won, the tactics of siege warfare and attacks on fortified places, surprise, ambushes, and a discussion of how to deal with defeat, and how to retreat.

The most interesting sections deal with counterinsurgency, and with the measures necessary to hold on to conquered territory, books viii and ix. We find here, couched entirely in terms of self-interest, untouched by any rhetoric of compassion, views that can be traced back to Renaissance authors such as Machiavelli and Don Bernardino de Mendoza, who had cautioned rulers against dealing too harshly with their own rebellious subjects. Santa Cruz opined that few insurrections occurred without mistakes having been made first by the local governors. Therefore he urged preventive measures against any abuse of power and poor governance. Government policies must be in the interest of the subjects, not merely those of the rulers. Thus insurgencies must be quelled by ruling with justice, assuring the full enjoyment by all citizens of their property, laws, freedoms, and religion. Respect for their customs, traditions, and even clothing, but also the local religion, must be shown. One's own troops must behave with extreme discipline and their misdeeds must be punished "with a public show of displeasure." If governors abused of their powers, they must be replaced with due emphasis that this was done to show justice, not for fear of the people. Justice, the just administration of the province, the just working of public law courts were in every way crucial to his argument. He recognized that inflation and food scarcity are common causes of insurgencies, especially if these were believed to be due to taxes, usury, or neglect on the part of the government.

Santa Cruz thought that *in extremis,* starving a population into submission was acceptable, and if military force was to be used, it had to be done quickly and overwhelmingly; clearly, the rebels needed to be disarmed. But long-term success required the rebel leaders to be punished—not turned into martyrs—and isolated from the population in general. This, in turn, must be given a massive stake in a peaceful settlement, "by building industry and commerce, through sciences, new schools and universities." The way to peace was for the legitimate rulers to forgive with all their "heart, without rancour or revenge: thus the courage of the peoples is rekindled, and one seeks their hearts and their love."

Descendents: The Marques' international activities since 1722 helped make both him and his works famous abroad in the 18th century. The *Reflexiones militares* were translated into French in 1735–1738 and reprinted in The Hague in 1739 and 1771. A comprehensive German translation was published in 1753, and an Italian translation in the 1750s. An abridged one-volume German edition of 1775 by Friedrich Wilhelm von Zanthier is by far the most legible, as Zanthier omitted most of the examples. After this, Santa Cruz de Marcenado's 11-volume work on war was relegated to oblivion, certainly due to its cumbersome format. The first translation into English (see below) was published only in 2010; parallels to his thinking in more recent works, especially on counterinsurgency, are thus a reinvention of his wheel.

Further Reading

Anes, Gonzalo, A. Castrillón, et al., *El Marques de Santa Cruz de Marcenado: 300 Años despues.* Oviedo: Instituto de Estudios Asturianos, 1985.

Don Alvaro de Navia Ossorio y Vigil, Vizconde de Puerto, Marques de Santa Cruz de Marcenado, *Reflexiones Militares* 21 Books in 11 volumes, of which vol. 1–10. Turin: Juan Francisco Mairesse, 1724–1727, vol. 11. Paris: Simon Langlois, 1730.

Madariaga, Juan de, ed., *Comentarios á la vida y escritos del General Marqués de Santa Cruz de Marcenado.* Madrid: Enrique Rubiños, 1886.

For excerpts, see Beatrice Heuser (ed. and trans.), *The Strategy Makers: Thoughts on War and Society from Machiavelli to Clausewitz.* Santa Barbara, CA: Praeger/ABC-CLIO, 2010.

Beatrice Heuser

Scharnhorst, Gerhard Johann David von and Gneisenau, August Wilhelm Anton Count Neidhardt von
(1755–1813 and 1760–1831)

Significance: Scharnhorst and Gneisenau were jointly responsible for the first delineation of the principle of civic militarism (often recognizable by other, synonymous names such as the "nation in arms") in Germany during the Napoleonic period. Although the concept of civic militarism was really embodied in a series of practical reforms rather than a major theoretical treatise or coherent doctrine, it ultimately resulted in a major revolution in warfare by the middle of the 19th century. In a modern context, Prussia first deployed it in modified form and on a massive scale in the wars of German unification and experienced phenomenal success. Ultimately the other great powers of Europe—with the exception of Great Britain, which maintained a small-scale professional force up to 1914—emulated Prussia and systematically deployed the concept of civic militarism in their own armies after 1871. By the outbreak of the World War I, the civilian adult male population of Europe was highly militarized and prepared to fight war on a scale almost unimaginable in Napoleon's time.

Context: Scharnhorst and Gneisenau experienced a meteoric rise to significance as a result of their service in the wars of the French Revolution and the Napoleon. In this period, a number of contemporary developments influenced the theories and ideas of the two men that later became embodied in the notion of militarizing all classes of the civilian population to secure the ultimate victory over Napoleon. Most significant among these were the general shift from more limited wars fought by professional armies to total war fought by masses of citizen soldiers; the rise and spread of modern nationalist ideas in Europe after 1792; and the larger spirit of rationalism originating from the Enlightenment. Following the disastrous collapse of the Prussian army at Jena and Auerstedt in the fall of 1806, these trends encouraged a series of military reforms pioneered by Scharnhorst and Gneisenau, who led the circle of officers working together on the Military Reorganization Commission to revolutionize the army in Prussia in the first decade of the 19th century.

Biography: Both Scharnhorst and Gneisenau rose from somewhat modest circumstances to become central figures in the military coalition that eventually defeated Napoleon. Scharnhorst, the elder of the two and initially the senior officer in their relationship, was the son of a prosperous farmer and veteran soldier. As a young man, Scharnhorst attended a military academy in the 1770s, learning the latest advances in military science and imbibing more generally the culture of the Enlightenment. He then taught briefly in Hanover and authored several military handbooks before taking up active duty in 1793. By the early 1800s, he had been promoted to the rank of colonel and fought in the Prussian army in the 1806 campaign. After playing a leading role on the Military Reorganization Commission, he served in various capacities in the Prussian army before once again taking up arms against Napoleon in 1813. He was wounded in an engagement outside Leipzig in June of 1813 and subsequently died of his wounds.

Gneisenau, the son of a commissioned officer from Saxony, served in various capacities early in his career, even seeing action in North America in the period of the American Revolution. He joined the Prussian army in 1785 and served as a company commander during many of the initial engagements of the Revolutionary and Napoleonic Wars after 1795, before being injured in skirmishing at Saalfeld that preceded the defeats at Jena and Auerstedt in 1806. Gneisenau then commanded the defenses at Kolberg and worked with Scharnhorst and others on the Military Reorganization Commission after 1808. He also fought with Blücher in the final campaigns of the Napoleonic period, most notably in the ultimate defeat of the French emperor at Waterloo in 1815. He continued to serve in the Prussian army after the Congress of Vienna, eventually dying of cholera in 1831.

Influences: There were a number of late 18th-century European influences on the development of the concept of civic militarism. Perhaps the most significant long-term factor was the canton system developed in Prussia during the 1730s under the "soldier king," King Frederick William I. Under the canton system, regiments in the Prussian army were assigned specific districts where all adult male residents were enrolled in regimental recruiting lists. These lists were then used to fill any gap between the number of actual volunteers for a regiment and the recruitment quotas set by the king. Although far from a system of universal military service in practice, the canton system was quite novel for its time. Nevertheless, Frederick the Great later eschewed the canton system in favor of using foreign mercenaries to fill the regimental quotas of the army. It was, in large measure, because of the failure Frederican organization and tactical doctrines during the Napoleonic Wars that it became obvious that the entire organizational principle behind the Prussian army had to be recast.

In a more immediate sense, the success of the emergency military measures—especially the *Levée en masse*—put into place by the French Republic after 1792 to combat the foreign enemies of the Revolution also had an obvious influence on the development of civic militarism by Scharnhorst and Gneisenau. Because universal conscription had proved spectacularly successful against Austria and Prussia, particularly when it was combined with the nationalist spirit of the Revolution, the Prussian military reformers sought to emulate the French reforms as a way of creating the conditions for success after 1806 with the adoption of universal service by Prussian "citizens." Finally, the humanitarian impulses of the Enlightenment played a role in the reform movement as it informed the attempts to rationalize and humanize discipline and punishments in the army.

The Theory: The theory of "civic militarism" was developed under the leadership of Scharnhorst and Gneisenau in the immediate aftermath of the disastrous Battles at Jena and Auerstadt in October 1806. Following those twin defeats, it became obvious that there was a vast gulf that separated the monarchy and the traditional base of power among the Junker nobility from the larger civilian population in the Prussian state. One of the most obvious defects of the campaign was the utter lack of popular support for the government during the campaign—a phenomenon that contrasted sharply with, for instance, the later attitude of the civilian population in Prussia during the 1813–1814 campaign, or the unwavering support of many Frenchmen in the emergency years of the mid-1790s. To remedy this defect and instill a new feeling of duty and obligation to the state, and patriotic feelings among the civic body more generally, Baron vom Stein, the king's chief minister, instituted a series of political, military, and social reforms beginning in 1807.

Baron vom Stein's larger program included a number of broader reforms aimed to inculcate patriotism and civic feeling in the population as a whole. The first major reform, embodied in the Reform Edict of October 1807, was a measure that abolished serfdom in Prussia three years hence. A series of like-minded reforms followed: the Municipal Ordinance (1808), which granted self-government to the cities; a measure abolishing the guilds and embodying free-market principles in the trades (1810); and the emancipation of Jews in Prussia (1812). Taken together, these measures were intended to improve the morale of the civilian population and fortify it for the renewal of the struggle with Napoleon.

Perhaps most significant for the subsequent history of Prussia, however, was the series of military reforms implemented under the leadership of Scharnhorst and Gneisenau as a part of the larger program of reform enacted by Stein. In July 1807, King Frederick William III created the Military Reorganization Commission, whose original mandate had included the investigation of the failures of 1806, the punishment of unbecoming conduct by officers in the campaign, and the drafting of a series of proposals to revamp operations, logistics, training, regulations, and the selection of officers. The Military Reorganization Commission was ultimately subsumed under Stein's larger reform program, implementing improvements and modifications in the army.

In the process of investigating the collapse of the army in 1806, Scharnhorst and Gneisenau drew the conclusion that the aristocratic stranglehold on the officer corps was the first deficiency requiring immediate remedy. The Junker monopoly on the officer corps had helped encourage a popular feeling of alienation from the army, which had seemed to many Prussians the primary means used by the monarchy to retain power. To obviate this sentiment, the Military Reorganization Commission—with the support of the king—decreed in 1808 that there should be a new system of officer selection based upon knowledge and education in peacetime, and bravery and effective leadership in wartime. This reform created for the first time a system based on merit and examination, as well as a reorganization of the military schools that would train the new officer class. In more practical terms, the measure was supplemented by a purge of several hundred officers—some of those let go were so antiquated they had served in the Seven Years' War under Frederick the Great—and the opening of the officer corps to men of all social backgrounds and classes, most significantly the bourgeoisie. Gneisenau and Scharnhorst created the War Academy at Berlin as a training ground for the new educated officer corps and appointed Carl von Clausewitz to oversee instruction there. Another highly significant and enlightened reform abolished corporal punishment in the army.

It was in the realm of organization and recruitment, however, that the move toward the "nation-in-arms" was most obvious. Under the Treaty of Paris (1808), Napoleon had demanded a measure that would permanently hamstring Prussia in international affairs by restricting the total number of peacetime soldiers to 42,000 men, effectively limiting the army to one very large division composed of six brigades. In addition, Napoleon had explicitly prohibited the formation of militias or other peacetime auxiliary forces to supplement the regular army.

These restrictions stood in direct contrast to the goals of the reformers, which leaned heavily in the direction of a system of universal military service, whereby all adult men would be subject, through a lottery system, either to direct service in the regular army or to emergency service in a national reserve militia. This plan would, in the eyes of the reformers, create a truly patriotic army that would instruct citizens in the duties and obligations of members of the nation, not only with regard to military service, but also in civic life as well.

From 1809 to 1811, the reformers tried to get around Napoleon's restrictions through the use of the so-called *Krümper* system, which rotated new recruits into the army by sending a small number of a regiment's older men home on leave. The principle of universal service was thus not fully implemented until 1813, when Prussia officially joined the final coalition that finally defeated Napoleon. Even then, King Frederick William III was somewhat hesitant to embrace the nation-in-arms fully. As a result, civic militarism was adopted in 1813 through the creation of a three-tiered system of service: the regular army run by the king; the *Landwehr,* composed of all able-bodied male citizens between the ages of 18 and 45; and the *Landsturm,* which included men who did not meet basic service qualifications because of age or physical fitness.

Application: The reforms implemented under the leadership Scharnhorst and Gneisenau had an immediate and revolutionary effect on Prussia's contribution to the Napoleonic wars. If the support of the civilian population had been anemic at best before 1806, the reforms inculcated a new feeling of patriotism that combined elements of monarchical sentiment, with budding nationalism and anti-French fervor. By the time of the outbreak of hostilities in 1813, Prussia had mobilized a total fighting force of roughly 280,000 men—though a significantly smaller number of those comprised the core force of 68,000 fully trained soldiers immediately ready for battle. A large portion of this force was ultimately put to good use at the Battle of the Nations at Leipzig, where more than a half million men were engaged and Napoleon was decisively defeated for the first time. Following Napoleon's attempt in 1815 to regain control of France in the Hundred Days, a Prussian army fought alongside the Duke of Wellington's army at the Battle of Waterloo and inflicted a final defeat on Bonaparte.

Descendents: Following the conclusion of the Napoleonic wars, most states in Europe returned to the ideal of small professional armies in lieu of mass citizen armies. In Prussia, on the other hand, although many of the reforms were deliberately rejected in the conservative period after 1815—for example, the Junker monopoly on the officer corps was reestablished—the larger principle of civic militarism continued in force, most importantly with the ideal of a modified form of universal, obligatory military service. By the time of German unification, this amounted to a system where soldiers served three years in the regular army, two years in the reserves, and another decade in the *Landwehr.* With the enlargement of the regular army during the Constitutional Conflict in the 1860s, the Prussian army became Europe's most effective fighting force, a fact displayed in rapid succession during the wars of German unification from 1864 to 1871. In the end, most of the other major powers in Europe adopted some variant of the Prussian model, so that by 1914 universal military service and the principle of civic militarism had become a military norm.

See also: Bonaparte, Napoleon; Clausewitz, C.; Moltke "the Elder", H.; Schlieffen, Alfred von

Further Reading

There is a very voluminous bibliography on the subject of the Wars of Liberation and the age of reforms in Prussia. Perhaps the most relevant English-language contributions are Walter M. Simon, *The Failure of the Prussian Reform Movement, 1807–1819* (1955), Charles E. White, *The Enlightened Soldier: Scharnhorst and the Militärische Gesellschaft in Berlin, 1801–1805* (1989), and Dennis E. Showalter, "Manifestation of Reform: The Rearmament of the Prussian Infantry, 1806–1813," *Journal of Modern History* (vol. 44, no. 3, Sept. 1972). More general, but still highly useful treatments include the relevant chapters in Gordon A. Craig, *The Politics of the Prussian Army, 1640–1945* (1955), Gerhard Ritter, *The Sword and the Scepter,* vol. 1 (1969), and, more recently, Robert M. Citino, *The German Way of War: From the Thirty Years' War to the Third Reich* (2005).

Nathan N. Orgill

III

Siege Warfare
and Artillery Theory

For the period before 1815, the understanding of how to take a fortified city, or how to correctly defend it, was a matter of vital interest to all states. Armies before the 19th century were simply not big enough to bypass cities, requiring them for lines of supply and communications. The writers here are generally engineers, or men who understood the more mathematical necessities of siege warfare and the use of weaponry. Artillery before the 1400s CE meant torsion weapons: catapults and trebuchets, as seen in the work of **Apollodorus,** for example. With the advent of effective gunpowder weapons in the 15th century, the nature of siege warfare changed.

Aineias, called Aeneas Tacticus
(fl. 360 BE)

Significance: Known for his book describing the ways to withstand a siege

Context: Classical Greece

Biography: Little is known about the identity of Aineias, because his only surviving text, the *Poliorketica* or "Siege Matters," does not contain an author page revealing his patronymic (his cognomen *Tacticus* was given to him by later writers) or place of origin. However, the numerous historical events cited as examples in that text do not include any after 350 BCE, and many are taken from the region of the Peloponnesus. For this reason, it is often assumed that the identification made by Renaissance scholar Isaac Casaubon of this Aineias with an Aineias the Stymphalian, an Arcadian general mentioned by Xenophon (*Hellenica* 7.3.1), is the correct one. This would give him military experience to lend weight to the advice he offers in the *Poliorketica* and in the several lost treatises referred to by Aineias himself and by Polybius (10.44).

The Theory: The *Poliorketica* is less a theoretical text than a manual on sieges, and although there are a few lines that advise how to conduct a siege, the majority of the work concerns how to withstand one. Topics covered include the selection of passwords and signals; how to post guards and conduct patrols; how to devise ways to destroy rams, siege towers, and artillery (including a formula for a mixture that will produce flames which it is claimed cannot be extinguished); and the best way to counter miners.

Slightly more interesting are his occasional tidbits involving the psychology of the common soldier. In one section, for example, he warns that leniency should be shown to men who have fallen asleep on watch if the army has recently been defeated, lest the troops become further demoralized. Most revealing of all, however, is the persistent concern for betrayal of the besieged city by traitors. Almost every section of the work in some way deals with these and the ways by which the potential damage they might inflict can be eliminated or minimized.

Descendents: The writings of Aineias are clearly influential upon Aelian, the author of a later text on military operations and siegecraft.

Aineias offers advice that is almost entirely practical rather than theoretical, and deals with his own culture and the technology available during his own time. As a result, much of his counsel has been rendered obsolete by the technological advances made in the intervening millennia; for example, his technique for stretching sails across the tops of city walls to catch arrows would be most ineffective against modern explosive projectiles. As a result, his text is now considered valuable less for the military guidance it provides than for the historical insights it offers, both in terms of the many examples he cites to illustrate the success or failure of certain tactics and for its indication of the fractious nature of Greek communities, ones whose tendency toward betrayal must have been actual and frequently encountered based on the emphasis he places on offsetting such activity.

Seth Lyons Kendall

Al-Tabari, 'Abd al-Rahman
(ca. late eighth century to early ninth century CE)

Significance: Archery master and author of several treatises on archery in Arabic, Abu Muhammad 'Abd al-Rahman Ahmad al-Tabari may be the single most influential figure in Muslim archery literature and history.

Context: During al-Tabari's lifetime, archery enjoyed great importance, both on the military level and within civilian society. Many archery guilds emerged and competitions in target archery and flight shooting thrived. This new culture was initiated by the advent of the 'Abbasids, with their infantry and horse archery (*see* Ibn Akhi Hizam), plus the shifting of the caliphal empire's center from Syria to

Iraq, with its deep-rooted traditions of archery. This shift made the bow the paramount military weapon within the Middle East.

Biography: Al-Tabari was still active in the early ninth century CE, but little else is known about him except that he was a devoted archer who travelled in greater Khurasan and Iraq seeking perfection in this art. He wrote all his books in Iraq, where he also apparently lived.

His designation of "al-Tabari" might indicate that he or his forebears originated from Tabaristan (today called Mazandaran, in northern Iran bordering the Caspian Sea). The designation was probably geographical rather than ethnic as there is sufficient evidence to suggest that he was of Arabic rather than Persian-Iranian origin (see below).

Influences: Al-Tabari was a veteran warrior, trained in the techniques of each of the three greatest early archery masters, al-Bawardi, al-Balkhi, and al-Rafa' by their respective disciples. He then formed his own synthesis of their techniques. Al-Tabari not only rejected contemporary Persians claim that archery and the hand bow originated with their ancestors, but also asserted that archery was first bestowed upon the Arabs as a divine gift and that the real inventor of the hand bow was Abraham. Al-Tabari also rejected the habitual Persian claims regarding the archery prowess of the pre-Islamic Sasanian kings; in particular discrediting their assumptions concerning the method of "squint-eyed binocular aiming" attributed to Bahram Gur (historically the Sasanian ruler Vahram V, ruled during 420–438 CE).

During the pre-Islamic period within Arabia, the bow occupied a marginal place in the Bedouin warfare. It was mainly used for hunting. In Arab poetry, the bow, unlike the sword and the lance, was rarely glorified. Killing an enemy at a distance was generally seen as a cowardly act, incompatible with Bedouin Arab values of courage tested in close-quarters combat. Although there were some exceptions, such as the Banu Tamim tribe, which was under Sasanid influence in Iraq, the bow was never seriously considered or used by the Arab Bedouin tribes as a mass-combat weapon. The situation was somewhat different with the sedentary Arabs of the Hijaz region who sporadically used it to defend fortified places.

The advent of Islam changed the situation radically, because the Prophet Muhammad insisted upon the importance of the bow as a tactical field weapon. He urged his fellow Muslims to practice archery almost as a religious duty, warning the Muslim Arabs that "the Persian is a better shot than you." By the time the Islamic conquests began under the first Rashidi Caliph Abu-Bakr (623–634 CE), the bow had become an indispensable part of the Muslim Arabs' military equipment.

The Arab war bow was "the long Hijazian bow" (*al-qaws al-hijaziyya al-tawila*), a wooden stave between 165 and 185 centimeters long trimmed to shape. It could be reinforced by adding another layer of wood, sinew, or horn. Nevertheless, it remained a simple bow. The true composite bow was not being used by the Arab peoples of the Arabian in pre- and proto-Islamic periods. As an infantry weapon, the Hijazian bow was, like the later English "longbow," highly effective in the hands of a skilled archer. Early Arab Muslims' archery skills were amply demonstrated during the conquests, and the Hijazian bow proved a worthy match for the Persian composite bow.

Due to a shortage of horses in Arabia, the Arab Muslim armies that engaged the Byzantines and Persians were infantry dominated. However, horses became so abundant after these initial conquests that, when the Rashidi Caliph Omar Ibn al-Khattab (r. 634–644) established the army register (*Diwan al-Jund*) around 640, virtually all of the Arab Muslim warriors enlisted as horsemen, or as warriors possessing a horse. According to Islamic law, a horseman was entitled to two or three portions of booty, whereas a foot soldier was entitled to only one portion. In the Koran, the Prophet Muhammad also accorded the horse the title of the ultimate instrument of Jihad. There was also a traditionally a special relationship between Arabs and their horses, and high prestige for horsemen within Arab—and especially Bedouin—society.

The transformation from an infantry-dominated to a cavalry force gave the Muslim armies greater strategic mobility, as was demonstrated in the conquest of Egypt in 640, only four years after the conquest of Iraq. However, the change did not immediately impact upon tactics. Arab Muslim mounted infantry, now mainly riding horses rather than camels, continued to play an important role on the battlefield throughout the rest of the Rashidun period (632–661). This trend would continue well into the early decades of the Umayyad period. The distinction between Arab Muslim infantry and cavalry corps was fading, initiating the decline of the long Hijazian war bow as a field weapon and the disappearance of ethnic Arab infantry archers as separate units.

Under the Umayyad caliphs, whose period witnessed important developments in Arab Muslim cavalry, military archery in the Arab region remained an *ad hoc* enterprise often carried out by poor and unmounted *mawali* (non-Arab Muslims affiliated to Arab tribes) or by relatively small contingents of mercenaries. The latter were mainly brought from Central Asia and greater Khurasan (eastern Iran) and were based solely in Iraq. They included the Bukharian and Qayqanid (from Sind, now in Pakistan) archers who finally settled in the city of Wasit between Basra and Kufa, which became the first Arabo-Islamic center for the manufacture of composite bows.

The main corps of the Umayyad army consisted of heavily armored Arab cavalrymen mainly using cut and thrust weapons, though some still carried a long Hijazian bow slung over their chest in bandolier fashion. This weapon only seems to have been used infrequently as the men had to dismount to shoot. It seems that the last Umayyad Caliph Marwan Ibn Muhammad tried to promote the systematic employment of infantry archers using both the long Hijazian bow and the composite Wasitian bow, but his dynasty was overthrown before he could put this reform into practice.

At the decisive battle of al-Zab in 749 CE (near Mosul in northern Iraq), which sealed the fate of the Umayyad dynasty, Marwan's army was largely composed of tribal Arab cavalry so heavily armored that they were described as "mountains of iron." They were nevertheless defeated by a smaller, though more determined and coordinated, 'Abbasid army consisting of a cavalry elite and a larger force of infantry who included pikemen and composite bowmen. These archers, like most of the early Kurasani 'Abbasid forces, were mainly recruited from Arab troops and settlers in greater Khurasan who had been influenced by Khurasanian culture and military traditions. Khurasani archers, both Arabs and non-Arabs, dominated 'Abbasid Archery. Their bow, known as the Khurasanian bow (*al-qaws al-khurasaniyya*) became one of the four major prototypes of composite bows that marked the history of Arabo-Islamic archery in the Middle East. The other three were the Wasitian bow, the Egyptian bow, and the Damascus bow. Each of these four prototypes represents a specific phase in the evolution of Arabo-Islamic archery, starting in the late 7th century with the Wasitian bow and concluding in the early 16th century with the Damascene bow.

Like all *furusiyya* arts that initially evolved under the 'Abbasids (see Ibn Akhi Hizam), Arabo-Islamic horse and foot archery synthesized individual contributions and collective efforts from various traditions, including Mesopotamian, Arabic, Central Asian, Persian, Byzantine, and Armenian. This process is documented in archery treatises written in Arabic from the late 8th to early 16th centuries CE.

Arabo-Islamic archery, as expounded in archery treatises, was exclusively based upon the composite bow. However, all Arab philological works on bows, classical Arab poetry, as well as the entire corpus of *hadith* religious traditions attributed to the Prophet Muhammad concerned with the merits of archery, focused upon the simple wooden hand bow. Nearly all the nomenclature pertinent to the simple Arab bow was adopted for the composite bow, which is referred to in the archery treatises as the *qaws* (bow) without further distinction. This can lead to confusion between the two types of bows, especially when we know that archery treatises usually begin with the relevant religious traditions (*sunna*) on archery, followed by the nomenclature and types of the simple bow as established by 'Abbasid philologists and coupled with appropriate verses from Arab poetry. As composite and simple bows differ fundamentally, confusion between them will render archery treatises incomprehensible and will deeply compromise our understanding of *furusiyya* arts and literature. Indeed, the essence of military *furusiyya* and the whole Mamluk institution (see Ibn Akhi Hizam) was based upon horse archery solely using the composite bow. Unless otherwise specified, all occurrences of the term "bow" hereafter denote this composite bow.

Practically all the basic archery texts were written in Arabic during the first two centuries of 'Abbasid rule. The authors were trained archers and their works recorded both their own experience and the techniques of their respective schools of archery (*madhahib al-rami*). These schools of archery emerged during the same period. The founders, who flourished in Iraq and Khurasan, were archery masters commonly referred to as *a'immat al-rami* (imams of archery) numbering no more than 10 principal figures. The most prominent were Abu Hashim al-Bawardi, Tahir al-Balkhi, Ishaq al-Raffa', Abu'l-Hasan al-Kaghadi, and Abu'l-Fath Sa'id Ibn Khafif al-Samarqandi. The latter, who was considered the greatest master of his time and the last of the "archery imams," was born in Baghdad in the second half of the ninth century and gained prominence under the Caliphs al-Radi (934–940) and al-Mustakfi (944–946). His father, Khafif al-Samarqandi, had been a confidant of the Caliph al-Mu'tadid. Under this caliph, 'Abbasid archery reached its apogee. Being an army commander, Abu'l-Fath Sa'id Ibn Khafif al-Samarqandi's *madhhab* in archery was entirely military. He was also the younger contemporary of Abu'l-Hasan al-Kaghadi who lived in Harat (now in Afghanistan), where he devoted his life and fortune to gaining excellence in archery. His school, which was based on target archery, was civilian.

Al-Bawardi, al-Balkhi, and al-Raffa were three celebrated great masters who were later consecrated as the truest masters of archery (*a'immat al-rami al-kibar*). Consequently it was they who largely dictated the nature of archery literature in the latter 'Abbasid and Mamluk periods. The first school, that of al-Bawardi, who was probably still alive in the first half of eighth century, was close to the old Sasanian school, which was principally based upon infantry archery. Al-Balkhi lived in the second half of the eighth century and his school represented 'Abbasid Khurasani infantry and horse archery. Ishaq al-Raffa flourished in Iraq in the first half of the ninth century and his school was a specifically 'Abbasid development. As such it remains extremely important for our understanding of the evolution of Muslim archery, especially in the Arab regions, where it was adopted by the majority of mounted and infantry archers from the 'Abbasid to Mamluk periods. Al-Raffa's school was often described as the middle school (*madhhab al-wasat*) for having allegedly taken a middle way in terms of archery techniques, between the schools of al-Bawardi and al-Balkhi. However, its importance lies in its contribution to the standardization of archery techniques. This is implied by the systemization of the 'Abbasid military training programme, which inevitably led to the standardization of the war bow, and consequently allowed its large-scale production. This development reached remarkable dimensions in Ayyubid Syria when Damascus became the largest center for manufacturing war bows within the Islamic world.

The Theory: Al-Tabari was the foremost authority on the schools of al-Bawardi, al-Balkhi and al-Raffa. He expounded their methods as well as his own eclectic approach in *Kitab al-wadih fi'l-rami,* "The Clear Book on Archery." This treatise apparently became so popular in Baghdad during the late 9th and 10th centuries that the author was confused with the famous Baghdadi historian Muhammad Ibn Jarir al-Tabari (838–923). The text became even more admired after the consecration of al-Bawardi, al-Balkhi and al-Raffa as the greatest masters of archery in the 12th century.

During the Mamluk period, al-Tabari, who was referred to as the "founder of the eclectic school" (*sahib madhhab al-ikhtyar*), became implicitly consecrated as the fourth "imam of archery" and his widely used *Kitab al-wadih* became an essential treatise for understanding Mamluk archery and its specialized literature. The *Kitab al-wadih* gained popularity from the 12th century onward, not only because it was the main source of information about the schools of the three great archery masters but also, and more importantly, because of its author's eclectic approach that had important technical and economic implications. Indeed, during the Ayyubid period, when the mass production of war bows in Damascus was standardized into three types, some Syrian authors and archers introduced the idea that the practices of the great masters represented three size categories: tall (Abu Hashim al-Bawardi), medium (Ishaq al-Raffa), and short (Tahir al-Balkhi). This categorization was too constricting because in practice a bow made for a tall man and the techniques for using it were not necessarily unsuitable for a man of medium or short proportions. Al-Tabari's diverse method thus provided a practical alternative and became a stabilizing influence and a release from overrigid classification.

Kitab al-wadih considered the fundamentals of archery according to the schools of the three great masters plus the author's personal views. By contrast, al-Tabari's most thorough work remained *Kitab al-shamil fi'l-rami,* "The Inclusive Book on Archery," which represents the oldest surviving comprehensive archery treatise and was probably the first of its kind in archery literature. It mainly deals with military archery and covers the types of bows, bowstrings, arrows, thumb-guards, training a novice, the perfection of archery techniques, target shooting, the faults and injuries to which an archer is exposed, bracing the bow, hints for archers on foot and on horseback, shooting techniques while carrying a shield, how infantry archers should behave if they were taken by surprise or were outnumbered, how to alternate between different weapons during combat, and shooting at an enemy in the dark. He also offered advice on camping at night, on shooting short arrows with an arrow guide, shooting incendiary projectiles, shooting small incendiary pellets with a handheld bow, as well as how to make such missiles, shooting at and from a fortress, and various other useful skills. *Kitab al-shamil* became a major source for subsequent general and thematic *furusiyya* treatises including treatises specifically concerned with archery, starting with the *furusiyya* treatise by al-Tabari's younger contemporary Ibn Akhi Hizam (v.q.). Other works by al-Tabari may not have survived and currently remains untraceable, though they are quoted in later archery treatises, especially those from the Mamluk period. These missing works include *Kitab nuzhat al-qulub* "The Heart's Joy Book (of Archery)," *Kitab al-kanz* "The Treasure Book (of Archery)," and *Kitab jami al-asrar* "The Book of (Archery) Secrets."

Descendents: After having flourished for more than eight centuries, Arab-Islamic archery literature died out when the Mamluk Sultanate of Egypt and Syria fell to the Ottoman Turks in 1517. The manufacture of war and competition bows in the Arab regions also came to a virtual standstill when the Ottomans deported Syrian bow makers *en masse* to Istanbul and turned their workshops complex, the *Qaysariyat al-Qawasin,* where the famous Damascene bow was manufactured, into a kitchen for Ottoman *yeni cheri* (Janissaries) troops in 1516. The Ottomans mostly recycled Arabic and especially 'Abbasid archery literature. Al-Tabari remained the point of reference, as attested in a 19th-century Ottoman archery treatise written by Qahwachi Bashi for Sultan Mahmud II (1808–1839 CE).

See also: Ibn Akhi Hizam, Muhammad Ibn Ya'qub al-Khuttali; Mubarakshah, Fakhr-i Mudabbir; Usama Ibn Munqidh

Shihab al-Sarraf

Apollodorus (Apollodoros), Architect

Significance: Apollodorus's treatise of offensive siege devices shows us some of the equipment used by the famed Roman legions at the apogee of the empire.

Context: Apollodorus's career belongs to the time when the Roman Empire achieved its greatest extent as a result of Trajan's (98–117 AD) offensive wars, and when his successor Hadrian (117–138 AD) put a stop to the conquests.

Biography: Apollodorus served as Trajan's chief engineer during his Second Dacian War (105–106 AD), becoming famous for his great bridge over the Danube, after which he served as architect responsible for the building of Trajan's Forum. According to ancient sources, Hadrian had Apollodorus first exiled and then executed for being too free with words, but some modern historians have doubted the veracity of this story.

Influences: Apollodorus's siege machines were based on existing models that he then adapted to the needs of the planned military campaign.

The Theory: As military theorist Apollodorus is most famous for his treatise of the building of the bridge over the Danube (lost) and for his manual of offensive siege machines called *Poliorketica.* The latter was dedicated to an emperor who was about to embark upon a military campaign. According to the *Parangelmata Poliorketica,* the emperor was Hadrian, but some modern historians have challenged this and would prefer Trajan. The authorship of the work has also been questioned.

   The purpose of the handbook was to give a list of offensive siege machines, which were easy to transport, light in weight, practical, and fast to assemble, together with instructions on how to use those. The offensive devices include: a fortified ditch; a wedge-shaped deflector; a light screen/shed; a shed for mining;

a drill for use against brick; a primitive flame-thrower; a device to crack stone; a shed with a ram and a separate shed for the personnel; a scout ladder; a siege tower with five possible attachments (a drawbridge, a double ram usable as drawbridge, a pivoted antipersonnel flail, a platform to level ground, and hosepipes for fire-fighting); interlocking ladders with possible attachments (an antipersonnel flail/cleaver, a device for pouring hot oil or liquid on the defenders, a ram, a double ram, and a ram with flail); and a floating bridge/raft.

The commentators have had mixed opinions of the practicality of the devices. The survival of the treatise and the inclusion of some its equipment in the Column of Trajan and Septimius Severus' Arch suggest that at least some of the devices were found useful. However, the usefulness of the floating bridge was already justifiably criticized by Syrianus Magister, because it could be used only in certain circumstances, and some of the modern commentators have also doubted the usefulness of the other devices. The treatise has also been criticized for not including defensive measures, but it should be kept in mind that the handbook was written only as a list of offensive siege devices to be employed during a particular military campaign.

Application: The portable devices mentioned by Apollodorus's treatise were used, for example, during Trajan's Dacian Wars (e.g., light ladders, wedge-shaped deflectors) and Septimius Severus' Parthian Wars. The later evidence also suggests that some of the devices continued to be used by the late Romans and Byzantines.

Descendents: The inclusion of Apollodorus's *Poliorketica* among the official collections of military treatises by the Byzantines proves that it was considered useful. It was also read as Syrianus Magister's negative comment regarding the floating bridge and the use of the treatise by the Pseudo-Heron of Byzantium as his principal source attest. Apollodorus's instructions remained helpful until the advent of gunpowder.

See also: Byzantine Military Doctrine

Further Reading
Burford, Alison, *Craftsmen in Greek and Roman Society*. London: Thames & Hudson, 1972.

Ilkka Syvänne

Archimedes of Syracuse
(ca. 287–212 BCE)

Significance: Known for his various machines used to drive off a besieging army.

Context: Second Punic War (218–202 BCE).

Biography: The significance of Archimedes in the history of science is vast: in addition to his many texts on mathematics and the physics of the simple machines, he was also one of the most important investigators and theorists on the properties of water. In addition to his intellect, however, Archimedes is somewhat unique in that he turned his scientific knowledge not only toward explaining the natural world, but also toward solving everyday difficulties encountered in it. For example, one of the most famous of the many anecdotes surrounding him involves his discovery of the properties of buoyancy; his delight in his having done so stems in part from the contributions he thereby made to natural philosophy, and also in part from the fact that it helped him solve a specific problem given to him by the ruler of Syracuse. Likewise, this same knowledge also allowed him to invent a functional and useful water-moving device, which is still called the "Archimedes screw."

It was this sort of real-world problem solving that led Archimedes to his most relevant interaction with military history. According to many sources (of which Polybius is the earliest but Plutarch is the most significant), Archimedes was at some point, prior to the year 213 BCE, commissioned by the ruler of Syracuse to apply his theories about the simple machines to the invention or improvement of siege engines. When the Romans determined to lay siege to Syracuse during the Second Punic War, these machines were used to frustrate them at every turn: the sources describe devices that dropped enormous weights on Romans, launched missiles at both short and long range, and a claw-like mechanism that picked up entire ships and either capsized them or dashed them to pieces. Later sources also mention some sort of "burning glass," which set fire to Roman vessels. Because of these apparatus, the Roman commander Marcus Claudius Marcellus was forced to find means other than frontal assault to take Syracuse. When he did, Archimedes was among those who died at the hands of the invading Romans; Plutarch reports that he was killed by a soldier when he refused to be led away to captivity before he had finished a mathematical proof, although he also records an alternative account which holds that Archimedes was attempting to surrender to a soldier who confused the scientific equipment he was carrying with him for treasure. Marcellus is said by that author to have been aggrieved by his death, and to have returned the scientist's body to his family with due honors.

The Theory: In spite of his unquestioned importance to the history of mathematics, science, and technology, Archimedes was not himself greatly influential on the history of warfare. In the first place, his engines delayed but did not prevent the capture of Syracuse. Moreover, he left behind no treatises describing the physics behind these, nor any guides for their tactical use or manufacture. Indeed, the engines themselves were apparently never duplicated (and perhaps could not be without their inventor's genius, which may help to explain the dismay of Marcellus at his death). An explanation for this can be found in the prevailing attitude in the classical world that technology was the reserve of craftsmen or *banausoi,* who were generally lower-class laborers, and not an appropriate endeavor for the wealthy upper-class men of the sort who were devoted to science. Plutarch records that Archimedes himself held this opinion, and refrained from writing about his inventions for precisely this reason. Thus, although artillery and siege engines were well known in the ancient world, they were almost always invented and improved upon by unknown technicians who knew how they worked, but not necessarily why. Scientists, for their part, very rarely applied their knowledge toward inventing or improving machines or processes of any stripe before Archimedes, and he himself was compelled to do so.

This attitude persisted throughout the classical period, and despite the fact that the machines invented by Archimedes were themselves would be of some interest to later scientists (most notably Hero of Alexandria, whose works *Belopoieka* and *Cheiroballista* describe the construction, maintenance, and use of war machines, specifically citing Archimedes), there are practically no references to other philosophers turning their expertise toward accomplishing military aims or surmounting military problems through machinery or other means. Archimedes was thus something of a singular case, one whose successes were not sufficient to lead to many imitators beyond Hero. Because this same attitude would persist throughout the Middle Ages, scientists would not regularly play a significant role in the development of military technology until modern times.

Descendents: Hero of Alexandria

See also: Hero of Alexandria

Further Reading
Burford, Alison, *Craftsmen in Greek and Roman Society.* London: Thames & Hudson, 1972.

Seth Lyons Kendall

Biton, Engineer

Significance: Biton's handbook of siege machines is the only extant treatise to give a full description of advanced nontorsion (i.e., tension) catapults (later called as bow ballistae).

Context: Biton wrote his handbook for a king of Pergamum. Pergamum faced many powerful enemies as a result of which its kings allied themselves with Rome.

Biography: Little is known of Biton besides that he was an engineer who dedicated his treatise to Attalus. It is usually thought that Biton meant Attalus I, king of Pergamum (241–197 BC), but Attalus II (159–138 BC) and Attalus III (138–133 BC) have also received support, and it has even been claimed that the whole work is a later forgery.

Influences: Biton's thinking was clearly influenced by the inherent practicality and reliability of the old traditional siege equipment at the time when new inventions were in vogue.

The Theory: Biton's handbook describes four tension bow catapults, a *helepolis* (city-taker = siege tower), and a *sambuca* (mechanical scaling ladder). The bow catapults consist of two stone throwers (small and large) and two bolt shooters (a medium "belly bow" and mountain "belly bow"). All of these designs had been invented by other famous engineers, and were old and tried at the time Biton wrote his treatise. For example, the tension catapults were easier to build and maintain than the torsion engines and therefore quite practical and reliable even in difficult conditions. However, Biton has unfortunately left out some of the details. For example, he does not mention how the bows were constructed as a result of which the opinions of modern commentators are divided into supporters of either steel or composite construction.

Application: All of the designs had seen use in the field before Biton included those in his treatise. We do not know whether Attalus employed them, but the designs were definitely used in numerous later sieges and naval battles.

Descendents: Biton's manual was later mentioned by Athenaeus, Hesychius, and Pseudo-Heron of Byzantium, and it was also included in the Byzantine canon of Greek military treatises. For example, the Byzantines used tension powered artillery on their ships evidently because those were less vulnerable to wet than the torsion artillery. This suggests that at least the Byzantines probably used steel or bronze springs rather than composite bows. Biton's instructions retained their relevance until the advent of gunpowder.

See also: Byzantine Military Doctrine

Further Reading
Haldon, John, *Byzantine Warfare* (*The International Library of Essays on Military History*). London: Ashgate Publ., 2007.

Ilkka Syvänne

Brialmont, Major General Henri Alexis
(1821–1903)

Significance: The most celebrated military architect of his day, Brialmont achieved international fame by modernizing the fortifications of several major cities, writing several textbooks on military engineering, and by publishing an enormous number of books, pamphlets, and articles on international affairs, defense policy, history, tactics, and biography. In his home country of Belgium, Brialmont is remembered as an eloquent advocate for a strong national defense and one of the few military thinkers of the 19th century who based his theories on the strategic problems faced by small nations.

Context: Brialmont's career coincided with a period of enormous progress in the realm of military technology. He saw the replacement of smooth-bore, muzzle-loading artillery pieces by rifled breechloaders, black powder cartridges by powerful smokeless propellants, spherical cast-iron shells by steel projectiles, low-power bursting charges by modern high explosives, burning lengths of match by sophisticated fuses, and traditional forms of masonry and brickwork by reinforced concrete. At the same time, Brialmont lived in an age when small standing armies of the middle years of the 19th century were evolving into the mass armies of the early 20th century.

Biography: Henri Alexis Brialmont was born on May 25, 1821, in Maagdenberg, a village near the city of Venlo, in the kingdom of the Netherlands. Educated at the Royal Military School (*Ecole Royale Militaire / Koninklijke Militaire School*) in Brussels, he was commissioned in 1843 as a second lieutenant (*sous lieutenant*) in the Regiment of Engineers (*Régiment du Génie*). In 1849, while employed as the private secretary to the minister of war, Brialmont published his first substantial piece of writing, a lengthy essay on the participation of field artillery batteries in the reclamation of marginal lands. This small book, which he wrote in partnership with Major General (*lieutenant général*) Alexis Michel Eenens (1805–1883), displayed the careful reconciliation of political, military, and technical considerations that would characterize his subsequent writings. The grand debut of Brialmont as a military writer in his own right, however, did not take place until 1850. In that year, he founded the *Journal of the Belgian Army (Journal de l'Armée Belge)*, published his first treatise on the subject of fortification, and came out with a remarkable monograph on the role played by fortresses in the international negotiations leading up to the creation of the Belgian state in 1831.

In the years that followed, Brialmont wrote a large number of books. These included a three-volume overview of Belgian defense policy (1851–1855), a biography of the Duke of Wellington (1856–1857), several works on the role that fortifications played in international affairs (1863), a study of the defenses of the kingdom of the Netherlands (1866), six books advocating the reform of the Belgian army (1866–1871), six works on improvised fortifications (1872–1880), two books on the impact of improved explosive shells on fortification (1888, 1890), and a history of the evolution of fortification in 17th, 18th, and 19th centuries (1890).

Brialmont's considerable literary output seems to have had a positive effect on his career. By 1868, he had attained the rank of colonel and the post of director of operations at the war ministry. Seven years later, he was a brigadier general (*général major*), inspector general of fortifications and chief of the Belgian engineer corps. In 1877, Brialmont was promoted to the highest rank then accorded by the Belgian army in peacetime, that of major general (*lieutenant général*). Brialmont spent much of the 1880s advising the governments of several foreign states (including Romania, Switzerland, Bulgaria, Greece, and the Ottoman Empire) on matters related to fortification. In 1888, however, he returned to Belgium to supervise the building of modern fortifications at Liège and Namur.

Influences: In the early years of his career, Brialmont took many of his ideas about fortification from the great military engineer of the 17th century, Sébastien Le Prestre, le Seigneur de Vauban (1633–1707). In particular, the young Brialmont advocated compact fortifications that were optimized for passive resistance to hostile artillery fire and the task of subjecting attacking infantry to heavy volumes of fire at very close ranges. By the late 1850s, however, Brialmont had discarded many of Vauban's ideas about fortification in favor of concepts made popular by the "father of modern fortification," Marc Réné, le Marquis de Montalembert (1714–1800.) Montalembert's ideas included straighter lines, longer fields of fire and a fondness for creating situations that placed attackers in a crossfire. (Because the straight lines gave fortresses the appearance of simple polygons, Montalembert's approach was often called the "polygonal method.")

The Theory: The starting point for Brialmont's theory of war was the axiom that the states of Europe were continuously engaged in a multisided contest. The dynamics of this contest were such that, if any given state overextended itself, other states would try to take advantage of its temporary weakness. For large states, this situation created a strong bias in favor of campaigns of rapid maneuver— operations that would result in a decisive military victory before other large states could react. For smaller states, the dynamics of this "concert of Europe" created a strong incentive against campaigns of rapid maneuver. Indeed, the armies of small states were well advised to play for time, to avoid decisive engagement until the action of third parties forced the aggressor to disengage. In other words, the chief task of a small army was not to win victory on the battlefield, but to maintain itself as an "army in being."

For Brialmont, an indispensable tool for avoiding defeat at the hands of larger army was the employment of a well-prepared refuge. Variously known as an "entrenched camp" (*camp retranché*) or the "national redoubt" (*redoute nationale*), this refuge was large enough to accommodate the field army of the state in question. The most important defenses of an entrenched camp were the detached forts that prevented hostile artillery from bombarding its interior. (Some advocates of entrenched camps argued that these detached forts could be improvised in time of war. Brialmont, however, believed that improvised forts took too long to build. Thus, although he advocated the extensive use of field fortifications, he saw these as a complement to fortresses built at leisure during times of peace.) In addition to this, entrenched camps were built around a central fortress. This served as a base of supply for the field army, as well as a means of stopping attacks by enemy troops that might infiltrate through the line of detached forts.

Brialmont's ideas about the proper size of an entrenched camp evolved over the course of his career. In the middle years of the 19th century, when the effective range of siege artillery was limited to a few thousand meters, he favored camps that were relatively small. Later, when the ability of siege artillery to hit distant targets improved, he became an advocate for substantially larger camps. In Brialmont's first plan for the entrenched camp of Antwerp, which dates from the 1850s, the detached forts that served to keep hostile siege artillery beyond effective firing range were only three or four kilometers away from the central fortress. Twenty years later, he began to propose the building of detached forts that were separated from the central fortress by a bare minimum of nine kilometers of intervening space.

The respect for the growing power of siege artillery that characterized Brialmont's ideas about entrenched camps extended the design of the detached fort. Brialmont was an early advocate of the use of armored plate to protect the defensive artillery of fortresses. In particular, he favored the placement of the most powerful ordnance of a fort in rotating armored turrets known as "cupolas" (*cupules*), as well as the extensive use of covered positions for supplementary weapons of various sorts. These, Brialmont believed, would allow a relatively small number of artillery pieces to provide a degree of coverage that would otherwise have required a much larger number of guns and howitzers.

To supplement the fire of detached forts, Brialmont advocated the building of intermediate batteries. These were protected positions for artillery pieces that were placed in the area between the central fortress and the detached forts. Because they were less likely to be exposed to the full weight of the fire of a besieging force, intermediate batteries did not have to be as well protected as detached forts. Intermediate batteries were located in positions that allowed them to bring effective fire to bear on any hostile force trying to take a detached fort. That is to say, they existed so that hostile forces attacking a detached fort would have to deal, not only with the defenses of the fort itself, but also with artillery fire coming from a number of different directions. (The detached forts were also located in a way that allowed them to bring fire to bear upon any hostile force that posed a danger to a neighboring fort.)

Application: Brialmont was able to apply his ideas to the defenses of Antwerp, other Belgian fortresses (such as Liège and Namur), and the defenses of Bucharest. Indeed, where Belgian fortifications were concerned, his career was sufficiently long to permit the periodic revision of many of his earlier projects. He thus avoided the sad fate of the theorists who see the incomplete ideas of their youth put into action and their mature conceptions ignored. In addition, many of Brialmont's ideas were employed by the designers of other contemporary fortresses, particularly those on both sides of the Franco-German border.

Descendents: During the first few weeks of World War I, many of the fortresses designed by Brialmont were quickly captured by German forces equipped with super-heavy siege howitzers, weapons such as the 420-mm "Big Bertha" and the 305-mm "Slender Emma." The ability of these pieces to reduce detached forts to so much rubble in a matter of hours, however, confirmed the validity of the principle underlying Brialmont's designs—the idea that the chief strength of a fortress lay less in its passive features than its artillery. Similarly, although the national redoubt of Antwerp did not function in accordance with Brialmont's original conception, it did permit the Belgian army to recover from its initial defeats. In addition, the German campaign to capture Antwerp employed resources that, if used elsewhere, might have resulted in decisive German victories. (In particular, siege artillery that was originally earmarked for the capture of Verdun, as well as divisions that would have been welcome in the "race to the sea" that followed battle of the Marne, were diverted to Antwerp.)

Because of the events of 1914, those who associated Brialmont with particular features of fortress design became convinced that his ideas had been rendered obsolete by changes in military technology. Those, however, who looked beyond the steel and concrete to see the underlying principles, were less eager to consign Brialmont to the dustbin of history. In particular, the designers of the many fortifications commissioned by the governments of Switzerland, the Netherlands, Belgium, and Czechoslovakia during the years after World War I drew a great deal of inspiration from Brialmont's work. The same could be said for the fortifications of the famous Maginot line, which were based on ideas that might well be described as logical extensions of those of Brialmont.

See also: Coehoorn, Menno Van

Further Reading

Brialmont lived at a time when most of the people with a serious interest in military engineering, international affairs, or Belgian defense policy could read French. Because of this, very few of Brialmont's works were translated into English. Those that were, moreover, tended to deal with subjects on the periphery of Brialmont's interests—such things as the defense of the British Isles (1860), field engineering (1872), and cavalry tactics (1893). The great exception to this rule is Brialmont's biography of the Duke of Wellington, which contains a great deal of his early thought on the relationship between the art of building fortresses, the course of major wars and the fate of small nations. (The verbatim translation of Brialmont's biography of Wellington, which was published in four volumes in 1858–1860, should not be confused with the many condensations and adaptations of the original work that appeared in subsequent years.)

Neither of the two "life and work" biographies of Brialmont, both of which were written by Paul B. Crokaert in the 1920s, have been translated into English. Because of this, the best way for Anglophone readers to study the works of Brialmont is through the many reviews of his books and commentaries on his designs that can be found in the back issues of the *Royal Engineers Journal* (United Kingdom) and the *Professional Papers of the Corps of Engineers* (United States). More recent commentary, with an emphasis on surviving examples of fortifications designed by Brialmont or his disciples, can be found in *Fort, the International Journal of Fortification and Military Architecture.*

Crokaert, Paul, *Brialmont,* Brussels: Dewit, 1928 (Biography).

Crokaert, Paul, *Brialmont, Eloge et Mémoires,* Brussels: Lesigne, 1925 (Comprehensive biography).

Duffy, Christopher, *Fire and Stone: The Science of Fortress Warfare, 1660–1860,* Mechanicsburg: Stackpole, 1996 (Background).

Kaufmann, J. E., and Clayton Donnell, *Modern European Fortifications, 1870–1950,* Westport: Praeger, 2004 (Bibliography).

Bruce I. Gudmundsson

Coehoorn, Baron Menno Van
(1641–1704)

Significance: Coehoorn made numerous innovations in siege warfare and fortification techniques.

Context: Coehoorn lived at a time of almost continuous war between Holland and France. The Dutch War of 1672–1679 had revealed weaknesses in the science of fortification, and Coehoorn applied himself toward remedying this situation.

Biography: Coehoorn was born at Leeuwarden in Friesland in 1641 into a Dutch army family of Swedish origin. He studied mathematics and fortification at the academy of Franeker and entered the army in 1657. He took part in the defense of Maastricht in 1673 and the siege of Grave in 1674, during the Dutch War of Louis XIV (1672–1679). In the same year, he gave his name to a man-portable mortar, useful for fighting in the trenches of sieges. He was promoted to colonel as a reward for his courage in the Battle of Seneffe in 1674, and he was also present at the battles of Cassel (1667) and Saint Denis (1678). His first book, *The Pentagonal Fortress with all its Outworks* (1682), convinced the Dutch government to commission him to redesign the major fortresses of the Netherlands.

In the Nine Years' War, also known as the War of the League of Augsburg (1689–1697), Coehoorn was a brigade commander. In 1690, he participated with distinction in the Allied defeat of Fleurus against the French general Luxembourg. In 1692, at his own fortress of Namur, Coehoorn was besieged by the great military engineer, Vauban. He was wounded by a bomb and forced to capitulate. There followed a pointed exchange between the two men, where Coehoorn boasted that he had forced the Frenchman to change the sites of his batteries seven times. Coehoorn retook the strengthened and supposedly impregnable fortress of Namur in 1695, after a fierce bombardment and a costly storming by Cutts's English infantry, but Vauban wrote off this effort as crude.

During the War of the Spanish Succession Coehoorn, now a lieutenant general, proposed a bold stroke into Brabant, but the Allies decided to winkle the French out of the Rhine and Maas forts in the old style. Coehoorn served as chief engineer to Marlborough at the siege of Venlo in 1702, and made very careful preparations, securing the city after a short but very violent cannonade. This was a major victory for the maritime powers, because, as Louis XIV himself admitted, Venlo was the key to Gelders and the Rhine fortresses, vital for the defense of France. This success was followed by the swift reduction of Bonn and Huy in 1703.

Coehoorn died of natural causes in 1704, at the height of the War of the Spanish Succession. In Amsterdam, stock exchange prices tumbled, as he was regarded as something of a lucky totem. He was indeed sorely missed by his friends and allies, Prince Eugene of Savoy saying of him, "I know that there can be no comparison between his ability and that of the horrible little men we have with us now."

Influences: Coehoorn adapted many of the details of his work from the 1630 work of his countryman Adam Freitag, and the 16th-century German engineer Daniel Speckle.

The Theory: Coehoorn's great work, *The New Method of Fortification,* was published in 1685. This work advocated the simplification of fortress design to the most geometrically elegant and efficient plan. Coehoorn's three "systems" emphasized different parts of the defensive structure: the first was a combined bastion and *fausse-braye* (a low earthen rampart); the second a continuous *fausse-braye*; and the third were large protecting ravelins and lunettes (triangular raised outworks). He also recommended reliance on alternate wet and dry ditches, narrow *orillons* (projecting shoulders on the bastions), and stubborn defense from hidden redoubts. His designs were well suited to the low lying and marshy terrain of this homeland, and he was able to adapt them to take account of local topographical peculiarities.

Coehoorn also recommended an aggressive defense to upset the besiegers. During siege operations, Coehoorn advocated concentrated fire on the enemy defenses rather than a desultory bombardment of the town within—this proved very successful during the War of the League of Augsburg, at the sieges of Kaiserswörth and Bonn in 1689.

Application and Descendents: Coehoorn's designs were incorporated into the defenses of Namur, and Coehoorn became engineer general of fortifications in 1695, working on the modernization of Bergen op Zoom and other fortresses such as Nijmegen, Breda, and Mannheim to the specifications of his first system. Timisoara and Belgrade in Eastern Europe were rebuilt according to his second system.

See also: Brialmont

Further Reading
The best modern works on fortification in this period are by Christopher Duffy: *The Fortress in the Age of Vauban and Frederick the Great, 1660–1789* (London: Routledge, 1985) and *Fire and Stone: The Science of Fortress Warfare, 1660–1860* (London: David and Charles, 1995).

Toby McLeod

Dionysios I
(Also Dionysios the Elder Greek)

Significance: He was the autocratic ruler of Syracuse that made use of mercenary troops.

Context: Dionysios fought a long campaign against Carthage and created the powerful fortifications for his city Syracuse.

Biography: A talented officer, Dionysios was elected the supreme commander of Syracuse's forces in 406 BC and then a year later became tyrant. Fond of literature and the arts, but absolutely ruthless, it was rumored that he was poisoned by his son, Dionysios the Younger.

Influences: The early Greek tyrants of the mainland.

The Theory: He made use of ruthless force to gain power and the construction of formidable walls to make Syracuse a local power.

Application: In 402 BC, Dionysius began construction of the great circuit walls of Syracuse, which were finished in 397 BC.

Descendents: Dionysius appears in Dante's *Inferno,* but it is unclear that he was a direct influence on any specific theorists.

Further Reading
Meier-Welcker, Hans, *Dionysios I., Tyrann von Syrakus* (Personlichkeit und Geschichte). Musterschmidt, 1971.

John Serrati

Gribeauval, Jean-Baptiste Vaquette de
(1715–1789)

Significance: From 1792 to 1815 the French artillery was the magic ingredient in victory. It had saved the Republic at Valmy in 1792 and played an important role in Napoleon I's performance.

Context: Improvements in iron foundry techniques and in metallurgy allowed Gribeauval to develop a lighter and stronger barrel for his artillery system. This, together with a light and strong twin trail carriage, combined good fire power with high mobility, and improved the ratio of weight of shot to overall weapon weight. Equally, the Briton John Wilkinson's invention, sold in France, of cannon boring machines, allowed more accurate and consistent calibers to be produced. This reduced "windage," the gap between the solid shot and the barrel's bore that had previously reduced accuracy.

Biography: Born in Amiens in 1715, the son of a judge, Gribeauval entered the *Royale Artillerie* regiment of the French army in 1732 and was commissioned in 1735, dividing his time between his military duties and scientific study. In 1752, he became the captain of a company of sappers.

After a trip to Prussia, he served in the Seven Years' War as a lieutenant colonel on attachment to the Austrian army as an artillery commander. He was mentioned in dispatches at the siege of Glatz and the defense of Schweidnitz. He was captured by the Prussians but soon exchanged and decorated by the Empress of Austria herself with the order of Maria-Theresa.

Having learned much, he returned after the peace to work on the improvement of his native artillery arm. Promoted to lieutenant general and inspector of artillery, and decorated with the order of St. Louis in 1764, he started on the rationalization of the service's equipment. He simplified the variety of different sizes of gun then in existence into three classified by weight of shot: 4, 8, and 12 pounder, firing round shot or canister. These were complemented by the 6.4- and 8-inch howitzer for bombardment with explosive shells. They were all designed to the same specification, with interchangeable wheels and other components that meant that if a piece was damaged or broken it could be repaired and back in action very quickly. Also, the pieces could be moved around very quickly by horses harnessed in pairs, or by the "prolong" method—by means of a rope hitched to the gun—without the need to limber and unlimber. Gribeauval's system even allowed the guns to be moved in action without horses, using the "*bricole*" system of ropes and a team of willing helpers. A new siege train was also created, containing heavier 24- and 32-pound pieces.

In 1776, Gribeauval was appointed inspector general of artillery. He began to create a cadre of specialist artillery officers (including Napoleon Bonaparte) and set in place a proper promotion and career structure. He improved pay for the gunners, as befitted a technical service, and paid much attention to the comfort and hygiene of their barracks. Gribeauval died on May 9, 1789, just before the outbreak of the French Revolution.

Influences: New tactics for the use of light artillery in battle had been suggested by Guibert and the Chevalier du Teil in 1778. The 4- and 8-pound guns of Gribeauval's system were ideal for use as battalion guns to support infantry at close range, and also for use by the horse artillery—a concept introduced by the Prussians in the 1760s. Horse artillery proved to be the most radical improvement. Although originally designed originally to advance with the cavalry, from the 1792 onward the horse gunners were increasingly used to support rapid infantry column attacks. General Jourdan gave a marvelous display of this technique at the battle of Wattignies in 1793, and successive French commanders built on this tactic.

The Theory: Gribeauval expanded the artillery system beyond the guns alone to include the whole doctrine of the employment of artillery and the training of gunners. The technical improvements such as lighter carriages, better horse harness, and mobile caissons meant that the guns could now keep up with the army's lead formations, rather than having to be sited in static batteries. Improved sighting using a screw at the breech, and an adjustable back sight meant that fire could be accurate concentrated on a single point of an enemy's defensive line.

Application: The Gribeauval system really came into its own when two or three batteries were massed together at divisional or more at corps level. When the French Revolutionary War broke out in 1792, the armies of the French Republic enjoyed an unrivalled technical superiority in the artillery arm, and they capitalized on this straight away. Artillery was seen as modern, efficient, and highly technical and quite in keeping with the revolutionary spirit. Its officers tended to be less aristocratic than the cavalry or infantry, as the *Royal Artillerie* in prerevolutionary days was not seen as a very fashionable regiment, consequently it suffered less from desertions and defections by officers of noble birth fearing for their necks in the wake of the fall of the Bastille.

As early as 1796 at Castiglione, Marmont had used an 18-gun battery to break the Austrian line. During the empire, from 1804 onward, the creation of the Imperial Guard brought into being a large reserve of artillery that could be deployed to defend a threatened potion of the line, or could be deployed forward aggressively to rupture an enemy's position. This worked marvelously well at Friedland in 1807, where Sénarmont combined all the artillery of one corps, some 38 pieces in total, into a single battery firing at a range of 200 meters, and then rushed them forward to a range of only 60 meters, opening fire with canister. This effectively shattered the Russian line, and was a remarkable offensive use of artillery made possible by the exceptional mobility of Gribeauval's design.

However, in the later period of the wars, Napoleon increasingly used massed artillery to make up for the declining quality of his soldiers, and there were occasions where it was not entirely successful, such as at Wagram (1809), and famously at Waterloo (1815).

Descendents: The result of Gribeauval's work was a century of French dominance in field artillery, and several generations of outstanding artillery officers and theorists.

See also: Bonaparte, Napoleon; Tartaglia (The Stammerer) (aka Niccolò Fontana); Teil de Beaumont, Jean du

Further Reading
Griffith, P., *French Artillery* (1976) and *The Art of War of Revolutionary France 1789–1802* (1998).

Toby McLeod

Hero of Alexandria
(fl. 66 CE)

Significance: Known for describing the construction and maintenance of artillery and siege engines.

Context: Roman Egypt during the time of Nero.

Biography: A mathematician, scientist, and inventor during the early days of the Roman Principate, Hero is the author of many texts describing the scientific and mechanical discoveries made by himself and others.

The Theory: One of Hero's extant works, the *Belopoieka,* describes the construction, maintenance, and use of war machines, as does a work often attributed to him, the *Cheiroballista.*

Influences: Archimedes, whose developments in military technology are cited by Hero.

Further Reading
Mardsen, E. W., *Greek and Roman Artillery* London: Oxbow Books,, 1971.

Seth Lyons Kendall

il Taccola, Mariano di Jacopo detto

(il Taccola, "the Crow," is a nickname)
(1382–ca. 1453)

Significance: Working in the first half of the 15th century, Mariano di Jacopo, called Taccola, was one of the earliest and most influential of the Italian "courtly engineers." In his two works, *De ingeneis* (On Engines) and *De machinis* (On Machines), he added his own artistic style to the depiction of military equipment made by earlier "courtly engineers," which combined some new artistic tendencies of Renaissance Italian art, although not necessarily perspective (despite his knowing this artistic practice), with more traditional two-dimensional portrayals of technology.

Context: Taccola's birth in northern Italy at the end of the 14th century put him at the center of a rapid growth of communal and personal wealth, greater accessibility to educational and artistic advancements and an increase in the awareness of technological innovations. At the same time, virtually all the various Italian states became involved in warfare, generally against each other and without the involvement of larger, more powerful state armies. The desire by the leaders of those states to acquire the latest in military (and nonmilitary) technology presented employment opportunities to several "courtly engineers," their manuscripts serving as job applications.

Biography: Marino was born in Siena in 1382. Almost all that is known about him comes from the two books he produced quite late in his life, in which he says little about his parents, family, upbringing, economic status, or even why he was called "the Crow." It is also not known how he acquired his engineering or artistic training, although, because he was a notary and university secretary in his early adulthood, he might not have been formally educated in these fields. There is no doubt that he was interested in technology from a young age, as his first book, *De ingeneis,* was begun sometime around 1419 and completed in 1433. No doubt it was this interest that led to his appointment as supervisor of roads and hydraulic engineering in Siena, a position that he held sometime during this period, and from which he retired in the 1440s.

From 1433 to 1449, Taccola continued to work on his first manuscript, updating and redesigning some of his initial drawings, while adding others. In 1449, his second book, *De machinis,* appeared. In it were several devices and machines that had appeared in *De ingeneis,* but also several new ones. As far as is known, Taccola did not continue his work beyond this second volume. He appears to have lived in Siena for his entire life, drawing a pension from the city for his administrative work until 1453, during which year he also joined the fraternal order of San Jacomo. After this year he disappears from Sienese records, likely indicating that he died sometime around this time.

Influences: There is little direct evidence that Taccola was influenced by earlier "courtly engineers," as he does not refer to any of them in his books. Nor is his artistic style directly descended from any predecessors.

The Theory: Taccola's two books depict hundreds of different machines, "ingenious devices," he calls them. Some have added written commentary, but others do not. The drawings are of a quality rarely seen in the work of other "courtly engineers"—and perhaps not duplicated until Leonardo's work—which has led to suggestions that some of even the most fantastical inventions have some credibility. But, like all other "courtly engineers," many of his drawings are realistic and others fantastic.

Application: There is no indication that Taccola ever tried to make any of his machines or engines, successfully or unsuccessfully. His autograph manuscripts are extant, although there are also copies. When they were made, or whether Taccola himself authorized any of these, is not known.

Descendents: Taccola's drawings seem to have been well known in Italy during the 15th and early 16th centuries, and their influence can be seen in the works of several later Italian "courtly engineers," including Buonacorso Ghiberti, Francesco di Giorgio Martini, and Leonardo da Vinci. They may also have influenced later inventions, including lifting machines and reversible-gear devices that were used by architects such as Filippo Brunelleschi. However, the texts were not printed until the 20th century.

See also: Valturio, Roberto; Vinci, Leonardo da

Further Reading
Prager, Frank D. and Gustina Scaglia, eds. *Mariano Taccola and His Book "De ingeneis."* Cambridge, MA: MIT Press, 1971.
Shelby, Lon R, "Mariano Taccola and His Books on Engines and Machines," *Technology and Culture* 16 (1975), 466–475.
Taccola, Mariano di Jacopo detto il, *Liber tertius de ingeneis ac edifitiis non usitatis.* Ed. J.H. Beck. Milan: Edizioni il Polifilo, 1969.
Taccola, Mariano, *De machinis: The Engineering Treatise of 1449.* Ed. Giustina Scaglia, ed. 2 vols. Wiesbaden: Dr. Ludwig Reichert Verlag, 1971.

Kelly DeVries

Kyeser, Conrad (Konrad)
(1366–post 1405)

Significance: After military service in an allied European Christian army fighting against the Ottoman Turks during the Nicopolis campaign of 1396, Kyeser, from the Holy Roman Empire, turned to military engineering, writing (in Latin), and illustrating what is one of the first treatises of the so-called "Courtly Engineers," the *Bellifortis*.

Context: Kyeser lived at a time when advances were being seen throughout Europe in education, engineering, technology, and art. Gunpowder weapons had become more numerous and more powerful. Their proliferation and effectiveness at sieges and on the battlefield necessitated changes in fortifications, strategy, tactics, logistics, and metallurgy. Leaders sought military engineers throughout Europe, many of whom advertised their talents in books of inventions, heavily illustrated with their designs. Kyeser dedicated the *Bellifortis* to King Ruprecht III of Germany, from whom he seems to have sought patronage.

Biography: Little is known about the early life of Conrad Kyeser, other than his birth date, August 28, 1366, his birthplace, Eichstätt, in Bavaria, that he lived in Padua in his early 20s, and that, at the age of 30, he fought in the Battle of Nicopolis against the Ottoman Turks in the Balkans. Nicopolis was a terrible disaster for the European Christian forces, with few of the major participants, cavalry men-at-arms, escaping capture and execution. Although Kyeser does not confirm this, he was likely not among those, but instead among the forces who remained as a rearguard, which fled from the battlefield after the initial cavalry charges failed. He may have been serving as an engineer on this campaign.

Kyeser's military service following this battle is not known, although during the years 1402–1403, he returned to Eichstatt, in exile from the court of Holy Roman Emperor Sigismund, although he does not reveal the reason for this. Sometime during or after this exile Kyeser composed his *Bellifortis,* its completion thought not to be later than 1405, the date given on the "presentation manuscript," Göttingen University, Cod. Ms. philos. 63.

Influences: Kyeser does not specify any influences on his work, although many of his technologies, even the more fantastical, are not original to him. Others appear for the first time, such as the chastity belt—interestingly juxtaposed on the same page as a horseshoe. He does note the influence of classical military strategists such as Vegetius and Frontinus on his ideas about siege tactics.

The Theory: The *Bellifortis* is, in a sense, a job application. Kyeser depicts offensive and defensive machines of war, which he claims that he can make if employed by Ruprecht. He also shows new tactics and strategy in using, and defending against, gunpowder weapons.

Application: The *Bellifortis* describes and illustrates many different military technologies: trebuchets; gunpowder artillery (of various sizes); rockets and incendiaries; battering rams, portable mantles and war machines; portable bridges; scaling ladders; wagons; ships; underwater breathing apparatus, crossbows and other handheld weapons; and armor, and other technological devices and machines.

Kyeser is often derided for the fantastical nature of many of his military technologies, and there is a certainty that some either could not be made, that is, several of his gunpowder pieces and war machines, or would likely not have functioned as he depicted they would, that is, his underwater breathing devices. However, other depictions suggest that he was not only aware of some of the most up-to-date gunpowder weapons, but also more traditional military machines, such as counterweight catapults and pontoon bridges. Artefactual and comparative artistic evidence confirms the accuracy of these depictions. Kyeser is often credited with the earliest depiction of an accurate handheld gunpowder weapon.

Although he most often tries to portray these devices being used "in action," some are depicted from a two-dimensional bird's-eye view. Kyeser is hampered by the lack of artistic perspective, a technique that had little influence north of the Alps at the time.

Descendents: It is thought that the single extant manuscript is a presentation copy of the *Bellifortis,* either from Kyeser's autograph work or a copy. Nor can it be determined if any of the later courtly engineers were able to look at the manuscript, let alone be influenced by it. Bertrand Gille has theorized that there were two schools of courtly engineers, German and Italian, and that Kyeser was of substantial influence among later German engineers. Italian courtly engineers, more numerous and famous, would have had difficulty seeing Kyeser's manuscript, but there are similarities in some of the illustrations that suggest a common precursor or precursors.

See also: il Taccola; Martini, Francesco di Giorgio; Vinci, Leonardo da

Further Reading

Gille, Bertrand, *Les ingénieurs de la Renaissance.* Paris: Hermann, 1964 ; trans. *The Renaissance Engineers.* Cambridge: MIT University Press, 1966.

Kyeser, Conrad, *Bellifortis* (facsimile of the Göttinger MS Philos. 63). Ed. Götz Quarg. 2 vols. Düsseldorf : VDI-Verlag, 1967.

Long, Pamela O, *Openness, Secrecy, Authorship: Technical Arts and the Culture of Knowledge from Antiquity to the Renaissance.* Baltimore: Johns Hopkins University Press, 2001.

White, Lynn Jr., "Kyeser's *Bellifortis:* The First Technological Treatise of the Fifteenth Century," *Technology and Culture* 10 (1969), 436–41.

Kelly DeVries

Martini, Francesco di Giorgio
(1439–1502)

Significance: At a time when fortification engineers were trying to counter increasingly more effective gunpowder weapons, Francesco di Giorgio Martini produced some of the most innovative designs, to be found especially in his heavily illustrated book, *Trattato di architettura, ingegneria e arte militare* (A Treatise on Architecture, Engineering and Military Arts), written under the patronage of the city of Siena and Federico da Montefeltro, Duke of Urbino

Context: By the second half of the 15th century, gunpowder artillery had increased in ballistic power and range. Cannons still had difficulty in subduing a fortified location, but their increasing threat often forced the besieged to surrender in anticipation of a destruction of economy and lives, especially when no relieving force could be counted on. Innovative engineers began to experiment with designs, the culmination of which was very late 15th/early 16th-century *trace italienne* fortifications. Among those who produced especially important contributions was Francesco di Giorgio Martini.

Biography: Born in Siena ca. 1439, Francesco di Giorgio Martini was raised in a place and during a period of intellectual greatness, where and when military technology developed alongside less violent creative outlets. Education was key, and Francesco seems to have been an adept pupil of fine arts, training in Siena initially as a painter under Francesco di Giorgio e di Lorenzo (most frequently called Vecchietta). But, it seems, his talent lay more in architecture than painting. By the 1460s he had begun designing and overseeing the building of city walls and other fortifications for Federico da Montefeltro. In these it is clear his training in symmetry and perspective was key. Around 1482, then one of the chief architects of Siena, Francesco published his *Trattato di architettura, ingegneria e arte militare,* which in the ensuing years was frequently copied and circulated. He seems to have held this position until 1502 when he died.

Influences: Although not explicitly indicated in his writings, Francesco di Giorgio Martini appear to have followed Leone Battista Alberti's and Filarete's architectural works, although he may also have read and profited from the books of earlier Italian courtly engineers, including those of Mariano di Jacopo detto il Taccola and Roberto Valturio.

The Theory: Although during a late medieval siege the advantage remained with the besieged, their fortifications able to stand against even the most extensive gunpowder artillery bombardment, by the second half of the 15th century it had become apparent that the future of more "medieval" defenses was limited. Francesco di Giorgio Martini was one of several architects who promoted the construction of entirely new fortification systems. These, known as *trace italienne* fortresses, completely altered traditional fortifications by introducing overlapping defensive structures, replacing long, straight, and high walls with angular and polygonal bastions that utilized flanking gunpowder artillery fire to defend the spaces immediately in front of them. Experimenting previously with numerous various designs, Francesco, in 1482, compiled the best of these in his *Trattato di architettura, ingegneria e arte militare,* the third section (or "book") of which is devoted to his concept of an ideally fortified city, protected by a large number of walls and bastions.

Application: By his death, it is estimated that Francesco's designs had been used to build more than 136 fortifications throughout northern Italy, but especially in lands controlled by the Duke of Urbino and the city of Siena.

Descendents: Francesco's *Trattato* was copied and later printed in several editions during the late 15th and 16th centuries. Its most immediate influence was on Leonardo da Vinci, whose drawings of fortifications are clearly derived from Francesco di Giorgio Martini's treatise.

See also: il Taccola; Valturio, Roberto; Vinci, Leonardo da

Further Reading
DeVries, Kelly, "The Impact of Gunpowder Weaponry on Siege Warfare in the Hundred Years War." In: *The Medieval City Under Siege.* Ed. I.A. Corfis and M. Wolfe. Woodbridge, 1995, pp. 227–44.
Gille, Bertrand, *Les ingénieurs de la Renaissance.* Paris: Hermann, 1964 (trans. *Engineers of the Renaissance.* Cambridge: MIT Press, 1966).
Giorgio Martini, Francesco di, *Trattati di architettura ingegneria e arte militare.* 2 vols. Milan: Electa, 1967.
Vasari, Giorgio, *The Lives of the Most Excellent Painters, Sculptors, and Architects.* Trans. Gaston du C. de Vere and Philip Jacks. New York: Modern Library, 2006.

Kelly DeVries

Tartaglia (The Stammerer) (aka Niccolò Fontana)
(1500–1557)

Significance: His literary works reveal the convergence of military architecture with mathematical theory that will be of great importance to understanding the development of artillery.

Context: Tartaglia theorized at a time when artillery first gained prominence on European battlefields.

Biography: Normally styled Tartaglia, this mathematician was active in Venice.

The Theory: Tartaglia makes the explicit claim that it is useful to set firing elevations in a way that refutes A.R. Hall's theory of the irrelevance of early efforts to aim guns. Although misled by the then current fashion of analyzing gravity by analogy to static balances, Tartaglia largely got trajectory and air resistance right.

Application and Descendents: Tartaglia's ideas helped the infant science of ballistics to develop in the West.

See also: Al-Tabari; Archimedes; Vitruvius

Further Reading
Tartaglia, Niccolò [Fontana], *Three Books of Colloquies* trans. Cyprian Lucar. London: I. Harrison, 1588.

Erik A. Lund

Teil de Beaumont, Major General Jean du
(1738–1820)

Significance: Use of mobile artillery as infantry support on the battlefield was one of the more significant aspects of Napoleonic tactics.

Context: Major reforms were carried out by France in the aftermath of the Seven Years' War (1756–1763). Among them, a new design of artillery, known as the "Gribeauval system," began to be implemented in 1765 in replacement of the "Vallière System" conceived in 1732 by Jean Florent de Vallière (1667–1759). Although numbers of calibers were already limited from anterior regulations, canons were yet too heavy for easy transportation. Jean-Baptiste Vaquette de Gribeauval (1715–1789), with knowledge of Swedish, Prussian, and Austrian new ordnance, especially the 1753 "Lichtenstein System," was in charge of these reforms. Field ordnance included howitzers (6 inches) and lighter field guns (4, 8, and 12-pounders) with new sighting devices. Ammunition caissons and other carriages were standardized and interchangeable. "New Artillery," experimentally tested in Strasbourg in 1764, was used for the first time in the field by Rochambeau's French forces during the American War of Independence (1775–1783).

Biography: Jean du Teil de Beaumont was born in 1738. At nine years old, he was enlisted as a *"Cadet"* in *"Royal Artillerie"* for his first campaign (Flanders, 1747). Later, although an aristocrat, he was promoted major general (*"général de division"*) during the French Revolution. Retired in 1814 after 66 years in the army, he died in 1820. His elder brother Jean Pierre (1722–1794), a general of artillery as their father too, was executed as a Royalist although he served in the Revolution.

Influences: Gribeauval was committed to the implementation of a new design of field artillery, especially suited to arms mutual support. Jacques-Antoine-Hippolyte,

Comte de Guibert (1743–1790), prophetically conceptualized (*"Essai général de tactique,"* 1770) a new way of warfare that was to be used in the Revolutionary and Napoleonic Wars. He probably encouraged chevalier Jean du Teil to publish his work.

The Theory: In the years following its implementation (1765–1777), the "New Artillery" was largely discussed by the military; du Teil was only one, among those who wrote about the controversy that opposed the conservative "Reds" to the modern "Blues" (so nicknamed because of changes in the colors of uniforms). As a "Red," Edme Jean Antoine du Puget d'Orval (1742–1801) published in 1771 *"Essai sur l'usage de l'artillerie dans la guerre de campagne et dans celle des sièges par un officier du corps."* As a "Blue" Philippe Charles Jean Baptiste Tronson du Coudray (1738–1777) wrote in 1772 *"L'artillerie nouvelle, ou Examen des changements faits dans l'artillerie française depuis 1765."* For the "Moderns," new artillery had to be used as an actual combat arm able to be quickly moved on the battlefield. Tactical coordination, for reciprocal support between artillery and infantry, was seen as the key to victory. Each infantry battalion in the line got two organic 4-pdr guns for direct support. Counter battery action was not a priority; enemy troops were the first target if within sight and range. Concentration of fire on decisive points was of first importance to prepare a successful infantry advance. "In attack or defense, no doubt about the decisive effect of a well placed and commanded artillery. By its support, artillery will make infantry advance easier; audacious tactical movements with lower casualties could so be carried on" (Jean du Teil, 1778).

Application: During French Revolutionary and Napoleonic Wars, Napoleon Bonaparte (1769–1821) joined the firepower of "New Artillery" to the moral strength of the revolutionary soldier. Quality of ordnance, the finest in the world, was sometimes unknown. For example, Muller's *Treatise of Artillery,* second edition (London, 1780) contained no mention of the "Gribeauval system," although it had already been described in von Scheel's *Mémoires d'Artillerie* (Copenhaguen, 1777).

Descendents: Bonaparte was a junior lieutenant in Artillery Regiment and School of Auxonne, under the orders of the elder brother Jean Pierre du Teil, whom he visited several times later in his castle of Pommier; the emperor gave by legacy 100,000 Francs to his descendents. Louis de Tousard (1749–1817), a French artillery officer commissioned in the U.S. artillery from 1795 to 1802, published *American Artillerist's Companion* in 1809.

See also: Bonaparte, Napoleon; Guibert, J.

Further Reading
M*** ci-devant Lieutenant au Corps Royal d'Artillerie, *L'artillerie nouvelle ou examen des changements faits dans l'artillerie française depuis 1765.* Liege, 1772.

Internet: http://ooks.google.com. The author is Philippe Charles Jean Baptiste Tronson du Coudray, dead by drowning during the American War of Independence.

Teil, Chevalier Jean du, *De l'usage de l'artillerie nouvelle dans la guerre de campagne; connaissance nécessaire aux officiers destinés à commander toutes les armes.* Metz (France): Marchal, 1778. Internet: Bibliothèque nationale de France, Gallica, http://gallica.bnf.fr/ark:/12148/bpt6k86513s.

Jean-Jacques Arzalier

Vinci, Leonardo da
(1452–1519)

Significance: Leonardo da Vinci conceived of a number of military designs over the course of his career. Many appear only in his private notebooks. He did submit designs for naval defenses to the Republic of Venice in 1499, and he worked as a military engineer for Cesare Borgia in the early 16th century.

Context: Leonardo's work must be understood in the context of Italian Renaissance humanism, as well as the political conditions of late Renaissance Italy. As a humanist and a polymath, he combined his considerable technical abilities with his work in the visual arts, natural philosophy, and the humanities. As a talented artist and designer in 15th-century Italy, his career illustrates the complex culture of patronage typical of the period, as well as the intricate politics of the time.

Biography: Leonardo was born in Tuscany in 1452, the illegitimate son of a notary and a peasant woman. He was trained in painting at the workshop of the Florentine master Verrocchio. Over the five decades of his adult life, he moved throughout Italy—Florence, Milan, Venice, the Romagna—working for various patrons. Renowned for his abilities as a painter, he also did significant work as a military engineer. His private notebooks reveal the great dimensions of his curiosity and creativity, as he explored subjects ranging from anatomy and optics to the design of weapons and fortifications. In his later years, he moved to France, and died in 1519 in the service of King Francis I.

Influences: Leonardo exhibits the intellectual priorities of Italian Renaissance Humanism: a respect for the classics and a sense of confidence in human beauty and potential. The intellectual energy of the late Renaissance certainly affected his own incredible fertility of mind. However, his remarkable combination of abilities makes his work unique.

The Theory: A study of his career and an examination of his notebooks reveal Leonardo's varied interests in military technology and fortification. In 1499, he submitted plans to the Republic of Venice for naval defenses: a temporary dam intended to direct ruinous floods toward an invading force, and underwater gear meant to allow for attacks on enemy ships. As a military engineer in the employ of

Cesare Borgia in 1502–1503, he addressed issues of fortification. His most well-known military works come from his notebooks; he conceived of a number of fascinating technical innovations including steam cannon, multibarreled firearms, and a type of armored vehicle. His drawings of different flying apparatus are quite famous. He also conceived of a covered siege engine for attacks on city walls, and varied methods of defending against sieges as well.

Applications: Most of Leonardo's military designs were never constructed (at least in his own day).

Further Reading
Strathern, Paul, *The Artist, the Philosopher, and the Warrior: The Intersecting Lives of Da Vinci, Machiavelli, and Borgia and the World They Shaped.* New York: Bantam, 2009.

Robert Kiely

Vitruvius, Marcus Pollio, Architect

Significance: Vitruvius is the most influential architect of the ancient world. His book *De Architectura* has not only inspired generations of civilian architects ever since its publication but also military architects and engineers.

Context: The late Republican Rome underwent a series of civil wars, which finally ended when Octavian (Augustus) defeated Mark Antony in 30 BC. Augustus maintained a façade of republican institutions, but in practice he became a dictator whose power rested on the personal control of the professional armed forces.

Biography: Vitruvius was born in ca. 90 BC. He served under Julius Caesar and Octavian (Augustus) as artillery officer, military engineer, and architect (*architectus*). Octavian granted Vitruvius a pension, which was then continued for life on the recommendation of Octavian's sister. Vitruvius died at about 20 BC.

Influences: Vitruvius learnt his trade as architect, military engineer, and artilleryman in the Roman army. Vitruvius's thinking was heavily influenced by Greek architecture and engineering Vitruvius had not only studied the works of great Greek architects such as Diades of Pella and Archimedes, but even his alma mater, the Roman army, had inherited most of its engineering techniques from the Greeks.

The Theory: The final form of Vitruvius's *De Architectura* probably dates from about 27 BC or after. It was dedicated to Octavian (Augustus) and consisted of a set of recommendations. The books 1–6 discuss the various aspects of urban design including military considerations such as locale and logistics. The book 7 focuses on the finishing of surfaces and decoration. The books 8 describes how to find, collect, transfer, and store water. The book 9 describes the workings of timepieces. The book 10 explains how various mechanical devises worked.

The architectural portion includes information of the way in which the Romans were to set up military colonies in such locales that were considered defensible and safe for the health of the occupants, and thereby contributed to the selection of suitable places for many cities and fortifications in Europe, Asia, and Africa. The instructions on how to set up defenses and how to build them served as a guide for the building of such structures until the fall of the empire and beyond. The sections describing how to obtain safe drinking water, how to build cranes, and how to measure distances also had military significance.

The sections 10.10–16 are devoted to military mechanics. Vitruvius began the discussion with a description of the torsion catapults/scorpions and ballistae. The former were arrow/bolt shooters, which came in various sizes (length of arrow determined the "caliber") and also included personal shooters. The latter were stone throwers, which also came in various sizes ("calibers" from a 2-pound stone up to 360-pound stone). The design and construction of both types was based on earlier Hellenistic models that had only received slight modifications to improve their performance.

Vitruvius's treatment of siege machines consists of a mix of historical examples and period practices. Vitruvius paid his respects to Diades, who was Alexander the Great's military architect/engineer, by devoting a significant portion of his text to the description of Diades's treatise. Diades's treatise included mobile towers (large and small) that could be taken apart, drill/borer, scaling machine, devastating raven/crane (not described because it was useless), wheeled battering ram, tortoise with a battering ram, but it did not include treatments of the scaling machine and machines used at sea. Even though Vitruvius probably included the discussion of Diades's treatise primarily to show off his own education, it still had a practical purpose because several of these siege machines were also used by the Romans. After this, Vitruvius proceeded to describe what he had learnt from his teachers and what he found practical. His list of equipment includes a tortoise (siege-shed) used for filling of ditches, another tortoise, tortoise to dig mines, and Hegetor's tortoise. The last was invented by Hegetor of Byzantium and also belonged to the equipment invented by the Greeks. It was a huge tortoise, which included the shed, scorpions/catapults, and a huge battering ram. Vitruvius did not include descriptions of ladders and other simpler devises because the soldiers could build those on their own initiative.

Vitruvius stressed the utmost importance of adapting the information provided by him to the type of enemy and situation. This Vitruvius also demonstrated with a list of various inventive methods used by defenders' architects against besiegers (creation of a swamp, countermining techniques, hot iron bolts shot with ballistae, defensive crane, incendiary missiles). In short, the retired Vitruvius asked Augustus to distribute his *De Architectura* to the military architects as a set of instructions on which they could base their own engineering works.

Application: Vitruvius appears to have been present at the famous siege of Massilia in 49 BC. In that siege Julius Caesar's military architects faced a very well prepared Greek city whose defenders were able to destroy the besiegers' mining works and siege engines on several occasions with their ingenuity and ruses forcing the besiegers to resort to the use of improvisation. The standard siege machines also proved unable to withstand the defender's artillery, which forced the attackers to build a brick tower and wall, and to reinforce their tortoises with protective brick coatings.

Descendents: The Romans continued to use the construction techniques described by Vitruvius until the fall of the empire. Vitruvius's construction techniques saw a new revival during the Renaissance period. However, the lifespan of Vitruvius's siege machines was shorter. Apollodorus, who was an architect of Trajan and Hadrian, already modified them significantly and further modifications occurred during the late empire until the advent of firearms made them entirely redundant.

See also: Apollodorus (Apollodoros), Architect; Caesar, Gaius Julius

Further Reading

Duncan B. Campbell's *Besieged* (Oxford, 2006) provides a good overview of the ancient siege warfare.

Ilkka Syvänne

IV

Tactical and Operational Theory

The term tactics means, for the reader, the deployment of men and equipment on the battlefield. In hand with that, the term "operations," although modern and not used before 1815, is helpful as it designates the concern writers placed on the movement of troops, animals, and equipment from one place to another, generally the point of contact with an enemy. Because tactics were considered more the realm of practice and the real application of a commander's abilities, there is less written about tactics before 1815 than about the general notion of war or strategy. For this reason there was no accepted approach to the field. Writers are diverse in the actual application of force and how to understand it. The Japanese sword and tactics master **Miyamoto Mushashi** is at times poetic and often opaque, displaying an indirect approach to the topic. The Prussian **Heinrich Deitrich von Bülow**, by direct contrast, developed a specific geometric formula for the deployment of troops to engage the enemy the near mathematic perfection. Or so he intended.

Arrian, Governor of Cappadocia, Lucius Flavius Arrianus (Arrianos) Xenophon

Significance: Arrian was a successful Roman commander of Greek origins who updated the Hellenistic tactical treatise with period material, described contemporary Roman cavalry exercises, and provided detailed instruction on how to array contemporary Roman army as a phalanx against cavalry. Arrian's treatment of these topics found favor among the Roman military elite, and his treatises survived and continued to be circulated. Arrian gives us a unique description of the period Roman tactics and of the changes taking place at the time.

Context: Arrian wrote his principal military works at a time when the Emperor Hadrian had instituted a number of military reforms that reflected the lessons learnt as a result of the prolonged military campaigns against the Dacians, Sarmatians,

Alans, Armenians, Parthians, and others. Arrian's descriptions of the Roman use of the phalanx and its cavalry exercises are an endorsement of these reforms. Arrian's preoccupation with phalanx and cavalry warfare manifested itself also in his interest in Alexander the Great whose biography he also wrote.

Biography: Arrian was probably born at Nicomedia (Izmit) between AD 85 and 92. During the first decade of the second century AD, Arrian attended the lectures of the famous Stoic philosopher Epictetus at Nicopolis in Epirus. He appears to have served in *legio VII Claudia* during Trajan's Dacian Wars. Arrian may also have taken part in Trajan's Parthian Wars in AD 114–117. At some point Arrian also befriended Hadrian, who on becoming emperor, elected him to the senate. In the early 120s Arrian served as a legate of a legion in the Danubian region and then became governor of the province of Baetica in Spain in about 125 and then suffect consul in 129 or 130. Arrian served as governor of Cappadocia from 130/131 to 137/138 in which capacity he repulsed the invasion of the Alans. In about 137/138 Arrian appears to have retired to Athens, where he reached the prestigious position of *archon* in 145/146. He died probably in the 160s.

Influences: Arrian's views on tactics were based on his own experiences gained as officer and commander in the Roman army, study of the Hellenistic military theory, and study of the Greek and Roman history. However, by far the most significant influence affecting Arrian's writing was his eagerness to please the Emperor Hadrian, who was also his friend and patron. On the basis of sound analysis of recent military campaigns Hadrian had introduced a number of reforms into the Roman army, and Arrian as a professional military man unabashedly sought to prove himself to be a faithful follower of Hadrian's reforms and therefore worthy of further promotion. For example, Arrian's theoretical treatise *Ars tactica* (Tactics) includes several direct references to Hadrian and his reforms as a form of personal flattery. The philhellene Hadrian was also interested in all things Greek, and the inclusion of the Hellenistic military theory as part of Arrian's treatment of tactics should also be seen as an attempt to please the emperor.

The Theory: Arrian wrote profusely of a multitude of subjects as was expected of a philosopher at the time, and this included the military topics. Eight of Arrian's works are still extant, and his fragmentary or lost works include eight or nine other works (the figure is disputed).

From the point of view of military theory the most important works are the *Acies* or *Ectaxis contra Alanos* (*Battle Formation against the Alans, Ektaxis kata Alanon,* AD 135–137), *Ars tactica* (*Tactics, Techne taktike,* 136/137), and *Anabasis Alexandri* (*Anabasis of Alexander, Alexandrou Anabasis,* date uncertain). Notably, Arrian's *Acies contra Alanos* is the earliest extant detailed treatment of the imperial Roman infantry phalanx in action. The origin and purpose of the *Acies contra Alanos* has caused plenty of speculation. It has been suggested that it was an extract from Arrian's lost *Alanike* or some other work, or that it was an extract from his campaign report to Hadrian, or that it formed a separate essay of the campaign report or some other work.

Arrian's *Ars Tactica* mixes Hellenistic military theory freely with contemporary Roman and foreign military practices and also introduces historical examples not present in the other so-called Hellenistic military treatises. Unsurprisingly, Arrian's descriptions of both the Roman (*Acies contra Alanos* 12ff; *Ars tactica* 11.4–12.5) and Hellenistic (*Ars tactica* 12.6ff.) versions of the phalanx formation simultaneously have caused modern historians to present widely divergent points of view. Some modern historians have claimed that Arrian's phalanx reflected Roman fetish for Alexander the Great; some have claimed that it was Arrian's own invention; others that the phalanx was used only in the East and not at all in the West; and still others that the Romans had always used the phalanx array as part of their repertoire of combat methods.

Ars tactica consists of two distinct sections. The first portion of the manual consists of Arrian's own reworking of the existing Hellenistic military treatises (1–32.2) and the second portion (32.3–44.3) describes the contemporary Roman parade ground drill. The contents of *Ars tactica* are: introduction (first half lost); classification of warfare; types of troops and their equipment; organization of the army; unit formations; movements; marching; commands; and Roman cavalry exercises. In each of the sections Arrian includes contemporary information and practices, and even those sections that are directly drawn from Hellenistic military theory, such as the types of cavalry (e.g., cataphracts, *contus*-spear bearers and mounted archers) include types of units employed by the Romans at the time. Unfortunately, we do not know why Arrian chose to update the Hellenistic portion of his *Ars Tactica* with contemporary material because the beginning of the treatise is lost. It may simply have been to provide as complete treatment of the military theory as possible within the constraints of the genre. Arrian lists the various types of heavy infantry (hoplite, Macedonian, Roman), peltasts ("medium infantry"), light infantry (archers, slingers, javelin throwers), cavalry (two horsed, cataphracts, various types of noncataphracts, Roman cavalry), elephants, and chariots. In short, Arrian's *Ars tactica* provides a very full list of various types of troops used both in the past and present.

Arrian's description of the Roman parade ground cavalry drills in *Ars tactica* celebrates the Roman readiness to copy from the enemies what was found useful. The drills include maneuvers borrowed from the Gauls, Spaniards, Getae, Alans, Armenians, and Parthians, and the details of the Roman cavalry parade ground drills given by Arrian are also confirmed by Hadrian's speech preserved at a monument in Lambaesis. The fragments of the same inscription also confirm the differentiation of arms among the legionaries found in the *Acies contra Alanos,* which stated that the first four ranks of the phalanx were armed with *kontoi* (long spears) and the following four with *logchai* (javelins). Arrian's treatise also proves that the Hellenistic *synaspismos* (locked shields) formation was for practical purposes the same as the Roman *testudo* (tortoise). The employment of the four front ranks of spearmen in the locked shields formation (later called *fulcum/foulkon/syskouton*) for both attack and defense remained one of the standard infantry tactics and can be found in one form or another in many later military manuals (e.g., Maurice, Syrianus Magister, Leo the Wise). The principal difference between the Roman phalanx on the one hand and the Macedonian phalanx on the other hand was that the former system was built around the use of the spear (later called *kontarion*), which was also usable as a throwing weapon. In other words, the Roman phalanx was more maneuverable than its Macedonian counterpart.

The various combat maneuvers of the phalanx in *Ars tactica* such as the out-flanking on one or both flanks, forward and rearward angled half-square forma-tions, oblique formations, wedge, hollow wedge, two-fronted phalanx, hollow oblong/square, etc., were continuously used by the Romans and Byzantines, and even the cavalry wedge was found useful for the purposes stated by Arrian. The only things missing from Arrian's description is the use of cohorts in such situa-tions when the legionaries were not deployed as phalanxes. It is possible that Ar-rian considered such tactics obsolete. Consequently, Arrian's *Ars tactica* gives an almost complete description of the period Roman tactics and tactical methods available to them. Even the portions that described the actual Macedonian pike phalanx could be found useful at times when the Romans experimented with the use of the actual Macedonian phalanx as happened, for example, during the reign of Caracalla (AD 211–217).

Application: The tactics described by Arrian were essentially those that were to be followed by the Romans and Byzantines at least until the 12th century, and can therefore be considered to have been highly practicable. It is prob-able but not absolutely certain that as governor of Cappadocia in 135 Arrian himself employed the marching formation and tactics he describes in his *Acies contra Alanos*. Arrian's tactical concept was to oppose the Alan cavalry with an infantry phalanx placed between the hills, and the hills were protected by detachments of infantry and torsion artillery. Light infantry were placed behind the heavy infantry and cavalry behind them. The formation was essentially a variation of the forward angled half-square. The enemy was to be received by a barrage of missiles shot by light infantry, artillery, and mounted archers fol-lowed up by a barrage of javelins thrown by the rear rankers of the phalanx. If this was not sufficient to deter the enemy, then the phalanx was expected to stop the enemy. This was to be followed up by the pursuit of the now-disordered enemy by the Roman cavalry that had been placed behind infantry. One half of the cavalry conducted the pursuit whereas the other half formed its reserve. The infantry also marched forward to protect the cavalry. This same tactical concept of placing a battle formation to the mouth of a valley was also subsequently used, for example, by Narses to overcome the Goths at Busta Gallorum in 552. The inclusion of the same tactics in the 10th century *De velitatione* (3–4, 23) of Nicephorus Phocas also shows the doctrinal continuity.

It is impossible to claim that either had copied their tactics from Arrian, but what is definitely known is that Arrian's texts were well known in the military circles at the time. The same can be said of the other forms of phalanx tactics described by Arrian. All of the variants mentioned saw continuous use in one form or another until the advent of firearms made them redundant. Arrian's descriptions of the phalanx and cavalry showed the way to the future. The time of the cohort tactics was almost over.

Descendents: Arrian's treatises were among the most copied texts of antiquity and were used as sources, for example, by Leo the Wise and Ouranos during the 10th century AD. Urbicius's *Tactica,* which is dedicated to the Emperor Anastasius I (491–518), is an epitome of the first part of Arrian's *Ars tactica.* This suggests that the tactical concepts of Arrian's treatise were considered to be particularly relevant at the time. Urbicius's *Tactica* in its turn was later copied and used by other authors as a source of information. In addition, new copies of Arrian's original military treatises were produced and certain portions of his other texts were also excerpted into other manuals as the inclusion of Alexander the Great's sieges of Tyre and Gaza in the Byzantine military compilation *Excerpta historica de proeliis et obsidionibus* shows. The general principles of Arrian's military treatises remained relevant as long as men were deployed in ranks and files. Arrian's *Anabasis Alexandri* has also inspired generations of military commanders, but in this instance one cannot really say that Alexander the Great's conquests would have always reflected Arrian's own military theories. Arrian had simply written a biography of Alexander.

See also: Asklepiodotos; Leo VI

Further Reading

Philip A. Stadter's *Arrian of Nicomedia* (Chapel Hill: The University of North Carolina Press, 1980) is a must. For a full analysis of Arrian's phalanx and its Roman background, see E. L. Wheeler ("The Legion as Phalanx in the Late Empire (I)," in *L'armée romaine de Dioclétien à Valentinien Ier,* eds. Yann Le Bohec and Catherine Wolff, Lyon, 2004, pp. 309–358; "The Legion as Phalanx in the Late Empire, Part II," *REMA 1* (2004): 147–175).

Ilkka Syvänne

Asklepiodotos (Asclepiodotus) the Philosopher

Significance: The exact influence of Asklepiodotos's *Techne taktike* (Tactical Theory) upon the other Hellenistic tactical treatises is not known with certainty. Two things suggest that it may have had influence upon later treatises: (1)

Asklepiodotos's treatise appears to have been used as a source by other military theorists; (2) It was included among the official imperial collection of military treatises during the reign of Constantine Porphyrogenitus (913–959).

Context: The exact context of when and how Asklepiodotos's treatise came into existence is not known with certainty, but the current consensus among the historians is that it was probably written as a philosophical treatise during the first century BC.

Biography: On the basis of Seneca's five citations, it is usually thought that the Asklepiodotos, who is mentioned as the author of the *Techne taktike* in the 10th-century Laurentian manuscript, was a pupil of the stoic philosopher Poseidonios (ca. 135–50 BC) and therefore not a military man. However, other possible identifications have also been suggested.

Influences: If the most commonly accepted identification is correct, the principal source for Asklepiodotos's tactical treatise was Poseidonios. In fact, it has been suggested that Asklepiodotos's treatise is a mere paraphrase or epitome of Poseidonios's treatise.

The Theory: Asklepiodotos's treatise is the earliest of the extant Hellenistic tactical manuals. It describes the fully developed tactical organization of the Seleucid army of the late second century BC. The source of this information was undoubtedly Poseidonios of Apameia, a Macedonian from the Seleucid Empire. The treatise includes all period arms of service: heavy infantry, light infantry, cavalry, elephants, and chariots. The Seleucid tactical organization was an amalgam of Macedonian and Persian military systems. Indian influence in the use of chariots and elephants is also quite evident. The late composition of the treatise is evident from the inclusion of Roman manipular tactics (the scattered formation) in the treatise, which suggests that the Seleucids had made an effort to copy their enemies' military tactics.

Asklepiodotos's treatise is the shortest of the extant Hellenistic military manuals, but still manages to include material missing from both Aelian and Arrian. The contents conform with the other Hellenistic treatises and include chapters on the types and sizes of various units, armament, evolutions and maneuvers, formations, marching, and commands. Asklepiodotos's treatise provides a short, but still complete overview of the late Hellenistic army and its phalanx formation.

Application: The basic phalanx organization described by Asklepiodotos with its accompanying tactical formations was later used by the Romans and Byzantines, but it is impossible to prove any direct connection between Asklepiodotos's tactical manual and the later usage because several later military treatises also include similar arrays.

Descendents: The basic organization and tactics described by Asklepiodotos were included in a great number of Byzantine military manuals, and remained in use until the fall of the Byzantine Empire. The advent of effective firearms made these concepts outdated.

Further Reading

N. Sekunda's analysis of the relationship between Poseidonios and Asklepiodotos in *Hellenistic Infantry Reform in the 160's BC* (Gdansk, 2006, pp. 125–134) is well worth reading.

Ilkka Syvänne

Bourcet, Lieutenant General Pierre-Joseph de
(1700–1780)

Significance: Bourcet conceived many developments later used by modern armies: the divisional system, multipronged offensive operations, and the general staff system. He organized one of the first modern staffs in 1766 and paved the way for Napoleon's offensive methods.

Context: Bourcet's ideas emerged within the context of French military defeat in the War of the Austrian Succession (1740–1748) and the Seven Years' War (1756–1763). Drawing on his extensive military experience in Italy and Germany, he promoted reforms that would remedy deficiencies that led to defeat.

Biography: Bourcet was born in 1700 and began his army career as an engineering and artillery officer. He saw action in northern Italy during the War of the Polish Succession (1733–1735). As a lieutenant, he fought under Maillebois in Germany and again on the Alpine frontier with Italy during the War of the Austrian Succession. Between 1745 and 1748, he advanced rapidly from lieutenant colonel to brigadier general. During the Seven Years' War, Bourcet served under Soubise as an artillery commander and fought at the battle of Rossbach (1757). He was promoted to lieutenant general in 1762 and made commander of the Order of Saint-Louis. In 1766, he organized one of the first general staffs, called the *Officers employees á la reconnaissance du pays,* and instructed staff officers at Grenoble (1764–1771). In 1769, he fought against the Corsican insurgency. He died in 1780.

Influences: Bourcet drew his inspiration from his own military experiences in Italy and Germany and French defeat generally. No single theoretical influence is discernible.

The Theory: Bourcet's theory is found in the unpublished *Principes de la guerre de montagnes,* which he used to instruct staff officers at Grenoble in 1766. Although the work deals with much more than mountain warfare, it was inspired by his experience defending the Franco-Italian Alpine frontier.

War is divided into two distinct forms: offensive and defensive. To wage offensive war, superiority of numbers was paramount. The role of commander was to assemble the army and draw up plans for the campaign, and to understand instructions received from his government. The principle for offensive war was called "the plan with branches." An army should be divided into many branches or columns and act along many routes to deceive the enemy as to your intentions and make the most efficient use of the terrain. The role of diversions is key. In doing so, one could upset the plans of the enemy, achieve surprise, and attack where least expected. One could discover the plans of the enemy based on his initial reactions to your dispositions. This frontage would equal about 25 to 30 miles. With the enemy paralyzed, the general would reunite his columns on the decisive point simultaneously and win the battle. Bourcet believed that these principles could be applied outside of mountain warfare.

Defensive warfare proved more difficult to theorize. To defend many points only weakened your ability across the entire front. One could not be equally strong everywhere. In a passive or static defense, fortresses must be used to augment the troops at the points that they occupy. The active defense enables the general to operate more freely when responded to the enemy, so long as he is well supplied and protected on the flanks, preferably by natural obstacles. The general had to divine the intentions of the attacker. Any misstep may prove fatal because the initiative was not his. Bourcet concludes that the offensive warfare is preferable to the defense.

Both forms of war required extensive preparations, which included the knowledge of the country, topography, preplanned positioning, and intelligence of the enemy's movements. This could only be realized through an organized staff under the direction of the general, who relied upon its preparations for his entire plan. His theory demanded the reorganization the unitary armies of the day into smaller divisions so they could be detached and act independently for a short time along their operational "branches."

Application: Bourcet's theory became a fundamental part of a French officer's education. Combined with Guibert's ideas on tactics, their combined effort produced the synthesis of the divisional structure in the French army and Napoleon's *corps d'armeé* operational art. The creation of the general staff to prepare officers for planning campaigns gave rise the modern staff system, most fully realized by the Prussian army after the Napoleonic Era.

Descendents: Bourcet's influence in the French army was great in his own lifetime and greater still during the Napoleonic Era, but it was not widespread throughout Europe. His treatise on mountain warfare was never published, and only printed privately in 1888. Bourcet's emphasis on the offensive spirit of war, modern divisional organization, and general staff planning make him ubiquitous as an ancestor of the modern professional officer and military planner.

See also: Bonaparte, Napoleon; Guibert, J.

Further Reading
Quimby, Robert S., *The Background of Napoleonic Warfare: The Theory of Military Tactics in Eighteenth Century France.* New York: Columbia University Press, 1979.

Patrick J. Speelman

Bülow, (Adam) Dietrich (Heinrich) Freiherr von
(1757–1808)

Significance: Bülow's work represents the *reduction ad absurdum* of warfare to the single independent variable space (including geography) and the dependent variable of the employment of armed forces as the function of that space.

Context: No longer an active officer at the time, Bülow witnessed the French Revolutionary and Napoleonic Wars indirectly.

Biography: Dietrich von Bülow was born in Falkenberg in Brandenburg in 1757, as the son of a Prussian envoy to Sweden and the daughter of a church musician. His older brother Friedrich Wilhelm would become a famous Prussian general and both brothers entered a cadet school in early youth to become military officers. Impatiently awaiting further promotion, Dietrich resigned his commission in 1790 to offer his services to the Austrians in Belgium, but the new employment failed to materialize. Nor did he succeed in founding a theatrical company. He travelled to North America twice, first in 1792, the second time in 1795 to seek his fortune in the glass trade, another enterprise in which he failed, losing his entire fortune. He returned to Europe, published on his experiences of the United States, but also several works on military matters. He tried, and failed, to find employment as a writer in London, and in 1804 he was living in Paris. He returned to Berlin, and still recognition of his works eschewed him. He seems to have got into a quarrel with the Russian envoy in Berlin, who had him arrested as a dangerous madman and sent to the Charité hospital for examination. As he was found perfectly sane, he was sent to prison in Colberg in 1806, and thence to Riga, then under Russian rule. He died there either in July 1807 or 1808, either from a cold he contracted in transit, or from wounds received in a fight.

Influences: Although there is no explicit mention of either of these, Bülow clearly tried to put warfare on a scientific footing based on mathematical formulae in the vein in which Newton had revolutionized physics, or Boyle, chemistry.

The Theory: Bülow's theory in his *Spirit of the New System of War* of 1799 (*Der Geist des neuern Kriegssystems aus dem Grundsatze einer Basis der Operationen.* (1st edn. Hamburg: Benjamin Gottlieb Hofmann, 1799; 2nd edn. ibid. 1806) which he claimed would finally turn the art of war into a mathematics-based science of war, consists of two linked concepts. The first is the attempt to calculate and prescribe the movement of military forces exclusively according to mathematical formulae emphasizing the distance to bases (depots, headquarters, etc.), and angles of operation. From this he deduced a second, considerably more interesting idea: that any strategy of defense would hold considerable advantages over the offensive, making conquest well-nigh impossible, simply because with a defensive posture, one would be closer to one's bases. Consequently he postulated that all states had a tendency to consolidate their territory, away from the medieval possession of patches of land here and there, to a coherent space bordered by natural obstacles (rivers, mountain ranges). In this competition for land, the stronger, bigger states would swallow up the smaller ones, until only a handful of large states would co-exist in Europe. Once this stage was attained, he argued, these states would stop expanding and would have the tendency to live in peace with each other. If one state tried to break out, he thought, the others would in a counterbalance of power game join forces against it to contain it and cut it back to its former size. In his second, revised edition of the work dating from 1806, he had to concede that conquest had not become impossible; he had to come to the revised—and unsurprising—conclusion that recent wars had favored the stronger and more numerous battalions. He also felt forced to concede that the best science of war might not find its systematic application because human weaknesses might get in the way of purely rational policy making.

Descendents: Bülow's *Spirit of the New System of War* was read widely, but was derided by contemporaries as dealing with "minor matters only" (Clausewitz) in its algebraic treatment of war, while missing out completely on the much more important political dimension. Although Clausewitz for one agreed on the greater strength of the defensive, and Jomini developed some interest in inner lines of defense, these and others used Bülow's views mainly as whetstone on which to sharpen their own, differing views.

Further Reading

Meerheimb, Richard von, "Bülow, Dietrich Heinrich Freiherr von," *Allgemeine Deutsche Biographie* Vol. III (1876, New impression). Berlin: Duncker & Humblot, 1967, pp. 515–517.

Palmer, R. R., "Frederick the Great, Guibert, Bülow: From Dynastic to National War," in Peter Paret (ed.), *The Makers of Modern Strategy.* Princeton, NJ: Princeton University Press, 1986, reprinted from Edward Mead Earle (ed.), *The Makers of Modern Strategy.* Princeton, NJ: Princeton University Press, 1944, pp. 49–74.

Beatrice Heuser

De Ligne, Charles Joseph, Prince
(1735–1814)

Significance: A native of the Austrian Netherlands, the Walloon Prince De Ligne was the greatest Austrian military philosopher of the 18th century. He remains the best source regarding the ethos of the Austrian army of the period.

Context: During the Seven Years' War (1756–1763) the Austrians and Russians fought Frederick II of Prussia to a standstill. Only the death of Czarina Elizabeth and the withdrawal of the new Czar Peter from the war averted the collapse of Prussia. The Austrian army, under commanders such as von Daun and Laudon, showed itself to be tough, resourceful, and well disciplined, if conservative.

Biography: At the age of 21, De Ligne was appointed a captain of infantry. His first battle was in Bohemia against the Prussian army of Frederick II. He was promoted to colonel after the battle of Hochkirch (1758). He distinguished himself at Maxen (1759) and at Torgau (1760). In 1788, he joined the Russian army and participated in the siege of the Turkish naval base of Ochakov. Then, with an Austrian army corps, he participated in the Danube Campaign of 1789, alongside A Suvorov. De Ligne admired the smart and practical Potemkin regulation uniforms, the spirit of the Russian soldiers, and the quality of the troops, especially the grenadiers. However, he criticized the crowds of camp followers attracted by the Russian army, the callous disregard for the soldiers' welfare and the ignorance in the Russian service of military science. This campaign was his last period of active military service, although he was promoted to field marshal in 1808.

Influences: As a young man, De Ligne read the Classics widely, including Livy's *History of Rome,* Caesar and Quintus Curtius's *History of Alexander.* He had studied and carefully annotated De Saxe's *Mes Rêveries* at the tender age of 22.

The Theory: The art of war was De Ligne's consuming passion, and between 1795 and 1811 he collected all his works into a *Military, Literary and Sentimental Miscellany.* There were three volumes on the Seven Years' War, one on his campaigns against the Turks and one military bibliography.

De Ligne asserts the superiority of the Austrian army in strategic affairs, but points out the failures of the high command in the Seven Years' War. He offers some solutions in a two-volume commentary, *Military Precedents and Fantasies,* published in 1780, and reprinted in 1795, 1827, and 1829.

He sees the arguments between proponents of the column and line formations as futile, pointing out that Frederick II of Prussia used both formations as the situation demanded. He considers the attack column very vulnerable to hostile fire—in four minutes, he calculates, a battalion would be swept by 32,000 bullets, preventing it from pressing home its assault. As far as the infantry mêlée with the bayonet was concerned, he reckons that it was limited to when two bodies of troops surprised one another, as had happened at Görlitz. As regards the Russian bayonet charges, he believed that the Russians took too long to reload their muskets, and that they succeeded because they were only facing swordsmen and not infantry armed with bayonets. Although he admires the oblique order, he warned that it was important not to get carried away by its ability to strike at an enemy's flank, as it just as often exposed one's own flank—as Frederick II found at Kolin (1757).

He is also very skeptical about the shock value of cavalry, and says that cavalry troopers were reluctant to hurl themselves headlong into hand-to-hand combat for fear of injury.

The second volume of *Military Precedents and Fantasies* discusses military dress, weapons, encampments, and battle deployments. Like De Saxe, De Ligne recommends mixing cavalry with infantry, and the use of *ordre mixte* (using columns and lines in a staggered formation). He is sarcastic about Vegetius's seven orders of battle, so beloved of educated officers, and suggest an eighth—none at all! Overall, his tone is practical, as opposed to pure concern with abstract theory.

On the strategic level, De Ligne is remarkably prescient: one must be clear on what one wants from the eventual peace; one should try to foresee every eventuality, even negligence or accidents, to examine the worst-case scenario, and be realistic about the performance of allies; one should seem outwardly audacious and offensive, while remaining inwardly cautious.

De Ligne disliked fixed fortresses: for him they are a waste of manpower and money but, like De Saxe, he maintains that fortified camps are useful, especially for the protection of magazines. These would be placed at the confluence of major rivers, and each army would have four of these "envelopes." Nevertheless, he recognizes that battles are now the order of the day: "I would rather fight straightforward battles for the protection of these 'envelopes'—genius would decide the day, and nowadays we live in the academy of genius."

In 1787, De Ligne published a French translation of Frederick II's *Secret Instructions to his generals,* which contains advice on patrols, reconnaissance duties assaulting enemy cavalry, protecting villages, and so on. As there is no surviving copy of the original *Secret Instructions,* some believe that De Ligne himself was the real author. This seems unlikely, because a copy was supposed to have been captured at the battle of Kossdorf in 1760, and translated into French by a Saxon lieutenant colonel called Faesch, becoming widely available throughout Europe by the end of 1762.

Application: The spirit of erudition and practicality espoused by De Ligne stood the Austrian army in good stead, and although bested on many occasions, it became an implacable and dangerous opponent during the Revolutionary and Napoleonic War, particularly after the reforms of Archduke Charles between 1805 and 1809.

Descendents: Emperor Joseph II (1741–1790) tried to modernize the Austrian army, especially the artillery under Kinsky, but met with resistance from vested interests. After the French Revolution of 1789 there was a retrenchment among reactionary and conservative elements in the army, which left it ill prepared for the vicissitudes of the French Revolutionary War.

See also: Crissé; Feuquières; Frederick II ("the Great"); Guibert, J.; Khevenhüller; Lloyd, H.; Lindenau; Saxe, M.; Vegetius

Further Reading
Duffy, Christopher, *The Army of Maria Theresa; the Armed Forces of Imperial Austria 1740–1780.* New York: Hippocrene, 1977.

Toby McLeod

Folard, Jean-Charles, Chevalier de
(1669–1752)

Significance: Jean-Charles de Folard was the most celebrated European military writer of the first half of the 18th century. He opposed the other great military theoretician of his time, Puységur, on many points, especially regarding the mechanical adherence to fixed orders of battle and the "cabinet strategy" defined at Versailles by courtiers.

Context: The armies of Louis XIV had, on the whole, performed poorly in the War of the Spanish Succession (1701–1715). Despite signal victories at Denain (1712) and Alamanza (1707), they were repeatedly beaten by the forces of the Grand Alliance commanded by John Churchill, Duke of Marlborough. In the 17th century, the French army had carried all before it, but there now seemed to be something wrong with the French system of making war. This called for a reassessment, a new model of war-making based on the science and rationalism of the European Enlightenment.

Biography: Folard was born at Avignon and studied at its Jesuit College. At age 16, he joined a regiment of infantry. After his baptism of fire in 1688, he decided to record his insights in a small manuscript treatise on the business of making war. Fighting in Italy from 1702 to 1706 during the War of the Spanish Succession, Folard developed a reputation as an intrepid officer, and was frequently entrusted with difficult missions. For example, on one occasion, with only a few dozen infantry, he successfully defended a farmhouse in the Po Valley, the Casino Boulino, against the assaults of 1,500 Austrian grenadiers.

In 1709, he took part in the terrible battle of Malplaquet, and was wounded. The following year he was taken prisoner and was presented to Prince Eugene, with whom he spent hours discussing the art of war. In 1716, he visited Charles XII of Sweden.

Folard's service record and his military skill were well known, but his aggressive style was often judged impetuous by French generals. His forthright manner and his lack of discretion also made him many enemies. The restoration of peace in 1715 allowed him to devote all his time to literary projects.

Influences: Like many of his contemporaries, Folard looked to the Ancients and their science of war. He initially toyed with a commentary on Xenophon, but decided on Polybius instead, because his work allowed Folard to compare the tactics of the Greeks and the Romans. As he knew no ancient Greek, Folard approached *Dom* Thuillier, a Benedictine monk and linguist from the order of St. Maur. The available French translation of Polybius, published by the royal historian Pierre du Ryer in 1648, was unsatisfactory, so *Dom* Thuillier produced a new translation, and Folard added his chapter-by-chapter commentaries. The first volume of the *Abrégé des commentaries de M. de Folard sur L'Histoire de Polybe* (*Commentaries on Polybius*) appeared in 1727, and there were to be eight volumes in all. These were republished in 1753 and 1774, and a German translation appeared in Vienna in 1760. A first abridged edition was published in Paris in 1754, thanks to Chabot de la Serre (1715–1780) of the Royal Volunteers. In the War of the Austrian Succession, de la Serre had distinguished himself at the siege of Prague (1742) and at the battle of Dettingen (1743), where a facial wound earned him the nickname "Scarface Chabot." He chased the Austrians and Piedmontese out of Provence in 1747, and was promoted as lieutenant general after participating in the Seven Years' War. Interestingly, de la Serre wrote a series of memoranda on the reorganization the army, notably recommending that it should have a national character.

The Theory: All of Folard's works began with a treatise on the infantry attack column, and the *Abrégé des commentaires* was no exception. Folard wished to improve French the infantry tactics he had seen in use at Malplaquet (1709), where Marshal Villars, following regulations and custom, had drawn up his battalions four ranks deep. Folard opined that the slavish attachment to the *ordre mince* (thin lines) paralyzed command. To maneuver, infantry had to be formed in columns.

> The true strength of a body of men is in its depth, or in the number of files, in their union, and the pressing of ranks at sword point. Depth makes the flanks almost as strong as the front. In this order of battle every battalion will be in a state to resist and break any opposing battalion not fighting according to this principle, and to move with much more ease and lightness than a body that fights on a wide front with little depth, and which can only maneuver with difficulty, and will not be able to escape the inevitable crowding of unwieldy formations. (*Abrégé,* vol. I p.2)

According to Folard, the column should be formed with one to six battalions, one behind the other. The frontage should vary between 24 and 30 files in open terrain. The column should rely on shock rather than firepower: it should then easily overwhelm the enemy with cold steel.

The most important thing was to combine shock action and firepower. Folard cites the columns of Gustavus Adolphus at Leipzig (aka Breitenfeld) in 1631, the wedge or "boar's head" formations of the Greeks and Byzantines, and the orders of battle of Epaminondas at Leuctra and at Mantinea as illustrations. At Leuctra, for example, Epaminondas wanted to make his main effort with the left wing of his army. He formed a column of 3,000 elite troops, 50-ranks deep, and the 300 men of the Sacred Band closed up the wing. The rest of his infantry, with the light troops, were spread out in a thin line three or four deep toward the right, and would try to avoid engagement. The right extreme of the line would not move, acting as a pivot for the rest of the line moving forward in a wide arc to smash into the enemy with the reinforced left. This order of battle is Vegetius' sixth, the so-called "oblique order."

Folard compares wars where armies were powerful and numerous, to those with limited forces. According to him, the former were too much admired, an error he ascribes to imaginations fired by titanic clashes of arms. However, large armies cannot avoid combat: "their fate is decided by battle." In contemporary wars, Folard believes, terrain rarely allowed such armies to fully deploy. At Malplaquet, four to six successive lines of battle were formed, but he claims that not all the lines could fight effectively. With small armies, science and intellect could be used, as seen in Caesar's campaign around Ilerda in 49 BCE and in Turenne's campaigns of 1674 and 1675. The desire to endlessly build up armies "only bears witness to a weakness in the art of war and in tactics."

Folard demonstrates that even Fabius "*Cunctator,*" Hannibal's cautious opponent in the Second Punic War, was a supporter of the column and shock action, even though he did not advocate seeking battle, but rather preferred maneuver and subterfuge. To this end Folard quotes Vegetius:

Great captains," he [i.e. Vegetius] says, "are not those who fight in open campaigns, where the peril is shared, but rather those who by dexterity and 'ruse de guerre', without losing a single soldier, try to undo the enemy, or at least to hold him in fear and in check. (the *Abrégé,* vol.II p.216)

Folard's *Commentaries* uses Polybius's history as a starting point to make practical suggestions. For example, in attacking entrenched army "to save men's lives and to quickly bring about the dangerous moment of decision," portable bridges, bundles of fascines, or large canvas bags filled with straw, leaves or manure could be constructed.

For Folard, art of war is the opposite of unrestrained violence, and the general's task (and his claim to courage) was to direct the blow most effectively (*Abrégé,* vol. II, p.216). Closing with the Roman disaster at Cannae, Folard blames Varro for having risked battle without thinking.

> Apart from the danger to the general's cause which was put at risk, did he value his men's lives so little that he would venture a useless battle? [...] This was the genius of M. de Turenne, and the finest point of his praise in the conversations of [knowledgeable] men. (*Abrégé,* vol II, pp.289–290)

Folard did not limit himself to tactics. He touched on what would soon be called strategy when he broached "the manner in which to establish the state of war." He had read in the Imperial general Montecúccoli's writings that Frontinus (ca. 40–103 CE) had written a *De constituendo statu belli,* but he was unable to find a copy of this text.

> Establishing the state of war is to describe the shape that one wants to give to it: offensive or defensive, careful or dashing, made up of sieges or battles. For this it is important to know its means, those of the enemy, and the country where operations will take place.

For Folard, this is the most important of the state's military preparations (*Abrégé,* vol. III, pp 68–74).

The *Abrégé des commentaires* closes with a *Treatise on the Attack and Defense of Ancient Fortresses.* Folard maintains that there is less art and science in the attack than in the defense of fortresses. He maintains that the easterners outstripped the Greeks and Romans in this regard.

Folard undertook a great piece of historical research, even becoming an amateur archaeologist when he shows reproductions of the arch of Septimus Severus and Trajan's Column, and describes the major sieges of the ancient world. Folard's research and work is remarkable. He rescued numerous ancient texts, which hitherto had only been understood by specialist scholars. He read enormously in order to edit Polybius, and he acted as a critic on many points of ancient military science. His observations on the battle of Zama (202 BCE), which he considers the apogee of the art of war, appeared in the *Commentaries,* and later in a *History of Scipio Africanus* by the *abbé* Seran de la Tour. Folard knew of a work, including a plan of the battle of Zama, by Louis of Nassau. However, the importance of the columns that Scipio formed at Zama had escaped Nassau. Folard maintained that Scipio's victory at Zama validated his own argument regarding the column.

The *Commentaries on Polybius* was republished in an abridged edition in 1761 in Berlin, Lyon and Leipzig, and it was widely distributed, but this was a substandard collection, which the publisher wanted to pass off as the work of Frederick the Great. Folard's erudite commentaries are edited so as to be unrecognizable, turning this edition into a mundane campaign manual.

Application: Folard's doctrine hardly influenced the tactical regulations of the French infantry during the last years of the reign of Louis XIV. However, in 1734, during the War of the Polish Succession, the *Duc* de Coigny and the *Duc* de Broglie, following Folard's suggestions, charged with their battalions in column at the battles of Parma and at Guastalla. By 1758, some generals were taking far more initiative, and some adopted Folard's ideas.

Folard initiated a great debate between European military pundits over the virtues of the column, and over aspects of ancient military history. These interests soon permeated all discussions of the art of war. Many have criticized Folard, yet others have defended him. His principal merit probably resides in the fact that he gave soldiers of his time a *dialectique du métier*—a spirit of professional debate.

Descendents: Folard's ideas greatly influenced the career and thoughts of Maurice de Saxe and many other military writers of his time.

See also: Guibert, J.; Puységur; Saxe, M.; Vegetius

Further Reading

Chandler, David, *The Art of War in the Age of Marlborough.* Tunbridge Wells, UK: Spellmount, 1990.

Nosworthy, Brent, *The Anatomy of Victory: Battle Tactics, 1689–1763.* New York: Hippocrene, 1992.

Toby McLeod

Frederick II ("the Great"), King of Prussia
(b. 1712, r. 1740–1786)

Significance: It would be an injustice to define this great monarch and general by one tactical idea. He was both an intellectual of the Enlightenment and a pragmatic soldier, who constantly tested his military thought through practice. Through war, he transformed Prussia from a vulnerable second-rank state to great power status. He became the most successful commander in Europe's "classical age" of limited war, 1713–1789.

Biography: Frederick was born in 1712 to Frederick William I, the king of Prussia. He inherited the throne in 1740 and then ferociously defended, and expanded, Prussian interests against a variety of major powers.

Influences: Although he rebelled against the barrack room mentality of his father, he inherited an army, a bureaucracy, and financial system that was remarkably efficient for its time. Frederick was an avid reader of military treatises, including those of Turenne, Montecúccoli, and Folard, and studied closely the campaigns of Prince Eugene of Savoy.

The Theory and Application: Frederick the Great is often associated with a tactical doctrine, the oblique order, which allowed him to concentrate the bulk of his army against the flank of a numerically superior enemy while refusing to commit the weaker wing. Employment of this tactic was often cited as the reason for his striking battlefield successes during the two Silesian wars against Austria in the 1740s and against a massive coalition of enemies during the Seven Years' War. However, the oblique order had been introduced by the ancient Theban general Epaminados. Nevertheless, it was dangerous to execute in the face of an enemy army for it meant marching across its front. The outstanding Prussian march discipline and Frederick's capacity to exploit the landscape allowed him to execute this tactic more effectively than anyone else. When Frederick was unfamiliar with the ground or had done poor reconnaissance, and as this tactic became predictable to the enemy, success was far from guaranteed. Only his victory over the Austrians at Leuthen in 1757 represents the unqualified success of the oblique order.

Over the course of his career, Frederick wrote extensively on military subjects, largely for the instruction of his generals. Although intended as secret, many of these documents fell into enemy hands and, once published in France, were intensely studied throughout Europe. The full body of his work was not published until 1846 in *Oeuvres de Frederick le Grande*. It consisted of 31 volumes, with volumes 28–30 devoted to military subjects. These works demonstrate Frederick's development from an aggressive young general in search of fame into a great commander and military thinker whose prudence had been forged in the hard school of experience.

Initially, Frederick's sense of Prussia's strategic weakness combined with the powerful army that he had inherited inclined him to aggressive war and preemptive strikes. Drawing upon his military role models, he stressed the need to seize the offensive. The Sieur de Folard had questioned the effectiveness of firepower and the linear tactics of the day, which he thought contributed to stalemate. Frederick seemed to agree. In 1747, he wrote that morale factors determined the outcome of battles and ordered that his infantry advance on the enemy with shouldered weapons. "It is not fire but bearing that defeats the enemy" (Frederick II, *Instructions for His Generals,* trans. Thomas Phillips (Harrisburg: Stackpole Press (1960), 99). Frederick's victories in the Silesian wars seemed to confirm the truth of this instruction, but they had come at the expense of a weak and unprepared Austria that was beset by other powerful enemies. Even so, the experience of these wars caused him to improve the quality of his cavalry and artillery, and to understand the importance of fortifications.

The Seven Years' War provided a changed context, in which he faced a powerful coalition led by a regenerate and vengeful Austria supported by France and Russia. If the survival of Prussia was not at stake, its great power status certainly was. Frederick's aggressive spirit remained evident when he launched the war by a preventive attack against Saxony, after which he drafted the entire Saxon army into his own. Confronted by overwhelming numbers on many fronts, he adopted an offensive–defensive strategy, exploiting interior lines to strike at his opponents in hopes of defeating them in detail. At best his often costly battlefield victories bought him time, a valuable asset against a coalition with differing goals and interests.

Frederick found it necessary to adapt to new conditions on the battlefield. Despite his disparaging comments about the Russians as inept savages, the fighting resolve of Russian soldiers came as a shock. His old enemies, the Austrians, manifested a new professionalism and demonstrated the merits of defensive tactics. Frederick's later treatises of 1758 and 1770 reflect his respect for these circumstances. He concluded that war had become more refined, more murderous, and required greater caution, and now recommended a war of positions rather than a search for decisive battle. Thus, he wrote favorably of the Austrians, who were masters of this kind of war with their new and deadly field artillery (designed by Prince Joseph Wenzel von Liechtenstein), their field fortifications and powerful encampments, and their shrewd exploitation of the terrain. He now recommended that his generals approach this form of warfare as if it were siegecraft.

It is worth noting that Frederick, in his writing, was not only willing to give the Austrians their due (if not the French and Russians), but also to recognize and learn from his mistakes. Although his military thought evolved through experience, Frederick never ceased to search for its underlying principles. In recommending Folard to his officers, he wrote:

> Every art has its rules and maxims. One must study them: theory facilitates practice. The lifetime of one man is not long enough to enable him to acquire perfect knowledge and experience. Theory helps to supplement it, it provides youth with premature experience and makes him skillful through the mistakes of others. In the profession of war the rules are never violated without drawing some punishment from the enemy who is delighted to find us at fault. (*Frederick the Great on the Art of War,* ed. Jay Luvaas (New York: Free Press, 1966, 54)

Frederick, nevertheless, recognized that great commanders possessed innate qualities that could only be partially compensated for by education. The quality termed *coup d'oeil* in the 18th century was essential. He believed that it consisted of two points: the ability to judge how many troops a position could hold and how best to exploit the terrain. We might say that it meant a general's quick grasp of a tactical situation and his immediate sense of what to do. This ability Frederick possessed in abundance, but he still attempted to convey its principles to his commanders. He instructed them to apply the rules of fortification to the battlefield as a means of understanding the best positions for an army.

Frederick was not alone among 18th-century commanders in seeking to apply the predictable, scientific practices of fortification and siegecraft as a means of imposing some clarity and order on the chaos of the battlefield. Much of

18th-century theoretical military debate focused on tactics and Frederick certainly made his contribution in this area. But as a soldier king his first concern was inevitably strategy. How was he to secure and increase the power of the state that was his inheritance? He believed in constant thought and preparation, even in time of peace. This required an accurate knowledge of politics, so as to understand the intentions of other monarchs (ironically, for the author of a treatise critical of Machiavelli, no one had a more realistic, perhaps cynical, view of his fellow monarchs, than did Frederick). He recommended that military leaders should understand the enemy's finances and their actual and potential military power. Detailed knowledge of their communications and of the geography were essential if one was to wage war in their countries—no easy matter in an age of poor roads and scarce and inadequate maps. Although Frederick did not coin the term friction of war, he certainly understood it. He urged his officers to always place themselves in the enemy's shoes, to anticipate his plans and to overcome the obstacles that the opponent would inevitably place in one's way. "Above all," one "must train his mind to furnish him with a multitude of expedients, ways, and means in case of need. For those who are destined for the military profession, peace must be a time of meditation, and war the period where one puts his ideas into practice" (Luvaas, 337).

Descendents: Frederick was the most admired commander of his time, and the Prussian army was held up as a model for others. Nevertheless, his long-term influence was ambiguous. Despite his efforts to educate his officers, the Prussian way of war depended upon his personal leadership at the highest level. With his death, the system ossified and proved unable to meet the challenges of the post-1789 revolutionary environment.

Frederick himself accepted two restraints upon his ability to make war. First was the international system of balance of power and coalition war that meant that the greatest military efforts might reap only the gain of a province. Second was Frederick's fundamental social conservatism. He relied for his officer corps upon a *Junker* service nobility on the assumption, widespread among the European nobility, that only they possessed the proper military spirit and culture of self-sacrifice. But there were not enough of these officers to sustain the bloodbaths of Frederick's wars. He recruited middle class officers out of necessity and eliminated them as soon as peace made it possible. In doing so, Frederick locked the Prussian officer corps into an increasingly anachronistic culture. His attitude toward the rank and file was similarly conservative. Prussia's small population required him to employ large numbers of mercenaries. Many foreigners were impressed into his service, which gave the army an evil reputation (most famously in *Candide*) as a gang of kidnappers. Lacking patriotic motives for service, the Prussian system became notorious for savage and inhumane discipline. Some of this was clearly caricature, but the Prussian method seem to have run against an increasing tide in the late 18th century of concern by military intellectuals for the humanity of the troops and for new ways motivating them as soldiers. These ideas lay outside Frederick's cynical worldview. He remained committed to the social and political system of his time.

Finally, although he was forced to detach independent commands to meet his wide circle of enemies, Frederick remained committed to a unitary army in operations in a specific theater. He does not seem to have experimented in the development of divisional and corps organizations, already underway in France before 1789, which would became a hallmark of Napoleonic warfare. He was the most successful practitioner of war within the context of his era, but he left the Prussian military unprepared for the challenges brewing for the future.

Nineteenth-century Prussian and German general staff officers drew upon Frederick as a model for preemptive war and offensive strategies. He also represented an ideal concentration of total military and political authority in a supreme warlord unconstrained by constitutional limits. This was a baleful legacy. One may argue that the Schlieffen Plan was a kind of Fredrecian preemptive strike, employing a version of the oblique order on a grand scale. But such conclusions also represented a misreading of Frederick's evolving thought. The later Frederick was much less eager for war than the youthful monarch of 1740. Prussia was exhausted by the efforts of the Seven Years' War and although Frederick was content to participate in two "peaceful" partitions of Poland, he fought only one more war, the War of the Bavarian Succession 1778–1779, sometimes known as the "Potato War" because the conflict between Prussia and Austria was dominated by a war of positions and logistics. Gerhard Ritter, describing the peaceful world of late Enlightenment Germany, believed that Frederick won a reputation as a "sovereign of peace." This Frederick had no place in the pantheon of the Great general staff. When the pro-Russian Voltaire, gulled by the blandishments of Catherine the Great, urged Frederick to join in her "crusade" against the Turks (which culminated in the Russo-Turkish War of 1787–1790), the king responded that he intended henceforth to cultivate his own garden.

See also: Folard; Montecúccoli, R.; Saxe, M.

Further Reading
Duffy, Christopher, *The Military Life of Frederick.* New York: Atheneum, 1986.

Armstrong Starkey

Genghis Khan (Personal Name: Temüjin)
(1167–1227)

Significance: Mobility, outflanking tactics, ambush and technological investment.

Context: At the end of the 12th century, the unification of the Mongol and the conquest of northern China set up the bases of the Mongol Empire.

Biography: Born in the Mongolian steppe from an aristocratic family, Temüjin lost his father Yisügei, poisoned by the Tatars, at the age of nine. Temüjin and his family were bereft of his father's wealth, and were abandoned by his clan. Temüjin found in this life hardiness the necessary strength to build back his own clan. He gained his military skills in the crucible of wars between Mongolia's tribes, showing a great talent in making alliances.

He was probably not the cleverest of the Mongolians of his time, but he was able to develop faithful friendships and efficient networks. Though he was illiterate, herders' life and hunting developed his knowledge of strategy, in the conduct of outflanking tactics, archery fire, and heavy and light cavalry interaction.

His reputation of loyalty attached him a growing number of Mongol leaders who joined him with their men, so that he eventually became one of the most powerful Khans of Mongolia.

During the war against the Jin Empire in north China (1211–1215), he learned siege warfare from his Khitan subjects. In a short time, the Mongol army, especially in Central Asia (1220–1221) and in China, was able to use siege machines, like the most advanced sedentary armies. This technological investment, and achievement, was also noticeable in the creation of a field artillery displayed in Hungary in 1241, and fireworks used in Korea in 1274, or even in Japan. Some years later, thanks to Chinese or Korean defectors, the descendents of Genghis Khan were able to build a true, efficient military navy, and the famous Qubilai attempted to conquer not only Japan (Kyushu), but also Vietnam, unsuccessfully, however.

Influences: Steppe warfare

The Theory: Mongol warfare relied on pragmatism, swarming tactics, mobility and art of swift maneuver, and the early development of a fierce, modern-styled discipline, scarcely seen elsewhere at the time.

Application: Campaigns of northern China, Central Asia, and southern Russia, then campaigns by Genghis descendents, in Korea, Japan, etc.

Descendents: Captain Liddel Hart praised the Mongol three-pronged columns that stormed Central Asia. The mobility of the Mongol horsemen inspired armored and mechanized tactics in various countries in the 20th century. Mongol influence is also perceptible, in operational art, combined armed doctrine, etc., though there is no direct filiations.

See also: Subotai, Baator (Sübedei Baatar)

Further Reading
Basil, Liddell-Hart, *Great Captains Unveiled.* London: William Blackwood and Sons, 1927.

Chambers, James, *The Devil's Horsemen: The Mongol Invasion of Europe,* New York, Atheneum, 1979.

Grousset, René, *L'Empire des Steppes* (The Empire of the steppes), Payot, Paris, 1952 (reed. Rutgers University Press, 1970).

Lococo, Paul, *Genghis Khan.* Washington, DC: Potomac books, 2008.

May, Timothy, *The Mongol Art of War.* Yardley, PA: Westholme, 2007.

Rachewiltz, Igor de, *The Secret History of the Mongols,* Boston: Inner Asian Library, 7: 1–2, 2004; 2nd ed., 2006.

Laurent Quisefit

Gustavus II Adolphus, King of Sweden
(1594–1632)

Significance: Gustavus Adolphus made revolutionary innovations in terms of combined-arms warfare and logistics.

Context: Gustavus's grandfather had introduced the Protestant faith to Sweden, and created a social, political, and economic change that influenced the Swedish army. Gustavus's military reforms were tested in several wars, including the Thirty Years' War (1618–1648).

Biography: Gustavus Adolphus became king of Sweden in 1611. He fought successfully against Russia and Poland and enlarged Sweden's territory. In 1630, Gustavus joined the Thirty Years' War to protect his territories in north Germany against catholic forces. He fought several engagements, including at Breitenfeld, Lech, Munich, and Lützen, where Gustavus was killed leading a cavalry charge.

Influences: Maurice of Nassau's reorganization of the Dutch army against the Spaniards in the late 16th century influenced Gustavus's military reforms. Maurice properly structured his forces and emphasized drill to create coherent military units. Gustavus also benefited from the reforms introduced in Sweden by his father and grandfather, which made it easier to raise a standing army.

The Theory: Gustavus fully developed the capabilities of gunpowder of his era. He reduced the number of pikemen and emphasized firearms, which changed the composition of is forces, increasing the ratio of musketeers to pikemen from the common 1:2 to 3:2. His infantry was deployed in six files, rather than in the Spanish-style *tercios* (squares). Three of the files were musketeers, allowing one file to fire whereas the others reloaded. This structure, together with the drill conducted in the Swedish army, meant that Gustavus's army could maneuver and fire more rapidly than its opponents. Gustavus furthermore realized the potential of artillery against the square formations of his opponents. He increased the number of cannons from one per thousand soldiers to eight. He also divided the artillery according to its military use—mobile close support, field, and siege artillery—with standard calibers. Gustavus organized his forces into small, standardized units with a special emphasis on combined arms. Thus, the brigade became the basic tactical formation, consisting of infantry, cavalry, and artillery. Gustavus put an emphasis on mobility, and he realized that a successful mobile campaign was based on discipline. Discipline, in turn, was based on efficient administration and leadership. Gustavus was able to raise a comparatively strong army by introducing a precursor system of conscription.

Application: Gustavus applied his modern tactics successfully in several battles conducted by him.

Descendents: Gustavus has been called the father of modern warfare and his ways and methods of waging war had a deep impact on future military leaders and the conduct of war. Napoleon identified Gustavus as the first great captain of the modern era.

See also: Bonaparte, Napoleon; Frederick II ("the Great"); Maurice of Nassau; Montecúccoli, R.

Matthias Strohn

Hannibal Barca
(247–183 BCE)

Significance: Hannibal's strategy for defeating Rome in the Second Punic War was based on winning enough battles to convince or compel Rome's Italian allies to defect to the Carthaginian camp. An isolated and disheartened Rome would then seek peace on terms favorable to Carthage. Although Hannibal smashed Roman armies in three major battles, these successes did not produce the desired result. He thus provides an early example of an oft-repeated strategic miscalculation: that winning on the battlefield will produce victory in war.

Context: Hannibal was a native of Carthage, a city-state located near modern Tunis. Founded in the ninth century BCE by Phoenician settlers, it became a military and economic power in the Western Mediterranean and, eventually, the chief rival of the region's other ascendant power, Rome. During the second and third centuries BCE, Carthage and Rome engaged in three separate conflicts collectively known as the Punic Wars (after *Poeni,* the Latin term for the people of Carthage). The First Punic War (264–241) was fought mainly at sea and ended with Carthage relinquishing Sicily to Rome. Carthage was also vanquished in the Second Punic War (218–202), but not before Hannibal brought Rome to the brink of collapse. In the Third Punic War (149–146) the Romans captured Carthage and destroyed it.

Biography: Hannibal was the eldest son of Hamilcar Barca, leader of Carthage's prominent Barcid family. In 237, Hannibal, age nine, accompanied his father to Iberia (Spain). In 222, he assumed command of the Carthaginian army in Iberia. War with Rome soon followed (218) and Hannibal took his army on an epic march across the Alps into northern Italy. His first three years in Italy saw him win several battles, destroying three Roman armies and ravaging the Italian countryside—but failing to force Rome's surrender. Hannibal and his army remained in Italy until 202, when they were recalled to North Africa. That same year he was defeated in the Battle of Zama and Carthage sued for peace. He spent his final years in exile in Bithynia, committing suicide at age 64 upon learning that Roman agents were seeking his arrest.

Influences: If it is true, as Polybius says, that Hannibal ranked Alexander the Great and Pyrrhus of Epirus as the world's first- and second-greatest generals (he ranked himself third), then it is safe to say that they had a major influence on his development as a general. Admiration for Alexander and Pyrrhus was common in Hannibal's times, and their thinking is discernible in Hannibal's generalship. He developed no new technology, but worked within a tactical framework that was circumscribed by the technology of edged-weapon warfare. His brilliance, at least as a tactician, was his ability to adapt his army to the circumstances of the battlefield—and also to create a battlefield that was suitable to his army. He was a master of manipulating prebattle events so that when battle was finally joined, it was on ground that maximized his army's strengths while minimizing its weaknesses. Later generations of military theorists would call this talent *"coup d'oeil"* (literally, "eye to the ground"). That said, it is revealing that he held Pyrrhus in such high esteem: like Hannibal, Pyrrhus won battles against the Romans; and like Hannibal, he lost his war with Rome.

Theory and Application: Hannibal's reputation for greatness was based largely on his performance in the first three years (218–216) of the 16-year Second Punic War (alternately, the "Hannibalic War"). His achievements in that period nonetheless did not produce decisive results. His superior practice of the operational art and his tactical brilliance were undeniable, enabling him to outmarch, outmaneuver, and outfight the Romans—but to no ultimate avail. He could defeat Roman armies; but he could not defeat Rome. After 216 he did not fight, much less win, any major battles on Italian soil even though he remained in Italy for 14 years. His next big battle, fought in North Africa (at Zama, near Carthage, in 202), was his last; and he lost it and thereby the war.

In 218, shortly after the outbreak of war between Rome and Carthage (the *casus belli* was a dispute over the Spanish city of Saguntum), Hannibal and his multiethnic, polyglot mercenary force began a 1,000-mile trek from Spain over the Pyrenees, across southern France, and finally across the Alps and down into the Po Valley. In France, at the Rhone River, he sidestepped Publius Scipio's

Roman army. All along the way he intermittently battled local tribes. He took his army over the Alps in late autumn when winter weather had descended on the high passes, and through it all he held his army together, which alone was a remarkable achievement.

Hannibal's invasion of Italy is one of the great military feats of the age, at once a masterpiece of operational maneuver, a textbook case of leadership in adversity, and a triumph of endurance. But the fact that Hannibal had to make the journey was evidence of a profound weakness in his, and Carthage's, war-waging capabilities, namely, the lack of an effective navy to provide seaborne support for her overseas armies. The Carthaginian navy had been largely destroyed in the First Punic War and in the 23 years that followed the city's oligarchy had given shipbuilding priority to merchant carriers over war galleys. In the meantime, the Roman navy had grown to dominate the seas. Hannibal took the land route to Italy because Rome and Carthage's elite left him with no other choice.

Rome's control of the Western Mediterranean prevented Hannibal from receiving meaningful reinforcements from either Spain, his primary source of fighting men, or North Africa. He tried to make good his losses by recruiting among the Celtic tribes of northern Italy. However, there were never enough Celts willing to join him and always too many Italians eager to oppose him; as a result, he always suffered manpower shortages and fought outnumbered.

Hannibal clearly recognized that Rome's numerical advantages would prove insurmountable in the long term, ruling out a lengthy war of attrition. He therefore formed a strategy that would enable him to win the war in a few years' time. He hoped to strike at the alliances that Rome had built with other Italian states, which provided Rome with the vast manpower reserves and material resources necessary to fight Carthage. The alliances system was, in modern parlance, Rome's strategic center of gravity.

Hannibal believed that many if not most of the allied states were only waiting on favorable circumstances to break away from Rome. Hannibal determined to create those circumstances by bringing Rome to battle early and often and by winning those battles convincingly. His victories would leave Rome too battered to retaliate against disloyal allies, causing them to defect. Eventually the defections would reach a critical mass and Rome's citizens would lose the will to continue the war. The Romans would then sue for peace and in the negotiated settlement that followed Hannibal would impose terms that would restore Carthage to parity with Rome.

Hannibal enjoyed initial success. Once in Italy he persuaded thousands of Celts to join his ranks, partly due to a successful skirmish at the River Ticinus. Shortly thereafter Hannibal smashed a Roman army at the River Trebia, killing 30,000 of the 40,000 Roman troops deployed. In the spring of 217, he again exhibited his gift for operational maneuver by crossing the Apennines and passing through the Arnus marshes, interposing his army between Rome and the bulk of Roman forces that were supposed to defend it in the north. The Romans' northern force hastened south and Hannibal ambushed and virtually annihilated it on the shore of Lake Trasimene, killing another 30,000 legionaries.

In the aftermath of the Lake Trasimene disaster the Roman Senate appointed Quintus Fabius as temporary dictator, putting him in charge of Rome's armies. Fabius avoided open battle with Hannibal. Instead, he implemented a strategy of mobile containment, attrition, and delay (hence his moniker, *Cunctator,* Latin for "delayer"), whereby several large forces shadowed the Carthaginian army, conducting fighting withdrawals when advanced upon, and otherwise harrying its rear and flanks. This so-called Fabian strategy prevented Hannibal from inflicting further crushing defeats on Roman armies. But it did not stop Hannibal from ravaging the countryside, and so was unpopular with the Romans. When in the spring of 216 Hannibal's army marched from its winter quarters, the Romans sacked Fabius, replaced him with two generals who were eager to fight, and gave them a mighty army numbering over 86,000 men and a mandate to destroy the invaders. Instead, at the Battle of Cannae, Hannibal maneuvered his outnumbered forces to execute a double envelopment of the Roman army. The Roman force was annihilated; more than 50,000 legionaries were killed.

Hannibal did not follow up on his victory by marching on Rome: according to Livy he paused for a day and a night to allow his troops, exhausted by the effort required to slaughter so many Romans, to rest. Marhabal, the Carthaginian cavalry commander, had urged Hannibal to seize the moment and attack the capital; when Hannibal refused Marhabal reproached his commander: "You know how to win victory, Hannibal, you do not how to use it" ("*vincere scis, Hannibal; victoria uti nescis*"). Marhabal's criticism was unfair and erroneous. Hannibal surely knew how to "use" victory; and although he must have known that moving on Rome would entail a lengthy siege, his army had no siege equipment. Nor did it have enough men to garrison its conquests in Italy while investing the city. A naval task force from Carthage or Spain might have delivered both the men and equipment Hannibal needed. But the Carthaginian navy was virtually defunct and Rome ruled the sea. Hannibal did not attack Rome directly; instead, he continued to pursue his previous strategic course, hoping that Cannae would induce more of Rome's allies to come over to Carthage. A number of allied states, notably Capua and Tarentum, did indeed defect, but overall the alliance held and Rome and its citizens remained stalwart in their prosecution of the war. The Romans again refused open battle, electing to merely contain Hannibal in southern Italy while striking at Spain. Hannibal's strategy had failed and in 202 he returned to North Africa, there to preside over Carthage's downfall.

Descendents: The Battle of Cannae was Hannibal's crowning achievement. In the modern age it has mesmerized military theorists and commanders, who regarded his tactic of double envelopment as a textbook example of how to win decisively on the battlefield against a numerically superior force. The Germans were particularly taken with the perceived efficacy of fighting a "battle of annihilation" (*Vernichtungsschlacht*) as a means of solving their perennial problem of waging war on multiple fronts. Writing in *On War,* German military theorist and philosopher Carl von Clausewitz asserted that the goal of land war was to destroy the enemy army. In the late 19th century, Count Alfred von Schlieffen, chief of the German general staff, became convinced that Cannae provided the model for destruction, a conclusion he reached after reading Hans Delbrück's account of the battle. Schlieffen himself penned a treatise on the subject (*Cannae*), calling it "the perfect battle," and commissioned the historical section of the general staff to produce a series of essays known as *Cannae Studies* that analyzed and extolled the virtues of the annihilating encirclement battle. As a result of Schlieffen's efforts, the "Cannae concept," as it came to be known, was elevated to the level of strategic doctrine (Delbrück called it *Niederwerfungsstragie,* "strategy of annihilation"). Schlieffen came to see war as a series of battles, each of which would ideally entail the envelopment and annihilation of the opposing army. Wars would be swiftly won by the victor of those battles, because the enemy would soon be left with no armies to fight them. Somehow Hannibal's experience, that a strategy predicated on winning battles decisively did not necessarily produce a quick, decisive victory in war, escaped Schlieffen's notice. Thus the form of battle became as important (if not more so) then the aim: victory and battle became one and the same, and the form, or technique, became all important. The Cannae concept would have a profound influence on German operational and strategic planning in both World Wars and helped to inspire the development of World War II *blitzkrieg* warfare in particular.

The battle-centric approach to warfare had its critics, the most prolific and articulate of whom was Friedrich von Bernhardi, a German general and military theorist. Bernhardi was particularly critical of Schlieffen's belief that the encirclement battle of annihilation should become every army commander's desiderata in every battle, to the exclusion of other methods (including penetration and breakthrough tactics).

In the World War II, Japan and Germany both proved adept, like Hannibal, at winning battles, only to lose the war. Especially notable in this regard are the battles that the *Wehrmacht* won in summer 1941 as part of Operation Barbarossa. In the course of Barbarossa the German army executed the greatest encirclement/annihilation battles of all time: for example, in the encirclement battles at Minsk and Smolensk (mid-July), Kiev (August 21–September 26), and Vyazma (September 30–October 7) the Germans bagged over 1.7 million prisoners—and this is to say nothing of all the Soviet soldiers killed in those battles. Nonetheless, the *Wehrmacht* failed to capture Moscow and Leningrad, key strategic goals, and by early December the Red Army could launch a massive counteroffensive that came within in ace of destroying the *Wehrmacht* and left it permanently weakened.

Perhaps the most trenchant commentary on the pitfalls of a battle-centric strategy was delivered by a North Vietnamese Colonel named Tu in a conversation with U.S. Army Colonel Harry Summers during the latter's 1974 trip to Hanoi to discuss the status of U.S. prisoners of war. Colonel Summers told Tu, "You know, you never beat us on the battlefield." To which Colonel Tu replied: "That may be so—but it is also irrelevant." Less than a year later, in April 1975, North

Vietnamese tanks rolled through Saigon, and the war in which U.S. forces had lost no major battles ended in victory for North Vietnam.

See also: Bernhardi, Friedrich von; Schlieffen, Alfred von

Further Reading

Daly, George, *Cannae: The Experience of Battle in the Second Punic War.* London: Routledge, 2003.

Lazenby, J. F., *A Military History of the Second Punic War.* Norman, Oklahoma: University of Oklahoma Press, 1998.

Steven Weingartner

Howe, George Augustus
(ca. 1725–1758)

Significance: George Augustus Howe introduced the concept of light infantry to the British army in the 18th century. His reforms made the force a more effective fighting unit in the terrain and conditions of North America and contributed to British success in the French and Indian War.

Context: The British army of the mid-18th century was organized to conduct wars in the more open terrain of the European continent. Howe quickly came to understand that the British army, as it was then trained and organized, was ill suited to fight in the challenging terrain of the North American frontier. In attempting to remedy this situation, Howe accompanied Captain Robert Rogers and a group of his Rangers on a scouting mission in the vicinity of Fort Carillon (Ticonderoga) in 1757. He paid particular attention to the Rangers' dress and methods.

On his return, Howe initiated a series of reforms in his own 55th regiment designed to make them more effective at wilderness fighting. These reforms included shortening the men's coats, cutting their long hair, and providing them with an ample food reserve of their own so that they would not be dependent on the long army supply train. Leading by example, as he was known to do, Howe modified his own dress accordingly and had his own hair cut. He likewise carried his own rations, which were the same as those of his men. In addition, he shortened the baggage train substantially by forbidding the officers to bring any superfluous materials along with them on campaign. All of these reforms combined to make the 55th a very effective unit in wilderness fighting.

Biography: George Augustus, 3rd Viscount Howe was the oldest of three brothers and an Irish peer. All three were well known British military leaders of the 18th century. George Howe served as a career officer in the British army, where he attained the rank of brigadier general. He is most known for his reforms to the British army made while on campaign in North America during the French and Indian War.

Born at Trout Brook, George Howe received his education at Westminster and Eton. He then entered the British army as an ensign in the 1st Regiment Foot Guards at age 20. He saw his first service on campaign in Flanders during the War of the Austrian Succession.

In 1746, George Augustus became an aide-de-camp to the William Augustus, Duke of Cumberland, leader of the Allied army in Flanders. The following year, he fought at the Battle of Lauffeldt near Maastricht in July 1747. As a result of his services in this conflict, George Augustus received a promotion to the rank of lieutenant colonel in 1749.

With the outbreak of the Seven Years' War, George Augustus, now a colonel in the 55th regiment, received orders to go with his unit to North America. His unit, among others, was dispatched in an effort to make up for earlier defeats suffered by British forces at the hands of the French. He arrived in Halifax, Nova Scotia, in July 1757. While fighting in the United States, George Augustus Howe was killed on July 6, 1758 in a skirmish just prior to the failed British assault on Forth Ticonderoga. There are monuments to him both in England and the United States.

Influences: The reforms initiated by George Howe in his own unit were certainly influenced by the practices of Robert Rogers, the U.S. ranger. By the same token, he may have been influenced by the exploits of other European continental forces, such as the Croats then in the service of the Austrian Empire, however, this is very difficult to substantiate.

The Theory: Howe believed that effective combat in North America required a more mobile and maneuverable infantry force. He sought to create this type of force through modifying the dress and training of his troops. The equipment of both officers and men was drastically reduced, as noted above. In addition, the men were trained to fight in open order, and to utilize aimed fire.

Application: George Howe's reforms quickly spread from the fifty-fifth to other British regiments fighting in North America.

Descendents: As a result of the success of Howe's unit in North America, the British army introduced the light infantry company to all regiments in the aftermath of the Seven Years' War.

Further Reading
Brumwell, Stephen, "Band of Brothers" *History Today* 58, 6 (June 2008): 25–31.
Fuller, J.F.C., *British Light Infantry in the Eighteenth Century.* London: Hutchinson, 1925.

Houlding, J. A., *Fit for Service The Training of the British Army, 1715–1795*. Oxford: Clarendon Press, 1981.

Williams, Noel St. John, *Redcoats along the Hudson: the Struggle for North America, 1754–1763*. London: Brassey's, 1998.

James R. McIntyre

Kikkuli the Mitannian

Summary of Theory: In the mid-14th century BC, a Mitannian horse master called Kikkuli entered the service of the king of Hatti (probably Suppiluliuma I) to train horses for the Hittite chariotry arm. While engaged in this task he authored a training manual that set forth a seven-month regimen designed to prepare young horses both physically and psychologically for chariotry combat. Preserved on four clay tablets (plus a fragment of a fifth tablet) and written mostly in the Hittite language, with Indo-Aryan and Luwian terms used liberally throughout, the cuneiform inscriptions that constitute the so-called Kikkuli text exhibit a genius for equine care and conditioning that anticipated by several thousand years the scientific methodologies of the modern era. Efficacy of results was its hallmark: Hittite chariotry, using horses trained in the Kikkuli method, proved a formidable force that contributed substantially to the growth and maintenance of Hittite power in Near East during the Late Bronze Age.

Context: In Kikkuli's time Tusratta was king of Mitanni, ruling an empire centered in the great bend of the Euphrates River in Upper Mesopotamia, an area known as the "Hurri lands." Formed in the 16th century BC by peoples of mixed Hurrian and Indo-Aryan stock, Mitanni swiftly became a dominant power in the region, expanding into northern Syria, parts of eastern and southeastern Anatolia, and Assyria. Conflict with Egypt in the 15th century over control of southern Syria was resolved generally in Egypt's favor, in part through warfare but chiefly through diplomacy driven by Mitanni's need to confront the more imminent and pressing threat posed by Hatti. The accession in 1350 of Suppiluliuma I to Hittite kingship marked the beginning of Mitanni's end: in a conflict lasting more than a decade the Hitties sacked Wassuganni (the Mitannian capital), conquered northern Syria, and fomented dynastic strife that led ultimately to the murder of Tusratta by one of his sons. Relegated to Hittite puppet status after losing its northern territories to the Assyrians, what remained of Mitanni eventually succumbed to further Assyrian aggression: thenceforth known as Hanigabat, it became first a vassal and then a province of Assyria, disappearing forever from the role of Near Eastern nations.

Biography: The Kikkuli text begins with an announcement: "Thus speaks Kikkuli, master of the horse from the land of Mitanni." Name, job title, country of origin: this is all that Kikkuli tells us about himself. The language of the text is more revealing. Significantly, "master of the horse" is rendered as *assusani,* an Indo-Aryan term, closely related to Sanskrit *aśva-sana.* Other Indo-Aryan terms appear frequently in the text, particularly in connection with training intervals, gaits, and classification of horses at their various training stages. These terms are often followed by an explanation in Hittite, necessitated by the absence of Hittite equivalents.

Kikkuli's use of Indic terminology is indicative of the Indo-Aryan strain in the Mitannian population and, perhaps, in Kikkuli himself. A subgroup of the Indo-European peoples, the Indo-Aryans entered the Hurri lands early in the second millennium as part of a larger pattern of migrations from the Indo-European homeland, reliably located on the South Russian steppe. Inasmuch as this region is also the native habitat of the horse, it is probably no coincidence that Indo-Europeans pioneered the domestication of horses and were among the first to use the horse in warfare. By the same token, t is likely (albeit arguable) that the spoke-wheel horse-drawn chariot is an Indo-European invention that Indo-Aryans introduced to the Near East, along with their methodologies of horse training and, crucially, the means for communicating them.

Initially establishing themselves as rulers in the Hurri lands, the Indo-Aryans were eventually absorbed by the more numerous Hurrians, an apparently amicable process—the two ethnic groups seem to have gotten along quite well. The Indo-Aryan–Hurrian symbiosis produced the kingdom of Mitanni, where kings with Indo-Aryan names (and, in all likelihood, bloodlines) reigned over a mostly Hurrian populace that spoke a Hurrian language with many Indic loanwords. In addition to the latter, the Hurrians also acquired the Indo-Aryan affinity for horses and the forms of warfare that horses made possible, so much so that in time Hurrians in general and Mitannians in particular became widely acknowledged by their contemporaries as experts at chariot combat and the closely related art of breeding and training chariot horses. Kikkuli talents as a "master of horse" must have been exceptional, even for a Mitannian, otherwise he would not have attracted the attention of the greatest of Hittite kings.

He is not, however, an exceptional writer. His presentation is terse, straightforward, and economical. The man is all business: there are no literary embellishments, no flowery phrases. He never uses two words where one would suffice. Nor does he express fondness, or any emotion whatsoever, toward his horses. Whether his lack of affect is a reflection of personality or an aspect (along with brevity and concision) of the stylistic convention for writing manuals is a matter for speculation. In substance, however, Kikkuli's instructions are informed by concern for the horses' welfare. Perhaps this was mere pragmatism at work: Kikkuli knew from experience that his training goals were more likely to be achieved if his horses were happy and healthy. But it is not too much of a stretch to believe that such concern was a practical application of Kikkuli's genuine love of horses.

Why Kikkuli chose to use his expertise in the service of a power hostile to Mitanni can only be guessed at. It may well be that choice had nothing to do with it: quite possibly Kikkuli was brought to Hatti as a captive taken in Suppiluliuma's wars with Mitanni. Alternately, Kikkuli might have gone to Hatti willingly, as part of deal struck with the Hittite king, a career-enhancing move sweetened by an extravagant benefits package in which riches and rank figured prominently. Whatever the circumstances of his employment, the Hittites got their money's worth. The horses Kikkuli trained were in large measure responsible for the combat effectiveness of a chariotry corps that played a key role in the wars and conquests of Suppiluliuma I and the kings that succeeded him.

Previous Theories Influencing the New Philosophy: Inasmuch as the use of chariots in Anatolia extends back to the early second millennium, it is reasonable to assume that protocols for the training of chariot horses existed well before Kikkuli entered history. Some years before Kikkuli arrived in Hatti—and, probably, before the reign of Suppiluliuma I—the Hittites produced several horse-training texts of unknown authorship. Because those documents lack the detail and breadth of knowledge found in Kikkuli's manual, it is doubtful that they had any influence on the latter's composition; indeed, it may well be the case that Suppiluliuma commissioned the Kikkuli test as a replacement for the earlier works. In all likelihood Kikkuli learned how to train horses from his own mentors, kinsmen and native-born Mitannians like himself.

Theory and Application: Kikkuli was not a philosopher but rather a skilled technician educated in a venerable tradition of horse breeding and training passed down to him by his Indo-Aryan forbearers. As such he was also the inheritor and steward of that tradition. Most of all, though, he was its practitioner.

Kikkuli's job was to condition young horses mentally and physically for the arduous task of pulling chariots in battle. He knew that the primary requirement for a chariot horse was endurance: the animal had to be strong, in both mind and body, to endure the extreme and terrible rigors that combat imposed on it. He also knew that such mind/body strength was not innate: it had to be developed in the horse's formative years when it was most open to instruction and discipline. In the nature versus nurture debate Kikkuli was firmly on the side of the latter, and a firm believer as well that concern for the horse's well-being was foundational to the nurturing process. He recognized that a young horse's tractability could prove its undoing in the hands of an inept handler: pushing it too hard or too fast in its training might harm it physically or psychologically. Either outcome could ruin its utility for military use.

Thus the training regimen bearing his name was crafted to address both the physiological and psychological needs of the horse. Implicit in its protocols is the recognition that the rates of physical and mental development differ, with the former advancing faster than the latter. Accordingly the regimen unfolds in three stages, with the first two emphasizing the development of the horse's mechanical–skeletal and cardiovascular systems, and the third focusing on the neuromuscular system. The process is one whereby physical development in the form of enhanced strength (especially in the legs) and heart–lung function also promotes self-confidence, which spurs mental (brain) growth, which matures fully in the third stage.

The workouts themselves featured the techniques of what is now known as interval training. Each workout consisted of several heats, or intervals, conducted at varying gaits—trot, canter, gallop—over different distances. Between heats the horse was briefly rested. During these pauses the heart rate dropped, but was not allowed to fall to pre-workout levels: the next heat was begun before full recovery (to the resting heart rate) was achieved. Thus, over the course of an entire workout involving several heat/pause cycles, the heart was always being stressed, but at different levels.

Modern science has shown that this alternating pattern of first raising the heart rate (through exercise) and then lowering it with brief pauses to allow partial recovery is optimal for aerobic, that is, endurance, training. Alternating the gait and distance of the heats within a workout session enhances the conditioning effect.

The horse would be put through as many as three workouts in a single day. Sometimes a workout or set of workouts was repeated over a period of several days. Horses were also given days off, as many as three in a row, and there were slow days where the workouts were short and easy.

In the early stages of the Kikkuli regimen the horse was tethered to a chariot and led through its workout. Eventually the horse graduated to pulling a chariot in harness with another horse.

Over the long haul, the intensity and difficulty of the workouts increased, while remaining basically the same in form. It is important to note, however, that the horse was never exercised to the point of mental or physical exhaustion. At all times the horse was allowed to develop at its own pace. If it needed additional days off or slow days, it got them; and when it returned to the training regimen, it picked up on the day it had left off. This is the reason why the number of days a horse actually spent in training probably exceeded the number of training days (214) stipulated in the text. It is also worth noting in this regard that the Kikkuli text is not complete—only the fragment of a fifth tablet exists—which almost certainly means that the program exceeded 214 days.

Other features of the Kikkuli method included a four-day culling process, during which horses unsuitable for further training would be identified and dismissed. Horses were also taught to swim, and a number of workouts were conducted at night. Meals (when, how much, what to feed the horse) were rigorously prescribed, as were warm-down and cooling periods, and rubdowns.

The Kikkuli regimen constituted merely the first phase of a chariot horse's education. Conditioning the horse was its sole objective. Teaching the horse how to perform on the battlefield, in harness with another horse and acting in concert with other chariots, would be undertaken after completion of the Kikkuli regimen. The horse would then learn to execute the moves characteristic of chariot warfare: fast starts and stops, sudden sharp turns, backing up, and linear advances at varying speeds. It learned to make these moves instantly, without thinking, on the chariot driver's command, which might be expressed vocally or by a distinctive tug of the reins.

The program of daily exercises aimed at building stamina also increased the horse's overall physical strength. The horses had to be strong to pull the Hittite chariot, a robust vehicle. The basis of comparison is the Egyptian chariot, Egypt being Hatti's chief rival in the Near East after the demise of Mitanni as a great power. The Egyptian chariot was a nimble machine, smaller, lighter, and faster than its Hittite counterpart, and more maneuverable due to the placement of the axle at the rear of the vehicle. The bigger, heavier Hittite chariot was less agile and slower; but it was also sturdier, able to carry more weight, and more stable, attributes conferred by placing the axle in the middle of the vehicle.

In time the Hittites figured out that the superior conditioning and strength of Kikkuli-trained horses would allow them to change their system of chariot combat in a way that substantially enhanced the tactical potentialities of their large, stoutly constructed vehicles and, by extension, their use of chariotry. This change entailed placing a third man in the chariot cab and was implemented less than 50 years after Kikkuli entered the employ of Suppiluliuma, during the early years of the reign Suppiluliuma's grandson, Muwattalli II.

The third mounted crewman was previously a "runner," a dismounted man-at-arms common to all Bronze Age chariotry forces. In chariotry clashes runners jogged into battle alongside their vehicle to perform a dual offensive/defensive role, protecting their vehicles from assault by enemy runners and chariots or attacking enemy chariots and their runners, as circumstances warranted. They could also help chariot drivers control panicking horses by seizing reins or cheek straps, an important function given the volatility of the equine temperament.

The three-man chariot opened up new possibilities for the conduct of chariot warfare, hence warfare in general. Men-at-arms riding in chariots did not tire as quickly as runners, and they could go anywhere their chariots went, effectively increasing the operating range of Hittite chariotry. This in turn allowed the Hittites to dispense with the conventions of the set piece or parallel battle, which had been the norm in warfare (and would remain so for the most part of three millennia). Set-piece battles are usually pounding affairs that by their very nature obviate tactical maneuver and surprise: the opposing forces line up opposite (i.e., parallel to) each other and advance to contact in the "battle space," where they slug it out until one or both cannot carry on any longer. But the ability of Hittite chariotry employing three-man vehicles to range beyond the battle space allowed the Hittites to mass greater numbers of chariots for a single engagement and to use large formations to fight a battle of tactical maneuver in which the principles of surprise and concentration of force could be applied.

Muwattalli unveiled his three-man chariots and the strategy and tactics developed for their use against an Egyptian army commanded by Pharaoh Ramesses II at the Battle of Kadesh in 1275 BC. It seems evident that Muwattalli planned the Kadesh campaign and its climactic battle with considerable care, to employ his new machines to their best advantage.

Of the two armies, Muwattalli's was the smaller, numbering about 15,000 combat troops of all types to Ramesses's 20,000. But Muwattalli had more chariots, perhaps as many as 3,000 machines (estimates vary), against 2,000 Egyptian. And most if not all of the Hittite chariots carried three men and were pulled by superbly conditioned horses trained in the Kikkuli method. In a set-piece battle where limited numbers of chariots clashed in the confines of a rectangular battle space, fighting what was essentially a battle of attrition, the larger Egyptian army would enjoy a distinct advantage. Muwattalli's goal, therefore, was to fight what would quite literally be a free-wheeling battle of tactical maneuver using massive chariotry formations. To that end he selected Kadesh as the venue of battle, because the terrain around the city was suitable for chariotry operations across a broad area.

Probably Ramesses expected to meet the Hittite army at Kadesh. Muwattalli accordingly undertook to convince his enemies he would be far away when the Egyptians arrived at the city. This he accomplished through the use of double agents, two Shosu (Bedouin) tribesmen who told the pharaoh on what proved to be the morning of the battle that the Hittite army could be found in the vicinity of Khaleb (Aleppo), some 125 miles north of the Kadesh. It was a lie: in fact the Hittite army had already moved down from Khaleb, massing just northeast of Kadesh. But Ramesses believed them.

Muwattalli had stolen a march on the Egyptians, a deftly executed piece of operational footwork, masked by deception, constructing a trap baited with Kadesh itself. Like all traps this one now depended on the actions of the intended prey to complete its work. It could be said that Muwattalli was gambling on Ramesses to do the wrong thing, but this would be to underestimate Muwattalli's acumen as a judge of character. For his plan to succeed, Ramesses had to be both gullible and rash. And Ramesses—as Muwattalli must have known—did not disappoint.

The pharaoh's army was at this juncture positioned to the southwest of Kadesh, well within a day's march of the city. It was organized into four combined-arms battle groups, each comprising about 5,000 men organized into an infantry brigade of 3,500 troops (mostly the heavy infantry of the phalanx, but also light skirmishers and archers) and a chariotry grouping of 500 machines with three-man crews (warrior, driver, and dismounted runner/man-at-arms) for a total of 1,500 effectives. In the van of the Egyptian host marched the Amun battle group with Ramesses in command, his royal person protected by a contingent of Sherden (or Shardana) swordsmen, the Pharaoh's elite bodyguard. Following Amun were, respectively, the Ra, Ptah, and Seth battle groups, each separated from the other by a distance of about two miles.

This configuration played right into Muwattalli's hands, insofar as it would allow the Hittites to engage the Egyptian battle groups in detail—a necessary precondition for fighting a maneuver battle with chariotry against a numerically superior foe. Here again Ramesses acted in complete if unwitting accord with Muwattalli's designs. Convinced by the Shosu that Kadesh was his for the taking, Ramesses ordered the Amun battle group to move on the double to the city.

The other battle groups would follow at their normal, and considerably slower, marching pace.

Ramesses and the Amun division forded the Orontes River near the village of Shabtuna and hastened north across the Kadesh plain, crossing a shallow canal linking the Orontes with what is now the village of El-Mukadiya and pitching camp just northwest of the city. Evidently the entire Hittite army, infantry and chariotry, was then concentrated on the other side (northeast) of the city, which concealed the Hittites' presence from the Egyptians. Fortunately for Ramesses the Hittites, thus situated, were not in position to attack the Amun division as it marched up from the Orontes. Had the Hittites struck Amun on the plain it is quite likely they would have destroyed the Egyptian battle group killed or captured the pharaoh, ending the battle—and the war—then and there. Perhaps in this instance the pharaoh's rashness had actually saved him. Spurred to action by the Shosu's report, Ramesses had moved faster and arrived at Kadesh sooner than Muwattalli expect, before he could array his forces. Which is to say: Ramesses had, however unwittingly, stolen a march on the Hittites.

Muwattalli adjusted his plan accordingly, moving his chariotry into attack positions south of the city, but keeping his infantry in position northeast of the city as a counter to the Amun battle group. Meanwhile the Amun troops, still oblivious to the presence and proximity of the Hittite army, were busy setting up camp—a task that notably entailed, among other endeavors, erecting a palisade of shields, implanted in the ground, around the camp's perimeter.

Around this time the Egyptians captured two Hittite soldiers lurking near the camp, a surprising development in light of what the Shosu had told Ramesses. Brought before the pharaoh and beaten severely, the Hittite soldiers revealed their army's true location. Ramesses, properly alarmed, knowing that a battle was imminent, immediately dispatched messengers to his other battle groups, informing their commanders of the situation and ordering them to get to Kadesh with all due speed. No doubt he also ordered the Amun troops to prepare for battle, fully expecting that the Hittites would try to overrun his camp before the arrival of Egyptian reinforcements.

But Muwattalli wisely elected to forego attacking the camp, at least for the time being. Why bother? The pharaoh and his troops weren't going anywhere. Muwattalli could dispose of them at his leisure. First he would deal with Amun's would-be rescuers.

Here again the Egyptians played into his hands. The Ra battle group had crossed the Orontes and was marching north in column of route across the Kadesh plain when Muwattalli unleashed his chariotry. Comprising some 2,000 machines, the Hittite chariotry grouping had previously forded a shallow stretch of the Orontes just south of Kadesh and had massed in a lightly wooded grove or orchard on the river's west bank, awaiting the signal to attack. The signal given, this enormous force emerged from the trees and advanced across the Kadesh plain, striking the Egyptian battle group in the flank before it could redeploy to meet the attack. The battle group quickly disintegrated, its troops scattering to escape the rampaging Hittite chariots.

Many of the Ra troops fled north toward the putative safety of the Amun camp, hotly pursued by the Hittite chariotry. Within minutes the Hittite forces had encircled the camp and were attacking it from every direction. Muwattalli probably did not sanction this action. Attacking a fortified position with chariotry unsupported by infantry was a highly problematic enterprise, the more so because the Egyptian battle group with 5,000 troops enjoyed a slight numerical advantage over the Hittite force (6,000 troops total but, excluding the chariot drivers, only 4,000 combatants). It is likely that Muwattalli meant for this chariotry to halt by the river to block the advance of the follow-on Egyptian battle groups, Ptah and Set; in the meantime he would attack and destroy the Amun camp with a combined-arms formation comprising his infantry mass and his reserve chariotry, which numbered about 1,000 machines.

But the Hittite chariotry troops, evidently intoxicated by their success in smashing Ra, could not be restrained. Their blood was up and burning hot: the bit was in their teeth and they were going to run with it. And run with it they most certainly did, driving hard to the Amun camp, their martial ardor fired by the prospect of killing the pharaoh and winning the battle outright. Not incidentally, in doing so they would also win glory for themselves and all the spoils of war to be gotten by looting the camp: a powerful incentive to keep moving, keep attacking.

Many of the Egyptian chariot warriors in the camp, terrified by the Hittite onslaught, infected with the contagion of panic spread by the fleeing troops of the Ra battle group, leapt aboard their machines and bolted from the camp. No doubt many Egyptian foot soldiers also took flight. Undaunted, Ramesses rallied his remaining troops, notably his bodyguard of Sherden swordsman, and, mounting his own chariot, led them in repeated counterattacks against the enemy host. A few Hittite chariots broke through the shield wall that the Egyptians had erected around the camp, but instead of pressing their advantage the crews paused for some impromptu battlefield looting and were all killed. Meanwhile Ramesses and his troops managed to hold the rest of the Hittite chariots at bay.

Realizing that he had lost control of his strike force, if not of the battle itself, Muwattalli committed his chariotry reserve to the fighting at the camp. The circumstances demanded that he do so: he had to eliminate the Amun battle group before the Set and Ptah battle groups arrived on the scene. The circumstances further demanded that he withhold his infantry from the fighting, keeping them in reserve but ready for immediate use against the reinforcing battle groups.

Perhaps, too, the Hittite king withheld his infantry because he had received reports that yet another Egyptian battle group, a combined-arms force of chariotry and infantry comprising troops called "Nearin" (or "N'rn," a Semitic loanword for "trained soldier"), which had previously landed on the Amurru coast at or near the mouth of the Eleuthros River, was approaching from the northwest through the river valley. It seems likely, however, that he had no prior knowledge of the battle group's existence: the prebattle disposition of his forces, which makes no allowance for the appearance of an enemy force on his right (north) flank, would seem to indicate that this was the case. Very tellingly in this regard, he had not positioned troops in the valley to block an Egyptian thrust from that direction. Conversely, one may argue that he knew about the Nearin but was hoping to destroy the Egyptian main force the battle group arrived, and that he had not placed troops in the valley because to do so would have revealed the presence of his army and thus spoiled the element of surprise upon which his victory over the main force depended.

But such speculation is all beside the point. The fact is, when the Nearin battle group arrived at Kadesh, Muwattalli was either unprepared or unable to prevent them from entering the fray. What's more, the Nearin had come to fight—they must have received news that a battle was either in the offing or in progress as they neared the city, and had prepared themselves accordingly. The attack of the Nearin, coinciding as it did with a counterattack by Ramesses and his Amun troops, drove the Hittite chariots back across the Orontes, effectively ending the battle.

This occurred late in the day, and neither the Egyptians nor the Hittites had the wherewithal, much less the will, to continue fighting. Both armies had suffered substantial losses and the survivors, men and horses alike, were exhausted. The arrival of the Set and Ptah battle groups obviated any further attempts by Muwattalli to reengage; by the same token the Egyptians, mindful of the presence of the Hittite infantry corps just north and east of the city, did not dare in their depleted state to exploit across the Orontes.

The Nearin had saved the day for Ramesses, and probably saved his life as well. But it had been a near-run thing. Because the Egyptians were still in possession of the battlefield when the fighting ended, Ramesses could and would declare victory. But it was a specious claim. A few days later his badly mauled army withdrew to the south, toward Egypt, with the Hittite army—also greatly reduced—following it, a slow and cautious pursuit. Subsequently the strategic objective of the Hittites, the kingdom of Amurru (located south of Kadesh), passed into their control: a clear victory for Muwattalli. The Egyptians may have won the battle (barely); but the Hittites had won the war.

The use of three-man chariots played a key role in gaining that victory. One would note that the distance from the grove where the Hittite chariotry emerged onto the Kadesh plain to the Ra battle group was a little over 400 yards; and from there to the Amun camp, about 650 yards. Thus, the Hittite chariotry drove over 1,050 yards from the grove to the camp and fought two battles in doing so—and this is to say nothing of the distances driven in the course of each battle, that is, during the melees with the enemy and the movement by the Hittite chariotry to encircle the Amun camp. One would further note that chariotry melees were probably quite similar in form to those of a polo match; and that in polo matches the exertions of the horses were such that they had be switched out about every eight minutes.

The Hittite horses, of course, were not switched out: those that went into battle fought and finished the battle without replacement. Certainly, the Hittite chariot crews must have rested their horses (and themselves!) periodically if briefly during the battle at the camp: after all the Battle of Kadesh in all its phases lasted several hours, and no horse or man is capable of sustained effort for that length of time without taking frequent breaks for rest and refreshment. But the point still stands: namely, that the Hittite horses were capable of movement over a considerable distance and of fighting prolonged battles of the utmost ferocity. One may also make the point that their recuperative powers were greater and faster than those of their Egyptian counterparts—recuperation from exertion being a hallmark of the Kikkuli method. Thus one may fairly conclude that Kikkuli, who instituted the training program for horses that made three-man chariots viable, was in no small way responsible for the Hittites' triumph.

Legacy: About a century after Kikkuli authored his training manual the first of four so-called Hippiatric texts were produced in Ugarit, a powerful Bronze Age city-state located on the coast of northern Syria. Addressed to professional trainers, these texts were concerned with diagnosing and curing sick horses, chiefly by dietary means.

Ten centuries after Kikkuli, the Athenian historian Xenophon wrote *On the Art of Equestrianism*. Written in lively and accessible prose, Xenophon's book is concerned solely with ridden horses, not horses in harness, and is addressed to civilians and amateurs as well as professional soldiers and cavalrymen.

Kikkuli's legacy lives on through the work of Australian horse breeder and endurance competitor Ann Nyland. In 1991, Nyland conducted what became known as the "Kikkuli experiment," using the Kikkuli text as her guide for training 10 Arabians—the breed that most closely resembles the Bronze Age chariot horses. During Kikkuli's seven-month training period, Nyland adhered scrupulously to his complex daily regimen of interval training, rest and feeding breaks, and other activities and exercises stipulated in the text. The ancient diet was replicated and the horses received the same pre- and post-workout care Kikkuli gave to his horses.

The results, confirmed by physical examinations and tests administered before and after the training period, showed substantial increases in fitness and performance. Significantly, these had been achieved without the use of drugs and food additives, and with no injury to the horses. Nyland also found that rates as well as levels of improvement were directly related to the horse's psychological state, which Kikkuli nurtured by allowing each horse to develop at its own pace, without approaching much less pushing beyond the animal's physical and mental tolerances.

Having realized that Kikkuli recognized the mind/body link in a horse's development and had crafted his training regimen accordingly, Nyland concluded that the Kikkuli method was superior to modern training programs and that trainers would be well advised to adopt it. She wrote about the benefits and modern applications of the Kikkuli method in a 1993 book chronicling her experiment. She has since digitized the book, with minor revisions to the text but not to her views, making it available on the Internet for downloading.

See also: Subotai, Baator (Sübedei Baatar)

Further Reading
Beal, Richard H., *The Organization of the Hittite Military.* Heidelberg: Carl Winter, 1992.
Gabriel, Richard A., and Karen S. Metz, *From Sumer to Rome: The Military Capabilities of Ancient Armies.* Westport, CT: Greenwood Press, 1991.
Nyland, Ann, *The Kikkuli Method of Horse Training.* Australia: Kikkuli Research Publications, 1993. Revised (2006) edition available online at http://www.kikkulimethod.com/.

Steven Weingartner

Maurice (Flavius Mauricius Tiberius Augustus)
(ca. 539–602 CE)

Significance: Emperor Maurice's military treatise depicts late Roman military organization and practice ca. 600 CE and has been called the most sophisticated combined-arms theory written before World War I.

Context: Maurice ruled the Roman (or Byzantine) Empire from 582 to 602, a period of constant struggle against "barbarian" invaders in the west and the Persians in the east.

Biography: Maurice was born in Cappadocia ca. 539 and became a successful general under the Emperor Tiberius II Constantinus, whose daughter he married. He became emperor in 582 on the death of his father-in-law. Although an excellent ruler, he was unable to prevent the further disintegration of the empire. The last outpost in Spain, Cordoba, was lost in 582, and Maurice failed to expel the Lombards from Italy. He temporarily checked, but did not halt, the incursions of the Slavs and Avars in the Balkans. In the east, he reinstated the legitimate Persian king, Chosroes II, in 591, and regained Armenia and eastern Mesopotamia. In 602, the armies, ordered to winter north of the Danube, revolted and Maurice was overthrown and executed along with his five sons by the usurper Phocas. His wife, Constantina, and three daughters were also later executed.

Influences: The tumultuous events of his own day influenced Maurice's military thought, but he knew the work of many Classical Greek and Roman military writers, such as Aeneas the Tactician, Arrian, Frontinus, and Vegetius.

The Theory: Maurice is the supposed author of the military handbook entitled *Strategikon,* although the work has been attributed to others, including his brother-in-law, Philippicus (d. 615). Written ca. 592–610 by an author with broad experience in the field, the treatise is divided into 12 books and covers military recruitment, organization, tactics, strategy, law, and logistics. In Book XII he prescribes methods for the close coordination of infantry and cavalry, or what we today call combined-arms warfare. The author also argues for the replacement of mercenary armies by a peasant militia, an idea promoted by Vegetius in the 4th century and Machiavelli in the 16th. Book XI provides an interesting characterization of the foes faced by the empire and their tactics.

Application: Maurice's prescriptions for the organization of military forces, their use in defensive and offensive operations, and their discipline and logistical support were the basis for reform of the Roman armies by Maurice and are reflected by his successors, such as the Emperors Heraclius (610–641 CE) and Leo VI (886–912 CE).

Descendents: The military system prescribed by Maurice lasted more than 300 years, the Byzantine armies described by the Emperor Leo VI in the 10th century being very similar to those described in the *Strategikon*.

See also: Machiavelli; Vegetius

Further Reading

Maurice's Strategikon: Handbook of Byzantine Military Strategy. Translated by George T. Dennis. Philadelphia: University of Pennsylvania Press, 1984.

Whitby, Michael, *The Emperor Maurice and his Historian Theophylact Simocatta on Persian and Balkan Warfare.* Oxford: The Clarendon Press, 1988.

Charles R. Shrader

Musashi, Miyamoto
(ca. 1584–1645 CE)

Significance: One of the greatest swordsmen in Japanese history, Musashi's text on fighting, *Go Rin No Sho* (*The Book of Five Rings*), is considered a fundamental Japanese work on strategy. Its relevance extends from personal combat to the large-scale organization of men into effective working units.

Context: Musashi witnessed and participated in the consolidation of a unified Japan under the rule of the Tokugawa Shogunate (1600–1853), although he fought on the losing side in several engagements. His experiences encompassed the gamut of samurai experience in a time of profound struggle and societal change.

Biography: Shinmen Musashi no Kami Fujiwara no Genshin (ca. 1584–1645), usually called Miyamoto Musashi, but known by a variety of other names during his lifetime, was the son of a renowned swordsmen and master of the *jitte,* Shinmen Munisai. Musashi's early history is uncertain, with many of the details of his childhood under debate. He was born a samurai, trained in martial arts, and educated—though to what degree is unknown. He won his first duel at the age of 13 against Arima Kihei, and went on to win some 60 odd duels over the course of his life. By his own count, he participated in a half-dozen battles, though never as the commander of any large unit. Musashi often used a wooden sword or staff in his duels, and also developed a sword style that used a short sword in one hand and a long sword in the other. He was also an accomplished painter. Musashi died peacefully of an illness in 1645.

Influences: Although he repeatedly claimed that he had no teachers, and rejected the practice of quoting from other texts in his writing, it is clear both that he had been trained in the martial arts and that he had some measure of education. His intellectual and spiritual positions reflect direct engagement with aspects of Zen Buddhism and a variety of Chinese texts, including Sun Tzu's *Art of War.* It would therefore be more accurate to say that although he had many teachers who profoundly influenced him, his ultimate outlook and practice was uniquely personal. Musashi was almost entirely unconventional in everything he did, particularly combat.

The Theory: Musashi composed his most famous work, *The Book of Five Rings,* at the end of his life. It summarized his ideas on life in general and combat in particular. It was closely followed by a much shorter work, *The Way of Walking Alone* (*Dokkodo*). He had also made earlier attempts to write down his overall ideas.

The basic conundrum of *The Book of Five Rings* is how to codify an unconventional approach. Musashi himself had spent his entire adult life physically and intellectually exploring his environment in a quest for personal enlightenment. That this was carried out, in part, through the medium of combat was in no way surprising for a man of his time and place. Combat is a very direct experience of the world, and success in it requires a great many skills and personal capabilities. As someone who had been undefeated in personal combat, Musashi proceeded from the reasonable assumption that he had somehow mastered something, without being sure what that was. Indeed, he tries to downplay his combat abilities at one point to argue that he really knows nothing, and that his victories did not indicate any profound insight. This was not just humility, however; it was an attempt to escape the problem of articulating the manner of reaching and understanding a profound spiritual state of being. The result was a terse and often obtuse text that makes constant reference to physical practice and thinking beyond that which he has set down. Musashi struggles in *The Book of Five Rings* to convince the reader to explore and consider things for himself, rather than stopping intellectually with what Musashi says.

Part of the difficulty for the modern reader in interpreting Musashi's work lies in initially evaluating its worth. *The Book of Five Rings* has not been universally accepted as a work of great value, and some Japanese scholars have even expressed doubts as to his capability as a swordsman. Many of the things he said had been said before, or were so commonplace as to be banal. Musashi was not a great thinker by any standard. Conversely, his work was directed at his own students, and was principally concerned with physical and spiritual development rather than intellectual analysis.

Musashi's comments on strategy as a whole are suspect, because they are based purely on his own, extremely limited, experience. Indeed, it is precisely his avowed skill in single combat that so distinguished him, rather than his understanding of battles between armies. However, even though his specific discussions of combat are obviously not pertinent to large unit actions, his general approach to conflict is still worthwhile. In particular, his focus on unconventional thinking, and the importance of psychology in fighting, is relevant to any student of warfare.

The key concept unifying Musashi's work is that of not allowing conventional thinking to interfere with the pursuit of victory. Any struggle involves the goal of defeating one's opponent, regardless of whether that opponent is an individual, a group, or an army. One should use every resource available to achieve that end. For example, he advocates using two swords in combat, for why would one not use both of the swords one was carrying (samurai typically carried both a long and short sword) in a life and death struggle? A fixed notion of how to fight can be fatal under the extreme conditions of combat.

However, Musashi also recognized the difficulties involved in his unconventional fighting technique—a *caveat* also applicable to maneuvering armies. Someone unused to wielding a sword in each hand would find it extremely difficult to do so effectively. It was therefore not possible to switch spontaneously to using two swords from the common practice of using the long sword with both hands. The ability to use two swords in combat developed through extensive practice; however, persistence through the initial period of struggle would pay off handsomely. Another warning also rears its head, and is again applicable to individuals as well as armies: practicing a technique so thoroughly that it becomes comfortable, also makes it conventional. Training is necessary to develop skills, but training by its very nature builds in a rigid system of actions and thought.

Musashi attempted to address the problem of training becoming a trap. After explaining how training could make a certain practice easy—in this case using a sword in each hand—he then advises the reader to use a two-handed stroke if that is necessary to kill an opponent. That is, he stresses that training to develop one skill should not foreclose the possibility of using another if the situation warrants it. He digresses to state that a two-handed stroke would probably not be necessary if one had fully developed the ability to use a sword in each hand, which not only illuminates the limitations of Musashi as a writer, but also the problem of *training to be unconventional*. Musashi has great difficulty in describing a program of training that results in a skilled, but flexible, fighter, capable of seizing any opportunity to achieve victory. His response is to describe and advocate specific techniques, while simultaneously pointing out that they are not always appropriate. This vacillation places a tremendous burden upon the practitioner somehow to do what is best in a given situation without real guidance from the master. Perhaps Musashi had difficulty communicating techniques that he intuitively invented during combat.

Musashi faces another conundrum: he somehow managed to do what was correct in combat, but he does not want his students to copy him exactly. He is forced to suggest practice that is not prescriptive in its response, although still functional. For example, he argues for taking the "middle position," a place or stance from which one can move in any direction, as circumstances require. This has broad application on every level of conflict. Musashi is clear, that the middle position is simply the starting point that leaves open the largest number of options, and that one will need to move in one direction or another. Indeed, as he points out in his discussion of fighting multiple opponents, one must attack, rather than receive an attack, to survive. The middle position is therefore a place from which one maintains the initiative. This is critical in combat, with respect to both oneself and one's opponent.

Psychology lies at the heart of Musashi's approach, and underlies most of his more specific suggestions on technique. Musashi repeatedly insists on self-discipline. He is at pains to confuse the enemy while remaining clear himself. This gives him the initiative in combat, allowing him to dictate the initial psychological state of the encounter. Musashi undermined the composure of his opponents on several occasions by arriving late to a scheduled duel. A number of scholars have denigrated Musashi's skills as a swordsman, attributing his success to such underhanded practices. Yet Musashi would have pointed out that the goal was to win the duel, not to somehow establish a "fair" contest between swordsmen. If his opponents were unable to cope with the psychological disruption caused by his tardiness, then surely that was also part of the contest of skills.

Musashi therefore does not recognize any moral or ethical restraints—the pursuit of winning should take precedence over any other consideration. By itself, this highly disruptive approach may well have accounted for a great part of his success in battle, but it formed part of his unconventional strategy. For example, he also often used a wooden sword in his duels. This was certainly unexpected, but it also had advantages. A wooden sword was lighter than a steel sword, and therefore faster to wield. Musashi could also use a longer weapon without slowing his stroke. He gained in reach and speed, without sacrificing lethal effect, because duels were not fought in armor. Musashi never attempted to contend with his opponent on an equal footing, seeing instead that the end justified the means. Form was far less important than function.

The psychological focus was therefore profound: Musashi directed his efforts at the mind of his opponent. This is consistent with Sunzi, though, given Musashi's decision not to quote from other texts in *The Book of Five Rings,* we cannot know if he arrived at this independently or through study. He argued that defeating an opponent in any situation requires the disruption of his plans, which ultimately leads back to the opponent's mind itself. Conventional thinking is a vulnerability to be exploited, and an unconventional action is a direct attack on the conventional conceptions of the opponent. This confuses the opponent under circumstances in which mental acuity is of life and death importance. Musashi creates a momentary mental fog within his opponent that provides him with a decisive combat advantage.

Seeing conventionality as vulnerability makes it clear why Musashi is so concerned that his students remain unconventional. Just as adoption of the middle position was a way to obtain and retain the initiative, an unconventional mind is necessary to exploit that initiative and avoid being mentally stunned by an unexpected action. Psychology cuts both ways, and one must retain mental flexibility for both attack and defense. Only a flexible mind is able to exploit an opportunity for victory, unconstrained by a preconceived notion of what an advantage looked like or how one could go about achieving victory. Conversely, a flexible mind would react correctly and unexpectedly to an unexpected attack. A flexible mental state can therefore transform an apparent disadvantage into an advantage. Musashi saw that this transformation took place not merely in the physical realm, but in the mental realm. It is within the combatant himself to change the circumstances of the battle.

The mentality of the combatant, be he a general or an individual warrior, is crucial to success. It is natural, on any level, for the mind to stop when confronted by something unexpected, or to become fixed upon a certain path. An open mind is always beneficial in a hostile situation. The nature of combat is unexpected change; the successful warrior or general is the one who is able to react correctly to that change. The path to that victory cannot be predetermined. Even surprise is not a guarantee of advantage if the opponent responds effectively. The ambushing force might itself fall into confusion if its expected advantage fails. Mental flexibility is vital, but it is one of the hardest capabilities to develop.

Not everyone, of course, can develop such mental flexibility. Most people possess limited capabilities, both in terms of skills and mentality. A commander cannot impose a system on a group that will erase their particular, individual, qualities. The wise commander must understand his subordinates and assign them to tasks appropriate to their respective natures. The example Musashi uses is the master carpenter, who is careful to assign men to tasks that suit their abilities. He assumes here that any leader will have to work with the men he has, rather than be able to choose only men of certain characteristics. This application of the correct man for the correct job extends to his discussion of weapons. One should use the appropriate weapon for the circumstance. Although this discussion seems astonishingly banal, it speaks of the sort of conventional thinking that he sought to overcome. For example, Musashi thought it necessary to argue that one should use a short sword in confined spaces, because warriors could become so fixated on using only their long swords.

Musashi's overall programme centers on exploiting, or compensating for, psychological rigidity. One must strive not to be rigid, while recognizing that everyone else is rigid. Most people can only be used effectively in specific circumstances, and it is the responsibility of the leader to correctly evaluate his subordinates and assign them appropriate tasks. Different tools and different men are appropriate for different tasks. Unfortunately, he does not provide any means to assess one's subordinates, beyond his general admonition to develop one's ability to perceive the truth in all matters.

The source of most of Musashi's knowledge of the world is his own observations and analysis. He repeatedly urges his reader to extrapolate from an individual case to the general, and thus gain broad knowledge without being specifically taught. Keeping in mind the tendentiousness of his own claim to be self-taught, this is not only a claim that one can learn for oneself, but also that the entire world is comprehensible if one is prepared to think things through.

Part of Musashi's insistence on extrapolation in the text is his desire to convince his students to be independent minded, and to go beyond his own pronouncements. If a student is unwilling to think for himself, or to take Musashi's training and text as a mere starting point, then he will become conventional. His mind will have stopped.

To stimulate the reader's thinking, Musashi is often terse to the point of obscurity. This forces the student to try to break through to personal understanding. Such effort only a valuable exercise if one believes that there is something worthwhile to be understood, and Musashi's own reputation is what convinces the reader to struggle with the text. However, the quandary remains—how can one adhere to *The Book of Five Rings* mantra of unconventionality, if one is simultaneously participating in a highly conventional exercise of replicating a master's published system?

In conclusion, it is striking that Musashi was adamantly against convention. As a man functioning in a highly conventional society, who wrote a text to transmit his own path to success in battle, it would seem he was faced with an impossible task. He tried to convey a nonmethod as a method of approaching combat. Even a talented writer and thinker would have been severely challenged by such a task, and Musashi was neither. He was a supremely successful duelist by virtue of his natural talents and unconventional approach to fighting. His life, combat methods, and teachings were, in their consistent opposition to convention, extremely un-Japanese. His emphasis on winning without regard for convention, being open-minded, and the psychological aspects of conflict are valuable lessons to keep in mind.

Because Musashi, unlike military thinkers writing for generals and statesmen, proceeded from personal combat to generalizations about all conflict, his approach centered on personal development, or even enlightenment. He has nothing to say about the purpose of war, how it fits into a larger context, or even how an army should be used. Perhaps uniquely among writers who discuss conflict at an abstract level, he speaks to the warrior and describes how the way of the warrior ramifies in larger battles. The challenge of Musashi, however, is how to understand him, how to achieve the state of mind he advocates, and whether that will, indeed, be useful beyond individual combat.

See also: War and Military Philosophy in Traditional Japan

Peter Lorge

Nelson, Vice Admiral Horatio
(1758–1805)

Significance: Nelson's leadership was critical to the maritime defense of Britain from Napoleonic forces.

Context: Nelson's success at Cape Trafalgar (October 21, 1805) against the French and Spanish fleets was critical to the defense of Britain from invasion by Napoleon.

Biography: Nelson went to sea at age 12 and attained command by 20. As Britain became involved with the French Revolutionary Wars, he participated in the capture of Corsica and the Battle of Calvi, where he lost his right eye. This was followed by the loss of his right arm at Santa Cruz de Tenerife (1797), the same year he defeated the Spanish at Cape Vincent. One year later, he engaged Napoleon's fleet at the Battle of the Nile, quashing French hopes for direct trade with India. Promoted as vice admiral in 1801, he won the Battle of Copenhagen after ignoring a signal to cease fighting, which he blamed on his missing eye. In his best known and final engagement at Cape Trafalgar, Nelson was felled by a French sniper.

Influences: Captain Maurice Suckling (maternal uncle, eventually comptroller of the navy) took Nelson to sea under his tutelage after the death of the boy's mother.

The Theory: Devoted to duty, Nelson eschewed strict adherence to orders and doctrine when extemporaneous shifts yielded opportunities to seize the advantage.

Application: British naval tactics.

Descendents: Mahan.

Further Reading
Coleman, Terry, *The Nelson Touch: The Life and Legend of Horatio Nelson.* New York: Oxford University Press, 2004.

Joe Caddell

Paré, Ambroise
(1510–1590)

Significance: Serving as a French military surgeon during the 16th-century Italian wars, Ambroise Paré was one of the most innovative military medical practitioners of the Early Modern world. One of the few surgeons in the period to write down his procedures, Paré penned a number of treatises devoted to medicine, principally in the fields of surgery, obstetrics, forensics, prosthetics, and psychology, with many of these correcting or improving previous, often lethal, practices.

Context: Living at a time when gunpowder weapons had improved and proliferated to such an extent that wounds by them began to outnumber those caused by sharp-edged weapons and archery, Paré's willingness to try new surgeries invariably proved sounder than previously practices.

Biography: Nothing is known about Paré's life before his military surgical service in the French army during the Italian Wars. He does not tell us what training he received, nor is there enough known about what education or practical training military surgeons had at the time to make generalizations. It might be concluded, however, from Paré's experiences at Turin in 1536, that some flexibility was allowed to individual surgeons in treating wounded soldiers.

Although it was battlefield surgery that brought Paré prominence, he later went on to write more works on other medical fields, which brought not only fame but also wealth. Despite being a Protestant, which put him at odds with the majority of French during the Wars of Religion, and that he could not keep King Henry II from succumbing to his tournament injury in 1559, Paré remained in royal surgical service until his death, at 80, in 1590.

The Theory: It is for his military surgical innovations that Paré is particularly known. Living at a time when gunpowder weapons had improved and proliferated to such an extent that wounds by them began to outnumber those caused by sharp-edged weapons and archery, Paré's willingness to try new surgeries invariably proved sounder than previously practices. His initial, and perhaps most famous, innovation came from necessity when he was serving in the French army at the siege of Turin in 1536. So numerous and severe were the wounds he was treating that he ran out of the oil that would be poured boiling hot into gunshot wounds to cauterize them. This had been a practice made famous in Giovanni da Vigo's *Practica in arte chirugica copiosa* (*The Extensive Practice of Surgical Arts*), one of the earliest and most popular printed surgical manuals of the time. Because of the quick onset of infection in wounds uncared for, military surgeons operating in warmer climate used cauterization to close the wound rather than suturing, a practice preferred by northern European military surgeons. It was also believed that these wounds had been poisoned by gunpowder, creating another need for cauterization. Paré was forced to cleanse and apply an ointment made of egg whites, rose oil, and turpentine to the wounds of those he was unable to treat with oil, only to discover the next day that a much greater number of those had survived the surgery and were recovering than those who had their wounds cauterized. He quickly changed his practice, with the result that his patients lived in far greater numbers than those of surgeons who continued using traditional procedures.

Application: Writing of this success first in a short work on gunshot wounds in 1545, Paré publicized his new treatments in the enlarged *La maniere de traicter les playes faictes par hacqeubutes, que par fleches: & les accidentz d'icelles, côme fractures & caries des os, gangrene & mortification: avec les traictz des instrumentz necessaires pour leur curation. Et la methode de curer les combustions principalement faictes par la pouldre a canon* (*The Treatment of Wounds Made by Arquebuses, and by Arrows, and their Effects, such as Fractures and Decay of Bones, Gangrene and Decay, with the Surgical Instruments Needed for their Care. And How to Care for Burns Principally Made by Gunpowder*), which appeared in 1552. One of the other innovations introduced in the treatise was the cauterization of any exposed and pierced arteries while repairing wounds.

Descendents: Initially, Paré's innovations made only slight differences in military medical proceedings, but eventually their wisdom was recognized and older traditions discarded.

Further Reading

Carbonnier, Jeanne, *A Barber-Surgeon: A Life of Ambroise Paré, Founder of Modern Surgery.* New York: Pantheon Books, 1965.

Malgaigne, J. F., *Surgery and Ambroise Paré.* Trans. Wallace B. Hamby. Norman: University of Oklahoma Press, 1965.

Paré, Ambroise, *The Apologie and Treatise.* Ed. and trans. Geoffrey Keynes. Chicago: University of Chicago Press, 1952.

Paré, Ambroise, *Ten Books of Surgery with the Magazine of the Instruments Necessary for It.* Ed. and trans. Robert White Linker and Nathan Womack. Athens: University of Georgia Press, 1969.

Kelly DeVries

Philip II
(382–336 BC)

Significance: Philip II was responsible for building a genuine Macedonian state that would later become the basis for the empire of Alexander the Great. In many respects, he laid the foundations upon which his son would conquer much of the world. In terms of military theory, Philip developed a novel approach to warfare, featuring powerful defensive spear formations and innovative offensive cavalry that proved unstoppable against barbarian and Greek enemies.

Context: The kingdom of Macedonia in 359 BC was more of a geographical expression than an actual state. The Argead dynasty, which had ruled the kingdom for the previous three and a half centuries, practiced neither primogeniture nor monogamy. The crown was elective within the family with election frequently being a cross between acclamation by the army and trial by ordeal. The dynastic history is a long chain of plots, assassinations, and civil wars. Macedonia's neighbors took advantage of this factionalism and instability to mount invasions and annex border regions.

The old Macedonian army consisted of aristocratic medium cavalry. They lacked the missile weapons of true light cavalry and the armor of heavy cavalry. They also lacked both stirrups and saddles. The horseman equipped and trained himself and fought as an individual warrior rather than in organized formations. The infantry were peasants with even less training, called up with whatever household weapons or tools they possessed. Put together they combined the worst features of a barbarian tribal host and the forces of a settled civilized society but were a good representative of Macedonia's state of development, a semicivilized collection of semimigratory upland herding clans and their lowland kin recently settled in agricultural villages.

In terms of the Greek world, Macedonia was a classic marcher state. It was on the fringes, barely accepted as being Greek. The Greeks and Persians both tended to not regard Macedonia as a state or a region. However, from a Macedonian standpoint, it was surrounded by enemies not just on the fringe of the Greco-Persian world; the Illyrians, Thracians, Sarmatians and other peoples of the Balkans were if anything greater threats to Macedonia than the Greeks were when Philip took the throne after his predecessor had been killed along with most of his army failing to turn back an Illyrian invasion. Overall, Philip spent nearly as many campaign months fighting his supposedly barbarian neighbors as fighting the Greeks.

Biography: Philip was born in 382 BC, the youngest son of King Amyntas III by one of his two legitimate wives. In his youth (368–365 BC) he was a hostage in Thebes. During this period he was given a Greek education, both cultural and military. He assumed power in 359, nominally as regent for his five-year-old nephew Amyntas IV, and was king in his own right from 357 onward.

Philip II took the throne after his predecessor had left the nation defenseless. The kingdom he inherited was on the verge of dissolution, with armed neighbors occupying nearly half the territory and the kingdom's army destroyed. Through skillful diplomacy he was able to buy time to create a new model army and fight his opponents in succession instead of all at once. This enabled him to take advantage of Macedonia's large manpower base and abundant raw materials, especially gold and silver.

By his death in 336, Philip had created a powerful Macedonian state covering most of the lower reaches of the Balkan Peninsula. In modern terms, this region included the Former Yugoslav Republic of Macedonia, Greek Macedonia, a fair part of northern Greece, most of Albania, and virtually all of modern Bulgaria. A still larger area was allied to him by conquest and diplomacy.

Influences: Philip II was forced to create a new model army essentially from scratch and in the midst of a period of continual war and threat of war. His predecessor had managed to have the prior army destroyed in the midst of a lost war. Our sources for how Philip did so are secondary and mostly backward looking, taking the army that Alexander the Great used to conquer Persia after Philip's assassination and treating its earlier iterations as way stations to a predetermined end. This evolutionary path may be true, but our sources are silent. We can intuit that some of Philip's ideas were extensive developments of Theban military concepts that he acquired during his period as a hostage student. We must presume he thought up the rest himself, although he may have had unnamed helpers that our few sources do not mention.

The Theory: Philip quickly established a new army based on an infantry phalanx of a new type. This 16-man-by-16-man box was Philip's basic unit. In round numbers it was a 250-man company. Four of these would be grouped under an officer for a battalion and four such battalions as a brigade. The main army consisted of such four 1,000-man blocks, when deployed at full strength.

Philip started with a two-handed pike, the sarissa. It was much longer than the Greek hoplite spear, although the exact length is subject to dispute. To this he added a deeper formation with successive rear ranks deploying their pikes over the shoulders of those in front of them. Approached from the front this hedge of pike points was extremely difficult to attack. Each hoplite would be, in effect, fighting multiple men, all thrusting at him from different angles. This square also required less training to maneuver as it could lift its pikes, turn left or right and move in a new direction. In its early iterations it could also make better use of untrained men as the weapon took strength and courage rather than intensive training to wield. By placing the best trained men on the outward-facing sides of the pike square, it also minimized the need for maneuver training, as the men in the interior of the box were largely carried along by just doing what everyone else was doing.

The cavalry was also reconceptualized. Borrowing a simple wedge formation from the Thracians and adding a lance (which was basically just a longer cavalry spear), plus a new model of sword better suited for hacking downward, Philip was able to create a cavalry force that could be used offensively against hoplite infantry. Prior Greek cavalry had been useless against formed hoplites, as a horse will not willingly charge an obstruction such as a line of spears. Macedonian cavalry did not charge in the manner of later knights. They trotted up to the infantry formation and used their height from the saddle and the longer reach of their lance as a thrusting spear to force gaps that they then rode into. This cavalry may be thought of more as mounted spearmen than traditional cavalry. For traditional light cavalry functions, Philip used allied horsemen from his northern and western frontiers.

The essence of Philip's tactics was the defensive strength of the new phalanx and the offensive strength of his new cavalry. As his reign progressed, further specialized units were layered on, until by the final war with Thebes and Athens in 338 BC, the full breadth of unit types employed by Alexander was there. This panoply included mercenary traditional hoplites, elite heavy infantry, javelin-armed light cavalry, light infantry skirmishers, and an engineering corps. Philip used, and over the course of his career perfected, a combined-arms approach to fighting at radical variance with the prior Greek pattern of essentially frontal pushes of near identical hoplite infantry armies.

Application: In more than two decades of near continuous warfare, Philip was defeated in battle twice, had two clearly unsuccessful sieges (others were raised for operational reasons), and suffered one ambush of operational significance, while returning from his Scythian Expedition of 339 BC. This is a record on par with Napoleon and other great captains of history, although not as perfect as that of his son, Alexander. How much of this was Philip's actual generalship and how much was a combination of both the superior military machine he created and his abilities as an operational commander will remain forever unknown.

Winning campaigns is much harder than winning battles, and Philip was even better at this level of warfare. Structurally, what Philip created was in the template of 18th-century Prussia, an army that had a state. The Greeks of his era had a mix of citizen forces, called up for a battle or a campaign but not expected to do continuous service, and mercenary units with no fixed loyalties. The surrounding barbarians had warrior levies built around the household troops of the chief or king. Philip created a field army of 25,000–40,000 professional soldiers. They served year-round for pay, as did the mercenaries, but were recruited from specific districts. This gave them a loyalty to Macedonia and the royal family that mercenaries lacked. Within each of these recruiting districts, the remaining men were trained as militia in similar drill with similar weapons to the standing army. New recruits fit easily into old units, keeping them at strength and reinforcing the loyalties.

Philip also kept a core of professional commanders who had trained under him for use as subunit commanders and as commanders of detached corps. Promotion was both by birth and merit. The higher aristocrats were kept as specialist cavalry fighting alongside the king, both to inhibit their ability to raise revolts and to create personal bonds to Philip as a fellow warrior. Junior officers could be promoted by merit. Philip inherited a page school that he turned into a de facto military academy. The page school served an additional function of turning the hostage sons of conquered neighbors into Macedonian nobles. Philip was the first to create a permanent engineering corps for sieges and a permanent intelligence staff. For a man dismissed until quite late in his reign as a semibarbarian by the other Greek states, Philip had a very Clausewitzian view of war. Campaigns were conducted for medium-term objectives rather than for glory and plunder. Battle was a means rather than an end in itself. Philip was quite content to use diplomacy, personal charisma and bribes where these would serve his aims of expansion.

Philip also systematized and professionalized the logistics of his army. He used pack horses instead of carts, thereby increasing both his operational range and operational possibilities, as horses could use worse roads in bad weather than could loaded carts. This combination worked operationally to provide several advantages. Philip could campaign through the winter, whereas his opponents could not. Philip could use lesser routes that his opponents could not, as when he was able to avoid Theban-held Thermopylae in 339 BC. Overall, Philip like Napoleon was capable of an operational tempo his opponents could not match. Greek warfare was geared to a tempo of citizen militias and mercenaries fighting at a pace that allowed a city to politic internally. Philip could move further and faster than they could and could keep the campaign moving faster than their decision cycles could readily cope with.

Descendents: The basic model of Philip's army was used by Alexander and his successors for several centuries with much success and relatively little change until the Roman legions destroyed the main successor states in the second century BC. Whether Alexander's failures in the Punjab were a function of the limits of this military system, or a more prosaic situation of a tired army very far from its homeland that simply wearied of perpetual campaigning, is another issue that will probably never be settled. The dynasty ended with Alexander, but the Macedonian state survived under his general, Antipater. Despite having seven wives (or possibly eight), Philip's direct line ends shortly after Alexander's death.

Philip's subjugation of Greece via the League of Corinth did not long survive Alexander's death at Babylon in 323 BC. The de facto union with Thessaly did survive making Macedonia so predominant over the remaining Greek states as to make it nearly hegemonic. The Balkan frontiers did fluctuate but this owed more to the Macedonian kings being preoccupied with contests with the other Hellenistic monarchs than with Macedonian ability to extend its power to the lower Danube. The structure of the state and army remained much as Philip created them for a period of two centuries. Whereas the other successor kings tended toward Asiatic- or Persian-style monarchies, Macedonia under the Antipatrid dynasty remained a warrior monarchy in the Indo-European tradition.

Further Reading

The most recent scholarship will be found in Richard A. Gabriel's *Philip II of Macedonia: Greater Than Alexander* (2010) and *Alexander the Great at War* (2011), edited by Ruth Shepard. Theodore Dodge's turn-of-the-century classic *Alexander* (reprinted 2004) will also be useful, as may be Victor Davis Hanson's *Carnage and Culture* (2001).

Scott Palter and Tristan Abbey

Puységur, Jacques-François De Chastenet, Marquis de
(1655–1743)

Significance: Puységur was a senior and experienced staff officer who expressed the official French view of the art of war at the beginning of the 18th century.

Context: Despite signal victories at Denain (1712), and Almanza (1707), the armies of Louis XIV had been repeatedly beaten in open battle by the forces of the Grand Alliance during the War of the Spanish Succession (1701–1715). Reassessment and a new model of conducting military business, based on the science and rationalism of the European Enlightenment, was required.

Biography: At first an officer in the senior French infantry *Régiment du Roi,* Puységur became an expert in campaigning—the science of marching and castrametation (the construction of army camps, a science in itself). He was frequently consulted by Louis XIV in his council of war, and became a successful quartermaster general to the Duke of Luxembourg. During the War of the Spanish Succession (1701–1715) he was one of France's leading commanders, and led the army in Spain in 1705, taking part in the siege of Barcelona in 1706. He was then posted to the Flanders front as an officer on the general staff, to face the Duke of Marlborough. However, at the defeat of Oudenarde (1708), he deferred to the opinions of the Duke of Burgundy, Louis XIV's grandson, rather than heed the advice of the experienced Marshal Vendôme, compounding the confusion in the French ranks. In 1734, he was made a marshal of France and set himself up as the leading military expert in France. No military operation was undertaken without consulting him.

Influences: Puységur's *Art of War* (1749) cites Homer, Xenophon, Thucydides, Arian, Polybius, Caesar, Vegetius, Daniel, Montecúccoli, and Turenne. For Puységur there are no finer writers on the subject of war than Caesar and Turenne.

The Theory: Puységur explicitly tried to emulate what Vauban had done for siege warfare, laying down a series of rules and principles for "the entire theory of war from the smallest part to the largest" in the *Art of War* (1749). In the final years of his life, he produced a collection of his notes on the conduct of war, but unhappy with what he had written he had most copies burnt. His son managed to find an extant version. It was published in 1748, and a second edition in 1749 was translated into Italian and German.

In the foreword, Puységur sets out to contradict the idea that only practice mattered. He wanted to show that "without war, without troops, without an army, without having to leave the house, by study alone, with a little geometry and geography, one can learn all the theory of campaign warfare." He sees the art and science of war as the same thing. The foremost part of the art of war is "to know how to form up in sound battle order, and to cause it to move and act in the most perfect evolutions." There is also a lengthy section on the drill book of 1703: various commands, including how to march past with a battalion and give a salute—all tightly choreographed like a giant ballet.

He goes on to discuss Vegetius's seven orders of battle, dismissing some as impractical, given the development of modern weaponry, and then describes marching and the construction of camps. The second volume describes a fictitious war between the Seine and the Loire: somewhat strange, because there had been no civil war in France since 1649, and the key theatres of war at that time were the frontier with the Low countries, the Rhineland, and northern Italy.

There is then a discussion of the memoirs of Turenne and particularly the second battle of Nördlingen or Allerheim (1645), where he looks at the mistakes made. With the glorious luxury of hindsight he recommends Vegetius's second order or battle, a right oblique attack, which he considers would have dislodged Mercy's entrenched imperial Bavarian army. He goes on to draw rather spurious comparisons between this battle and Pharsalus in 48 BCE, where Caesar routed the numerically superior forces of Pompey for trifling losses. He claims that Frontinus says that Caesar's reserves were drawn up obliquely to his front line and that these fell on the flank of Pompey's cavalry as they broke through Caesar's flank, and that this tactic should have been tried at Nördlingen.

For Puységur the rules of war that lead to victory "consist of knowing the lie of the land and how it is suited to attack and defense, outnumbering the enemy, deploying them in greater strength and bringing a greater number to bear than your enemy, and combining this with superior courage." He says that has seen many die uselessly because of a lack of knowledge of the art of war, and that it is better to win with the brain than the sword, as Caesar did at Ilerda in 49 BCE, or Turenne during the uprisings of the Frondes (1643–1649).

Application: Although many of Puységur's ideas were interesting, he was a product of his time. War was changing, and innovators such as Frederick II of Prussia and Maurice de Saxe were to radically alter the accepted perception of military operations that Puységur cherished so dearly. His over-reliance on historical precedent serves as proof of the old adage that it is always dangerous to prepare for the last war rather than the next one. His conservatism and love of abstract theory epitomizes much of what was wrong with the traditional conception of war in the 18th century.

Descendents: De Saxe's *Mes Rêveries* was written as a direct rebuttal to Puységur and in reaction to the "cabinet wars"' of the late 17th and early 18th centuries, of which Puységur was such a great exponent.

See also: Saxe, M.; Vegetius

Further Reading

No modern author really covers Puységur adequately; he is referred to in passing in David Chandler's *Art of War in the Age of Marlborough* (1990).

Toby McLeod

Subotai, Baator (Sübedei Baatar)
(1175?–1248?)

Significance: Emphasis on reaching superiority through superior maneuver.

Context: The Mongol conquests of the 13th century.

Biography: Subotai, the most able of Genghis Khan and his successor Ögedei Khan commanded in more than 20 campaigns, subjugating 32 nations, and winning 65 battles.

Influences: As Temüjin's (Genghis Khan) servant, Subotai learned in detail strategy and decision making, being present in most Mongol military council.

The Theory: Subotai advocated dispersed advance and concentration for battle, operational art, long-time raids and false retreats, outflanking operations, deception, ambushes. He used also siege warfare when needed.

Application: He applied these principles in the conquest of the Chin(Jin) Empire in China in 1211–1215, then all of Genghis Khan's campaigns. He led a raid in southern Russia in 1223. In Eastern Europe in 1241, he destroyed the armies of Hungary and Poland, through a combination of maneuver and remote command of detachments and army columns.

Descendents: Mongol warfare exerted fascination on many military thinkers, in Russia and the Soviet Union, England, and the United States. Modern combined-arms doctrine also shows a certain affinity with Mongol warfare.

See also: Genghis Khan

Further Reading
Gabriel, Richard A., *Genghis Khan's Greatest General: Subotai the Valiant.* Westport, CT: Praeger, 2004.

Laurent Quisefit

Sutcliffe, Matthew
(ca. 1550–1629)

Significance: Matthew Sutcliffe's *The Practice,* stands out among the wave of publications engendered by the Anglo-Spanish War both in England and Spain, which tended to focus on tactical matters. *The Practice* contains what would today be called an integrated strategic concept, which ranges from considerations on how to finance the campaigns and ships, and the recruitment of soldiers to grand strategy (including questions of alliances), strategy in a narrower sense (an offensive strategy aiming to capture and hold Spanish territory to cut off Spain from its vital transatlantic revenue), and down to tactical issues. As such, it is peerless in its century.

Sutcliffe is also of modern significance in urging a strategy to pacify conquered areas by winning over the support of the local population through good governance and efforts to increase their prosperity. Generally, he advocated measures to win the hearts and minds of the locals, as this would be called later. His work also contains a famous list of rules issued to soldiers, including terms of engagement concerning the behaviour in war with regard to combatants and noncombatants, and the restraints that were imposed, an early codex of *ius in bello*.

In advocating the conquest and permanent holding of territory overseas, Sutcliffe at once stood at the end of centuries in which the English monarchs owned land on the European continent (mainly in France): it was during his youth that Calais was lost, but England still had garrisons in Flemish ports in support of the Dutch rebels in their Eighty Years' War of Independence against the Spanish. At the same time, he was a prophet of colonialism, in that he recognised the potential of naval lines of communication for the capture and holding of land at greater distances from England, from a fortified town or city to more extensive lands, with which England would communicate only by sea. In his own time, the lines of communication were still extremely vulnerable to storms and piracy, as contemporary naval expeditions showed. But like Douhet with regard to airpower, Sutcliffe realized the potential of naval power way ahead of the precarious possibilities of his own times.

Context: The context of this work is the more general Catholic–Protestant strife throughout Europe in the 16th century, and specifically, the Anglo-Spanish War of 1585–1604, which had the British Isles (including Ireland), Flanders, the Channel, the Atlantic, its islands, and its American and European coasts as its theatre. Sutcliffe's *The Practice* was written not long after the famous Spanish Armada of ships was repelled by England in 1588. Sutcliffe was writing as the importance of navies was increasing sharply, and as the Americas, and the transatlantic trade routes, were acquiring enormous political and economic significance for all of Europe.

Biography: Matthew Sutcliffe was the son of commoners from Melroyd in the parish of Halifax. He studied at Cambridge: in 1568 he was elected a scholar of Trinity, stayed on as a fellow until 1580. Sutcliffe claimed several times to have seen military action himself, in France, Italy, Flanders, and Portugal, and he claims that Essex showed him "singular fauour" in this last context.

Sutcliffe was appointed Archdeacon at Taunton in Somerset in the winter of 1586–1587. Taunton was represented in Parliament in 1586 by Essex's future employee, Francis Bacon, also of Trinity College. In 1587–1588, Sutcliffe was a judge martial (or advocate general) among the "officers serving in the Low countries" of Elizabeth's army, receiving an income of 40 pounds. Due perhaps to Francis Bacon's intercession or to that of Essex, Sutcliffe was subsequently appointed dean at the Cathedral of Exeter until his death in 1629. He continued for some time to take an interest in England's defense: in 1598 he was made captain of a unit of horsemen in his diocesis. He was simultaneously vicar of Welt Alvington in Devonshire, and became one of the Queen's chaplains, managing to keep this position under King James who also became his patron.

Otherwise, "Sutlivus" (as he rendered his name in Latin) published on issues of theology in English and Latin, not only taking a strong anti-Catholic stance, but also quarrelling with other factions within the Church of England. He founded a short-lived theological college in Chelsea, dedicated to anti-Catholic diatribes. In keeping with his argument in *The Practice,* he proved a prophet of the capacity of naval power to establish lines of communication that would enable England, as previously it had Spain and Portugal, to establish and hold territorial bases far away; he thus later supported the English colonization of North America.

Influences: Sutcliffe was hostile to mercenaries as Machiavelli had been. There is no evidence of direct influence by Machiavelli, as by the time Sutcliffe was writing, echoes of Machiavelli could be found in many publications, and this view was widespread. Sutcliffe quoted his Spanish contemporary Sancho de Londoño, whose views on the need for good governance for a conquered people tallied with his own. No other contemporary writer is quoted in *The Practice;* Sutcliffe preferred to use evidence from the classics to support his views, and he cited current customs in other countries.

The Theory: Like many Roman Catholic authors before him, Sutcliffe, although an English Protestant theologian, underscored the importance of a just cause in war, and of clemency in victory, and good governance to be practiced toward a defeated population. *The Practice* is an important source for the laws of war as applied in his times by England, especially under the Earl of Essex, as Sutcliffe provides a catalogue of offenses and their punishment. In this emphasis on observance of the *ius ad bellum* and the *ius in bello,* he illustrates the continuity between Catholic thinking on war and that which was developed within the Church of England, as opposed to more radical Protestant sects.

An original twist is given to this standard reasoning by Sutcliffe's advocacy of preemptive attacks. As strategic intelligence was very slow in his times—a Spanish Armada could sail against England and appear on its coasts before news of this enterprise had reached London—Sutcliffe argued that it would be more advantageous for England to preempt another Spanish invasion by striking first, and destroying Spanish ships in port before they were deployed against England. He went further still, however: a strong supporter of England's budding navy and its possibilities, he advocated capturing the key Atlantic ports of the Iberian Peninsula, establishing garrisons there, and holding them, much as England at the time held ports in Flanders.

Strikingly, there follow passages in which he emphasises the need to pacify the local population and win their support by ruling them "by fortitude, industrie, and justice"—that is, practicing good governance. This approach that is in the interest of both sides, the conquerors and the conquered, is seen as vital by him to prevent the conquered people from rebelling against the new rule, and wishing for the return of the previous regime. In this, Sutcliffe put forward a leitmotif for successful counterinsurgency strategy: "For no people can long like a government, wherein they are [de]spoyled, vexed, injured, and to lay all in one word, pill[ag]ed and tyrannised."

Like Machiavelli before him, Sutcliffe favored the employment of soldiers who were subjects of Queen Elizabeth over that of mercenaries, as the latter would be more expensive. He devoted much space to the issue of financing campaigns, and proposed measures to reduce abuses of the English mustering system due to cheating officers. With considerable examples of alliance warfare available in recent years, when England had sided with the Dutch rebels and King Henry IV of France against the Spanish, namely, Catholic factions, Sutcliffe considered the advantages and drawbacks of alliance warfare as force multiplier. In this context, he wisely warned against joining a coalition war with insufficient means and forces inferior to those of allies, as automatically, this would leave the supreme command to those allies, and these in turn would be prone to sacrifice the smaller ally's forces before their own. Also, under-staffing one's forces meant that these might end up sitting in fortified places, using up resources, instead of venturing out to fight enemy forces in the countryside, which might be impossible if their own numbers were too small. This pattern identified by Sutcliffe has been all too often confirmed over the following centuries.

Application: When he was at Cambridge, Sutcliffe presumably tutored Robert Devereux, Second Earl of Essex (1565–1601), 15 years his junior. Essex had a scholarly bent and sought out scholars to give him guidance. Sutcliffe's subsequent career unfolded under the patronage of the young Earl. Essex and Sutcliffe were on the side of the hawks in Elisabeth I's wars with Spain. Sutcliffe probably accompanied Essex and his stepfather, Robert Dudley, Earl of Lester, on a campaign to Flanders in 1585/1586. In 1593, Sutcliffe dedicated *The Practice* to the Earl of Essex. Essex's Cádiz expedition three years later was designed by Essex to follow aims—the permanent conquest and occupation of Spain's main Atlantic sea ports—which fully fit Sutcliffe's prescriptions in *The Practice*. Sutcliffe's ideas thus had some impact on government policy through the influence his ideas had on the Earl of Essex. Essex's plans were thwarted, however, by the strict orders of Queen Elizabeth and her Council not to attempt to hold Cádiz and the other ports, which Essex's co-commanders adhered to loyally, so Sutcliffe's prescriptions were not applied due to intragovernmental disagreements about strategy.

Descendents: Although Sutcliffe's theological works in Latin were read widely in Spain, there is little evidence that *The Practice* was read much outside England or indeed by later generations.

Further Reading

Sutcliffe, Matthew, *The Practice, Proceedings and Lawes of Armes.* London: C. Barker, 1593.

For excerpts, see Beatrice Heuser (ed. and trans.), *The Strategy Makers: Thoughts on War and Society from Machiavelli to Clausewitz.* Santa Barbara, CA: Praeger/ABC-CLIO, 2010.

Beatrice Heuser

Suvorov, Alexander Vasilievich
(1729–1800)

Significance: Suvorov was the most dynamic of the Russian commanders of the French Revolutionary wars and famous for always attacking.

Context: The Russo–Turkish Wars (1787–1972) and the Wars of the French Revolution.

Biography: Suvorov was the son of an important Russian noble and, joining the Life Guard Semeyonovsk Regiment at the age of 12, served his entire life in the army. He served in the Seven Years' War, the Russian wars against the Ottomans, and finally against the French in during the Wars of the Revolution. His greatest moment of fame came when, at the age of 68, he led a Russian army across the Alps in 1799. Immediately after this Suvorov feel afoul of Tsar Paul and was dismissed and disgraced. He died shortly thereafter in 1800.

Influences: He gained his primary experience and preference for the operational and tactical offensive in Russia's war with Frederick of Prussia.

The Theory: Simply put, Suvorov believed that a commander must move his army directly at the enemy and attack immediately, if possible with the bayonet.

Application: In 1762, as commander of the Sudzal infantry regiment he wrote the *Sudzal Regimental Code.* Suvorov created three maxims. First, quickly look to assess enemy strength and the terrain. Second, always try and gain the element of surprise. Third, move to close, preferably with the bayonet.

Descendents: Russian commanders in the Napoleonic era and after often ascribed to the preference for direct assault with the bayonet.

Further Reading
Longworth, Philip, *The Art of Victory: The Life and Achievements of Field Marshal Suvorov, 1729–1800.* New York: Holt, Rinehart and Winston, 1966.

Lee W. Eysturlid

Tukulti-Ninurta II
(890–884 BCE)

Significance: Tukulti-Ninurta II (890–884 BCE) of Assyria is strongly associated with the invention of horse cavalry. He was the first to integrate cavalry squadrons into an army of the ancient world.

Context: The records from Tukulti-Ninurta's reign contain the first known reference to warriors mounted on horseback. The expansion of the Assyrian Empire forced it to fight in mountainous and difficult terrain (today's Iran, Turkey, Syria, Lebanon), where the chariot proved of little tactical use. It was probably the need to conduct operations under these new conditions that led the Assyrians to abandon the chariot for the horse.

Biography: Tukulti-Ninurta was the second of the four great Assyrian kings (Adad-nerari II, 911–891 BCE), Ashurnasirpal II, 883–859 BCE), and Shalmaneser III, 858–824 BCE) who created the Assyrian Empire in the ninth century BCE. His conquests in the northern regions around Lake Van and beyond the eastern Taurus Mountains gave him access to the horse-raising country occupied by tribal peoples. This provided the Assyrians with a large and inexpensive supply of horses.

Influences: Assyrian mounted combat was initially strongly influenced by chariot warfare methods employed in the Fertile Crescent. At first, Assyrian "cavalrymen" still fought in the manner of the old chariot system of driver and archer, operating in pairs with one "charioteer" riding his horse while holding the reins of another, upon which sat the chariot archer with his composite bow. The "charioteer" managed both horses, leaving the archer free to concentrate on shooting, just as if he were in a chariot. The "charioteer" was armed with a spear, and both he and the archer wore the standard armor, helmet, and other equipment of the Assyrian chariot team. The Assyrians used these cavalry teams for almost 50 years before the individual horseman armed with spear and bow made his appearance under Shalmaneser III (858–824 BCE). This gave rise to the true horse cavalryman.

Although early Assyrian cavalry imitated the chariot in employment and tactics, it is likely that the Assyrians adopted the use of the lance and bow from horseback from the tribal peoples of Iran and Kurdistan, whom they often fought.

The Theory: Cavalry was very valuable to ancient armies, and could do everything a chariot could do, including acting as reconnaissance scouts. However, cavalry could act and range further and over rougher terrain than could the chariot. On the march, cavalry units could move further and faster in a day than chariots, and provide flank security through forested terrain where chariots could not go. Without the horseshoe, horses in antiquity often went lame, but cavalry horses were put out of action far less often than chariot horses, which were useless when the chariot broke down. A single cavalryman armed with the lance and bow provided more fighting power than a chariot crew, and could maneuver much more quickly than chariots on the battlefield. Cavalry's ability to assemble and reassemble for attack after attack made cavalry a far more flexible combat instrument than chariots. Assyrian cavalry later became expert lancers and bowmen; as horse archers they are mentioned in the Bible as the "hurricanes on horseback."

The Assyrian cavalryman (*qurubuti sha pithalli*) of Shalmaneser's time wore the standardized equipment of the Assyrian chariot units, comprising a pointed helmet of polished iron, short corselet of lamellar armor, short-sleeved linen tunic, wrap-around kilt, and high boots with long socks. The emphasis on personal protection suggests that most Assyrian cavalrymen fought dismounted, at least initially. Later, the Assyrians developed light cavalry equipped with less personal protection and used mostly for reconnaissance. Assyrian heavy cavalry were equipped with both a thrusting spear (*azmaru*) 3.5 meters in length and a short angular composite bow (*qashtu akkadu*). A short iron sword was suspended from a leather baldric over the cavalryman's right shoulder. The horse was sometimes protected by a coat of textile armor.

Neither the saddle nor the stirrup were yet invented in antiquity, and Assyrian cavalry and others who came later used the blanket, saddle girth, crupper, and breast strap to stabilize the rider. The cavalryman controlled their mounts with their legs and the heel pressure of their boots, the spur having not yet been invented.

Application: Without the stirrup and saddle to provide stability for the horseman, cavalry could not deliver sufficient shock to break disciplined infantry formations. Infantry therefore remained the combat arm of decision for all later armies of antiquity (Persia, Rome, Carthage, Greece, China, and India). Cavalry was relegated to hovering on the wings of the battlefield until the infantry broke the enemy formations, upon which the cavalry could engage in pursuit. Often, cavalry-to-cavalry engagements ended in both sides dismounting and fighting as infantry. Other times, one side's cavalry would retreat whereas the other side pursued it all over the countryside, having no influence at all on the outcome of the battle.

Descendents: Philip II of Macedon was the first to employ cavalry as a combat arm of decision, using his phalanx infantry as a platform of maneuver to fix the enemy in the battle space while his cavalry turned a flank or exploited a gap in the enemy line. His son, Alexander, developed this tactic to a high art. With Alexander's death, the armies of antiquity returned to an emphasis on infantry, and cavalry once more came to occupy a secondary role. It was only after the barbarian invaders (Goths, Germans, Parthians, and Huns) destroyed the Roman infantry armies that the horse once more came to occupy an important place on the battlefield.

Further Reading

Gabriel, Richard A., "The Iron Empire of Assyria," in Gabriel, *Empires at War* vol. 1. Westport, CT: Greenwood Press, 2005, 177–204.

Saggs, H.W.F., *The Might That Was Assyria.* London: Sidgwick and Jackson, 1984.

Richard A. Gabriel

Valentini, Lieutenant General Georg Wilhelm Freiherr von
(1775–1834)

Significance: Valentini wrote the *Abhandlung über den kleinen Krieg und den Gebrauch der Leichten Truppen* (Treatise in small wars and the use of light troops).

Context: Valentini's theory was based on service in the French Revolutionary Wars (1792–1799).

Biography: Valentini served in the Prussian army, and eventually became chief of its educational service.

Influences: Frederick II of Prussia had written on the use of light troops, but he had disapproved of them. Valentini also gained ideas from Colonel Andreas Emmerich's *The Partisan in War or the Use of a Corps of Light Troops to an Army in London* (1789) and Johann von Ewald.

Theory and Application: Valentini believed that the deployment of light troops could be decisive in the last resort. He used the example of the winter campaign of 1793, where the French *tirailleurs* had harassed the Austrian forces, forcing their retreat without a single battle.

Descendents: The deployment of light infantry in regular armies, and modern guerrilla warfare, all descend from the school of small war.

See also: Bourcet; Clausewitz, C.; Ewald; Frederick II ("the Great"); Howe; Jomini; Lemière de Corvey; Rogers

Matthias Strohn

Vegetius (Publius Flavius Vegetius Renatus)
(fl. 385–435 CE)

Significance: Vegetius's *Epitoma Rei Militaris* (Epitome of Military Science) remained the most complete compilation and manual of Roman military practices to survive from antiquity. The *Epitoma's* greatest contribution related not to any particular theory but to its preservation of earlier writings dating back to the middle Republic, circa 250 BCE. Some of these writings are no longer extant. Vegetius advised engaging infantry and cavalry battles only when topographical features favored one's forces. Vegetius counseled that care must be taken to mitigate harmful effects of wind, sun, and dust. Lines should deploy to permit more lightly armed forces maximum flexibility while enjoying the protection of the more heavily armed front two lines of soldiers. Above all, commanders need to keep in reserve adequate troops both to counter the enemy and to deploy in specialized formations. Siege warfare required advanced preparation and knowledge of enemies, hydrology, and civic engineering.

Context: Rome incorporated larger numbers of barbarians into its military in Vegetius's era. Roman forces had already suffered major defeats, including at Adrianople (378 CE), where the emperor, Valens (364–378 CE), perished. Depending upon when Vegetius wrote, Rome's "fall" to Alaric's Gothic forces (410 CE) might have also occurred. The *Epitoma* responded by seeking to train full Roman legions comprising Roman citizens. It says little about training barbarian auxiliaries. In fact, it says little about late-Roman military organization, which by Vegetius's time had broken into *comitatenses* and *palatini* (more elite units) in the field and *limitanei* and *ripensis* (along border and riparian systems). Vegetius wanted to reestablish the old legionary model as a remedy. The *Epitoma* also bears testimony to the Christianization of Roman forces in its call for recruits to love the emperor second only to God, Christ, and the Holy Spirit.

Biography: Vegetius remains mysterious. He composed both the *Epitoma* and a *Digest of Veterinary Medicine,* which concerned equine and livestock health. Named *Publius Flavius Vegetius Renatus,* the use of "*Flavius*" signified Vegetius's status as a civilian imperial official. He is considered a "Spaniard" connected to Theodosius I (379–395 CE), the emperor from Spain who brought capable Hispano-Romans to Constantinople. Vegetius indicated he compiled his work from previously existing material as a bureaucrat, and thus not as a military officer. Dating both Vegetius's life and the *Epitoma's* composition remains difficult. Vegetius concluded the *Epitoma* sometime between 383 and 450 CE, but scholars cannot further agree about dates. Whenever it was finished, Vegetius dedicated it to the emperor. Vegetius mentioned that he sought remedies for the present in the past, and he strongly believed that Rome was better off with citizen soldiers as opposed to employing barbarians. As a Christian, his religion posed no personal problems for enthusiasm for the military.

Influences: Fortunately, Vegetius revealed the influence of authors and historical documents informing his work, including most prominently: Cato the Elder "Censor" (234–149 BCE), Sallust (86–35 BCE), Marcus Terrentius Varro (116 BCE–27 BCE), Aulus Cornelius Celsus (25 BCE–50 CE), Sextus Julius Frontinus (40–103 CE), Tarruntenus Paternus (ca. 179 CE), the Emperors Trajan (98–117 CE) and Hadrian (117–138 CE), and Augustus's and Hadrian's *constitutiones*. Unfortunately, not all of their works survive. Vegetius found in these sources testimony to ancient Roman praxis, including the training of recruits, the organization of the legions, mundane issues such as the establishment of a camp and its sanitary standards, and all other topics implied by the term "military science," which he thought applied to cavalry, infantry, and navy. Vegetius related in the preface to Book II that the emperor had commissioned him to report on the training and recruitment of military recruits, which informed Book I. Lamenting the decline in training standards, Vegetius especially consulted Cato and Frontinus. His faithfulness to Cato cannot be gauged because Cato's military writings are not extant. It was considerable based on what can be discerned. Other influences included lessons from Roman history. Scipio Africanus's example in Numantia in 133 BCE reminded Vegetius that leaders skilled in disciplining their troops could command a defeated army, reverse its fortunes, and emerge victorious through the implementation of a training regimen. Another lesson from Scipio—through Frontinus—concerned treatment of surrounded enemies: give them an escape route to cut them down in flight instead of facing trapped men with nothing to lose.

The Theory: Vegetius intended the *Epitoma Rei Militaris* to address several problems at once: recruitment of citizen soldiers; training and restoration of discipline within the Roman military; revival of Rome's old strategies, which included infantry, cavalry, and naval tactics; and defending cities from barbarian sieges. Vegetius seemingly had not despaired of the military situation in the western empire.

The *Epitoma's* recommendations for recruitment and training remained practical. Some reflected the prejudices of the time. Recruiters should prefer rural over urban people. Those from temperate climates make better soldiers because colder climates produce less intelligent warriors. Recruits with a background in physical labor and hunting make better soldiers than those in softer trades such as baking. Stronger and fit recruits will make better soldiers than bigger but lazy ones.

Training remained the operative theme throughout the *Epitoma*. Vegetius insisted upon running, jumping, swimming, marching, and carrying heavy loads. He further insisted upon extensive practice. Every soldier should know how to use all weapons and should further display the ability to mount and dismount a horse while carrying arms. His stress on knowledge of weapons derived in part from the natural advantages of certain topographical features. An intelligent and well-trained soldier could take advantage of his surroundings. For example, all recruits should drill with stone weapons because certain regions in Europe were abundant with rocks. Vegetius recorded Cato's saying that any soldier's deficiencies could be corrected over time, but the battlefield permitted no forgiveness for negligence of training. Vegetius thought military camps should be constructed with careful planning and learned preparation. Such knowledge included camp layout, fortification, appropriate size, and location. He concluded the section on training with a critique of hiring barbarian warriors. Training one's own citizens was both preferable and more cost effective.

Because Vegetius considered the infantry the most significant of the three branches of the military, it is not accidental that his *Epitoma* spent the most time addressing it. Classical legionary formations were preferred above all. This meant the cavalry arrayed on the outside wings, with the typical right, center, and left infantry lines comprised the most experienced and effective fighters. Archers, javelin hurlers, and others followed behind but could deploy in front to launch weapons before safely retiring behind the front lines. Trailing behind these were: the carriage ballistic devices capable of catapulting weapons at great range into the enemy; those with crossbows; those with slings to hurl rocks; and lastly, the *triarii,* the infantry reserves of the Roman Republic capable of deployment depending upon battlefield outcomes.

In addition to considering the state of his men, the commander ought to use nature to his advantage. Namely, a battle was more auspiciously fought from higher ground, with wind and sun at the back of Roman forces. Vegetius also recorded what many consider Cato's tactical advice for facing enemies who boasted superior numbers. These tactics included but were not limited to: forming a rectangle; holding back one's left wing while commencing hostilities with one's right wing so that the opponent's left wing could be outflanked by cavalry; attacking with both wings preceding the front line in a sudden burst of speed; making heavy use of archers in front of a weakened center line while simultaneously attacking with the wings; and utilizing wedges or pincers of the strongest soldiers to create holes in enemy lines. No matter how many soldiers were present, the *Epitoma* always emphasized that the quality of soldiers mattered more than their sheer numbers.

The *Epitoma* recorded surprisingly little about cavalry tactics. Vegetius's strategies for countering elephants and camels, although important, were likely to apply more to the eastern empire, where Roman forces occasionally encountered Persian armies with war pachyderms. Vegetius suggested that horses laden with protective armor could be countered because their weight slowed them down. Lassos and nooses could be used to yank riders from horse's backs, and horses could be subjected to additional counter measures. Another reason for Vegetius's brevity on the cavalry is his admission that cavalry fighting had changed so much from antiquity that there was little useful to add from the ancient authors.

Vegetius recognized the importance of preparation for military strategy, and the *Epitoma* revealed the lessons for naval warfare. Preparation affected even the quality of material used to construct ships. Poorly built ships might sink at open sea, condemning crews to near certain death. Preparation extended from the quality of construction to the quality of ship captains and pilots, who needed familiarity with harbors and routes. Officer skill and the sheer muscle of those rowing the oars usually determined the battle's outcome. Tactical advice drifted toward common sense. It took even more types of armaments to wage naval warfare. Shields needed to be larger, the armor heavier, and armaments specialized for ship to ship fighting. Vegetius's sources suggested that the Roman fleet should utilize the deeper and more open water while attempting to force opponents toward shore, where ease of maneuverability decreased. Vegetius recognized that river patrol craft had advanced in use and theory to the point that ancient authors could not offer anything useful.

Vegetius's thought turned increasingly to the demands of siege warfare. The sheer quantity of words devoted to protecting cities from sieges testified to the topic's growing importance. If examples were needed, Vegetius had only to think about the aftermath of the Battle of Adrianople, when Romans succeeded in withdrawing inside the confines of their walled cities. Because food was stored inside city walls, they resurrected Gothic hunger and within a few years reached a negotiated settlement with the Goths. Even the Gothic chieftain, Fritigern (d. 380), said he kept peace with walls of cities.

Much of Vegetius's advice appealed to common sense. Cities and forts ought to take advantage of nature's gifts such as hills, rivers, and other natural impediments to hostile forces. The ground in front of the city's walls should include a deep and broad trench. The trench creates difficulties for besiegers, it can be flooded, and it makes the wall seem taller. A circuit of two interior walls ought also to be constructed. Vegetius advised that the dirt excavated from the exterior trenches should then be used to partially infill the interior walls. The interior ground would thus be considerably higher than the ground outside of the exterior wall, but more importantly, the compacted dirt makes it almost impossible to batter in the walls from the outside.

Vegetius's stress on preparation served the protection of cities in numerous ways. First, water supplies ought to be guarded, and a well should be dug within city walls if at all possible. Second, all provisions for the nourishment of the city's inhabitants ought to be made: cured meats, animal fodder, and anything else that might be dragged into the city. He advised burning anything that might be left outside the walls and used as food by the enemy. Third, defensive weapons needed to be stockpiled. This included above all incendiary supplies capable of burning siege engines, stones and boulders, wood for arrows, supplies for catapults, and large wooden beams and planks.

To counter various mobile devices equipped with fire retardant animal skins, Vegetius proffered these countermeasures: making a risky sortie from inside the city walls to the device, pull off the fire protection, and ignite the machine; launching incendiaries from catapults; shooting flaming darts, arrows, and spears; adding height to the walls even as the enemy besieges it; secretly tunneling under the city walls and into the paths of the enemy's wheeled devices in the hope that the tunnels will sink and crash the devices; utilizing catapult devices, against which few mobile systems can be defended; trying to capture the battering ram with a noose; and should a breach of the outer walls happen, retreating within the interior walls to continue fighting.

Assessment of the strengths and weaknesses of Vegetius's military thinking is difficult. His work demonstrates cognizance of problems in the late western Roman Empire. His thinking on citizen soldiers continued to resonate throughout history, but it revealed a cultural prejudice and an unrealistic view of political and military dynamics for his time. Notwithstanding his prejudice against barbarians, the empire's survival depended upon the very barbarians he seemed to dislike. The half-Vandal half-Roman Stilicho (d. 408 CE) rose to the highest level of military authority in the West. The Roman general, Aetius (d. 454 CE), was only able to defeat the Huns and their Ostrogothic allies at the Battle of the Catalaunian Plains (451 CE) with the help of his own Frankish, Visigothic, and other barbarian allies. Indeed, the Visigoths supplied the majority of the troops and suffered the death of their king in the battle. Vegetius omitted diplomacy from his discussion on military affairs. That is a shame because Rome had succeeded for centuries in militarily playing its barbarian neighbors against each other. The real significance of Vegetius rests not only in his preservation of ancient advice but also in the influence his *Epitoma* wielded in the medieval world.

Application: Vegetius's thought surfaced with great frequency in the Middle Ages and Renaissance. It is an open secret that the *Epitoma* ranked among the more frequently copied texts in medieval history. It certainly was the most popular military book. It had broad appeal to many elements of society. For example, even monks admired the stress upon discipline and training. Similar to newly enrolled monks who underwent the rigors of a novitiate, Vegetius's new recruits withstood a rigorous training regimen to make them stronger. Although monastic houses succeeded in copying the text, the greater levels of application fell to those who fought and ruled in the secular realm. One example will be given here and a second in the next section to highlight different applications and influences.

Giles of Rome (*dgidius Romanus, 1243–1316 CE*) reflected the transition of Vegetius's text from monastic house to the decidedly more secular realm when he composed the *De Regimine Principum* (*On the Mirror of Princes*) in 1280 CE, for Philip the Fair (1268–1314), who later became King Philip IV in 1285. Although Giles made significant use of Aristotle, he referred to Vegetius well over a dozen times. The third book (of three) was the most important in terms of Vegetius's influence. Giles, relying upon Aristotle and Aquinas, argued that monarchy remained the best form of government and the one most to be preferred. There was nothing unusual in this assertion in either philosophical or even practical terms considering that monarchies were just beginning to find the power to reassert themselves against the nobility. Successful monarchs, however, relied upon a vigorous military. It was here that Vegetius appeared in Giles's text with typical themes: rural people represented potentially better recruits because they were naturally most accustomed to strenuous exercise; training and practice remained vital; all soldiers should practice with different weapons because even the cavalry might find itself without a horse and compelled to engage in hand to hand combat; combat should be engaged with topography favoring the strength of one's army.

Assessing the exact impact of Giles's work upon Philip IV—and therefore that of Vegetius—is not completely possible. However, Philip became king at the age of 17 in 1285, and he managed to survive until his death in a hunting accident in 1314. Philip committed himself vigorously to solidifying his monarchy. To that end he strengthened not only his military but also the bureaucracy. He utilized competent administrators and preferred for them to deal with problems generated by administrative decisions. His administrators mirrored Giles's advice and Vegetius's soldiers: prepared, professional, calculating.

Descendents: One of Vegetius's biggest descendents lived at the other end of the medieval era, over a millennium later, in the Renaissance. Vegetius's appeal to Renaissance thinkers is understandable given the epoch's emphasis, especially in Italy, on militias comprising citizens. Vegetius's text thus found great resonance with Machiavelli, who emphasized citizen militias in both his *Art of War (Arte della guerra)* and the *Prince (Il Principe)*. In the *Prince,* Machiavelli blamed the weakness of some Renaissance city-states on their excessive use of mercenary armies led by *condottieri.* This had already been attempted in northern Italy, and Italian intellectuals and political leaders found these mercenary armies deficient in many ways. They were also expensive. It was more than Vegetius's ideas about citizen militias that appealed to Machiavelli, however. Significant portions of the *Arte della guerra* found resonance in Vegetius's *Epitoma.* Machiavelli saw in Vegetius's words to the emperor the ideal for Renaissance princes. That idea chiefly related to military knowledge and preparedness. Without adequate knowledge of military matters, the leader could not hope to create, let alone lead, a military force capable of trust. A prince well versed in military matters could also ensure that his soldiers received the adequate preparation about which Vegetius wrote. The tactics of war had obviously changed, but the lessons behind the tactics remained the same: preparations and foresight, physical conditioning, and constant drilling as an infantry body. Many Renaissance writers, Machiavelli included, hoped that a nascent patriotism would inspire these citizen militias to greater heights of military effectiveness and courage.

See also: Constantine, "the Great" (Flavius Valerius Aurelius Constantinus Augustus); Frontinus; Machiavelli

Further Reading
Allmand, Christopher, *The De Re Militari of Vegetius: The Reception, Transmission, and Legacy of a Roman Text in the Middle Ages.* Cambridge: Cambridge University Press, 2011.

Charles, Michael, *Vegetius in Context.* Stuttgart: Franz Steiner Verlag, 2007.
Reeve, M. D. "The Transmission of Vegetius's *Epitoma Rei Militaris,*" *Aevum* 74 (2000): 243–354.

Richard Rawls

Xenophon of Athens
(ca. 430–354 BC)

Significance: The first Westerner to theorize coherently about tactics, Xenophon studded his many writings with keen observations on fighting the Persians successfully, laying the groundwork for the military efforts of Philip II of Macedon and his son Alexander the Great.

Biography: An aristocratic Athenian, Xenophon joined the army of Cyrus the Younger invading the Persian Empire and was one of those who led the Greeks in a fighting retreat to the Black Sea after Cyrus's death. He then fought as a Spartan mercenary in Anatolia before settling in Sparta and writing his memoir of the epic retreat, a pseudo-historical life of Cyrus, a continuation of Thucydides's *Peloponnesian War,* a study of cavalry command and a eulogy of King Agesilaus, the Spartan commander, all of them studded with his military observations and conclusions.

Previous Theories: The Greek experience of fighting to Xenophon's time focused primarily on the use of heavy infantry (hoplite) units armed with spears clashing with one another in masses 8- to 12-files deep (phalanxes) on a short front. Javelin-armed light infantry (peltasts) were employed (if at all) primarily as skirmishers while cavalry fought on the flanks as mounted hoplites.

The Theory: To Xenophon, Cyrus's victory at Cunaxa reinforced the lesson of the Battle of Marathon that Persian troops could not stand up to Greek hoplites in a direct clash. In the retreat from Persia, when his hoplites were harassed by slingers and archers in mountainous territory where phalanxes were ineffective, Xenophon made a virtue of necessity and converted troops from Rhodes, where skill with the sling was common, into skirmishers to take the chief role in the fighting. The retreat also impressed him with the need for careful logistical planning, undeveloped by the Greeks because at home they didn't have to move their armies great distances.

Fighting in the army of Agesilaus, Xenophon observed not only the use of peltasts to harry hoplites on the line of march but also the inability of cavalry to protect the army while tied closely to the infantry. In recommending that the cavalry take on new roles in scouting, skirmishing, and pursuit, Xenophon ran headlong into the aristocratic tradition of cavalry that made it resistant to the kind of direction from other commanders, so he wrote a treatise on cavalry emphasizing the role of competition in training and even the hiring of mercenary cavalry to solve the problem.

Although there must have been some systematic tactical training in various of the armies of his time, Xenophon felt that the success of Spartan armies proved the superiority of the rigorousness of their training and argued for increased training of Greek armies along the Spartan model. In any case, the cooperation of hoplites, peltasts, skirmishers, and cavalry that he envisioned could only be achieved through a revolution in training methods.

Legacy: Before Xenophon, the different types of military units fought essentially separate battles. His vision of their cooperation percolated through Greek military circles for four decades until Philip II organized a new army that drew much from Xenophon's ideas.

Further Reading

Anderson, J.K., *Military Theory and Practice in the Age of Xenophon.* Los Angeles: University of California Press, 1970.

Joseph M. McCarthy

V

General Essays

Because much of humanity in the period before 1815 lived in preliterate settings that precluded the writing of theories about war, does not mean that they did not engage in warfare. Rather, the guide on "how" to fight was driven by cultural norms and traditions. The overview essays collected in this section will allow the user to get at practices of war that are often ignored or overlooked except in specialist monographs. This can be seen by reading the complementary essays of "Western Just War Theory" and "The Hindu Notion of Just and Unjust War." The essays allow the user to see that non-Western cultures are not driven by change that must originate from technological innovation, but from change in social structure, as seen in "War and Military Philosophy in Traditional Japan."

Byzantine Military Doctrine

Significance: The Byzantines have left us with a very rich inheritance of various types of military treatises ranging from the ancient Greco-Roman treatises to their own sophisticated treatises.

The Byzantine military treatises include tactical treatises, treatments of siege equipment and/or siege techniques, naval treatises, treatises of foreign policy and diplomacy, and general treatises dealing with these all.

The Byzantine military theories were built upon the foundations laid by the Greeks and Romans on top of which they themselves added new practical tactical innovations, new types of military equipment, as well as further conceptual and practical improvements in the use of diplomacy and foreign policy to obtain military goals without the use of force.

Context: The Byzantine Empire saw many ups and downs during its 1,000 year existence: In 395, Rome was divided; west Rome faded away in the fifth century; much of the west was reconquered during the reign of Justinian (518–565); Muslims conquered most of the empire after ca. 636; the empire resumed the offensive after 842 and reached it apogee in 1025; weak emperors followed; most of Anatolia was lost to the Seljuk Turks after 1071; the Komnenian revival (1081–1185) ended in disaster when the Latin Crusaders conquered Constantinople in 1204; Michael Palaiologus retook Constantinople in 1261; and slow decline of the Greek Byzantium followed; Constantinople fell to the Ottomans in 1453. These various ups and downs are obviously visible in the Byzantine military thinking. Most of the military treatises were written when the Byzantines were on the offensive.

Influences: The Byzantines inherited and preserved the vast body of ancient military texts that were divided into the following categories: *taktika* (military terminology, formations, and maneuvers); *strategika* (generalship); *poliorketika* (siege warfare); *naumachika* (naval warfare); and *strategemata* (stratagems). However, the Byzantines were not mere copyists. They produced a whole new genre of even more sophisticated military manuals. The four principal sources of inspiration were: (1) The Greco-Roman military treatises; (2) Roman military inheritance; (3) imitation of enemies, allies, and other foreigners; and (4) innovations. The proportion of each of these varied according to the purpose of the author and treatise. There were military manuals that were mere copies or paraphrases of old texts or were compilations or epitomes of old material, and then there were treatises that presented author's personal inventions, but the vast majority of the treatises included all of these in varying proportions. The Byzantines also inherited a well trained and expensive professional army, which affected their ideas of what was possible and what was not in terms of military tactics and strategy.

The Theory: The Byzantine Empire did not possess any military academy in the modern sense. The closest thing to an academy was service in the imperial bodyguard units. Members of the aristocratic military families learnt their military skills from their elders, from military treatises and histories, and while serving in the armed forces. However, it was still possible for gifted soldiers to rise through the ranks to high-ranking positions and it was also possible for foreigners to attain high positions if their standing among their own people was high enough. The officers were usually expected to be able to read orders and drill manuals, and to possess adequate background knowledge of ancient treatises. The role of the military treatises and histories was very important in the transmission of military skills from one generation to the next. The military treatises and narrative histories served as the grounding of military skills, but with the expectation that the officers were not to follow those blindly but to use those as sources of inspiration.

The fact that the vast majority of the Byzantines spoke Greek ensured better survival of Greek military treatises as well as their greater influence upon their military thinking than was the case with the Latin treatises most of which are therefore no longer extant. However, this was not yet the case during the fifth and sixth centuries. For example, in 450, a copy of Vegetius's *Epitoma rei militaris* was produced in Constantinople and John Lydus (*De magistratibus* 1.47) still mentions many texts written in Latin alongside with the Greek texts. Only Vegetius's treatise dates from this period and despite being antiquarian in nature, it still does include some typically late Roman and Byzantine features. Vegetius acknowledged the increased effectiveness of cavalry as a result of which there was no need to imitate the ancients in cavalry warfare. It was the infantry that supposedly needed to be reformed along the old lines. Vegetius's treatise also promoted the cautious approach in warfare as well as the use of guerrilla warfare, which were to become typical aspects of Byzantine military thinking.

The Greek treatises preserved in the Byzantine tradition consist of the works of Biton, Philon of Byzantium, Athenaeus, Heron of Alexandria, Asclepiodotus, Onasander, *Definitiones/Hermeneia,* Apollodorus, Aelian, Arrian, *De constructione helepoleos,* Polyaenus, Julius Africanus, *Hypotheseis, De epistolis secreto mittendis, De arcus usu,* and Interpolations of Aelian. In addition, there were also other military treatises that are no longer extant as well as lexica and etymologies with military content, some of which are still extant. The Byzantines regarded the ancient texts useful for a good reason. Those served as sources of inspiration and emulation. For example, the Greek tactical treatises maintained their relevance as long as men were deployed in ranks and files, the siege manuals remained relevant until the advent of gunpowder, and the collections of stratagems could give ideas for new ruses.

Urbicius' *Taktikon* and *Epitedeuma,* dating from the reign of Anastasius I (491–518), are the first extant treatises that are definitely of Byzantine origin. The former is an epitome of the first part of Arrian's *Ars Tactica* with the implication that Urbicius considered the vocabulary of phalanx relevant for period warfare. The latter treatise, which is dedicated to Anastasius, advocates the use of some kind of *chevaux-de-frise* invented by Urbicius for the protection of infantry against barbarian cavalry charge. The implication is that the period infantry was in need of such protective devices.

In the sixth century the increased importance of cavalry caused heated opposition among the traditionalists. For example, *De scientia politica dialogus* from the reign of Justinian (527–565) includes a book on military science that claims that the infantry remained the queen of the battlefields although Procopius felt it necessary to defend the use of cavalry. The *Peri Strategikes,* which is now attributed to Syrianus Magister together with *Rhetorica militaris* and *Naumachiae,* also concentrates most of its attention to infantry warfare. Syrianus's treatises are traditionally dated to the sixth century on the basis of their contents, but the use of certain words has now caused some historians to prefer a middle Byzantine date. Syrianus's comprehensive military treatise includes discussions of: social structure; duties of officials; definition of strategy (general defeats the enemy by his defensive or offensive strategy); defensive structures (guards, signal fires, building easily defended cities, forts, terrain, diversionary invasions, use of enemy's enemy against them, stratagems, concluding peace); offensive structures (infantry and cavalry phalanx, formations and tactics); marching and camping; night attacks and ambushes; espionage and reconnaissance; archery training; naval warfare; and rhetoric. Syrianus drew most of his material from earlier Hellenistic treatises, but at the same time he also updated it with period material (archery has a prominent role) and own observations. Syrianus's phalanx tactics were relevant for the period infantry warfare, but he still failed to take into account properly the increased importance of cavalry making the treatise a statement in favor of the infantry warfare. However, the traditionalists were not entirely wrong, because infantry did perform very important roles in both offense and defense, but they still failed to acknowledge the increased importance of cavalry in mobile warfare.

By far the most important and influential of the Byzantine military manuals was the *Strategikon,* which has traditionally been attributed to the Emperor Maurice (582–602). It is the first extant treatise to fully acknowledge the increased importance of cavalry and all the new military practices. The treatise consists of two parts: (1) The cavalry treatise and other material (Books 1–11); (2) The infantry treatise (Book 12). The author used as his sources drill manuals, contemporary practices, and earlier treatises. The influence of foreign equipment and tactics is also obvious. Cavalry warfare receives most of the attention, but not at the cost of infantry, because the author saw both arms of service as complementary. The treatment of the topics is very comprehensive. The author included discussions of organization, training, morale, law, tactics, spying, reconnaissance, duties of officers and men, marching and fortified camps, supply, surprise attacks, night attacks, ambushes, river warfare, guerrilla warfare, stratagems, fighting in difficult terrain, sieges, strategy, bribery and diplomacy, etc. The *Strategikon* also includes the first extant analysis of the enemies and how to fight them. The treatise does not include instructions for naval warfare probably because the Byzantines faced no naval threats at the time. There are also no real instructions on how to deal with internal threats, because it was the emperor's duty to keep his subjects happy. This is actually the area in which Maurice and many other emperors failed. Most of the disasters in the history of the empire resulted from enemy invasions at the times of civil wars.

The *Strategikon* stressed the cautionary approach in warfare. It was better to defeat the enemy with ambushes, stratagems, and bribery rather than by fighting battles. It was not wise to endanger expensive professional soldiers needlessly. If it was necessary to fight a battle, the author favored the use of cavalry formations with reserves as well as the use of the traditional infantry phalanxes. The *Strategikon* favored the pragmatism above all and also approved of the use of opportunistic surprise invasions whenever the enemy was weak. The *Strategikon* is also the first source to mention the iron stirrups. This was not the only advance in military technology that had taken place. From other sources we learn that the Byzantines were already using traction trebuchets more effectively than their enemies. The Byzantine professional army described by the *Strategikon* was the most versatile and flexible armed force of its era. The short *De militari scientia* contains much of the same information as the *Strategikon,* but with some significant differences in terminology and details. Unfortunately, this treatise cannot be securely dated at the moment.

For the next 300-plus years the Byzantines followed the principles laid out by the *Strategikon.* It should be kept in mind, however, that how well such principles were followed in practice always depended upon the personality of the emperors, generals and officers, and the situation. Furthermore, it was during this period that the military organization was reorganized as a result of the Muslim conquests and the Greek fire came into use in naval warfare. The treatises needed updating and it has been speculated that there must have been other treatises that are no longer extant. In addition, a new Interpolation of Aelian, an extract of Maurice, and the *Excerpta historica* were written at some unknown point in time.

The next extant treatises that can be securely dated are Leo VI the Wise's (886–912) *Problemata* and *Taktika.* The former consists of questions that are then answered by extracts from the *Strategikon.* The latter is a compilation that consists of material mainly taken from the *Strategikon* and Onasander, but all of which are updated with period material. Of particular value are Leo's descriptions of: the period military organization; the Muslim enemy and the tactics to be employed against them; his naval treatise; and his cynical call to imitate the Muslims in the use of religion for military purposes. He is also the first author to mention the use of hand-held siphons to shoot liquid fire. Leo wrote his *Taktika* as a set of instructions for his generals and officers and can therefore be considered as an expression of his military doctrine. The anonymous *De obsidione toleranda* as well as Leo Katakylas' treatise (only a fragment exists) also belong to this period. The former describes how to defend cities. It is a collection of earlier but still relevant siege techniques together with period practices such as the use of siphons to shoot Greek fire. Such instructions together with naval treatises were particularly relevant at the time when the Arabs were able to conquer even the coastal city of Thessalonica in 903.

The first treatise to step out of the shadow of the *Strategikon* was the *Sylloge tacticorum.* The date and authorship of this treatise are contested. The treatise bears Leo VI's name with the date 903–904, but it has also been suggested that it was written by Leo's brother Alexander. However, the current consensus among the historians is that the *Sylloge* is a forgery dating from ca. 950. The treatise is a mixture of old and new material. It is the first treatise to describe the new cavalry and infantry formations (hollow square; cavalry in three lines and cataphract wedge) and new types of equipment and tactics that were used to good effect in offensive warfare throughout the 10th century. The information provided by the *Sylloge* stand as the first indication of the increased importance of infantry on the battlefield. Infantry was needed in the offensive wars of the 10th century.

The reign of Constantine VII Porphyrogenitos (913–959) saw a veritable renaissance of compilations, collections, excerpts, and encyclopedias of military treatises and histories. It was then that most of the now extant ancient treatises were collected together into manuscripts. The compilations and excerpts that were probably written during Constantine's reign include the so-called *Apparatus bellicus, Praecepta de re militari, Quomodo Saracenis debelletur, De moribus diversarum gentium,* and *Ad Basilium Patricium Naumachica.* The two anonymous treatises, *Parangelmata poliorketika* and *Geodesia,* that are attributed to Heron of Byzantium (ca. 925–950), reflect the new offensive spirit of the Byzantine military policies. The first is an updated version of Apollodorus's (Trajan's architect) and Athenaeus's (first century BC?) treatises of offensive siege equipment with some borrowings also from other sources. The second is a treatise for measuring various things, which uses Heron of Alexandria's *Dioptra* as its main source. Four treatises bearing the emperor's own name, the *Praecepta imperatori, De ceremoniis* (especially 2.44–45), *De administrando imperio,* and *De thematibus* have military significance. The first, drawing on earlier sources, including Leo Katakylas, gives details on how to organize an imperial expedition. The second, likewise using earlier sources, gives details on how to organize a naval expedition. Also drawing on earlier sources the third gives details on how to conduct foreign and military policies. The fourth lists the military districts (themes) of the empire. According to Constantine, the emperor's personal baggage was to include military treatises (especially Polyaenus and Syrianus), books on siege machines and artillery, and histories, which once again stand as a good indication of the continued relevance of the old treatises.

The offensive spirit of the Byzantine military thinking saw its apogee during the reigns of Nikephoros Phokas (963–969), John Tzimiskes (969–976), and Basil II (963–1025). The *Praecepta militaria,* either written by Nikephoros Phokas or someone at his behest, describes how to conduct offensive campaigns in northern Syria with cavalry and infantry. One of its sources was the *Sylloge.* The treatise describes in great detail and realistically how to fight pitched battles in different circumstances. The fighting of battles was obviously necessary when the intention was to conquer territory. *De velitatione* describes how to defend Asia Minor and how to conduct guerrilla warfare like Bardas Phokas. This manual was commissioned by Nikephoros in case there would be a need for the use of defensive warfare again in the future. Both of these manuals were highly practical. *De re militari,* which probably dates from the reign of Basil, describes realistically how to conduct imperial campaigns (scouts, supply, marching, units, equipment, etc.) in particular in the Balkans. According to Psellus (1.33), Basil did indeed use formations borrowed from books, and also invented new ones himself. The *Taktika* of general Nikephoros Ouranos is the last major treatise (ca. 1001–1011) of the golden age of Byzantine military writing. It is a compilation consisting of Leo's *Taktika, Praecepta militaria,* and many other older treatises, and discusses all aspects of warfare on land and water. Despite being a compilation, the author also updated the *Praecepta* and included personal observations such as that his generation had tried many of the ancient offensive siege devices, but had found out that the most useful method was the use of mining, and included instructions on how to conduct military operations in northern Syria.

During the 10th and early 11th centuries a great number of new excerpts, paraphrases, compilations, and epitomes of existing manuals were also produced together with a new "edition" of the *Strategikon*. These included: Paraphrase of Onasander, *Conciones militares, Strategemata Ambrosiana, Corpus nauticum Ambrosianum, De navali proelio* of Leo VI, *Excerptum nauticum* of Leo VI, Paraphrase of *De fluminibus traiciendis,* "*Mémorandum sur la defense des places,*" *Syntaxis armatorum quadrata, Excerptum tacticum* of Leo VI, and *Parecbolae.* The old texts and excerpts were clearly still found useful for a great variety of uses, one of which must have been to serve as lists of things to keep in mind for the generals and admirals.

Only two new treatises are known to have been written after Ouranos during the 11th century. The rest were new "editions" of old texts consisting of: (1) ancient siege treatises with *De obsidione toleranda;* (2) other ancient manuals (Onasander, Aelian, Julius Africanus); and (3) Byzantine texts (*Strategikon,* Leo's *Taktika, De velitatione, De re militari*). Psellos's treatise was based on Aelian leaving Kekaumenos's *Strategikon* (ca. 1075–1078) as the only original military treatise of the period, but even in this case the military treatise forms only a part of a much longer book of advice for his son. As a general of a theme, the son was instructed to pay particular attention to spying, reconnaissance, stratagems, and security in military operations. Notably, Kekaumenos also recommended the reading of the Bible as a source of military instruction. He did not offer any particular advice on the use of military arrays, but rather referred his son to study the earlier treatises, which were considered sufficient. Consequently, the Byzantines appear to have reverted back to their earlier military practices and used treatises such as Aelian's *Taktika* (Anna Komnena 15.3.6) and Leo's *Taktika* as their main sources of inspiration during the Komnenian revival.

After the fall of Constantinople to the Latins in 1204, the Byzantines faced a serious problem. It gradually became increasingly difficult for them to follow the traditional military practices when the resources of the empire had diminished beyond recovery, since those demanded a well-trained professional army. This does not mean that the Byzantines would not have tried to revive their old tactics; it just means that the Byzantines were not as successful in this as they had been with greater resources and better-trained armies. The last of the "Byzantine" military treatises was written by Theodore Palaiologos (1291–1338), but his work already reflected Italian practices, as befitted marquis of Montferrat, and was therefore actually better suited to the prevailing conditions than the traditional Byzantine military manuals.

Application: The history of Byzantine Empire offers several very good examples of how their commanders put into practice the methods described by the military treatises, while also offering examples how some generals chose to ignore the sound advice with predictably disastrous consequences. For example, when the

Persians invaded in 576 the Byzantines resorted to the use of guerrilla warfare until the Persians started to retreat and then assembled their army at Melitene to block the Persians' route of retreat. The Byzantines fooled the Persians into believing that the Byzantines used only one cavalry line with the result that they were able to outflank the Persians with their second line. All of these practices were subsequently included in the *Strategikon*. The victory was only delayed because one of the commanders failed to follow the military doctrine and allowed his men to start looting the enemy camp, but the subsequent night attack against retreating Persian column brought a complete victory. The siege of Dyrrachium by the Normans in 1081–1082 offers a good late example of the continuing relevance of the practices described by the ancient siege treatises (siege machines, blockade, naval forces, relief army, betrayal, etc.).

Descendents: The Byzantine military practices saw a sort of rebirth when Maurice of Nassau used Aelian and Leo's *Taktika* alongside with other old military treatises as his sources of inspiration for the reform of the Dutch armies from 1594 onward. However, it is not only Aelian, but also the other Greek military texts preserved in the Byzantine military tradition that have had a profound influence on many generations of military thinkers, and now the interest in the actual Byzantine treatises has also grown immensely mainly thanks to the new critical editions and translations of the texts.

See also: Apollodorus (Apollodoros), Architect ; Arrian; Maurice of Nassau; Vegetius

Further Reading

Alphonse Dain's posthumous article (Les stratégistes byzantins, *TM* 2, 1967) forms the basis of all modern studies of Byzantine military treatises. Ilkka Syvänne's *The Age of Hippotoxotai* (Tampere 2004) analyzes the early Byzantine art of war, whereas E. McGeer's *Sowing the Dragon's Teeth* offers a very comprehensive analysis of the 10th-century military thinking. *The Age of the Dromon* (Leiden, Boston, 2006) by J. H. Pryor and E. M. Jeffreys includes a thorough analysis of the Byzantine naval treatises. *The Grand Strategy of the Byzantine Empire* (Cambridge, London, 2009) by E. N. Luttwak analyzes the Byzantine military thinking from the perspective of a modern strategy analyst.

Ilkka Syvänne

Chinese Naval Theorists
(549 BCE–1895 CE)

Significance: China has been viewed predominantly as a land power rather than a naval power. Its political leaders have usually been preoccupied with internal stability than expansion, with foreign ventures such as Zheng He's (or Cheng Ho) 15th-century voyages into Southeast Asia and the Indian Ocean seen as brief departures from the norm. This impression has been overturned in the last 20 years by studies demonstrating substantial Chinese maritime interests. This essay surveys Chinese naval history until the defeat inflicted upon China by Japan in 1894–1895, which serves as a convenient marker between China's historical and modern naval history. Until then, Chinese naval operations had been predominantly driven by internal models and ideas. Thereafter, China would have to borrow external technology and approaches.

Context: Profitable maritime trade meant that pro-trade factions in court were usually dominant, or unimpeded by xenophobic rivals realizing commerce's importance to state coffers. This pro-trade inclination did not stimulate a permanent, substantial state naval power tied to national overseas trading interests, as was the case in early modern Europe. Rather, Chinese naval power consisted of a small naval core that could be supplemented from the enormous civilian maritime sector. Until the 19th century, China's neighborhood contained no significant naval powers capable of dominating its coastal waters or overthrowing its rulers by seaborne invasion.

Approaches and Application: The first recorded Chinese naval battle occurred in 549 BCE when the Chu kingdom attacked its rival Wu. Wu also faced naval threats from the kingdom of Yue. Naval operations featured during the Warring States Period (475–221 BCE). Fleets transported forces, raided enemy territory, and confronted rival forces at sea or on rivers. Fighting was conducted by marines armed with spears, long-handled axes, grappling hooks and bows assembled on the upper decks of multi-decked vessels (*louchuan,* or castled ships) propelled by oarsmen. The decks, up to three in number, had protective hide or leather sides, some of which had openings to launch missiles. Upper decks might also house trebuchets. The equipment and vessels were designed for ram and boarding tactics, perhaps preceded by projectile bombardment—tactics that continued down to the 15th century.

The Southern Song was China's most maritime-orientated dynasty, located as it was in the heart of China's maritime regions with its capital at Hangchow. Although seaboard and riverside states had maintained small navies, and the earlier Han, Sui, and T'ang dynasties had raised fleets for overseas campaigns, the Southern Song were the first dynasty to establish a substantial permanent navy to guard their river and canal encrusted land border on the Yangtze, and extensive seacoast from Jurchen and Mongol invasions. The Southern Song fleet expanded from 11 squadrons with 3,000 men in 1130 to 20 squadrons with 52,000 men in 1237. The Song's expertly designed and handled ships carried projectile stores, trebuchets, gunpowder bombs delivered by catapult, rockets, flamethrowers and incendiary arrows, and were protected by iron-resistant bulwarks and counterincendiary devices. Cash rewards for naval innovation and the threat of invasion prompted more naval experiments, including a treadmill-powered paddlewheel vessel, variations of existing galleys and rams, and cotton sails instead of the heavier bamboo mat sails. Song fleets dominated the waters of China for over a century.

The rival Mongol Yuan dynasty, however, developed a competitive fleet between 1268 and 1270, based on the remnant of Northern Song equipment and expertise. It consisted of 5,000 warships carrying 70,000 men. This force defeated the last of the Song naval forces at Yai-shan in 1279. The Mongols attempted to invade Japan in 1274 and 1281. On both occasions, problems with maritime supply routes led to withdrawals after landing in Japan. The second invasion force of 140,000 men was the largest amphibious operation in world history until then, but was neutralized by a Japanese defensive wall and a typhoon that destroyed much of the fleet. A combined land and sea operations against Vietnam between 1283 and 1288 also failed, although 1,000 vessels sent against Java in 1292 had more success.

Coastal regions were difficult for Chinese emperors to control, especially south of the Yangtze, because of the rugged inland terrain, islands, and distance from the centers of political power, usually located away from the coast. The first recorded instance of rebellion by maritime areas occurred in 17 CE in Shandong Province. Another rebellion centered on the Liaodong Peninsula between 109 and 111 CE. Subsequently, several tenacious maritime rebellions occurred south of the Yangtze.

The decline of the Yuan dynasty in the mid-14th century prompted rivals within China to assert their independence. Two fleets based in Zhejiang and Jiangsu provinces, respectively, disrupted Yuan grain shipments from the south to the north, forcing the Yuan to offer an amnesty to the rebels. The Ming dynasty succeeded the Yuan after a series of large-scale naval and siege operations between the Han, Wu, and Ming kingdoms in the Yangtze River system in the 1360s. Fighting focused on sieges, with armies moving along convenient waterways. A large naval battle occurred on the vast Poyang Lake in August 1363 as the Ming fleet attempted to relieve a city besieged by the Han fleet. The ships featured multiple decks, boarding bridges, catapults, and firebombs. The largest vessels were capable of carrying 500 men as well as horses.

By the 15th century the Ming maintained 48 coastal naval bases and a fleet of over 1,000 large warships. The most impressive naval achievements of the Ming era were the seven voyages of Zheng He from 1405 to 1433. In 1403, the Ming began construction of more than 2,000 large seagoing vessels. The seven expeditions carried between 25,000 and 30,000 men each. The first expedition sailed in 62 large *baochuan,* or treasure ships, and 255 smaller vessels. One of the tasks undertaken by Zheng He's fleet was to defeat a southern Chinese pirate fleet based in Sumatra.

Periodic Ming attempts to impose restrictions on trade to restrict Western influence proved hard to enforce. Many coastal people engaged in clandestine trading voyages, smuggling, and collaboration with foreigners. Piracy also flourished among fisherfolk and farmers where arable land was limited, crops failed, and where coastal waters crowded with Chinese and Western merchant vessels, rarely traveling in convoys, offered tempting targets. Many local government officials were complicit and profiting from the trade. Maritime piracy and raiding culminated in the early 1500s in the sacking of Quanzhou and the siege of Nanjing in 1555.

Unable to block raiders at sea, the Ming authorities resorted to constructing a series of coastal beacon stations from Jiangsu to Guangdong, and to using the army to try and catch their more mobile foe on land. The Ming also established regional military guards known as *wei*. *Wei* units ideally mustered 5,600 men and around 50 ships and were assigned to coastal localities centered on major ports. They were subdivided into units based at coastal forts or small naval bases to maximize coastal surveillance and coverage. When a major threat arose, *wei* could be concentrated. Thinly stretched and often inadequate government forces meant that the emperor might also appoint a special official to recruit and lead temporary forces (*yongying*). Perhaps the most notable example was Qi Jiguang who was sent to Zhejiang Province in the mid-1550s to counter rising piracy and succeeded through reorganizing local coastal defense units and supporting them with mobile reserve fleets and a land force. Many coastal people organized self-defense militias, fortified their villages, or even hired mercenaries. Others maintained friendly relations with pirates.

The Ming dynasty was supplanted by the Qing (Ching) in the 17th century. Between 1644 and 1683, Ming loyalists resisted Qing rule by operating out of island and coastal enclaves. Between 1647 and 1654, their naval superiority allowed them to brush aside Qing fleets and raid coastal cities from Guangdong to the mouth of the Yangtze at will, and to besiege cities along the Yangtze. They are reputed to have mustered 170,000 men and to have commanded 8,000 vessels. They seized Taiwan from the Dutch in 1661 and held it for two decades. From their bases in Taiwan, Quemoy, and the Pescadores Islands the rebel fleet dominated the Taiwan Strait and raided the southeastern coast of China. The Qing fortified coastal ports and sought to control the coastal population so as to deny the pirate rebels supplies and recruits. Much of this naval domination was based on the tactical sophistication of their leader Zheng Chenggong (or Koxinga). Harking back to naval tactics used successfully by the Koreans against Japan in the 1590s and right back to doctrine advocated by the great Chinese thinker Sun Tzu, Zheng's fleets relied on diamond-shaped battle formations. Fleets were typically divided into five squadrons mirroring Sun Tzu's quinary system of north (forward), south (rear), east (right), west (left), and center. The commander's vessel was positioned in the center rather than well to the traditional rear of battle lines to improve control over the fleet, although most formations seem to have broken up once fighting moved to close quarters.

Europeans probably did not match Chinese ship technology until the 15th century. Thereafter, China failed to develop men-of-war and European vessels increasingly outgunned and outmaneuvered Chinese naval vessels. The Chinese realized the advantage cannon and firearms conferred and sought them through trade, after which they began casting their own initially poor imitations. In 1524, a Spanish observer based in Macao noted that Chinese naval cannon were small and their powder weak, and Chinese arquebuses could not penetrate European cuirasses. Most crew seemed to be armed with iron-tipped bamboo pikes and swords, and their main tactic against European vessels was to isolate and overwhelm with greater numbers after blinding the crew by throwing powdered lime from ships to windward. Jesuit missionaries later assisted the Chinese in establishing foundries that produced better quality weapons. Although Western vessels plying China's coastal waters in the 1600s and 1700s were never numerous enough to threaten China as a whole, the Qing restricted the length and locations of their visits. They also exploited European rivalry. The Qing even made alliances with Western naval forces, such as in 1679, when Emperor Kangxi invited the Dutch to join him against their mutual enemy on Taiwan.

These measures restricted European inroads until Britain forcibly opened China's ports in the First Opium War (1839–1842). The Chinese relied primarily on coastal fortifications in these campaigns, as they were heavily outgunned at sea—in 1840, the British flat-bottomed iron hulled *Nemesis* with two 32-pounder guns decimated a Chinese fleet of 15 larger wooden junks armed with Congreve rockets and poor quality firearms. The Chinese *haifang* or coastal defense consisted of trying to lure the enemy into traps set in shallow or narrow nearshore waters where they could be further restricted by sunken boats or chains and systematically destroyed by firepower from forts on shore and or fireships. By then Europeans possessed iron-clad battleships whose armor, shallower drafts, and self-contained energy source made them far more capable of penetrating China's nearshore waters and rivers than wooden sail ships, even when faced with fortified coastal batteries. The Chinese practiced passive coastal defense again in the Second Opium War of 1856–1860, and the Sino-Franco War of 1883–1885.

Meanwhile, the Chinese sought to rectify their clear naval inferiority. The respected scholar Wei Yuan urged the immediate purchase of foreign military technology until such time as high-quality local production could be established using foreign advisors. An arsenal was constructed on the lower Yangtze to manufacture modern weapons and was in production by 1865. New shipyards built modern warships from 1866 with the assistance of Western technicians. The first modern warship was produced in 1868. French instructors were employed to train Chinese naval officers at the newly established Majiang naval academy in 1867. By 1900, China had established five such academies. From 1876 Chinese cadets were also sent abroad to study at European naval academies and shipyards. Imperial coffers were insufficient to finance these developments and they were only sustained through "voluntary subscriptions" imposed upon the provinces. The result, by 1875, was a modern navy of Western-style iron warships manned by sailors and officers trained along western lines. However, this was still an essentially conservative embrace of foreign ways. One of the leading naval reformers, the scholar and general Zuo Zongtang who commanded the crucial maritime Fujian and Zhejiang Provinces, still urged caution in embracing outside ideas or resources as it could result in foreign domination. Zuo went on to command forces in Sinkiang and focused on the Russian threat to China's inland territory. His chief rival in the national defense debate, Li Hongzhang, emphasized coastal defense, arguing that Japan posed the greatest threat to China. Li also remained a conservative, however, in emphasizing coastal onshore defense ahead developing a modern fleet.

The new Western-style fleet failed its first test when advisors became enemies in the Franco-Sino War of 1884. The French fleet attacked the Fujian fleet, anchored in the Min River, and sunk 22 naval vessels in half an hour, before leveling the Fuzhou dockyards. The fleet was rebuilt through a costly purchase programme emphasizing steam-powered ironclads. However, it aimed at nearshore defense rather than developing local construction capacity and a blue water fleet in keeping with Li's conservative outlook. The new fleet remained largely untested until the Sino-Japanese War of 1894–1895. Sweeping changes to the antiquated command and training structure of the navy involving greater use of foreign advisors were also implemented in the late 1880s, but these problems had not been effectively dealt with by 1894.

As war broke out, naval planning and direction was still incoherent. Chinese deficiencies were exposed in the Battle of the Yalu River in September 1894. Although the Chinese forces fought bravely, the Japanese fleet had superior ships, training, and leaders. The Chinese force steamed toward the Japanese in an uncoordinated line ahead formation and were overwhelmed by superior Japanese firepower as the Japanese fleet steamed across their front in column, bringing more guns to bear. The Chinese also only discovered in the heat of battle that much of their ammunition was unsuitable for firing. The Japanese lost no ships and suffered only 240 casualties whereas every Chinese ship was badly damaged or sunk, with heavy casualties. The battleship *Dingyuan* sustained 200 direct hits, losing much of its superstructure, every officer was killed or wounded and 600 of the crew. The battle did not end the war, but it ended the illusion that China could use Western naval technology selectively and on its own terms and still preserve its national sovereignty.

See also: Li Ching; Li Ch'üan; Shang Yang; Sima Qian; Southeast Asian Naval Warfare; Sun Tzu; Thai Military Culture (Ramathibodi II); Tran Hung Dao; Zeng Guofan

Further Reading

Antony, Robert J., *Like Froth Floating on the Sea: The World of Pirates and Seafarers in Late Imperial South China,* Berkeley, CA: Institute for East Asian Studies, 2003.

Deng, Gang, *Chinese Maritime Activities and Socioeconomic Development, ca. 2100 BCE–1900 CE,* Westport, CT: Greenwood Publishing, 1997.

Deng, Gang, *Maritime Sector, Institutions, and Sea Power of Premodern China,* Westport, CT: Greenwood Publishing, 1999.

Kierman, Frank A. Jr., & John K. Fairbank (eds.), *Chinese Ways in Warfare,* Cambridge, MA: Harvard University Press, 1974.

Leonard, Jane Kate, *Wei Yuan and China's Rediscovery of the Maritime World,* Cambridge, MA: Harvard East Asian Monographs 111, 1984.

Levathes, Louise, *When China Ruled the Seas: The Treasure Fleet of the Dragon Throne 1405–1433,* New York: Oxford University Press, 1994.

Lo, Jung-Pang, "The Emergence of China as a Seapower during the Late Sung and Early Yuan Periods," *Far Eastern Quarterly,* vol. 14 (4), 1955, pp. 489–503.

Murray, Dian H., *Pirates of the South China Coast 1790–1810,* Stanford, CA: Stanford University Press, 1987.

Swanson, Bruce, *Eighth Voyage of the Dragon: A History of China's Quest for Seapower,* Annapolis, MY: Naval Institute Press, 1982.

Paul D'Arcy

Ethiopian Military Culture
(Fifth century CE–1941)

Significance: Ethiopia in northeast Africa survived doggedly for one-and-a-half millennia as an isolated Christian kingdom with a distinct military culture on the crossroads between Islamic states to the north, west, and east, Red Sea traders to the east and black African societies to the south. From the later 19th century Ethiopia modernized militarily, enabling it to stave off European colonization until 1936.

Context: The rugged mountains and fertile plateau of the Ethiopian highlands, which are bisected by the Great Rift Valley and its many lakes, have long sustained a sedentary, agricultural population living in villages of round, thatched huts. The highlands, with their temperate grasslands and rich volcanic soils, slope downward in all direction to the surrounding, arid lowlands, which are suitable only for nomadic pastoralists. These sparsely inhabited zones effectively cut Ethiopia off from the rest of sub-Saharan Africa. Ethiopia is consequently much more closely linked down the Nile to North Africa, and across the Red Sea to southern Arabia. In ancient times trade and cultural exchanges with Egypt and the Hellenistic and Roman worlds were strongly established. The kingdom of Aksum (now northeastern Ethiopia and Eritrea), which in the early centuries of the Christian era was the major commercial and military power on the Red Sea, adopted Christianity in about 350 CE as its official religion to facilitate trade relations with the eastern Roman Empire. The Christianity Aksum embraced was the monastic, Monophysite form then prevalent in Egypt, which meant the Ethiopian Church has always remained attached to the Egyptian Coptic Church. With the rise of Islam in the seventh century CE there was no sudden Muslim conquest of Aksum as there was of Egypt in 642, but a gradual infiltration by Muslim nomads and merchants until by the 1250s the eastern highlands and all the territory to the east and north of the Christian kingdom were Muslim or strongly influenced by it. With the coast lost to Islam, and contact with the Red Sea and the Indian Ocean attenuated, the people of Aksum, who spoke the Semitic Tigrinya and Amharic languages, turned inland. They set about conquering and converting the Cushite speakers of the highlands to the south of them to Christianity, and building the new kingdom of Ethiopia.

The Approach and Its Application: In 1270, Yekunno-Amlak, a lord (or *ras*) from Showa in the south of Ethiopia, seized the throne from the last of the ancient Zagwe dynasty. The new dynasty is called "Solomonid" because it kings claimed legitimacy through the Aksumite kings as the descendent of the Old Testament King Solomon of Judea and the Queen of Saba (Sheba). This gave them the sanction of the Bible, established Ethiopia as the new Zion, and privileged their subjects as God's chosen people. Surrounded as Ethiopia was by hostile non-Christian or Muslim states, this ideology was crucial in defining Ethiopian identity. All Christians were expected to carry signs of their faith on their clothes and even on their ploughs. The spread of political control and Christianity therefore remained synonymous, and campaigning over the 14th and 15th centuries steadily extended the Solomonic kingdom and reduced smaller states along its periphery to tributaries.

Colonies of Christian soldiers, settlers and communities of monks helped the Ethiopian king rule his new territories and he rewarded them with land grants called *gwult*. The gwult holder was not entitled to cultivate the land himself, and the rights stayed with the peasants from whom he collected tribute in kind. This effectively institutionalized the practice whereby the king permitted his army to requisition its food from the peasantry, and created a military, office-holding class of administrator dependent on royal favor. Gwult holders strove to make land awards permanent, and certain great families succeeded in building up hereditary estates and regional power bases reinforced by dynastic marriages. When a king was weak, these great nobles inevitably posed a threat to the state. To overawe the regional nobles, the Solomonid kings kept no fixed capital but lived as military leaders in great camps of over 5,000 tents close to the current scene of military operations and required the attendance of the great men of the realm.

The high ideal of Ethiopian society was the *tellek saw,* or the superior man who was expected to prove his worth to the people through deeds of valor or generosity. Thus a nobleman was expected to live lavishly, dress ostentatiously, and be openhanded to a fault with his retainers. He could never touch a plough, but was expected to be both a bearer of arms and a man of culture and refined etiquette. Pride of blood and defense of honor in single combat were obligatory, causing endemic feuds and vendettas. This honor code persisted into modern times and fostered a sense of the Old Testament warrior of God smiting the heathen. King, nobles, and officers of state were expected to be active warriors, and all sought visibility through their bright clothes and accouterments. From an early age noble youths, unless destined for the church, learned the arts of war and horsemanship, besides being instructed in reading, music, and the scriptures. Their defining step into manhood was marked by a first kill of man or beast.

Honor came from horse combat, and cavalry continued to dominate the Ethiopian battlefield until it was broken in 1848 by an Egyptian army modernized by Muhammad Ali. A nobleman identified with his horse and might adopt its name to be used in praise-songs. Warriors might praise themselves when parading before battle, reporting victories, or throwing down trophies taken from the enemy. This equestrian warfare was highly individualistic, and single combat was the route to honor and office, even for lowly warriors. Nevertheless, warfare had its rules. Honor demanded that armies fight hand to hand in the open field with sword, spear, and shield despite the mountainous country's obvious suitability for fortifications and guerrilla tactics. Enemy who attacked from ambush or at night were considered treacherous. Etiquette required commanders to communicate courteously with each other before battle while their troops traded insults. Devotion to the death in battle might be admired, but was not expected, and it was not dishonorable to preserve one's life by flight from a stronger enemy.

These professional men-at-arms and their mounted retainers constituted the core of the Ethiopian army, and were called up for service by the king. From the 14th until the mid-19th century they were supplemented by mercenaries because, until the military reforms of the 19th century, Ethiopian peasants of military age were generally not expected to form part of the army, though they could be called out in time of major crisis.

The Solomonid kings were not only continually challenged by overmighty nobles and their armed retainers, but were also increasingly sucked into a struggle with Muslim states to the east for control of the trade route along the Awash Valley that connected the Ethiopian highlands to the Red Sea. In the 1520s the charismatic Ahmad Ibn Ibrahim al-Ghazi gained control in the Muslim state of Adal on the Harar plateau and built a powerful coalition of Muslim forces, including the warlike Somali nomads of the lowlands. In 1527, Ahmad proclaimed a *jihad* against the Solomonic kingdom. At the battle of Shimbra-Kure in 1529, he shattered a great Ethiopian host and his armies marauded northward through the heartlands of Ethiopia destroying monasteries and churches and enforcing conversion to Islam.

In 1505, the Portuguese had arrived in strength on the east coast of Africa, and soon were in a struggle for control of the Red Sea with the Ottomans, who had conquered Egypt in 1517. The Ottomans saw Ahmad of Adal as an ally. In 1540, they sent musketeers supported by artillery to help him gain final control of the Ethiopian highlands, though he still relied primarily on his mounted nomads. The Portuguese countered by sending musketeers of their own to aid the Christian Ethiopians. Though suffering heavy losses on the way, the Portuguese contingent eventually joined the Ethiopian army and defeated and killed Ahmad on February 22, 1543, at Woina Dega near Lake Tana. With Ahmad's death his *jihad* collapsed.

Ethiopia and Adal were both prostrated by years of war, and the Cushite-speaking Oromo (Galla) to the south seized the opportunity. Some of the Oromo were agriculturalists and others pastoralists, but they shared a common belief in the sky god and a social and political system centered on *gada,* or age-grade sets. They began to infiltrate the areas devastated and dislocated by war and abandoned by their long-standing frontier garrisons of local militia. Armed with spears (and not initially mounted on horses as they would be later), they raided by night and avoided the large, set-piece battles favored by the Ethiopians. Eventually the people they were raiding were left with no option but to accept Oromo protection. They were then absorbed into Oromo society, adopting its culture and ethnicity. Through these effective methods of armed encroachment the Oromo gained control over much of the south-central Ethiopian highlands by the end of the 16th century.

In the diminished and now chronically unstable Solomonic kingdom King Fasilidas established his capital at Gondar on the north side of Lake Tana in 1632, thus writing off the old southern territories to the Oromo. The attempt to maintain the Portuguese connection to gain access to their weaponry and military expertise founded on the Portuguese insistence in return on converting Ethiopia to Roman Catholicism. In the consequent backlash the Portuguese presence in Ethiopia was eliminated by 1638, and the country was left more isolated than ever.

The wars against Adal and the Oromo nevertheless led to some rearmament and expansion of the Ethiopian army. By 1634, the army had some 1,500 matchlocks, though for lack of training and discipline they could not withstand a charge by mounted spearmen such as the Oromo who had by now adopted the horse. Military predominance in the king's army thus still lay with his 5,000 horsemen and their aristocratic code of honor. Threatened on all sides, the Ethiopian kings began to rely on walled defenses built on flat-topped mountains. Oromo infiltration that continued throughout the 17th and 18th centuries, combined with the growing autonomy of the great regional lords so weakened royal authority that by the end of the 18th-century Ethiopia was a single kingdom in name only. The regional lords continued to recognize the ritual authority of the ineffectual kings at Gondar and pay him nominal allegiance, but the chaotic period of provincial autonomy between 1769 and 1855 came to be known as the *Zamana Masafint,* or era of the princes.

The warlord who seized the throne as Tewodros II (1855–1868) attempted to restore the Solomonic kingdom and bring the regional lords to heel. Early in his career disastrous encounters against Egyptian regulars armed with modern weapons convinced Tewodros that to safeguard Ethiopia it was necessary to adopt Western statecraft and military technology, and that artillery was necessary to reduce the mountain forts of his rivals. He began importing arms and foreign technicians and launched a domestic weapons industry. Tewodros was still battling his rivals when on April 10, 1868, at the battle of Aroge, a British expeditionary force from India (dispatched to rescue the British consul whom Tewodros had imprudently imprisoned) overwhelmed a charge of foot soldiers armed with muskets with volley firing from breech-loading rifles.

The *ras* of Tigré province in the north, who had been allied to the British, seized the throne as Yohannes IV (1868–1889). Using military equipment provided him by the British, he curbed rebellious provincial nobles. In 1875 and 1876, he defeated European-trained and officered Egyptians armies attempting to advance from the Red Sea enclaves they had taken over from the declining Ottoman Empire. These successes were due more to weight of numbers and the enemy's blunders rather than to new tactics and weaponry, but Yohannes looted the Egyptians' modern rifles, artillery, and Gatling guns (which captured Egyptian gunners taught the Ethiopians to use) and integrated them effectively into his army. With this modernizing force he successfully prosecuted campaigns against recalcitrant rivals, and at Dogali, in 1887, Yohannes's general, Ras Alula, repulsed the Italians who were trying to push westward from their Eritrean enclave gained in 1885. In 1888, Yohannes died in a minor engagement against Muslim Mahdists who were raiding from the Sudan to the west, and the throne passed to Menelik II (1889–1913), the *ras* of Showa and his longtime southern rival.

Menelik saw the need for even more rapid military modernization if Ethiopia were to survive the accelerating partition of Africa by the colonial powers. So although he retained 5,000 cavalry recruited from the social elite, the core of the late 19th-century Ethiopian army was formed by 500 professional, drilled riflemen. In addition, by 1902 Menelik had an army of 30,000 mounted infantry armed with repeating rifles mainly supplied by the French to spite their colonial rivals, the Italians. Through training by European specialists and experience on many battlefields Menelik's riflemen knew how to maneuver to maximize the impact of their weapons, to aim carefully, and to minimize exposure to enemy fire through taking cover or lying prone. This central army also had quick-firing artillery (partly served by Russian artillerymen sent by the Tsar to preserve Christian Ethiopia from the Muslims), and machine guns. It could be reinforced by about 300,000 provincial troops and peasant militia, many of whom carried a musket or rifle as a matter of honor. Thus in the campaign of 1896 against the Italians the Ethiopians were able to field 100,000 reasonably well equipped and trained men, 70,000 of whom bore modern rifles. The rest of the army still carried swords, spears, and buffalo-hide shields.

The reformed army also had weaknesses, particularly logistical. It lived off the land, and its very size meant it could not survive long in the field before disintegrating for lack of supplies. The Ethiopians only gained their great victory over the Italians at Adwa (Adowa) on March 1, 1896, through skillfully drawing the Italian expeditionary force out of its prepared defenses and bringing its three separated and disorganized columns to battle before they themselves were forced to disperse through hunger. Although the Ethiopian victory might have owed as much to effective deployment, overwhelming advantage of numbers, and traditional courage and panache as to modern weaponry, its consequences were dramatic. The Italians temporarily gave up their Ethiopian ambitions, freeing Menelik to throw his victorious army into the brutal conquest of mainly non-Christian people around the southerly fringes of the Ethiopian core: the Oromo, the Muslims of the eastern highlands, and the Somali speakers of the Ogaden. The very size of this greatly enlarged empire, coupled with the military prestige won at Adwa, secured Ethiopia international recognition as a nation-state and preserved it for 40 years from further attempts at colonization.

However, Menelik was unable to maintain a monopoly over all the modern arms entering the country, and the great regional nobles also acquire them and continued to challenge central authority. Yet in the campaigns of 1929–1930 when the Showan noble, Ras Tafari, who had been the regent since 1916 and would became Emperor Haile Selassie in 1930, crushed his rivals, victory was not simply a matter of larger and better-led armies. It was the result of superior communications through Haile Selassie's earlier installation of government telegraph and telephone lines, and the purchase of machine guns and even some air support. During the 1930s Haile Selassie continued to try and build up a real European-style army through the foundation of military academies and the acquisition of more modern weaponry.

Yet the Ethiopian army remained a small professional force supported by a mass of peasant levies and irregulars who still subscribed to antique notions of honorable face-to-face conduct in battle. They proved no match for the Italians when they invaded again in 1935–1936 with their superior weapons, mechanical transport, airplanes, and poison gas. After the defeat of their conventional army, some 25,000 Ethiopians turned to guerrilla warfare that, although it contravened the hallowed military traditions of open warfare, nevertheless exploited the culture of heroic single combat. Women (this was without precedent in Ethiopia) also took up arms in the insurgency, which the Italians never suppressed entirely. In 1941, the surviving "patriots" cooperated with British forces and Haile Selassie's poorly equipped army to defeat the Italians and restore the emperor to his throne. Ethiopia, with its strong sense of cultural solidarity, which found expression in its ancient Christian monarchy, and with its deeply rooted military ethos honed by centuries of dogged resistance against enemies from every side, had survived once more.

Descendents: The military junta (or *Dergue*) that overthrew Haile Selassie in 1974 and instituted a Marxist dictatorship revolutionized the entire structure of Ethiopian society. The ancient cultural bonds that had held Ethiopia together were severed, and the country entered a new era. In the bitter wars from 1974 to 1991 against Somali, Tigrean, and Eritrean separatists, much of the fighting took the form of modern counterinsurgency operations. In the large-scale conventional clashes in the Ogaden desert and in Eritrea the Ethiopians were supported by military aid from the Soviet bloc including tanks, fighter jets, military advisers, and technicians, and even Cuban troops. The Dergue ordered a mass mobilization of Ethiopian peasants (by the 1980s the Ethiopian army had grown to 300,000 men, the largest in Africa), and these raw troops were thrown into the front line. There (and again in 1998–2000 in renewed fighting against Eritrea) their courage and tenacity suggest that the old warrior ethos has not been entirely obliterated by revolution and the changed circumstances of warfare.

Further Reading
Iliffe, John, *Honour in African History*. Cambridge: Cambridge University Press, 2005.
Marcus, H. G., *A History of Ethiopia*. Berkeley: University of California Press, 1994.
Rubenson, S., *The Survival of Ethiopian Independence*. London: Heinemann, 1978.

John Laband

Forest Kingdoms of West Africa
(ca. 1500–1900)

Significance: In the forest region of West Africa, sophisticated kingdoms competed between the 16th and 19th centuries for power and economic control. The Atlantic slave trade distorted the economic and political dynamics of the region, whereas firearms transformed its military culture.

Context: In West Africa the savannah gives way toward the coast to thick tropical rainforest. For epidemiological and practical reasons this environment limited cavalry warfare. Armies of mixed cavalry and infantry operated only in the Gap of Benin, where the savannah penetrates the forest almost to the coast. Nevertheless, though this was open country, horses could not long survive the diseases of the wet season. The coast has no natural harbors, but along the Gap of Benin and to its east inland lagoons, lakes, and rivers allowed marine infantry operations.

Approaches and Application:

The Gold Coast

The Akan States (Asante)

The Gold Coast (the region immediately west of the Gap of Benin and the Volta River), was dominated by Akan-speaking people. In the 16th and 17th centuries, dozens of states abounded, each dominated by a town. From the 1470s European traders made treaties with coastal Akan states and established trading castles. Initially the trade was in local gold, but by the 18th century slaves dominated exports. These slaves were the victims of wars between the Akan states, and had long been used in mining. It is debatable how far European economic demand accelerated the taking of slaves. Certainly, to further their own economic interests, Europeans became embroiled in coastal politics, though they were never powerful enough to dictate proceedings. The African import of firearms and the need to pay for them with slaves increased the slave trade and the scale of the warfare, but in participating in this cycle, Africans were not simply responding to European traders, but had their own motives.

During the 17th century larger, expansionist Akan states emerged. By 1750, Asante emerged as the inland power. It was a military union in which six confederate chiefdoms were surrounded by a circle of incorporated Akan speakers, and then by a periphery of conquered tributary peoples. Asante attempted to break out of the forest and to secure control of the coast and its trade, but it was thwarted by the Fante kingdom. The Asante faced repeated revolts by their subject peoples, and found an answer in the royal "golden stool," which embodied the ties of kinship that bound the people together and mystically subordinated the ceremonial stools of district governors to that of the *asantehene,* or king. Nationhood was also instilled through songs and rituals that stressed the common origin of all the people of the empire. The national army, which was a conscripted militia, also promoted common loyalty among recruits from all parts of the country.

By the 18th century only the English, Dutch, and Danish maintained a presence on the Gold Coast and were contained by Asante and Fante. The Asante army was the only one in West Africa to defeat Europeans repeatedly, most notably humiliating the British in 1824 and 1864. The end of the Atlantic slave trade was a blow to the Asante economy, but it switched successfully to "legitimate" trade in gold, kola nuts, and palm oil. Tightening British control along the coast, and its threat to Asante trade, precipitated a disastrous war. After a successful punitive British expedition in 1873–1874 the empire fragmented, and in 1896 Britain occupied the country, suppressing a determined revolt in 1900.

Throughout the 16th and 17th century, the Akan states fielded exclusively infantry forces. The noble elite and their trained retainers carried swords, javelins (often poisoned), and shields. This heavy infantry were often organized in professional military associations. The peasant militia and slaves (who might belong to nobles or to the king) fought with bows and javelins. Akan armies were still small, and were augmented by mercenaries and allies from neighboring states, and Europeans. Because of the fertile region's burgeoning population and resultant forest clearing, much of the rainforest consisted of impenetrable secondary growth transected by narrow paths, where armies were vulnerable to ambush, and small forces could defy much larger ones. Consequently, towns of the Gold Coast (except in the more open country merging into the Gap of Benin) were left unfortified because the forest formed their defense. Operations typically took the form of sudden raids. Major wars were rare, and were generally preceded by a period of skirmishing. The occasional set-piece battles could only take place in agreed-upon forest clearings, and became accompanied by much ceremony. The heavy infantry advanced in dense masses, throwing their javelins, while to their rear militia and slave archers kept up volleys of arrows over their heads. Hand-to-hand combat decided the day.

Gunpowder weapons procured from the Europeans transformed Gold Coast warfare, though the transition only proved decisive at the end of the 17th century when flintlock muskets replaced matchlocks. By the 1650s, corps of several hundred musketeers were common. They skirmished ahead, still leaving the final encounter to the heavy infantry. When flintlocks became common, musketeers became front line soldiers, until by the early 18th century whole armies consisted of them. These soldiers fought as waves of skirmishers making much use of cover, and engagements were decided entirely by musket fire.

The gunpowder revolution also changed the composition of Akan armies. The elite heavy infantry and archers were replaced by less-skilled militia and conscript troops carrying their own muskets and raised by local notables. The larger conscript armies began to face severe problems of supply, which limited the length of campaigns and capped the size of field armies. Armies outpaced the women or boys who accompanied them with food and then exhausted their own dry rations, compelling them to forage. Moreover, the forest environment still defined tactics. Armies had to advance in several columns strung out along the forest tracks, hoping to concentrate if a rare pitched battle threatened. Usually, though, campaigns were wars of position dependent upon intelligence and speed that allowed an army to blockade an enemy in the forest paths until it was weakened by disease or starvation.

The purpose of war in Akan culture was to ruin an enemy state by destroying its trade and agriculture, by killing or enslaving prisoners, or by relocating and incorporating conquered communities to reduce the enemy state's population and military potential. Control over people was more important than extent of territory. By the late 17th century, the vast European demand for slaves made the wholesale depopulation of an enemy feasible for the Akan, who used frontier raiding rather than full-scale war to achieve the desired effect. The Asante emerged as the masters of this form of warfare and in the later 18th century built the great roads through the forest that connected strategic points and allowed the rapid passage of their armies and captive slaves.

The Asante went to war (as did all soldiers of the region) ritually strengthened by religious ceremonies, magic, and protective amulets. They emphasized courage and unflinching endurance of pain. Heroism could bring promotion and prestige. Cowardice could mean death, a fine, or public humiliation. Disobedience could mean death. Special units placed to the rear of the army drove forward with whips anyone attempting to retreat. Unsuccessful commanders faced ignominious dismissal, or preferred to commit ritual suicide.

The Asante's established strategy of blockade did not succeed in 1874 against superior British logistical organization and firepower. The Asante fared better in 1900, when they adopted guerrilla warfare.

The Slave Coast

The Yoruba (Oyo)

State formation among the Yoruba-speaking peoples inland from the Slave Coast began in the 11th century, each centered on individual fortified cities. The greatest of the Yoruba states was Oyo, placed strategically across the north–south trade routes. It occupied only marginal horse country, but in the mid-16th century the rulers (*alafins*) of Oyo copied the militaries of the successful cavalry king-doms of the savannah. Oyo's predominantly cavalry army, armed with swords and spears, often went without saddles or stirrups and made little use of defensive armor. Nevertheless, it built up a large conquest state. With many of the horsemen being slave warriors imported from the Muslim Hausa states to the north, Oyo was influenced by Islamic civilization and its institutionalized military slavery. War leaders appointed by the *alafin* recruited their own soldiers from the free popula-tion, as well as from slaves. In the late 18th century the *alafins* began recruiting slaves for a mounted palace guard. War captives became slaves on the royal farms that were the economic basis of Oyo's economic power. By the 17th century Oyo had overcome Nupe, its great rival, and because its cavalry could not operate in the forest, it turned its attention southwest to the open country of the Gap of Benin.

The Edo (Benin)

South of Oyo and Ife, deep within the forest, the Edo-speaking people were also in the 11th century developing a centralized city-state called Benin. By the early 16th century, Benin was a large walled city with a powerful standing army guarding an empire dominating the coast west from the Niger Delta to the Lagos Lagoon. In the 16th century, the Portuguese established diplomatic relations with Benin, and served as mercenaries in its army. Fortified European posts followed, and European attempts to monopolize commerce, particularly in slaves, contrib-uted to the instability of the coastal region. Benin suffered a disastrous civil war between 1689 and 1732 and was replaced by smaller regional powers.

Dahomey

The 18th century was a period of unremitting warfare for the region. In the southern part of the Gap of Benin the dominant state was Dahomey. In the mid-17th century, Aja people had founded a centralized state with a strong cult of kingship that required annual human sacrifices from war captives. In the 1720s Dahomey began a drive to the coast to control the slave trade. Local rulers wel-comed the European coastal forts as places of refuge against Dahomey, though they regularly fell to mining operations, surprise, and direct assault. However, Da-homey lacked the naval resources to control the coastal waterways. The navies of states such as Warri on the western side of the Niger Delta, commanded enough paddled watercraft, carrying up to a hundred marines, to force the region's islands into submission by cutting off trade and food supplies. Dahomey did not have the craft similarly to dominate the waterways, but by 1774 it learned how to build causeways to contain enemy naval action and to storm the islands.

Oyo took advantage of Dahomey's attempt to subdue the coast by invading the north of the Gap and challenging Dahomey's hegemony. Its horsemen humbled Dahomey's infantry in 1728. Yet, because Oyo could not maintain its cavalry in the Gap on account of infection with trypanosomiasis and lack of forage, it had to be content with regular raiding rather than annexation. Dahomey and Oyo continued to compete inconclusively for control of the broken countryside in the north of the Gap in unprofitable campaigns of blockade against fortified natural fastnesses. A new factor was added in the late 18th century when both clashed with the expansionist Asante.

In all these Slave Coast states, military forces were recruited largely from the peasantry by local notables, and also from professional mercenaries and bandits. Some commanders tried to recruit troops from their own clan network, although in times of civil war the state army might divide along such lines. Dahomey attempted to transfer the loyalty of its soldiers to the king, and important state officials and military officers were provisionally appointed at the king's pleasure. Defeated commanders were not expected to return alive and ransomed soldiers might be executed for surrendering in the first place. The Dahomean kings created units of royal guards with uniforms and the best firearms available. These politically dependable guards were replenished by levies of boys. As a warlike but relatively small state, Dahomey lacked sufficient manpower for its ambitions and women were employed in many military roles. When his regular soldiers took heavy casualties during the Oyo invasion of 1728, King Agaja recruited women and eunuchs. This was likely the origin of the notorious "Amazon" elite corps of women who and were finally destroyed by the French in 1892–1894.

As on the Gold Coast, in the 16th-century swords, javelins, and animal-hide shields that covered the whole body were originally common armaments, as well as throwing clubs and bows. Armies clashed in loose formations, first launching projectiles and then engaging in hand-to-hand encounters. The victors sought to enslave as many fugitives as possible. By 1650, these weapons began to be augmented by gunpowder weapons obtained from Europeans in exchange for surplus war captives. By the later 18th century muskets had widely replaced other missile weapons, and battles took place between maneuvering bodies of skirmishers. Dahomey in particular embraced firearms, and to procure them it became deeply involved in the slave trade. This made double sense. Firearms allowed Dahomean infantry to withstand the cavalry of Oyo, who still preferred their traditional spears and swords, from behind field fortifications. Even if this technological edge never gave Dahomey the final victory over Oyo, it was enough to secure its survival. Also, as a beleaguered state desirous of reducing its enemies' manpower, Dahomey was wary of keeping prisoners of war or allowing them to remain in conquered territory, and saw the ideal solution in selling them on as slaves to the coast.

The Age of Confusion

The Yoruba call the 19th century the "Age of Confusion." In the late 18th century Oyo was weakened by internal power struggles, and in 1796 the revolt of the vassal state of Ilorin initiated the breakup of Oyo's empire. The end of the Atlantic slave trade meant the economic ruin of Oyo, and led to the faltering of royal authority and an inability to afford expensive imported warhorses. The army broke into the personal followings of individual commanders, and during the 1830s and 1840s, Oyo disintegrated in civil war. The attack in 1835 from the north by the Fulbe cavalry of the jihadist Sokoto Caliphate introduced a dimension of religious war. The Oyo abandoned their capital and reconstructed their state southward in the forest where Sokoto's cavalry could not operate. Fighting was now conducted increasingly with flintlock muskets with forces firing in an advancing succession of ranks, charging home with their swords. Less trained soldiers defended the many walled towns. The introduction in 1881 of breech-loading rifles ended the old hand-to-hand fighting. Soldiers learned to fight exclusively from behind cover, including trenches. Strong notions of honor still prevailed, with men fighting to the death or committing suicide to avoid capture, but the Age of Confusion also condoned easy switches of loyalty and alliances. What counted most in terms of a man's honor was success. The main victims of the continuous warfare were the ordinary people.

After the Berlin conference of 1884–1885 decreed that the colonial powers had to demonstrate effective occupation of the regions they claimed in Africa, the British moved to consolidate their hold over the territory between the Niger Delta and the Gap of Benin. Most of the Yoruba states were conquered in 1892–1893 and the Emirate of Ilorin in 1897. Benin fell in 1897.

See also: Ethiopian Military Culture; Sub-Saharan Military Responses to European Invasion

Further Reading
Smith, Robert S., *Warfare and Diplomacy in Pre-Colonial West Africa,* 2nd ed. Madison, Wisconsin: University of Wisconsin Press, 1989.
Thornton, John K., *Warfare in Atlantic Africa 1500–1800.* London: UCL Press, 1999.
Vandervort, Bruce, *Wars of Imperial Conquest in Africa 1830–1914.* London: UCL Press, 1998.

John Laband

Hindu Tradition of Just and Unjust War
(ca. 500 BCE–900 CE)

Significance: Indian philosophy contains two polar opposite concepts regarding warfare. The concept of *dharmayuddha* (just war) evolved from the Vedic era. It gave rise to laws of armed conflict based on the principle of "humanity" and humanitarian considerations, designed to limit the suffering caused by warfare. In contrast, *kutayuddha* or *adharma yuddha* (unjust war) emphasizes psychological warfare, spying, and use of special forces (equivalent to 20th century's commando forces) for covert operations. The more prudential trend of *kutayuddha* remained marginal in Indian statecraft.

Context: Ancient and medieval India produced few theoretical treatises on strategy. Unlike in the Classical West, it was not customary in ancient India to note down day-to-day political and military events. Nor did any generals or warlords of ancient India write memoirs. Specialist technical monographs on military affairs are also absent. However, ancient India generated vast amounts of literary works in Sanskrit, which, although mainly romantic, idealistic, and imbued with a deep sense of spiritual vision, also contains a lot of practical wisdom. One therefore has to distill ancient India's military philosophy from the classical Sanskrit texts.

The main proponent of *kutayuddha* was Kautilya, who flourished under the patronage of Chandragupta Maurya (317–293 BCE), the founder of a pan-Indian empire. In 256 BCE, Chandragupta Maurya's grandson Asoka invaded Kalinga (Orissa). After witnessing the suffering that occurred during the conquest, he renounced violence and turned to Buddhist pacifism. Asoka's edicts and inscriptions provide empirical data regarding the formulation of *dharmayuddha.*

The geographical insularity of India made the Indian monarchs more interested in establishing their sway inside the subcontinent rather than in invading foreign countries. Warfare within the same ethno-cultural group further encouraged the growth of a ritualized combat. This brought about the dominance of *dharmayuddha* in India until the ninth century CE, when Islamic forces invaded from the northwest.

The Theory: Kutayuddha means warfare through unfair means. The term *dharmayuddha* could be translated as "just war" or "virtuous war" and means making warfare in the righteous way, with an emphasis on moral injunctions. The objective is to limit the "injustice" inherent in warfare.

The term *dharmayuddha* is derived from *dharma,* the code of conduct accepted by the pious to sustain the good order in the cosmos. Virtuous actions and piety characterize *dharma,* and a devout and a benevolent ruler is supposed to wage *dharmayuddha.* The *Vedas* (religious literature produced between 1200–500 BCE. The important *Vedas* are *Rig, Yajur, Atharva* and *Sama Veda*) laid down certain rules for conducting *dharmayuddha.* The argument is that a *dharma raja* (a righteous king), whose duty is to uphold virtue, justice and truth, should always implement fair play and conduct *dharmayuddha,* even for defending his territory. The *dharmashastras* are idealistic: for example, the date and place of battle must be decided beforehand by the parties involved. *Dharmayuddha* also rejects night attack, and assaults on the wounded soldiers and soldiers engaged in praying. Enemy warriors whose stocks of weapons had been finished were not to be attacked, and the use of poisoned and barbed arrows was not sanctioned. The *Puranashastras* mention that war should not be waged with deceitful machines. In general, the theory of warfare propounded by the *Vedas* provided no place for treachery and clandestine operations: the emphasis was on clear-cut battles fought by the *Kshatriyas* (warrior caste).

The *Bhagavad Gita,* a prime example of Vedic literature, was composed around 500 BCE. Most interpreters argue that it merely uses the imagery of war to portray the struggle between good and evil within one's own soul. The *Bhagavad Gita* is presented as a collection of *slokas* (hymns in poetic forms) by anonymous sages put into the mouth of Lord Krishna, who was acting as the driver of Arjuna's chariot during the battle between the Kurus and the Pandavas described in *Mahabharata.* The philosophy enunciated in *Bhagavad Gita* is somewhat fatalistic. The *karma* theory asserts that regardless of consequences, one must go on doing one's duty as ordained in the *shastras.* The death of the warriors is accepted as natural, and the profession of killing is legitimized.

Heroic warfare (*dvandvayuddha*) is best exemplified in the combat between Arjuna and Karna, one of the *senapatis* (commander in chiefs) of Duryodhana (cousin of Arjuna and chief of the confederacy that was opposing the Pandavas; the principal warrior on Pandava side was Arjuna). The *Bhagavad Gita* describes combat in the Mahabharata War: in the morning, the battle started with the blowing of conch shells. The principal heroes (all *Kshatriyas*) of both sides advance toward each other by chariot and shoot arrows at their opponents. With sunset, all hostilities cease till the next morning.

Kautilya, in *Arthashastra,* rejected the ideology of just war as propounded in the Vedic literature, and enunciated the concept of *kutayuddha. Dvaidhibhava* (duplicity) constitutes the core of *kutayuddha:* self-interest and self-aggrandizement motivates this sort of warfare. Kautilya claims that each state only considers its own interests as supreme and in their defense often resorts to apparently unethical actions. Kautilya is extremely pragmatic, and attacks the normative model prescribed by the theorists of *dharmayuddha.*

Bhedniti (divide and rule policy) is one of the mechanisms for conducting *kutayuddha.* If necessary for the survival of the state, the ruler should enter into a treaty even with his natural enemy, so that the enemy may be outwitted latter. Such a short term, self-interested diplomatic alliance is known as *karmasandhi.* The king should pursue *sandhi* (alliance/treaty/cease-fire/truce) with one king and *vigraha* (war) with another king simultaneously. Between *sandhi* and *vigraha,* there is another option, *asana* (the policy of waiting in expectation that the enemy would grow weak or might be involved in war with others). When the enemy is weak, the king should attack him. When the king is stronger than his enemy, the king should negotiate from a position of strength and force upon the latter a disadvantageous treaty. The objective in the long run, says Kautilya, is to grow stronger than the enemy.

To cope with external threats, *Arthashastra* prescribes direct and indirect warfare. Every possible unorthodox technique ought to be followed to confuse and tire the enemy. Instead of a battle, it is better to ambush the enemy force at a propitious moment. But, at times when battles become necessary, unorthodox techniques must be pursued. The basic objective is not the pursuit of honor and glory but to take full advantage of the enemy's vulnerabilities.

As far as battle tactics of *kutayuddha* is concerned, Kautilya says that the main force should be directed against the weak and unreliable portions of the enemy's army. Frontal attacks are rejected. A tactical retreat should be conducted to bring the enemy in an unfavorable terrain and then a counterattack should be launched. Nocturnal attack is another favorite tactic. The enemy's force should be kept awake by night forays and then attacked during the day when they are drowsy. In the field of battle, a double should impersonate the king to confuse the enemy's sharpshooters. In the battlefield, says Kautilya, special forces should be used to spread false news, kill enemy leaders, and attack the rear and baggage of the enemy.

Arthashastra says that, instead of a siege operation, psychological warfare should be waged against the besieged enemy. *Kutayuddha* includes covert operations for taking enemy strong points. The idea is to infiltrate "commando" units inside enemy's fortifications with the aid of double agents. Such infiltration compared to frontal attacks (direct warfare) lowers the risk and cost in terms of men and material. This can be done either by tricking the enemy into opening the gates or by gradually building up a clandestine armed unit inside the fort. Alternatively, the conqueror may make peace with the enemy and lull him into a false sense of security. Infiltration into the enemy's fort may be facilitated using escorts of trading caravans, bridal parties, horse traders, equipment sellers, grain merchants, disguised monks, or envoys. The enemy's supplies may also be poisoned.

A weak state fighting a strong state is particularly advised to engage in indirect warfare involving "unjust" techniques—a form of irregular warfare. Methods include inciting troubles within the domains of the enemy state by bribing enemy officials, initiating intrigues, kidnapping relatives of the enemy rulers, and hiring assassins. For eliminating rebel warlords, *Arthashastra* authorizes the use of prostitutes and assassins. Kautilya takes a new step in advocating the use of young and beautiful women as secret agents and contract killers. Secret agents can also gain the confidence of the *sunyapala* (regent or governor in the enemy king's territory) and spread misinformation about conspiracies by the regent among the enemy soldiers. Disinformation may be spread among invading troops. Special forces should be send into the enemy territory to carry out political murders and terrorize the civilians.

Forty years after Kautilya's death, in the third century BCE, the concept of just war made a strong comeback under Emperor Asoka. *Ahimsa* (the doctrine of nonviolence in thought, speech and action) assumed importance in Buddhist and Jain literature.

The Jain work *Nandisutra* says that *Arthashastra* belongs to the tradition of *mithyasutras* (false doctrine). Buddhism emphasizes that no injury should be inflicted on either human beings or animals. Further, it ordains that rigid morality should be observed not only in personal life but also in national life. According to Buddhism, it is possible to exercise good governance without hurting others and without conquest. The *dharmika dharmaraja* (lord of righteousness) is encouraged to lay aside his sword and to rule through righteousness. Asoka accepted Buddhism and raised *ahimsa* and pacifism from acts of personal virtue to state policy. Under Asoka, the concept of *digvijaya* (conquest of the known world by sword) was replaced by the idea of *dhammavijaya* (conquest by spiritual force of nonviolence).

These ideas were taken up by other thinkers, for example, Bhartrihari, who lived in the first century CE. His Sanskrit work, *Atha Nitishatakam* (literal meaning *On Polity and Human Behavior in a Civilized Society emphasizing Prudence and Wisdom*) throws light on polity and human behavior both in the private and public spheres. Bhartrihari emphasizes that those who tread not the path of *dharma,* are a burden on this mortal world. Armed forces occupy a secondary position in Bhartrihari's scheme. Bhartrihari advocates *dharmayuddha* and he believes in the *karma* theory. He claims that it is the duty of warriors to fight bravely, but that a warrior ought to be *yudhi vikramah* (chivalrous). He asserts that, just as the sun illuminates the whole world with its powerful rays, a warrior by dint of his valor can conquer the enemies. The *Atha Nitishatakam* continues that truthful and glorious men consider it better to lay down their lives than to renege on their promises and surrender their ideals. Good conduct and unblemished moral character are required from both the warriors and the kings.

The debate regarding just and unjust war was, however, not concluded. The *Panchatantra,* a collection of didactic fables came into existence around 500 CE under the direction of Vishnusarma. The *Panchatantra* accepts that warfare is inevitable and says that friendship can only occur among equals. Inequality in power between the various polities results in warfare. To an extent, it ordains *kutayuddha,* arguing that a soldier who goes to battle does not think about right and wrong. The general message is that the remnants of an enemy, such as debt, may grow again if allowed to unite. Therefore, an enemy should be utterly obliterated. However, the message of *Panchatantra* remained marginal and the ritualistic combat propagated by Manu and Kamandaka in the post-Kautilyan era held sway.

Ethnic and racial ties circumscribed the worldview of the intellectuals propagating *dharmayuddha.* They were almost exclusively interested in *Aryavarta* (the land of the Aryans). Beyond the orbit of *Aryavarta* was *Mlechchhadesa,* the land of the non-Aryans, who were categorized as barbarians. The limits of *Aryavarta* were the Himalayas and Sind. The doctrine of *dharmayuddha* criticized efforts to engage states outside *Aryavarta,* even for ensuring external security, although the Mauryan rulers certainly had the power to interfere beyond the border of India in an aggressive manner. This strategic myopia caused trouble for the Hindu kings from eighth century CE onward, when the Arabs and the Turks invaded India from Sind and Afghanistan. In the ninth century CE, Sukra (also known as Sukracharya, the author of *Sukranitisara* written around ninth century CE) realized that *dharmayuddha* had become obsolete in the face of Islamic steppe nomads poised to invade India. It was already too late.

Application: Abu Zaid, an Arab who lived in ninth century CE, wrote in *Geography of the East* that the Indian kings' objective of war was limited. They did not aim at permanent annexation or restructuring of the enemy's administration, but merely to replace the existing ruler with another from the same clan, preferably a family member of the fallen prince, who was to carry on the government in the name of the conqueror. Victories in war brought no radical new policies but merely regime change. Because the goal of war was restricted, the effects of war were also limited. Systematic depredations were not carried out against the conquered people. Such ritualistic and limited warfare did not require the maintenance of trained standing armies.

The armies of the Indian rulers, operating within the rules of *dharmayuddha,* were at a disadvantage in relation to the Eurasian steppe nomads. Chivalry had unforeseen consequences, in that it encouraged personal vanity even at the cost of policy and expediency. Hindu warriors carried some just war maxims, such as to spare a prostrate foe, to excess. *Dharmayuddha* maxims from early Vedic India (e.g., the practice whereby defeated enemy soldiers were not executed but were abused and then released) preempted the laws of chivalry enunciated in the Rajput code of warfare after 800 CE. The influx of chivalric ideas partially caused Rajput battles to degenerate into hand-to-hand combats. Bardic literature fostered the growth of chivalrous code of conduct, and the ideal of chivalry, an essential ingredient of *ksatra-dharma,* attained its full bloom in the early medieval era. Eventually, the elephant-centric armies and positional warfare centered on forts, a major facet of the just war propounded by Hindu theoreticians, collapsed in the face of maneuver warfare, backed by the dogma of *jihad,* waged by the mounted followers of Muhammad. For example, when Muhammad Ghori invaded north India, Prithviraj Chauhan, the leader of the Rajput Confederacy, defeated him at the Battle of Tarain in 1191 CE. For both cultural and practical reasons, the defeated Muslim army was not pursued and annihilated by the victorious Rajputs: first, in accordance with the creed of *dharmayuddha,* a defeated enemy ought to be provided a safe passage; second, the country-bred ponies of the Rajputs could not match the steppe horses of Ghori's army in speed and endurance. Ghori escaped, reorganized his army and returned India the next year to defeat Prithviraj's forces at the second battle of Tarain.

Descendents: In the early 20th century, Jawaharlal Nehru and Mahatma Gandhi drew upon Asoka's policy of pacifism. Nehru portrayed himself as a just warrior. He was much influenced by Asoka's ideal of winning peace to avoid war, and in 1949, proclaimed a fully defensive strategy. Nehru's peace-loving posture was partly shaped by economic reality: he admitted that India's military weakness was shaped by economic backwardness. To balance military weakness, Nehru used diplomacy. In 1952, he revealed his nonalignment policy: that is, nonalignment with the power blocs of the Cold War era and an attempt to maintain friendly relations with all countries. This was antithetical to the *bhedniti* (divide and rule) principle of *kutayuddha.*

By contrast, Jaswant Singh, foreign minister of the Bharatiya Janata Party (BJP), a right-wing Hindu party that remained in power in India until mid-2005, implemented *bhedniti* by trying to win friendship of post-Taliban Afghanistan. He hoped to establish *bheda* (division) between Kabul and Islamabad. The BJP's defense minister also initiated a program in the ministry of defense for analyzing the techniques of *kutayuddha* derived from *Arthashastra*.

See also: Bana; Indian Use of Chariots; Kamandaka; Kautilya; Manu

Further Reading

Sarkar, Jadunath, *Military History of India.* 3rd ed. New Delhi: Orient Longmans, 1970.

Sinha, Manoj Kumar, "Hinduism and International Humanitarian Law." *International Review of the Red Cross,* 87 (2005): 285–94.

Yadava, B.N.S., "Chivalry and Warfare." In Jos J.L. Gommans and Dirk H.A. Kolff, eds. *Warfare and Weaponry in South Asia: 1000–1800.* New Delhi: Oxford University Press, 2001, pp. 66–98.

Kaushik Roy

Incan Approaches to War
(1438–1532)

Significance: The Inca forged the largest empire of the Americas between 1438 and 1532. Their domain extended from present-day Ecuador to central Chile, some 4,000 kilometers from north to south. Covering an estimated three million square kilometers, the empire encompassed complex environments, ranging from desert coastlines to Andean highlands and valleys, to tropical rainforests. Military and political control over this range of ecologies allowed the Inca to dominate an estimated 12–32 million subjects.

Context: The word "Inca" refers to the hereditary ruler of the city of Cuzco, and by extension that city's ruling class. They referred to this domain as *Tawantinsuyu,* or the "four corners of the world." Greater Cuzco, sitting in the Andes at an elevation of 3,450 meters, had an estimated population of 100,000–150,000. This included the Inca royalty, an extensive bureaucracy, and also retainers, artisans, and laborers. Three successive rulers made victorious military incursions from Cuzco to subdue distant peoples.

Description: The primary goal of Inca expansionism was the acquisition of outlying lands, resources, and labor. As the empire matured, acquisition turned into consolidation. Insurrections and unstable frontiers became persistent problems. The empire's extraordinary expansion was probably due, in part, to the custom of mummifying each deceased ruler and dedicating his subject lands and tributes to his cult. The following ruler, therefore, arrived empty handed, and was required to conquer new lands to finance his government.

The keys to rapid Inca military success lay in efficient organization and military infrastructure. The army was manned by peasants conscripted as warriors when needed. There was no standing army. Because the empire was composed of numerous ethnic and language groups (as many as 160), these warriors were grouped under their own lords. They were massed in units of 10; 100; 1,000; and 10,000. Some accounts claim that the Incas could field armies of more than 100,000 for a single campaign. There were a few military specialists: high-ranking officers and the ruler's highly trained personal guard.

The armies used an elaborate military infrastructure. An estimated 40,000 kilometers of well-maintained, primarily military roads traversed the Inca domain. Transport utilized human porters and llama pack trains. Bridges compensated for the rugged terrain, and warehouses stored provisions for armies on the march. Way stations were established every two kilometers and housed runners who could carry messages, relay style, as quickly as 300 kilometers in 24 hours. Massive fortifications protected Cuzco, as well as frontier borderlands.

High-ranking officers went to battle arrayed in colorful and distinctive military adornments. Inca weapons consisted of spears, slings, bows, bronze maces, and wooden clubs. They wore armor of quilted cloth and metal plates, and cane helmets. Notably absent from their arsenal were the wheel and the extensive use of metal weapons. Llamas could carry only light loads and would frequently balk.

Politics and religion were closely intertwined, and each military victory was celebrated with royal feasting and ceremonies. Defeated enemies, particularly important ones, were humiliated and sometimes sacrificed. Courageous warriors were presented with status-laden gifts and privileges. Conquered regions were obligated to serve the Inca with labor drafts and military service.

Application: Thupa Inka Yupanki (r. 1471–1493 CE) was the most aggressive of the three Inca imperial rulers. His unrelenting conquests have earned him the sobriquet "Alexander the Great of South America." He was decisive and personally led numerous difficult campaigns. He is also credited with establishing the regional storehouses and creating the way station–messenger system.

Legacy: The great weakness of Inca rulership became obvious just as Francisco Pizarro arrived in South America: the rules of hereditary succession were uncertain. A bloody, five-year war erupted between two royal brothers claiming the Inca throne. Pizarro took advantage of a weakened rulership, imprisoning and executing the victor Atawallpa. The Spaniards placed puppet Inca rulers on the Cuzco throne while facing violent resistance and insurrections throughout the Inca Empire. These were suppressed, and the last Inca ruler was executed by the Spaniards in 1572.

Further Reading
D'Altroy, Terence N., *The Incas.* Oxford: Blackwell Publishing, 2003.
Kaufmann, H.W. and J.E. Kaufmann, *Fortifications of the Incas 1200–1531.* Oxford: Osprey Publishing. 2006.

Frances F. Berdan

Indian Use of Chariots
(1500 BCE–170 BCE)

Significance: The *rathas* (chariots) allowed the Aryans to defeat the Dravidians in India. The chariot was queen of the battlefield in the Vedic age (1500 BCE–500 BCE), and was the monopoly of the warriors belonging to the noble classes.

Context: Archaeological excavations and ancient Hindu literature throw light on the use of *rathas* in ancient Indian warfare. Both China and north India gained chariot technology through Central Asia. From the Ganga Valley, the use of war chariots reached south India.

Description: During the Early Vedic age (ca. 1500 BCE) the warrior was also the charioteer. By 500 BCE, the function of the driver, who drove the horses with whips and reins, was differentiated from that of the warrior. The Indian armies during the Vedic age were composed of *pattis* (foot soldiers) and *rathins* (chariot warriors) and during battle, infantry supported the chariots. The chariots offered three advantages over the foot soldiers. First the warrior in his chariot carried more weapons than a foot soldier. Second, the chariot warrior, being on an elevated position, enjoyed physical and psychological advantages over the *pattis*. Third, the warrior riding his chariot arrived in the battlefield relatively free from fatigue—unlike the marching *pattis*. The Indians fought from the chariots with bows and arrows, and chariots also functioned as command vehicles. The *Agni Purana* (Brahmanical religious literature composed after 500 BCE) says that the chariot of the commander had a pole to which a banner was attached, and which acted as a rallying point. The chariot was made of wood and each wheel had about four to eight spokes. Around 400 BCE, most chariots had two wheels and were drawn by two horses. Over time, the chariots became bigger with four wheels.

Application: Besides mythological sources, we have little historical data to show successful use of chariots in actual battles. Problems are, however, highlighted in Greek sources. For example, at the Battle of Jhelum in June 326 BCE, Paurava deployed 300 heavy chariots. Each such chariot was drawn by four horses and carried six men, of whom two carried shields to protect the two archers. Two were drivers who, when not driving the chariots, also threw missiles at the enemy. Heavy rainfall occurred in the day before the battle. On the next day, the chariots got stuck in the mud. When the drivers whipped the horses to pull the vehicles out of the quagmire, many chariots overturned. These chariots proved useless against the Greek phalanx.

Descendents: The Mauryans used chariots against the second-class powers of south India. The last use of *rathas* was by the conqueror Kharavela of Orissa in 170 BCE. By this time, elephants were displacing chariots as the dominant weapon system in the Hindu armies.

See also: Bana; Kamandaka; Use of Elephants in Indian Warfare

Further Reading
Chakravarti, P.C., *The Art of War in Ancient India,* 1941, reprint, Delhi: Low Price Publications.

Kaushik Roy

Indigenous Southern African Military Cultures

Significance: During the 19th century, southern Africa witnessed wide-ranging military adaptations by its African peoples that were partly in response to long-term European colonial settlement on a scale unique to sub-Saharan Africa, but that also accompanied state formation by indigenous peoples. Those indigenous societies most receptive to the adoption of firearms, horses, and associated military innovations were those already in the habit of defensive tactics against raiding African neighbors. The latter, secure in their aggressive military systems, responded less effectively to European invasion.

Context: Much of southern Africa is open grassland, suitable for grazing, and horsesickness is relatively confined. Yet horses had not survived the prehistoric, southward-bound migrations of the Bantu-speaking peoples through the equatorial forests. So warfare in the region was entirely a matter for infantry, until the horse was introduced in the mid-17th century by the Dutch settlers at the Cape. The combination of firearms, cavalry, and on occasion defensive *laagers* (formations of wagons used as mobile fortifications, reminiscent of the Hussite *wagenburg*) posed a significant threat to indigenous cultures, which adapted in diverse ways. In the early decades of the 19th century a number of centralized states emerged in southern Africa out of a period of considerable tumult, its precise causes still a matter for unresolved historical debate. Some of these kingdoms were of Nguni-speaking people, and the military systems of the Zulu, their northern neighbors the Swazi, and the Ndebele (who split off from the Zulu and migrated north into what is now Zimbabwe) were all intimately bound up with the very structure of their new states.

Approaches and Application: The Zulu king, Shaka kaSenzangakhona (ca. 1787–1828), was long credited with initiating the revolutionary changes associated with these militaristic states. Historians now view them more as the accelerated culmination of long evolving developments in the chiefdoms that would later constitute the Zulu kingdom. Warriors had usually been raised by regional chiefs and, when called out by the paramount chief, had fought in local contingents under their own chiefs. By the early 19th century, they were instead placed in the sole service of the monarch (*inkosi* in Zulu) who thus took control of the kingdom's manpower. Young men of the same age cohort from across the entire kingdom were banded together into regiments (*amabutho*) and stationed for part of the year in royal barracks (*amakhanda*) strategically situated around the kingdom to assert the king's authority. These regiments collected tribute, herded the royal cattle, and fought as the king's soldiers in time of war. When not thus directly serving the king, the warriors went home and pursued their own economic and domestic tasks.

Other regional powers were not as centralized. The Nguni-speaking Xhosa, Mpondo, and Thembu living along the coast to the south of the Zulu, were not organized into kingdoms, but consisted of clusters of chiefdoms acknowledging the loose authority of a number of paramount chiefs. In war, each local chief commanded his own following, which depended for its size on his prestige as a leader.

The Sotho- and Tswana-speaking chiefdoms of the interior had also been severely dislocated in the early 19th century, and a number of powerful groupings, such as the southern Sotho and Pedi kingdoms, emerged from the chaos. Unlike the Zulu and associated polities, these were more conglomerates of allied chiefdoms than tightly controlled kingdoms. In them, the regimental system did not become the central agent of state power. Although youths were banded together into regiments based on their initiation sets (the brutal initiation rites trained them in courage and endurance), they were not placed at the king's direct command, but were mobilized in the service of their local chiefs. In turn, chiefs who gave their allegiance to a ruler were expected to supply contingents from these regiments to support him in time of war.

If age-grade units were fundamental to military organization in all these societies, so was the ritual associated with war. Before going on campaign, warriors required purification and strengthening by symbolic medicines administered by war doctors. These rituals, and amulets worn on campaign, protected them from the mystical pollution of homicide, secured supernatural ascendancy over their enemies, and rendered them safe from their weapons. Success in a warlike enterprise also depended on the favor of the spirits of the ancestors, and these had to be placated with generous sacrifices of cattle. After combat the ritually contaminated warriors had once again to be purified and protected against the vengeful spirits of the slain before they could reenter normal society. Culturally, the observance of these rituals was essential, but they inevitably delayed or disrupted the conduct of campaigns.

In these societies where every man was a part-time warrior, courtesy, virility, and personal prowess in battle were all highly regarded and cowardice deeply despised. The heroic ethos was reflected in elaborate military costume, in athletic dance, and in praise-singing, which exalted courage, ferocity, and unbending courage. Among the Zulu and Ndebele, the emphasis was on hand-to-hand combat on foot, using the stabbing spear and large cow-hide shield. The classic maneuver was to envelop the enemy with two rapidly deploying "horns" while the "chest" closed in for the kill. Such tactics bred contempt among the Zulu for the Swazi, who avoided the open field and took refuge in their mountain fastnesses. The Zulu also disparaged foes who preferred missiles, even when, like the Xhosa, they could cast their long-shafted spears with enviable skill and accuracy up to 50 yards. Thus the Zulu and Ndebele never regarded firearms as anything but secondary weapons: they even feared that their adoption would change their tried methods of warfare, upset the nature of their military system and, by extension, undermine the very political, social, and economic structure of their kingdoms.

Other societies embraced change more readily. The Tswana chiefdoms of the interior obtained firearms from traders and missionaries and initially used them defensively to beat off raids by traditional foes such as the Ndeble. Later, when threatened by colonial rule, they retreated to their fastnesses in the Langeberg Mountains and in 1896–1897 employed firearms effectively against the Cape forces. The Xhosa fought nine Frontier Wars between 1779 and 1878 with the European colonists of the Cape eastern frontier, British troops, and allied indigenous peoples. As Xhosa land was progressively seized and their society threatened, Xhosa resistance became ever more bitter. They laid aside their hide shields, replaced throwing spears with firearms by the 1830s, and abandoned their traditional Zulu-like tactic of encircling the enemy on the open battlefield. Instead, they adopted guerrilla warfare, ambushing the enemy from their strongholds deep in the mountains and bushy river valleys. They were finally defeated only through ruthless scorched earth tactics and deprivation.

In the mid-19th century, the southern Sotho in their mountainous kingdom began adapting their existing military system to deter raids for slaves and cattle by mounted gunmen from the northern Cape Colony, and to fight off Boer settlers of the Orange Free State encroaching on their agricultural lands. They gradually adopted their enemies' guns and horses, though until the 1870s they neither possessed modern firearms in sufficient quantities nor had mastered handling them well enough to abandon their traditional battleaxes and long spears (although they jettisoned their distinctive winged shields designed to deflect thrown spears). Instead of large, traditional regiments, firearms, and mountain warfare required a decentralized pattern of mobile, mounted bands (similar to the mounted infantry of the Boer commandos and the Griqua) that excelled at firing from cover, laying ambushes, skirmishing, raiding, and defending their rocky strongholds. Dress became increasingly Europeanized, with high-crowned straw hats in imitation of Boer headgear. Sotho military innovations ultimately proved successful, and in the long series of wars between 1858 and 1881, first against the Boers and then the British, earlier failures were reversed, and the Sotho secured effective independence for a diminished kingdom.

The Pedi, living in the mountains that bounded the northeastern Transvaal settled by the Boers, had originally organized and armed their forces much like the Sotho to the south. They too changed their military culture as whites impinged on their lands. The prevalence of horsesickness in their territory prevented them from embracing mounted warfare as had the southern Sotho. However, by the 1860s they had been drawn into the migrant labor system of neighboring white-ruled territories where, like the southern Sotho, they used their wages to obtain firearms. Like the Xhosa, Tswana, Shona, and other African societies the Pedi struggled to secure firearms that were not obsolete, to obtain ammunition and the means to maintain their weapons, but professional hunters among them who had been trained in the service of Europeans helped change their outlook and firearms came increasingly to dominate their military thinking. When the Pedi went to war with the Transvaal in 1876 they resolutely defended their strongholds on the rocky hills, fortified with stone breastworks and rifle pits, until defeated in 1879 by British troops and Swazi auxiliaries.

North across the Limpopo River, the Shona, who were raided annually by the Ndebele, responded by falling back to the security of their stockaded caves and rocky hilltop fortresses and abandoning their traditional bows and arrows for traded firearms. They consequently became adept at defensive warfare, and in the 1896–1897 rising severely tested the forces of the British South Africa Company.

By contrast, the Zulu and the Ndebele were essentially raiding states that were wedded to offensive warfare, preferably in their enemy's territory, and had no tradition of guerrilla or defensive warfare. When invaded by Europeans neither proved flexible enough to adapt their habitual way of war to new challenges and they were comprehensively defeated. The Zulu were vanquished by the Boers in 1838 and again by the British in 1879 when their mass attacks broke against all-round defenses and volley fire, followed up by mounted pursuit. The British completed their victory by fragmenting the Zulu kingdom and dismantling the military system upon which it was built. The Ndebele likewise, deceptively secure behind the depopulated zone they had created between themselves and their enemies, remained confident in their traditional weapons and offensive tactics. In the 1880s they began to secure firearms, but it was too late to modify their customary way of war. In 1893, the Pioneer Column, armed with modern rifles, Maxim guns, and some field guns, and secure in their laagers, repulsed all Ndebele assaults.

Descendents: In none of the cases mentioned above was military modernization a guaranteed means by which the African states of southeastern Africa could maintain their independence from colonial conquest, but the more complete the change of military culture, the greater was the chance was of doing so.

Further Reading

Etherington, Norman. *The Great Treks. The Transformation of Southern Africa, 1815–1854*. London: Longman, 2001.

Maylam, Paul. *A history of the African People of South Africa: From the Early Iron Age to the 1970s*. London: Croom Helm, 1986.

Wilson, Monica, and Leonard Thompson, eds. *The Oxford History of South Africa*. 2 vols. Oxford: Oxford University Press, 1969.

John Laband

Just War Theory (Western)

(ca. 600 BCE–1800 CE)

Significance: The idea that war can and should be just is a middle position between realism (the refusal to impose any moral restraints on the waging of war) and pacifism (the rejection of all warfare as immoral).

Context: The theory of the just war emerged gradually in the Western world from the confluence of Greek philosophy, Roman law, and the Hebrew–Christian scriptural tradition.

Description: The principles of just war theory in its mature form fall into two main categories. The first category is *ius ad bellum,* or justice in declaring war, and the second is *ius in bello,* or justice in the conduct of war. Although just war theory has evolved over time and significant differences exist among the many thinkers in the just war tradition, one may roughly summarize the theory's principles as follows: for the decision to go to war to be just (*ius ad bellum*), (1) it must be made by a lawful authority (e.g., a duly constituted national government); (2) it must be a response to a grave injustice committed by the enemy (e.g., an unprovoked attack or seizure of territory); (3) peaceful means of resolving the dispute (e.g., arbitration) are unlikely to work or have been tried and failed; (4) the rectification of the injustice must be important enough to justify the damage likely to ensue from the war (e.g., one ought not to go to war if one is unlikely to win, or if the retaking of captured territory will lead to the devastation of an even larger area); and (5) the intention in waging war must be morally upright (e.g., imperialistic ambition or the lust for vengeance must not be motives). For the actual waging of the war to be just (*ius in bello*), (6) no more force than necessary may be used to achieve the just objectives of the war, and (7) noncombatants must not be targeted directly.

Application: The history of just war theory may be divided up into four eras: (1) ancient Greco-Roman (fifth to first centuries BCE); (2) patristic and medieval (2nd to 14th centuries CE); (3) early modern (15th to 17th centuries); and (4) modern (18th century on). The following survey will cover the first three of these periods.

Greco-Roman Period

A consistent theme in the thought of Socrates (470–399 BCE) and his student, Plato (427–347 BCE), is that moral virtues such as justice must govern all human acts. Socrates and Plato alike maintain that death is preferable to unjust action. Thus Socrates and Plato emphatically reject the cynical realism about war that Thucydides (ca. 460–400 BCE) attributes to the Athenians in his history of the Peloponnesian War. Plato's student, Aristotle (384–322 BCE), shared his teacher's conviction that war-making should be subordinated to, and guided by, the demands of justice, a conviction that led Aristotle to criticize the militaristic culture of the Spartans. A second key belief shared by Socrates, Plato, and Aristotle is that natural human reason can discover an objective moral order against which human laws and customs must be measured.

The ancient Romans, too, developed a tradition of applying standards of justice to the waging of war. The Romans considered a war to be just when carried out in strict adherence to legal and religious norms, especially the *ius fetiale* or fetial law, whereby a special college of priests (the *fetiales*) had responsibility for ensuring that the Romans did not enter into an unjust war with any city in alliance with them. Roman law required that war be a response to a grave injustice and that peaceful means of resolving the dispute be tried first.

Among Roman thinkers, Cicero (106–43 BCE) stands out for his contributions to reflection on the ethics of war. Influenced both by Roman law and by Greek philosophy, Cicero argues that war must be a response to a grave wrong; it must be preceded by a formal declaration; it must be declared only after reasonable demands for redress have gone unheeded. Cicero is also notable for his insistence that there is a law of nature, knowable by all human beings and rooted in our common human nature, that obliges us to consider the interests of all human beings, simply because they are human beings.

Patristic and Medieval Period

While developing its own ethic based on the Gospel, Christianity was also eager to appropriate what it could from Greek philosophy and Roman law. From the death of Jesus (ca. 30 CE) until the conversion of Constantine (312 CE), Christians were persecuted outsiders, often skeptical about military service and leaning toward a moderate pacifism (see, e.g., Tertullian, ca. 160–220, and Origen, ca. 185–254), but generally not embracing absolute pacifism. After the conversion of Constantine, mainstream Christian thought shifted decisively in favor of the idea that war can be just. Ambrose of Milan (ca. 340–397), heavily influenced by Cicero, argued that war could be justified in self-defense or as punishment for wrongdoing. Augustine of Hippo (354–430) endorsed the same position and formulated what became for centuries the standard trio of just-war principles: wars are just only if they are declared by a competent authority, for a just cause, and with an upright intention. Augustine also affirms the existence of an eternal law of nature against which human laws are to be measured. Finally, Augustine set a fateful precedent when he endorsed the view that the police powers of the state should be used to punish Donatist heretics and compel their return to orthodoxy. Augustine would become the most influential theologian in the Western (Latin) church, quoted extensively as an authority by future generations of theologians and canon lawyers.

Later medieval and early modern theologians worked within the Augustinian framework, but that framework allowed much room for further development. By the 13th century, for example, as seen in thinkers such as Raymond of Penafort, William of Rennes, and St. Thomas Aquinas, the principle of proportionality had become a standard aspect of the just war: no more violence than necessary should be used to achieve the just aims of war. Pope Innocent IV (1180–1254), one of the foremost canon lawyers of his time, established an important precedent by arguing that mere difference of religion is not a just cause for war, since by natural law unbelievers have a right to dominion and sovereignty. Innocent argued for the justice of the crusades on the grounds that occupation of the Holy Land by the Saracens was illegal and the Saracens were persecuting Christians. However, like Augustine, he insisted that unbelievers may not be converted to Christianity by force, since faith must stem from free choice.

Early Modern Period

The Italian Dominican theologian and cardinal, Thomas de Vio Cajetan (1468–1534), introduced what would become a common distinction in just war discussions, namely, between defensive and offensive war. Defensive war is an immediate response to a violent attack, and by natural law all people have a right to such self-defense. Offensive war is the attempt to impose punitive justice across international frontiers; not being a matter of urgent necessity, offensive war must meet a higher standard to be justified.

The Spanish Dominican theologian, Francisco de Vitoria (1492–1546), wrote and lectured on war between nations in the context of Spain's conquest of the Americas. Often called "the father of international law," Vitoria followed Pope Innocent IV in arguing that by natural law, non-Christians have a right to sovereignty over their own lands, so that mere religious difference cannot be just cause for war. War against native Americans could only be justified if the natives violated the natural rights of Spaniards, for example, rights to trade, safe passage, or missionary activity, and even then war must be a last resort and directed only at the guilty, not the innocent. (In fact, Vitoria took a very dim view of the military campaigns of the *conquistadors*.) One of Vitoria's achievements was to highlight the logical connection between the principles of just cause and noncombatant immunity: war is justly waged only to stop attacks or punish injuries, so we may not use the sword against those who have done us no harm; to kill the innocent is prohibited by the natural law.

Two Spanish Jesuits, Luis de Molina (1535–1600) and Francisco Suarez (1548–1617), made contributions to just war thinking both as original thinkers and as systematizers. Molina questioned the view of war as punishment, for the wrongdoers who provoke war may be "invincibly ignorant" that they are doing wrong and hence not culpable (that is, they be "materially" but not "formally" guilty of wrongdoing). Suarez accepted Cajetan's distinction between defensive and offensive war and argued that the latter is only justified if it has an overwhelming probability of success. He also upheld a right of rebellion by subjects against tyrants (as had medieval thinkers such as John of Salisbury and Thomas Aquinas). He insisted on the value of arbitration as an alternative to war. He also argued at some length that religious differences are not a just basis for war and that Christian and non-Christian rulers alike must base the decision to wage war on the natural law.

The Protestant reformation had no significant impact on the just war tradition. Though some radical reformers adopted pacifism, the mainstream reformers Luther and Calvin opted instead for the just war position. Indeed, some of the most significant contributions to just war discourse would be made by Protestants such as Hugo Grotius (1583–1645), Samuel von Pufendorf (1632–1694), and John Locke (1632–1704). Protestants, like Catholics, embraced the idea of natural law and scripture as complementary bases of ethics. Thus, Locke's key assertions— that there is a law of nature; that reason teaches that law to all human beings; that natural law commands the preservation of human life but allows self-defense against unjust attacks; and that natural law permits punishment of wrongdoers and rebellion against tyrants—can all be found in the Catholic natural law thinkers of the medieval and early modern periods.

Descendents: Western thought on just war may be compared with traditions in other great civilizations (cf. "See also" and "Further Reading" sections below). (*Note: major thinkers on just war post-dating 1800 have been given their own entries.*)

See also: Clausewitz, C; Dunant, J.; Fanon; Gandhi, M.; Hindu Tradition of Just and Unjust War; Jomini; Kant; Kautilya; Lieber, F.; Marx, K.; Muhammad; Al-Shaybani; Sun Tzu; Usama Ibn Munqidh

Further Reading

Aquinas, St. Thomas, *On Law, Morality, and Politics.* William P. Baumgarth and Richard J. Regan, S. J., editors. Indianapolis/Cambridge: Hackett Publishing Co., 1988.

Grotius, Hugo, *The Rights of War and Peace.* Richard Tuck, editor. Indianapolis: Liberty Fund, 2005.

Locke, John, *Second Treatise of Government.* C. B. Macpherson, editor. Indianapolis/Cambridge: Hackett Publishing Co., 1980.

Panzer, Joel S., *The Popes and Slavery.* New York: Alba House, 1996.

Ramsey, Paul, *War and the Christian Conscience.* Durham, NC: Duke University Press, 1961.

Reichberg, Gregory M., Henrik Syse, and Endre Begby, editors, *The Ethics of War: Classic and Contemporary Readings.* Oxford: Blackwell Publishing, 2006.

Russell, Frederick H., *The Just War in the Middle Ages*. Cambridge: Cambridge University Press, 1975.

Suarez, Francisco, *Selections from Three Works of Francisco Suarez, SJ*. Gwladys L. Williams, translator. *The Classics of International Law*, Vol. II. Oxford: The Clarendon Press, 1944.

Vitoria, Francisco de, *Political Writings*. Anthony Pagden and Jeremy Lawrence, editors. Cambridge: Cambridge University Press, 1991.

Joseph S. Spoerl

Mesoamerican Cultures of War
(1200 BCE–1521 CE)

Significance: Mesoamerica encompasses the area roughly extending from northern Mexico to northern Honduras and El Salvador. From approximately 1200 BCE until 1521 CE, this region supported several sophisticated civilizations. Although evidence for warfare can be detected as early as 1200 BCE with the Olmecs, this essay will focus on the best documented Mesoamerican civilizations: the Classic Maya (250–900 CE) and the Aztec Empire (1428–1521 CE), among whom warfare was a conspicuous activity.

Context: The political building blocks of both the Classic Maya and the Aztecs were numerous, relatively small city-states. Each city-state was characterized by its own dynastic leadership, founding legend, territory, and patron deity. Tropical forest Maya states rarely (and only briefly) expanded into larger conquest states. The Aztecs (or Mexica) came to dominate a variety of ecological zones throughout central and southern Mexico during only 91 years of military expansion, creating the largest empire in Mesoamerican prehistory.

Intensive cultivation of maize, beans, squashes, and chilies provided these groups with their basic subsistence. City-states with populations of 10,000–30,000 were typical, with a few exceeding those numbers (Tenochtitlan, the Aztec/Mexica capital city, may have housed as many as 250,000 people, and Tikal in the Mayan lowlands up to 60,000). Classic Mayan and Aztec city-states were linked through trade networks, elite marriage arrangements, political alliances, and common religious performances.

These civilizations were characterized by overt social hierarchies, resembling castes rather than classes. Elite positions were solidified by military and political control, and symbolized by extravagant material displays. Some of this was financed through tribute obtained through military conquest. Political control was expressed through religious rituals, including human sacrifice.

Description: The ancient civilizations of Mesoamerica shared traditions and faced circumstances that affected their approaches to warfare.

Technologically, these ancient peoples relied on stone and wood for weaponry; on cotton fibers for armor; and on cane, cotton, leather, maguey fiber, and feathers for shields. Common projectile weapons included bows, spears, atlatls, and slings. Warriors also used thrusting spears and the *macquauitl,* a wooden sword studded with sharp obsidian blades. Quilted cotton body armor, approximately five- to eight-centimeters thick, covered the torso but left the limbs vulnerable to injury. The head was also vulnerable, although some groups used helmets, perhaps also made of light-weight quilted cotton. A warrior typically carried a shield made from canes lashed together with maguey fibers and covered with cotton, leather, and/or decorative feathers. The decorative shields carried status information, and many of them were presented to successful warriors. Also laden with status symbolism were highly stylized and distinctive feathered warrior costumes, with their accompanying headdresses or back devices.

Although the Tarascans in western Mexico did develop axes and points made of copper and copper alloys, overall, the Mesoamericans lacked metal weapons and armor manufactured from iron, steel, or bronze. They also lacked firearms and gunpowder, crossbows, large domestic animals, wheeled vehicles, naval vessels, and sails for watercraft.

This situation had important logistical consequences. All travel and transport was on foot or canoe. With no large animals to help with transport, Mesoamerican armies carried all of their needs on their backs: an image from an Aztec codex depicts a well-heeled warrior with his apprentice in tow laden with a basket full of provisions and a shield. Progress would have been relatively slow across mountains or through dense rain forests, and is estimated at just over 11 miles in an eight-hour day. If a target city-state were close, as among the Classic Maya, it could be reached in just a few days, with the forces still relatively fresh and well provisioned. However, more ambitious campaigns, such as those undertaken by later Aztec armies, required a more extensive support system. Aside from pillaging the countryside as it passed through, such an army might rely for provisions on tenuously allied city-states or garrisons established along their travel route. Another important practical consideration was timing. It was normally necessary to plan military campaigns during the dry season (December–April) when roads and paths would be passable, and also when the bulk of commoner warriors would not be engaged in critical agricultural pursuits. This meant that wars were somewhat predictable for both adversaries.

Defensive walls and ditches existed at several Classic Mayan sites, and many city-states in central Mexico were situated on high ground. Fortified outposts and garrisons were established along volatile borderlands, such as that between the Aztec and Tarascan domains. Given the lack of heavy artillery and siege weaponry, defensive barriers involved relatively little effort to construct and usually consisted of masonry or wooden walls, ditches, or even rows of spiny plants. Often these did not encompass the entire city, but protected a palace group or ceremonial precinct.

There were no standing armies. Among the Classic Maya, elites personally engaged in warfare. There is still uncertainty about the extent to which commoners served as warriors among the Classic Maya, although commoners apparently served as warriors in Postclassic Mayan times (900 CE–early 16th century). No such doubt exists for the later Aztecs, for all men, regardless of social status, were trained in the martial arts and could be mobilized for war on short notice.

Among the Aztecs, rulers were expected to excel on the battlefield. It was usual for a new ruler to solidify his exalted position by spearheading an important conquest. Postconquest celebrations, including human sacrifice of captured warriors, validated each ruler's capability to rule. The ruler went to battle accompanied by warriors from all walks of life. Some highly accomplished warriors gained high military titles and martial responsibilities, and some entered specialized knightly orders: Jaguar, Eagle, *Otomí,* or *Cuachic* ("shorn ones"). These orders were full-time military occupations.

Little is known about provisioning for Classic Maya engagements, but abundant evidence exists for Aztec campaigns, some of which were conducted at great distances. Prior to setting out, the ruler distributed weapons from his armory. It is not entirely clear if all warriors obtained their arms in this fashion, or if this only pertained to the elite warriors and knightly orders. Some of this equipment in the ruler's arsenal was obtained through tribute from already-conquered city-states. Little in the way of manufactured weaponry was paid in tribute to the Aztec emperors: perhaps these rulers disliked encouraging weapons production in conquered but potentially rebellious provinces. As for food supplies, the "market folk" were called upon to provide subsistence provisions for the army on the march. When these gave out, the warriors had to rely on allies to provide them with sustenance. To this end, the empire established client states astride major transport routes and along hostile borderlands.

Based on somewhat controversial hieroglyphic readings, it appears that Classic Maya warfare ranged from "capture" (of an enemy ruler or city-state) and "destruction" (perhaps of an enemy dynasty), to full-scale defeat of one city-state by another. It also appears that warfare waged for territory and tribute became increasingly important as the Mayan Classic period drew to a close. Among the Aztecs, warfare was overwhelmingly conducted for the purpose of conquest and tribute. One possible exception involved the renowned Flower Wars. These ritualized encounters were reportedly pursued to provide sacrificial victims and warrior training. The most common example of this is the endless war between the Aztecs and the nearby Tlaxcallans and their allies. However, it is just as likely that these wars were serious Aztec attempts to conquer these powerful enemies—their description by the Aztecs as Flower Wars may have served as political excuses for repeated failures.

Warfare was accompanied by political posturing whereby city-state rulers vied for allies to augment their military strength. The Aztec Empire was a Triple Alliance of three city-states (Tenochtitlan, Texcoco, and Tlacopan). In addition, as each conquest was made, warriors from conquered city-states swelled the empire's ranks for increasingly distant campaigns. In a world where technology and tactics were similar among all adversaries, the ability to field a large army provided a significant military advantage.

Warfare in Mesoamerica had social, political, economic, and religious ramifications, particularly among the Aztecs. Aztec warriors who captured enemies on the battlefield gained economic and symbolic rewards for their achievements. By offering their captives for sacrifice, they helped maintain cosmic stability while announcing the power of the empire. Military conquest established dominance over other city-states and especially over their resources and specialized manufactures. Tribute payments were typically demanded, and some of these resources supported further military incursions. The symbol for military conquest was a burning temple (i.e., one god defeating another), battlefield tactics were geared toward capturing enemy warriors for later sacrifice, and warfare was supported by religious and mythological underpinnings where warfare emerges as a frequent theme.

These themes are less obvious among the Classic Maya. City-state rulers were glorified for their military victories and conquests, thereby enriching their local and even regional prestige. Prisoners were ritually sacrificed, thus contributing to both the power of the victorious city-state and to the symbolic maintenance of the universe. However, extensive burning and destruction of defeated city-states suggests that extended tributary or political relations were not commonly sought or achieved.

Application: The Aztecs employed different strategies to gain sacrifices, conquest, or tribute. These strategies were purposeful, planned, and based on historical traditions, although each military and political incursion was somewhat unique. Each Aztec ruler placed his own stamp on the military enterprise. Axayacatl (r. 1468–1481) established many client states during his reign—this approach required little direct military action. Motecuhzoma Ilhuicamina (r. 1440–1468) and Ahuitzotl (r. 1486–1502) favored overt military encounters, even where the establishment of client states may have been a more strategically sound and less expensive option. These latter two punctuated their victories with great and flamboyant ceremonies.

Legacy: In the indigenous Mesoamerican world of war, city-state met city-state on a relatively even playing field. This style of warfare came to an abrupt end with the Spanish conquest of the region in the early 16th century CE. The Spaniards arrived not only with a different military technology, but also with different goals, tactics, and strategies. Technologically, the Spaniards brought the use of metal swords, firearms, and crossbows, of which the swords were the most effective weapon. Horses provided mobility and some initial "shock value," and large dogs, trained to attack, struck terror into the hearts of the native warriors. Tactically, the Mesoamerican focus on capturing enemies worked against them on a battlefield where their adversary was determined to kill. Additionally, Spaniards ultimately employed sieges (notably at Tenochtitlan), a style of warfare for which the native city-states and armies were not prepared (and during which epidemic diseases took their toll). As the Spaniards sought to conquer Mesoamerica's greatest empire, the Aztecs' enemies, subjects, and even allies who shifted their allegiances to the new arrivals, provided the small Spanish forces with an abundance of well-trained manpower.

Further Reading

Brown, M. Kathryn and Travis W. Stanton, eds., *Ancient Mesoamerican Warfare*. Walnut Creek, CA: Altamira Press, 2003.
Hassig, Ross, *Aztec Warfare*. Norman, OK: University of Oklahoma Press, 1988.
Pohl, John and Charles M. Robinson III, *Aztecs and Conquistadores*. Oxford: Osprey Publishing, 2005.
Schele, Linda, and David Freidel, *A Forest of Kings*. New York: William Morrow and Company, 1990.

Frances F. Berdan

Pacific Islander Culture of War, Including Maori

Significance and Context: The Pacific Islands are sometimes referred to collectively as Oceania. They are generally divided into three geographical areas: Melanesia, Micronesia, and Polynesia. Polynesia consists of all the islands east of a line running along the west coast of New Zealand to Fiji and up to the western end of the Hawaiian chain. Micronesia consists of all the islands from Palau, Yap, and the Mariana Islands in the west across to Kiribati in the east. Melanesia stretches from Fiji to New Guinea.

Approaches and Application: Throughout Oceania, all adult males could potentially be called upon to fight for their communities. However, in more hierarchical societies such as Hawaii and Tonga in Polynesia, the brunt of any fighting fell upon a relatively small cadre, occasionally supplemented by levied forces. In these societies, any chief of standing maintained a retinue, including many who constantly trained in the use of weaponry. These chiefly retinues formed the nearest equivalent that the Pacific Islanders had to standing armies. Relatives were an important part of any chiefly retinue. They were also bolstered from further afield. In Hawaii, for example, training exercises were used in part to reveal potential fighters who were taken into the retinues and trained and brought up as warriors.

Military prowess was important for social and political status. Chiefs figure prominently in traditional accounts of battles, with the death of an important chief often cited as the turning point in a battle. Although Pacific Islanders occasionally fought for control of land and resources, the overwhelming motivation for war recorded in their traditions was to seek revenge for physical harm or insults received. Status mattered. Much of that status centered on the ability to demonstrate that gods and ancestors favored one. Success in a range of human endeavors was an indication of this favor. Misfortunes such as defeat in battle and natural disasters on the land were seen as indications of the gods' withdrawing of support. The fear of being seen to back away from the challenges of battle in front of one's comrades, many of whom were kin, acted as another powerful incentive to warriors' bravery and group coherence.

Most traditional fighting consisted of hand-to-hand combat with clubs, spears, and daggers, occasionally preceded by an initial exchange of projectiles. The main defensive asset of combatants was their skill at dodging and parrying blows and projectiles. Although the bow and arrow was used in Melanesian warfare, its use was restricted in more hierarchical societies elsewhere in Oceania because its higher velocity compromised the fighting skills upon which so much status rested. Single combat between champions was not an uncommon way for battles to begin. In much of Melanesia, fighting was largely limited to stealthy raids to avenge deaths by slaying the first member of the offenders' group encountered. Open confrontations also occurred. Across Oceania, battle varied from prearranged clashes with set rules and few casualties to all out confrontations that only ended with the rout and possible destruction of one side. In all circumstances, much importance was placed upon drawing first blood. Such an achievement was seen as an indication of the gods' support, and could have a decisive effect on the morale of both sides. However, sometimes the issue was only decided by the clash of massed battle lines. Even then, unless one side dissolved rapidly, combat usually broke up into a series of personal duels.

Tactical sophistication varied considerably within the Pacific Islands. Ambushes and surprise attacks were the most common tactic across the Pacific Islands. The siege of fortified settlements was really only prominent in warfare in New Zealand and Fiji, although fortifications and inaccessible refuges did exist elsewhere. The most detailed indigenous accounts of pre-European tactics concern New Zealand Maori, Tahitians, and Hawaiians. Common tactics in Maori traditions include ambushes on narrow paths through forests, mock retreats to draw pursuers into prepared ambushes, and open battles along the lines described below. Tahitians made little use of fortifications beyond a number of fortified refuges in the mountainous interiors of their islands. Land warfare was usually decided by set battles in which both forces fought in lines or serried ranks, with the judicious use of reserve lines sometimes deciding the issue. Hawaiian warfare occasionally featured ambushes, but more usually involved open battles. These centered on clashes between elite groups drilled to fight in unison using long pikes, supported by lighter armed levies armed with projectiles. Where rugged terrain ruled out such controlled maneuvering, the armies might fight in detached groups seeking out opponents of equal social status.

Although most of the population lived in the interior of the large islands of Melanesia, naval power played a significant role elsewhere in this most oceanic of human habitats. Poor overland communications and no beasts of burden meant that sea power conferred mobility. Canoes were the only bulk carriers of men and supplies. With a fleet, the center became less remote in perception and reality to those contemplating rebellion. Those with naval forces could harass enemy coasts at will if not met by naval forces of comparable strength. Although an army could contest landings, canoe-borne opponents could soon outdistanced them, and move on to attack unguarded coasts. The fragmentation of power meant that quite small polities with naval capacity could exercise significant influence. They were often based on small islands off large islands, and included groups distinguished as "sea people." Bau in Fiji and Borabora in the Society Islands were good examples. Sea people were renowned for ferocity and skill as assassins.

Naval activities varied between localities. Sea battles were more decisive than those on land, as the vanquished party lacked the option of fleeing to safe havens like the mountain refuges used on land. Naval warfare was most developed in Fiji. Huge double-hulled, and outrigger canoes carrying hundreds of men each, served as troop transports. Other canoes were designed specially for fighting at sea. Known as *tabilai,* they combined hulls tipped with several feet of solid wood at either end to enable ramming, with wind-driven speed and maneuverability.

Fijian naval battles were on the whole bloodier than land operations, which generally consisted of indecisive sieges. Fleet movements were coordinated by commanders in canoes distinguished by battle flags flown from the mast. Naval tactics usually consisted of attempts to run down or ram opponents to sink or disable them. Once this was achieved, the victors would board and finish off the occupants of the disabled canoe, or kill the survivors in the water. Approaching an enemy vessel from the windward side was crucial, as it exposed their outrigger. The enemy crew could not venture on to the outrigger to defend it without the risk of capsizing their vessel.

Naval warfare in the eastern Pacific aimed to kill enemy personnel rather than disable their canoes. Naval operations in Hawaii mostly involved transporting troops and supplies, although there are also references to major naval battles, and coordinated attacks from the sea and the mountains against coastal enemies. Fighting at sea consisted of exchanges of projectiles followed by attempts to board. Tahitian battle fleets in the 1770s consisted of specialist war canoes supported by sailing canoes in transport roles. The main fighting vessel was a double canoe with high hulls and bulky fronts for ramming. It was propelled by paddlers, and had a raised fighting stage in the front for warriors. Paddlers were armed with slings and sling-stones. Tahitian traditions refer to fleets fighting in coordinated battle lines, with canoes sometimes lashed together to provide a more stable platform, and to prevent retreat.

Geography, economic, and social organization curtailed political consolidation of military victory. Kin-based loyalties present problems to rulers seeking to consolidate or expand power. Unless frequent visits were made to areas away from the paramount chief's power base, local rulers might be tempted to assert their independence or even challenge the paramount. These dangers were enhanced by communication problems. Most land routes consisted of narrow trails, vulnerable to disruption by bad weather. Sea travel was also determined by the weather, especially in the absence of fringing reefs. These problems were exacerbated in larger polities. Political expansion increased the resource base, but ran the risk of overextending the realm. More resources might be needed to maintain coherence than were gained through expansion. The structure held together, in part, because the ruler's demands did not intrude too deeply into parochial worlds. Chiefly rights of expropriation were based on their sacred status, and could not be pushed too far without putting that status at risk. To increase their military capacity, rulers needed to get enough food to their army for sustained periods in an essentially dispersed economy without placing too high a burden on any locality.

See also: Southeast Asia Naval Warfare

Further Reading

Clunie, Fergus, *Fijian Weapons and Warfare.* Suva: Fiji Museum, 1977.

D'Arcy, Paul, "Fluid Frontiers: the sea as a contested space," in *The People of the Sea: Environment, Identity and History in Oceania.* Honolulu: University of Hawai'i Press, 2006, pp.98–117.

D'Arcy, Paul, "Warfare and State Formation in Hawai'i: The Limits on Violence as a Means of Political Consolidation," *Journal of Pacific History,* 38 (1), 2003, pp. 29–52.

Knauft, B., "Melanesian Warfare," *Oceania,* 60 (4), 1990, pp. 250–311.

Meggitt, Mervyn, *Blood is Their Argument: Warfare among the Mae Enga Tribesmen of the New Guinea Highlands.* Palo Alto, CA: Mayfield Publishing Company, 1977.

Oliver, Douglas L., "Warfare and Killing," in *Oceania: The Native Cultures of Australia and the Pacific Islands,* 2 vols. Honolulu: University of Hawai'i Press, 1989, vol. 1, pp.423–500.

Vayda, A. P., *Maori Warfare.* Wellington: Polynesian Society, 1960.

Paul D'Arcy

Southeast Asian Naval Warfare

Significance and Context: Southeast Asia is a vast and diverse region sitting between the Indian subcontinent and China. The region's naval history has been influenced by both Indian and Chinese ways of war and doctrine; it also developed distinct characteristics based on its unique geography and political institutions. Mainland Southeast Asia, stretching from Burma to Vietnam, was characterized by large centralized fleets conducting essentially conventional naval warfare on the regions' large rivers and near-shore coastal waters. Island Southeast Asia, stretching from Aceh in Western Sumatra to the Philippines, combined both conventional naval warfare and more irregular naval tactics in the form of raids and piracy at sea. Even today, most global piracy is centered on this region that is ideally suited to this form of naval warfare because of the numerous lairs within its mangrove and forest-lined islands and shorelines, and significant bottlenecks which funnel and concentrate maritime commerce.

Approaches and Application: Forested, rugged terrain combined with a number of navigable rivers meant that waterborne transport was usually plentiful. While some polities such as Arakan and Thailand launched war fleets numbering thousands of vessels at various times during their histories, most maritime powers had fleets numbered in the hundreds rather than thousands. Such fleets consisted of specialist war galleys and more general-purpose transports. The latter were often requisitioned from subjects during times of war. Areas with particular shipbuilding skills such as the teak-rich districts of Southern Vietnam or villages along rivers might be made to pay tribute in vessels or ordered to construct them in preparation for expeditions requiring the movement of armed forces overseas or along rivers. The importance of waterborne transport meant that such skills were widespread so that large fleets could be constructed rapidly by spreading the burden across many villages.

Fighting between vessels was most common in river warfare. Grappling hooks up to six meters in length were used to latch onto enemy vessels so that boarding could be attempted by the fighting contingents of the vessel. This was a common and longstanding tactic recorded in ancient Khmer reliefs through to Dutch records of naval struggles with Cham vessels from Southern Vietnam in the 17th century. Ramming and boarding tactics were also common in river warfare, with many vessels armed with metal rams in their prows. These rams seem to have worked more to impale enemy boats in preparation for boarding or dragging back towards one's own supporting vessels than to sink them. Massed vessels in crowded rivers tended to come into contact prow to prow rather than being rammed side-on. Another tactic for disabling enemy vessels was to pull in oars just before passing the side of the enemy vessel so that the hull sheared off the enemy's oars. The introduction of cannon and muskets onboard in the 16th century allowed enemy crews to be disabled before boarding and also made boarding all the more hazardous. Massed vessels in narrow rivers offered great scope for fireboats to be used to break up or force retreat upon enemy fleets by those with the wind at their backs or the upstream advantage.

While naval operations in mainland Southeast Asia were largely limited to coastal waters and rivers, the coastal states of Island Southeast Asia built larger sea-going war galleys that were more suited to this archipelagic environment. Some 16th and 17th century Achenese war galleys could carry up to 400 men. Cannon, either wooden or metal, became features of many fighting vessels from the 16th century under the influence of Portuguese vessels that began to contest these waters. Early cannons were particularly positioned in the prow of fighting galleys, although through time swivel guns and cannon were also positioned on the sides of vessels. Oars were the main form of propulsion for military vessels because of the need to travel upstream on occasion, or against or without the wind at sea. Sails were carried to take advantage of winds and to rest oarsmen when the opportunity arose. The use of slaves or war captives as rowers was feasible for river warfare, but warfare at sea required skilled rowers and sea fighters best drawn from specialist seafaring communities. Warfare and sea raids could therefore either replenish or destroy the pool of rowers to power naval war machines of the region. The Burmese conquest of coastal regions severely curtailed the potential of Burmese naval power by dispersing the coastal Mons across the region as refugees, while victory against the Thai kingdom supplied captive rowers to power Burmese vessels.

Most maritime operations were conducted in conjunction with land operations, and involved the transport of armies, the blockade of ports, or the defense of river mouths and harbors. The Achenese, for example, attempted unsuccessfully to besiege Portuguese Melaka (Malacca) a number of times in this manner during the 16th and 17th centuries to restore their control of the strategic Straits of Melaka. Southeast Asian fleets had more success in blockading river mouths by means of massed vessels, occasionally linked together with rope or oars. Iron chains were also used to block access by hostile forces to rivers and harbors, for example, by the Kingdom of Srivijaya against pirate raids and by the Burmese against British forces moving up the Irrawaddy River in 1885. Major fleet operations at sea declined after the 17th century as European navies took control of the region's seas. European sailing ships deeper hulls and greater broadside firepower made them the masters of blue water actions, while the shallower drafts and tighter maneuvering capacity of indigenous vessels gave them the advantage in rivers until Europeans introduced more, smaller, shallow draft gunboats and armed steam ships in the 19th century.

Only the Iranun and Balangingi of the Sulu Archipelago in the southern Philippines persisted with sea operations into the 19th century. In this century, however, European naval actions also curtailed their widespread raids of predation in search of plunder and slaves across the breadth of eastern Southeast Asia from Singapore to Western New Guinea. These raiders used the element of surprise and the speed of their oared vessels to hit isolated vessels or coastal towns and villages with overwhelming force. They also cultivated their well-deserved reputation for ferocity to terrorize many opponents into surrendering prematurely or not resisting as resolutely as they might have.

See also: Chinese Naval Theorists; Thai Military Culture (Ramathibodi II); Tran Hung Dao

Further Reading

Charney, Michael W., *Southeast Asian Warfare, 1300–1900*. Leiden: Brill, 2004.

Manguin, Pierre-Yves, "The Vanishing Jong: Insular Southeast Asian Fleets in Trade and War (Fifteenth to Seventeenth Centuries)," in Anthony Reid (ed.), *Southeast Asia in the Early Modern Era: Trade, Power, and Belief.* Ithaca: Cornell University Press, 1993, pp. 197–213.

Quaritch Wales, H. G., *Ancient South-East Asian Warfare*. London: Bernard Quaritch Ltd., 1952.

Tarling, Nicholas, *Piracy and Politics in the Malay World: A Study of British Imperialism in Nineteenth-Century South-East Asia*. Melbourne: F.W. Cheshire, 1963.

Warren, James Francis, *The Sulu Zone 1768–1898: The Dynamics of External Trade, Slavery, and Ethnicity in the Transformation of a Southeast Asian Maritime State*. Singapore: Singapore University Press, 1981.

Paul D'Arcy

Sub-Saharan Military Responses to European Invasion

(1500–1900)

Significance: In the late 19th century, the limited European involvement in sub-Saharan Africa accelerated into a scramble to divide up the region between the colonial powers. Colonial armed forces enjoyed an unprecedented technological and organizational edge over African armies. The African response varied, but was always conditioned by prevailing military culture. Although some societies clung unsuccessfully to their traditional fighting methods, others adopted innovations that made their resistance more effective, if ultimately unavailing.

Context: The Muslim states of North Africa had remained integrated to the European experience. The rest of Africa was largely separated from the Mediterranean by the Sahara Desert, and from antiquity, the East African coast was integrated into the Indian Ocean network. European contact with sub-Saharan Africa largely waited until the late 15th century. Most penetration of the interior only occurred well into the 19th century.

Approach and Application:

Introduction: The European Partition of Africa

Until the late 18th century, Europeans established on the African coastline remained sea bound, content to export commodities from the African interior. Settlement was confined to enclaves, primarily in southern Africa. In 1879, more than 90 percent of the continent was still ruled by Africans, yet by 1912, only Ethiopia and Liberia remained independent from European powers. The reason for this change was that in the later 19th-century European states began expressing their economic and political rivalries through rapid colonial expansion, often driven along by ambitious officers and officials on the spot. The years 1891 and 1902 saw the high point of this "scramble for Africa." The Berlin Conference (1884–1885) had required that claims to colonies or protectorates should be backed by the establishment of effective colonial authority. This agreement staved off armed conflict between the European powers, but sparked a rush to lay physical claim to vast territories.

The Means of European Conquest

How Were Europeans to Conquer a Continent?

In conquering Africa, the European conundrum hardly changed between 1450 and 1880: how was a handful of Europeans with limited technological means to traverse a comparatively inaccessible and disease-ridden continent and conquer a numerically superior and often sophisticated enemy? Initially, Europeans lacked much of an edge. For example, the arrival of the Portuguese in the 1480s in what is now northwestern Angola upset the local dynamics of the sophisticated, trading kingdoms of Kongo and Ndongo. The Portuguese became embroiled in the local wars, but were not strong enough to dominate. Instead, they remained a disruptive factor, adopting local African military culture and operating as a disciplined core in large African armies still mainly engaging in traditional hand-to-hand combat.

The stateless Khoi pastoralists living at the Cape of Good Hope had originally welcomed trading contact with passing European ships, but they resisted when the Dutch occupied the Cape in 1652 and pushed inland. In 1659–1660, their spears were a good match for Dutch muzzle loaders, but the Khoi could not take the Dutch fortress. Soon thereafter, the Khoi were decimated by smallpox brought by the foreign ships. The Dutch settlers exploited this catastrophe, and using firearms and mounted infantry, drove the Khoi into the interior. The technological edge in weaponry, when coupled with the flexible adaptation of European military prac- tices to African conditions and the exploitation of favorable circumstances, could compensate for inferior settler numbers.

Colonial wars in Africa were largely campaigns against nature: disease, dis- tance, nonexistent roads and bridges, difficult terrain, and lack of supplies. These difficulties were only ever partially overcome, despite the eventual introduction of quinine, railways, and steam-driven river boats, but by the later 19th century, organizational ability, logistical edge, and medical knowledge better matched su- periority in weaponry. Professional military intelligence also improved, as did better maps and an understanding of how to exploit local divisions.

African Collaboration

Imperial military expeditions were expensive and hard to justify to domestic opinion, and there was always concern when home garrisons were drawn upon for African service, especially because European troops were decimated by tropical diseases. The British and French responded by recruiting, on average, two indig- enous African troops to every European soldier toward the end of the 19th century. Untrained tribal levies could prove troublesome, but African troops trained along European lines dominated colonial armies everywhere except southern Africa, where white settlers distrusted their loyalty, and themselves provided volunteer mil- itary units. Large numbers of African auxiliaries served field forces in support roles.

The colonial conquest of Africa was thus only made possible through the co- operation of Africans. Motivation was complex. African kingdoms were built by conquest and incorporation, and there were usually rival claimants to the throne. Consequently, for collaborators there was the lure of plunder or revenge. Once their own state had been defeated, warrior classes could maintain their honor and prestige through military service with the conqueror, and the many African slave soldiers believed they had exchanged their African owners for better masters. Non- combatant auxiliaries participated for pay rather than through compulsion.

How Crucial Was the Technological Gap?

Indigenous African societies failed to organize a successful resistance to the colonial advance. This has generally been explained more in terms of technological lag than, say, of a chronic inability of rival states to cooperate militarily. On many occasions, imperial or settler forces were defeated because Africans employed terrain, superior tactics, or surprise and negated any technological advantages the colonial troops may have enjoyed. Especially in West Africa's wet coastal climate, the Europeans' muzzle-loading guns made no appreciable impact on African warfare until the more effective flintlocks were introduced. Then, as in southern Africa in the early 19th century during the wars of conquest fought by Boer settlers against the Xhosa, Ndebele, Zulu, and Sotho, the musket and wagon laager provided a decisive advantage.

As early as the 1830s the Xhosa chiefdoms of the Eastern Cape abandoned their spears for muskets to wage effective irregular warfare in the thick bush and mountains against impinging white settlers. In the same region, trans-frontiersmen of mixed Khoisan, slave, and white descent—the Kora, Oorlams, and Griqua (who originally called themselves "Basters" or Bastards)—adopted aspects of white settler culture, including their guns and horses, and in the early 19th century, raided the Tswana and Sotho communities.

This "intermediate" technology of muskets, which were easy to repair and used simple black powder and projectiles, was rendered obsolete between the 1860s and the 1880s. Breech-loading rifles, bolt-action rifles with metal cartridges, and finally magazine rifles were standard by 1890 and were superior to muskets in range, accuracy, rapidity of fire, and stopping power. The adoption in 1892 of smokeless cordite improved visibility and accuracy, but also kept an adversary concealed. The era of the empty battlefield had dawned in Africa wherever Africans, such as the white irregulars of the two Boer republics of South Africa during the South African War (1899–1902), had access to the new rifles and ammunition and took up position in trenches and rifle pits.

Some 16 million firearms entered Africa during the 1800s, mostly obsolete muzzle loaders such as the Tower Musket ("Brown Bess") or the "Long Dane." Modern rifles were sold in much smaller numbers. The Zulu used them against the British (1879) and the Dahomeans against the French (1892). But modern rifles required an advanced technology to manufacture spare parts and bullets. Most Africans (with a few exceptions like the gunsmiths in Samori's West African empire whose spies had learned the techniques from the French in Senegal) became dependent on European suppliers, and were always short of ammunition. In 1890, the European powers agreed to stop selling modern arms to Africans. This measure was only partially successful, but it did ensure at least that artillery stayed out of African hands, except for the white-dominated Boer republics.

The weight of the heavy, muzzle-loading artillery of the 17th to 19th centuries made it a liability on remote African battlefields. Then from the 1840s light mountain guns that could be disassembled and carried on pack animals became available. By the 1870s small, breech-loading artillery pieces were firing both shrapnel and impact shells. Artillery fire in battle could be very effective if the enemy massed as the Mahdists did in the Sudan at Tel-el-Kebir in 1882 and Omdurman in 1898. But the effect on dispersed forces was more psychological than physical. In contrast, the stone and mud fortresses of the Muslim states and the stockades of the West African forest kingdoms were all vulnerable to modern artillery. Where possible, as at Zanzibar in 1896, battleships played a deciding role. On the Nile in 1885 and 1898, gunboats provided fire support to troops on land.

The machine gun gave Europeans an undoubted defensive advantage. Earlier versions, such as the Gatling, were unwieldy, and jammed at crucial moments, as at Ulundi (1879). The breakthrough came with the lighter, more reliable Maxim gun adopted by the British army in 1891. In 1893, it was used with devastating effect by the Chartered Company against the Ndebele of what is now southern Zimbabwe. Nevertheless, they were usually too few to decide a campaign.

African Options in the Face of Invasion

By the late 19th century Europeans decidedly enjoyed a military edge over Africans because of superior technology and discipline combined with improved logistics and organization. Africans had the choice between conventional military resistance by the army, opportunistic alliance with the invaders against other Africans, submission on favorable terms, guerrilla warfare, or a flexible combination of all of these.

Clinging to the Old

Military resistance required a further choice between adherences to traditional forms of fighting or innovation. To innovate was to subvert many cultural norms, which not all societies could tolerate. Ironically, the relative political and military sophistication that made states like the Zulu kingdom, Asante, or Dahomey so formidable in the African context rendered them more vulnerable to European conquest. In these societies, armies and warfare were enmeshed in precise political, economic, social, cultural, and religious structures, so to change a military culture meant an unacceptable societal revolution. Besides, armies were designed for slave and cattle raiding, or for short campaigns of annexation. Fighting a series of battles over an extended campaign against relentless Europeans placed intolerable strains on the royal armies.

Traditionalist armies such as the Zulu or the mounted Mahdist host of the Sudan emphasized the imposing spectacle of ceremonial warfare, in which war cries and aggressive massed charges (fatal against prepared, defensive positions) were intended to break the will of the enemy before contact. Envelopment of the enemy was the tactical objective, so that warriors' heroic qualities could be brought out in hand-to-hand fighting. It was difficult to embrace a new way of fighting that contradicted accepted notions of honor and bravery. So, although firearms were increasingly carried (e.g., by Zulu infantry and Sokoto cavalry), their novel military potential was ignored and tactically they were handled like any other ancillary projectile weapons.

This combined with a tragically repeated failure to appreciate the overwhelming effect of disciplined, concentrated fire on mass attacks in the open, for example, the Zulu (1838 and 1879), the Ndebele (1836–1837 and 1893), and the Ngoni (1895–1899), however bolstered by notions of personal honor. The massed cavalry charges of the Sikoto Caliphate and the Mahdist Sudan also failed disastrously.

Supernatural Protection

Religion contributed vitality and moral strength to African resistance. In Muslim states, especially in the jihadist ones such as the Sokoto Caliphate, warriors went to war assured of the holiness of their cause. Islam proved an important focus of resistance that survived initial conquest. Armies in centralized states with traditional religions went to war invoking gods or ancestors through the sacrifice of animals (or even of humans at times of great crisis, as in Benin in 1897), and "strengthened" by ceremonies and potions administered by "war-doctors." During the Ndebele and Shona resistance in 1896–1897, the leadership of religious spirit-mediums nearly succeeded in expelling the white settlers. In German East Africa (now Tanzania), the determined Maji Maji rising of 1905–1907 saw numerous ethnic groups, mostly stateless people without strong military traditions, brought together by prophets who purported to render warriors invulnerable to bullets through the ritual administration of water medicine (Maji Maji), which inspired them to suicidal bravery. Millenarianism could be disastrous, however. In 1857, a young woman prophet persuaded the Xhosa that if they destroyed all their livestock and crops, a wind would sweep all the invading white settlers into the sea. Starvation followed, and Xhosa resistance was fatally weakened.

The Adoption of Guns, Horses, and Irregular Tactics

When confronted by European invasion, some African societies responded innovatively. In South Africa, the southern Sotho responded to the aggression of their Griqua and white neighbors by adapting their traditional military system to incorporate their enemies' guns and horses, and by laying ambushes, skirmishing, raiding, and defending their rocky strongholds. After several wars between 1858 and 1881, first against the Boers and then the British, the Sotho secured effective independence.

The Pedi, living in the mountains that bounded the Boers' Transvaal, also changed their military culture. The prevalence of horse-sickness prevented them from embracing mounted warfare, but they tried to secure good firearms. When the Pedi went to war with the Transvaal in 1876, they defended rocky hills, fortified with stone breastworks and rifle pits, until defeated in 1879 by British troops and Swazi auxiliaries.

Innovation and Resistance in Dahomey and Asante

Dahomey, after the first clash with the French in 1890, urgently bought breech-loading rifles, machine guns and field guns, and hired instructors. So when the

French invaded in 1892 they had first to overcome stoutly defended entrenched positions, and then to fight a long bush campaign.

The most striking adaptation to technological change in West Africa occurred among the Asante. The British punitive expedition of 1873–1874 exposed the ineffectiveness of Asante skirmishing tactics with outdated muskets. Britain annexed Asante in 1896 without resistance, but in the rebellion of 1900 the Asante adopted major tactical changes. They first constructed forest stockades to blockade the British, and when these fell to direct assault, they conducted a guerrilla resistance.

Resistance by the Professional Soldiers of the West African Savannah

In the West African savannah, warfare had been dominated for centuries by the likes of the *ceddo* of Senegal, professional warriors with long experience in firearms, elaborate codes of honor, and supporting structures of powerful kingdoms. The French invaded the Senegal Valley in 1855 and took 50 years to subdue the *ceddo*. The Tukulor Empire of the upper Senegal and Niger Valleys that had been founded by a jihad launched in 1852, fielded a formidable army consisting of a core of disciplined Muslim warrior zealots supported by military slaves. Although their flintlocks and traditional weapons were outmoded, their morale and tactical cohesion were high. Between 1889 and 1890, the French took their border fortresses and broke their field army. The Tukulor army conducted a fighting retreat and only gave up in 1893 because the French exploited their political divisions.

Samori Touré's Mande-speaking empire, established in the 1860s between the Niger River and the forest edge, resisted the French between 1891 until 1898. Except for an elite corps of cavalry, Samori's army consisted of select and highly disciplined slave soldiers, armed with the latest breech-loading, magazine rifles and trained to fight exactly like the French. Samori emphasized mobility and long survived French attack by refusing to meet them in the open field. Instead, he abandoned fixed positions, ordered a scorched-earth policy, and withdrew east with his people. He only surrendered when he could retire no further because of the hostile British presence in Asante, and when famine finally destroyed his troops.

Guerrilla Warfare: The Key to Sustained Resistance

Colonial military theorists recognized that guerrilla operations usually formed a final phase of the struggle in Africa. All African societies could conduct irregular warfare, but not all were prepared to sustain a war of attrition that would bear heavily on the civilian population. This was especially the case if the conquerors made clear they did not plan to drastically alter the existing structure of society. Thus, for centralized states such as the Zulu kingdom, the defeat of the army in 1879, coupled with the amicable submission of the senior chiefs and the capture of the king ended resistance. Furthermore, once the state had collapsed, there were also dangers for the former rulers if popular resistance continued. The

Sokoto Caliphate never attempted guerrilla warfare, not least because the elite feared a popular insurrection by the exploited Hausa peasantry and the slave populations.

Stateless Societies and the Willingness to Adopt Guerrilla Tactics

Colonial commanders were right to dread guerrilla tactics. They nullified the invaders' technological advantages, and permitted small bodies of mobile—if poorly armed—soldiers to resist successfully for years. The isolated and acephalous societies (stateless people with no recognized chief) of East and West Africa had little experience with firearms and no state armies with which to resist colonial invasion. Yet these lightly armed people exploited mountainous and forest regions to fight on for years because of their local knowledge, experience of small-scale warfare, guerrilla tactics, hostility to government, and lack of established leadership whose elimination would end the fighting. It took the British between 1892 and 1900 to suppress Igbo resistance in southeastern Nigeria. The Baoule people of the Côte d'Ivoire and the Hehe in central German East Africa, among others, proved equally determined. The Turkana adopted modern rifles after 1902 and kept fighting for 22 years.

The Dire Consequences of Failed Guerrilla Resistance

Guerrilla fighters depend upon civilians for sustenance and camouflage. Unable to identify enemy operatives unequivocally, counterinsurgency forces punish all inhabitants of the area of operations. In all the African counterinsurgency campaigns during the latter stages of the "scramble for Africa," atrocities took place, sometimes systematically. The two most notorious exemplars were the Anglo-Boer War of 1899–1902 and the Herero-Nama uprisings of 1904–1907.

The war between Britain and the two independent Boer republics for supremacy in South Africa began conventionally with sieges and battles. But having been defeated on the battlefield, in early 1900 the Boers adopted mounted guerrilla warfare that took the British until 1902 to suppress. To do so they divided the country with barbed wire and blockhouses into compartments that they systematically pacified. To deny guerrillas support, the British confined over 150,000 Boer civilians and over 100,000 of their African laborers to concentration camps where the high death rates through disease engendered a bitter legacy.

In German southwest Africa the uncoordinated revolts by the Herero and Nama in 1904 took the form of guerrilla warfare. The Germans nearly exterminated the Herero, pushing the whole community into the waterless desert. Many survivors, both fighters and civilians, as well as the Nama who also surrendered in 1906, were sent to "labor camps" that became death camps. Less than a quarter of the Herero survived, and only half the Nama.

Rather than the original campaigns of colonial conquest and conventional warfare, it is these indiscriminate guerrilla struggles that resonate most vividly in the collective memory of Africans, and inspired the movements of armed resistance to colonial rule that gathered momentum after the Second World War.

See also: Ethiopian Military Culture; Forest Kingdoms of West Africa; Indigenous Southern African Military Cultures

John Laband

Thai Military Culture (Ramathibodi II)
(1491–1529)

Context and Influences: The Thai developed their own written text on warfare in the early 16th century when King Ramathibodi ordered military knowledge to be written down in 1518. The result was the first *Treatise on the Art of War*. It borrowed heavily from earlier Khmer texts, which in turn probably derived from Indian texts. Two contemporary Indian texts on warfare were also influential, and Thai literate elites had access to translations of Chinese military classics. Others followed the original Thai treatise, with certain elements added and removed according to new experiences and priorities. Ceremonial and ritual aspects diminished over time to be replaced by practical battle and campaign tactics and strategies. A new treatise produced in 1798, for example, combined predominantly the latter elements of the original Ramathibodi treatise with knowledge of Burmese military tactics acquired by King Naresuan of Thailand in the 16th century.

Approaches and Application: The bulk of Thai armies were made up of a small core of elite warriors supplemented by peasant levies conscripted at the outbreak of hostilities. The most important weapons in indigenous warfare were swords, spears, daggers, and bows. Armies consisted of elephants, cavalry, and infantry. Elephants were viewed as the supreme weapon and the Thai state maintained thousands of them in readiness for war.

Armies were led by aristocrats who received advanced weapons' training and instruction in military formations and tactics from a cumulative body of imported and local knowledge.

Thai military manuals outlined an array of marching and battle formations and tactics for various circumstances such as attacking or defending hills, defending in open plains, and assaulting small, medium, and large forces. Each was named after objects, animals, or mythological creatures such as the eagle, garuda, buffalo, lion, and demon. The battle formations were represented by fixed illustrations of the creatures they were named after. The creatures illustrated were divided into sections allocated to different elite warriors or units of troops. These represent fixed positions rather than maneuvers and so may represent starting positions for different contingencies. Outstretched flanks represent formations suited to attack, such as the horned buffalo formation used against smaller armies. More compact formations, such as the circle or wheel, were designed for defense.

The manuals also discuss methods of mobilizing and provisioning an army for war, and the use of trickery and deception to achieve victory. Stealth and deception were important weapons in the arsenal of Thai commanders and so it is not surprising that the manuals offered an itemized list of stratagems to achieve surprise. Spells, incantations to assist the securing of victory were also outlined, as were omens in the natural world such as cloud formations and the behavior of animals. This is not surprising when it is realized that Ramathibodi and his successors relied heavily on astrologers to ascertain the most auspicious moments to prepare for war or to seek battle.

These treatises need to be viewed in the social and political context of warfare. There were limits on the lethality of Thai warfare. Armies were made up essentially of localized levies fighting for their immediate overlords, who were reluctant to risk losing too many men in battle as their power and wealth derived from manpower and labor intensive agricultural productivity.

See also: Southeast Asian Naval Warfare; Sun Tzu; Tran Hung Dao

Further Reading

Charney, Michael W., *Southeast Asian Warfare, 1300–1900.* Leiden: Brill, 2004.

Quaritch Wales, H. G., *Ancient South-East Asian Warfare.* London: Bernard Quaritch Ltd., 1952.

Reynolds, Craig J., *Seditious Histories: Contesting Thai and Southeast Asian Pasts.* Seattle: University of Washington Press, 2006.

Paul D'Arcy

Use of Elephants in Indian Warfare
(1000 BCE–1943 CE)

Significance: Elephants are one of only a few domesticated animal species used *en masse* in warfare. They were also employed differently from more maneuverable species such as horses, asses, and camels.

Context: Elephants were used in Indian warfare from 1000 BCE onward. The *Mahabharatha* (Indian epic describing the struggle within the Aryan tribes) describes how the army of the ruler of Assam used elephants. The Achaemenid Empire and the Seleucids copied the use of elephants from the Indians. From the Seleucids, the Ptolemids gained elephant technology, and the Ptolemids were in turn imitated by the Carthaginians. From the Carthaginians and the Ptolemids, the use of war elephants spread in the Balkans. In third century BCE, King Pyrrhus of Epirus used elephants against the Romans in southern Italy. After the Second Punic War, the Roman Republic employed elephants while fighting Macedonia. The technique of controlling elephants in battle by using *ankush* (iron rods with hooks) also spread from India. Under the Roman Empire, the use of elephants in warfare died out in the West.

Description: The Indian subcontinent saw the highest development of elephant-based warfare. We can reconstruct the vital role played by elephants in premodern Indian warfare using Greek accounts, treatises by the classical Hindu theorists and Muslim chroniclers of medieval India, coins issued by the Indian dynasties, and miniature paintings in Mughal manuscripts. Although elephants were militarily ineffective when used in isolation, integrating them with cavalry and infantry proved effective. Elephants were also useful as beasts of burden during siege operations, for crossing rivers, and for making roads when an army was campaigning in forested and mountainous terrain. Before the arrival of internal combustion engines, elephants were the biggest animals available for hauling heavy guns and military stores.

Even after war elephants passed into history elsewhere, their use continued in South Asia. First, elephants were not available in large numbers outside India, but here they were obtained from Bihar, Orissa, Bengal, Assam, Konkan, Malabar, Gujarat, and the forests in the Vindhya Mountains and in the deep south. Second, Indian war elephants were bigger and more easily tamed than the African forest elephants. The conservatism of the Hindu military philosophers also meant a continued overemphasis on elephants in battle. In fact, in premodern India an elephant was a sign of royalty. To legitimize his rule, a king had to inspect the troops while riding an elephant and the ruler had to command his army in the battlefield from an elephant's back.

The climate and terrain of India was not suitable for breeding good horses. The ruling dynasties of India, whether they were Hindu in ancient period or Muslim during the medieval era, had to import horses from Arabia and Central Asia. Whenever these supply lines were severed due to external invasions, the monarchs of India were forced to depend on elephants.

Application: The Achemenid Emperor Cyrus conquered western Punjab and incorporated elephants into his army, and at Gaugemela in 331 BCE, Darius deployed 15 elephants. However, only at the Battle of Hydaspes in 326 BCE, the West was really exposed to large-scale elephant warfare. Porus deployed 85 elephants, each carrying three fighters and a driver. Each elephant was deployed 100 feet from the other and the gaps between the elephants were filled with infantry. Initially, the noise and smell of the elephants frightened Alexander's cavalry. Many cavalrymen were plucked from their horses by the elephants, which also crashed into the phalanx and trampled many phalangites. In response, Alexander deployed his light infantry that killed the drivers by throwing darts. The driver-less elephants then ran amok, trampling friends and foes alike. Alexander won the day at the cost of 280 cavalry and 700 infantry.

Though the Macedonians were victorious, the large beasts of India impressed Alexander's generals. Greek historians noted that the Macedonian army had suffered more losses at Hydaspes compared to Gaugemela and Issus, and that most of the casualties suffered against Porus were caused by the elephants. The fact that, at the time of Alexander's invasion, the Nanda emperor possessed 8,000 elephants certainly deterred further expansion by the Macedonians east of the Punjab.

In 305 BCE, Chandragupta Maurya gave 500 elephants to Seleucus in return for present-day Pakistan and eastern Afghanistan. He retained overwhelming superiority in this branch of warfare—the Mauryan army had about 9,000 elephants. After the secession of Bactria from the Seleucid Empire in 244 BCE, the latter's land link with Mauryan India was cut. Thereafter, the Seleucids faced problems in acquiring elephants from India. Moreover, the climate of Syria was unsuitable for elephants. The Indo-Bactrian kings of Kabul also maintained an elephant corps, but by the first century CE, they were overthrown by the Sakas and Parthian horse nomads.

While in the Middle East and Central Asia elephants were vanishing from the battle order, the elephants' importance continued to grow in India. Chandragupta Maurya's success at halting Seleucus increased the status of the elephant arm both in Hindu military theory and practice. Kautilya, Kamandaka, Bana, and Sukra all emphasized cooperation between the battle-winning elephants with supporting infantry. The *Purananuru,* one of the anthologies of poems of the Sangam era (between first and third centuries CE) describes the use of elephants both as a battlefield weapon and as a siege weapon in south India. From north India, the use of war elephants spread to south India especially among the Chola and Chera armies. Elephants were used as a battering ram against the wooden doors of the enemy forts, and to cross ditches and filling moats.

Several Islamic writers provide snap-shots of the use of elephants in India. Abu Zaid, an Arab who lived in ninth century CE, tells us in his *Geography of the East* that the king of Assam and Bengal maintained 50,000 elephants. Zaid probably referred to the potential number of elephants that could be raised in these two regions, rather than the actual number of war elephants deployed by these two kings in campaigns.

Al-Masudi's book titled *Murujul-Zahab* (*Meadows of Gold*), written in 10th century CE, throws light on the military confrontations between the Muslims and the Hindus, and how terrain shaped the force structure. The Rashtrakuta army was reliant on elephants because they mostly campaigned in mountainous central India, where elephants were more effective than the locally bred ponies. However, an elephant-centric army posed certain logistical constraints during operations. Sulaiman, an Arab merchant from the ninth century CE, wrote that the rulers of Assam and Bengal, who relied on elephants in battle, could move only during winter when the elephants could endure thirst.

Elephant-centric Hindu armies were no match for Muslim horse archers using stirrups. The Arabs invaded Sind in 711 CE and moved up along River Indus. In June 712 CE, naphtha fire (probably Greek fire) and 6,000 Syrian armored cavalry shredded Dahir's elephant-centric army. The great power and unpredictability of elephants also made them a double-edged sword. For example, in 1009 CE, Mahmud Ghazni confronted the confederacy of north Indian kings under Anandpal near Peshawar. Mahmud's cavalry was in dire straits due to the attack launched by the Rajputs, in which Gakkar spearmen penetrated both the flanks of

Mahmud's army and reached the center. At this critical juncture, Anandpal's personal elephant mount took fright due to a barrage of arrows and naptha balls. As the elephant fled back in panic, the Rajput army lost heart and broke.

Technological improvements in cavalry warfare undermined the elephant as the primary weapon system on Indian battlefields. Muslim mounted archers began using four-foot-long composite bows capable of piercing elephant hide. The effective range of such bow was 250 yards. Nailed horseshoes further raised the effectiveness of Muslim cavalry. In 1193 CE, Muhammad Ghori, using horse cavalry, defeated Raja Jai Chand of Kanauj and captured 300 of his elephants. Once the Turks settled in India, they absorbed the Hindu culture of using war elephants from the Rajputs. For example, Sultan Mahmud Ghazni used elephants against the Central Asian Turks, and the Delhi Sultanate (1210 CE–1525 CE) also maintained elephants. When the sultanate expanded into central India, deployment of elephants was more effective than cavalry due to forested and rocky terrain. Elephants were also useful for crossing rivers.

The advent of gunpowder finally sounded the death knell of elephant-based warfare. In the First Battle of Panipat fought on April 21, 1526 CE, Ibrahim Lodhi deployed 1,000 armored elephants. Since the Lodhi Sultanate had lost control over northwest India, it did not possess horse archers. Babur's mounted archers attacked the enemy at both flanks and in the rear, and their arrows forced the elephants to retire. In addition, the guns deployed at Babur's center unnerved the elephants. Eventually, Ibrahim's soldiers and elephants were massed in such a crowd and unable to either fight effectively or retreat in an organized manner. Ibrahim died on the battlefield and Babur captured Delhi.

The Second Battle of Panipat was fought on November 5, 1556 CE, between the Hindu warlord Hemu and the Mughal army under Bairam Khan. Abul Fazl emphasizes the destructive capacity of Hemu's battle elephants, whose charge almost routed the Mughal cavalry, before Hemu was killed by an arrow. This was the last major use of elephants in battle. Under the Mughals, mounted archers and field guns became the principal components of the army. Rather than elephants, gunpowder was used to blast the fortifications. The elephants were now used as command vehicles and as beasts of burden.

In the first half of the 18th century CE, the elephants were used for pushing heavy guns with their heads over difficult passages. The East India Company's army used elephants for dragging the siege guns and mortars while campaigning along the roadless northwest frontier. The last use of elephants as carriers of military supplies occurred in 1943 when Field Marshal Slim's Fourteenth Army was campaigning in Arakan. In 1944, Dakotas replaced the elephants.

See also: Bana; Kamandaka; Kautilya

Further Reading

Gommans, Jos, "Warhorse and Gunpowder in India c. 1000–1850." In Jeremy Black, ed., *War in the Early Modern World.* 1999, reprint, London/New York: Routledge, 2004, pp. 105–27.

McCrindle, John W., *Ancient India as described by Megasthenes and Arrian: Being a translation of the fragments of the Indika of Megasthenes collected by Dr. Schwanbeck, and of the first part of the Indika of Arrian.* 1926, reprint, New Delhi: Munshiram Manoharlal, 2000.

Kaushik Roy

War and Military Philosophy in Traditional Japan
(ca. 600–1868 CE)

Significance: Japan's ethnically homogenous society, strong sense of cultural continuity, and for some periods of its history, cultural insularity, makes it a fascinating case study of a highly complex and unique military culture.

Influences: Japan generated little significant dialogue of its own on the purpose of armies and war. It drew instead on the prodigious volume of theoretical work on war produced in China during the later Chou era (722–221 BCE). This included both specialized works on military theory and strategy and more general works by Legalist, Taoist, Confucian, and other philosophers. This Chinese canon formed a base to which Japanese military thinkers returned for inspiration throughout the premodern and early modern epochs.

Chinese political theory cast the state as a conduit for expressing the will of the sovereign, who was himself the earthly agent and custodian of the cosmic order, with authority over and responsibility for his subjects analogous to those of a father for his children. The emperor's role in the social order applied equally to domestic and foreign affairs, which formed a continuum with the emperor at the center of a radial series of zones of influence. Any disruptions of the social order, from petty crimes and familial disputes in the capital to armed conflicts abroad, were thus transgressions against the proper cosmic order and deserving of imperial attention.

When all was as it should be, the virtuous and proper conduct of the ruler exerted an edifying effect on his subjects, driving them toward righteous behavior without further need for coercion, just as ideal children acquire moral rectitude from their parents' example. But where, owing to shortcomings on the part of the ruler or the subjects, this was insufficient, the monarch encouraged virtuous conduct by reward and discouraged misbehavior by punishment. Recourse to violent coercion, including war, was justifiable when—but only when—all else had failed.

Thus war, in the Chinese scheme of things, could be pursued only by the rightful sovereign, and only if conducted as a matter of last resort. At the same time, the righteousness and the justice of *any* military action the emperor and his ministers deemed it necessary to pursue could not be questioned. The success of any military venture was in itself proof that the campaign had been in accord with the cosmic order, and therefore by definition right and just.

Approaches and Application:

Just War in Classical Japan (ca. 600–1200)

Chinese ideas about war made their way into Japan along with other bits of Chinese culture over the course of the fifth, sixth, and seventh centuries, providing the framework for the military institutions of the imperial (*ritsuryō*) state. Thus the Japanese court, like its Chinese paragon, laid claim to an authority whose boundaries often exceeded its real power, and whose implications left scarce room for debate concerning the parameters of just war. The *ritsuryō* polity equated its existence, and the sociopolitical structure over which it reigned, with morality and the cosmic order. Military actions undertaken to preserve—or enhance—the imperial order were—must be—just war, while any and all other recourses to force of arms were by definition selfish, particularistic, and unjust. And, following the Chinese model, the Japanese court viewed warfare with foreign powers and peoples, and domestic law enforcement as essentially the same activity. Outside the capital, military defense and police functions were carried out by the same units and officers, following the same procedures. Military adventures outside the boundaries of the state were justified with the same rhetoric as police actions within it.

By the mid-10th century, the court had discarded most of the elaborate, Chinese-inspired military apparatus established under the *ritsuryō* codes, an excision that in part facilitated and was in part facilitated by the birth and rapid growth of a new order of professional fighting men—most commonly referred to in English as the samurai—in the capital and the countryside. From this time forward, the court maintained no armies of its own, depending instead on the members of this emerging warrior order deputized to act as its "claws and teeth."

For more than two and a half centuries, the samurai obediently fought the court's battles for it, until Minamoto Yoritomo laid the foundations for warrior rule in Japan with his creation of a military government, or shogunate, in the eastern village of Kamakura at the end of the 12th century. The Kamakura shogunate was in essence a government within a government, exercising authority delegated to it by the emperor and his court in Kyoto. Under its successor regime, established in 1336 in the Muromachi district of Kyoto, however, warriors came not only to dominate the countryside, but also to overshadow the imperial court as well.

Nevertheless, samurai acquisition of a monopoly over the *means* of armed force did not lead quickly or directly to warrior autonomy in the *application* of force. For in contrast to Europe, where knights and feudal lordship arose together from the confusion of the waning Carolingian Empire and the onslaughts of Norse marauders, the wellspring of samurai warfare lay within a secure and still-vital imperial state structure. The principle that final authority and formal control rested with the central government remained a key feature of Japan's military and police system from the late seventh century until well into the medieval era: the state jealously guarded its exclusive right to sanction the use of force throughout the Heian

(794–1184) and Kamakura (1185–1333) periods and attempted to do so, albeit with ever-lessening success, under the Muromachi regime (1336–1573) as well.

"Private War" in Medieval Japan (ca. 1000–1600)

Thus Japanese law made an unambiguous distinction between lawful military action, in which one (or more) of the parties involved possessed a legal warrant, and unlawful, private fights. Nevertheless, legalities notwithstanding, it is clear that warriors did engage in fighting for reasons other than being called to service on behalf of the state, that they were doing this from the very beginning of their history, and that they felt morally justified in doing so.

One of the most important forms of private warfare during the late classical period was samurai involvement in the political intrigues of the upper court aristocracy. Although political authority during this era still derived from the emperor through the *ritsuryō* bureaucracy, real power took an oligarchic form in which various courtier houses, major shrines, and temples ruled through a combination of public and private assets and channels. The competition between these court houses and institutions for wealth and influence was often intense. And in this struggle, control of martial resources of one sort or another could be a crucial asset. Dramatic or large-scale examples of recourse to arms in pursuit of political aims were rare, but attempts at assassination and intimidation were common enough that military retainers were needed to protect the persons, as well as the status of the top courtiers and their heirs. The great houses and religious institutions, accordingly, assembled private military forces and pressed for control of state military resources.

From the perspective of the warriors involved, military actions undertaken on behalf of aristocratic employers were not, of course, very far removed from actions conducted in possession of warrants. In either case the warrior acted on orders from above. From the mid-ninth century public and private rights and responsibilities with respect to many key government functions were becoming increasingly hard to separate. Under such circumstances, warriors probably made little practical distinction between orders from state officials and (private) orders from courtier patrons.

But not all private warfare was initiated by or for the aristocracy. Warriors were also taking to the saddle in their own interests. Early samurai had a highly developed sense of personal and familial honor, and were rarely averse to bloodshed to protect or advance it. Warriors were also sometimes drawn into the quarrels of their vassals and retainers. Overt attempts at self-aggrandizement by armed force provided yet another source of unsanctioned military encounters. Such skirmishes were a minor, albeit ongoing, phenomenon from the 10th century, and became increasingly commonplace during the Kamakura and Muromachi periods.

In principle, the state's exclusive right to sanction violence ought to have robbed private war of any rectitude; but clearly it did not. Instead, the notion of just war seems to have broadened over the course of the 10th to 13th centuries, making increasing room for the existence of legitimate battle, even in the absence of formal legality. Not surprisingly, the state's willingness to tolerate military activities conducted for enhancing or preserving personal profit grew at a pace just a few steps behind the court's dependence on private warriors for law enforcement.

The government's increasingly liberal attitude toward private conflicts between samurai can be seen in the punishments meted out to violators of the peace. Tenth- and 11th-century warriors engaged in private fighting at their peril, and the court was only slightly more lenient when unauthorized military actions coincided with the public interest. But the Kamakura shogunate, forced to maintain a delicate balancing act between satisfying its mandate from the court to maintain law and order and not alienating the vassals on whose support it depended for continued existence, was much more tolerant than the imperial court of small-scale private warfare in the provinces. In Kamakura times armed incursion into neighboring lands and use of force to extort estate residents and proprietors alike became commonplace. Although shogunal edicts described attempts at self-aggrandizement through force of arms as "outrages" (*ranbō*), "evil acts" (*akugyō*), or "depredations" (*rōzeki*), severe punishments were almost never imposed.

The Kamakura regime fell in 1333 as a result of events spawned by an imperial succession dispute, which also gave rise to the six-decade long Nambokuchō ("southern and northern courts") era, the longest and most significant dynastic schism in Japanese history. During this interval, the existence of rival imperial courts made it impossible to distinguish public from private war, inasmuch as both courts claimed to be issuing public calls to arms. This enabled samurai to justify almost any recourse to violence as public and lent an unprecedented legitimacy to feuding, with the predictable result that violence became endemic. At the same time, the inability of any central authority to provide meaningful protection for property rights, or to secure public safety, made warriors increasingly reliant on their own resources for resolving disputes. Sixty years of this sort of ambiguity reified the custom of warrior self-help, and the Muromachi shogunate found itself unable to recover control of the situation, even after the era of two courts ended, in 1392.

Fifteen Ashikaga shoguns reigned between 1336 and 1573, when the last, Yoshiaki, was deposed; but only the first six could lay claim to have actually ruled the country. By the mid-1400s, although both the court and the shogunate remained nominally in authority, real power in Japan had devolved to a few score feudal barons, called daimyō, whose authority rested first and foremost on their ability to hold lands by military force. There followed a century and a half of nearly continuous warfare as daimyō contested with one another and with those below them to maintain and expand their domains. The spirit of this Sengoku (literally, "country at war") age is captured in two expressions current at the time: *gekokujō* ("the low overthrow the high") and *jakuniku kyōshoku* ("the weak become meat; the strong eat").

The proliferation of private warfaring that occurred over the course of the medieval period reflects a fundamental change in Japanese definitions of just war, one that centered on the replacement of courtier values with those of the samurai themselves. Although the former focused narrowly on central government sanction, the latter broadly embraced the right of warriors to fight on the personal authority of courtier or warrior patrons, as well as in pursuit or defense of private profit or matters of honor. Nevertheless, although central authorities were forced, with increasing frequency, to look the other way during private squabbles between warriors, they never dropped their pretense that such activities were criminal. And even the samurai themselves took great pains to cloak their quarrels under the mantle of state authority. This habit persisted even in the late 16th century, long after central government power had all but ceased to exist. Daimyō continued—insofar as it was possible—to invoke the authority of the court or the shogunate to justify their campaigns, even as lesser lords cited daimyō domanial authority for theirs.

Private warfare in medieval Japan thus corresponded closely to what European legal scholars termed "*guerre couverte,*" or covert war: private war between two lords who held their lands from the same sovereign. In such conflicts no legal rights attached to any captured property. Similarly, the *formal* legal structure of medieval Japan made only minimal allowance for the pursuit of private ends through violence. This made the affixing of one's private disputes to some public cause attractive to the point of being imperative, for it was the public sanction—irrespective of whether or not the "sanctioning" authority was even aware of one's participation—that rendered the violence legitimate.

In any event, the instability of the Sengoku age could and did not continue indefinitely. Daimyō quickly discovered that the corollary cliché to "might makes right" is that "he who lives by the sword, dies by the sword," and that many were spending as much time and energy defending themselves from their own ambitious vassals as from other daimyō. During the late 16th century, the most able among them began searching for ways to reduce vassal independence. This in turn made possible the creation of ever-larger domains and hegemonic alliances extending across entire regions. At length, the successive efforts of Oda Nobunaga (1534–1582), Toyotomi Hideyoshi (1536–1598), and Tokugawa Ieyasu (1542–1616) eliminated many of the daimyō and unified the rest into a nationwide coalition.

In 1603, Ieyasu assumed the title of shōgun and established Japan's third military regime. The new polity, a kind of centralized feudalism, kept the peace in Japan for the better part of three centuries, before at last succumbing to a combination of foreign pressure, evolution of the nation's social and economic structure, and decay of the government itself.

Military Thought in Early Modern Japan (ca. 1600–1868)

The advent of the Tokugawa shogunate and the ensuing Pax Tokugawa marked the transition from medieval to early modern Japan, which brought with it profound changes for the samurai. In the medieval age, warriors had constituted a flexible and permeable order defined primarily by their activities as fighting men. At the top of this order stood the daimyō, some of whom were inheritors to family warrior legacies dating back centuries, whereas others had clawed their way to this status from far humbler beginnings. Below these were multiple layers of lesser lords, enfeoffed vassals, and yeoman farmers whose numbers and service as samurai waxed and waned with the fortunes of war and the resources and military needs of the great barons. But the early modern regime froze the social order, drawing for the first time a clear line between peasants, who were registered with and bound to their fields, and samurai, who were removed from their lands and gathered into garrisons in the castle towns of the shogun and the daimyō. The samurai thus became a legally defined, legally privileged, hereditary class, consisting of a very few enfeoffed lords and a much larger body of stipended retainers, whose numbers were now fixed by law. Daimyō were stripped—by formal law enforced through a variety of new administrative measures—of any authority to make war or forge alliances independently of the shogunate. And, without wars to fight, the military skills and culture of this class inevitably atrophied. The samurai rapidly evolved from sword-wielding warriors to sword-bearing bureaucrats.

One effect of these developments was to turn the role and behavioral patterns of warriors into a topic of extensive philosophical musing for the samurai, who had stationed themselves at the top of the sociopolitical hierarchy, and yet effectively did no real work, inasmuch as there were no longer any wars. This new reality and the rapid spread of literacy among the samurai during the Tokugawa period gave rise to a substantial genre of widely circulated manuals and treatises pontificating on warrior identity and samurai morality. Most were written from Neo-Confucian perspectives, penned by scholar bureaucrats within the government, as well as by conservative or progressive pundits and educators unaffiliated with the shogunate or any daimyō.

Modern observers most commonly refer to the subject of this discussion as "*bushidō*" ("the way of the warrior"), but the term is problematic, insofar as it suggests orthodoxy and a consensus of opinion that simply did not exist. For although there was considerable debate, there was little agreement; the opinions of the would-be arbiters of samurai mores differed on both basic principles and practical applications thereof. Indeed, even the term *bushidō* itself was scarcely used prior to the 20th century, appearing in only a handful of late medieval and Tokugawa period texts.

Ballooning literacy rates and the peacetime environment of the Tokugawa period gave rise to an unprecedented volume of writing on the craft, as well as the ethical imperatives, of being a samurai. Two overlapping genres of schools and treatises on strategy and tactics emerged, both heavily influenced by Japanese analyses of ancient and medieval Chinese texts.

The first of these, styled *gungaku* ("military studies) or sometimes *gunpō* ("military methods"), focused on battlefield tactics and the organization of armies. Shogunal advisors, including Obata Kagenori (1572–1663) and Hōjō Ujinaga (1609–1670), and independent scholars such as Yamago Sokō

(1622–1685) combined idealized reconstructions of Sengoku era battles with a theoretical base culled from the Chinese military canon (primarily the Chou period texts Sun Tzu's *Ping fa* ["Art of War"], T'ai Kung's *Liu t'ao* ["Six Secret Teachings"], Huang shih-kung's *San lue* ["Three Strategies"], the *Wu-tzu* ["Book of Master Wu"], *Ssu-ma Fa* ["Methods of the Ssu-ma"], and *Wei Liao-tzu* ["Book of Master Wei Liao"]; and the seventh-century *T'ang T'ai-tsung Li Wei-kung Wen-tui* ["Questions and Replies Between T'ang T'ai-tsung and Li Wei-kung"]) to stimulate the emergence of a half-dozen or so schools of military science. The most prominent among these were the Kōshū-ryū, the Echigo-ryū, the Hōjō-ryū, the Takeda-ryū, the Yamaga-ryū, the Naganuma-ryū, and the Kusunoki-ryū.

The second genre focused on the methods and goals of individual training, providing a philosophical framework for the schools of swordsmanship, spearmanship, archery, and other martial arts (*bugei*) that mushroomed across the landscape during the Tokugawa period. It drew its inspirations from an exotic mixture of Buddhist (primarily Esoteric, or *Mikkyō*, Buddhism, and Zen), Taoist, Neo-Confucian, and nativist (Shintō) cosmology.

Organized schools (*ryūha*) of martial art first appeared around the turn of the 15th century, as veteran warriors began to codify their knowledge and experience and to methodize its study, in keeping with a broad trend of the age toward systemization of knowledge and teaching in various applied arts. During the Tokugawa period, martial art instruction became professionalized, and in some cases, commercialized; training periods became longer, curricula were formalized; and elaborate systems of student ranks developed.

More intriguingly, the motives and goals underlying practice were refined. The curricula of *ryūha bugei* had, in fact, been militarily anachronistic from its inception; its purpose was less to teach prosaic battle skills than to convey more abstract ideals of personal development. With the onset of peace under the Tokugawa regime, the notion of martial training as a vehicle for physical and spiritual cultivation of the self took on a new emphasis and reached new levels of development. Samurai, who no longer expected to spend time on the battlefield, sought and found a more relevant rationale for studying martial art.

Seventeenth-, 18th- and 19th-century texts on swordsmanship and other martial art describe extraordinarily complex phenomena in which various physical, technical, psychological, and philosophical factors intertwine and interact; and in which expertise in personal combat and spiritual illumination are interdependent developments—inseparable aspects of the whole—to be experienced simultaneously. This perspective rested on a compelling paradox that equated perfection of the arts of violence with perfect nonviolence. By the mid-Tokugawa period, absolute, flawless proficiency in combat came to be identified as a state in which one rose above all possible opponents by deactivating all possible opposition. The ultimate warrior was seen as one in such perfect harmony with the natural order that he transcended both any interest in fighting and any need to fight.

In this respect the conclusions reached by *bugei* philosophers dovetailed neatly with the goals and exhortations of sociopolitical leaders seeking to bring the ideals of the medieval warrior into line with those of a peaceful, stable and orderly realm. Nevertheless, although the evolution of the *bugei* was part and parcel to the overall transformation of the samurai in early modern Japan, it was driven by an internal logic of its own, one that allowed exponents to believe that they were pursuing exactly the same goals as their ancestors had. Tokugawa samurai were enjoined not to repudiate violence or abandon the world, the way a monk does, but to raise the quest for perfect martial skill to a level of sophistication that impelled them to transcend it. According to this ideal, which turns on the indivisibility of pragmatic military, moral and psycho-spiritual concerns in a worldview that stresses the interpenetration of all things and all actions, a perfect warrior is still a warrior, performing the functions of a warrior by mastering violence and becoming able to defend the realm and serve justice without needing to fight.

Legacy: In 1868, combined armies from two daimyō domains in southwestern Japan forced the resignation of the last shōgun and declared a restoration of all powers of governance to the emperor. This event, known as the Meiji Restoration, marked the beginning of the end for the samurai as a class. By the 1890s Japan was a modernized, industrialized nation ruled by a constitutional government and defended by a conscript Imperial army and navy that drew their ideological frameworks from a volatile—and oft-times quixotic—mixture of German and British tactical and organizational models with carefully selected bits and pieces of samurai—particularly early modern *gungaku* and "bushidō"—traditions.

See also: Just War Theory (Western); Hindu Tradition of Just and Unjust War; Kautilya; Li Ching; Li Ch'üan; Muhammad; Musashi, Miyamoto; Shang Yang; Sun Tzu

Further Reading

Bay, Alexander R, "Bugei and Heihō: Military Skills and Strategy in Japan from the Eighth to Eleventh Centuries." MA thesis, University of Oregon, 1998.

Conlan, Thomas Donald, *State of War: The Violent Order of Fourteenth Century Japan*, Michigan Monograph Series in Japanese Studies. Ann Arbor: University of Michigan Center for Japanese Studies, 2003.

Farris, Wm Wayne, *Heavenly Warriors: the Evolution of Japan's Military, 500–1300*. Cambridge: Harvard University Press, 1992.

Friday, Karl, "Bushidō or Bull? A Medieval Historian's Perspective on the Imperial Army and the Japanese Warrior Tradition." *The History Teacher* 27 no. 3 (1994): 339–49.

Friday, Karl, *Hired Swords: the Rise of Private Warrior Power in Early Japan*. Stanford, CA: Stanford University Press, 1992.

Friday, Karl, "Off the Warpath: Military Science & Budō in the Evolution of Ryūha Bugei." In Alexander Bennett, ed., *Budo Perspectives*, vol. 1. Auckland, New Zealand: Kendo World Publications, 2005, 249–68.

Friday, Karl, *Samurai, Warfare & the State in Early Medieval Japan*. London: Routledge, 2004.

Friday, Karl with Seki Humitake, *Legacies of the Sword: The Kashima-Shinryū & Samurai Martial Culture*. Honolulu: University of Hawaii Press, 1997.

Futomaru Nobuaki, *Senryaku senjutsu heiki jiten Chūgoku kodai hen*. Vol. 1 of Gurafikku senshi shiriizu. Tokyo: Gakushū kenkyūsha, 1996.

Futomaru Nobuaki, *Senryaku senjutsu heiki jiten Chūgoku chūsei/kindai hen*. Vol. 7 of Gurafikku senshi shiriizu. Tokyo: Gakushū kenkyūsha, 1999.

Graff, David A, *Medieval Chinese Warfare, 300–900*. Warfare and History. Ed., Jeremy Black. London and New York: Routledge, 2002.

Hurst, G. Cameron III, *Armed Martial Arts of Japan: Swordsmanship & Archery*. New Haven, CN: Yale University Press, 1998.

Hurst, G. Cameron III, "Death, Honor, and Loyalty: The Bushidō Ideal." *Philosophy East and West* 40 no. 4 (1990): 511–27.

Ikegami, Eiko, *The Taming of the Samurai: Honorific Individualism and the Making of Modern Japan*. Cambridge, MA: Harvard University Press, 1995.

Kierman, Frank A. Jr. and John K. Fairbank, eds. *Chinese Ways in Warfare*. Cambridge, MA: Harvard University Press, 1974.

Sato, Hiroaki, *Legends of the Samurai*. Woodstock, NY: Overlook Press, 1995.

Tien Chen-Ya, *Chinese Military Theory*. Oakville, Ontario: Mosaic Press, 1992.

Yates, Robin D.S., "Early China." In *War and Society in the Ancient and Medieval Worlds: Asia, the Mediterranean, Europe, and Mesoamerica*. Ed., Kurt Raaflaub and Nathan Rosenstein. Cambridge, MA: Center for Hellenic Studies, Harvard University, 1999, 7–46.

Karl Friday

Warfare in the Western and Central Sudan
(14th to 20th centuries CE)

Significance: The African savannah region south of the Sahara has, for centuries, been a meeting ground between largely Islamic North Africa and Black African cultures. The diversity of the landscape, and the wide range of cultures and ethnic groups that inhabit it, has made this a melting pot for military cultures and techniques.

Context: In the region of Africa known as the western and central Sudan, open grasslands with patches of woodland stretch from the Atlantic coast to the foothills of Ethiopia. To the north of this savannah is the semiarid grass steppe and acacia thornveld of the Sahel, which gives way to the Sahara Desert; to the south is the rain forest and the tropical coast. The peoples of the western Sudan generally speak languages of the Niger–Congo group that extends through central and southern Africa, and those of the central Sudan speak either the languages of the Nilo-Saharan or Afro-Asiatic groups, the latter being related to Arabic. For at least a thousand years BCE, Berber intermediaries carried on trade and fostered cultural exchanges across the Sahara between this region and the Carthaginians and subsequently the Romans of Africa's Mediterranean shore. The introduction of the camel by the fifth century CE greatly facilitated trans-Saharan contacts. By the ninth century Islam had crossed the desert and gained a foothold in the sophisticated Iron Age kingdom of Ghana (in modern-day Mali), which reached its apogee in the 11th century CE, and in its successor, the empire of Mali, whose ruler in the 14th century made the pilgrimage to Mecca.

Approach: Evidence is fragmentary, but it seems war leaders south of the Sahara for reasons of prestige had long ridden the small, local breed of horse introduced from North Africa in the first millennium BCE. By the 14th century cavalry had begun to dominate warfare in Mali, although large warhorses suitable for carrying heavily armed warriors were rare on account of the equatorial diseases of the savannah, and had to be imported at great expense across the Sahara from North Africa, or bought from the nomads of the Sahel and Sahara fringe where they were bred. The shock tactics generally favored by cavalry required firm saddles and stirrups. Though evidence is scant, it seems indigenous saddles were in use at least by the 14th century. Certainly, by the 17th century—doubtless as a result of ongoing contacts with the Maghreb—the horsemen of the central Sudan had adopted the heavy Arab-style stirrups that protect the whole leg and have sharp cutting edges at toe and heel. Riders carried hide shields and by the 16th century the elite wore chain mail and helmets. Heavy cavalry with cumbersome thick quilted cloth armor for both horses and riders were common in the central Sudan and served as bodyguards for rulers and shock forces to break enemy formations. Light cavalry, which were better suited to the terrain and climate, scouted and harassed the enemy. Weapons were the lance, sword (often scimitar shaped) and 10 to 20 javelins carried in a quiver. In most societies horsemen favored close combat and despised those who used missile weapons, though the Fula (Fulani/Fulbe) pastoral clans of the more broken terrain of the western Sudan, where bows and arrows had long been the principal weapon, operated effectively as mounted archers against their lightly armored foes. Warriors normally went to war with at least one spare horse, essential for a rapid withdrawal. Not to do so was an indication of a resolve to fight to the death.

   Although all fighters were cavalry in the desert, mixed cavalry and infantry were the norm in the disciplined armies of the states of the savannah such as those of the Songhai Empire, the kingdom of Borno, and those of the Hausa city states. Possession of a horse entailed military obligation, which thus fell upon all nobles and state officials, as well as on their mounted clients and slaves. Infantry were recruited from slaves. The slave units and free mounted clients typically received their armaments from the state and formed the nucleus of the army. Until conscription became common in the *jihadi* states that arose in the 19th century, the peasantry usually had no rigid military obligations although the lure of booty usually persuaded many to volunteer. The ratio of infantry to cavalry was about 10:1, with the infantry component becoming ever larger as grassland gave way to forest, where horses could not long survive because of disease. On larger rivers, such as the Niger, watercraft of shallow draft powered by paddles were manned by marines. A typical infantryman carried a leather shield with no other armor, a javelin, sword, and a bow and arrows with poisoned, barbed heads. Battle formation generally had infantry massed in the center, typically deployed in squadrons and lines with shield-bearing foot in front and on the flanks, and with archers behind shooting over them. The cavalry were on the wings and in reserve, though they might be posted in the vanguard for their shock effect. Generally, horses were too valuable to be readily risked in charging home but, if the enemy infantry broke, the cavalry rode them down in pursuit and determined the battle.

Villages were usually left undefended and their inhabitants scattered into the surrounding countryside or fled to nearby towns if attacked. On the west coast, people took to building wooden fortification in the 18th century under the influence of the French trading settlements. However, elsewhere in the savannah, the practice of surrounding towns with mud brick fortifications and towers was long established. By the end of the 18th century the growing prevalence of firearms meant that clay and stone fortifications, loopholed and constructed for fighting with gunpowder weapons, were becoming more common, and besiegers were devising sophisticated networks of trenches, towers, and other siege works.

States such as Songhai often called in nomad desert horsemen to harass an enemy without cost to them or to take part in major campaigns and civil wars. Local raids against villages by mixed forces of foot and horse were very common because they were an effective means of weakening an enemy and capturing slaves to pay for horses and weapons. In large-scale declared wars, the weaker army might retire to the safety of a fortified town where it was invested while the enemy ravaged the countryside and enslaved whole populations. The western and central Sudan were still underpopulated regions and the power of a state was measured not in its extent of territory but in the number of productive people (such as farmers, traders, and slaves) it controlled.

The advent of firearms did not put an early end to the predominance of cavalry in the western and central Sudan. European traders at the coast introduced reliable flintlocks at the end of the 17th century, and firearms also came from across the Sahara. By the mid-18th century the nomad cavalry of the desert had abandoned their bows and javelins for flintlocks, though guns were more slowly adopted by cavalry at the eastern end of the desert zone, and traditionally armed cavalry in the floodplain south of the Niger remained more than a match for nomad cavalry with firearms. Infantry continued to carry javelins and bows, though by the 18th century, as these were increasingly supplemented by firearms, traditionally tight infantry formations gave way to looser ones. It has been argued that by the late 19th century detachments of slave musketeers with their slave commanders grew in significance as the core of standing armies and the instrument of centralizing state power against the traditional (and mounted) nobility. This might well have been so, but in battle infantry long remained reluctant to engage hand to hand, and relied on maneuver and firepower (or simply the loud report of a discharge) to break their opponents or frighten away horsemen. The successful cavalry charge therefore remained decisive well into the late 19th century, so although infantry as always bore the brunt of savannah warfare, the prestige and ethos of the horseman persisted. Horsemanship and social distinction remained synonymous, and for the nobleman, war was a means of enrichment and the acquisition of honor.

Application:

Mali

In the great empire of Mali, which reached its height in the 14th century, society was divided into freemen, slaves, and craftsmen. Slaves had been exported northward since at least the eighth century, and the warhorse made it easier for Mali to capture slaves from the surrounding agricultural peoples. As with other future powerful states of the savannah, Mali's army was built around a core of full-time royal guards (mainly mounted slaves) and numerous infantry levies drawn from conquered or allied provinces and supplied through tribute.

Songhai

When Mali weakened in the late 15th century, it was supplanted by the Songhai Empire, which dominated the middle Niger Valley. In Songhai, the equestrian nobility bought their warhorses from the north with slaves. They conducted warfare like a dangerous sport governed by a strict code of chivalric honor and fear of being shamed. After Moroccan invaders fragmented Songhai in 1591, the chief heirs to their military traditions in this turbulent region were the Songhai-speaking Zarma groups, a society highly stratified between noble freemen, commoners, and slaves. The brutally arrogant noble Zarma horsemen were notorious up to the 19th century for their slave raids.

Borno

In the central Sudan, further to the east, in the 16th century the Sefawa dynasty of the kingdom of Borno northwest of Lake Chad created an equestrian military class that owed military service for their fiefs of land. Borno was primarily a slave-owning society, so the army included many slave infantrymen, heartily despised by the noble cavalrymen in their rich clothing and chain mail. Borno maintained strong relations across the Sahara with the Ottoman Empire in North Africa, and employed Ottoman musketeers as a striking force whose tactics inevitably influenced the deployment of Borno's armies. Trade in slaves and cola nuts bought muskets for use in further slaving. Borno was often at war with the Hausa city kingdoms to its west, where in the 15th century, a dominant equestrian nobility had also emerged. These Hausa states were interminably at war with each other over trade routes and the capture of slaves.

Fula

The Fula pastoral clans, who spread eastward from the Senegal Valley on the Atlantic coast as far east as Borno, and who had adopted horses, regarded themselves as freeborn noblemen, superior to the agriculturalists they conquered and exploited. Ancestry determined both rank and behavior. The most distinctive social group were the professional warrior horsemen who—whether freemen or royal slaves—were deeply engaged in slave-raiding. They followed an austere heroic code of honor, called *pulaaku,* never violating the rules of hospitality nor displaying weakness of any sort, but instead stressing self-control, courage, loyalty, and truthfulness, as well as grace of manner and generosity.

Sinnar, Segu, and Kaarta

In the state of Sinnar at the furthest eastern fringes of the savannah below the Ethiopian highlands, the aristocratic order of armored, sword-wielding horsemen was undermined in the early 18th century by the Sultan of Sinnar's creation of a slave army. This was similar to a development in the western Sudan. Here, the two kingdoms of Segu and Kaarta, which had arisen in the 17th century on the ruins of Songhai, had built their power on the novel institution of a standing army of slaves who fought not as cavalry, but as archers, and increasingly in the 18th century, as musketeers. But by then, all through the savannah the heroic tradition (which went back in oral tradition to at least the 13th century CE) of the noble warrior on horseback in search of fame and honor was being undermined by armies of Muslim zealots.

Influence of Islam (including Futa Jallon, Sokoto Caliphate, Masina Caliphate, Tukulor Empire)

The equestrian aristocracy, stretching from Jolof in the western Sudan through Hausaland to Borno and Sinnar in the east, was distinguished culturally from their subjects by their early conversion to Islam. North African and Berber merchants brought Islam south across the Sahara and by the 11th century rulers and their nobles began to convert to Islam because it represented intellectual sophistication and cosmopolitanism. This was a type of "mixed Islam," in which "pagan" elements of the ancient, polytheistic religions of the peasant majority (which were proscribed by strict Islam) were nevertheless accommodated. The sacral nature of kingship still made it essential for rulers to maintain the religious rituals of kingship necessary to fulfill their subjects' cultural expectations and maintain their allegiance. This "mixed Islam" had little impact on the traditional warrior ethos of the savannah. But Muslim zealots rejected many aspects of pagan warrior culture and wished to substitute respect for the Prophet for glorification of the warrior hero, and the ideals of Muslim virtue and respectability for the crass pursuit of rank and reputation.

In the late 17th and early 18th centuries, Muslim clerics (*marabouts*) in several states of the Senegambia region in the far western Sudan encouraged *jihad* (or holy war of religious reform) against rulers. Most spectacularly, Fula herders set up their new state of **Futa Jallon,** based on Islamic ideals. Nevertheless, this too remained a warrior society, in which the traditional, heroic aristocratic ethos blended with Muslim virtue. The new aristocracy regularly raided the small-scale societies of the west coast for slaves in the guise of *jihad* against nonbelievers.

Over the course of the 18th and 19th centuries a number of West Sudanese *marabouts* organized further *jihad* that created fundamentalist Muslim states and built a strong and abiding Islamic identity in the region. The *jihadi* armies prayed before they marched out, regularly while on the march, just before giving battle and in thanksgiving afterward. This strict regimen of prayer imposed discipline over the otherwise unruly host, raised morale, and discomforted the enemy. The *jihad* of 1804 that created the **Sokoto Caliphate** was the model for militant Islam in the region. *Marabouts* had settled in Hausaland before the 16th century and by the late 18th century were aggressively attempting to convert the peasantry and bring the Hausa rulers to a more orthodox Islam. One *marabout,* Usuman dan Fodio, declared a *jihad* on the Hausa kingdom of Gobir. His army was a new phenomenon in Hausaland, being composed almost entirely of light infantry. Though mobile, the *jihadi* infantry were at a disadvantage against traditional cavalry on open ground until they found a tactical formation that neutralized it. At Tabkin Kwotto in 1804 they formed up in a square and the archers drove the Hausa cavalry from the field. Usuman's son, Muhammad Bello, fought 47 major campaigns in conquering Hausaland and forcing the sultans to obey the new Islamic authority of the Sokoto Caliphate.

However, the original egalitarianism of the jihad movement faded away and the highly stratified society of Hausaland was perpetuated in the Sokoto Caliphate. The Fula elite insisted on their ethnic dominance over the conquered blacks who were forbidden arms and horses, and created a noble class differing from the old only in scrupulous adherence to Islamic law. Adoption of Hausa culture included traditional cavalry warfare, and the *jihad* armies were soon dominated by horsemen and their distinctive ethos. The expensive horse (which could often only be bought with slaves) became once again the sign of rank and wealth. The dominance of cavalry in Sokoto survived the introduction of firearms in the late 19th century and remained intact until the British conquest in 1902.

In **Masina,** the pastoral floodplain of the Niger in the central Sudan, another *marabout,* Shehu Amadu, proclaimed a *jihad* in 1818 in emulation of Sokoto and established another caliphate. Though by the 1850s the infantry of Masina had acquired some poor-quality firearms, traditional cavalrymen with their lances and ancient, heroic ethos remained dominant in battle, and their tactics were sufficient to defeat Masina's immediate neighbors.

To the west of Masina, in Senegambia, al-Hajj Umar Tal (1794–1864) launched a new *jihad* in 1853 of Tukulors, who were Fula from Futa Toro, with contingents from all surrounding people. The fanatical *talaba,* Umar's disciples, formed the elite corps in the **Tukulor** army and served as mounted shock troops. The infantry were zealous Islamic volunteers, recently converted animists (*sofas*), and conscript levies (*tuburru*). The *sofas* also worked as servants to the *talaba* and did all the chores of camp, but enjoyed the right to plunder the enemy with their masters. *Tuburru* were forbidden booty. The Tukulors were well equipped with modern firearms and artillery bought from English and French traders at the coast with donations by the faithful and the revenue of captured gold mines. These gave them superiority over less well-equipped foes and allowed them to breach the walls of fortified cities. Gunsmiths maintained the weapons, though they lacked the means to manufacture more themselves. Unusually for the armies of the savannah, Tukulor cavalry and infantry could maneuver well in formation, which gave them additional advantage in combat, though the *talaba* cavalry still dominated the battlefield. Arguably, though, the real strength of the Tukulor army lay in its zeal to crush pagans and infidels and in Umar's promise of heaven for death on the battlefield.

The Tukulor army overran the kingdoms of Kaarta and Segu between 1854 and 1858 and the Masina Caliphate in 1862, making the Tukulor Empire the most powerful state in the western Sudan. However, social tensions began to surface in the Tukulor army and religious zeal inevitably evaporated. Under Ahmadu Seku, Umar's successor, the puritanical *talaba* emerged as the new ruling class, provoking revolts and defections. The Tukulor Empire nevertheless survived until the French, advancing inland from Senegal on the coast, brought it down in a drawn-out struggle between 1883 and 1891.

The last indigenous empire to be formed in the western Sudan was not a revolutionary *jihad* state, and respected traditional society. **Samori Touré** (1830–1900) had begun as a mercenary leader. By the 1880s he had put together a sprawling, multiethnic, religiously mixed empire in the politically fragmented Guinea Highlands that was marked by administrative efficiency and military modernization. Samori was guarded by an elite of 500 *sofas* armed with modern repeating rifles. Each of the eight districts of the empire had an army corps of 5,000 with a nucleus of 300 veteran *sofas* who, in peacetime, spent half their time working in the fields. The rest of the army consisted of conscripts (10% of the empire's males, rising to 50% in time of war). There was a very active external trade in slaves, mainly to Futa Jallon, and revenues were used to buy horses from the north and rifles and ammunition from the French on the coast. By the 1890s the army, which in sub-Saharan Africa was next only to the Ethiopian in its armaments, was equipped with breech-loading rifles. Sophisticated arsenals produced ammunition and spare parts, and even manufactured breech-loading rifles. Samori's army was the first since that of the Sokoto Caliphate to rely primarily on infantry rather than cavalry. The *sofas* lived off the land and carried only their arms (rifle, sabre, and dagger) and were dressed with recognizable uniformity. Samori's state, like the Tukulor Empire, stood in the road of French expansion. It put up a superb resistance, resorting to effective guerrilla warfare before finally falling in 1898.

Descendents: During the subsequent decades of colonial rule many thousands of men of the western and central Sudan enlisted in the French and British colonial armies and served gallantly in two World Wars. After independence, long periods of military rule in the new states perpetuated the prestige of the soldier in African society. Although African soldiers now go to war with the most modern weaponry their states can afford, in the savannah horses are still associated with royalty and the descendents of the rulers of Sokoto and other kingdoms continue to ride with their mounted guards on ceremonial occasions.

Further Reading

Iliffe, John, *Honour in African History.* Cambridge: Cambridge University Press, 2005.
Smith, R. S., *War and Diplomacy in Pre-Colonial West Africa.* London: Methuen, 1976.
Thornton, John K., *Warfare in Atlantic Africa 1500–1800.* London: UCL Press, 1999.

John Laband

Western Naval Warfare
(1450–1850)

Context or Significance: According to some historians, naval warfare created the very foundations of the modern world. Specifically, much recent work has focused specifically on the role of European navies in the formation of the modern state. By 1790, the Royal Navy had 145 battleships each carrying between 50 and 100 guns, along with 131 cruisers or frigates. Such an instrument of war cannot be built and sustained without enormous financial investment and administrative oversight and, more broadly, the consent and investment of at least a significant part of the population. National navies also supported and protected the western European empires and global trade networks from which the modern world system emerged. Indeed key naval battles through the ages seem to punctuate the account of rising Western power. In 1509, at Diu, in India, a small Portuguese fleet defeated the Sultan of Gujarat and Egyptian allies and imposed their control over the seaborne trade in the area, a key step in the development of the first major European empire in the Indian Ocean. At the battle of Lepanto in 1571, the combined forces of Spain, Venice, the Papacy and others destroyed the Ottoman fleet, in what was the last major battle between fleets made up primarily of Mediterranean galleys. This has traditionally been seen as a key moment in the decline of the Turkish threat and the rise of the Christian West. Equally, England's victory over the Spanish Armada, sent into the Channel in 1588 to facilitate an invasion, is seen by some as the triumph of Protestant, mercantile powers over the older Catholic monarchies that to date had dominated the seas. By the time of the Seven Years' War (1756–1763), Britain was able to use control of the seas to beat France and Spain emphatically and to win an unparalleled overseas empire on all continents. Although it was subsequently unable to use its sea power to retain the American colonies, which won their independence by 1783, Britain still retained its naval superiority and dominated world trade. The value of sea power was demonstrated most clearly in the French Revolutionary and Napoleonic Wars (1792–1815), as Britain was able to inflict heavy defeat at sea, notably at Trafalgar in 1805, and to put pressure on the French Empire that eventually contributed to its defeat. In the years of relative peace that followed, Britain's ability to project and to support military power over great distances by sea was maintained, as demonstrated by the success of the international effort led by Britain to check Russian expansion in the Crimean War (1853–1856). With its unchallenged naval strength, Britain was able to maintain the balance of power in Europe and to guarantee the global security necessary to promote, and to dominate, the world's burgeoning trade in the 19th century.

Explanation: Most of what has been written about the strategic context of early modern naval warfare comes from, or is directly influenced by, the pens of a small number of late 19th- and early 20th-century theorists. As Andrew Lambert has insisted, it is essential to bear in mind the perspective of these writers on their past and the purposes for which they were writing. Mahan, Corbett, Laughton, and others were writing in an uncertain time of rising international tension, militarism, and rapid technological change. Coming after a long period of relative stability in naval warfare, they had to look back to the exploits of past eras to form theories and to draw lessons that could be applied to their current service education needs and to prepare their governments for the possible outbreak of large-scale naval war. Consistent with the current military thought of the age dominated by Clausewitz and Jomini, they saw, each in his different way, the historical success of the British Empire and the Royal Navy as an important lesson on the basis of which they made a plea for greater preparation and investment in naval power.

Certainly, the relationship between naval warfare and the power of modern states appears to have been a long and a close one. For example, Henry V's campaign in France leading up to victory at the battle of Agincourt in 1415, where greater ruthlessness matched his greater political ambitions, arguably marks the beginning of a shift from medieval notions of chivalry toward the escalation of modern warfare. At sea, this was accompanied by a sudden increase in English naval strength, with 36 royal warships and a fleet of over 1,500 vessels of all sizes transporting his troops and conducting the initial siege of Harfleur. In the same year, the Portuguese were taking their first tentative steps in North Africa, with the capture of Ceuta, which would eventually lead them down the African coast and into the Indian Ocean.

Over the next four centuries, the evolution of naval power continued to mirror the development of both modern warfare and Western imperialism. The use of heavy cannons in the late 15th century, which led to the development of *trace italienne* fortifications on land had a similar effect on ship design. Heavier ships were needed to cope with the recoil of heavy guns (and with enemy fire). Instead of simply hiring merchant ships and temporarily outfitting them for war when needed, states soon required purpose-built warships. The introduction of hinged gun ports, which could be closed when not in use, allowed for more guns placed on lower decks for stability. The new "galleons" of the 16th century combined as much as possible the sleek lines of the traditional Mediterranean galley with the needs of heavy artillery. Other changes, including the development of smaller, faster frigates, and the wider use of cast iron cannons, which were much cheaper to produce than the traditional bronze cannon, further improved the fighting capacity of the warship by the early 17th century.

Battle tactics soon evolved to maximize the offensive power of guns, which were, necessarily, fixed on the broadsides of ships. By forming into long, uniform, disciplined lines, a fleet could keep its guns fixed in one direction and thus onto the enemy's line. These "line ahead" tactics were common by the mid-century and were quickly formalized in the fighting instructions of different nations' navies. This occurred at about the same time that northern European armies were introducing similar tactics on land, with long lines of infantry, well organized and drilled, providing more continuous volley fire. This escalation on the battlefield was identified as the key change in what Michael Roberts famously referred to as the military revolution in early modern warfare. Much more than on land, however, the fixed, line-ahead tactics, and the emphasis on firepower in battle took hold at sea, becoming doctrine from which European navies rarely deviate. In a parallel with the reputation of 18th-century warfare generally for large scale but limited battles of maneuver, fleets spent much of their time trying to get the right position with respect to the wind, maintaining proper formation, and trying to engage the enemy. Given the enormous expense of building large warships, it was often very difficult to engage a reluctant enemy who did not want to take the risk. When battle did begin between relatively equal forces, it could end up as a pointless exchange of fire.

Though not the only one to innovate, Nelson's leadership, and his bold strategic vision, have been credited with largely transcending the limitations of 18th-century naval tactics by breaking enemy lines in bold offensive moves and pursuing a strategy of annihilation. He built his fame in the destruction of opposing fleets at Aboukir Bay in Egypt (1798), Copenhagen (1801), and most famously, four years later, at Trafalgar. Napoleonic warfare is usually credited with introducing strategies of annihilation and escalation that Clausewitz witnessed as the basis of his theories of modern warfare. Nevertheless, Napoleon's defeat came, to some extent at least, by parallel strategic thinking by Nelson.

However, this picture of warfare at sea as the mirror image of the development of modern warfare more generally exaggerates the role of set-piece battles between opposing fleets in naval warfare. These occurred only rarely. As Julian Corbett recognized, decisive battle is only one aspect of the successful application of sea power. To affect war on land, where people's interests actually lie, a more complete strategy of sea control must be pursued. Navies can also be used to blockade foreign ports, for example, or to attack enemy trade. Unlike war on land, which is usually between contiguous neighbors with a tendency to escalation, Corbett said, war at sea is mainly about controlling lines of communication and supply and denying the use of the sea to the enemy. All of these Corbett saw, along with the dramatic victory over the French invasion forces at Quiberon Bay in 1759 by the 23 ships of the line under Edward Hawke, as the source of British success in the Seven Years' War and the foundation of its global power.

Theorists such as Corbett, however, tended to assume a coherent strategic outlook in the past, which was not necessarily there. In fact, British naval policy, such as it was, appears to have been rather ad hoc. There had been no plan at the start of the war to win as much territory as they acquired by the terms of the peace, and not everyone thought it was a good idea. Many felt that extending the empire territorially was dangerous, for it would now be difficult to govern and defend, and it represented a fatal departure from its essentially commercial nature to date. For many, the real challenge was not global imperial competition but protecting Britain from absolutist France and a Catholic restoration. Indeed throughout the 18th century, British naval forces remained overwhelmingly in European waters, defending the approaches to the English Channel. Only once did the main fleet fight overseas, at the Battle of the Saintes in 1782. Although victorious in battle, Britain lost the larger War of American Independence. Overall, the navy was primarily defensive, and it was most successful when it attacked its enemies in Europe.

The three Anglo-Dutch Wars, 1652–1654, 1665–1667, 1672–1674, had been fought between two maritime nations who needed to protect their overseas trade and fisheries and who competed in a relatively narrow stretch of sea. It is perhaps not surprising that in these wars battleship tactics and design developed. Heavy artillery fights were common between fleets that operated close to home ports. By the time of the wars against Louis XIV in the following decades, large navies had become essential elements of national strength. This is not to say that naval strategy had become fixed, however. Despite having built the largest navy in Europe, France decided quite suddenly in the 1690s largely to set aside its battle fleets, leasing warships to individual privateers, and pursuing a more piecemeal *guerre de course,* or commerce raiding strategy. It made sense to limit investment in battleships and to try to harm the British economy directly, especially given the continental commitments of the French crown in the War of the Spanish Succession (1702–1714).

Britain emerged from the war strengthened at sea, most notably having taken Minorca and Gibraltar, which they relied upon to maintain their naval presence in the Mediterranean. Yet the use of private violence at sea was no French innovation. It has always been common and was a key part of British strategy too. People in Britain looked back fondly to their victory over the Spanish Armada in 1588. Then, the nation had been saved from invasion by the collective action of what were essentially privateers who preyed on Spanish shipping. Many in 18th-century Britain felt, therefore, that this defined the nature of British naval power and that it should be conducted aggressively as an overseas business making venture against Spanish interests rather than as a formal instrument of foreign policy or territorial expansion. Such opinion mattered a great deal, because to be effective, navies had to reflect the interests, not just of government, but of the seafarers, taxpayers, and investors of a society. Dutch success in the 17th century, for example, reflects the fact that the navy had been designed to protect trade. It was not centralized but actually the cooperative effort of five local admiralties.

The French navy reflected the nature of absolutist France in a similar way. Although there was certainly private initiative in France, the navy was largely an instrument of royal policy serving the crown's military needs in Europe and supporting its more territorial, integrationist empire overseas. As the largest monarchy in Europe, it could often afford to build great navies, but the expense was enormous, and when people felt that they did not have sufficient stake in it, it became difficult to sustain financially. The greatest advantages the British enjoyed were a population with a close connection to the sea, which helped to meet the enormous manpower challenges of outfitting a major navy and, perhaps more importantly, a balance of interests in naval power. Everyone wanted protection from invasion by Catholic France, and those people with a financial interest were happy to invest in a navy that protected trade and Britain's essentially commercial empire. As a result, stable banking and investment in the navy were priorities in Britain. It could afford to develop its system of support, with the effect that crews became better fed and organized, and fleets could be maintained longer at sea. Effective blockades of distant enemy ports could, therefore, be sustained for longer.

Though France and Spain competed, especially in the late 18th century with large ship-building programs, Britain maintained the greatest navy in the world, and this proved to be an essential weapon against the threat that Napoleon soon posed to Europe. Nelson's victories, however, did not open a new era of fleet battles, which were, in fact, even rarer in the 19th century. Instead, naval warfare continued in its traditional role of supporting warfare on land, usually with the transportation of troops or materials. Coastal bombardments and blockades, however, continued to be effective, and they helped Britain to put enormous economic and military pressure on the United States during the War of 1812 allowing it to concentrate on Napoleon.

Two features dominate the post-1815 environment in naval warfare. The first is the unquestioned supremacy of the Royal Navy and the global, international trade that it protected, a system often referred to as the *Pax Britannica*. The Royal Navy was certainly still effective in war, but it was most useful in deterring smaller powers and in policing the seas, suppressing the now illegal slave trade and piracy and promoting British financial interests. Fighting against the Spanish and the Portuguese, the radical Thomas Cochrane helped the South American colonies to exploit the waning of Iberian sea power in their fight for independence. Later, he led Greek radicals in their fight for independence from the Ottoman Empire, which culminated in the Battle of Navarino of October 20, 1827. Control of the sea was the key in this victory by the British, French, and Russians over the Turkish and Egyptian forces. Although other powers clearly had an interest in maintaining naval strength, none could compete with Britain. With a series of coastal operations and an effective blockade, Britain again took the international lead putting an end to Egyptian occupation of Syria in 1840. It had not just been Egyptian aggression, this time against Ottoman interests, which alarmed the British, but the threat to British trade the occupation represented.

The other feature of the post-1815 period is significant technological change. With the development of the screw propeller by 1837, the chief weakness of the early experiments with steam power could be overcome. With no large paddles interfering with the warship's traditional broadside gunnery, the way was open for the technological arms race between Britain and France that characterized the whole of the 19th century. Britain introduced the screw-propelled frigate, which was soon copied and improved by France. Similar technological competitions later occurred, most notably with the launch of the French frigate the *Gloire* in 1859, the first ironclad warship. Such French innovations led, later in the century, to a school of thought known as the *Jeune École,* which advocated what was essentially a commerce raiding strategy. To use small torpedo boats, which could exploit their technological sophistication to attack larger British capital ships, was seen as a more appropriate strategy than attempting to compete directly with British naval strength.

Technological innovation in this age of industrialization certainly changed the face of naval warfare. It did not significantly affect its strategic context, however. In a spectacular effort to open markets on the other side of the world, Britain used some steamships in the First Opium War (1839–1842). With a number of coastal bombardments and an audacious raid up the Yangzte, Britain was able to force the Chinese into a humiliating concession. As useful as steam had been, however, it was the broader commitment to the use of sea power to commercial ends and the political and popular will to maintain the infrastructure and the global system of supply and support that had made the difference. The British Empire was the product not just of policy makers and military planners but the growing capitalist interests in the city of London. The value of such combined effort was demonstrated very clearly in the Crimean War (1854–1856), the first major war with a large naval element since 1815. The attempt by Britain and France to cooperate in taking the Russian naval base at Sevastopol in the Black Sea turned into a long war of attrition in which Britain's ability to control the sea and put pressure on Russian logistics there, and to threaten St. Petersburg itself from the Baltic, led the Russians to seek peace, thus preserving the European balance of power.

The history of naval power is varied. Private seafarers, trading companies, and states had all used sea power in different ways through the centuries, but there was never one, single theory covering its use. As valuable as the writings of the main strategists still are, it is essential for historians and for today's policy makers to keep in mind the context in which they were writing. We must always question our strategic assumptions and ask what purpose navies in the past had and how they were used before reflecting on their use in the future.

Further Reading

Black, Jeremy, *Naval Power*. Houndmills: Palgrave, 2009.

Dull, Jonathan R, *The Age of the Ship of the Line*. Lincoln: University of Nebraska Press, 2009.

Glete, Jan, *Navies and Nations*. Vol.1: Stockholm: Almqvist and Wiksell, 1993, p.278.

Glete, Jan, *Warfare at Sea, 1500–1650*. London: Routledge, 2000.

Harding, Richard, *Seapower and Naval Warfare, 1650–1830*. London: Taylor and Francis, 1999.

Lambert, Andrew, *The Foundations of Naval History*. London: Chatham, 1998.

Rodger, N.A.M., *The Command of the Ocean*. London: Allen Lane, 2004.

Rodger, N.A.M., *The Safeguard of the Sea*. London: Harper Collins, 1997.

Sondhaus, Lawrence, *Naval Warfare, 1815–1914*. London: Routledge, 2001.

Alan James

About the Editors and Contributors

Editors

Daniel Coetzee attended Pembroke College, Cambridge, where he obtained a PhD in history. He is a freelance researcher and author.

Lee W. Eysturlid attended Purdue University, where he obtained a PhD with a focus in military history. He teaches at the Illinois Mathematics and Science Academy, Aurora, Illinois, and is author of *The Formative Influences, Theories, and Campaigns of the Archduke Carl of Austria* (Greenwood, 2000).

Contributors

Tristan Abbey is a senior editor at *Bellum: A Project of the Stanford Review*. He graduated with honors from Stanford University and the Security Studies Program at Georgetown University's School of Foreign Service.

Shihab al-Sarraf, independent scholar.

Jean-Jacques Arzalier (MD) is colonel in the French Army Health Department (Reserve) and has a Master in military history and defense studies (Aix-en-Provence, Political Studies Institute, 1992).

Frances F. Berdan, California State University, San Bernardino.

Joe Caddell, North Carolina State University.

Mark Danley, University of Memphis Libraries.

Paul D'Arcy, Australian National University.

Morgan Deane, Brigham Young University Idaho, served for five years as infantry rifleman, squad leader, and intelligence analyst in the U.S. Marine Corps and

National Guard. He was named as a Marshall Scholar by the George C. Marshall Foundation at the Virginia Military Institute.

Kelly DeVries, Loyola College.

Saeid Edalatnejad, Encyclopaedia Islamica Foundation, member of the Scientific Board.

Karl Friday, professor emeritus, University of Georgia and Center Director, IES Abroad Tokyo Center.

Richard A. Gabriel, distinguished visiting professor, Department of History and War Studies, Royal Military College of Canada, Kingston, Ontario.

Ioannis Georganas is a researcher (Antiquity) at the Foundation of the Hellenic World. He holds a PhD in archaeology from the University of Nottingham and his main area of interest is the study of ancient Greek weapons and warfare, especially during the Late Bronze and Early Iron Ages.

David A. Graff, Kansas State University.

Bruce I. Gudmundsson, Marine Corps University.

Muhammed Hassanali, independent scholar.

Dietmar Herz, Universitaet Erfurt.

Beatrice Heuser, chair of international relations, Department of Politics and International Relations, University of Reading.

Carl Cavanagh Hodge, Okanagan University College/No Kelowna, political science.

Alan James, King's College, London.

Seth Lyons Kendall is assistant professor of history at Georgia Gwinnett College, specializing in the history of the Roman Republic.

Robert Kiely, School of the Art Institute of Chicago.

John Laband, Wilfrid Laurier University, Department of History.

Peter Lieb, Royal Military Academy, Sandhurst.

Peter Lorge, Vanderbilt University, assistant professor of history.

Erik A. Lund received his PhD in history from the University of Toronto in the spring of 1997.

Joseph M. McCarthy has a PhD in history and philosophy of education with distinction, Boston College. He is emeritus professor of education and human services/history, Suffolk University, and is the author of several books.

James R. McIntyre, Moraine Valley Community College.

Toby McLeod, University of Birmingham, Medieval and Modern History Department.

David Nicolle, honorary research fellow, Institute of Medieval Studies, History Department, Nottingham University, United Kingdom.

Nathan N. Orgill, George Gwinnett College.

Scott Palter is president of Final Swords Production, LLC, and a senior editor at *Bellum: A Project of The Stanford Review.*

Laurent Quisefit (PhD) is a lecturer in Korean studies at Paris Denis Diderot University (Paris, France). He wrote articles about East Asian history, usually focusing on Korean culture, internal relations and military topics.

Richard Rawls is an associate professor of history at Georgia Gwinnett College in Lawrenceville (suburban Atlanta, Georgia). He is currently working on a two-volume history of the conversions of the Goths. In 2004, he won the Nickel Excellence in Teaching Award.

Kaushik Roy, associate professor, Department of History, Jadavpur University and senior researcher at the Centre for the Study of Civil War (CSCW) at Peace Research Institute Oslo (PRIO), Norway.

John Serrati, Classics and History Department, Abbott College.

Jeffrey M. Shaw is a professor in the Department of Strategy and Policy at the United States Naval War College.

Charles R. Shrader, U.S. Army (retired).

Claiborne Skinner, Illinois Mathematics and Science Academy.

Patrick J. Speelman, College of Charleston, History Department.

Joseph S. Spoerl, Professor, Philosophy Department, Saint Anselm College.

Armstrong Starkey, Adelphi University, history department.

Matthias Strohn, senior research fellow in modern war studies, University of Buckingham.

Ilkka Syvanne (Syvänne) is vice chairman of the Finnish Research Society of Byzantium. He has written extensively on ancient and medieval military topics and is the author of *The Age of Hippotoxotai: Art of War in Roman Military Revival and Disaster 491–636* (2004). In 2006, he won the *Society of Ancients'* Ian Greenwood Price (The Best Research Article 0–1000 AD).

William J. Walsh, University of Chicago.

Steven Weingartner is a writer and editor specializing in military history and military affairs. He latest book is *Faithful Warriors: A Combat Marine Remembers the Pacific War* (with Dean Ladd, Naval Institute Press, Winter 2008).

Corbin Williamson is a graduate student in history at Texas Tech University.

Index

Note: Page numbers in **boldface** reflect main entries in the book.